Handbook of Research on the Interplay Between Service Quality and Customer Delight

Sarmistha Sarma
Institute of Innovation in Technology and Management, India

Neha Gupta
IBCS, SOA University (Deemed), India

A volume in the Advances in Marketing, Customer Relationship Management, and E-Services (AMCRMES) Book Series

Published in the United States of America by
IGI Global
Business Science Reference (an imprint of IGI Global)
701 E. Chocolate Avenue
Hershey PA, USA 17033
Tel: 717-533-8845
Fax: 717-533-8661
E-mail: cust@igi-global.com
Web site: http://www.igi-global.com

Library of Congress Cataloging-in-Publication Data

Names: Sarma, Sarmistha, editor. | Gupta, Neha, 1985- editor.
Title: Handbook of research on the interplay between service quality and
  customer delight / Sarmistha Sarma, and Neha Gupta, editor.
Description: Hershey, PA : Business Science Reference, [2023] | Includes
  bibliographical references and index. | Summary: "Customer delight has
  been the goal for all companies small and big around the world. The
  present book is an effort to analyse the nuances of marketing efforts
  put forward by companies to achieve customer delight and sustain it in a
  fiercely competitive marketing environment. The book proposes to have
  chapters from around the world giving a global perspective to
  understanding the concept of customer delight"-- Provided by publisher.
Identifiers: LCCN 2022039823 (print) | LCCN 2022039824 (ebook) | ISBN
  9781668458532 (hardcover) | ISBN 9781668458556 (ebook)
Subjects: LCSH: Customer services. | Customer relations. | Quality control.
  | Marketing.
Classification: LCC HF5415.5 .G56 2023 (print) | LCC HF5415.5 (ebook) |
  DDC 658.8/12--dc23/eng/20220929
LC record available at https://lccn.loc.gov/2022039823
LC ebook record available at https://lccn.loc.gov/2022039824

This book is published in the IGI Global book series Advances in Marketing, Customer Relationship Management, and E-
Services (AMCRMES) (ISSN: 2327-5502; eISSN: 2327-5529).

British Cataloguing in Publication Data
A Cataloguing in Publication record for this book is available from the British Library.

For electronic access to this publication, please contact: eresources@igi-global.com.

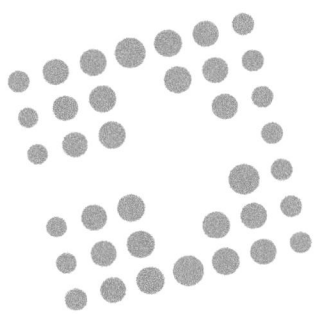

Advances in Marketing, Customer Relationship Management, and E-Services (AMCRMES) Book Series

Eldon Y. Li

National Chengchi University, Taiwan & California Polytechnic State University, USA

ISSN:2327-5502
EISSN:2327-5529

MISSION

Business processes, services, and communications are important factors in the management of good customer relationship, which is the foundation of any well organized business. Technology continues to play a vital role in the organization and automation of business processes for marketing, sales, and customer service. These features aid in the attraction of new clients and maintaining existing relationships.

The Advances in Marketing, Customer Relationship Management, and E-Services (AMCRMES) Book Series addresses success factors for customer relationship management, marketing, and electronic services and its performance outcomes. This collection of reference source covers aspects of consumer behavior and marketing business strategies aiming towards researchers, scholars, and practitioners in the fields of marketing management.

COVERAGE

- CRM strategies
- Legal Considerations in E-Marketing
- Customer Relationship Management
- Cases on Electronic Services
- Mobile Services
- Web Mining and Marketing
- Telemarketing
- Social Networking and Marketing
- Relationship Marketing
- CRM and customer trust

IGI Global is currently accepting manuscripts for publication within this series. To submit a proposal for a volume in this series, please contact our Acquisition Editors at Acquisitions@igi-global.com or visit: http://www.igi-global.com/publish/.

Titles in this Series

For a list of additional titles in this series, please visit: http://www.igi-global.com/book-series/advances-marketing-customer-relationship-management/37150

Handbook of Research on the Future of Advertising and Brands in the New Entertainment Landscape
Blanca Miguélez-Juan (University of the Basque Country, Spain) and Gema Bonales-Daimiel (Complutense University of Madrid, Spain)
Business Science Reference • © 2023 • 441pp • H/C (ISBN: 9781668439715) • US $295.00

Promoting Consumer Engagement Through Emotional Branding and Sensory Marketing
Monika Gupta (Chitkara Business School, Chitkara University, India) Priya Jindal (Chitkara Business School, Chitkara University, India) and Shubhi Bansal (Indian Institute of Technology, Indore, India)
Business Science Reference • © 2023 • 298pp • H/C (ISBN: 9781668458976) • US $250.00

Marketing and Advertising in the Online-to-Offline (O2O) World
Hesham Osama Dinana (American University in Cairo, Egypt)
Business Science Reference • © 2023 • 310pp • H/C (ISBN: 9781668458440) • US $250.00

Global Agricultural and Food Marketing in a Global Context Advancing Policy, Management, and Innovation
Aluwani Maiwashe-Tagwi (University of South Africa (UNISA), South Africa) Ailweli Solomon Mawela (University of South Africa (UNISA), South Africa) and Phineus Khazamula Chauke (University of South Africa (UNISA), South Africa)
Business Science Reference • © 2023 • 315pp • H/C (ISBN: 9781668447802) • US $250.00

Promoting Organizational Performance Through 5G and Agile Marketing
José Duarte Santos (Accounting and Business School, Polytechnic of Porto, Portugal) and Bruno Miguel Sousa (Polytechnic Institute of Cávado and Ave, Portugal)
Business Science Reference • © 2023 • 316pp • H/C (ISBN: 9781668455234) • US $225.00

Cases on Social Justice in China and Perspectives on Chinese Brands
Youssef El Haoussine (Beijing Normal University-Hong Kong Baptist University United International College, China) and Lulu Wang (Sinotrend Consulting, China)
Business Science Reference • © 2023 • 335pp • H/C (ISBN: 9781668449554) • US $215.00

Building a Brand Image Through Electronic Customer Relationship Management
Arshi Naim (King Kalid University, Saudi Arabia) and Sandeep Kumar Kautish (Lord Buddha Education Foundation, Asia Pacific University, India)
Business Science Reference • © 2022 • 360pp • H/C (ISBN: 9781668453865) • US $250.00

701 East Chocolate Avenue, Hershey, PA 17033, USA
Tel: 717-533-8845 x100 • Fax: 717-533-8661
E-Mail: cust@igi-global.com • www.igi-global.com

List of Contributors

Table of Contents

Detailed Table of Contents

Chapter 1

Sudeshna Dutta, Biju Patnaik Institute of Information Technology and Management Studies,
India
Dhananjay Beura, Biju Patnaik Institute of Information Technology and Management
Studies, India

Rising income is driving the demand for online trading services across all income brackets. After the demand of online trading, many brokers have entered the cutthroat competition, high customer expectation, and dynamic technological changes have forced brokers to thrive on service quality. Online brokerage service as opted as an appropriate research framework for two main reasons. First, online brokerage is a service-intensive, fast-growing industry that is well suited for current research purposes. Second, there are few empirical studies measuring quality of service aspects and customer satisfaction and switching intention in the context of online securities. A relevant conceptual framework was outlined from extant literature which reveals an association between overall e-service quality, customer satisfaction and switching intension. Key dimensions were identified in the research which will add to the existing body of literature of service marketing. The finding of the research adds more depth in the body of literature of e-service quality in the online brokerage sector.

Chapter 2

Jigna Chandrakant Trivedi, Shri Jairambhai Patel Institute of Business Management and
Computer Applications, Gandhinagar, India
Bindiya Kunal Soni, Anand Institute of Management and Information Sciences, India

This study is carried out to analyze how SERVQUAL factors together with customer satisfaction and customer trust to influence the purchase intention for the insurance industry in Gandhinagar, Gujarat. The primary data for the study was collected through a self-administered questionnaire. 379 responses were collected from the households of the selected region through the convenience sampling method. Exploratory factor analysis (EFA) and confirmatory factor analysis (CFA) were employed to check how tangibility, reliability, responsiveness, assurance, empathy, customer satisfaction, and customer trust influence the purchase intention of the households. The structural equation modelling (SEM) revealed that empathy, tangibility, reliability, and customer satisfaction positively influence the purchase intention of the respondents for the insurance policies.

Chapter 3

Sagarika Mohanty, KIIT University, India
Shahni Singh, Biju Patnaik Institute of Information Technology and Management Studies,
*   India*
Jitendra Mohanty, KIIT University, India

Digital banking (DB) promotes the digital growth of the economy. Digital growth leads to an improved ecosystem. The present paper gives more significant experiences into all the selected key factors, such as service quality (SQ) and behavioral intention (BI) to use digital banking; perceived usefulness (PU) and perceived risk (PR) in digital banking adoption; performance expectancy (PE) and effort expectancy (EE) with the prospect of customer satisfaction in digital banking. This paper also analyzes different models and related theories of SQ, BI, PU, PR, PE, and EE in the prospect of the adoption of digital banking, and summarizes the gaps and limitations of this topic. To give more insightful information, these studies develop network analysis and temporal analysis in accordance with keywords. The sole sector of the economy covered by this study is banking. Thus, the findings also give a new path to analyze in other areas. Further studies can be done in large-scale review by taking other key factors like grievance handling, customer dissonance and customer experience, and others.

Chapter 4

Pfano Mashau, University of KwaZulu-Natal, South Africa
Mathews Smangaliso Shange, University of KwaZulu-Natal, South Africa
Andrisha Beharry-Ramraj, University of KwaZulu-Natal, South Africa

The Consumer Protection Act (CPA) of 2008 was developed with the intention to protect consumers and promote fair dealings and responsible conduct of retailers in the marketplace. However, consumers continue to suffer in the marketplace due to defective products, unfair dealings, and poor service despite there being a CPA that was developed to protect their rights. Studies revealed a reduction in the number of registered complaints and an unchanged market environment for retail consumers pertaining to handling their consumer disputes. A quantitative study was conducted with a random sample of 95 retail furniture consumers who visited five furniture retail shops at Kwa Mnyandu Mall in the Umlazi township. Furniture retail consumers in Umlazi are aware of the CPA, however, they have reasonably less or no knowledge of the consumer rights contained in the CPA. Identified shortcomings in the use of the CPA to handle customer complaints is also explored. It was evident from the findings that retail consumers know that there is a CPA but they are unclear on how it is supposed to protect them when dissatisfied with a product.

The Covid-19 crisis has propelled no small extent of changes in the attitude and behavior of people all over the world. This has created a challenge for the consumers' consumption on different categories of products. Consumers' behavior on the basis of their personalities, like emotional and cognitive, is the key area to study during the pandemic. Affect and cognition have profound impacts on behavioral pattern of consumers in all times. The pandemic changed purchase behavior and made consumers behave with cognition and emotion. The study has verified a deviation in consumer behavior on consumption of essential goods. The result is based on the brand consciousness and price sensitivity of both cognitive and emotional consumers during the purchase of essential commodities. Structural equation modeling utilized to study the extent of deviations in behavior during the purchases.

This study looked into how customer empowerment affects a company's performance (i.e., a bank). The relationship between customer empowerment and the firm's performance of banks in India's Delhi and NCR region has been studied, and innovation and customer satisfaction have been found to mediate this relationship. 439 bank employees, both male and female, were chosen for this study. Confirmatory factor analysis was used to analyze the data, and it was discovered that the variables met the requirements of path analysis. Customer empowerment has been found to have a significant impact on firm performance (i.e., a bank) as well as a negligible impact on customer satisfaction and customer retention. Therefore, this research differs from earlier studies that demonstrate that customer empowerment has a significant impact. It suggests a comprehensive framework that explains the connections between customer empowerment, innovation, customer satisfaction, customer retention, and business performance.

Customer delight is defined as exceeding client expectations through an experience that is truly differentiated. Customer delight is not limited to delivering service quality, but it is also about how the service is delivered and customer experience of the service provided. Customer experience will traverse seamlessly across the virtual and physical worlds with the evolution of the metaverse resulting in 'innovative disruption'. As the new playing field for corporates and engagement with consumers, it will transform customer experience. This will be augmented by turning historical notifications and transactions into real-time personalized communications. In this chapter the authors look at key pillars of how the metaverse will impact customer experience and delight. Through a literature survey, this chapter identifies the key pillars of the metaverse that will impact customer experience. The study then further drills into how customer experience is likely to be shaped in the metaverse for key sectors including retail, technology, and banking.

Chapter 8

Devesh Bathla, Chitkara Business School, Chitkara University, Punjab, India
Raina Ahuja, Kurukshetra University, India

Human capital analytics transforms this information into significant understanding which reveals deeper insights. HR analytics is the utilization of systematic procedure to determine the HR issues. Starting from discovering best fit candidate until his retention, businesses are taking a stab at a lot of keen choices. The choice of selection in HR for the majority depends on trust and dislike in other verticals in the organisations. In the author's analytical view, human resource is an abundantly disregarded field by and large when contrasted with different business verticals, however the right fit candidates are required for each business unit for better outcomes. Be that as it may, after the recession time frame of later half of first decade of the 20th century, the majority of the associations perceived the need of evidence based human resource management. To come up with better decision making in the field of HR, evidence based HRM driven by information and data should rehearse with analysis, making choices, and critical thinking.

Chapter 9

Shilpa Arora Narang, Institute of Innovation in Technology and Management, GGSIP
University, New Delhi, India
Sarmistha Sarma, Institute of Innovation in Technology and Management, GGSIP University,
New Delhi, India
Ashita Raveendran, National Council of Educational Research and Training, New Delhi,
India
P. D. Subhash, National Council of Educational Research and Training, New Delhi, India

Global citizen education (GCED) is a strategic area of UNESCO's education sector program and builds on the work of peace and human rights education. It may prove to be a key area of focus for school education services around the world. India has always been a key stakeholder in implementing the SDGs in its policies. The education sector plays a pivotal role in realizing the SDG targets, and GCED curriculum implementation plays are strategic roles in realizing this target of achieving SDG in education. India has played an active role in making efforts to implement GCED in school education. This chapter focuses on GCED practices, traces its origin, its prospective arrival in the Indian education scenario, and the state of affairs at present in terms of its implementation in prominent states around the country. Therefore, the chapter describes GCED implementation in Indian school system and its contribution to making the school education system a delightful and sustainable practice.

Chapter 10

Ritika Sharma, KIIT University, India
Pallabi Mishra, Utkal University, India

Over the last few years, the digital technologies have grown at a rapid pace and have become a part of the daily lives of billions of people across the world. The advancements in the field of telecommunications and the availability of devices with enhanced capabilities have a major role to play in this growth. Numerous studies have also addressed and explained about this emerging trend in the entertainment and media industry in many parts of the world. Over-the-top services, commonly known as OTT, are delivered directly through a stable internet connection. Consumers are spending more time on the internet than ever before. The internet has become an essential part of their lives, and so is the usage of OTT. There has been a shift in the habits of consumers, particularly young consumers, between the age group of 16-34 years. For OTT players to continue and succeed further, a combination of ad-based models and subscription-based models seem viable. Here the authors have tried to understand the major factors responsible for the adoption OTT services among Indian consumers.

Chapter 11

Priyabrata Panda, Gangadhar Meher University, India
Manisha Satapathy, Gangadhar Meher University, India
Satyabrata Acharya, Gangadhar Meher University, India

Customers prefer a bank that can be easily accessed from the point of view of the location, staff coordination, service delivery, etc. In this context, the present study tries the factors stimulating ease of access to banks by customers. The study also focuses to assess the relationship of personal interest of staff, coordinated approach of staff, and customer support approach with prompt service delivery to customers. Data has been collected through scheduled questionnaires from SBI customers. The study is confined to the western part of Odisha, India. Exploratory factor analysis, multiple linear regression, and canonical correlation have been applied for data analysis. It is found that service quality, staff behaviour, and gender have a significant impact on the ease of access to the bank. It is also revealed that the personal interest of staff and coordinated approach of staff have a significant relationship with prompt service to customers. The findings of this research work will be helpful to banks to revamp their strategy for long-term endurance.

Chapter 12

Parul Singh, Indian Institute of Foreign Trade, India
Areej Aftab Siddiqui, Dubai Business School, University of Dubai, UAE

Online crowdsourcing is a concept which is gaining momentum among business organizations for various reasons. It is a modern age digital marketing tool. It may be considered as a tool for gathering information, views, opinions, work, assigned task, ideas, solution to problems generally from crowds (a group of people) via the internet. This has enabled organizations to save resources such as time and money by utilizing different skills and expertise of people globally. Realizing the numerous benefits that crowdsourcing offers to organizations, they are adopting online crowdsourcing models not only to engage customers for co-creation, co-engagement, and collaboration but also for brand building and creating customer satisfaction. Organizations in a crowdsourcing model throws a contest, task, or a problem in hand to the crowd. The interest lies in understanding what motivates crowd to participate in such contests, which offers them delight, perceived value, and satisfaction.

FinTech refers to the introduction of technology into the financial sector as a result of the development of digital technology. FinTech uses technology-savvy financial innovations to create business models that are advanced, operations, or new products/services. This has led to the development of new types of services, improved financial markets, and better financial institutions. India is moving towards a powerful environment that provides a platform for FinTech startups to become billion-dollar unicorns. FinTech in India has several goals, from opening new divisions to exploring overseas markets. India's economy, typically money-driven, has seen tremendous growth in FinTech by capitalising on the opportunities presented as a result of growth in e-commerce and greater smartphone penetration rates. Hence, based on a thorough literature review by using exploratory research method, this chapter seeks to study the growth and evolution of FinTech in India, with special reference to the COVID-19 pandemic.

This chapter discusses theories that explain how microfinance interacts with service quality and customer delight globally. It also identifies moderating elements between satisfaction and service quality. Microfinance provides services to low-income, self-employed, and financially disadvantaged people who don't have access to formal banking. The concept of "service" is the provision of an intangible act or performance by one party to another without ownership. Microfinance services are categorized into financial and non-financial services. And the service quality parameters are reliability, tangibility, responsiveness, assurance, and empathy. Customer delight means customers are happy with a product or service if it exceeds their expectations. Moreover, institutional affiliations (religious or secular), adaptability of new technologies, and geographical (regional) concerns moderate the relationship between service quality and customer satisfaction level.

    Jyotisankar Mishra, KIIT University, India
    Pruthiranjan Dwibedi, KIIT University, India

The authors conducted a bibliometric study of the aforesaid area of interest since healthcare service quality is becoming more important in the literature. Its goal is to look at the trends and patterns that have been observed in the literature on healthcare service quality. R Software is used for analysis. Performance analysis and science mapping programs of the software have been used for the study. Using the Scopus database, the publication pattern from 1996 to 2022 was examined. Two thousand one hundred seventeen articles in the subject area were found, retrieved, and used in the study. The most successful and well-known authors were recognised. Analysis of co-authorship and co-occurrence was done. The leading nations publishing of papers relating to healthcare service quality according to the results of co-authorship and co-occurrence have been analysed. The bibilometric study was carried out to find trends in the healthcare sector's service quality. The study's findings revealed a publication tendency that was perhaps growing and would continue to grow.

    Lingam Naveen, Biju Patnaik Institute of Information Technology and Management Studies
        (BIITM), India
    Rabi N. Subudhi, KIIT School of Management, KIIT University, India

The world of retail is very dynamic and interesting. The evolution of retail as an industry withholds immense richness in terms of research literature. This study has adopted a review research design to study the retailing literature of last two decades. The bibliometric database Scopus was used to extract the list of studies. The central constructs considered for the study are service quality (SQ), customer satisfaction (CS), and customer delight (CD). A systematic literature review approach was undertaken along with PRISMA framework. Multiple rounds of screening were done to finalize a total of 92 documents for the review. To identify, evaluate, and study various themes and variables related to the central constructs, several research tools were used like network analysis, temporal analysis, citation analysis, and mind maps. The findings of the study would help both retail researchers and practitioners to understand consumer behavior concerning retail sector and devise the future course of action to develop higher levels of customer loyalty and retention.

    Amandeep Singh, Chitkara Business School, Chitkara University, Punjab, India
    Devesh Bathla, Chitkara Business School, Chitkara University, Punjab, India
    Amrinder Singh, Jain University (Deemed), India

The most important objective of service quality is the retention of the customer to provide repeatability of services through customer satisfaction. Since customer perceptions and expectations affect the service quality, this study helps to understand and identify the service quality gaps in services provided by cab aggregators to customers in India using SERVQUAL Gap Analysis between perception and expectation.

The main objective of this chapter is to understand, study, and compare the customer perception and expectations from customers using services of the cab aggregators within India to identify the areas of service quality gaps. Primary data was collected from 495 respondents from various cities across different demographic variables such as gender, age, income, education, and occupation. The responses were taken using Google Forms, which is consolidated in an Excel sheet. It is suggested to also create a service quality framework for cab aggregators on the basis of service quality gaps identified in the current study.

Financial product marketing requires the use of well-researched techniques to achieve investor satisfaction. The intention of this study is to examine elements that affect investor satisfaction while keeping the aforementioned debate as its central concept. Investor is the term used for customer of financial products. The factors that contribute most to it have been discovered to be safety, profitability, and liquidity. It was discovered after looking at a variety of schools of thought and literatures that there has been little research on investor satisfaction, and the work aims to examine the impact of financial products' liquidity, profitability, and safety (specifically, the SLP approach) on investors' satisfaction. Data is analysed using Tukey's test, principal component analysis, correlation, regression, and ANOVA. This study contributes that investor satisfaction is a valuable intangible asset that is primarily produced by the financial instrument's safety, security, and liquidity features using the SLP technique.

Preface

Research in the field of service quality and consumer behaviour has developed in many dimensions in the past decade. Satisfaction studies were the highlights in these researches. A number of models have been developed to determine the factors leading to satisfaction. Scholars such as Zeithmal, Parsuraman, Groonros and Dhabolkar are some of the pioneers in the satisfaction studies. However, in the past few years scholars have proved that satisfaction is not sufficient to leave a strong mark in the minds of the customers. Scholars such as Keiningham, Vavra and Kano have proved that customer delight is the key to customer retention.

In the present time, the emphasis is on Customer Delight (CD), so as to exceed customer's expectations. Delight resulting from high level of surprisingly positive disconfirmation can satisfy customers only when it is experienced but does not dissatisfy when it is not experienced. The important aspect of service contributing to Customer Delight is how a customer is treated in a service industry, i.e., with politeness, respect, friendliness and other similar considerations because caring attitude adds more value to Customer Delight than the service quality dimensions being maintained, like tangibility, responsiveness, reliability and empathy.

Customer Delight provides a distinct advantage to the company that does it first and does it well and thus create a desire for pleasurable performance in the future. Companies attempt to go beyond just meeting customer expectations in order to enjoy proportionately greater gains as delighted customers buy more, complain less spread positive word of mouth ensure loyal customer base and repeat purchases. Many studies assert that a delighted customer is "very satisfied" whereas a very satisfied customer is not necessarily delighted. Although, additional cost of designing implementing and marketing the delighted product /service features generate loyalty, there is a tendency that customers may forget delight with the passage of time if it is not maintained forever. Such value-add ups raise expectations of the customers and then it becomes difficult to maintain the similar delight level for the future. However, delight creates a desire for future recurrence of pleasurable surprising performance and thus instigates the customer to return to the service provider. Service quality and customer delight have been the buzzwords in the business world in recent times as scholars have proven that customer delight is the key to customer retention.

Handbook of Research on the Interplay Between Service Quality and Customer Delight considers how companies around the world in a cross-cultural environment are dealing with service quality and customer delight and proposes a global outlook on the current trends, tactics, and opportunities. Covering key topics such as buyer funnels, consumer dissonance, and digital solutions, this reference work is ideal for business owners, managers, industry professionals, researchers, scholars, practitioners, academicians, instructors, and students.

The book encompasses a rich collection of diverse chapters. Each one of the chapters has enriching insight into the concept of customer satisfaction and delight. In the following paragraphs a detailed write up is given on the each chapter and a summery of the same.

Chapter 1

Chapter 1 talks about E- Service quality in the online brokerage sector. Rising income is driving the demand for online trading services across all income brackets. After the demand of online trading, many brokers have entered the cutthroat competition, high customer expectation, and dynamic technological changes have forced brokers to thrive on service quality. Online brokerage service as opted as an appropriate research framework for two main reasons. First, online brokerage is a service-intensive, fast-growing industry that is well suited for current research purposes. Second, there are few empirical studies measuring quality of service aspects and customer satisfaction and switching intention in the context of online securities. A relevant conceptual framework was outlined from extant literature which reveals an association between overall e-service quality, customer satisfaction and switching intension. Key dimensions were identified in the research which will add to the existing body of literature of service marketing. The findings of the research adds more depth in the body of literature of e-service quality in the online brokerage sector.

Chapter 2

This study is carried out to analyze how SERVQUAL factors together with customer satisfaction and customer trust influence the purchase intention for the insurance industry in Gandhinagar, Gujarat. The primary data for the study was collected through a self-administered questionnaire. 379 responses were collected from the households of the selected region through the convenience sampling method. Exploratory Factor Analysis (EFA) and Confirmatory Factor Analysis (CFA) were employed to check how tangibility, reliability, responsiveness, assurance, empathy, customer satisfaction, and customer trust influence the purchase intention of the households. The Structural Equation Modelling (SEM) revealed that empathy, tangibility, reliability, and customer satisfaction positively influence the purchase intention of the respondents for the insurance policies.

Chapter 3

This chapter talks about how digital banking (DB) promotes the digital growth of the economy. Digital growth leads to an improved ecosystem. The present paper gives more significant experiences into all the selected key factors, such as service quality (SQ), behavioral intention (BI) to use digital banking, perceived usefulness (PU), perceived risk (PR) in digital banking adoption, performance expectancy (PE) and effort expectancy (EE) with the prospect of customer satisfaction in digital banking. This paper also analyzes different models and related theories of SQ, BI, PU, PR, PE, and EE in the prospect of the adoption of digital banking and summarizes the gaps and limitations of this topic. To give more insightful information, these studies develop network analysis and temporal analysis in accordance with keywords. The sole sector of the economy covered by this study is banking. Thus, the findings also give a new path to analyze in other areas. Further studies can be done in large-scale review by taking other key factors like grievance handling, customer dissonance and customer experience and others.

Chapter 4

The study is done with the intention to protect consumers and promote fair dealings and responsible conduct of retailers in the marketplace. consumers continue to suffer in the marketplace due to defective products, unfair dealings and poor service despite there being a CPA that was developed to protect their rights. Studies revealed a reduction in the number of registered complaints and an unchanged market environment for retail consumers pertaining to handling their consumer disputes. A quantitative study with a random sample of 95 retail furniture consumers who visited five furniture retail shops at Kwa Mnyandu Mall in the Umlazi township. Furniture retail consumers in Umlazi are aware of the CPA, however, they have reasonably less or no knowledge of the consumer rights contained in the CPA. Identified shortcomings in the use of the CPA to handle customer complaints. It was evident from the findings that retail consumers know that there is a CPA but they are unclear on how it is supposed to protect them when dissatisfied with a product.

Chapter 5

COVID-19 crisis has propelled in no small extent of changes in the attitude and behavior of people all over the world. This has created a challenge for the consumers' consumption on different categories of products. Consumers' behavior on the basis of their personalities like emotional and cognitive is the key area to study during the pandemic. Affect and Cognition have profound impact on behavioral pattern of consumers in all times. Pandemic changed purchase behavior and make consumers to behave with cognition and emotion. The study has verified a deviation in consumer behavior on consumption of essential goods. The result is based on the brand consciousness and price sensitivity of both cognitive and emotional consumers during the purchase of essential commodities. Structural equation modeling utilized to study the extent of deviations in behavior during the purchases.

Chapter 6

This study looked into how customer empowerment affects a company's performance (i.e., bank). The relationship between customer empowerment and the firm's performance of banks in India's Delhi & NCR region has been studied, and innovation and customer satisfaction have been found to mediate this relationship. Four hundred thirty-nine bank employees, both male and female, were chosen for this study. Confirmatory factor analysis was used to analyze the data, and it was discovered that the variables met the requirements of path analysis. Customer empowerment has been found to have a significant impact on firm performance (i.e., bank) as well as a negligible impact on customer satisfaction and customer retention. Therefore, this research differs from earlier studies that demonstrate that customer empowerment has a significant impact, as it is in the present study. It suggests a comprehensive framework that explains the connections between customer empowerment, innovation, customer satisfaction, customer retention, and business performance.

Chapter 7

Customer delight is defined as exceeding client expectations through an experience that is truly differentiated. Customer delight is not limited to delivering service quality, but it is also about how the service is delivered and customer experience the service provided. Customer experience will traverse seamlessly across the virtual and physical worlds with the evolution of the Metaverse resulting in "Innovative Disruption". As the new playing field for corporates and engagement with consumers, it will transform Customer Experience. This will be augmented by turning historical notifications and transactions into real time personalized communications. In this chapter we look at key pillars of how Metaverse will impact Customer Experience and Delight. Through Literature survey, this chapter identifies the key pillars of Metaverse that will impact Customer Experience. The study then further drills into how customer experience is likely to be shaped in the Metaverse for key sectors including Retail, Technology and Banking.

Chapter 8

The paper aims at studying the importance of Human Capital Analytics and how transforms this information into significant understanding and improves efficiency of organisation. HR analytics is the utilization of systematic procedure to determine the HR issues. Starting from discovering best fit candidate till his retention, businesses are taking a stab at a lot of keen choices. The choice of selection in HR for the majority depends on trust and dislike how in other verticals in the organisations. In my analytical view, Human Resource is abundantly disregarded field by and large when contrasted with different business verticals however the right fit candidates are required for each business unit for better outcomes. Be that as it may, after the recession time frame of later half of first decade of the 20th century, the majority of the associations perceived the need of evidence based human resource management. To come up with better decision making in the field of HR, evidence based HRM driven by information and data should rehearse with analysis, making choices and critical thinking.

Chapter 9

GCED is a strategic area of UNESCO's Education Sector programme and builds on the work of Peace and Human Rights Education. It may prove to be a key area of focus for school education services around the world. India has been always a key stakeholder in implementing the SDGs in its policies. The education sector plays a pivotal role in realizing the SDG targets and GCED curriculum implementation plays are strategic role in realizing this target of achieving SDG in education. India has played an active role in making efforts to implement GCED in school education. This chapter focuses on GCED practices, traces its origin, its prospective arrival in the Indian education scenario and the state of affairs at present in terms of its implementation in prominent states around the country. Therefore, the chapter describes GCED implementation in Indian school system and its contribution to making the school education system a delightful and sustainable practice.

Chapter 10

Over the last few years, the digital technologies have grown at a rapid pace and have become a part of the daily lives of billions of people across the world. The advancements in the field of telecommunications and the availability of devices with enhanced capabilities have a major role to play in this growth. Numerous studies have also addressed and explained about this emerging trend in the entertainment and media industry in many parts of the world. Over-the-top services, commonly known as OTT, are delivered directly through a stable internet connection. Consumers are spending more time on internet than ever before. The internet has become an essential part of their lives, and so is the usage of OTT. There has been a shift in the habits of consumers, particularly young consumers, between the age group of 16-34 years. For OTT players to continue and succeed further, a combination of ad based models and subscription based models seem viable. Here the authors have tried to understand the major factors responsible to adopt OTT services among Indian consumers.

Chapter 11

Customers prefer a bank that can be easily accessed from the point of view of the location, staff coordination, service delivery, etc. In this context, the present study tries out the factors stimulating ease of access to banks by customers. The study also focuses to assess the relationship of Personal Interest of Staff, Coordinated Approach of Staff, and Customer Support Approach with prompt service delivery to customers. Data has been collected through scheduled questionnaires from SBI customers. The study is confined to the western part of Odisha, India. Exploratory factor analysis, multiple linear regression, and canonical correlation have been applied for data analysis. It is found that Service Quality, Staff Behaviour, and gender have a significant impact on the ease of access to the bank. It is also revealed that the Personal Interest of Staff and Coordinated Approach of Staff have a significant relationship with Prompt Service to Customers. The findings of this research work will be helpful to banks to revamp their strategy for long-term endurance.

Chapter 12

Online crowdsourcing is a concept which is gaining momentum among business organizations for various reasons. It is a modern age digital marketing tool. It may be considered as a tool for gathering information, views, opinions, work, assigned task, ideas, solution to problems generally from crowd (a group of people) via the Internet. This has enabled organizations save resources such as time and money by utilizing different skills and expertise of people globally. Realizing the numerous benefits that crowdsourcing offers to organizations, they are adopting online crowdsourcing models not only to engage customers for co-creation, co-engagement, and collaboration but also for brand building and creating customer satisfaction. Organizations in a crowdsourcing model throws a contest, task, or a problem in hand to the crowd. The interest lies in understanding what motivates crowd to participate in such contests which offers them delight, perceived value and satisfaction.

Chapter 13

FinTech refers to the introduction of technology into the financial sector as a result of the development of digital technology. FinTech uses technology-savvy financial innovations to create business models that are advanced, operations, or new products/services. This has led to the development of new types of services, improved financial markets and better financial institutions. India is moving towards a powerful environment that provides a platform for FinTech startups to become billion-dollar unicorns. FinTech in India has several goals, from opening new divisions to exploring overseas markets. India's economy, typically money-driven, has seen tremendous growth in FinTech by capitalizing on the opportunities presented as a result of growth in e-commerce and greater smartphone penetration rates. Hence, based on a thorough literature review by using exploratory research method, this chapter seeks to study the growth and evolution of FinTech in India, with special reference to the Covid-19 pandemic.

Chapter 14

This chapter discusses theories that explain how microfinance interacts with service quality and customer delight globally. It also identifies moderating elements between satisfaction and service quality. Microfinance provides services to low-income, self-employed, and financially disadvantaged people who don't have access to formal banking. The concept of "service" is the provision of an intangible act or performance by one party to another, without ownership. Microfinance services are categorized into financial and non-financial services. And the service quality parameters are reliability, tangibility, responsiveness, assurance, and empathy. Customer delight means customers are happy with a product or service if it exceeds their expectations. Moreover, institutional affiliations (religious or secular), adaptability of new technologies, and geographical (regional) concerns moderate the relationship between service quality and customer satisfaction level.

Chapter 15

Main aim of bibliometric study of the aforesaid area is to look at the trends and patterns that have been observed in the literature on healthcare service quality. R Software is used for analysis. Performance analysis and science mapping programs of the software have been used for the study. Using the Scopus database, the publication pattern from 1996 to 2022 was examined. 2117 articles in the subject area were found, retrieved, and used in the study. The most successful and well-known authors were recognised. Analysis of co-authorship and co-occurrence was done. The leading nations publishing of papers relating to healthcare service quality, according to the results of co-authorship and co-occurrence have been analysed. The bibilometric study was carried out to find trends in the healthcare sector's service quality. The study's findings revealed a publication tendency that was perhaps growing and would continue to grow.

Chapter 16

The world of retail is very dynamic and interesting. The evolution of retail as an industry withholds immense richness in terms of research literature. This study has adopted a review research design to study the retailing literature of last two decades. Bibliometric database, Scopus was used to extract the list of studies. The central constructs considered for the study are service quality (SQ), customer satisfaction (CS) and customer delight (CD). A systematic literature review approach was undertaken along with PRISMA framework. Multiple rounds of screening were done to finalize a total of 92 documents for the review. To identify, evaluate and study various themes and variables related to the central constructs, several research tools were used like network analysis, temporal analysis, citation analysis and mind maps. The findings of the study would help both retail researchers and practitioners to understand consumer behavior concerning retail sector and devise the future course of action to develop higher levels of customer loyalty and retention.

Chapter 17

The most important objective of service quality is the retention of the customer to provide repeatability of services through customer satisfaction. Since customer perceptions and expectations affect the service quality, so this study helps to understand and identify the service quality gaps in services provided by cab aggregators to customers in India using SERVQUAL Gap Analysis between perception and expectation. The main objective of this research paper is to understand, study and compare the customer perception and expectations from customers using services of the cab aggregators within India to identify the areas of service quality gaps. Primary Data was collected from 495 respondents from various cities across different demographic variables such as gender, age, income, education and occupation. The responses were taken using Google Forms, which is consolidated in an excel sheet. it is suggested to also create a service quality framework for cab aggregators on the basis of service quality gaps identified in the current study.

Chapter 18

Financial product marketing requires the use of well-researched techniques to achieve investor satisfaction. The intention of this study is to examine elements that affect investor satisfaction while keeping the aforementioned debate as its central concept. Investor is the term used for customer of financial products. The factors that contribute most to it have been discovered to be safety, profitability, and liquidity. It was discovered after looking at a variety of schools of thought and literatures that there has been little research on investor satisfaction and the work aims to examine the impact of financial products' liquidity, profitability, and safety (specifically, the SLP Approach) on investors' satisfaction. Data is analysed using Tukey's test, Principal Component Analysis, Correlation, Regression, and ANOVA. This study contributes that investor satisfaction is a valuable intangible asset that is primarily produced by the financial instrument's safety, security, and liquidity features using the SLP technique.

Sarmistha Sarma
Institute of Innovation in Technology and Management, India

Neha Gupta
IBCS, SOA University (Deemed), India

Chapter 1
A Conceptual Framework for E–Service Quality:
Special Reference to Switching Intention in Online Trading

Sudeshna Dutta

Biju Patnaik Institute of Information Technology and Management Studies, India

Dhananjay Beura

 https://orcid.org/0000-0001-6370-2139

Biju Patnaik Institute of Information Technology and Management Studies, India

ABSTRACT

Rising income is driving the demand for online trading services across all income brackets. After the demand of online trading, many brokers have entered the cutthroat competition, high customer expectation, and dynamic technological changes have forced brokers to thrive on service quality. Online brokerage service as opted as an appropriate research framework for two main reasons. First, online brokerage is a service-intensive, fast-growing industry that is well suited for current research purposes. Second, there are few empirical studies measuring quality of service aspects and customer satisfaction and switching intention in the context of online securities. A relevant conceptual framework was outlined from extant literature which reveals an association between overall e-service quality, customer satisfaction and switching intension. Key dimensions were identified in the research which will add to the existing body of literature of service marketing. The finding of the research adds more depth in the body of literature of e-service quality in the online brokerage sector.

DOI: 10.4018/978-1-6684-5853-2.ch001

INTRODUCTION

The Indian financial market is showing the world its exemplary growth story for the last few decades. It has been one of the most remunerative markets to investor. Indian financial market is not only limited to domestic investors but for also for foreign investors as well, in the form of FPI (Foreign Portfolio Investors) and FII (Foreign Institutional Investors).

It is known that during the introductory days, the transaction of sharing trading was concluded in physical form. The entire mechanism was time consuming, boisterous, and physically taxing. On to top of the mentioned complications, there were abundant chances in the physical mode of trading for malpractices and fraudulence. To overcome this kind of obstacles and for appropriate utilisation of time and fund, online trading/ internet trading first initiated in India around 2000. The National Stock Exchange of India was first of its kind to start the internet trading/ online trading in India. Data revealed by NSE (National stock exchange) states that nearly 2.3 million online traders are registered by SEBI (Security exchange board of India). The SEBI (Security exchange board of India) commissioned on Internet -Based Securities Trading and Services as approved the use of internet as an order routing system (ORS) for registered stockbrokers to execute trades on behalf of clients.

Steadily online trading gained momentum and with the benefits of convenience, transparency, ease of doing business and time saving for end users.

Stockbrokers are essentially institutions/ individuals who complete transactions mainly the buying and selling of stocks on behalf of their clients. Thus, it can be concluded that Brokers are trading members who execute the fundamental functions in the Indian stock market. In return for this, they charge a brokerage commission. Stockbrokers also endeavour services such as margin trading facilities. The fee-based financial advisory services offered by equity brokers are clearly of great value to existing investors, businesses, the banking sector, and financial institutions. Its purpose is to inform investors of the relative potential for a particular income investment to be hit or lost compared to various other rated assets or securities.

Further. stockbrokers can be parted in three different ways. First are the Full-service brokers are suitable for clients who need advice in the form of an account manager appointed by the full-service broker. Account managers accompany new investors at every stage of their financial journey. Such services require a personal relationship with the broker. Those who need call and trade services or who feel they need to go to a broker's branch / office. Generally full-service brokers have offices in most of the cities in the country. Full-service brokers offer a wide range of financial services, including Call n trading facilities, margin trading, research reports and trading platforms with technical indicators. Therefore, it is suitable for investors who want to invest in various financial products and are looking for better services. However, expertise and extensive experience in this area can be considered beneficial to the client. Traditionally, stockbrokers deal stocks directly or otherwise over the phone. In recent years, the number of traders in the stock market has increased significantly, and problems such as location restrictions, telephone line congestion, and communication shortages are increasing at securities brokerage offices. Further information technology has helped stockbrokers resolve state. For the year 2022, the maximum performing full time brokers according to their active clients include ICICI Direct, Sharekhan, HDFC Securities, Sharekhan, Angel One and Axis Bank.

Second categories are Discount stockbrokers, who are largely are online brokers specifically expert only in stock and commodity trading services. However, discount stockbrokers do not offer add-ons assistances like advisory and research-based services. They also do not have branch support and neither deal with PMS (Portfolio Management Services) and wealth management services for the clients. For the year 2022, the top performing discount brokers according to their active clients include Upstox, 5 paisa, Zerodha.

The last and third category are Robo Advisors. Robo-advisers are computerized digital platforms that offer financial advice to clients by using algorithms and require very limited human regulation. The mechanism is simple, that is, before investing the client has to provide all necessary information regarding them and accordingly the Robo Advisors guide the client. This category is even cheaper that Discount brokers, however they also offer limited services to clients. They mainly transact in Mutual Funds.

BACKGROUND

Rising income is driving the demand for online trading services across all income brackets. After the mounting demand of online trading, many brokers have entered the Cutthroat competition, high customer expectation, and dynamic technological changes have forced brokers to thrive on service quality. Aforementioned, the stock trading system in in India works according to the guideline issued by SEBI (Security Exchange board of India). SEBI (Security Exchange board of India) plays a vital role in terms of investors protection, Rules and regulation regarding trading mechanism. While most of the services by brokers are not much different from each other, as they are governed by SEBI, the only scope of success is from providing enhanced service quality.

The service quality has gained significance in the last few decades as a momentaneous of its distinctive characteristics of immateriality, inseparability, variability, and perishability. Unlike products, measuring service quality is very intricate because of its structures. These unique characteristics make the procedure of service purchase and delivery very complex for both customers and brokers. According to different geography, ethnic group, strategy to emphasis and to put forward a particular dimension of service becomes tricky. Researchers are working hard to evaluate and understand service quality more precisely as it is a prime gateway for customer satisfaction. Exceptional service quality is not a discretional competitive approach nowadays, but it is prerequisite for corporate profitability and growth.

All the brokers who are trading in stocks, commodity, and forex etc, are under the vigilance of SEBI. The maximum ceiling of brokerages, operations, margin money and timelines are all governed by the central body. Thus, most of the services offered by the are more or less similar in nature, like relationship management, portfolio management services and wealth management etcetera. Recognizing and continuous improvement of service quality is the only way to differentiate one brokers from another.

The association between service quality and customer satisfaction has been submitted to intense investigation by foremost service quality researchers (Bitner and Hubbert, 1994; Boulton and Drew, 1994). Understanding the significance of service quality on customer satisfaction and corporate profitability, many researchers have developed instruments to measure the same. SERVQUAL developed by Parasuraman et al. (1985) is the pioneer and remains the most widely used instrument to date. Although the skeleton for measuring service quality dimensions may be same, but with distinctive features of online services, it is the appropriate time to understand and develop service quality dimensions which are specifically suitable for online service. Online services dependency is hugely on features like browsers, encryption, database etc. Moreover, online service related to finance services has huge impact of security and privacy

Technological innovations are significant driver for increasing participations of investors in equity market. The online trading system allows traders to enter orders directly into the system via electronic media immediately and directly. Therefore, service quality dimensions for online trading plays a significant role in ensuring loyalty, trust and retention of customer. Emerging research stresses that customer satisfaction of product and service quality is not the only factor for customer satisfaction, switching barriers also plays a significant role. The quality of service provided by company will greatly influence the investor's behaviour and enhances the value and volume of trade. There are several tools like SERVQUAL, E SERVQUAL, WEBQUAL, SITEQUAL etc. are available to measure the service quality of an online trading platform. Online firm operate in an environment consisting of web-based technologies, network systems and digital information. The purpose of the study is to evaluate the concepts developed by various researchers about expected and perceived service quality of individual share traders to assess the service quality gap in an online trading platform. This research aims to explore the essence of e-SERVQUAL model applied for online trading customer satisfaction leading to customer retention& loyalty. This study attempts to answer a significant question: What are the factors which influence the customer satisfaction in an online trading platform or e brokerage environment.

Although the skeleton for measuring service quality dimensions may be same, but with distinctive features of online services, it is the appropriate time to understand and develop service quality dimensions which are specifically suitable for online service. Online services dependency is hugely on features like browsers, encryption, database etc. Moreover, online service related to finance services has huge impact of security and privacy. Therefore, with passage of time it become important to understand and explore service quality dimensions related to online services. Specially it was found to the best of knowledge that few research have been done in case of online broking system.

We chose an online brokerage service as our research framework for two main reasons. First, online brokerage is a service-intensive, fast-growing industry that is well suited for current research purposes. Second, there are few empirical studies measuring quality of service aspects and customer satisfaction in the context of online securities. Thus, this provides ample opportunity for further empirical research to be conducted in this area. The major contribution of this research is in the area of understanding the factors of service quality pertaining to the online trading platform.

Data from the Securities and Exchange Board of India (Sebi) shows that between April 2020 and January, the number of new dematerialized or demat accounts added reached an all-time high of 10.7 million. This signifies an increase of more than double the 4.7 million new accounts opened in FY20. In FY19 and FY18, correspondingly, there were additional about 4 million new accounts.

Service expectations of online trading platform are different from different markets. This research extended the understanding of service quality due

The research is of academic as well as practical business significance. It will add and enrich the works of existing literature in service quality, particularly in an Indian online broking context. For brokers, this study will help them to understand the priorities in the dimensions of service quality. It will guide them to strategies on customer segmentation, strong customer relationship, which will certainly lead to increased profitability and better brand value.

LITERATURE REVIEW

Extensive research on traditional SQ has been conducted during the past 20 years in different industries to measure the service quality applying the SERVQUAL model. (Parasuraman & Zeithaml 2002 for a review). In this section, we briefly overview the relevant aspects of traditional SQ and describe the reasons why such research needs to be carried out in the stock brokerage firms in India. One of the main research instruments for measuring quality in service industries is the SERVQUAL model, developed by Parasuraman and Zeithaml (1985; 1988), Markovic and Raspor (2010). The model contains five specific dimensions, under which there are 22 items as indicators for assessing customer expectations and perceptions regarding the service quality. The SERVQUAL model is based on five service quality dimensions, namely Tangibles (Appearance of physical facilities, equipment, personnel, and written materials), Reliability (ability to perform the promised service dependably and accurately), Responsiveness (willingness to help customers and provide prompt service), Assurance (employees' knowledge and courtesy and their ability to inspire trust and confidence) and Empathy (caring, individualized attention given to customers). Customers determine the perceived value of service based on their experience with the service delivered. Ghobadian, Speller and Jones (1994) stated that customers' expectations, service delivery process and service outcome have an impact on perceived service quality (Markovic & Raspor, 2010). During the last few years, a variety of service quality studies have been conducted (Ladhari, 2008). Among them, service quality was measured in: accounting and audit firms (Ismail, 2006). Higher education (Russell, 2005; Marković, 2006), public-transport (Sánchez-Pérez et al., 2007), etc. Despite its wide usage, the model has been criticized by a number of academicians (Carman, 1990; Babakus & Boller, 1992; Teas, 1994). However, there is a general agreement that SERVQUAL items are reliable predictors of overall service quality (Khan, 2003) (Markovic & Raspor, 2010). Customer's favorable and unfavorable experiences, as well as their positive and negative emotions play a big impact on perceived service quality.

Electronic service quality (e-service quality) has been in the focus of researchers for the past decade or so. However, it is generally acknowledged that research is still at a relatively early stage. A noticeable effort to develop a measurement instrument is E-S-QUAL, which has been proposed by Parasuraman et al. (2005). This team of researchers also developed SERVQUAL (Parasuraman et al., 1988), an instrument which played a pivotal role in measuring conventional service quality (Ladhari, 2009).

In order to examine the quality of electronic services with respect to internet banking several aspects have been considered in research during the past (Slu & Mou, 2003). The very proper primary description of web servqual, or e-ServQual, was presented by Zeithaml, Parasuraman, and Malhotra (2000). Researchers defined e-SQ as "the degree to which a web page supports efficient and effective goods & service shopping, purchase, and delivery." Liu and Arnett (2000) conducted a study of Fortune 1000 webmasters to determine the characteristics that influence web site performance with customers. The second most significant component, according to them, is e-service quality, which includes prompt responses along with assurance and empathy including follow-up. Many researchers have created techniques to assess the quality of eservices. To explore how customers rate quality of electronic service, Zeithaml, Parasuraman, and Malhotra (2000) created the measure of electronic service quality termed eSERVQUAL. They selected four categories to gauge customers' opinions of service quality supplied by online retailers: efficiency, dependability, fulfilment, and privacy.

WEBQUAL is a twelve-dimensional scale developed by Lociacono, Watson, and Goodhue (2000). With respect to notions derived from both the quality of service and retailing article, Wolfinbarger and Gilly (2002) have established the comQ measurement scale, which has four components: Web site design, dependability, privacy or can be known as security, and service of customer (cited by Slu & Mou, 2003).

Website Design: In business to consumer electronic commerce, satisfaction depicts to the comprehensive contentment with an experience through online consumption, having a spectrum from access to website data to navigation and perception of a website that which is well designed (Cyr, Kindra, and

Dash, 2008; Anderson & Srinivasan, 2003). The term "fulfilment" refers to the correctness of service claims, having the products in stock, and product delivery on schedule. The technical functionality of the site, specifically the degree to which it is available and performing effectively, is linked to reliability. The guarantee that online behavioural data is not disclosed and protected is part of the privacy component. The capacity of e-tailers to offer proper information to consumers when an issue arises, provide systems for managing refunds, as well as provide online warranties is measured by responsiveness. (Zethaml et al., 2002).

Reliability: The capacity of a service provider to complete the stated duties consistently and precisely is referred to as the servqual scale. Undoubtedly, one of most crucial consideration for clients when choosing between brokerage firms is services reliability. Due to the high level of unpredictability in the financial markets, a reputable broker not only works as a resource for asset allocation throughout the procedure of making a decision by the customer, on the other hand one who executes the plan by executing transactions on the client's behalf. One of the biggest worries that a consumer has in the brokerage sector is if the brokerage firm maintains proper accounting. Proper recordkeeping and timely distribution of transaction notifications do, in fact, indicate a company's degree of customer service reliability.

Responsiveness: In trading stocks, hardly a firm could guarantee customer profits. Yet, in the continuous changing stock market, rapid response to client order requests increases the prospect of an enhanced performance outcome. Servicing responsiveness for a major brokerage firm's customer necessitates connectivity to the management of the firm and also the brokers engaged. Furthermore, a timely brokerage business most likely has an excellent assistance by the back-office team. Brokerage services are known for having a high level of interaction (Parasuraman, Zeithaml, & Berry 1985).

Privacy: Referencing security as a person's confidence in security kept with their own financial information, as well as their conviction of nonavailability or not utilised by unauthorised persons (Flavian et al. 2006). The term "privacy" relates about an individual's perceptions of the dangers and possible negative repercussions of disclosing personal information over the internet (Baruh et al., 2017). The same is type of finding is found in the research conducted by Bulgurcu et al. (2010). Amidst current discussion about whether there is a distinction between privacy and security (Gogus and Saygin, 2019; Braber, 2016; Dinev et al., 2011). Belanger et al. (2002) certify that highlighting security of the website to customers is an important attribute, rather than the statements of privacy on the website. Researchers suggest that security as well as privacy need to be considered separately. See Table 1 for a summary of literature.

Table 1. Summary of literature

Sr No	Instrument	Developed by	Dimensions
1.	WEBQUAL	Loiacono et al. (2000)	Information fit to task, interaction, Trust, Response time, Design, Intuitiveness, Visual appeal, innovativeness, Flow, Integrated communication, business processes and substitutability
2.	E.SQ	Zeithaml et al (2000)	Reliability, Responsiveness, Access, Flexibility, Ease of navigation, Efficiency, Assurance, Security, price knowledge, Site aesthetics and personalization
3.	SITEQUAL	Yoo and Donthu (2001)	Ease of use. Processing speed, Aesthetic Design and interactive responsiveness
4.	E-SQUAL	Zeithaml et al (2002)	Tangibility, Reliability, Responsiveness, integration of communication, Assurance, Quality of information, Empathy
5.	E-S-Qual &RecSQual	Parasuraman et al. (2005)	Efficiency, System Availability, Fulfilment, Privacy & Responsiveness, Compensation, Contact

E-RecS-QUAL is used by Zeithaml et al. (2002) as an e-service quality's recovery scale. It is used to evaluate the e-service quality when there is a problem in providing service to the clients. E-service quality has many dimensions additional explanations about them are mentioned below. Scales for questioning the service problems that consumers encounter and their perceptions regarding the solution of these problems (i.e. service recovery) did not exist until Parasuraman et al.,2005 developed the E-RecS-QUAL. Yet, they called for future research because: "the E-RecS-QUAL Scale should be viewed as a preliminary scale because the small samples of customers with recovery-service experience at the sites used in later stages of scale testing did not permit a comprehensive psychometric assessment of that scale" (Parasuraman et al., 2005, p.229). One dimension customer recovery to the aforementioned four dimensions that is particularly salient when a service failure takes place. Customer recovery refers to the effective handling of problems by the online service company. It includes not only the availability of assistance through telephone or online representatives, but also correct and quick responses through the site when the customer has experienced any trouble (Parasuraman et al., 2005; Collier and Bienstock, 2006).

SITEQUAL focuses on consumers' perceptions of quality. In this study, we are interested in developing a way to measure the perceived quality of an Internet shopping site (referred to as SITEQUAL hereafter), that is, the quality of an Internet shopping site as perceived by consumers. There has been little research to develop a psychometrically sound measure of Internet shopping sites. In developing SITEQUAL, we emphasize three aspects of Internet shopping sites' perceived quality. First, consumers are the ultimate judges of the quality of a site. It is their perception that we are interested in capturing, so we do not force a definition of quality on the consumers. Second, Internet site quality is described in the common consumer's vernacular rather than in formal academic language or the technical vocabulary of web designers (e.g., information content or stickiness). Third, Internet sites without shopping features (such as pure promotional or informative sites) may develop a different definition of quality and are not included in the SITEQUAL domain. A nine-item survey instrument used to assess e-commerce web site quality. The instrument includes four dimensions: aesthetic design, ease of use, processing speed, and security.

Online customers are end-users of both information and networked systems (DeLone and McLean, 1992; Stockdale and Standing, 2002). With the intent of measuring end-users' satisfaction with information systems, Doll and Torkzadeh (1988) devised a 12-item scale that assesses ðve quality dimensions that have been determined to inñuence end-user satisfaction. The ðve dimensions are content, accuracy, format, ease of use, and timeliness. The reliability and validity of this scale have been veriðed in several studies (Doll et al., 1994; Hendrickson and Collins, 1996). (Yang and Fang, 2004)

Service Quality Dimensions and Customer Satisfaction:

Researchers have paid much attention to the close relationship between service quality and customer satisfaction (e.g. Bitner et al., 1990; Parasuraman et al., 1988). Oliver (1993) suggests that service quality is a more speciðc judgment, which can lead to a broad evaluation, customer satisfaction. The question is: how exactly will particular service quality dimensions inñuence customer satisfaction formation? Johnston (1995) has found that the causes of dissatisfaction and satisfaction are not necessarily the same. Some service quality attributes may not be critical for customer satisfaction but can signiðcantly lead to dissatisfaction when they are performed poorly. Drawing upon Herzberg et al.'s (1995) research on work motivation, Johnston (1997) has further classiðed all dimensions into enhancing (satisðers), hygiene (dissatisðers), and dual factors. Enhancing factors are those which will lead to customer satisfaction if they are delivered properly but will not necessarily cause dissatisfaction if absent. In contrast, hygiene factors are those which will lead to customer dissatisfaction if they fail to deliver, but will not result in satisfaction if present. Dual factors are those that will have an impact on both satisfaction and dissatisfaction. Johnston (1995) identiðed attentiveness, responsiveness, care, and friendliness as the main source of satisfaction in banking services, and integrity, reliability, responsiveness, availability, and functionality as the main source of dissatisfaction.

Empirical findings of previous studies provided insights about the critical dimensions of service quality, which could be categorized under two groups as follows: Functional quality dimensions: This included five SERVQUAL (Parasuraman, Zeithaml and Berry, 1988) dimensions, namely, (reliability, responsiveness, assurance, empathy, and tangibles). Further, few items related to 'convenience' and 'complaint handling' were also incorporated (Negi, 2009). Technical quality dimensions: In the context of cellular mobile communication, this dimension is related to customer perceived network quality. The measures related to this dimension were derived from literature and the subsequent feedback gained during the exploratory interviews. These included items relating to network coverage (on highways, inside buildings, and basement), voice clarity, call drop, and network congestion.

In the context of online securities brokerage services, Yang and Fang (2004) undertake a study to examine the reviews of brokerage firms by adopting the methodology of content analysis. Results of this exploratory research showed that there are similarities in the primary service quality dimensions between online customer satisfaction and traditional services however, the key factors leading to online brokerage service dissatisfaction is linked to information systems quality.

Service Quality and Traditional and Internet Settings

Service quality in traditional service contexts has been the focus of research since the 1980s. The roots of service quality occur in expectancy disconfirmation theory (Collier & Bienstock, 2006). Many studies adopted this theory as the base for measuring service quality. This concept is usually understood as a measure of how well the level of the delivered services matches customer's expectations (Santos, 2003). As an example, the definition of Gronroos (1984) outlines perceived service quality, as "the outcome of an evaluation process, where the consumer compares his expectations with the service, he perceives he has received". Parasuraman et al. (1985) stated that service quality is the degree and direction of discordance between perceptions and expectations of customers, in terms of different but relevant dimensions of service quality that can affect their behavior in the future.

Colby and Parasuraman (2003) defined e-services as "all services delivered via an electronic medium (usually the internet) and comprising transactions initiated and largely controlled by the customer". E-services differ from traditional services, in a sense that customers interact with the organization usually through a web site, relying on sight and sound, in comparison to traditional services, where they use all their senses (Rowley, 2006). The way that people apprehend service quality in internet-based settings differs from service quality in traditional settings, because they tend to have different beliefs about technology, a fact that makes them accept and use technologies in a different manner (Parasuraman et al., 2005). In recent years, the well acknowledged relationship between service quality and business performance has also increased interest in e-service quality (Rowley, 2006). E-service quality has been defined by Zeithaml (2002) as "the extent to which a Web site facilitates the efficient and effective shopping, purchasing and delivery".

E-S-QUAL, which was developed by Parasuraman et al. (2005) and forms the basis of the present study, provides a more comprehensive approach, since it supports the measurement of both pre- and post-e-service quality aspects. Furthermore, E-S-QUAL dimensions were developed by processing data provided by qualified respondents, who had effectual experience on internet shopping. Therefore, when compared to other studies that used convenience samples of students, E-S-QUAL provides more representative information in terms of e-service quality (Kim et al., 2006). E-S-QUAL includes the following four dimensions:

1. **Efficiency:** The ease and speed of accessing and using the site. Efficiency is considered very important in e-commerce, since convenience and saving of time are generally considered as the main reasons for shopping online (Ranganathan and Ganapathy, 2002).
2. **Fulfillment:** The extent to which the site's promises about order delivery and item availability are fulfilled. Fulfillment is one of the most vital factors for the judgment of the quality of an online shop, since keeping service promises and accurate order fulfillment are elements of service quality that lead to customer satisfaction or dissatisfaction (Yang and Fang, 2004).
3. **System availability:** The correct technical functioning of the site. When consumers purchase from an online shop or they are just surfing, function problems like non-working buttons or missing links, disappoint customers and can lead to exiting. As a result, the retailer loses the opportunity to enhance customer loyalty (Wachter, 2002).
4. **Privacy:** The degree to which the site is safe and protects customer information. Many people are still not willing to purchase products from the internet because of the risk that is related to maltreat of personal information. Online retailers are becoming more acquainted of the importance of providing consumer privacy (Ranganathan & Ganapathy, 2002). Privacy has been shown to have a strong effect on intention to purchase (Loiacono et al., 2002), customer satisfaction (Szymanski & Hise, 2000) and overall site quality (Yoo & Donthu, 2001).

Parasuraman et al. (2005) also developed a complementary scale, called E-RecS-QUAL, aiming to capture the effects of problems encountered during an online transaction on customers' perception of e-service quality. The dimensions of E-RecS-QUAL are responsiveness, compensation and contact. This scale is only applied in cases of customers that have questions or encounter problems and was not included in the research presented in this study

Switching Intention

Literature on customer switching (or churn) has investigated its potential antecedents (e.g., Dick & Basu, 1994; Bolton et al., 2004), where Keaveney (1995) was the first to introduce the model of customer switching behaviour, containing eight main casual factors that are critical to switching behaviour, namely, pricing, inconvenience, core service failures, service encounter failures, employee responses to service failures, competitive issues, ethical problems and involuntary factors. Among these antecedents, pricing problem emerged as the most influential factor for switching, followed by service failures and denied services (Colgate &Hedge, 2001). Although, relationship quality is an important driver of switching intentions, but switching costs and attractiveness of switching are its significant determinants (Wieringa &Verhoef, 2007).

Switching behaviour also appears in economic theory, where economic scholars approach switching costs as a mean for keeping customers in relationships (Wieringa & Verhoef, 2007), regardless of their satisfaction with the provider (e.g., Jones et al., 2000; Lee et al., 2001; Burnham et al., 2003; Bansawl et al., 2004; White & Yanamandram, 2007). More particularly, procedural switching cost enhances calculative commitment, which subsequently increases repurchase intention and decreases undesirable emotions, negative word-of-mouth and ultimately, switching (Jones et al., 2007; Khan et al., 2010). This becomes essential because if customers were able to switch easily, operators would be less inclined to charge excessively high prices or supply poor quality of services (Xavier &Ypsilanti, 2008). Probing further, Burnham et al. (2003) asserted that switching costs generate passive loyalty, while switching barriers prompt relationship-improving investments (Yen, 2010). Moreover, switching barriers are not only positively affecting the customer retention but also performing an adjustment effect on core service quality and satisfaction on the one hand (Chen &Wang, 2009) and satisfaction and loyalty on the other (Ranaweera & Prabhu, 2003; Kim et al., 2006). Beside relational investments, service recovery and alternative attractiveness, switching costs is also one of the most important categories of switching barriers (Colgate et al., 2001).

Extant literature reveals that the nature and extent of switching behaviour in the banking sector has not been passably studied. A good deal of research work has been restricted to various relational factors, thus neglecting other side of switching behaviour (Bansawl et al., 2004; Yavas et al., 2004; Jones et al., 2007; Chen &Wang, 2009; Liang et al., 2009). While studies such as Keaveney (1995); Colgate and Hedge (2001); Burnham et al. (2003); Wieringa and Verhoef (2007); Matos et al. (2009); Khan et al. (2010); constrained themselves to one or the other aspect of switching. Within this wide range of researches, very little attention has been given to why and when exchange relationship ends, especially with reference to customer relationship in services (Halinen & Tahtinen, 2002; Akerlund, 2005). However, study conducted by Bansawl et al. (2005) is an exception, which empirically explored the applicability of push-pull-mooring (PPM) paradigms. Within this large paradigm, customer loyalty has been neglected, which is a basic component of switching behaviour. Further, they restricted their study to auto repair and hair styling services, findings of which cannot be generalised to the financial sector.

Keaveney (1995) defined switching intention as one's attitude toward replacing the current brand with another. Shen and Li (2010) pointed out that switching intention was the intention to betray or exit an existing relationship. It depends primarily on customers' decision to stop buying or receiving the primary services from a service provider. Chih et al. (2012) showed that initial (discrepancy between service failure expectation and service performance) and recovery (discrepancy between recovery expectation and recovery performance) disconfirmations could affect switching intentions through satisfaction. Kim et al. (2006) proposed four items of consumers' intention for email switching. They suggested that intention for email switching depended on consumers' decision to terminate or cancel their subscription to the primary service of a company and use the alternative service of another company. Shen and Li (2010) explored the antecedents to switching and their relationship with customer loyalty. They found a negative relation between switching intention and customer loyalty.

CONCEPTUAL FRAMEWORK

Conceptual framework basically lies down the foundation upon which the research chapter will be directed forward. It is a schema which represents the characteristics of variables, and their relationship with each other. From the extant literature conceptual framework has been crafted according to the nature, scope, purpose of the research.

One of the most important features of service is that while delivering, service interaction between the service provider and the consumer becomes vital. The service delivery process itself is crucial, as it is part of service consumption as well. Before buying any products, it is easy to appraise them, as a buyer can touch, see and feel it. On the other hand, it is difficult to evaluate service before they are consumed. There are a few basic differences between manufactured products and services. Unlike products, services are intangible in nature. Thus, pricing becomes very difficult. There is a direct and significant impact on the service provider as services are inseparable in nature. (Parasuraman et al.,1985). SERVQUAL has been used widely throughout years to measure service quality in different industries. However, it is very much implied that in the context of changing time and dynamic market condition same measurement can't be applied every aspect. In case of online interface, the major challenge is the interaction are between customer and website interface. While the traditional model to measure service quality has always been customer and the service provider personnel. To bridge this gap researchers are working to measure service quality particularly for online interface. Several aspects have been considered in the previous years to investigate the dimensions of service quality for online purchase (Slu & Mou 2003).

It was found from extensive literature review that there many attributes which together form overall e-service quality. In early research by Dabholkar (1996) regarding e- service quality, and referred to five dimensions of overall e- service quality that is ease of use, speed of delivery, reliability, enjoyment and control. However out of the five dimensions ease of use, control and enjoyment are the attributes of over e-service quality. With passage of time many and fast-growing interface with customers many researchers continued to measure e- service quality. Few of the well-suited models are WebQual established by Barnes and Vidgen (2002) and Loiacono et al. (2002), eTailQ perceived by Wolfinbarger and Gilly (2003), E-S-Qual conceived by Parasuraman et al. (2005), and the newest classified model of e-service quality proposed by Blut (2016), and a refined version of the same model by Paulo Rita et al. (2019).Since the present research is about online trading where customers investment are at stake, most appropriate models have been considered based on factual investigation.

Website Design

Website design is one of the most significant dimensions in overall e- service quality and has been conferred by many researchers. Wolfinbarger and Gilly (2003), Parasuraman et al., (2005), Blut (2015) and Paulo Rita et al. (2019). A well organised website should comprise three main content groups: information-oriented, transaction-oriented, and customer-oriented (Cox & Koelzer, 2004). Online customers evaluate their practice of using a website to judge an online store's overall service quality. Therefore, it is very much evident that an efficient website design should accentuate us- ability by providing the aesthetics of the design, reñecting a strong and associative image to the brand, and being able to attract customers to visit it (Díaz & Koutra, 2013). According to Blut (2015), website design raises to all fundamentals of the customer experience related to the website, including information quality, web- site aesthetics, purchase process, website convenience, product selection, price offerings, website personalization, and system availability.

Security and Privacy

According to Holloway and Beatty (2008) it was found that online customers are insecure about their information like address and phone might be shared after their transaction. This particular dimension has a very prominent role to play in terms of online trading. Security/privacy refers to the security of credit card payments and privacy of shared information (Blut, 2016) The website must assurance and security to upsurge the website credibility and service quality. Schmidt et al. (2008) showed that an effective website must feature privacy and security (Fortes & Rita, 2016). The study by Rita et al. (2019) confers that security and privacy has a positive impact on overall e- service quality.

Fulfillment

Preceding literature has established an important relationship between e-service quality and customer satisfaction (Blut et al., 2015; Gounaris et al., 2010; Kitapci et al., 2014; Udo et al., 2010). Gounaris et al. (2010) argue that e-service quality has a positive effect on satisfaction. It can be referred as which refers to the online store' ability to ensure that customers receive what they thought they ordered. (Blut 2016). This dimension states that customers have already positioned their order, and they want to experience what they expect to receive. Hence, attributes related to accuracy of order fulfilment, order timing, and the condition of delivered products are of utmost importance. (Bauer, Falk, and Hammerschmidt, 2006). The recent study by Rita et al. (2019) confirms that in order of ranking fulfilment ranks number one on having an impact on overall e- service quality. Fulfilment essentially comprises of timeliness of delivery, order accuracy and delivery conditions.

Traditional Service Quality

Although with the passage of time the customer expectation from the service providers is changing, but from the study of extensive literature it was found that reliability and responsiveness are the attributes which stand strong irrespective of online and offline usage. As per the need of the hour, very significant model was established by Zeithaml, Parasuraman, and Malhotra (2000) created the measure of electronic service quality termed Servqual. To understand customers opinion of service quality for online retailers four groups were created: Reliability, Responsiveness, Access, Flexibility, Ease of navigation, Efficiency, Assurance, Security, Price Knowledge, Site aesthetics and Personalization. According to Loiacono et al. (2002) in their model of Webqual revealed that response time is an important attribute that impacts service quality. Similarly, reliability and responsiveness came out as distinctive and significant attribute. Kaynama & Black (2000), Zeithaml et al. (2001); Zeithaml et al. (2002); Wolfinbarger and Gilly (2002); Yang & Jun (2002). While reliability essentially refers to the firms' ability to execute the service accurately and consistently, responsiveness refers to the willingness and readiness of the personnel. It involves timeliness of the service. Parasuraman et al., (1988)

Customer Satisfaction

From the 1980s precisely, the importance of customer satisfaction has been valued. Vast research are carried out to understand the different perspective of customer satisfaction. Imperative progress has been made in the theory and research on consumer satisfaction including Oliver (1980), Churchill and Surprenant (1982)

Oliver (1980) described customer satisfaction as the judgment that emerges out of comparing pre –purchase expectation with the post- purchase evaluation of a product or service experience.

"Satisfaction, conceptually, could be thought as a consequence of purchase and use that is the outcome of the customer's comparison of the advantages and prices concerned in obtaining any product or service experience in relevance with the expected results, whilst, in operational terms, satisfaction is analogous to the perspective whereas it can be accessed as the accumulated satisfaction experiences with the various attributes of the product. (Churchill & Surprenant, 1982, pp. 491-504)

In a study by Spreng & Singh (1993) confirms that higher the level of service quality implies higher customer satisfaction. Similarly, Pitt et al. (1995) found that service quality is a significant aspect to measure customer satisfaction. They further established that if service quality improves apparently customer satisfaction also increases. Similarly, a study was carried out to examine the relationship between different forms of service quality and customer satisfaction with conventional and Islamic banks (Awan et al., 2011).

With the passage of time and referring from the relevant literature it has been established that a noteworthy association between e-service quality and customer satisfaction Gounaris et al. (2010); Blut et al., 2015; Gounaris et al., 2010; Kitapci et al., 2014; Udo et al., 2010). Although wide and practical in character, the extant literature provides useful information for the current study, which focuses on overall e- service quality and their connections to customer satisfaction.

Switching Intention

According to Keaveney (1995), switching intention is the intention to switch from one brand to another. According to Shen and Li (2010), switching intention is the desire to end or betray a current relationship. It mainly depends on the decision made by clients to quit purchasing from or using a service provider's key services. According to Chih et al. (2012), initial disconfirmations (differences between expectations and actual service performance) and recovery disconfirmations (differences between expectations and actual recovery performance) can influence switching intentions through satisfaction. Four items were suggested by Kim et al. (2006) as consumers' intentions for switching from email. They argued that consumers' choice to stop using or cancel their membership to a business's main service and move to an alternative service determined their desire to switch to email providers. Figure 1 is a conception model of this.

Figure 1. Conceptual Model

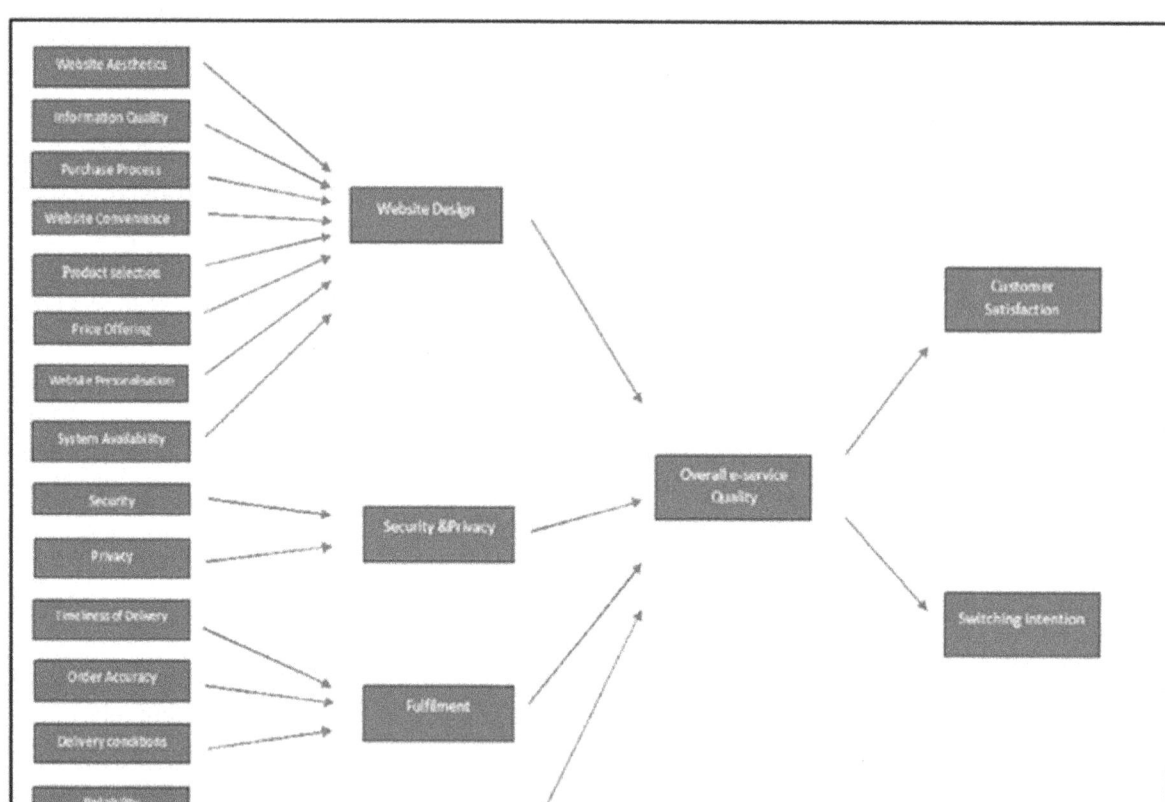

CONCLUSION

The online transaction scenario has changed drastically in the past few years. Earlier there were broking firms who operated physically. The online brokers have created distinctive need to study service quality. The online brokers are operated under the strict guidelines by Security Exchange Board of India. The basic product features by the online brokers are mostly predetermined by Security Exchange Board of India like limit to margin money, charges, cut off time for transactions etcetera. There is very diminutive difference between on; line brokers. Naturally, customers uncover hardly any difference in the products. As a result, the current problem in India with regards to online brokerage is to survive on matchless service delivery. This is the only alternative remaining under stiff competition and cutthroat survival strategy.

In this backdrop, it becomes important to study dimensions of service quality according to the customer's perspective. Firstly, if the dimensions are understood accurately and identified, then the job of the brokers becomes easy. Accordingly, brokers can improve service quality and manage the satisfaction level. Customer satisfaction can be described as to what extent customers perceive service quality. Thus, customer satisfaction will result in customer retention and ultimately profit maximization of a firm. Secondly, switching intention is a big barrier in case of online trading. For customers switch cost is very negligible and doesn't require huge investment. Thus, they can immediately decide on to switch between brokers if they are not satisfied.

Customer switching was a particularly critical issue in service sectors like insurance, banking, public services, healthcare, and mobile communication, according to Keaveney and Parthasarathy (2001). According to Ganesh et al. (2000), customers' post-purchase assessment of a product or service had a direct impact on their desire to switch or repurchase it. Despite the large number of surveys and studies on internet purchases, the majority of the current research remains concentrated on the fundamentals of online trade or shopping, and little study has addressed the needs contentment and customer satisfaction of securities traders online. Consequently, this study examined the most relevant and most appropriate attributes of overall service quality of online trading that investors in securities should consider and reconnoitre their relationship with customer satisfaction and switching intension.

Thirdly, discussed earlier in the study with reference to online brokerage, this field is a service-intensive, fast-growing industry that is well suited for current research purposes. Moreover, there are few empirical studies measuring quality of service aspects and customer satisfaction in the context of online securities

Using proven models from the fields of service marketing and new age technology, this study creates a comprehensive conceptual framework. In the process researchers came to many dimensions that has different relation among each other from different perspective, identify few of them from a vast ocean of literatures and how they affect both satisfied and dissatisfied customers. The results both theoretical and practical contributions to the body of knowledge about online service quality and the relevance to internet service providers.

Several measures that conceptualise the idea differently are provided in the literature on e-service quality. The current study improves upon these metrics and creates a brand-new metric that corrects for a number of issues. In accordance with the construct validation processes established by MacKenzie, Podsakoff, and Podsakoff, (2011); Blut (2016); Rita et al. (2019) the current study creates a conceptualization and assessment of the construct that is more thorough than previous scales. The present study issues to a recent

need to establish a new measurement containing all four dimension (sixteen sub dimensions) that characterise a great service quality of the online brokerage and switching intentions that increases the prediction capacity of the measurement by merging best performing items from previous scales. Previous research extracted from relevant literature continue to use WebQual, SERVQUAL, and E-S-QUAL assessment to assess the quality of e-services. Since, it strengthens the adoption of e-commerce, the present research united the model of overall e-service quality with customer satisfaction and furthermore with switching intention. Preceding studies only looked at the hierarchical model using WOM, repurchase intention, and satisfaction. To the best of knowledge, this is the first occurrence in which the overall model and switching intention have been integrated.

For online businesses such as securities brokerage services, the incorporation of traditional services and relevant e-service quality dimensions are critical. According to Zhilin Yang, Xiang Fang (2004) "well-trained and technically competent representatives are desirable in order to provide responsive and dependable services" It is also imperative to sustaining high levels of system reliability and responsiveness. For maintain the efficiency, the transaction process should be smooth and rapid, from logging onto the website, getting a quote, and taking every step to make a trade to receiving order confirmation. As the online trading system trading systems is so minute and suspectable to technical failures, internet speed etcetera., a human response must be on reserve to closely monitor and support virtual transactions as needed.

To the best of knowledge, the association between e- quality of service aspects, customer satisfaction and switching intention have not been explored yet. As a result, there is ample opportunity for additional empirical research in this area. The main contribution of this research is in the area of understanding the e-service quality factors related to the online trading platform with switching intensions as well. The findings of the research provide a layout for the measurement of dimensions of e-service quality in the context of online brokerage industry. Key dimensions were identified in the research which will add to the existing body of literature of service marketing. The finding of the research adds more depth in the body of literature of e-service quality in the online brokerage sector. Various researches are carried out to understand the impact of e- service quality on customer satisfaction. However, it entails more specification when it comes to the dynamic relationship in the context of switching intention, customer satisfaction and over e-service quality.

The service expectations of an online trading platform vary by market. This study widened our understanding of service quality as a result of market inequity and contextual factors. In reference to managerial implication cutthroat competition, and utmost requirement of differentiating one from another has compelled online brokers to rethink about measuring service quality from time to time. Hence online brokers require understanding dimensions of e-service quality, and how they can differentiate themselves from others. Moreover, the importance of research and evaluation of service quality with satisfaction and switching intentions cannot be neglected.

REFERENCES

Åkerlund, H. (2005). Fading customer relationships in professional services. *Managing Service Quality*.

Anderson, R. E., & Srinivasan, S. S. (2003). E-satisfaction and e-loyalty: A contingency framework. *Psychology and Marketing*, *20*(2), 123–138. doi:10.1002/mar.10063

Awan, H. M., Bukhari, K. S., & Iqbal, A. (2011). Service quality and customer satisfaction in the banking sector: A comparative study of conventional and Islamic banks in Pakistan. *Journal of Islamic Marketing*.

Babakus, E. and Boller, G.W. (1992) An Empirical Assessment of the SERVQUAL Scale. *Journal of Business Research, 24,* 253-268.

Bansawl, H. S., Irving, P. G., & Taylor, S. F. (2004). A three-component model of customer commitment to service providers. *Journal of the Academy of Marketing Science, 32*(3), 234–245. doi:10.1177/0092070304263332

Barnes, S., & Vidgen, R. (2002). An Integrative Approach to the Assessment of E-Commerce Quality. *Journal of Electronic Commerce Research, 3,* 114–127.

Baruh, L., Secinti, E., & Cemalcilar, Z. (2017). Online privacy concerns and privacy management: A meta-analytical review. *Journal of Communication, 67*(1), 26–53. doi:10.1111/jcom.12276

Bauer, H. H., Falk, T., & Hammerschmidt, M. (2006). eTransQual: A transaction process-based approach for capturing service quality in online shopping. *Journal of Business Research, 59*(7), 866–875. doi:10.1016/j.jbusres.2006.01.021

Belanger, F., Hiller, J. S., & Smith, W. J. (2002). Trustworthiness in electronic commerce: The role of privacy, security, and site attributes. *The Journal of Strategic Information Systems, 11*(3-4), 245–270. doi:10.1016/S0963-8687(02)00018-5

Bitner, M. J., Booms, B. H., & Tetreault, M. S. (1990). The service encounter: Diagnosing favorable and unfavorable incidents. *Journal of Marketing, 54*(1), 71–84. doi:10.1177/002224299005400105

Bitner, M.J., & Hubbert, A.R. (1994). *Encounter Satisfaction versus Overall Satisfaction versus Quality: The Customer's Voice.* Boulton and Drew.

Blut, M. (2016). E-service quality: Development of a hierarchical model. *Journal of Retailing, 92*(4), 500–517. doi:10.1016/j.jretai.2016.09.002

Blut, M., Chowdhry, N., Mittal, V., & Brock, C. (2015). E-service quality: A meta-analytic review. *Journal of Retailing, 91*(4), 679–700. doi:10.1016/j.jretai.2015.05.004

Bolton, R. N., Lemon, K. N., & Verhoef, P. C. (2004). The theoretical underpinnings of customer asset management: A framework and propositions for future research. *Journal of the Academy of Marketing Science, 32*(3), 271–292. doi:10.1177/0092070304263341

Braber, S. (2016). *Security and privacy perceptions of Millennials (18-24) and Non-Millennials (36-50) on Facebook* [Bachelor's thesis, University of Twente].

Bulgurcu, B., Cavusoglu, H., & Benbasat, I. (2010, January). Quality and fairness of an information security policy as antecedents of employees' security engagement in the workplace: An empirical investigation. In *2010 43rd Hawaii International Conference on System Sciences,* (pp. 1-7). IEEE.

Burnham, T. A., Frels, J. K., & Mahajan, V. (2003). Consumer switching costs: A typology, antecedents, and consequences. *Journal of the Academy of Marketing Science, 31*(2), 109–126. doi:10.1177/0092070302250897

Carman, J. M. (1990). Consumer perceptions of service quality: An assessment of the SERVQUAL dimensions. *Journal of Retailing, 66*(1), 33–55.

Caro, L., & Martinez, J. (2007). Measuring perceived service quality in urgent transport service. *Journal of Retailing and Consumer Services, 14*(1), 60–72. doi:10.1016/j.jretconser.2006.04.001

Chang, H. H., Wang, Y. H., & Yang, W. Y. (2009). The impact of e-service quality, customer satisfaction and loyalty on e-marketing: Moderating effect of perceived value. *Total Quality Management, 20*(4), 423–443. doi:10.1080/14783360902781923

Chih, W. H., Wu, C. H. J., & Li, H. J. (2012). The antecedents of consumer online buying impulsiveness on a travel website: Individual internal factor perspectives. *Journal of Travel & Tourism Marketing, 29*(5), 430–443. doi:10.1080/10548408.2012.691393

Churchill, G. A. Jr, & Surprenant, C. (1982). An investigation into the determinants of customer satisfaction. *JMR, Journal of Marketing Research, 19*(4), 491–504. doi:10.1177/002224378201900410

Colby, C. L., & Parasuraman, A. (2003). Technology still matters. *Marketing Management, 12*(4), 28–28.

Colgate, Mark & Hedge, Rachel. (2001). An investigation into the switching process in retail banking services. *International Journal of Bank Marketing, 19*, 201-212. doi:10.1108/02652320110400888

Collier, J., & Bienstock, C. (2006). Measuring Service Quality in E-Retailing. *Journal of Service Research, 8*, 260-275. . doi:10.1177/1094670505278867

Cox, B., & Koelzer, W. (2004). *Internet Marketing in Hospitality*. Pearson Prentice Hall.

Cyr, D., Kindra, G. S., & Dash, S. (2008). Web site design, trust, satisfaction and e-loyalty: The Indian experience. *Online Information Review, 32*(6), 773–790. doi:10.1108/14684520810923935

Dabholkar, P. A. (1996). Consumer evaluations of new technology-based self-service options: An investigation of alternative models of service quality. *International Journal of Research in Marketing, 13*(1), 29–51. doi:10.1016/0167-8116(95)00027-5

Díaz, E., & Koutra, C. (2013). Evaluation of the persuasive features of hotel chains websites: A latent class segmentation analysis. *International Journal of Hospitality Management, 34*, 338–347. doi:10.1016/j.ijhm.2012.11.009

Dick, A. S., & Basu, K. (1994). Customer loyalty: Toward an integrated conceptual framework. *Journal of the Academy of Marketing Science, 22*(2), 99–113. doi:10.1177/0092070394222001

Dinev, T., Xu, H., Smith, J. H., & Hart, P. (2013). Information privacy and correlates: An empirical attempt to bridge and distinguish privacy-related concepts. *European Journal of Information Systems, 22*(3), 295–316. doi:10.1057/ejis.2012.23

Flavián, C., Guinalíu, M., & Gurrea, R. (2006). The role played by perceived usability, satisfaction and consumer trust on website loyalty. *Information & Management, 43*(1), 1–14. doi:10.1016/j.im.2005.01.002

Fortes, N., & Rita, P. (2016). Privacy concerns and online purchasing behaviour: Towards an integrated model. *European Research on Management and Business Economics, 22*(3), 167–176. Advance online publication. doi:10.1016/j.iedeen.2016.04.002

Ganesh, J., Arnold, M. J., & Reynolds, K. E. (2000). Understanding the customer base of service providers: An examination of the differences between switchers and stayers. *Journal of Marketing, 64*(3), 65–87. doi:10.1509/jmkg.64.3.65.18028

Ghobadian, R., Speller, S., & Jones, W. (1994). Service Quality Concepts and Models. *International Journal of Quality Management, 11*, 43–66.

Gogus, A., & Saygın, Y. (2019). Privacy perception and information technology utilization of high school students. *Heliyon, 5*(5), e01614. doi:10.1016/j.heliyon.2019.e01614 PMID:31193323

Grönroos, C. (1984). A service quality model and its marketing implications. *European Journal of Marketing, 18*(4), 36–44. doi:10.1108/EUM0000000004784

Halinen, A., & Tähtinen, J. (2002). A process theory of relationship ending. *International Journal of Service Industry Management, 13*(2), 163–180. doi:10.1108/09564230210425359

Holloway, B. B., & Beatty, S. E. (2008). Satisfiers and dissatisfiers in the online environment: A critical incident assessment. *Journal of Service Research, 10*(4), 347–364. doi:10.1177/1094670508314266

Ismail, A. (2006). Is economic value added more associated with stock return than accounting earnings? The UK evidence. *International Journal of Managerial Finance*.

Jones, G., Hanton, S., & Connaughton, D. (2007). A Framework of Mental Toughness in the World's Best Performers. *The Sport Psychologist, 21*(2), 243–264. doi:10.1123/tsp.21.2.243

Jones, M. A., & David, L. (2000). Switching barriers and repurchase intentions in services. *Kournal of Retailing, 76*(2), 259–274. doi:10.1016/S0022-4359(00)00024-5

Kaynama, S. A., & Black, C. I. (2000). A proposal to assess the service quality of online travel agencies: An exploratory study. *Journal of Professional Services Marketing, 21*(1), 63–88. doi:10.1300/J090v21n01_05

Keaveney, S. M. (1995). Customer switching behavior in service industries: An exploratory study. *Journal of Marketing, 59*(2), 71–82. doi:10.1177/002224299505900206

Keaveney, S. M., & Parthasarathy, M. (2001). Customer switching behavior in online services: An exploratory study of the role of selected attitudinal, behavioral, and demographic factors. *Journal of the Academy of Marketing Science, 29*(4), 374–390. doi:10.1177/03079450094225

Khan, M. M., & Su, K. D. (2003). Service quality expectations of travellers visiting Cheju Island in Korea. *Journal of Ecotourism, 2*(2), 114–125. doi:10.1080/14724040308668138

Kim, M., Kim, J. H., & Lennon, S. J. (2006). Online service attributes available on apparel retail web sites: An E-S-QUAL approach. *Managing Service Quality, 16*(1), 51–77. doi:10.1108/09604520610639964

Kitapci, O., Akdogan, C., & Dortyol, İ. T. (2014). The impact of service quality dimensions on patient satisfaction, repurchase intentions and word-of-mouth communication in the public healthcare industry. *Procedia: Social and Behavioral Sciences, 148*, 161–169. doi:10.1016/j.sbspro.2014.07.030

Ladhari, R. (2008). Alternative measures of service quality: A review. *Managing Service Quality, 18*(1), 65–86. doi:10.1108/09604520810842849

Lee, C., Lee, K., & Pennings, J. M. (2001). Internal capabilities, external networks, and performance: A study on technology-based ventures. *Strategic Management Journal, 22*(6-7), 615–640. doi:10.1002mj.181

Liang, D., Ma, Z., & Qi, L. (2013). Service quality and customer switching behavior in China's mobile phone service sector. *Journal of Business Research, 66*(8), 1161–1167. doi:10.1016/j.jbusres.2012.03.012

Liu, C., Arnett, K. P., & Litecky, C. (2000). Design quality of websites for electronic commerce: Fortune 1000 webmasters' evaluations. *Electronic Markets, 10*(2), 120–129. doi:10.1080/10196780050138173

Loiacono, E. T., Watson, R. T., & Goodhue, D. L. (2002). WebQual: A measure of website quality. *Marketing theory and applications, 13*(3), 432-438.

MacKenzie, S. B., Podsakoff, P. M., & Podsakoff, N. P. (2011). Construct measurement and validation procedures in MIS and behavioral research: Integrating new and existing techniques. *Management Information Systems Quarterly*, *35*(2), 293–334. doi:10.2307/23044045

Markovic, S., & Raspor, S. (2010). Measuring Perceived Service Quality Using SERVQUAL: A Case Study of the Croatian Hotel Industry. *Management*, *5*, 195–209.

Matos, C. A., Ituassu, C. T., & Rossi, C. A. (2007). Consumer attitudes toward counterfeits: A review and extension. *Journal of Consumer Marketing*, *24*(1), 36–47. doi:10.1108/07363760710720975

Negi, R. (2009). Determining Customer Satisfaction through Perceived Service Quality: A Study of Ethiopian Mobile Users. *International Journal of Mobile Marketing*, *4*, 31.

Oliver, R. L. (1993). Cognitive, affective, and attribute bases of the satisfaction response. *The Journal of Consumer Research*, *20*(3), 418–430. doi:10.1086/209358

Parasuraman, A., Zeithaml, V. A., & Berry, L. (1988). SERVQUAL: A multiple-item scale for measuring consumer perceptions of service quality. *1988, 64*(1), 12-40.

Parasuraman, A., Zeithaml, V. A., & Berry, L. L. (1985). A conceptual model of service quality and its implications for future research. *Journal of Marketing*, *49*(4), 41–50. doi:10.1177/002224298504900403

Parasuraman, A., Zeithaml, V. A., & Malhotra, A. (2005). E-S-QUAL: A Multiple-Item Scale for Assessing Electronic Service Quality. *Journal of Service Research*, *7*(3), 213–233. doi:10.1177/1094670504271156

Pérez, M. S., Abad, J. C. G., Carrillo, G. M. M., & Fernández, R. S. (2007). Effects of service quality dimensions on behavioural purchase intentions: A study in public-sector transport. Managing Service Quality: An International Journal Pitt, L. F., Watson, R. T., &Kavan, C. B. (1995). Service Quality: A Measure of Information Systems Effectiveness. *Management Information Systems Quarterly*, *19*(2), 173–187. doi:10.2307/249687

Ranaweera, C., & Prabhu, J. (2003). The influence of satisfaction, trust and switching barriers on customer retention in a continuous purchasing setting. *International Journal of Service Industry Management*, *14*(4), 374–395. doi:10.1108/09564230310489231

Ranganathan, C., & Ganapathy, S. (2002). Key dimensions of business-to-consumer web sites. *Information & Management*, *39*(6), 457–465. doi:10.1016/S0378-7206(01)00112-4

Rita, P., Oliveira, T., & Farisa, A. (2019). The impact of e-service quality and customer satisfaction on customer behavior in online shopping. *Heliyon*, *5*(10), e02690. doi:10.1016/j.heliyon.2019.e02690 PMID:31720459

Rowley, J. (2006). An analysis of the e-service literature: Towards a research agenda. *Internet Research*, *16*(3), 339–359. doi:10.1108/10662240610673736

Russell, C. (2005). An overview of the integrative research review. *Progress in Transplantation (Aliso Viejo, Calif.)*, *15*(1), 8–13. doi:10.1177/152692480501500102 PMID:15839365

Sánchez-Pérez, M., Sánchez-Fernández, R., Marín-Carrillo, G. M., & Gázquez-Abad, J. C. (2007). Service quality in public services as a segmentation variable. *Service Industries Journal, 27*(4), 355–369. doi:10.1080/02642060701346771

Santos, J. (2003). E-service quality: A model of virtual service quality dimensions. *Managing Service Quality, 13*(3), 233–246. doi:10.1108/09604520310476490

Shen, Q. L., & Li, Y. T. (2010). Explore antecedent factors of switching costs and intentions and their impact on customer loyalty. The *13th Conference on Interdisciplinary and Multifunctional Business Management, 13*, (pp. 271-288). Semantic Scholar.

Slu, N. Y. M., & Mou, J. C. (2003). *A study of service quality in internet banking*. Hong Kong Baptist University.

Spreng, R. A., & Singh, A. K. (1993). An empirical assessment of the SERVQUAL scale and the relationship between service quality and satisfaction. *Enhancing knowledge development in marketing, 4*(1), 1-6.

Szymanski, D. M., & Hise, R. T. (2000). E-satisfaction: An initial examination. *Journal of Retailing, 76*(3), 309–322. doi:10.1016/S0022-4359(00)00035-X

Teas, R. K. (1994). Expectations as a comparison standard in measuring service quality: An assessment of a reassessment. *Journal of Marketing, 58*(1), 132–139. doi:10.1177/002224299405800111

Udo, G. J., Bagchi, K. K., & Kirs, P. J. (2010). An assessment of customers' e-service quality perception, satisfaction and intention. *International Journal of Information Management, 30*(6), 481–492. doi:10.1016/j.ijinfomgt.2010.03.005

Wachter, K. (2002). Longitudinal assessment of web retailers: Issues from a consumer point of view. *Journal of Fashion Marketing and Management, 6*(2), 134–145. doi:10.1108/13612020210429476

White, L., & Yanamandram, V. (2007). A model of customer retention of dissatisfied business services customers. *Managing Service Quality, 17*(3), 298–316. doi:10.1108/09604520710744317

Wieringa, J., & Verhoef, P. (2007). Understanding Customer Switching Behavior in a Liberalizing Service Market: An Exploratory Study. *Journal of Service Research, 10*(2), 174–186. doi:10.1177/1094670507306686

Wolfinbarger, M., & Gilly, M. (2002). comQ: dimensionalizing, measuring, and predicting quality of the e-tail experience. *Marketing Science Institute Report,* (02-100).

Xavier, P., & Ypsilanti, D. (2008). Switching costs and consumer behaviour: Implications for telecommunications regulation. *Info, 10*(4), 13–29. doi:10.1108/14636690810887517

Yang, Z., & Fang, X. (2004). Online service quality dimensions and their relationships with satisfaction: A content analysis of customer reviews of securities brokerage services. *International Journal of Service Industry Management, 15*(3), 302–326. doi:10.1108/09564230410540953

Yang, Z., & Jun, M. (2002). Consumer perception of e-service quality: from internet purchaser and non-purchaser perspectives. *Journal of Business strategies, 19*(1), 19-42.

Yavas, U., Benkenstein, M., & Stuhldreier, U. (2004). Relationships between service quality and behavioral outcomes: A study of private bank customers in Germany. *International Journal of Bank Marketing*, *22*(2), 144–157. doi:10.1108/02652320410521737

Yen, Y., & Horng, D. (2010). Effects of satisfaction, trust and alternative attractiveness on switching intentions in industrial customers. *International Journal of Management and Enterprise Development*, *8*(1), 82–101. doi:10.1504/IJMED.2010.029762

Yoo, B., & Donthu, N. (2001). Developing and validating a multidimensional consumer-based brand equity scale. *Journal of Business Research*, *52*(1), 1–14. doi:10.1016/S0148-2963(99)00098-3

Zeithaml, V. A., Parasuraman, A., & Malhotra, A. (2002). Service quality delivery through web sites: A critical review of extant knowledge. *Journal of the Academy of Marketing Science*, *30*(4), 362–375. doi:10.1177/009207002236911

Zeithaml, V. A., Rust, R. T., & Lemon, K. N. (2001). The customer pyramid: Creating and serving profitable customers. *California Management Review*, *43*(4), 118–142. doi:10.2307/41166104

Chapter 2
A Study on Factors Influencing the Purchase Intention of Insurance Products Amongst Urban Households of Gandhinagar City

Jigna Chandrakant Trivedi

Shri Jairambhai Patel Institute of Business Management and Computer Applications, Gandhinagar, India

Bindiya Kunal Soni

Anand Institute of Management and Information Sciences, India

ABSTRACT

This study is carried out to analyze how SERVQUAL factors together with customer satisfaction and customer trust to influence the purchase intention for the insurance industry in Gandhinagar, Gujarat. The primary data for the study was collected through a self-administered questionnaire. 379 responses were collected from the households of the selected region through the convenience sampling method. Exploratory factor analysis (EFA) and confirmatory factor analysis (CFA) were employed to check how tangibility, reliability, responsiveness, assurance, empathy, customer satisfaction, and customer trust influence the purchase intention of the households. The structural equation modelling (SEM) revealed that empathy, tangibility, reliability, and customer satisfaction positively influence the purchase intention of the respondents for the insurance policies.

DOI: 10.4018/978-1-6684-5853-2.ch002

INTRODUCTION

Service sector plays a dominant role in Indian economy for its potential for creating employment and its contribution to the national income along with manufacturing and agriculture sector. Insurance sector is an integral part of financial services and creates the base for sustainable economic growth. The insurance sector in India has witnessed dynamic growth historically. As per the Insurance Regulatory and Development Authority of India (IRDAI) annual report 2020-2021, insurance penetration in India grew by 11.7% (from 3.76% in 2019-20 to 4.20% in 2020-21). India is having the potential for becoming most prominent emerging insurance markets globally and is one of the fifth largest life Insurance market in the world. There are several growth drivers for insurance industry in India. In 2021, the FDI limit for India's insurance industry has been increased from 49% to 74% in 2021 by government of India. This move has opened up the doors for the foreign players in India's insurance industry. This will help us achieve product innovation and higher insurance penetration. As per the KPMG report, 2022, the insurance industry has evolved due to factors including the recent pandemic, advancements in the financial services space, digitalization, the advent of insure-techs etc. Apart from these, young working demographic, growth in the nuclear family structures and channelising the household savings into financial system have also added to the growth of insurance. The under penetration of insurance and the efforts of IRDAI for spreading the awareness and adoption of insurance are also largely responsible for the growth of the insurance sector in India. Further, India's robust start-up ecosystem would facilitate the new-age start-ups in India's insurance industry, and this would further fuel the growth of Indian insurance market.

At the same time, with so many insurance products and options, the insurance industry has become saturated. As per the updated list of insurers of IRDAI August 2022, there are 24 life insurers and 31 non-life insurers operating in India. The insurance industry is experiencing aggressive competition. Despite the economic growth and that of insurance industry, this industry still faces many challenges for its inclusive development. With the COVID pandemic, insurance has transformed from being sold to being bought. With sophisticated customers and intensified competition, it has become the need of the hour for insurers to deliver superior service quality. Delivering quality service refers to fulfilling the expectations of the customers in an articulate manner and it is the result of consumer expectation with actual service performance (Paposa et al., 2019). In recent times, service quality for insurance providers has become the focal point for a sustained business and customer retention (Devi et al., 2018). As per the findings documented in the State of Connected Customer report (2019), out of 8000 customers surveyed across the world, 84% said that the experience a company provides is as important as its products or services. However, there is a considerable gap between the user expectations and the actual delivery. Further, the research insights from IBM Institute of Business Value (*Elevating the insurance customer experience*, 2020) highlighted that on the demand side, 42% of customers did not fully trust their insurer, and on the supply side, 60% of insurers agreed that there is a lack of customer experience strategy in their organizations. Thus, though many reforms have been introduced in the insurance industry resulting in better penetration, when it comes to providing quality services, the insurance providers lack behind. This results into customer dissatisfaction. Further, it has been observed that customer experience positively influences customer satisfaction (Pei et al., 2020). In fact, IRDAI mentions customer satisfaction as one of the keywords in its objective. In fact, customer satisfaction is a key to attract new customers and retain existing customers and thus creates a loyal customer base (Kotler et al., 2013). In today's time, service providers attempt to retain the existing customers rather trying to find the new ones as it is more expensive for them (Chimedtseren & Safari, 2016). Ideally, to improve customer satisfaction, insurance providers should measure and improve the approaches to delivery of service (Siddiqui & Sharma, 2010).

As services are intangible and it becomes challenging to assess the quality of service as compared to goods. The quality of goods purchased can be identified with the help of parameters such as design, style, hardness, color, feel, package etc. However, such parameters cannot be applied in case of services and insurance is no exception. One way to measure the service quality is measurement of customers' perception for service quality. Considering this, an attempt has been made through this study to measure the service quality for insurance through five SERVQUAL dimensions namely tangibility, reliability, responsiveness, empathy and assurance along with customer satisfaction and customer trust if they can influence purchase intention for insurance.

LITERATURE REVIEW

As discussed above, service providers can attract and retain customers with recognition of service quality. The SERVQUAL model is applied largely to measure perceived service quality (Saeedpoor et al., 2015). The first method developed and applied to evaluate the quality of services has been SERVQUAL. It is worth noting that all other methods have been developed starting from the SERVQUAL conceptual architecture (Bente, 2021). This model has diverse applicability and is widely used by the researchers for its robust and well-defined structure (Siddiqui & Sharma, 2010). Based on service quality model, i.e., the gap between expectations and management perception (gap I), gap between management perception and service quality specifications (gap II), gap between service quality specifications and service delivery (gap III), gap between service delivery and external communication (gap IV) and gap between perceived service and expected service (gap V); researchers identified five determinants of service quality i.e. Reliability, Responsiveness, Assurance, Empathy, and Tangibility. Based on these five factors, the researchers developed the 21 item SERVQUAL scale. Subsequent researchers have extended the model (Kotler et al., 2013). The academicians and researchers have applied the SERVQUAL model to assess the service quality in various industries including the insurance (Saeedpoor et al., 2015; Bala et al., 2011; Tsoukatos and Rand, 2017; Kumar et al., 2018; Siddiqui & Sharma, 2010; Kumar & Singh, 2010; Sandhu & Bala, 2011; Arokiasamy & Tat, 2014; Jajaee & Ahmad, 2012; Khurana 2012, Tsoukatos, Simmy, Rand, 2004; Haque & Sultan, 2019; Siami & Gorji, 2012; Wells & Stafford, 1995; Paposa et al., 2019). In this study, along with the five factors of SERVQUAL model customer satisfaction and trust were also considered for checking the influence on purchase intention.

Tangibility

Insurance services are intangible in nature (Pathak, 2018). However, tangible here refers to physical evidence of the service (Sahoo et al., 2019). Tangibility aims to provide excellent service to the insurance industry customers (Chimedtseren and Safari, 2016). Physical facilities, equipment, and the appearance of the personnel (Panda and Das, 2014), communication materials and presence of other customers in the service facility (Sahoo et al., 2019) are included in the tangibility aspect of the service industry. Physical facility includes the ambience and spatial layout of the place in which the service is produced or delivered. The equipment parameter includes internet connectivity, printing or photocopy machines, card access systems, time clocks etc. The overall dressing, grooming and appearance of the employees delivering the service are also included in tangibility aspect. Lastly, the materials refer to the resources associated with the services like brochures, business card, furnishing etc. These materials and artifacts help in corporate branding and are found to be visually appealing (Paposa et al., 2019). Many studies have hypothesized a positive relationship between tangibles and customer satisfaction (Arokiasamy & Tat, 2014; Jajaee & Ahmad, 2012; Khurana 2012).

Reliability

According to Parasuraman et al. (1985), reliability means consistency of performance and dependability. It also refers to ability to perform services precisely and trustworthy (Shreenivasan et al., 2018). When the firm performs its services right for the first time and is able to honour its promises, the services are said to be reliable. In Insurance, the dimensions of reliability include clarity in contract terms, error-free documents, no delays in settlement of claims, and showing interest in solving the customers' problems (Tsoukatos & Rand, 2017; Bala et al., 2011). Delivering services on time to satisfy the needs of the customer is highly essential (Paposa et al., 2019). According to the research findings, there is a positive relationship between the reliability of the services and customer satisfaction (Upadhyay & Adhikari, 2021, Getnet, 2020, Arokiasamy & Tat, 2014).

Responsiveness

This dimension of service quality basically concerns the willingness and readiness of employees to provide service. Delivering the service on time is an integral part of responsiveness. Precisely, the responsiveness construct includes mailing a transaction slip immediately, calling the customer back quickly, and rendering prompt service by giving appointments quickly (Parasuraman et al., 1985). Previous studies documented the positive influence of responsiveness on customer satisfaction (Arokiasamy & Tat, 2014; Upadhyay & Adhikari, 2021; Ramadhan & Soegoto, 2020; Chege, 2021; Sivesan, 2019). Few studies documented the negligible impact of this dimension on customer satisfaction (Khurana 2012, Getnet, 2020).

Empathy

Empathy means providing individual attention by service providers toward customers in delivering services (Saeedpoor et al., 2015). In the service industry, the employees need to have an empathetic approach to servicing the customers. Once the customers feel they are attended individually and qualitatively, the likelihood of them giving the business again to the company increases (Suki, 2013). Specific to insurance, besides paying attention, this construct includes variables such as having convenient operating hours, having the customers' best interests at heart, and understanding the specific needs of customers by the staff (Tsoukatos & Rand, 2017). If the staff is not able to provide person attention, it found negatively correlated to service quality (Chimedtseren & Safari, 2016). There are the studies that have found the influence of empathy on customer satisfaction (Alemayehu & Dalega, 2019; Chege et al., 2019, Bahadur et al., 2018, Suki, 2013; Upadhyay & Adhikari, 2021).

Assurance

Assurance indicates employees' knowledge, courtesy, and the ability of the firm to inspire trust and confidence in the customers. It includes variables such as competence, courtesy, credibility, and security (Iwaarden et al., 2003). Extant research found a positive influence of assurance on customer satisfaction (Ramadhan & Soegoto, 2020, Getnet, 2020, Siddiqui & Sharma, 2010, Alauddin et al., 2019, Marsrurul, 2019).

Customer Satisfaction, Trust, and Purchase Intention

Kotler (2004) defined customer satisfaction as a person's feeling of pleasure or disappointment from comparing the actual performance of the product with the expectations. It is an overall attitude of a customer towards a provider of a service. In case of purchasing life insurance policy, the outcomes of are not immediate. Because of this reason, purchasing insurance policy may not lead to quick customer satisfaction. Further, future benefits of buying the insurance are difficult to anticipate and may take a long time to show its effects. Therefore, the understanding and interaction between the employees of life insurance company and the customers become very crucial to ensure customer satisfaction (Paposa et al., 2019). According to Parasuraman et al. (1985), the SERVQUAL model can be applied to measure service quality and prior studies have established a positive relationship between service quality with customer satisfaction (Terblanche & Boshoff, 2006; Cronin & Taylor, 1992; Zeithaml et al., 1996; Chimedtseren & Safari, 2016).

As customers' behavior can be predicted with the help of their intention, it is equally important to understand purchase intention (Bai et al., 2008). Purchase intention signifies the willingness of the consumers to purchase (Park et al., 2021). It is the probability associated with buying the product actually. Positive purchase intention helps the firms to increase its sales (Chimedtseren & Safari, 2016). It has been established in previous the research that Customer satisfaction judgments were more closely related to the formation of consumers' purchase intentions (Cronin & Taylor 1992, Taylor et al. 1997, Bai et al., 2008, Park et al., 2021, Gera et al., 2017). Khatoon et al. (2020) found that customer satisfaction plays a vital role as a mediator and the predictor of customer purchase intention, especially in the banking sector. Besides purchase intention, customer satisfaction affects service continuance as well (Salim et al., 2017).

Customer trust has been widely studied with respect to different fields, especially with respect to e-commerce and online shopping behavior (Jadil et al., 2022; Ling et al. 2010; Thinh et al., 2017; Huy et al., 2019, Jeon et al., 2021, Alharthey, 2019). Customer trust is formed when the customer expects that the service provider is dependable and can be relied on to deliver on its promises (Sirdeshmukh et. al., 2002). For any sustainable relationship, trust is very essential (Heffernan et al., 2008). The most important factor for customer satisfaction in the Iranian insurance industry is customer trust. Thus, the insurance service providers must adhere to their obligations as promised (Vazifehdust & Farokhian, 2013). The findings of a meta-analysis of the empirical literature on customer trust in salesperson highlighted that trust has a moderate but beneficial influence on the development of positive customer attitudes, intentions, and behavior (Swana et al., 1999). This was further validated in the findings of a Meta-analytic analysis of 19 studies Wang et al. (2022). As per the outcome of this research, trust positively influences consumers' purchase intentions. In nutshell, it can be said that while buying insurance policies, apart from financial aspects, all service-related dimensions of SERVQUAL model as discussed above are equally important.

Hypotheses for the Study

H$_{11}$: Tangibility positively influences the purchase intention of insurance policies.
H$_{12}$: Reliability positively influences the purchase intention of insurance policies.
H$_{13}$: Responsiveness positively influences purchase intention of insurance policies.
H$_{14}$: Empathy positively influences the purchase intention of insurance policies.
H$_{15}$: Assurance positively influences the purchase intention of insurance policies.
H$_{16}$: Customer Satisfaction positively influences purchase intention of insurance policies.
H$_{17}$: Customer Trust positively influences purchase intention of insurance policies.

The conceptual framework of the model is depicted in Figure 1.

Figure 1. Conceptual Framework
(Source: Based on Review of Literature)

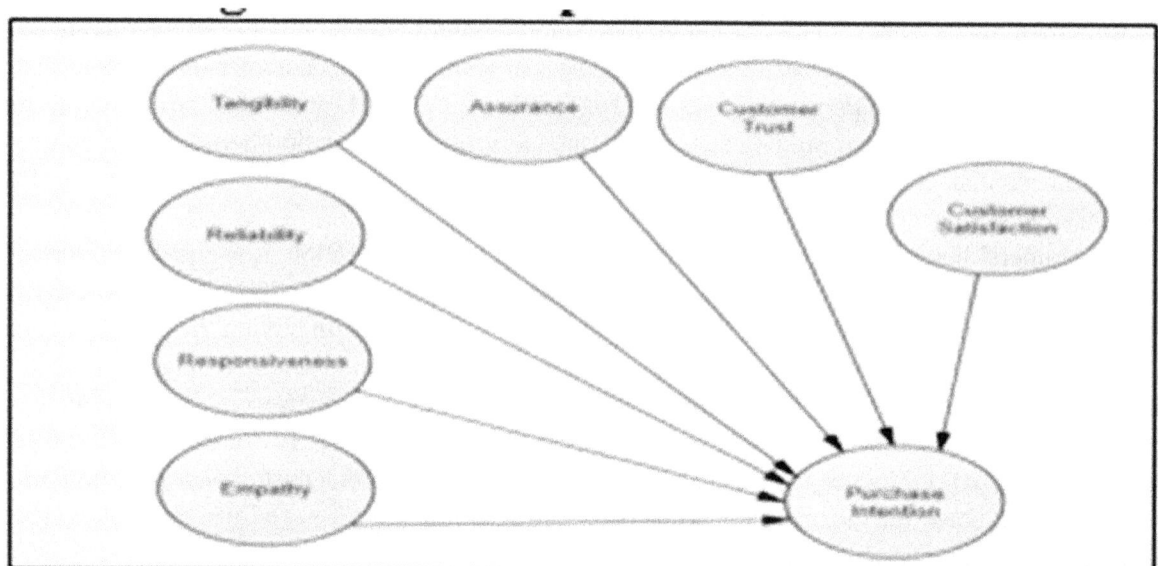

METHODOLOGY

The details pertaining to sample, data collection, and measures are discussed in the section.

Sample and Data Collection

The urban region of Gandhinagar (capital of Gujarat) was selected for the study. The population consisted of households dwelling in the urban or city area of Gandhinagar. As per the Directorate of Census Operations (2011), the number of households in the urban area of Gandhinagar city was 28,224. Based on the sample size calculator, at the confidence level of 95% and margin error of 5%, the sample size was determined at 379 households. The formula used in determination of sample size was n = Z^2* p* q

/e², i.e. $(1.96)^2 * (0.5) (0.5)/ (0.05)^2$. According to Kyriazos (2018) the sample size of 379 surpasses the thumb rule of N>200, which is treated feasible and also justifies the statistical power of data analysis. The head of the family (either male or female) of the household was contacted for the survey. On a sample of 30 respondents a pilot testing was performed, to ensure the proper usage of measurement scales and also comprehension of the questionnaire. The questionnaire required around 10 minutes of filling time. The survey was conducted from December 2021 to February 2022.

The researcher personally contacted 379 households to fill-up the paper-pencil-based survey. The respondent who had purchased either life or non-life insurance, were asked to fill up the survey. The questionnaire was handed over to the respondents, to avoid response bias (Jong, 2016). 82 respondents had just filled the demographic part of the questionnaire. 50 respondents had just filled the second part of the questionnaire. 30 Outliers response were eventually dropped from the survey, based on the Mahaloanobis Distances method, where the probability values were less than 0.001 (Statistics Solutions, n.d.). Nine respondents provided same liner response, so it was also discarded from the data-set. Thus, the final usable samples were 208, representing a 55% response rate. The demographic characteristics of the sample are discussed in Table 1.

Table 1. Demographic characteristics of the sample (n=208)

Attributes	Categorical Classification	Frequency	Percentage
Gender	Male	140	67
	Female	68	33
Age (in years)	Below 25	35	17
	25-30	19	09
	31 to 39	70	34
	40 to 49	63	30
	Above 50	21	10
Education Qualification	Below Graduate	61	29
	Graduate	143	69
	Post-Graduate	04	02
Occupation	Private	70	34
	Public	18	08
	Business	70	34
	Others	50	24
Yearly Income (Rs.)	Less than 5,00,000	109	52
	5,00,001-10,00,000	81	39
	10,00,001-20,00,000	14	07
	Above 20,00,000	04	02

(Source: Primary Data)

It may be inferred that as high as 67% of respondents were male. 34% of respondents were in the age group of 31 to 39 years. 69% of respondents were graduate. Each 34% of respondents were engaged in business and private jobs. 52% of respondents had income less than Rs.5,00,000.

Measures

The questionnaire was divided into two parts viz., demographic questions and measurement of Service Quality (SERVQUAL) questions, additional variables and Purchase Intentions. Five demographic questions consisted of questions based on gender (dichotomous), and ordinal questions related to age, educational qualification, and yearly income. The occupation question was measured on a nominal scale. The SERQUAL questions consisted of constructs such as Tangibility (five items); Reliability (five items), Responsiveness (four items), Empathy (four items), and Assurance (nine items). Two additional variables, Customer Trust (four items) and Customer Satisfaction (four items) were also included in the study. The dependent variable Purchase Intention (four items) construct was also used in the study. All the items of the construct were measured on the five-point Likert Scale, where 1 represented strongly disagree and 5 represented strongly agree. All the items of the construct were adapted from the scholarly work of Panigrahi, Azizan, &Waris (2018). Further, the descriptive statistics and normality of the questionnaire items are discussed further.

Table 2. Descriptive statistics and normality of the questionnaire items

Item Code	Item	Mean	Std. Deviation	Skewness	Kurtosis
TN1	Facilities provided by the insurance companies are visualized	3.96	0.59	0.01	-0.07
TN2	Employees of insurance companies are neat and well appeared.	4.03	0.67	-0.14	-0.44
TN3	Materials used for visualized services are clearly managed.	3.91	0.68	-0.18	-0.12
TN4	It is more convenient to use the service of the insurance companies.	4.06	0.71	-0.16	-0.73
TN5	Insurance Company has modern looking equipment.	4.01	0.62	-0.01	-0.35
RE1	Insurance companies keep their promises on time	3.85	0.64	0.14	-0.60
RE2	Service providers solve the problems with sincere interests.	3.95	0.70	0.07	-0.94
RE3	Insurance Company performs the right service in the first go itself.	3.98	0.66	0.02	-0.66
RE4	Services are provided at an appropriate time as it is promised to do so.	3.95	0.67	0.06	-0.76
RE5	Employees must be focused on providing error free services to the customers.	4.01	0.66	-0.01	-0.66
RS1	Employees inform customers about when the service will be delivered.	3.89	0.67	-0.28	0.23
RS2	Prompt service is provided by the employees to us.	3.96	0.79	-0.49	0.27
RS3	Employees are always willing to help,, whenever it is required.	3.98	0.76	-0.60	0.77
RS4	Employees always respond to the requests.	3.90	0.69	-0.34	0.24
EM1	Individual attention is provided by the employees	3.99	0.70	-0.43	0.34
EM2	The operating hours that the company provides is convenient.	4.05	0.74	-0.45	-0.04
EM3	Employees give you personal attention.	3.96	0.77	-0.45	-0.04
EM4	Companies have best interest at heart to provide services.	3.97	0.78	-0.54	0.46
AS1	Customer's specific requirements are understood by the employees.	3.58	0.85	-0.38	0.22
AS2	The behavior of employees brings confidence in customers.	3.66	0.81	-0.37	0.58
AS3	Customers feel secure while performing transactions for the insurance products.	3.60	0.74	0.03	-0.32
AS4	Employees are courteous with the customers continuously.	3.63	0.74	0.13	-0.41
AS5	Employees have the knowledge to answer your questions.	3.67	0.83	-0.43	0.52
AS6	Employees take initiative to step up and take action to solve problem.	3.67	0.83	-0.32	0.13
AS7	Employees do not give up easily while solving the issues.	3.60	0.83	-0.25	0.09
AS8	Employees help to tackle challenges in the competitive markets.	3.65	0.78	-0.15	0.02
AS9	Employees are committed to quality customer services.	3.73	0.84	-0.55	0.62
CT1	Customers are concerned about security while purchasing insurance products	4.05	0.67	-0.06	-0.76
CT2	Customers have trust in words and promises.	4.03	0.69	-0.04	-0.86
CT3	Employees must be able to fulfil obligations to customers to increase their trust.	3.96	0.62	0.02	-0.34
CT4	I rely on the insurance products.	3.89	0.67	0.14	-0.79
CS1	I would like to repeat my purchases of insurance products.	3.89	0.67	-0.28	0.23
CS2	I would like to talk about my experience about insurance products.	3.96	0.79	-0.49	0.27
CS3	I think I made the correct decision to buy the insurance product.	3.98	0.76	-0.60	0.77
CS4	Overall, I am satisfied with the insurance products.	3.90	0.69	-0.34	0.24
PI1	I would intend to purchase insurance products.	4.05	0.67	-0.06	-0.76
PI2	My willingness to purchase insurance products is high.	4.03	0.69	-0.04	-0.86
PI3	I am likely to purchase the insurance products.	3.96	0.62	0.02	-0.34
PI4	I have high intention to purchase insurance products.	3.89	0.67	0.14	-0.79

(Source: Authors' Adaptation)

From table 2, it may be observed that the SD of all items of the construct is less than one, indicating a consensus in the responses provided by the respondents. The normality of the data may be ensured by the skewness and kurtosis falling in the range of -1.00 to +1.00 (Mostafa and Elseidi, 2018).

Tools for Data Analysis

The frequency and percentage were computed using the software Statistical Package for Social Sciences (SPSS 20.0). Mean, SD, Skewness, and Kurtosis for each item of the construct and the construct itself were calculated from SPSS. Cronbach Alpha α coefficient was computed to ensure the reliability of the tool i.e. questionnaire. Inter-correlations and multivariate outliers were also calculated for better data clarity. Confirmatory Factor Analysis (CFA) was applied using Analysis Of Moment Structures (AMOS 21.0). To check the adequacy of the measurement and for confirming the reliability, convergent validity, and divergent validity of the questionnaire were also computed. The Maximum Shared Variance (MSV), Average Shared Variance (ASV), Average Variance Extracted (AVE), Composite Reliability (CR), Discriminant Value, and Heterotrait-Monotrait (HTMT) Ratio was computed using Excel 2007.

Results

Figure 2 depicts the Confirmatory Factor Analysis (CFA) used for the present study.

Figure 2. Confirmatory Factor Analysis (CFA)
(Source: AMOS Output)

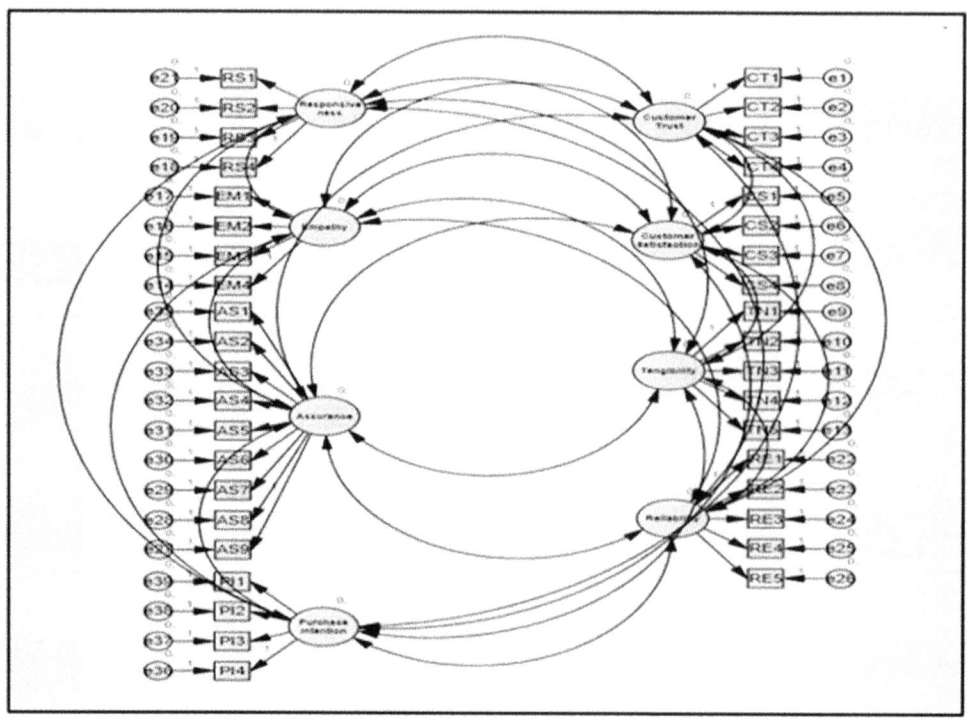

Internal Reliability Testing and Analysis of the Measurement Model

In order to assess the scale reliability and internal consistency, Cronbach Alpha also was computed (Brown, 2002). From table 3 it may be observed that the Cronbach Alpha value is exceeding the benchmark value of 0.6 (Hair et al., 2010 and Bernardi, 1194;), it lies between 0.76 to 0.89. The Cronbach Alpha Value of eight constructs and all the 39 items is 0.86. A measure of Alpha value greater than 0.80 indicates very good reliability (Ursach et al., 2015).

Table 3. Confirmatory factor analysis results

Item Coding	Factor Loadings	R-Square	P-value	Cronbach Alpha
TN1	0.76	0.43	***	
TN2	0.76	0.48	***	
TN3	0.74	0.45	***	0.79
TN4	0.70	0.44	***	
TN5	0.69	0.40	***	
RE1	0.75	0.54	***	
RE2	0.81	0.58	***	
RE3	0.78	0.40	***	0.81
RE4	0.73	0.37	***	
RE5	0.49	0.41	***	
RS1	0.67	0.42	***	
RS2	0.58	0.54	***	0.77
RS3	0.86	0.36	***	
RS4	0.63	0.51	***	
EM1	0.76	0.50	***	
EM2	0.53	0.49	***	0.81
EM3	0.89	0.41	***	
EM4	0.74	0.64	***	
AS1	0.75	0.57	***	
AS2	0.67	0.53	***	
AS3	0.79	0.46	***	
AS4	0.71	0.39	***	
AS5	0.85	0.49	***	0.89
AS6	0.56	0.51	***	
AS7	0.78	0.51	***	
AS8	0.78	0.47	***	
AS9	0.64	0.52	***	
CT1	0.83	0.57	***	
CT2	0.78	0.52	***	0.77
CT3	0.74	0.45	***	
CT4	0.68	0.32	***	

Continued on following page

Table 3. Continued

Item Coding	Factor Loadings	R-Square	P-value	Cronbach Alpha
CS1	0.68	0.45	***	
CS2	0.76	0.50	***	
CS3	0.80	0.38	***	0.76
CS4	0.75	0.50	***	
PI1	0.84	0.57	***	
PI2	0.81	0.49	***	
PI3	0.74	0.45	***	0.77
PI4	0.59	0.34	***	
Overall Cronbach Alpha is 0.86				

(Source: SPSS Output)

In order to check the load of the items on their respective construct, a Confirmatory Factor Analysis (CFA) was run using AMOS. The eight reflective constructs used in the study were Tangibility, Reliability, Responsiveness, Empathy, Assurance, Customer Trust, Customer Responsiveness and Purchase Intention. CFA was run using Maximum Likelihood (ML) Estimation because it is an appropriate method in the case of missing datasets (Anderson, 1957) and it identifies the probability distribution and parameters that would best explain the observed data (Brownlee, 2019). The Convergent and Discriminant Validity are best estimated by using the ML estimation. It may be observed that the items measure the same construct that is related (Mostafa & Elseidi, 2018). The p-value of all the items of the construct was less than 0.05, indicating that all the items were statistically significant at 95% level of confidence. The squared multiple correlation R-Square represents the percentage variance explained by the predictor variables (Gaskin, 2013). The factor loadings of each item of a construct were greater than 0.50 (Hair et al., 2010). The unidimensionality of the factor may be ensured from the range of standardized loadings ranging from 0.53 to 0.86 (Awang, 2012).

Validity of Measurement Model

If the instrument's intention to measure and the ability to measure is the same, then it may be inferred that the instrument used in the study is valid. When the Fitness Indexes meets the benchmark indexes, it is believed that the construct validity has been attained (Awang, 2012). From the AMOS output, it may be inferred that the CFA goodness-of-fit indices value was χ^2=292.77, df= 149, p=0.02<0.05, indicating statistically insignificant. The Chi-Square measure is sensitive to a sample size exceeding 200, and hence it may be ignored (Awang, 2012; Hair et al., 2010; Joreskog & Sorbom, 1984; Schumacker and Lomax, 2010). The researcher resorted to other fit indexes to ensure the validity of the construct. An absolute fit measure such as Root Mean Square Error of Approximation (RMSEA) and Goodness of Fit Index (GFI), was respectively, 0.03 <0.08 and 0.91>0.90. The Comparative Fit Index (CFI) and the Tucker-Lewis Index (TLI), a measure of the Incremental Fit Index were 0.97 and 0.96 respectively, which were greater than the cut-off value of 0.90. Chiq/df a measure of the Parsimonious fit index was 4.61<5.0. As all the fit indexes were in the acceptable range depicting the validity of the CFA model (Awang, 2012).

Construct Reliability and Validity Estimates

The reliability of the tool explains how reliable the tool is in measuring the intended latent construct. The internal reliability of the instrument i.e., the questionnaire was assessed using Cronbach Alpha. It is executed after the pilot testing but before the final commencement of the survey, which has been discussed above as per the statistics mentioned in table 3. The measure of reliability and internal consistency for the latent construct used in the study was assessed through CR. The average percentage of variation, which is explained by the measuring items of a construct was calculated using the AVE. AVE is a tool that measures the convergent validity when all the items in the measurement model are statistically significant. In order to ensure that the tool used in the model is free from redundant items, the discriminant validity (DV) was also computed. Supporting measures such as MSV and ASV were considered in the paper to measure the DV. Discriminant validity justifies that the constructs which are not supposed to be related are actually unrelated (Zhu, 2000). Results of different measures such as X, SD, CR, AVE, ASV, MSV and DV are represented in Table 4.

Table 4. Correlation coefficients and discriminant validity of the construct

Constructs	Mean	SD	MSV	ASV	AVE	CR	CT	CS	TN	EM	RS	RE	AS
CT	3.98	.51	.08	.03	.58	.77	**.68**						
CS	3.93	.56	.23	.07	.56	.77	.14	**.68**					
TN	3.99	.49	.35	.10	.53	.80	-.17	.36	**.66**				
EM	3.99	.60	.49	.20	.55	.81	.10	.03	.10	**.71**			
RS	3.93	.56	.46	.16	.50	.77	.20	-.09	.00	.72	**.68**		
RE	3.93	.52	.15	.08	.52	.81	.03	.48	.59	.02	-.04	**.68**	
AS	3.64	.60	.01	.01	.53	.90	.28	-.05	-.16	.51	.68	-.09	**.70**
PI	3.98	.51	.15	.06	.57	.77	.14	.20	.36	.18	.14	.39	.01

(Source: Excel Output)

The consolidated mean value of all eight constructs is nearer to four, which depicts agreement in the responses. The consolidated value of SD of each construct is less than one, which means there is a strong consensus in the response. The CR for all the constructs surpasses the test threshold value of 0.60, which depicts the internal reliability and consistency of the latent construct (Awang, 2012; Bagozzi & Yi, 1988). The AVE value of all the eight constructs is either equal to or greater than 0.5, which surpasses the test of convergent validity and internal consistency (Awang, 2012; Fornell & Larcker, 1981). The discriminant validity was further confirmed when the MSV and ASV were compared with AVE. It was noted that MSV and ASV both were smaller than AVE, indicating the discriminating validity (Alumran et al., 2014). The DV indicates that one construct differs from the other construct. As per Fornell and Larcker (1981) the square root of AVE for each construct is greater than the correlation coefficient (r) between each pair of constructs, indicating adequate discriminant validity in the majority of the cases except EM-RS and RS-AS. To overcome this difficulty, the modern method i.e. HTMT ratio, was used to assess the DV. HTMT ratio examines the correlations of items across the constructs (heterotrait) to the correlations of items within (monotrait) a construct. If the HTMT value is less than 0.90, then the discriminant validity is established between the two reflective constructs (Fawad, 2021)(see table 5).

Table 5. HTMT ratio

Construct	PI	AS	RE	RS	EM	TN	CS
PI							
AS	0.01						
RE	0.39	-0.08					
RS	0.14	0.68	-0.04				
EM	0.18	0.52	0.02	0.72			
TN	0.36	-0.16	0.59	0.00	0.10		
CS	0.20	-0.05	0.48	-0.09	0.03	0.36	
CT	0.14	0.28	0.03	0.20	0.10	-0.17	0.14

(Source: Excel Output)

All the values of HTMT Ratio were less than the benchmark value of 0.90, thus it indicates that there are no discriminant issues with the construct. The construct is not highly correlated with each other and are actually distinct. Thus, the singular identity of each construct is confirmed from the DV. The measurement model has a good fit because the unidimensionality, convergent validity, construct validity, discriminant validity, internal reliability, composite reliability, AVE, MSV, ASV and HTMT ratio are as per the pre-defined benchmark value.

Structural Model

Before running the SEM model (figure 3), the multicollinearity statistics and Variance Inflation Factor (VIF) were checked (table 6). It was checked from the perspective of outer values and inner values.

Table 6. Outer and inner collinearity statistics

Items	Tolerance	VIF	Item	Tolerance	VIF
TN1	0.66	1.51	RE1	0.58	1.72
TN2	0.63	1.59	RE2	0.54	1.85
TN3	0.65	1.53	RE3	0.67	1.49
TN4	0.67	1.50	RE4	0.70	1.43
TN5	0.69	1.44	RE5	0.71	1.40
RS1	0.68	1.46	EM1	0.60	1.67
RS2	0.64	1.56	EM2	0.63	1.59
RS3	0.70	1.43	EM3	0.63	1.58
RS4	0.64	1.57	EM4	0.53	1.88
AS1	0.46	2.16	CT1	0.59	1.69
AS2	0.52	1.94	CT2	0.63	1.59
AS3	0.57	1.74	CT3	0.68	1.48
AS4	0.60	1.66	CT4	0.75	1.33
AS5	0.51	1.97	CS1	0.71	1.42
AS6	0.56	1.80	CS2	0.66	1.52
AS7	0.50	2.00	CS3	0.69	1.45
AS8	0.57	1.77	CS4	0.65	1.54
AS9	0.55	1.83	Tangibility	0.74	1.35
Reliability	0.76	1.32	Responsiveness	0.56	1.79
Empathy	0.66	1.52	Assurance	0.63	1.60
Customer Trust	0.90	1.11	Customer Satisfaction	0.84	1.19

(Source: SPSS Output)

It may be noted that the outer and inner Tolerance value is greater than 0.20 and the VIF value is less than 5, which indicates there is no multi-collinearity problem between the independent variables (Kumar, 2020).

CONCLUSION

Figure 3. Structural Equation Model (SEM)
(Source: AMOS Output)

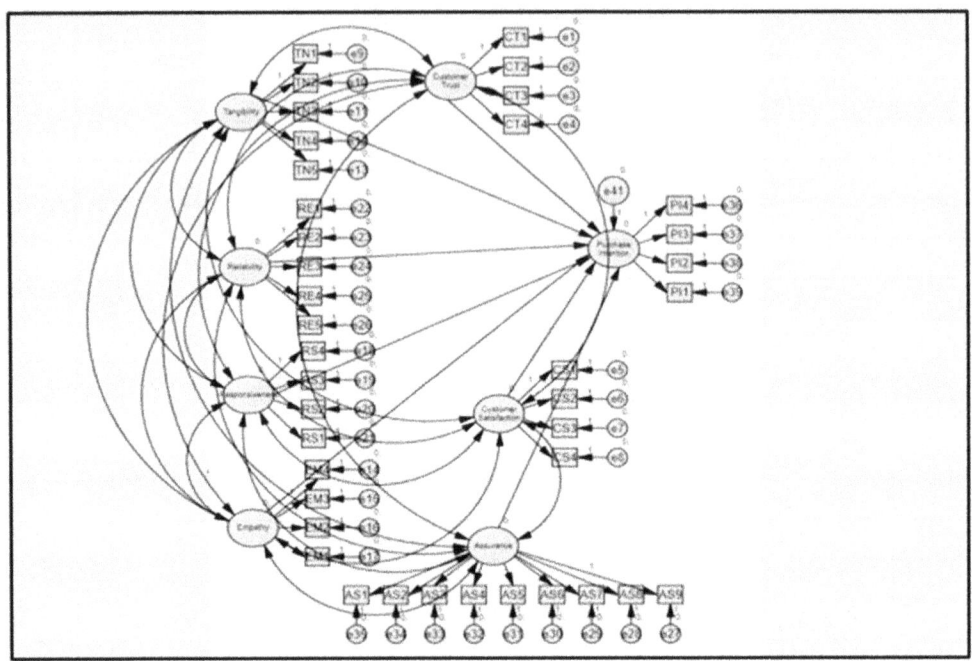

The statistical test administered on the factors highlights, the role each independent factor plays in influencing the dependent factor (see table 7).

Table 7. Status of the alternate hypothesis

Hypothesis	Supported or Not Supported
H_{11}: Tangibility positively influences the purchase intention of insurance policies.	Supported
H_{12}: Reliability positively influences the purchase intention of insurance policies.	Supported
H_{13}: Responsiveness positively influences the purchase intention of insurance policies.	Not-Supported
H_{14}: Empathy positively influences the purchase intention of insurance policies.	Supported
H_{15}: Assurance positively influences the purchase intention of insurance policies.	Not-Supported
H_{16}: Customer Satisfaction positively influences purchase intention of insurance policies.	Supported
H_{17}: Customer Trust positively influences purchase intention of insurance policies.	Not-Supported

(Source: Authors' Compilation)

The findings of this research on tangibility (Arokiasamy & Tat, 2014; Jajaee & Ahmad, 2012; Khurana, 2012), reliability (Upadhyay & Adhikari, 2021, Getnet, 2020, Arokiasamy & Tat, 2014), empathy (Alemayehu & Dalega, 2019; Chege et al., 2019, Bahadur et al., 2018, Suki, 2013; Upadhyay & Adhikari,

2021), and customer satisfaction (Terblanche & Boshoff, 2006; Cronin & Taylor, 1992; Zeithaml et al., 1996; Chimedtseren & Safari, 2016) are in line with the findings of previous researchers. Responsiveness (Khurana 2012, Getnet, 2020) and assurance (Ramadhan & Soegoto, 2020, Getnet, 2020, Siddiqui & Sharma, 2010, Alauddin et al., 2019, Marsrurul, 2019) do not influence the purchase intention and deviate from the findings of the previous researchers. As depicted in the survey 60% of the respondents are of less than 40 years of age, and in the one-to-one discussion, it was noted that they believe in online transactions for payment of insurance premiums and other requests. In the online mode of transactions, the receipts, and submission confirmation are quickly auto-generated, in such a case the human intervention becomes minimum, and, hence responsiveness and assurance do not play a vital role in providing service satisfaction. The findings of the present research deviate from the past researchers' findings on the construct of customer trust. Customer trust does not positively influence purchase intention. With the advent of the online ratings and review mechanism and grievance redressal with IRDA, the customers might feel that if anything goes wrong, then the insurance company may easily, be made to pay for, the mistakes or improper services on their part. Moreover, with the services of web aggregators such as policy bazaar, it has become easy for the customers to cross-compare the premium amount and ratings of the insurance company before the purchase. Maybe a third-party endorsement of the insurance company influences the purchase intention, which creates an absence of sole trust in the insurance company.

It may be noted that statistically, tangibility, reliability, empathy, and customer satisfaction positively influence the purchase intention of the insurance policies. The correlation between tangibility, reliability, empathy, and customer satisfaction has a moderate positive relation with purchase intention. Customer Trust, responsiveness, and assurance have a weak positive relation with purchase intention, but it is statistically not significant. Based on the path analysis it may be observed that 98% of the purchase intention prediction is based on the independent factors discussed in the study. In other words, tangibility, reliability, empathy, and customer satisfaction predict the purchase intention of insurance policies. Responsiveness, assurance, and customer trust do not support the intention to purchase insurance policies.

Managerial Implications

Insurance companies must emphasize the visibility of their existence, in the form of leaflet advertisements hoardings, or print advertisements. A virtual tour on the website may also be considered for showcasing the tangibility of the insurance company. Usage of modern equipment at office premises often lures the customers. The use of artificial intelligence (AI), and robotics may further help to attract customers. The management of the insurance companies must organize soft-skill training for their employees, in which the emphasis is provided on the learnings related to empathy and reliability. The employees must be well-trained to understand the needs and perspectives of the clients. The employees handling the clients directly must ensure that he or she does not give false promise to the clients. The employees must be well-trained in handling client queries and they should not be liberal to mention workdays or process days needed to either fulfill the claim or process any requests. Thus, all the employees must properly know the standard operating procedure (SOP) adopted by the company in solving clients' requests and claims. Prompt web services and offline services is a key to customer satisfaction. The company may encourage customers to write a review on their insurance products and services, which may act as a decision signal for others.

The purchase intention of any product or service is dependent on a variety of factors. Each factor of the SERQUAL tool is quite prominent in measuring the purchase intention, especially for the brick-

and-mortar setup i.e. physical outlets. The external environment is quite dynamic and, hence the importance of SERQUAL to predict purchase intention is questioned in this research. The study identifies that with the changing time the impact of SERQUAL factors on purchase intention changes. Out of the five SERQUAL factors, three factors, such as Tangibility, Reliability, and Empathy were noted to be significant in predicting purchase intention, which was consistent with the findings of the majority of the past researchers. All three independent factors explained 98% of the dependent variable i.e. Purchase Intention. Responsiveness and Assurance do not significantly predict purchase intention, which is inferred to deviate from the findings of previous research scholars. It might have differed, because many of the customers have shifted to the online purchase of insurance, especially during and post-COVID times. Online purchase of insurance not only makes the transaction quick but also relieves one from the physical paperwork and submissions. The ease of purchase and selection of low premium deals, often lure the customers to buy online insurance.

The present research tried to add two more constructs such as customer satisfaction and customer trust to check whether it influenced the purchase intention. Customer Satisfaction positively influenced purchase intention, but customer trust did not influence purchase intention. With the advent of social media activeness, a company's image and its services are always evaluated by the customers before they purchase it. Thus, a good review and higher gratification ratings from the satisfied customer may serve as a benchmark for prospective customer satisfaction. Good ratings from secondary sources such as web aggregators also motivated the prospective customer to buy a specific company's insurance policy. This study can be useful for insurance companies, both life, and non-life to pitch their services.

Limitations and Future Research

The present study is just limited to Gandhinagar city, it may be extended to Gujarat level or India level. The sample size may also be increased. The study could have been conducted by creating two groups such as online insurance buyers and offline insurance buyers, to establish a comparison and develop better insights. The study might also be segregated for comparison of life insurance buyers vis-à-vis non-life insurance buyers. The same study might have been done for only one segment such as life insurance (or non-life insurance), and a comparison might have been made between online versus offline buyers.

The future scope of research could be the comparison of the Technology Acceptance Model (TAM) and the SERQUAL Model. A separate study for identifying the factors influencing, purchase intention of online buyers, using TAM model may be proposed. Customer Satisfaction and Customer Trust could be treated as mediating variables to SERQUAL, for predicting purchase intention. A new construct such as endorsement of web aggregators influencing purchase intention may also be studied. The mediating role of web aggregators' endorsement may also act as a future scope for research. The role of social media reviews or electronic word of mouth (E-WOM) may be considered as mediating variable to study the purchase intention of life or non-life insurance products. Similarly, the WOM variable may be included as a mediator in understanding the purchase intention of life or non-life insurance products. The gender and age variables may be considered as moderating variables to study the purchase intention of life and non-life insurance products.

REFERENCES

Alauddin, M., & Ahsan, S., Md., Mowla, M., Islam, Md., Hossain, M. (2019). Investigating the relationship between service quality, customer satisfaction and customer loyalty in the hotel industry: Bangladesh perspective. *Global Journal of Management and Business Research*, *19*(1), 29–35.

Alemayehu, A., & Dalega, D. (2019). Impact of Service Quality on Customer Satisfaction in Insurance Companies: A Study Conducted on Wolaita Zone. *Journal of Marketing and Consumer Research*, *63*, 1–6. doi:10.7176/JMCR/63-01

Alharthey, B. (2019). Impact of Service Quality on Customer Trust, Purchase Intention and Store Loyalty, with Mediating Role of Customers' Satisfaction on Customer Trust and Purchase. *British Journal of Marketing Studies*, *7*(2), 40–61.

Alumran, A., Hou, Y. X., Sun, J., Yousef, A., & Hurst, C. (2014). Assessing the construct validity and reliability of the parental perception on antibiotics (PAPA) scales. NCBI. https://www.ncbi.nlm.nih.gov/pmc/articles/PMC3909352/

Anderson, J., & Gerbing, D. (1988). Structural equation modelling in practice: A Review and Recommended Two-Step Approach. *Psychological Bulletin*, *103*(3), 411–423. https://psycnet.apa.org/buy/1989-14190-001. doi:10.1037/0033-2909.103.3.411

Arokiasamy, A., & Tat, H. (2014). Assessing the Relationship between Service Quality and Customer Satisfaction in the Malaysian Automotive Insurance Industry. *Middle East Journal of Scientific Research*, *20*(9), 1023–1030. doi:10.5829/idosi.mejsr.2014.20.09.12029

Awang, Z. (2012). *Structural Equation Modeling Using Amos Graphic*. Penerbit Universiti Teknologi MARA.

Bagozzi, R. P., & Yi, Y. (1988). On the Evaluation of Structural Equation Models. *Journal of the Academy of Marketing Science*, *16*(1), 74–94. doi:10.1007/BF02723327

Bahadur, W., Aziz, S., & Zulfiqa, S. (2018). Effect of employee empathy on customer satisfaction and loyalty during employee–customer interactions: The mediating role of customer affective commitment and perceived service quality. *Cogent Business & Management*, *5*(1), 1–21. doi:10.1080/23311975.2018.1491780

Bai, B., Law, R., & Wen, I. (2008). The impact of website quality on customer satisfaction and purchase intentions: Evidence from Chinese online visitors. *International Journal of Hospitality Management*, *27*(3), 391–402. doi:10.1016/j.ijhm.2007.10.008

Bala, N., Sandhu, H., & Nagpal, N. (2011). Measuring Life Insurance Service Quality: An Empirical Assessment of SERVQUAL Instrument. *International Business Research*, *4*(4), 176–190. doi:10.5539/ibr.v4n4p176

Bente, C. (2011). Service Quality in Insurance Companies. *The Annals of the University of Oradea. Economic Sciences*. http://anale.steconomiceuoradea.ro/volume/2021/n1/018.pdf

Bernardi, R. A. (1994). Validating Research Results when Cronbach'S Alpha is Below. 70: A Methodological Procedure. *Educational and Psychological Measurement, 54*(3), 766–775. doi:10.1177/0013164494054003023

Brown, J. (2002). The Cronbach alpha reliability estimate. *Shiken:JALT Testing & Evaluation SIG Newsletter, 6* (1), 17-19. https://hosted.jalt.org/test/bro_13.htm

Brownlee, J. (2019, November 5). A Gentle Introduction to Maximum Likelihood Estimation for Machine Learning. *Machine Learning Mastery.* https://machinelearningmastery.com/what-is-maximum-likelihood-estimation-in-machine-learning/

Chege, C. (2021). Examining the influence of service reliability on customer satisfaction in the insurance industry in Kenya. *International Journal of Research in Business and Social Science, 10*(1), 259–265. doi:10.20525/ijrbs.v10i1.1025

Chege, C., Wanjau, K., & Nkirina, S. (2019). Relationship between empathy dimension and customer satisfaction in the insurance industry in Kenya. *International Journal of Research in Business and Social Science, 8*(6), 357–366. doi:10.20525/ijrbs.v8i6.577

Chimedtseren, E., & Safari, M. (2001). Service quality factors affecting purchase intention of life insurance products. *Journal of Insurance and Financial Management, 1*(1), 1–12.

Cronin, J. Jr, & Taylor, S. (1992). Measuring Service Quality: A Reexamination and Extension. *Journal of Marketing, 1992*(56), 55–68. doi:10.1177/002224299205600304

Devi, P., & Prabhakar, C. (2018). Assessing the Service Quality Gaps in the Life Insurance Sector. *International Journal of Pure and Applied Mathematics, 119*(15), 1639–1648.

Directorate of Census Operations. (2011). *District Census Hand-book.* DCO. https://gujecostat.gujarat.gov.in/uploads/mediafiles/2406-PART-B-DCHB-GANDHINAGAR.pdf

Elevating the insurance customer experience. (2020). IBM. https://www.ibm.com/downloads/cas/AAV81JLZ

Fawad. (2021, November 26). *SEM|SPSS AMOS|Assess Discriminant Validity|Heterotrait Monotrait Ratio* [Video]. [Youtube]. https://www.youtube.com/watch?v=XlYU6z5f8aI&t=70s

Fornell, C., & Larcker, D. F. (1981). Evaluating structural equation models with unobservable Variables and Measurement Error. *JMR, Journal of Marketing Research, 18*(1), 39–80. doi:10.1177/002224378101800104

Gaskin. (2013, October 13). *Standardized Estimates and R-Square in AMOS* [Video] Youtube. https://www.youtube.com/watch?v=3KHULVuCSh0

Gera, R., Mittal, S., Batra, D., & Prasad, B. (2017). Evaluating the Effects of Service Quality, Customer Satisfaction, and Service Value on Behavioral Intentions with Life Insurance Customers in India. *International Journal of Service Science, Management, Engineering, and Technology, 8*(3), 1–20. doi:10.4018/IJSSMET.2017070101

Getnet, B. (2020). The Impact of Service Quality on Customer Satisfaction in Case of Selected Insurance Companies in Bale Robe Town. *Research on Humanities and Social Sciences*, *10*(11), 40–48. doi:10.7176/RHSS/10-11-04

Hair, J. F., Black, W. C., Babin, B. J., Anderson, R. E., & Tatham, R. L. (2010). *Multivariate Data Analysis* (7th ed.). Pearson Education Inc.

Haque, M., & Sultan, Z. (2019). A Structural Equation Modeling Approach to Validate the Dimensions of SERVPERF in Insurance Industry of Saudi Arabia. *Management Science Letters*, *9*, 495–504. doi:10.5267/j.msl.2019.1.012

Heffernan, T., O'Neill, G., Travaglione, T., & Droulers, M. (2008). Relationship Marketing. *International Journal of Bank Marketing*, *26*(3), 183–199. doi:10.1108/02652320810864652

Huy, L., Thinh, N., Pham, L., & Strickler, C. (2019). Customer Trust and Purchase Intention: How Do Primary Website Service Quality Dimensions Matter in the Context of Luxury Hotels in Vietnam? *International Journal of E-Services and Mobile Applications*, *11*(1), 1–23. doi:10.4018/IJESMA.2019010101

IRDAI. (2021). *The IRDAI Annual Report, 2020-2021*. IRDAI. https://www.irdai.gov.in/admincms/cms/uploadedfiles/annual%20reports/Annual%20Report%202020-21.pdf

Iwaarden, J., Ton, W., Ball, L., & Millen, R. (2003). Applying SERVQUAL to Web sites: An exploratory study. *International Journal of Quality & Reliability Management*, *20*(8), 919–935. doi:10.1108/02656710310493634

Jadil, Y., Rana, N., & Dwivedi, Y. (2022). Understanding the drivers of online trust and intention to buy on a website: An emerging market perspective. *International Journal of Information Management Data Insights.*, *2*(1), 1–12. doi:10.1016/j.jjimei.2022.100065

Jajaee, S., & Ahmad, F. (2012). Evaluating the Relationship between Service Quality and Customer Satisfaction in the Australian Car Insurance Industry. *International Conference on Economics, Business Innovation*, *38*, (pp. 219-223). Macrothink.

Jeon, H., Kim, C., Lee, J., & Lee, K. (2021). Understanding E-Commerce Consumers' Repeat Purchase Intention: The Role of Trust Transfer and the Moderating Effect of Neuroticism. *Frontiers in Psychology*, *12*, 1–14. doi:10.3389/fpsyg.2021.690039 PMID:34140923

Jong, J. (2016). Self-Administered Surveys. *Cross Cultural Survey Guidelines*. https://ccsg.isr.umich.edu/chapters/data-collection/self-administered-surveys/

Joreskog, K. G., & Sorbom, D. (1984). LISREL-VI User's Guide (3rd ed.). Scientific Software.

Khatoon, S., Zhengliang, X., & Hussain, H. (2020). The Mediating Effect of Customer Satisfaction on the Relationship between Electronic Banking Service Quality and Customer Purchase Intention: Evidence from the Qatar Banking Sector. *SAGE Open*, *10*(2), 1–12. doi:10.1177/2158244020935887

Khurana, S. (2012). Relationship between Service Quality and Customer Satisfaction: An empirical study of Indian Life Insurance Industry. *Journal of Research in Marketing*, *1*(2), 35–42.

Kotler, P., Keller, K., Koshy, A., & Jha, M. (2013). *Marketing Management—A South Asian Perspective* (13th ed.). Pearson.

KPMG. (2022). *Outlook for the year - Insurance sector in India*. KPMG. https://home.kpmg/in/en/blogs/home/posts/2022/01/insurance-ecosystems-outlook-growth-mantra.html

Kumar, R., Jothimurugan, T., & Anbuoli, P. (2018). Importance of SERVQUAL dimensions in leveraging service quality in insurance industry from the perspective of different cultural and socioeconomic environment – a SEM approach. *International Journal of Services and Operations Management*, *30*(1), 98–119. doi:10.1504/IJSOM.2018.091442

Kumar, R., & Singh, M. (2010, July). Using SERVQUAL Model for Comparative Service Quality Analysis of the Indian Non-Life Insurance Sector. *Paradigm*, *14*(2), 56–63. doi:10.1177/0971890720100207

Kumar, S. (2020, March 8). How to do Multi-collinearity test?/|Tolerance test|VIF| [Video]. Youtube. https://www.youtube.com/watch?v=W4o_HWrnk2Q

Kyriazos, T. (2018). Applied Psychometrics: Sample Size and Sample Power Considerations in Factor Analysis (EFA, CFA) and SEM in General. *Psychology (Irvine, Calif.)*, *9*(8), 2207–2230. doi:10.4236/psych.2018.98126

Ling, K., Chai, L., & Piew, T. (2010). The Effects of Shopping Orientations, Online Trust and Prior Online Purchase Experience toward Customers' Online Purchase Intention. *International Business Research*, *3*(3), 63–76. doi:10.5539/ibr.v3n3p63

Marsrurul, M. (2019). Impact of service quality on customer satisfaction in Bangladesh Tourism Industry: An empirical study. *Advances in Management*, *12*(1), 136–140.

Mostafa, R., Elseidi, R. (2018). Factors affecting consumers' willingness to buy private label brands (PLBs). *Spanish Journal of Marketing-ESIC*, *22* (3), 341-361. . doi:10.1108/SJME-07-2018-0034

Panda, T., & Das, S. (2014). The Role of Tangibility in Service Quality and Its Impact on External Customer Satisfaction: A Comparative Study of Hospital and Hospitality Sectors. *The IUP Journal of Marketing Management*, *13*(4), 53–69.

Panigrahi, S., Azizan, N., & Waris, M. (2018). Investigating the Empirical Relationship Between Service Quality, Trust, Satisfaction, and Intention of Customers Purchasing Life Insurance Products. *Indian Journal of Marketing*, *48*(1), 28. doi:10.17010/ijom/2018/v48/i1/120734

Paposa, S., Ukinkar, V., & Paposa, K. (2019). Service Quality and Customer Satisfaction: Variation in Customer Perception Across Demographic Profiles in Life Insurance Industry. *International Journal of Innovative Technology and Exploring Engineering*, *8*(10), 3767–3775. doi:10.35940/ijitee.J9970.0881019

Parasuraman, A., Zeithaml, V. A., & Berry, L. L. (1985). A Conceptual Model of Service Quality and Its Implications for Future Research. *Journal of Marketing*, *49*(4), 41–50. doi:10.1177/002224298504900403

Park, W., Lee, S., Park, C., Jung, S., & Kim, H. (2021). The Effect of Service Quality of Internet Insurance on Intention to Purchase Online. *International Journal of Smart Business and Technology*, *9*(1), 63–70. doi:10.21742/IJSBT.2021.9.1.06

Pathak, B. (2018). *Indian Financial System*. Pearson Education.

Pei, X.-L., Guo, J.-N., Wu, T.-J., Zhou, W.-X., & Yeh, S.-P. (2020). Does the Effect of Customer Experience on Customer Satisfaction Create a Sustainable Competitive Advantage? A Comparative Study of Different Shopping Situations. *Sustainability, 12*(18), 7436. doi:10.3390u12187436

Ramadhan, A., & Soegoto, D. (2020). The Factor Influencing Customer Satisfaction in Health Insurance Companies. *Advances in Economics. Business and Management Research, 112*, 117–121. doi:10.2991/aebmr.k.200108.028

Saeedpoor, M., Mobin, M., & Rastegari, A. (2015). A SERVQUAL Model Approach Integrated With Fuzzy Ahp and Fuzzy Topsis Methodologies to Rank Life Insurance Firms. *Proceedings of the American Society for Engineering Management 2015 International Annual Conference*. Research Gate. https://www.researchgate.net/publication/282819370_A_SERVQUAL_MODEL_APPROACH_INTEGRATED_WITH_FUZZY_AHP_AND_FUZZY_TOPSIS_METHODOLOGIES_TO_RANK_LIFE_INSURANCE_FIRMS

Sahoo, S, Misra,S., Ray, K. (2019). Customer Perception of Service based on Servqual Dimensions: A Study of Indian Life Insurance Companies. *Parikalpana - KIIT Journal of Management*. 166-182. . doi:10.23862/kiit-parikalpana/2019/v15/i1-2/190181

Salim, T., Onyia, O., Harrison, T., & Lindsay, V. (2017). *Effects of perceived cost, service quality, and customer satisfaction on health insurance service continuance. Journal of Financial Services Research*. Macmillan Publishers.

Sandhu, B. (2011). Customers' Perception towards Service Quality of Life Insurance Corporation of India: A Factor Analytic Approach. *International Journal of Business and Social Science, 2*(18), 219–231.

Schumacker, R. E., & Lomax, R. G. (2010). *A Beginner's Guide to Structural Equation Modeling* (3rd ed.). Routledge. https://usermanual.wiki/Pdf/ABeginnersGuidetoStructuralEquationModeling3rded.967768708/help

Shreenivasan, K., Thiyagarajan, S., Kasthuri, A., & Abinaya, J. (2018). Customer Perception of Service Quality in the Insurance Sectors. *International Journal of Pure and Applied Mathematics, 119*(10), 1307–1316.

Siami, S., & Gorji, M. (2012). The measurement of service quality by using SERVQUAL and quality gap model. *Indian Journal of Science and Technology, 5*(1), 1956–1960. doi:10.17485/ijst/2012/v5i1.30

Siddiqui, M., & Sharma, T. (2010). Analyzing customer satisfaction with service quality in life insurance services. *Journal of Targeting. Measurement and Analysis for Marketing, 18*(3/4), 221–238. doi:10.1057/jt.2010.17

Siddiqui, M., & Sharma, T. (2010). Measuring the Customer Perceived Service Quality for Life Insurance Services: An Empirical Investigation. *International Business Research, 3*(3), 171–186. doi:10.5539/ibr.v3n3p171

Sirdeshmukh, D., Singh, J., & Sabol, B. (2002). Consumer trust, value and loyalty in relational exchanges. *Journal of Marketing, 66*(1), 15–37. doi:10.1509/jmkg.66.1.15.18449

Sivesan, S. (2019). Impact of Service Quality on Customer Satisfaction in Life Insurance Companies in Sri Lanka. *Global Journal of Management and Business Research: E Marketing.* 19 (5).

Solutions, S. (n.d.). Identifying Multivariate Outliers in SPSS. *Statistics Solutions.* https://www.statisticssolutions.com/identifying-multivariate -outliers-in-spss/?__cf_chl_jschl_tk__=3f161d0bfbc0bb2f449f3 b6184003a98e29964ca-1624273684-0-Aa4yMWgrdSqehH0tXjJ2w0ze4u3 u1fsu4LyudGXWzrsL7N58ett1pw70Vq83Y07EQrgLUMG6xTOHw7PFoQdj9LE xjbWvByaDMsQQj9

Suki, N. (2013). Customer Satisfaction with Service Delivery in the Life Insurance Industry: An Empirical Study. *Jurnal Pengurusan, 38,* 101–109. doi:10.17576/pengurusan-2013-38-09

Swana, J., Bowers, M., & Richardsona, L. (1999). Customer Trust in the Salesperson: An Integrative Review and Meta-Analysis of the Empirical Literature. *Journal of Business Research, 44*(2), 93–107. doi:10.1016/S0148-2963(97)00244-0

Taylor, S., Nicholson, J., Milan, J., & Martinez, R. (1997). Assessing the Roles of Service Quality and Customer Satisfaction in the Formation of the Purchase Intentions of Mexican Consumer. *Journal of Marketing Theory and Practice, 5*(1), 78–90. doi:10.1080/10696679.1997.11501752

Terblanche, N. S., & Boshoff, C. (2006). The relationship between a satisfactory in-store shopping experience and retail loyalty. *South African Journal of Business Management, 37*(2), 33–43. doi:10.4102ajbm. v37i2.600

Thinh, N., Huy, L., & Son, N. (2017). The Impact of Website Service Quality on Customer Trust and Purchase Intentions in the Hotel: Theoretical Approach. *International Journal of Applied Business and Economic Research, 15*(23), 479–498.

Tsoukatos, E., & Rand, G. (2017). Path analysis of perceived service quality, satisfaction and loyalty in Greek insurance. *Managing Service Quality, 16*(5), 501–519. doi:10.1108/09604520610686746

Tsoukatos, E., Simmy, M., & Rand, G. (2004). Quality Improvement in the Greek and Kenyan Insurance Industries. *Archives of Economic History, 16*(2), 93–116.

Upadhyay, J., & Adhikari, P. (2021). Impact of Service Quality on Customer Satisfaction and Firm Performance in Nepalese Life Insurance Companies. *International Journal of Engineering and Advanced Technology, 10*(3), 110–115. doi:10.35940/ijeat.C2191.0210321

Ursach, G., Horodnic, I., & Zait, A. (2015). How reliable are measurement scales? External factors with indirect influence on reliability estimators. *Procedia Economics and Finance, 20,* 679–686. doi:10.1016/ S2212-5671(15)00123-9

Vazifehdust, H., & Farokhian, S. (2013). Factors influencing customer satisfaction with the success factors identified in the insurance industry. *African Journal of Business Management, 7*(21), 2026–2032. doi:10.5897/AJBM11.2051

Wang, J., Shahzad, F., Ahmad, Z., Abdullah, M., & Hassan, N. M. (2022). Trust and Consumers' Purchase Intention in a Social Commerce Platform: A Meta- Analytic Approach. *SAGE Open*, *12*(2), 1–15. https://journals.sagepub.com/doi/pdf/10.1177/215824402210912 62. doi:10.1177/21582440221091262

Wells, B. P., & Stafford, M. R. (1995). Service Quality in the Insurance Industry. *Journal of Insurance Regulation.*, *13*(4), 462–478.

Zeithaml, V., Berry, L., & Parasuraman, A. (1996). The Behavioural Consequences of Service Quality. *Journal of Marketing*, *60*(2), 31–46. doi:10.1177/002224299606000203

Zhu, W. (2000). Which Should it Be Called: Convergent Validity or Discriminant Validity? [PubMed]. *Research Quarterly for Exercise and Sport*, *71*(2), 190–194. doi:10.1080/02701367.2000.10608897

Chapter 3
A Systematic Literature Review of Customer Satisfaction on Digital Banking

Sagarika Mohanty
KIIT University, India

Shahni Singh
Biju Patnaik Institute of Information Technology and Management Studies, India

Jitendra Mohanty
KIIT University, India

ABSTRACT

Digital banking (DB) promotes the digital growth of the economy. Digital growth leads to an improved ecosystem. The present paper gives more significant experiences into all the selected key factors, such as service quality (SQ) and behavioral intention (BI) to use digital banking; perceived usefulness (PU) and perceived risk (PR) in digital banking adoption; performance expectancy (PE) and effort expectancy (EE) with the prospect of customer satisfaction in digital banking. This paper also analyzes different models and related theories of SQ, BI, PU, PR, PE, and EE in the prospect of the adoption of digital banking, and summarizes the gaps and limitations of this topic. To give more insightful information, these studies develop network analysis and temporal analysis in accordance with keywords. The sole sector of the economy covered by this study is banking. Thus, the findings also give a new path to analyze in other areas. Further studies can be done in large-scale review by taking other key factors like grievance handling, customer dissonance and customer experience, and others.

DOI: 10.4018/978-1-6684-5853-2.ch003

INTRODUCTION

One of the most common research areas in e-commerce and marketing studies is customer satisfaction. Customer satisfaction means how satisfied customers feel after utilizing a product or service. When the word customer comes into any field of study, it is always considered the king of the field. Customer satisfaction is the prime concern of every industry. A contrast between expectations and experiences leads to a psychological state of satisfaction (Oliver, 1980). It is the customers' feelings and perceptions after consuming the product. Every business has to analyze the preferences of the customers and fulfill their demands for longer survival in the market. Customer attitude and buying behavior are key factors of customer satisfaction that fluctuate as indicated by individual attributes like age, gender, and experience (Eriksson & Nilsson, 2007; Egala, 2021). In this sense, customer happiness is a powerful response to purchasing circumstances that is crucial in retail banks. According to a number of academic research, satisfaction with mobile banking is a factor that influences its outcomes (Sampaio et al., 2017; Mohammadi, 2015).

Digital banking (DB) is one of the ways ahead to transform the banking sector. DB is one of the facilities provided by the banks to their clients to operate all the banking transactions with the help of the internet by using electronic gadgets like cell phones, computers, laptops, etc (Yoon, 2010). According to the RBI report, adopting online banking has generated more profits for banks. Although the operational cost of technology adopted by banks is comparatively more, this figure is much less than profits earned from electronic banking. The development of the COVID-19 pandemic provided some stimulus for the adoption and use of digital channels. As a result, there was an increased reliance on virtual banking application services, notably during the period of customer's mobility restrictions (Egala, 2021). Different researchers have given different terms to digital banking. However, according to findings, it is observed that digital banking has been denoted by a different term like m-banking (Comninos et al., 2008), internet banking (Cheng et al., 2006; Alsajjan & Dennis, 2010; Lai & Li, 2005), online banking (Dauda et al., 2015; Aladwani, 2001; Pikkarainen et al., 2004), mobile banking (Lee & Chung, 2009; Sampaio et al., 2017), and electronic banking (Gan et al., 2006).

Poon (2008) found that factors such as ease of use, banking content, speed, availability of features, and cyber security were important in influencing the users whether to opt for e-banking services or not in a Malaysian internet banking environment. Confidentiality and security were cited as the main reasons for dissatisfaction, whereas ease of use, accessibility, convenience, design, and content was cited as the key sources of satisfaction (Calisir & Gumussoy, 2008; Poon, 2008). In case of service failure, clients with high and low perceived fairness had considerably varied effects of given advantages on customer satisfaction (Shih & Fang, 2004). In order to fully understand customer satisfaction, it is important to pinpoint the essential elements (Harb et al., 2022). A study in Thailand showed the advantage of online banking services and found that customer satisfaction is attained by providing a wide range of banking services (Rompho & Unyathanakorn, 2014). Ahmad and Al-Zu'bi (2011) in their study observed that convenience, accessibility, and privacy directly impact the customer satisfaction. Brazil, the United States, and India's tendency to avoid uncertainty had little influence on the study's results (Sampaio et al., 2017). The effectiveness of the banking website is a crucial component of the quality of the internet banking services. The results showed a substantial correlation between the satisfaction of e-customer, loyalty, and the quality of digital banking services (Amin, 2016). Results from the structural model also indicate a strong and favorable correlation among users satisfaction and opinions of the overall digital banking services quality (Rod et al., 2009; Alalwan et al., 2005). The findings emphasize the significance of enhancing "customer satisfaction" through improved "DB experience" offers, demonstrating the link between the two (Mbama et al., 2018). Customer satisfaction or fulfillment in digital banking refers to the assessment of whether the service provided by digital banks has met the customers' requirements (Chauhan et al., 2022).

The structure of the current review article is as follows: first, the "Introduction part", precisely discussed the background of digital banking. The objectives of the present studies are signified in the second part. The third part is "methodology, "summarized with the PRISMA flowchart. The fourth part is the "Analysis and Findings" which is focused on a brief outline of variables chosen for the studies followed by conceptions, models, theories, network analysis, and temporal analysis, and the last part is addressed with the " Discussion, Limitations & Future Research, Conclusion and References".

Objectives

- To identify various research variables like service quality (SQ), behavioral intention (BI) to use digital banking, perceived usefulness (PU), perceived risk (PR) in digital banking adoption, performance expectancy (PE), and effort expectancy (EE) with the prospect of customer satisfaction in digital banking.
- To analyze different models and related theories SQ, BI, PU, PR, PE, and EE pertaining to the topic of online banking in customer satisfaction.
- To summarize the gaps and limitations of this topic.
- To develop network analysis in the context of keywords
- To analyze country-wise paper publications, their citations, and their total strength link.
- To examine the published documents with the help of temporal analysis.

METHODOLOGY

Figure 1. PRISMA flowchart (Liberati et al., 2009)

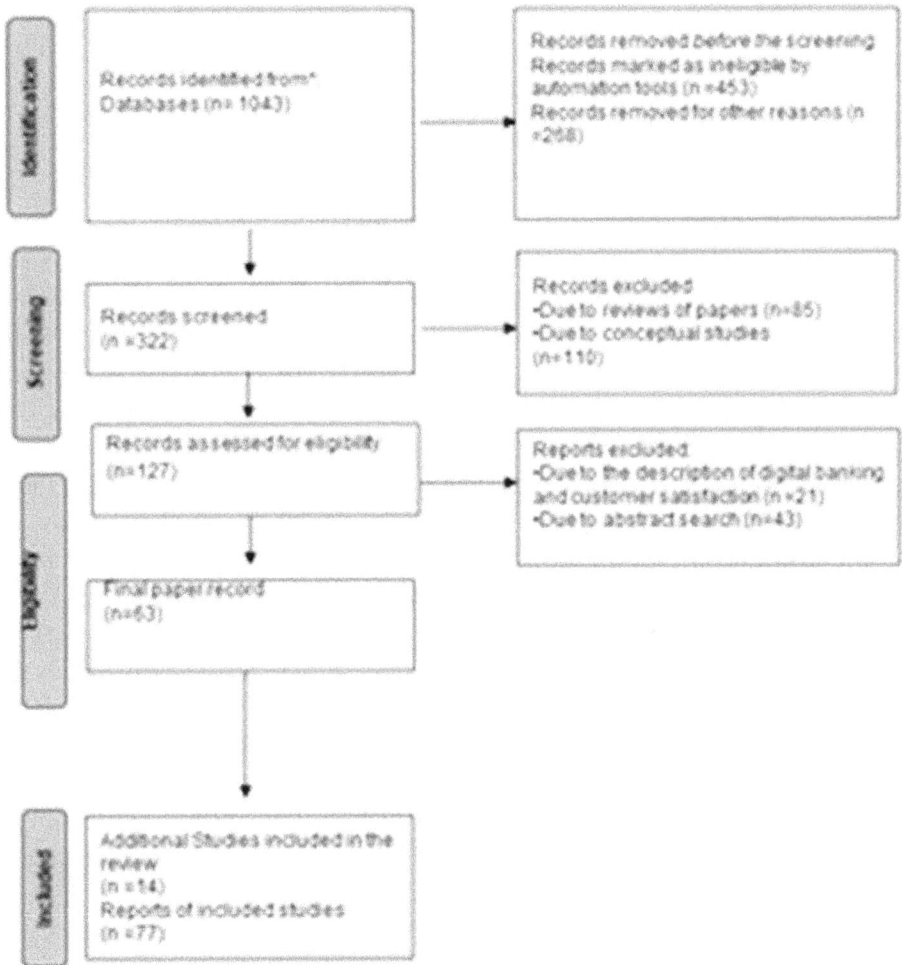

The present paper is based on a systematic literature review (SLR). The SLR is a kind of writing literature survey that gathers and fundamentally investigates numerous research papers in a systematic way. The reason for an SLR is to give comprehensive information about the research question. PRISMA technique is used for systematic literature review. For the sources of documents, the SCOPUS, Ebsco, Emerald, Google scholar, Sage Journals, Web of Science, and Taylor & Francis journal publications database are adopted. The period from 2000 to 2023 around 23 years involved papers are considered for the study. More than 1500 articles were found while searching keywords like, "digital banking" AND "customer satisfaction". On the basis of the area of research and language, 1043 papers were chosen. After the conceptual studies and subject matter, 322 papers are taken for analysis but 127 papers fulfilled the eligibility criteria on the consideration of careful screening of abstracts. However, 63 papers were made available in the full-text studies that correspond to the goal of the current investigation. Additionally,14 more papers from different databases have been included in the study. Thus, a total of 77 papers have been adopted for review of the recent paper. In order to provide more pertinent insights into the research, the current paper has been developed with an action plan that includes several graphs, network analysis, and a tabular presentation. Figure 1 is a visual of this flow.

Analysis and Findings

Selected Variables Study: Service Quality (SQ)

SQ could be stated as a customer's opinion of a bank's presentation, which may be positive, prevalent, or unfavorable. If the bank's SQ is satisfactory, the customer would prefer to repeat the same service; however, if the bank is unable to give satisfactory assistance to its clients, then, at that point, it would lead to adverse consequences (Ma & Zhao, 2012). According to Parasuraman et al. (1988), SQ is the difference between what a company offers its clients and what they expect from it. An interactive service among clients and financial institutions using the internet is characterized as a digital service (Rowley, 2006). The study by Parasuraman et al. (2005), reported that digitalized services are a means of communication between a firm and its customers, and as such, the institutions must guarantee the competence and acceptability of its services. According to Santos (2003), service quality digitally is a technique for customer assessment. In the past years, various conceptual ad empirical research examinations have been to find out the vital traits of SQ to digital service, and SERVQUAL has been broadly acknowledged and utilized in estimating data of SQ (Van Dyke et al., 1997). Joseph et al. (1999) took into consideration banks' SQ regarding innovation use, i.e., ATMs, phone, and the web, and recognized six aspects.

Behavioral Intention (BI)

Behavior intention (BI) is estimated by getting some information about customers' intentions and plans to utilize the innovation. Al-Somali et al. (2009) identified that to assess usage behavior (UB), users' genuine frequencies of internet banking were measured. The literature of (Alalwan et al., 2018; Nasri & Chrfeddine, 2012) observed that BI is an important factor among the principal antecedent constructs and consumer utilization of self-service technology (SST).

Perceived Usefulness (PU)

PU is a most prominent element that examined the impact of PEU (Perceived Ease of Use) and belief on customers' usage of digital banking with the aid of using Estonian customers (Eriksson et al., 2005). Afterward, Eriksson and Nilsson (2007) supported PU in improving each customer's willingness to adopt online banking and multichannel consumer satisfaction in the context of Estonian customers. Chiou and Shen (2012) accepted that PEU and PU are the key elements predicting clients' attitudes towards IB (Internet banking) usage. Perceived Usefulness is an important factor for user recognition of information technology. Moon and Kim (2001) discovered that PEU have a great impact on customers' attitude than PU, and an intrinsic motivational factor i.e. perceived playfulness has a greater emphasis placed on attitude than external motivation. i.e. perceived usefulness.

Perceived Risk (PR)

PR is described as the chance of customer bearing losses in pursuit of the favored effects of making use of internet banking (Featherman & Pavlou, 2003). Many researchers found unique interest in problems that might be involved with PR (Curran & Meuter, 2005). The biggest barrier to the uptake of online banking appears to be a security risk (Alsajjan & Dennis, 2010). The components associated with PR had broadly appeared as an important negative factor for customers' intentions and internet banking (Laukkanen et al., 2008; Al-Jabri, 2015; Flavián et al., 2006). The willingness to use mobile banking is found to be significantly impacted by compatibility and PR (Gerrard et al., 2006).

Performance Expectancy (PE)

PE is characterized as how much a man/woman trusts that making use of the innovation will assist that person to achieve profits in work execution (Venkatesh et al., 2003). With respect to digital banking, customers accept that utilizing this help will bring about redefining the model of banking structure, design of navigation, variety of web pages visited, and variety of exchanges executed (Dwivedi et al., 2017; Chiu et al., 2009; Mathew et al., 2020). Mir et al., (2022) and Zhou et al., (2010) discovered using UTAUT that PE significantly affects the continuous use of M-Banking.

Effort Expectancy (EE)

EE implies the number of attempts a customer needs to provide for utilizing the virtual service. Customers will now no longer experience comfort if the device is simply too complex to apply. Digital services of the financial institution must not be difficult to use. EE was one of the important factors (Venkatesh et al., 2003). Tsourela and Roumeliotis (2015) additionally observed that EE is having an optimistic impact on the customer in the case of innovative service. EE is characterized as "the degree of simplicity associated with the utilization of a device" (Ozturk et al., 2016; Kumar & Reinartz, 2006). The smooth accessibility of technology encourages customers and creates them to undertake the technology (Dwivedi et al., 2017). Thus, while updating the technological service automatically, customers must not face problems during the use of the technology (Oliveira et al., 2014).

Theories and Models

Technology Acceptance Model (TAM)

TAM is created by Davis et al. (1989). The Theory of Reason Action model serves as its foundation. TAM is useful to provide an explanation for why human beings use technology (Chui et al., 2009). The essential objective of TAM is to figure out the factors for accepting innovation. TAM might be suitable to expand the behavior and experience of the consumer in the event of the latest innovation (Davis et al., 1989). There are 2 determinants in TAM i.e. PU and PEU (Davis, 1989). These determinants create a favorable BI towards using the information technology that frequently impacts self-reported use. TAM states that the attitude of a person towards adopting a system and PU mutually determine BI (Davis et al., 1989). Hou (2016) conducted a study that determines which model may best explain consumer satisfaction, retention, and loyalty. That observation uses different models which include the Expectation confirmation model, TAM, and synthesized model. The study's findings demonstrate that other models, such as EMC, are superior to TAM because PEOU has no real effect on the consumer. TAM assumes that people act in certain ways because they consider the advantages and want to get certain outcomes (Dishaw & Strong, 1999). Mathieson (1991) observed that TAM is better than TRA and TPB in explaining the intention and attitudes of customers using information technology. Chang (2008) utilized TAM to find the customers' acceptance of intelligent agent technology. King & He (2006) led a factual meta-evaluation of TAM and tested it in different areas utilizing eighty-eight distributed investigations and the outcomes demonstrated TAM to be a strong, profoundly dependable, legitimate, and vigorous predictive model.

Theory of Reasoned Action (TRA)

The way a human behaves is impacted by the BI, this is explained by TRA. TRA is a BI model developed by Fishbein, Ajzen, and Belief (1975) which explained the reasons of behavior such as outside and inside factors. The author suggested that expectation is "the prompt determinant of the corresponding behavior", which is separated into "attitude toward behavior", and "emotional standard concerning behavior". The TRA is one of the most important theories used to present a cause of human behavior (Venkatesh et al., 2003). Davis (1989) set in TAM that the two hypothetical constructs, PU and PEU are essential determinants used in an association. These constructs additionally offer higher measures for predicting and explaining systems. The appropriate change ought to be taken into consideration to propose a new study as there is no decision on various parts of the TRA (Sheppard et al., 1988).

Theory of Planned Behavior (TPB)

To overcome the limitations of TRA, TPB was developed by Martin and Ajzen (1980). To solve the TRA issue, Ajzen (1991) used perceived behavioral control as a prerequisite of BI. Consequently, in TPB, an individual's overall performance of positive conduct relies upon his/her purpose towards that conduct, the intention is predicated on the basis of attitudes, subjective norms & perceived behavioral control. Ajzen (2006) characterizes PBC as "individuals' view of their capacity to play out a given way of behaving", and empirical proof indicates that it improves predictions of intentions. Vijayasarathy and Jones (2000) indicated that perceptions might vary as per the sort of conduct, others might also additionally fluctuate in step with the form of conduct, and similarly, Hartwick and Barki (1994) display that subjective norms sizeable impact on intentions for the obligatory system. Davis et al. (1989) neglect to see a huge connection between subjective norms and intentions.

Unified Theory of Acceptance and Use of Technology (UTAUT)

UTAUT is the most relevant hypothesis which can make a change in BI and the use of innovation (Neufeld et al., 2007). UTAUT has 4 constructs such as PE, SI, EE and FC (Martins et al., 2014). PE (Performance Expectancy) shows the number of benefits that customers are getting from the usage of technology (Raza et al., 2020). EE indicates how the amount of customer needs to apply different technology (Alalwan et al., 2018). In accordance with SI (Social influence), Al-Somali et al. (2009) identified that the acceptability and usage patterns of early adopters of new ITs are significantly influenced by social factors. The last component is FC (Facilitating Conditions) which shows customers' sources as the technology performance depends upon customers' device and technology (Chauhan et al., 2022; Alsajjan & Dennis, 2010). UTAUT is utilized to find out the employees' capacity of acknowledgment towards new innovation. Alvesson and Kärreman (2007) discovered that there is a need to be a few adjustments in the event that they need to use this idea to realize consumers' behavior. UTAUT2 has 3 extra variables i.e. habit, price, and hedonic motivation than UTAUT. Hedonic motivation refers back to enjoyment. Kim et al. (2005) tested propensity for innovation usage could be a fundamental variable as customers will feel all right with ordinary use and they will have the option to use these advancements better step by step. Chin et al. (2003) expressed PLS is perhaps of the best technique which was utilized to figure out the impact of various factors in UTAUT2. Morris et al. (2005) found that elderly individuals can't utilize innovation like the youth. Venkatesh and Moris (2000) observed that ladies are not dynamic in the event of innovation use.

Other Models of Adoption

Most of the studies were related to digital banking which adopted SEM (Structural Equation Model). SEM is a statistical technique that measured the relationship among the observed variables. It is linked with different variables or constructs chosen by different researchers. The structural model helps to determine the beta coefficient (β), which demonstrates the relationship link between variables or constructs (Mathew et al., 2020; Rod et al., 2009; Sampaio et al., 2017; Alalwan et al., 2018). A Random Utility Model (RUM) is also used to analyze customer preference regarding banking services, future banking service attributes, and possible perceived utility (Varian, 2003). In order to examine the consumers' preferences for prospective future online banking services in the Nigerian banking industry, this study combined stated preference methodologies and conjoint analysis with a discrete choice model (Dauda et al., 2015). CFA and EFA are applied to analyze the relationship of chosen variables (Sampaio et al., 2017; Mir et al., 2022; Alalwan et al., 2018).

Methods Utilized

The previous studies were based on several data collection methods which includes qualitative; quantitative and mixed methods (Mir et al., 2022; Egala, 2021; Amin, 2016; Rod et al., 2009; Chauhan et al., 2022). The most frequently used method for data collection regarding digital banking adoption is the survey method (Martins et al., 2014; Dauda et al., 2015; Aladwani, 2001). The survey included a structured questionnaire method and mailed questionnaire method, the 7-Likert scale for measurement which raging from totally disagree (1) to totally agree (7) for collecting responses from informants (Mathew et al., 2020; Boon-itt, 2015; Mir et al., 2022). For example, Sampaio et al. (2017) conducted survey methods where 383 questionnaires were collected to analyze customer satisfaction with m-banking apps. DBSQual scale is also used to measure the chosen factors and constructs (Mir et al., 2022). The interview method was also adopted by previous studies to identify the constructs (Mathew et al., 2020).

Network Analysis

Figure 2. The visualization of keywords network map- Occurrence of identified documents (from 2010-2023)
(Source: produced by the authors using VOSviewer s/w and the Scopus database)

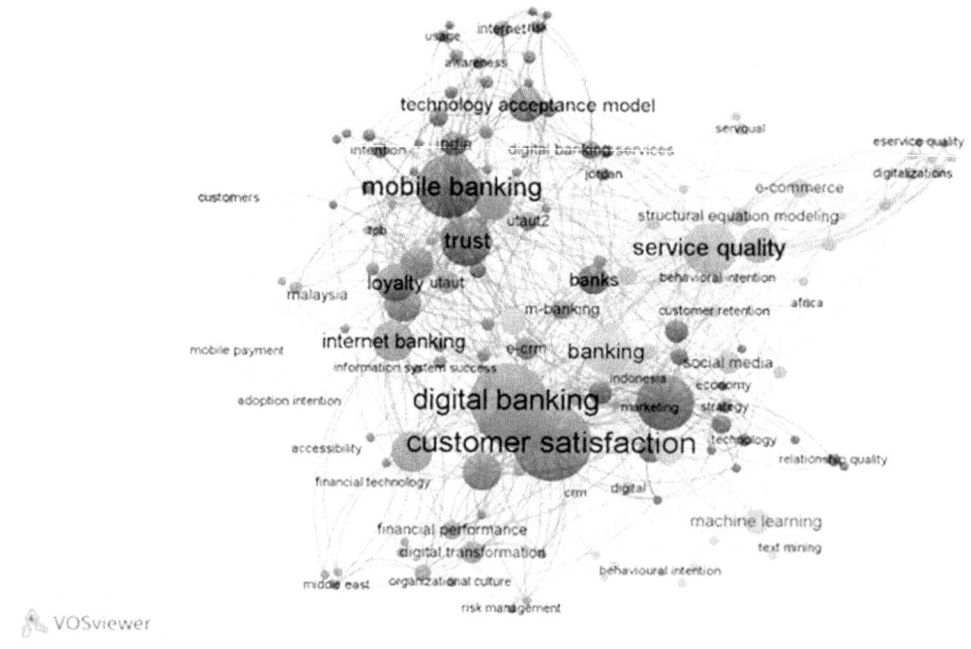

The keywords network map in Figure 2 is demonstrated in 12 clusters which are shown in 12 different colors. Examining the most significant cluster i.e. red cluster which specified digital banking, 868 connections between the keywords were found. The keywords are customer satisfaction (Eriksson & Nilsson, 2007), mobile banking (Comninos et al., 2007), customer experience (Kotler & Keller, 2012), internet banking (Alalwan et al., 2018), m-banking (Sampaio et al., 2017), service quality (Joseph et al., 1999), perceived value (Lee, 2009), trust (Järvinen 2014), e-banking services (Poon, 2008), loyalty (Kumar, 2006), etc. It is evident that one of the important variables was customer satisfaction and use of digital banking, which is connected to m-banking (Lee & Chung, 2009), service quality, trust and customer experience, etc. According to the network analysis, it is concluded that digital banking has more links with keywords of customer satisfaction, service quality, trust, mobile banking, and technology acceptance model (Lai & Li, 2005) and less connection with the keywords of risk management (Pyle, 1999), cryptocurrency (Eyal, 2017), digital transformation (Malar et al., 2019), financial performance (Chiou & Shen, 2012), etc.

The papers from the top 20 countries are presented in a table together with their citation counts and link popularity (see table 1).

Table 1. Presentation of top 20 countries' papers with their citations and total link strength

Country	Citations	Documents	Total link strength
United Kingdom	501	25	18
Saudi Arabia	375	13	16
India	301	75	15
Jordan	254	12	9
China	191	12	11
Finland	165	6	4
United States	163	15	7
Spain	150	9	0
Indonesia	125	24	2
Pakistan	103	12	10
Malaysia	85	20	17
Taiwan	80	10	7
Germany	71	7	3
South Korea	63	9	5
Romania	52	5	2
Viet Nam	44	13	5
Tunisia	43	6	1
South Africa	38	12	7
Thailand	35	6	1

(Source: produced from Scopus database)

The table 1 is a tabular presentation of the top 20 countries' papers on digital banking and customer satisfaction that highlights the country-wise highest number of citations, no. of papers published, and the overall strength of the relationships between the papers. According to the data, it found that the highest no. of citations scored by the United Kingdom with a figure of 501 and followed by Saudi Arabia and India with a figure of 375 and 301, respectively. From the table, it is concluded that India (75) has the highest no. of documents published, followed by the United Kingdom (25) and Indonesia (24). Romania has the lowest no. of published digital banking and customer satisfaction documents. As per the table, it is evicted that, the total strength link of digital banking and customer satisfaction papers are more in United Kingdom (18) and no connection is found in Spain.

Temporal Analysis

Figure 3. Temporal analysis of no. of documents published from 2010 to 2023
(Source: generated from Scopus database)

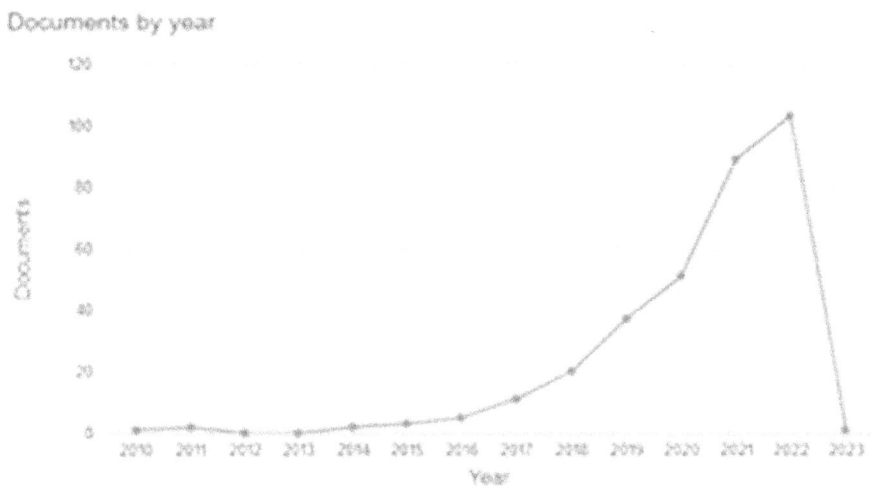

The temporal analysis is completed and displayed in figure 3 for a better interpretation of the current review study. Data for the analysis were gathered from the Scopus database, with the time frame for this particular study being from 2010 to 2023. The graph shows that customer satisfaction and digital banking were initially low, but with time, they have gradually improved. The period from 2019 to 2022 is remarkable as the graph has increased tremendously. The paper reached a peak in the year 2022, with 103 published papers and followed by the years 2020 and 2019 with 89 and 57 no. of publications respectively.

DISCUSSION

The importance of high-quality digital banking services in emerging nations has been highlighted by this study. The findings of Egala (2021), showed a strong correlation between customer retention choices and satisfaction with digital banking services. The findings also showed that consumer happiness and intent to stay with a brand are impacted by the quality characteristics of digital banking services such as usability, effectiveness, privacy/security, and reliability. Eriksson and Nilsson (2007) observed that multichannel satisfaction has an unfavorable effect on customers' willingness to keep using online banking & that customers face problems to differentiate between the banking services offered through online mode and other modes. It also analyzed that personalization, website design, user-friendliness, and digital efficiency are all 4 individual dimensions which showed that each of the four aspects of the online banking service quality has a substantial positive link with the other dimensions (Amin, 2016; Boon-itt, 2015; Raza et al., 2020). DB provides more precise and superior service quality to bank users (Mbama et al., 2018; Lee & Chung, 2009). According to the study by Kaur et al., 2021, north Indian customer satisfaction and the quality of their digital banking services are significantly correlated. They employed five service quality metrics for the analysis, and it was found through the CTA (Confirmatory Tetrad Analysis) that these metrics—reliability, assurance, tangibility, empathy, and responsiveness have a significant impact on customer satisfaction with digital banking services (Van Dyke et al., 1997; Parasuraman et al., 1991). Users are more likely to be thrilled with their online service and, as a result, more delighted with their banks when the overall quality of the internet banking service in New Zealand is judged to be excellent. This is supported by the substantial positive connection between customer satisfaction and overall internet banking service quality (Rod et al., 2009). The total service quality of digital banking services is directly linked with the quality of online information technology, banking service products, and online customer support, all of which have a favorable effect on customer satisfaction (Jun & Cai, 2001; Rod et al., 2009; Han & Baek, 2004).

The study by Martins et al. (2014) identified that age is a demographic factor that elucidated behavior intention of adoption of internet banking services and also concluded that older respondents will employ more frequently to access digital banking. Al-somali et al. (2009) observed that social influence also had a small but significant impact on BI, indicating that our respondents' intentions to utilize internet banking are influenced by external variables like friends' opinions. Behavioral intentions have such a big impact on user behavior (Chiu et al., 2005). Online banking customers are much more inclined to access the system if they are meant to do so (Nasri & Charfeddine, 2012). As a result, the use of IB by Jordanian banking customers will expand due to their behavioral intentions (Alalwan et al., 2018). According to his findings, perceived trustworthiness and usability as well as perceived usefulness are important factors in predicting behavioral intention in mobile banking. The overview of the study by Gu et al. (2009) suggested that there are major significant paths that lead to behavioral intention i.e., perceived usefulness → self-efficiency → perceived ease-of-use → structural assurance → trust → behavioral intention.

Perceived usefulness directly influences the attitudinal intention of digital banking users proved by conceptually and empirically (Alsajjan et al., 2010). According to the investigation of Cheng et al. (2006) implied that PU significantly affects the propensity to use internet banking. Additionally, it indirectly affects the behavioral use of online banking through attitude. The findings show that performance risk has a considerable negative impact on perceived usefulness (Lee, 2009). According to Kesharwani and Bisht (2012), identified that users in India were more likely to access online banking when perceived simplicity of use was acknowledged as a relevant factor that influence PU. A substantial favorable association between perceived utility and convenience of adoption and the attitude of customers toward self-service channels of banks was confirmed by Berger and Bouwman (2009) in Germany. However, the perceived internet banking to be has a favorable influence on the customer's attitude and their purpose to use it (Suh & Han, 2002; Alalwan et al., 2018; Nasri & Charfeddine, 2012; Eriksson & Nilsson, 2007; Moon & Kim, 2001; Lee, 2009). As per the conclusion from a study by Gu et al., (2009), perceived usefulness has been positively impacted by perceived ease of use, trust, and system quality and not impacted by social influence. As per the study of Yiu et al. (2007), internet banking of Hongkong users has been positively connected with perceived usefulness and customer satisfaction. Additionally, it showed a link between consumer satisfaction and perceived usefulness in digital banking, with higher perceived usefulness leading to higher customer satisfaction levels in the long run (Chiu et al. 2005). Bhattacherjee (2001) used EDT to investigate the role that cognitive belief and affect play in a person's intention to continue utilizing online banking services. According to his findings, customer satisfaction was significantly influenced by perceived usefulness. In research to gauge customer satisfaction with the e-commerce channel, Devaraj et al. (2002) concluded the evidence that perceived usefulness and perceived ease of use are important factors in determining customer satisfaction. They drew inspiration from the TAM, TCA, and SERVQUAL frameworks, three widely used ones.

There are several risks associated with the perceived risks. Such them are social risk, transactional risk, psychological risk, financial risk, security risk, performance risk, and time risk (Littler & Melanthiou, 2006; Lee, 2009). The cognitive inclination of an individual to risk varies among cultures and is likely to have an impact on how they perceived and assessed risks. Risks associated with performance, social, financial, time, and security risk have unfavorable influences on the intention to utilize online banking have revealed by a study by Lee (2009). The purpose of Jordanian users to adopt online banking will decline as a result of perceived risk (Alalwan et al., 2018). The utilization of IB in Hong Kong is directly concerned to PR (Yiu et al., 2007). Experience and brand are dependent on "perceived risk," which is related to "brand trust" (Mbama et al., 2018). Perceived risk has a direct relationship with attitude toward digital banking adoption and indirectly connected with the perceived benefit and behavioral intention to adopt digital banking (Lee, 2009). It has also been proved from the study of Martins et al. (2013) that perceived risk directly influences the PU, PE and effort EE, and BI of using digital banking. Perceived risk in digital banking also directly affects the customer experience and indirectly influences customer loyalty, financial performance, and customer satisfaction (Mbama et al., 2018).

The phrase "the degree to which an individual believes that using the technology will assist him or her in achieving advances in job performance" is used to define performance expectancy (PE). It was proven to be one of the best indicators of actual user behavior and concluded that PE significantly and favorably affects the BI of M-banking users (Baabdullah et al., 2019). The study by Alalwan et al. (2018) observed that there has a significant connection between customer expectancy and behavior. The statistical findings strongly suggested that PE has a remarkable impact on the cost-benefit analysis of using digital banking (Martins et al., 2014; Suh & Han, 2002). To put it another way, users who operate internet banking as a useful tool that improves their everyday life and provides a number of benefits, such as effectiveness, convenience, and more highly than the price they paid and vice versa (Ho & Ko, 2008). As per the UTAUT model, EE positively affects PE. When customers experience that IB is simple to apply and doesn't require lots of attempts, they will have excessive expectations in the direction of obtaining the anticipated overall performance; otherwise, their overall PE can be low (Zhou et al., 2010). Hariyanti et al. (2020b) found in their research that PE has a favorable and considerable impact on the BI of mobile banking users.

According to Venkatesh et al. (2003), when people get more expertise using the targeted technology, there is a higher likelihood that effort expectancy will have no effect. Theoretically, several researchers have found that effort expectancy has a negligible effect on performance (Chauhan et al., 2022; Mathew et al., 2020; Martins et al., 2014; Hanafizadeh et al., 2014). The likelihood that Jordanian customers will embrace internet banking (IB) will grow with effort expectations. The expected effort will raise IB performance expectations (Alalwan et al., 2018). EE has little impact on access to M-Banking (Baabdullah et al., 2019). The considerable connection among EE and BI to adopt internet banking has been confirmed by the empirical findings. Therefore, if respondents believe using these technologies is simple and requires little work, they are more inclined to want to put IB into practice (Amin, 2015; Venkatesh et al., 2012). Hariyanti et al. (2020a) covered in their study that EE is having a positive and significant effect on BI. Fauzi et al. (2018) concluded that BI, PE, FC & EE have a considerable indirect impact on the behavior use of customers.

LIMITATIONS AND FUTURE RESEARCH

The current review is based on 77 articles. To get more insightful outcomes, further research can be done on the large-scale review by enhancing the database. This paper focused on the study of 6 variables only. So, further research can be included other variables like customer relationship management (CRM), information technology (IT), grievance handling (GH), and others. Future research can be narrowed down to digital banking application, their design structure, banking products available in digital banking apps, etc. This study concluded with different variables with customer satisfaction. Thus, further study can be elucidated with the study of the relationship between different variables with behavioral usage, customer intentions, and customer dissonances about digital banking services. This research is limited to the only banking industry. Thus, the findings also give a new path to analyze in other areas.

CONCLUSION

Digital Banking is a program for banks that let users to access and use their financial transactions (such as fund transfers, balance inquiries, and opening different bank accounts like FD, RD, etc. via the internet (Shih & Fang, 2004). Our study is focused on the review of customer satisfaction on digital banking adoption. After a careful analysis of previous literature on customer satisfaction on digital banking, it concluded that to find out variables or constructs, several researchers applied TAM, TRA, UTAUT and TPB models. It has also been found that to link the different variables or constructs, most of the studies applied the SEM model. Thus, from the above literature, it is clearly reviewed that all the chosen factors, SQ, BI, PU, PR, PE, and EE with the prospect of customer satisfaction in digital banking. After the analysis of chosen variables, it summarized that the impacts of PE and EE on behavior intention were significant, indicating that people are concerned with the results of utilizing internet banking and the effort required to use it (Alalwan et al., 2018; Baabdullah et al., 2019; Hanafizadeh et al., 2014). Venkatesh et al. (2003) further claim that if PE and EE are included as major predictors of behavioral intention, then the affecting function of enabling situations on behavioral intention is more likely to disappear. Performance expectations had a substantial influence on customers' willingness to utilize internet banking (Dwivedi et al., 2017; Tsourela and Roumeliotis, 2015). According to statistical findings, performance expectancy significantly affects the cost-benefit analysis of using internet banking (Ho and Ko, 2008). Although there is concern over perceived risk issues, investment banks may be able to reduce them and protect digital channels by making the necessary expenditures (Martins et al., 2014; Littler & Melanthiou, 2006). Additionally, it was discovered that there has a favorable relationship between customer satisfaction and service quality (Raza et al., 2020). As per the analysis by Rod et al. (2009), observed that the internet banking services quality is favorably linked with the effectiveness of digital systems and client service in New Zealand. The purpose to use such services is significantly impacted by perceived risk in both direct and indirect ways (Yiu et al., 2007; Curran & Meuter, 2005). Theoretically, our findings indicate that perceived risk boosts the UTAUT model's ability to predict intention. The key predictors of customer intention and usage of internet banking have been investigated and confirmed for a number of variables. For instance, Martins et al. (2014) discovered PE; EE & social influence are the major variables that influence customers' desire to use online banking based on the data collected from two hundred and forty-nine bank customers in Portugal. Shih and Fang (2004) also observed a substantial correlation between behavioral intention and actual internet banking usage. PE; EE; playfulness and website design were found to be the important drivers of the consumer's intention in Oman (Riffai et al., 2012). Al-Somali et al. (2009) claimed that perceived simplicity of use has a significant impact in enhancing both customer attitudes and PU towards online banking, and have supported these findings. The fact that there is a strong correlation among the effectiveness of digital customer service and the overall effectiveness of internet services suggests that banks place a premium on customer care when it comes to online banking (Chin et al., 2003). Customers still value dependability, responsiveness, tangibles, and empathy even in the absence of face-to-face contact. Customers' satisfaction with the quality of the overall internet banking experience is directly impacted by these factors, which in turn determine how satisfied they are with the bank as a whole (Egala, 2021).

REFERENCES

Ahmad, A. E. M. K., & Al-Zu'bi, H. A. (2011). E-banking functionality and outcomes of customer satisfaction: an empirical investigation. *International journal of marketing studies, 3*(1), 50-65.

Ajzen, I. (1985). From intentions to actions: A theory of planned behavior. In *Action control* (pp. 11–39). Springer. doi:10.1007/978-3-642-69746-3_2

Ajzen, I. (1991). The theory of planned behavior. *Organizational Behavior and Human Decision Processes, 50*(2), 179–211. doi:10.1016/0749-5978(91)90020-T

Ajzen, I. (2006). *Behavioral interventions based on the theory of planned behavior*. UMass.

Al-Jabri, I. M. (2015). The intention to use mobile banking: Further evidence from Saudi Arabia. *South African Journal of Business Management, 46*(1), 23–34. doi:10.4102ajbm.v46i1.80

Al-Somali, S., Gholami, R., & Clegg, B. (2009). An investigation into the acceptance of online banking in Saudi Arabia. *Technovation, 29*(2), 130–141. doi:10.1016/j.technovation.2008.07.004

Aladwani, A. M. (2001). Online banking: A field study of drivers, development challenges, and expectations. *International Journal of Information Management, 21*(3), 213–225. doi:10.1016/S0268-4012(01)00011-1

Alalwan, A. A., Dwivedi, Y. K., Rana, N. P., & Algharabat, R. (2018). Examining factors influencing Jordanian customers' intentions and adoption of internet banking: Extending UTAUT2 with risk. *Journal of Retailing and Consumer Services, 40*, 125–138. doi:10.1016/j.jretconser.2017.08.026

Alsajjan, B., & Dennis, C. (2010). Internet banking acceptance model: Cross-market examination. *Journal of Business Research, 63*(9-10), 957–963. doi:10.1016/j.jbusres.2008.12.014

Alvesson, M., & Kärreman, D. (2007). Constructing Mystery: Empirical Matters in Theory Development. *Academy of Management Review, 32*(4), 126. doi:10.5465/amr.2007.26586822

Amin, M. (2016). Internet banking service quality and its implication on e-customer satisfaction and e-customer loyalty. *International Journal of Bank Marketing, 34*(3), 280–306. doi:10.1108/IJBM-10-2014-0139

Baabdullah, A. M., Alalwan, A. A., Rana, N. P., Kizgin, H., & Patil, P. (2019). Consumer use of mobile banking (M-Banking) in Saudi Arabia: Towards an integrated model. *International Journal of Information Management, 44*, 38–52. doi:10.1016/j.ijinfomgt.2018.09.002

Berger, A. N., & Bouwman, C. H. (2009). Bank liquidity creation. *Review of Financial Studies, 22*(9), 3779–3837. doi:10.1093/rfs/hhn104

Bhatiasevi, V. (2016). An extended UTAUT model to explain the adoption of mobile banking. *Information Development, 32*(4), 799–814. doi:10.1177/0266666915570764

Bhattacherjee, A. (2001). Understanding information systems continuance: An expectation-confirmation model. *Management Information Systems Quarterly, 25*(3), 351–370. doi:10.2307/3250921

Bhattacherjee, A. (2012). *Social science research: Principles, methods, and practices*. CreateSpace Independent Publishing Platform.

Boateng, H., Adam, D. R., Okoe, A. F., & Anning-Dorson, T. (2016). Assessing the determinants of internet banking adoption intentions: A social cognitive theory perspective. *Computers in Human Behavior, 65*, 468–478. doi:10.1016/j.chb.2016.09.017

Boon-itt, S. (2015). Managing self-service technology service quality to enhance e-satisfaction. *International Journal of Quality and Service Sciences, 7*(4), 373–391. doi:10.1108/IJQSS-01-2015-0013

Brown, R. D. (2001). E-commerce: Customer service success factors. *Futurics, 25*(3/4), 18.

Bussakorn, J., & Dieter, F. (2005). Internet banking adoption strategies for a developing country: The case of Thailand. *Internet Research, 15*(3), 295–311. doi:10.1108/10662240510602708

Calisir, F., & Gumussoy, C. A. (2008). Internet banking versus other banking channels: Young consumers' view. *International Journal of Information Management, 28*(3), 215–221. doi:10.1016/j.ijinfomgt.2008.02.009

Casaló, L. V., Flavián, C., & Guinalíu, M. (2008). The role of satisfaction and website usability in developing customer loyalty and positive word-of-mouth in the ebanking services. *International Journal of Bank Marketing, 26*(6), 399–417. doi:10.1108/02652320810902433

Chan, S., & Lu, M. (2004). Understanding Internet banking adoption and use behavior: A Hong Kong perspective. *Journal of Global Information Management, 12*(3), 21–43. doi:10.4018/jgim.2004070102

Chang, H. H. (2008). Intelligent agent's technology characteristics applied to online auctions' task: A combined model of TTF and TAM. *Technovation, 28*(9), 564–577. doi:10.1016/j.technovation.2008.03.006

Chauhan, S., Akhtar, A., & Gupta, A. (2022). Customer experience in digital banking: A review and future research directions. *International Journal of Quality and Service Sciences, 14*(2), 311–348. doi:10.1108/IJQSS-02-2021-0027

Cheng, T. E., Lam, D. Y., & Yeung, A. C. (2006). Adoption of internet banking: An empirical study in Hong Kong. *Decision Support Systems, 42*(3), 1558–1572. doi:10.1016/j.dss.2006.01.002

Chin, W. W., Marcolin, B. L., & Newsted, P. R. (2003). A Partial Least Squares Latent Variable Modeling Approach for Measuring Interaction Effects: Results from a Monte Carlo Simulation Study and an Electronic-Mail Emotion/Adoption Study. *Information Systems Research, 14*(2), 1. doi:10.1287/isre.14.2.189.16018

Chiou, J. S., & Shen, C. C. (2012). The antecedents of online financial service adoption: The impact of physical banking services on Internet banking acceptance. *Behaviour & Information Technology, 31*(9), 859–871. doi:10.1080/0144929X.2010.549509

Chiu, C.-M., Chang, C.-C., Cheng, H.-L., & Fang, Y.-H. (2009). Determinants of customer repurchase intention in online shopping. *Online Information Review, 33*(4), 761–784. doi:10.1108/14684520910985710

Chiu, C. M., Hsu, M. H., Sun, S. Y., Lin, T. C., & Sun, P. C. (2005). Usability, quality, value and e-learning continuance decisions. *Computers & Education, 45*(4), 399–416. doi:10.1016/j.compedu.2004.06.001

Comninos, A., Esselaar, S., Ndiwalana, A., & Stork, C. (2008). Towards evidence-based ICT policy and regulation m-banking the unbanked. *Externo.* http://externo.casafrica.es/aeo/pdf/english/ overview_part_2 _09_aeo_09.pdf

Curran, J. M., & Meuter, M. L. (2005). Self-service technology adoption: Comparing three technologies. *Journal of Services Marketing, 19*(2), 103–113. doi:10.1108/08876040510591411

Dauda, S. Y., & Lee, J. (2015). Technology adoption: A conjoint analysis of consumers′ preference on future online banking services. *Information Systems, 53*, 1–15. doi:10.1016/j.is.2015.04.006

Davis, F. D. (1989). Perceived Usefulness, Perceived Ease of Use, and User Acceptance of Information Technology. *Management Information Systems Quarterly, 13*(3), 319–340. doi:10.2307/249008

Davis, F. D., Bagozzi, R. P., & Warshaw, P. R. (1989). User acceptance of computer technology: A comparison of two theoretical models. *Management Science, 35*(8), 982–1003. doi:10.1287/mnsc.35.8.982

Devaraj, S., Fan, M., & Kohli, R. (2002). Antecedents of B2C channel satisfaction and preference: Validating e-commerce metrics. *Information Systems Research, 13*(3), 316–333. doi:10.1287/isre.13.3.316.77

Dishaw, M. T., & Strong, D. M. (1999). Extending the technology acceptance model with task–technology fit constructs. *Information & Management, 36*(1), 9–21. doi:10.1016/S0378-7206(98)00101-3

Dwivedi, Y. K., Rana, N. P., Jeyaraj, A., Clement, M., & Williams, M. D. (2017). Re-examining the unified theory of acceptance and use of technology (UTAUT): Towards a revised theoretical model. *Information Systems Frontiers.* doi:10.100710796-017-9774-y

Egala, S. B., Boateng, D., & Mensah, S. A. (2021). To leave or retain? An interplay between quality digital banking services and customer satisfaction. *International Journal of Bank Marketing.*

Eriksson, K., Kerem, K., & Nilsson, D. (2005). Customer acceptance of internet banking in Estonia. *International Journal of Bank Marketing, 23*(2), 200–216. doi:10.1108/02652320510584412

Eriksson, K., & Nilsson, D. (2007). Determinants of the continued use of self-service technology: The case of Internet banking. *Technovation, 27*(4), 159–167. doi:10.1016/j.technovation.2006.11.001

Eyal, I. (2017). Blockchain technology: Transforming libertarian cryptocurrency dreams to finance and banking realities. *Computer, 50*(9), 38–49. doi:10.1109/MC.2017.3571042

Fauzi, A., Widodo, T., & Djatmiko, T. (2018). Pengaruh Behavioral Intention Terhadap Use Behavior Pada Penggunaan Aplikasi Transportasi [The Effect of Behavorial Intention on Use Behavior in the Use of Transportation Applications]. *Studi Kasus Pada Pengguna Go-Jek Dan Grab Di Kalangan Mahasiswa Telkom University [On the Use of Online Transportaion Applications (Case Study on Go-Jek and Grab Users Among Telkom University students]*. E-Proceeding of Management.

Featherman, M. S., & Pavlou, P. A. (2003). Predicting e-services adoption: A perceived risk facets perspective. *International Journal of Human-Computer Studies, 59*(4), 451–474. doi:10.1016/S1071-5819(03)00111-3

Fishbein, M., Ajzen, I., & Belief, A. (1975). Intention and Behavior: An introduction to theory and research. *International Journal of Advanced Engineering and Science.*

Flavián, C., Guinaliu, M., & Torres, E. (2006). How bricks-and-mortar attributes affect online banking adoption. *International Journal of Bank Marketing, 24*(6), 406–423. doi:10.1108/02652320610701735

Gan, C., Clemes, M., Limsombunchai, V., & Weng, A. (2006). A logit analysis of electronic banking in New Zealand. Int. J. Bank Mark. 24 (6), 360–383. Gerrard, P., Cunningham, J. B., and Devlin, J. F. (2006). Why consumers are not using Internet banking: A qualitative study. *Journal of Services Marketing, 20*(3), 160–168.

Gerrard, P., Cunningham, J. B., & Devlin, J. F. (2006). Why consumers are not using internet banking: A qualitative study. *Journal of Services Marketing, 20*(3), 160–168. doi:10.1108/08876040610665616

Gu, J. C., Lee, S. C., & Suh, Y. H. (2009). Determinants of behavioral intention to mobile banking. *Expert Systems with Applications, 36*(9), 11605–11616. doi:10.1016/j.eswa.2009.03.024

Han, S. L., & Baek, S. (2004). *Antecedents and consequences of service quality in online banking: An application of the SERVQUAL instrument.* ACR North American Advances.

Hanafizadeh, P., Behboudi, M., Koshksaray, A. A., & Tabar, M. J. S. (2014). Mobile-banking adoption by Iranian bank clients. *Telematics and Informatics, 31*(1), 62–78. doi:10.1016/j.tele.2012.11.001

Harb, A., Thoumy, M., & Yazbeck, M. (2022). Customer satisfaction with digital banking channels in times of uncertainty.

Hariyanti, A. O., Hidayatullah, S., & Prasetya, D. A. (2020a). Analysis of the Acceptance and Use of Mobile Banking Services Using the Unified Theory of Acceptance and Use of Technology *International Research Journal of Advanced Engineering and Science, 5*(1), 254–262.

Hariyanti, A. O., Hidayatullah, S., & Prasetya, D. A. (2020b). Analysis of the Acceptance and Use of Mobile Banking Services Using the Unified Theory of Acceptance and Use of Technology (Case Study of Bank Jatim Pasuruan Branch). *Research Journal of Advanced Engineering and Science, 5*(1), 254–262.

Hartwick, J., & Barki, H. (1994). Explaining the role of user participation in information system use. *Management Science, 40*(4), 440–465. doi:10.1287/mnsc.40.4.440

Ho, S. H., & Ko, Y. Y. (2008). Effects of self-service technology on customer value and customer readiness: The case of Internet banking. *Internet research*. https://www.statista.com/

Järvinen, R. A. (2014). Consumer trust in banking relationships in Europe. *International Journal of Bank Marketing*.

Joseph, M., McClure, C., & Joseph, B. (1999). Service quality in the banking sector: The impact of technology on service delivery. *International Journal of Bank Marketing*, *17*(4), 182–193. doi:10.1108/02652329910278879

Jun, M., & Cai, S. (2001). The key determinants of internet banking service quality: A content analysis. *International Journal of Bank Marketing*, *19*(7), 276–291. doi:10.1108/02652320110409825

Kaur, B., Kiran, S., Grima, S., & Rupeika-Apoga, R. (2021). Digital banking in Northern India: The risks on customer satisfaction. *Risks*, *9*(11), 209. doi:10.3390/risks9110209

Kesharwani, A., & Bisht, S. S. (2012). The impact of trust and perceived risk on Internet banking adoption in India: An extension of technology acceptance model. *International Journal of Bank Marketing*, *30*(4), 303–322. doi:10.1108/02652321211236923

Kim, S. S., Malhotra, N. K., & Narasimhan, S. (2005). Two Competing Perspectives on Automatic Use: A Theoretical and Empirical Comparison. *Information Systems Research*, *16*(4), 418–432. doi:10.1287/isre.1050.0070

King, W. R., & He, J. (2006). A meta-analysis of the technology acceptance model. *Information & Management*, *43*(6), 740–755. doi:10.1016/j.im.2006.05.003

Kotler, P., & Keller, K. L. (2012). *Marketing management*. Pearson Education.

Kumar, V., & Reinartz, W. J. (2006). *Customer relationship management: a databased approach*. Wiley.

Lai, V. S., & Li, H. (2005). Technology acceptance model for internet banking: An invariance analysis. *Information & Management*, *42*(2), 373–386. doi:10.1016/j.im.2004.01.007

Laukkanen, P., Sinkkonen, S., & Laukkanen, T. (2008). Consumer resistance to internet banking: Postponers, opponents and rejectors. *International Journal of Bank Marketing*, *26*(6), 440–455. doi:10.1108/02652320810902451

Lee, K. C., & Chung, N. (2009). Understanding factors affecting trust in and satisfaction with mobile banking in Korea: A modified DeLone and McLean's model perspective. *Interacting with Computers*, *21*(5-6), 385–392. doi:10.1016/j.intcom.2009.06.004

Lee, K. C., & Chung, N. (2011). Exploring antecedents of behavior intention to use Internet banking in Korea: Adoption perspective. In *E-adoption and socioeconomic impacts: Emerging infrastructural effects*. IGI global. doi:10.4018/978-1-60960-597-1.ch003

Lee, M. C. (2009). Factors influencing the adoption of internet banking: An integration of TAM and TPB with perceived risk and perceived benefit. *Electronic Commerce Research and Applications*, *8*(3), 130–141. doi:10.1016/j.elerap.2008.11.006

Liberati, A., Altman, D. G., Tetzlaff, J., Mulrow, C., Gøtzsche, P. C., Ioannidis, J. P., Clarke, M., Devereaux, P. J., Kleijnen, J., & Moher, D. (2009). The PRISMA statement for reporting systematic reviews and meta-analyses of studies that evaluate health care interventions: Explanation and elaboration. *Journal of Clinical Epidemiology*, *62*(10), e1–e34. doi:10.1016/j.jclinepi.2009.06.006 PMID:19631507

Littler, D., & Melanthiou, D. (2006). Consumer perceptions of risk and uncertainty and the implications for behaviour towards innovative retail services: The case of internet banking. *Journal of Retailing and Consumer Services*, *13*(6), 431–443. doi:10.1016/j.jretconser.2006.02.006

Ma, Z., & Zhao, J. (2012). Evidence one-banking customer satisfaction in the China commercial bank sector. *Journal of Software*, *7*(4), 927–933.

Malar, D. A., Arvidsson, V., & Holmstrom, J. (2019). Digital transformation in banking: Exploring value co-creation in online banking services in India. *Journal of Global Information Technology Management*, *22*(1), 7–24.

Martins, C., Oliveira, T., & Popovič, A. (2014). Understanding the Internet banking adoption: A unified theory of acceptance and use of technology and perceived risk application. *International Journal of Information Management*, *34*(1), 1–13.

Mathew, S., Jose, A., Rejikumar, G., & Chacko, D. P. (2020). Examining the relationship between e-service recovery quality and e-service recovery satisfaction moderated by perceived justice in the banking context. *Benchmarking. International Journal (Toronto, Ont.)*.

Mathieson, K. (1991). Predicting user intentions: Comparing the technology acceptance model with the theory of planned behaviour. *Information Systems Research*, *2*(3), 173–191.

Mbama, C. I., Ezepue, P., Alboul, L., & Beer, M. (2018). Digital banking, customer experience and financial performance: UK bank managers' perceptions. *Journal of Research in Interactive Marketing*.

Mir, R. A., Rameez, R., & Tahir, N. (2022). Measuring Internet banking service quality: An empirical evidence. *The TQM Journal*.

Mohammadi, H. (2015). Investigating users' perspectives on e-learning: An integration of TAM and IS success model. *Computers in Human Behavior*, *45*, 359–374.

Moon, J. W., & Kim, Y. G. (2001). Extending the TAM for a World-Wide-Web context. *Information & Management*, *38*(4), 217–230. doi:10.1016/S0378-7206(00)00061-6

Morris, M. G., Venkatesh, V., & Ackerman, P. L. (2005). Gender and Age Differences in Employee Decisions about New Technology: An Extension to the Theory of Md Masum Miah – Users' Satisfaction of Digital Banking Services in Finland Planned Behaviour. *IEEE Transactions on Engineering Management*, *52*(1), 69–84.

Nasri, W., & Charfeddine, L. (2012). Factors affecting the adoption of Internet banking in Tunisia: An integration theory of acceptance model and theory of planned behavior. *The Journal of High Technology Management Research*, *23*(1), 1–14.

Neufeld, D. J., Dong, L., & Higgins, C. (2007). Charismatic Leadership and User Acceptance of Information Technology. *European Journal of Information Systems*, *16*(4), 49.

Oliveira, T., Faria, M., Thomas, M. A., & Popovic, A. (2014). Extending the understanding of mobile banking adoption: When UTAUT meets TTF and ITM. *International Journal of Information Management, 34*(5), 689e703.

Oliver, R. L. (1980). A cognitive model of the antecedents and consequences of satisfaction decisions. *JMR, Journal of Marketing Research, 17*(4), 460–469.

Ozturk, A. B., Bilgihan, A., Nusair, K., & Okumus, F. (2016). What keeps the mobile hotel booking users loyal? Investigating the roles of self-efficacy, compatibility, perceived ease of use, and perceived convenience. *International Journal of Information Management, 36*(6), 1350–1359.

Parasuraman, A., Berry, L., & Zeithaml, V. (1991). Refinement and reassessment of the SERVQUAL scale. *Journal of Retailing, 67*(4), 420–450.

Parasuraman, A., Zeithaml, V., & Malhotra, A. (2005). E-S-QUAL a multiple-item scale for assessing electronic service quality. *Journal of Service Research, 7*(3), 213–234.

Parasuraman, A., Zeithaml, V. A., & Berry, L. L. (1988). SERVQUAL: A multiple item scale for measuring customer perceptions of service quality. *Journal of Retailing, 64*(1), 12–40.

Pikkarainen, T., Pikkarainen, K., Karjaluoto, H., & Pahnila, S. (2004). Consumer acceptance of online banking: An extension of the technology acceptance model. *Internet Research, 14*(3), 224–235.

Poon, W. C. (2008). Users' adoption of e-banking services: The Malaysian perspective. *Journal of Business and Industrial Marketing.*

Pyle, D. H. (1999). Bank risk management: theory. In *Risk Management and regulation in banking* (pp. 7–14). Springer.

Raza, S. A., Umer, A., Qureshi, M. A., & Dahri, A. S. (2020). Internet banking service quality, e-customer satisfaction and loyalty: The modified e-SERVQUAL model. *The TQM Journal.*

Riffai, M. M. M. A., Grant, K., & Edgar, D. (2012). Big TAM in Oman: Exploring the promise of online banking, its adoption by customers and the challenges of banking in Oman. *International Journal of Information Management, 32*, 239–250.

Rod, M., Ashill, N. J., Shao, J., & Carruthers, J. (2009). An examination of the relationship between service quality dimensions, overall internet banking service quality and customer satisfaction: A New Zealand study. *Marketing Intelligence & Planning.*

Rompho, N., & Unyathanakorn, K. (2014). Factors Affecting Customer Satisfaction in Online Banking Service. *Journal of Marketing Development and Competitiveness, 8*(2), 50–60. http:// www.digitalcommons.www. na-businesspress.com/JMDC/ R omphoN_Web8_2_.pdf

Rowley, J. (2006). An analysis of the e-service literature: Towards a research agenda. *Internet Research, 16*(3), 339–359.

Sampaio, C. H., Ladeira, W. J., & Santini, F. D. O. (2017). Apps for mobile banking and customer satisfaction: A cross-cultural study. *International Journal of Bank Marketing.*

Santos, J. (2003). E-service quality: A model of virtual service quality dimensions. *Managing Service Quality*, *13*(3), 233–246.

Sheppard, B. H., Hartwick, J., & Warshaw, P. R. (1988). The theory of reasoned action: A meta-analysis of past research with recommendations for modifications and future research. *The Journal of Consumer Research*, *15*(3), 325–343.

Shim, S., Eastlick, M., Lotz, S., & Warrington, P. (2001). An online prepurchase intentions model: The role of intention to search. *Journal of Retailing*, *77*, 397–416.

Suh, B., & Han, I. (2002). Effect of trust on customer acceptance of Internet banking. *Electronic Commerce Research and Applications*, *1*(3-4), 247–263.

Tan, M., & Teo, T. S. H. (2000). Factors influencing the adoption of Internet banking. *Journal of the Association for Information Systems*, *1*(1).

Tsourela, M., & Roumeliotis, M. (2015). The moderating role of technology readiness, gender, and sex in consumer acceptance and actual use of Technology-based services. *The Journal of High Technology Management Research*, *26*(2), 124–136.

van Dyke, T. P., Kappelman, L. A., & Prybutok, V. R. (1997). Measuring information systems service quality: Concerns on the use of the SERVQUAL questionnaire. *Management Information Systems Quarterly*, *21*(2), 195–208.

Varian, H. R. (2003). Innovation, components, and complements. *October*.

Venkatesh, V., & Davis, F. D. (2000). A theoretical extension of the technology acceptance model: Four longitudinal field studies. *Management Science*, *46*(2), 186–204.

Venkatesh, V., Morris, M., Davis, G., & Davis, F. (2003). User acceptance of information technology: Toward a unified view. MIS Q. 27 (3), 425–478. .

Venkatesh, V., & Morris, M. G. (2000). Why Do not Men Ever Stop to Ask for Directions? Gender, Social Influence, and Their Role in Technology Acceptance and Usage Behavior. *Management Information Systems Quarterly*, *24*(1), 115.

Venkatesh, V., Ramesh, V., & Massey, A. P. (2003). Understanding usability in mobile commerce. *Communications of the ACM*, *46*, 53–56.

Venkatesh, V., Thong, J. Y. L., Xu, X., Walker, R. H., & Johnson, L. W. (2006). Why consumers use and do not use technology-enabled services. *Journal of Services Marketing*, *20*(2), 125–135.

Vijayasarathy, L. R., & Jones, J. M. (2000). Intentions to shop using internet catalogues: Exploring the effects of product types, shopping orientations, and attitudes towards computers. *Electronic Markets*, *10*(1), 29–38.

Wire, B. (1995). Stanford federal credit union pioneers online financial services. *Business Wire, June, 21*.

Yiu, C. S., Grant, K., & Edgar, D. (2007). Factors affecting the adoption of Internet banking in Hong Kong – Implications for the banking sector. *International Journal of Information Management*, *27*(5), 336–351.

Yoon, C. (2010). Antecedents of customer satisfaction with online banking in China: The effects of experience. *Computers in Human Behavior*, *26*(6), 1296–1304.

Yu, C. S. (2012). Factors affecting individuals to adopt mobile banking: Empirical evidence from the UTAUT model. *Journal of Electronic Commerce Research*, *13*(2), 104.

Zhou, T., Lu, Y., & Wang, B. (2010). Integrating TTF and UTAUT to explain mobile banking user adoption. *Computers in Human Behavior*, *26*(4), 760–767.

ADDITIONAL READING

Azjen, I. (1980). *Understanding attitudes and predicting social behavior*.

Cooil, B., Keiningham, T. L., Aksoy, L., & Hsu, M. (2007). A longitudinal analysis of customer satisfaction and share of wallet: Investigating the moderating effect of customer characteristics. *Journal of Marketing*, *71*(1), 67–83. doi:10.1509/jmkg.71.1.067

Courneya, K. S., Plotnikoff, R. C., Hotz, S. B., & Birkett, N. J. (2000). Social support and the theory of planned behavior in the exercise domain. *American Journal of Health Behavior*, *24*(4), 300–308. doi:10.5993/AJHB.24.4.6

Cronin, J. J. Jr, & Taylor, S. A. (1992). Measuring service quality: A reexamination and extension. *Journal of Marketing*, *56*(3), 55–68. doi:10.1177/002224299205600304

Dabholkar, P. A., Thorpe, D. I., & Rentz, J. O. (1996). A measure of service quality for retail stores: Scale development and validation. *Journal of the Academy of Marketing Science*, *24*(1), 3–16. doi:10.1007/BF02893933

Dodds, W. B., Monroe, K. B., & Grewal, D. (1991). Effects of Price, Brand, and Store Information on Buyers. *JMR, Journal of Marketing Research*, *28*(3), 30.

Foresee results survey (2005). Online banking: Customer satisfaction and its implications for building loyalty and influencing buying behavior. *Forbes*. http://pdf.forbes.com/adinfo/OnlineBankingSurvey2005.pdf

Hernandez, B., Jimenez, J., & Martín, M. J. (2008). Extending the technology acceptance model to include the IT decision-maker: A study of business management software. *Technovation*, *28*(3), 112–121. doi:10.1016/j.technovation.2007.11.002

Jaruwachirathanakul, B., & Fink, D. (2005). Internet banking adoption strategies for a developing country: The case of Thailand. *Internet Research*, *15*(3), 295–311. doi:10.1108/10662240510602708

Kimenyi, M., & Ndung'u, N. (2009). Expanding the financial services frontier: Lessons from mobile phone banking in Kenya. *October*.

Moe, W. W., & Fader, P. S. (2001). Uncovering patterns in cybershopping. *California Management Review*, *43*(4), 106–117. doi:10.2307/41166103

Moore, G. C., & Benbasat, I. (1991). Development of an instrument to measure the perceptions of adopting an information technology innovation. *Information Systems Research, 2*(3), 192–222. doi:10.1287/isre.2.3.192

Nayak, R. (2018). A conceptual study on digitalization of banking-issues and challenges in rural India. *Journal, 8*(6). http://www. ijmra. us

Revathi, P. (2019). Digital banking challenges and opportunities in India. *EPRA International Journal of Economic and Business Review, 7*(12), 20–23.

Saini, G. S. (2014). Mobile banking in India: Issues and challenges. *Sai Om Journal of Commerce & Management, 1*(3), 30–37.

Sharma, P., & Singh, P. (2009). Users' perception about mobile banking-with special reference to Indore & around. *Review of Business & Technology Research, 2*(1), 1–4.

Shih, Y. Y., & Fang, K. (2004). The use of a decomposed theory of planned behavior to study Internet banking in Taiwan. *Internet Research, 14*(3), 213–223. doi:10.1108/10662240410542643

Snoj, B., Korda, A. P., & Mumel, D. (2004). The relationships among perceived quality, perceived risk and perceived product value. *Journal of Product and Brand Management, 13*(3), 156–167. doi:10.1108/10610420410538050

Tashkandi, A. N., & Al-Jabri, I. M. (2015). Cloud computing adoption by higher education institutions in Saudi Arabia: An exploratory study. *Cluster Computing, 18*(4), 1527–1537. doi:10.100710586-015-0490-4

Taylor, S., & Todd, P. A. (1995). Understanding information technology usage: A test of competing models. *Information Systems Research, 6*(2), 144–176. doi:10.1287/isre.6.2.144

Wang, Y. S., & Shih, Y. W. (2009). Why do people use information kiosks? A validation of the unified theory of acceptance and use of technology. *Government Information Quarterly, 26*(1), 158–165. doi:10.1016/j.giq.2008.07.001

Wang, Y. S., Wang, Y. M., Lin, H. H., & Tang, I. (2003). Determinants of user acceptance of internet banking: An empirical study. *International Journal of Service Industry Management, 14*(5), 501–519. doi:10.1108/09564230310500192

Yang, J., Whitefield, M., & Boehme, K. (2007). New issues and challenges facing e-banking in rural areas: An empirical study. *International Journal of Electronic Finance, 1*(3), 336–354. doi:10.1504/IJEF.2007.011503

Yang, Z., & Jun, M. (2002). Consumer perception of e-service quality: From internet purchaser and non-purchaser perspectives. *The Journal of Business Strategy, 19*(1), 19–41. doi:10.54155/jbs.19.1.19-42

Chapter 4
Attitudes, Awareness, and Use of the Consumer Protection Act Among Retail Furniture Consumers in the Umlazi Township, South Africa

Pfano Mashau
University of KwaZulu-Natal, South Africa

Mathews Smangaliso Shange
University of KwaZulu-Natal, South Africa

Andrisha Beharry-Ramraj
University of KwaZulu-Natal, South Africa

ABSTRACT

The Consumer Protection Act (CPA) of 2008 was developed with the intention to protect consumers and promote fair dealings and responsible conduct of retailers in the marketplace. However, consumers continue to suffer in the marketplace due to defective products, unfair dealings, and poor service despite there being a CPA that was developed to protect their rights. Studies revealed a reduction in the number of registered complaints and an unchanged market environment for retail consumers pertaining to handling their consumer disputes. A quantitative study was conducted with a random sample of 95 retail furniture consumers who visited five furniture retail shops at Kwa Mnyandu Mall in the Umlazi township. Furniture retail consumers in Umlazi are aware of the CPA, however, they have reasonably less or no knowledge of the consumer rights contained in the CPA. Identified shortcomings in the use of the CPA to handle customer complaints is also explored. It was evident from the findings that retail consumers know that there is a CPA but they are unclear on how it is supposed to protect them when dissatisfied with a product.

DOI: 10.4018/978-1-6684-5853-2.ch004

INTRODUCTION

It is the duty of the South African government to protect its citizens from being abused by businesses through activities that violate their rights. Various legal frameworks were set up in the past to try to enforce such protection. Consumer movements (CM) also performed key tasks in protecting consumer rights through activism and organising public protests. However, their efforts to assist consumers were limited to protest campaigns rather than to holding businesses accountable for supplying defective, unsafe and harmful products. Thus, the CPA was introduced in March 2011 and signed into law in April 2011. The CPA seeks to regulate all consumer related matters in the marketplace but consumers still experience difficulties in obtaining redress when faced with retailers' unfair dealings. Nonetheless, the crucial point to consider is why consumers continue to be exploited by unscrupulous retailers despite there being a consumer law called the Consumer Protection Act. It is therefore important to examine whether the rights of ordinary consumers are protected by the CPA or not.

According to Keller and Swaminathan (2020), consumers purchase products to satisfy a need. Terblanche et al. (2016) expressed the view that consumers anticipate purchased products to be of excellent quality, in working order, able to satisfy their needs and exceed their expectations. Nonetheless, defective products are still being sold to consumers. Often, consumers do not detect product imperfections until the product has been used (Loubser & Reid, 2012). Defective goods should be returned to the retailer for either exchange or refund (Otto et al., 2014) but complaints of this nature irritate retailers who are reluctant to refund or exchange goods at the expense of their profits (Otto et al., 2014). According to De Stadler (2016), many consumers are not keen to complain to retailers as they think that nothing will be done to address their grievances. Unresolved consumer complaints may, at times, compel consumers to replace defective products at their own cost. This behaviour indirectly relieves the retailer of accountability. Such acts contribute to the infringement of consumer rights by retailers with no backlash from consumer protection legislation.

The aim of the chapter was therefore to examine the attitudes, awareness and the use of CPA by retail consumers in Umlazi township in South Africa. The chapter was imperative to ascertain whether the establishment of the CPA made consumer protection a reality or whether it became one of the government's futile exercises.

Consumer Protection Act

The CPA was promulgated in March 2011 and signed into law in April 2011. Its aim was to protect consumer rights in the marketplace (Phora, 2017). According to Devi and Rao (2016), the intention of the Act was to protect consumers' rights when they enter into business transactions with retailers or suppliers. The CPA is meant to encourage open and transparent business activities and enhance the ethical conduct of retailers in the market (Terblanche et al., 2016). Nevertheless, the plight of consumers in obtaining justice through retail complaint processes continues to exist in the retail sector, especially when a consumer has purchased a defective product. Magobo and Malunga (2015) claim that furniture retail consumers continue to struggle to obtain justice when the furniture they buy is defective.

Consumer Movements

Van Schalkwyk et al. (2015) define consumer movements (CM) as organised consumer groups whose values on the rights of consumers are held in high regard by consumers and society. Consumer movements were formed in the early 1960s due to the expansion of goods and services in the market (Weijo et al., 2018). The influx of dangerous goods and the complexity of information about goods made consumers more vulnerable. According to Weijo et al. (2018), concerns for consumer safety led to the emergence of consumer activists advocating for consumers' rights and their entrenchment as legal rights. The legal framework that protected consumers against exploitation and ensured their well-being began with CMs. The CMs used creative public performances to promote their cause and to effect change in what was considered an unfair consumer market (Weijo et al., 2018). CMs worked effectively in protecting consumers' rights if they were supported by government institutions (Pretorius, 2016). Therefore, it was crucial that consumer activists take part in the process of formulating the CPA in South Africa. The success of the CPA development relied on the collaboration between consumer movements and government (Pretorius, 2016).

Consumer Protection Act (68 of 2008)

Although all South African citizens' rights are protected under the South African Constitution, comprehensive consumer legislation was needed to protect all consumers. Thus, the CPA was established and signed into law in April 2011. The CPA consists of the following consumer rights: the first consumer right is to equality in the consumer market and protection against discriminatory marketing practices, the second right is privacy, the third right is being able to choose, while the fourth right is access to information, the fifth is the right to fair and responsible marketing, the sixth is the right being succumbed to fair and honest dealing, the seventh is the right to fair, just and reasonable terms and conditions, the eighth right is fair value, good quality and safety and final right is accountability coming from the suppliers (Van der Oordt, 2015). The CPA was constituted to regulate retail business actions and safeguard the interest of consumers in the market (Sharrock, 2016). Poor quality or unsafe products supplied in the market could endanger the lives of consumers. Consumer Protection Act, No.68 of 2008 purported that the CPA was constituted to improve consumer protection by effecting a legal framework that prohibits unjust business dealings and transactions in the South African consumer market. It was in the study's interest to understand how consumers seek redress when a defective product is supplied. Therefore, examining the CPA to see whether it has eventually managed to provide protection to ordinary retail consumers or whether it was just an idealistic documents was of great importance for the study.

BENEFITS OF CONSUMER RIGHTS

Township consumers are susceptible to unfair dealings from retailers due to limited access to information, education and a lack of knowledge of their rights (Van der Oordt, 2015). Thus, they easily fall victim to consumer rights violations by retailers. The CPA was intended to bring injustices in the marketplace to an end and rid it of errant retail business people. Each consumer right contained in the CPA was established with the intention of addressing specific consumer disputes. It is vital to understand how each of these rights benefits retail consumers. According to Van Schalkwyk et al. (2015), the following benefits are associated with using the consumers' rights as contained in the CPA:

- **The Right to Equality in the Consumer Market and Protection against Discriminatory Marketing Practices:** Retailers are not allowed to discriminate against consumer groups on the basis of skin colour, culture, gender and age or sex orientation when conducting their business activities.
- **The Right to Privacy:** Consumers are allowed to refuse access to marketing activities, reject meeting offers and demand the protection of their private information.
- **The Right to Choose:** Consumers have the right to search, compare and select products that will satisfy their needs.
- **The Right to Disclosure of Information:** Consumers can request cost-related information from suppliers to avoid being overcharged.
- **The Right to Fair and Responsible Marketing:** Direct marketing firms are not allowed to target consumers through their campaigns and bind them to their service product agreements without their consent.
- **The Right to Fair and Honest Dealing:** Consumers may ask for refunds for consumer goods that the supplier failed to deliver in time.
- **The Right to Fair Value, Good Quality and Safety:** Consumers have a right to return poor quality goods to retailers as well as those products that they deem unsafe to utilise.
- **The Right to Accountability from Suppliers:** Consumers have a right to compel suppliers to assume liability for any losses in the case where inferior quality goods were supplied.

Consumer Attitudes

Consumer attitudes emanate from acquired experiences on how to behave in a consistently favourable or unfavourable way towards the market-related situation (Kotler & Keller, 2016). This suggests that attitudes (good or bad) are shaped through experience with the service or product. Clow and Baack (2018) state that bad experiences evoke negative attitudes and emotions in the consumer and these in turn create a negative attitude towards the product. The study explores consumers' attitudes to establish how they hinder the functioning and the use of the CPA by consumers in the marketplace.

Consumer Awareness

Consumer awareness entails the consumer's ability to recognise the product under different conditions (Baines et al., 2017). Awareness occurs as the results of the marketing information that the consumers have been exposed to (Keller & Swaminathan, 2020). It is key to building consumer product knowledge. Thus, it is vital to identify how a lack of awareness affects the use of CPA by retail consumers in the marketplace.

Consumer Complaint Behaviour

Complaint behaviour refers to the process consumers undertake to register their complaints with the retailer concerned when they are dissatisfied with poor quality of service or with a product (Zeithmal et al., 2016). Products sometimes fall short of a consumer's expectations due to poor quality or performance (Wirtz & Lovelock, 2016). Thus, a consumer may decide to either to launch a complaint or to do nothing to voice his dissatisfaction with a product. Resolved consumer complaints enhance the consumer buying experience and develop long term relationships with retailers or service providers (Baines et al., 2017), while unresolved complaints are likely to create hostility or chase consumers away (Wirtz & Lovelock, 2016). Magobo & Malunga (2015) argue that unclear and tedious retail complaint processes discourage aggrieved retail consumers from lodging their complaints. It was vital to examine consumer complaint behaviour to find out how it influences the decision to use the CPA to handle complaints.

Consumer Forum on Complaints

According to Debnath and Mazurmdar (2015), consumer forums are redress platforms, such as the Consumer Commission and the Tribunal, that are available to consumers for the escalation of grievances. The Consumer Commission is a statutory body that was established as stipulated in the CPA (Woker, 2016). In cases where the retailer has failed to resolve a consumer dispute, the consumer has the right to refer the matter to the Commission (Koekemoer, 2017). Consumers who complain usually consider their complaints important and it affects them if they do not obtain redress (Donoghue & Van der Oordt, 2016). These forums do not function well as they are often criticised for being unable to resolve consumer disputes quickly, efficiently and at a low cost (Koekemoer, 2017). Very few consumers understand how to follow the legal processes required to lodge a complaint with the alternative dispute resolution channel (Woker, 2016). This is due to very little transparency in the activities of the forums. According to Naude (2018), consumer frustration is further exacerbated by some of the alternative dispute resolution decisions which are not binding on the retailer. It is therefore crucial to understand the effort made by consumer complaint forums in assisting aggrieved consumers to obtain justice as stipulated by the CPA

Consumers' Use and Application of the CPA

Application refers to the consumer's ability to use the product or service as set out in the terms and conditions as well as understand the instructions (Keller & Swaminathan, 2020). Consumers have to be exposed to the service information for them to utilise the firm's services (Wirtz & Lovelock, 2016). Donoghue and Van der Oordt (2016) reiterate that consumers must know how the CPA functions to effect the protection of consumers against ill-treatment by retailers. Sufficient CPA knowledge allows consumers to use the Act when the need arises but insufficient knowledge affects and prevents the use and application of the Act in consumer disputes. It is vital that the study establishes when and how consumers use the CPA. The study also takes into account the factors that impact the use of the CPA by retail consumers to settle their disputes with retailers.

Figure 1. Framework to Guided the Research Study
Source: Adapted from Pretorius (2016)

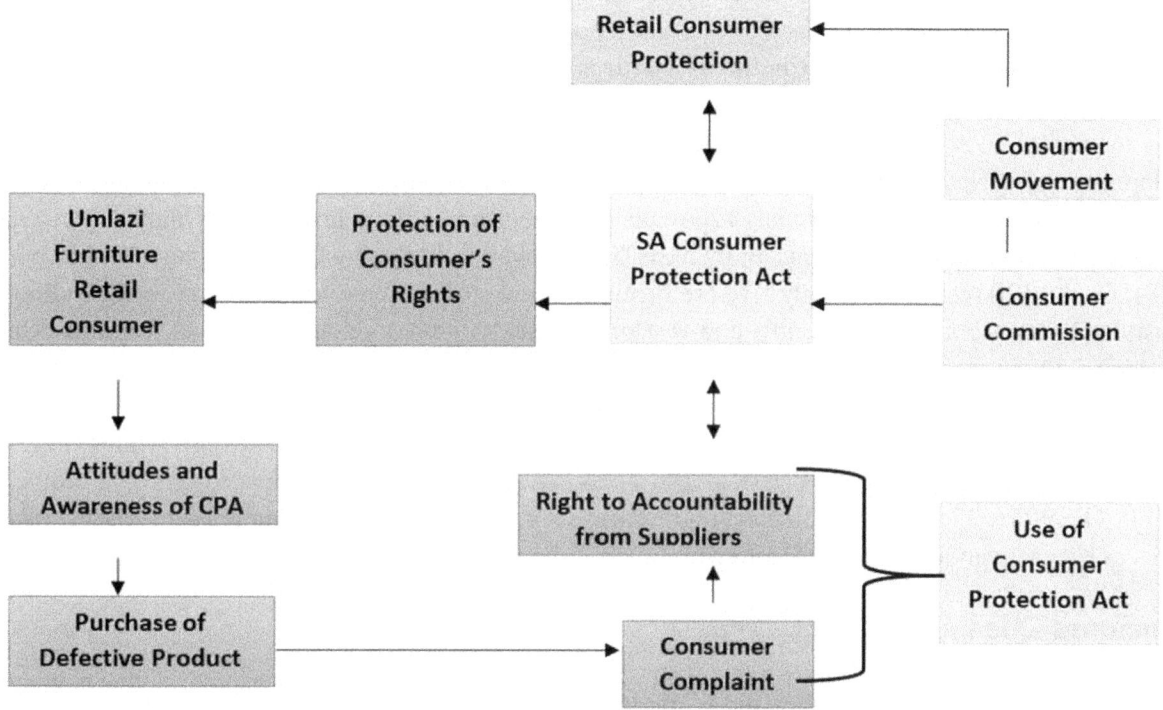

CONCEPTUAL FRAMEWORK GUIDE TO THE RESEARCH STUDY

This is an adapted conceptual framework that was used to guide the study and develop the questionnaire. Figure 1 shows the steps in the conceptual framework regarding how the CPA supposed to work based on the principles on which it was developed. The diagram illustrates how consumer movements have been actively protecting consumers since early 1960 (Van Schalkwyk et al., 2015). Consumer movements educated consumers about their rights and mobilized civil action in an attempt to protect consumers against exploitation by businesses (Bernard, 2015). The National Consumer Commission serves as the redress channel responsible for the enforcement of the CPA to safeguard consumer well-being (Sharrock, 2016). Hence, poor CPA enforcement results in consumers being exploited by retailers. The purchasing of defective products is still a source of dissatisfaction among consumers (Van der Linde, 2017). When a defective product is purchased from the retailers the CPA must protect the consumer to hold the supplier accountable for the damage suffered (Saleem et al., 2015).

However, that is not possible if consumers lack conscious awareness of the CPA and possess the bad attitudes towards the Act. When consumers complain about a defective product they are 25 empowering themselves to demand quality goods from retailers while at the same time protecting their rights. It is common knowledge that consumers often rely on the retail discretion to resolve their complaint. Thus, they overlook the protection offered by the Consumer Protection Act.

Research Methodology

The chapter is based on a research study approach using the probability sampling technique of which 80 respondents were randomly selected. The study population was furniture retail consumers who were visiting KwaMnyandu Shopping Centre. The instrument used for collecting data was a questionnaire which included questions on demographic information, awareness questions, attitude and opinions and lastly the use of CPA. The data were collected, cleaned, coded and analysed. Some of the information gathered was descriptive while the rest of the information was used for inferential analysis.

KwaMnyandu Shopping Centre has 120 retail stores located on three levels of the mall and they are visited by 8 700 retail customers on a daily basis (KwaMnyandu Shopping Centre Management Report, 2018). Of the 120 retail stores, only five are furniture retail stores. These are Sleepmasters, Bradlows, Lifestyle Discount furniture, Russell's and @ Home. Thus, the research study targeted furniture retail consumers who were visiting these furniture retail stores.

The number of selected sample units or objects is referred to as the sample size (Creswell & Creswell, 2018). In estimation that a population of 100 people visit the selected stores and specifying a level of significance of .05 and a margin of error of .05, it was calculated that the minimum sample size required was 80. Therefore, 95 people were a good representative of the population who visited the furniture retail stores at KwaMnyandu Shopping Centre.

Structured Questions

Structured questions are frequently used in marketing research and they are pre-formulated (Saunders et al., 2016). The researcher chose to use structured questions as they are appropriate for a quantitative research study approach. These are multiple choice questions used to collect quantitative data (Rahman, 2020). When questions are structured and concise respondents tend to be motivated to take part in the survey. The structured nature of these questions limits the participants' choice of answers (Rahman, 2020). The use of close-ended questions would allow the researcher to collect quantified data and use statistical analysis to analyse it. The structured nature of these questions also limits the researcher's influence because the respondents choose from a set list of answers.

Descriptive statistical analysis refers to statistically describing, aggregating and presenting collected data. The statistical software program called SPSS is often used to analyse collected data (Rahman, 2020). Inference analysis is a statistical procedure that is used to generalise the research findings of the sample to the general population (Gabriel et al., 2019). The researcher therefore chose the statistical analysis technique to analyse the data collected in the study and used inference analysis to reveal data patterns and to describe mode, standard deviation and range of data (Burns et al., 2019).

For inferential statistics, a univariate test was utilised on a categorical variable to assess whether any of the response options were selected substantially more or less often than the others. The null hypothesis assumed that all responses are equally chosen while the binomial test assessed whether a significant proportion of respondents selected one of a possible two responses. The data collected with more than two responses or binary responses was used to capture various responses from the respondents. The t-test was used to assess whether the mean score was significantly different from a scalar value. In the light of that, factor analysis was used to explore the structure of the collected data and to determine latent factors.

DATA PRESENTATION AND DISCUSSION

The respondents were asked to indicate on the questionnaires their level of awareness of the CPA. The research results outline the respondents' ratings of the statements on the Likert scale to identify significant agreements or disagreements. The following discussion of the research results is based on the questions that were asked of the respondents.

The respondents were asked to indicate their level of awareness of the CPA. They had to select the option applicable to them.

Figure 2 explains the overall responses of the respondents on the level of awareness of the CPA.

Figure 2. Level of Awareness

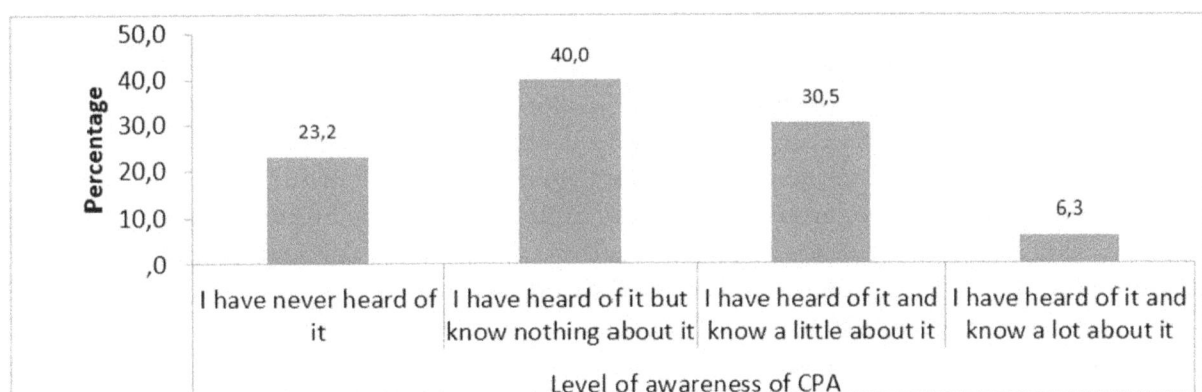

Results from a chi-square goodness-of-fit test show that a significant number of respondents the sample indicated that they have heard of the CPA but know nothing about it. About 30.5 per cent have heard of it but know a little about it while 6.3 per cent of the respondents have heard of it and know a lot about it. About 23.2 per cent have never heard of it. The responses were then split into two groups - those who have heard of the CPA and those who have not heard of it. Results of a binomial test on these two groups show that a significant 77 per cent have heard of the CPA. This implied that for consumers to be able to use the CPA to resolve consumer disputes they need to be consciously aware of the Act. The responses 1 and 2 (know nothing about) and 3 and 4 (know something about) were also grouped to test if a significant proportion know anything about the CPA. The research results show a significant number, 63 per cent, know nothing about the CPA. This shows that more consumers have no knowledge of the CPA. Respondents were asked to how often they search for Consumer Protection Act information.

Figure 3. Search for CPA Information

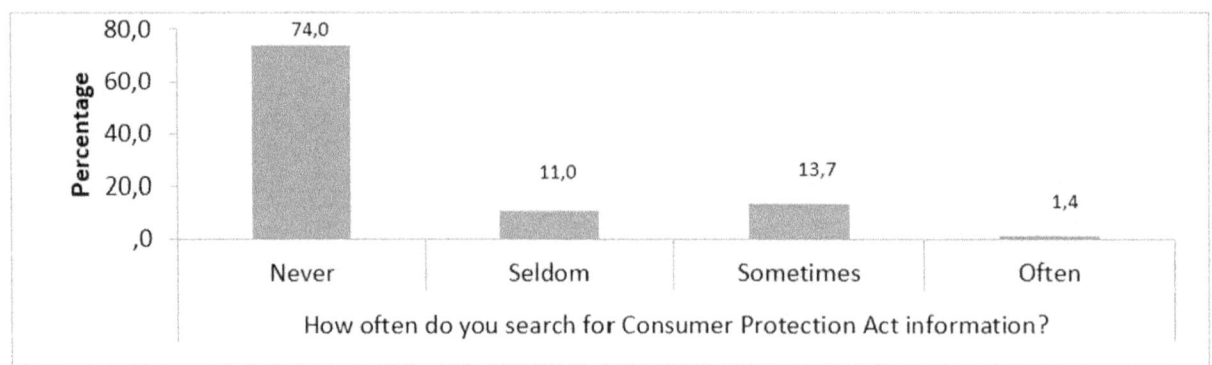

Figure 3 shows that more respondents never search for CPA information. The findings reveal that the least number of respondents often search for CPA information. About 11 per cent seldom search for CPA information while 13.7 per cent of the respondents sometimes search for CPA information. An insignificant number of respondents seldom search for CPA information. Bernard (2015) states that a lack of CPA information leaves consumers vulnerable to exploitation by errant business people. Therefore the results indicate that respondents who never search for CPA information will not have the relevant information to inform their consumer decision-making processes.

The respondents were asked to respond True, False or Unsure to each statement about the CPA. The statements were intended to provide an understanding of the respondents' overall knowledge of the CPA.

Figure 4. Correct and Incorrect Responses for Five Questions

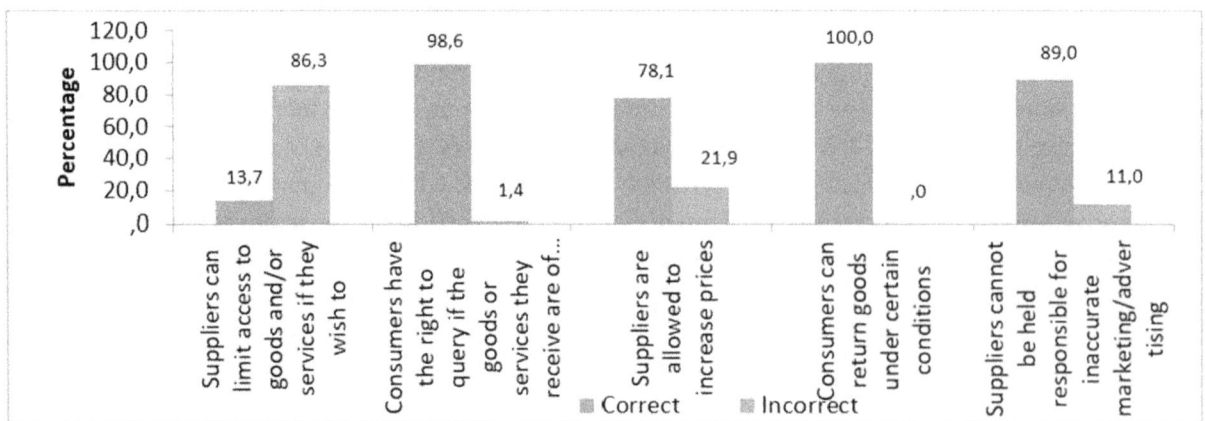

Figure 4 summarises the overall outcome of the answers to the five questions that were used to determine consumer knowledge. In response to the first question more respondents were incorrect while for the other four questions more respondents were correct. The correct responses to the four questions suggest that the respondents possess minimal knowledge of what is generally accepted as right or wrong in the marketplace.

The respondents were asked to indicate their level of agreement with the statements regarding the CPA. They had to state whether they strongly disagree, disagree, neutral, agree and strongly agree with each statement. The statements were intended to discover the respondents' opinions about the CPA. Figure 4.6 outlines the statements used to determine the respondents' opinions with regard to the CPA. This section in the questionnaire consisted of twelve statements regarding the CPA. It also examined respondents' possible attitudes towards the CPA. A one-sample t-test was used to test for significant agreement or disagreement with each item. Further analysis was conducted to test the groupings of these 12 items. Bartlett's test was applied to test the correlation between the items.

Figure 5. Furniture Retail Consumers' Opinions towards CPA

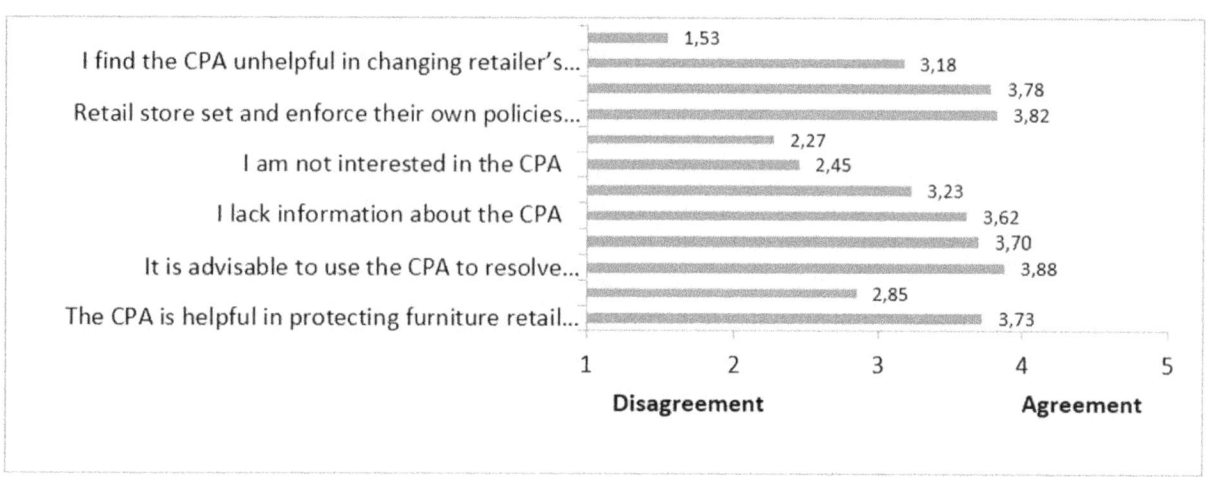

Figure 5 shows that there is significant agreement that 1. The CPA is helpful in protecting furniture retail consumers, M=3.73, p<.0005.Factor analysis with promax rotation was applied to these 12 items to explore the structure/groupings of these items. A Kaiser-Meyer-Olkin (KMO) value of 0.633 shows that the information was sufficient for impact and reliable extraction. In addition, a significant Bartlett's test (p<.05) indicates that relationships between items were not too low for reliable extraction. Two factors were extracted which account for 47.23 per cent of the variance in the data. These factors were tested for reliability using Cronbach's alpha. Alpha>.7 is considered an indication of a reliable measure, while values between 0.6 and 0.7 are considered acceptable. Items 2, 5 and 12 were dropped from this process because they either did not load strongly enough onto any factor or they negatively affected the reliability of the composite measure.

Table 1. Attitudes towards CPA

Factor	Construct name	Label	Items included	Cronbach's alpha
1	Positive attitude towards CPA	POS	1 3 4 10	0.694
2	Negative attitude towards CPA	NEG	6 7 8 9 11	0.641

Composite measures are formed for POS and NEG by calculating the average of the items in the groupings. These composite variables were used in further analysis (see Table 1). The one-sample t-test to test for significant agreement/disagreement was conducted. This result suggests that there is significant agreement that the CPA is helpful in protecting the furniture retail customer. Thus, the research findings show positive attitudes of the respondents towards the CPA. The research findings indicate that, despite a lack of awareness, respondents do have positive attitudes towards the CPA. The significant disagreement in the findings also implies that negative opinions about the CPA inhibit the effective functioning and use of the CPA by retail consumers. The existence of negative opinions about a product has a direct effect on the consumer decision-making process and behaviour (Koekemoer, 2014). Unless retail consumers possess favourable opinions and attitudes towards the CPA, it will be difficult for consumers to use the CPA to protect their rights in the marketplace.

Further opinions were investigated, here respondents were asked to indicate their agreement with the four statements. They had to indicate whether they strongly disagree, disagree, are neutral, agree and strongly agree with each statement.

Figure 6. Summary of Statements for Further Opinions

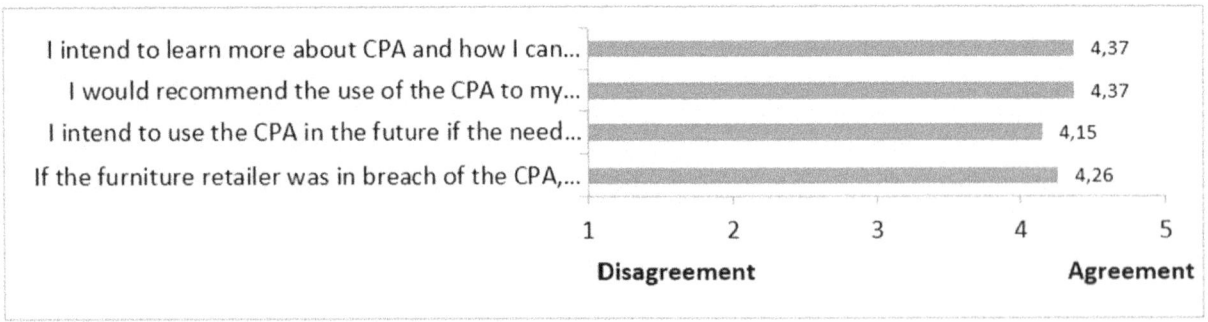

Figure 6 gives an outline of statements of further opinions regarding respondents' intention to use the CPA in the future. Responses above 3 revealed that there was significant agreement while anything below 3 suggested significant disagreement. For instance, there is significant agreement that: 1. I intend to use the CPA in the future if the need arises, M=4.15, p<.0005; 2. I intend to learn more about the CPA and how I can apply it when I purchase goods from a store, M=4.37, P<0005. In this regard, more respondents rated the statements regarding their intention to use the CPA in future above the scale of

4. These results also reveal that there is willingness to learn about the CPA and an emerging positive attitude towards using it in the future. Furthermore, a factor analysis with promax rotation was applied to these four items to explore the structure/groupings of these items.

Four items were dropped in this process because they either did not load strongly enough onto any factor or negatively affected the reliability of the composite measure. These four items were combined for a reliable single measure for intention to use the CPA as Cronbach's alpha was = .851. Table 4.9 shows that Cronbach's alpha values were below >7 which is an indication of reliability. A one-sample t-test was also done to test for significant agreement/disagreement on the intention to use the CPA in the future. The results are summarised in table 2.

Table 2. Intention to use CPA in future

Factor	Construct name	Label	Items included	Cronbach's alpha
	Intention to use	ITU	4	.851

The analysis of the single factor using a t-test showed a positive intention to use CPA in future. Therefore, it can be concluded that there was significant agreement that the respondents might use the CPA in the future, $p<.0005$ (see Table 2). These findings suggest that there was also a positive sentiment among respondents around the use of the CPA and learning more about it in the future.

This section in the questionnaire assessed the typed of consumer complaint in the furniture retail sector. The respondents were asked to indicate if any of the complaints stated resulted in them registering a complaint about a furniture retailer.

The respondents had to choose the statement that describes the reasons for them registering a customer complaint about a furniture retailer (figure 7). A binomial test was used to test if a significant proportion of the respondents cited any of the reasons mentioned in the statements. Figure below illustrate the aspects that the respondents have complained about regarding a furniture retailer.

Figure 7. Reasons for Registering a Complaint

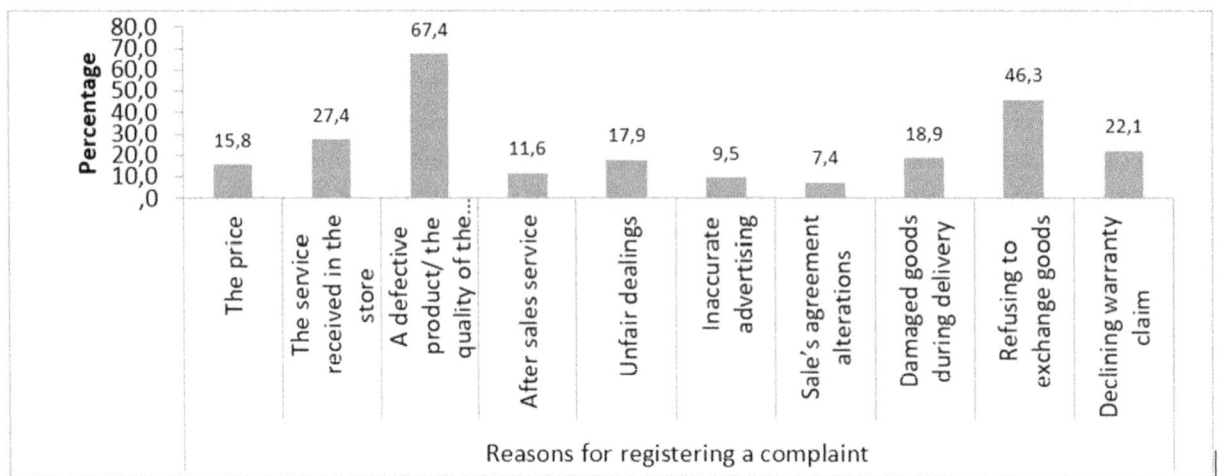

These results pertain to the full sample and a binomial test was conducted to test if a significant proportion had cited any of these reasons. The only reason that was cited by a significant proportion of the sample is 'a defective product/quality of the product', p=.001. It was found that more of the respondents have complained about a furniture retail shop concerning a defective product.

The respondents who have registered a complaint were also asked to indicate how often they follow up on their complaint and satisfactorily settled.

Figure 8 provides a summary of complaint follow up and those that were satisfactorily settled.

Figure 8. Summary of Complaint Follow up and Settlement

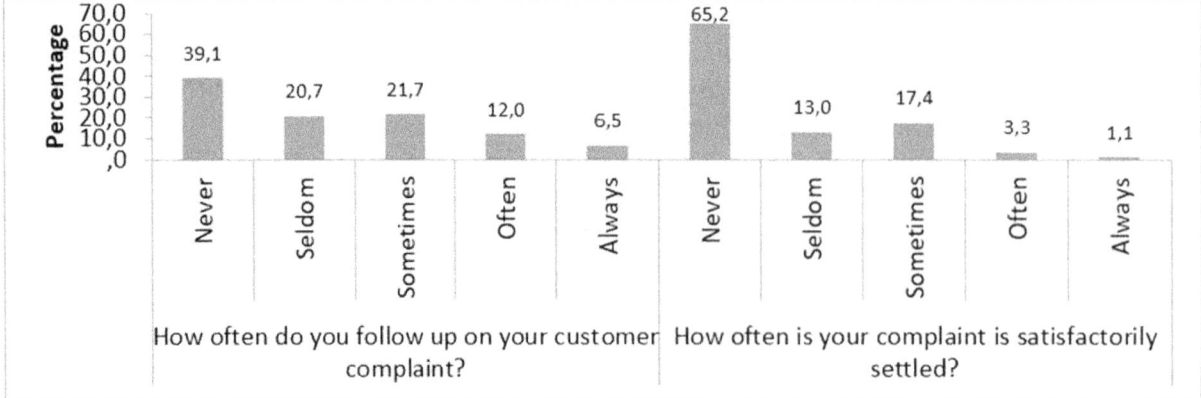

These results pertain to those who have registered a complaint. The chi-square test was conducted and the research findings show that more respondents never followed up on their complaint and in addition, that their complaint was never satisfactorily settled. The dissatisfaction among respondents could be the reason for not knowing the outcomes of their complaints or the retail reactions towards it.

The respondents were asked if they have ever used the CPA to handle a furniture retail complaint. Table 3 outlines the use of CPA among the respondents.

Table 3. Used the CPA to handle a furniture retail complaint

	Frequency	%
Yes	17	23.3
No	56	76.7
Total	73	100

From table 4 it is evident that a significant number of respondents (77 per cent) have not used the CPA to handle a furniture retail complaint, while 23 per cent have used the CPA to handle a furniture retail complaint. The results reveal that a larger number of respondents do not exercise their consumer rights contained in the Act when seeking redress. The majority of the responses reveal that the respondents have never used the CPA.

Those who have use it they had to indicate how often they have used the CPA with complaints regarding a furniture retailer.

Table 4. Number of times the CPA was used to handle a complaint

	Frequency	%
1 time	9	52.9
2-3 times	5	29.4
4-5 times	1	5.9
No response	2	11.8
Total	17	100

From table 4 it is evident that a significant number, 52.9 per cent, of the 17 respondents have used the CPA once with one complaint regarding a furniture retailer, p=.041. The findings reveal that few respondents have used the CPA once or more than once to handle furniture retail complaints. This shows that there is an emerging willingness to use the CPA to settle consumer disputes with retailers. Although a few respondents have used the CPA to handle furniture retail complaints, more respondents have never used the CPA to handle furniture retail complaints

Actual Attitudes, Awareness And Use Of Consumer Protection Act

The comprehensive data presentation as well as the discussion with respect to the research questions that the study intended to answer were presented in Chapter 4. Therefore, this section discusses the research results pertaining to the research objectives. This is a crucial step where findings are evaluated to ascertain if they have addressed the research objectives so that conclusions can be drawn.

The Levels of CPA Awareness Among Furniture Retail Consumers in Umlazi

The results from a chi-square goodness-of-fit test showed that more respondents indicated that they have heard of the CPA but know nothing about it. There were fewer respondents who had heard of the CPA but either knew little or more about it. The research results revealed that there is a certain level of CPA awareness among retail consumers but this does not translate into how much the respondents know about the CPA. Consumer rights awareness and knowledge safeguards consumers from being exploited (Usman et al., 2015). Therefore, the respondents' awareness of the CPA may not be sufficient to protect them from exploitation if they know very little about the Act. Donoghue and Van Oordt (2016) state that lack of profound consumerism knowledge contributes to the consumer's inability to engage formal complaint channels to obtain redress. In other words, consumers cannot be assertive about their consumer rights if they are not aware of or do not understand their rights.

Poor information searching skills contribute to a lack of awareness and knowledge (Davi & Rao, 2016). Sound consumer decisions are made based on the information obtained during the cognitive and affective stages of consumer buying behaviour (Clow & Baack, 2018). The findings of this study suggest that the respondents are unable to make informed decisions on whether or not to use the CPA because they lack CPA-related information. Although awareness of the Act may be necessary, relevant CPA information is also vital to influencing prospective furniture retail consumers as to whether or not to use the Act to deal with their complaints

The Views of Furniture Retail Consumers in Umlazi Towards the CPA

The one-simple test for significant agreement/disagreement was conducted and the research results imply that there is significant agreement that the CPA is helpful in protecting the furniture retail customers. Opinion is the view that the customers hold about the product or service (Keller & Swaminathan, 2020) and Clow and Baack (2018) claim that attitude is the mental position taken towards a product, event or person. The responses from the respondents indicate that they hold positive opinions on the CPA. However, the amount of CPA marketing communication exposure influences the consumer's attitude to the Act. Another crucial finding was the opinions of respondents regarding their intention to use the CPA in the future. They had to answer by indicating whether they agree, strongly agree, are neutral, disagree and strongly disagree. The results of the t-test indicate a positive intention to use the CPA. Therefore, it can be concluded that there is a significant agreement that the respondents will use the CPA in the future. These findings suggest that furniture retail consumers hold positive opinions on the use of the CPA when the need arises.

Complaints -- Furniture Retail Shops

The study aimed to set out the reasons respondents lodge a complaint against a furniture retailer. Statements relating to the reasons were provided and, in order to test whether a significant proportion cited any of the reasons, a binomial test was conducted. A defective product/quality was found to be the only reason cited by a significant proportion of the respondents. The research results revealed that furniture retail consumers do complain when a defective product is purchased. A defective product refers to any manufacturing imperfection that renders the product less useful and unable to meet the customer's expectations (Van Der Linde, 2017). Thus, poor product quality culminates in many product failures which subsequently lead to customer dissatisfaction. Furthermore, the findings relating to those who had filed a complaint showed that more respondents had never followed up on their complaint with the furniture retailer. The results also showed that furniture retail consumers lodge complaints about defective products but they do not use the CPA to claim redress. Suppliers should be held responsible for supplying defective or harmful products to consumers (Barnard, 2017). Saleem et al. (2015) consider that product quality is vital to achieve customer satisfaction. The lack of follow-up and use of CPA among furniture retail consumers leads to unresolved complaints and exempts the furniture retailer from accounting for the supply of defective products.

The Use of the CPA Among Furniture Retail Consumers in Umlazi to Protect Themselves

The respondents were asked questions about their use of the CPA and had to indicate their answer with 'yes' or 'no'. The binomial test that was conducted showed that more respondents had not used the CPA to handle furniture retail complaints. Fewer respondents indicated that they have used the CPA at least once to handle a furniture retail complaint. This implies that more respondents do not use the CPA to claim redress from furniture retailers. Despite the respondents' poor use of the CPA to get redress however, they have a strong intention to use the CPA in the future. To defend themselves against retail exploitation, consumers must have in-depth information and knowledge about their rights and how to handle disputes (Donoghue & Van Oordt, 2016). The power of the consumer arises from the effective use and enforcement of the CPA in the marketplace. Consumers should familiarise themselves with the complaint processes laid down by the NCC. Very few consumers understand how to follow the legal processes required to lodge a complaint with the consumer commission (Van Oordt, 2015).

RECOMMENDATIONS

The research results pointed out areas that inhibit the effective use of the CPA by furniture retail consumers in the marketplace. Although the findings show that there is awareness of the CPA, poor knowledge still hinders the effective use and application of the Act by retail consumers. The recommendations have been drawn from the literature used in chapter two and research outcomes. Therefore, the following actions are recommended:

- For consumers to use the CPA effectively they must have a full understanding of the clauses on consumer rights. The literature shows the steps involved in the consumer decision-making process.

Information search and knowledge are the primary influencers of the consumer decision-making process. Making CPA information available has the potential to change consumer behaviour towards the Act. Employing the services of a promotional agency to disseminate the CPA information among communities is vital to provide access to CPA information. Educational activities that speak about the role of the CPA and its functions could be created and incorporated into promotional programmes. These programmes must be implemented and rolled out on platforms like the internet, retail workshops, retail trade shows, workers' union forums, schools and universities' forums and community forums to educate consumers about the CPA. Such programmes could be led by volunteers from communities working together with government representatives. These interventions will not only educate but also improve CPA awareness among retail consumers.

- Government institutions such as the DTI, NCC and NCT must establish intervention programmes to make them visible and known to consumers. Such interventions involve outlining the structure, functions, procedures, branches, designated consumer court and expected role of consumers when dealing with such institutions. The literature revealed that the effective use of the CPA depends on consumers' understanding of the customer complaint process and available redress channels. Therefore, making communities part of the CPA programmes will raise consumer confidence in using the Act in the future.

- The success of the CPA cannot be achieved without the involvement of manufacturers, suppliers and retailers. Therefore, open communication channels directed to these stakeholders are important and should be developed. The literature shows that consumers are not keen to complain if they believe nothing will be done about their complaint. The research findings also showed that more respondents do not follow up on their complaints. A communication tool could be developed in the form of an outsourced website managed by CPA custodians. This intervention would ensure that consumer well-being in the marketplace is safeguarded at all times. Communication on the outcomes concerning the enforcement of the CPA must be shared among stakeholders as a deterrent to stop errant businesses from exploiting consumers.

CONCLUSION

The chapter reveal that furniture retail consumers in Umlazi are aware of the CPA, however, they have little or no knowledge of the consumer rights contained in the CPA. The findings suggest that there is a need to bridge the CPA information and knowledge gap among retail consumers in Umlazi. Positive opinions were expressed by furniture retail consumers regarding the use of the CPA to resolve customer complaints and they displayed their intention to use the CPA in the future. This suggests that consumers who are aware of the CPA and have positive attitudes are more likely to use the CPA to protect themselves against exploitation and to safeguard their interests. However, easy access to CPA information is vital to build the knowledge capacity of consumers on how the Act is applied. Well informed consumers will know how to follow complaint processes and can identify situations where the CPA applies.

The research results also identified shortcomings in the use of the CPA to handle customer complaints. The findings suggest that retail consumers know that there is a CPA, but they are unclear on how it is supposed to protect them when they are dissatisfied with a product. A significant number of retail consumers do complain but fail to follow up on their complaints. Thus, they never know whether their complaint was resolved or not. There is disparity between what retail consumers do when dealing with their complaints and what is stipulated in consumer grievance processes in consumer law. Such behaviour contributes further to their continued suffering and exploitation in the marketplace. Furthermore, poor use of the CPA, limited access to CPA sources, and lack of knowledge all hinder the Act's progress in protecting consumers. Thus, the CPA remains untested on whether it can effectively protect retail consumers or not. In addition, such consumer protection is impractical if consumers' rights in the marketplace are not enforced.

REFERENCES

Baines, P., Fill, C., & Rosengren, S. (2017). *Marketing* (4th ed.). Oxford University Press.

Barnard, J. (2017). *The Role of Comparative Law in Consumer Protection Law: A South African Perspective*. South Africa Mercantile Law Journal.

Bernard, J. (2015). Consumer rights of the elderly as vulnerable consumers in South Africa: Some comparative aspects of the Consumer Protection Act (68 of 2008). *International Journal of Consumer Studies*, *39*(3), 223–229. doi:10.1111/ijcs.12170

Burns, A. C., Veeck, A., & Bush, R. F. (2017). *Marketing Research* (8th Global Edition). Pearson Education Limited.

Clow, K. E., & Baack, D. (2018). *Message strategies and execution framework', Integrated Advertising, Promotion, and Marketing Communications* (8th ed.). Pearson Education Limited.

Constitution of the Republic of South Africa Act, No. 108 of 1996. Bill of Rights. (1996). https://www.justice.gov.za/legislation/constitution/chp02.html

Consumer Protection Act, No. 68 of 2008. (2008). https://www.gov.za/sites/default/files/gcis_document/201409/321864670.pdf

Creswell, J. W., & Creswell, J. D. (2018). *Research Design* (5th ed.). Sage Publication Inc.

De Stadler, E. B. (2016). *The scope of the application of the Consumer Protection Act 68 of 2008 in the context of the sale of defective goods in comparative perspective*. The University of Cape Town.

Debnath A. & Mazumdar. (2015). An Evaluative study on consumer rights in the context of business. *International Journal of Humanities and Social Science Studies, 1*(4).

Donoghue, S., & de Klerk, H. M. (2014). Consumers' anger and coping strategies following appraisals of appliance failure. International Journal of Consumer Studies.

Donoghue, S., & van der Oordt, C. (2016). *Consumers' subjective and objective consumerism knowledge and subsequent complaint behavior concerning consumer electronics*. The University of Pretoria.

Keller, K. L., & Kotler, P. (2016). *Marketing management* (15th ed.). Pearson Education Limited.

Keller, K. L., & Swaminathan, V. (2020). *Strategic Brand Management: Building, Measuring and Managing Brand Equity* (5th ed.). Pearson Education Limited.

Koekemoer, L. (2014). *Advertising and Sales Promotion*. Juta and Company Limited.

Koekemoer, M. (2017). South African Complaint Forums in the Retail Industry: a Survey of Literature and Some Lessons from the EU. Journal of consumer policy, 40. Springer Science Business Media.

Loubser, M., & Reid, E. (2012). Product Liability in South Africa. Juta and Company.

Mugobo, V., & Malunga, P. (2015). Consumer Protection Act in South Africa. Challenges and Opportunities for Furniture Retailers in Cape Town, South Africa. [MC Ser Publishing Rome, Italy.]. *Mediterranean Journal of Social Sciences*, 6.

Naude T. (2018). Dissemination of Consumer Law and Policy in South Africa. *Journal of Consumer Policy*. Springer Science and Business Media. doi:10.1007/s10603-018-9381-4

Otto J., Van Heerden C., and Barnard J. (2014). Redress in terms of the National Credit Act and the Consumer Protection Act for defective goods sold and financed in terms of an instalment agreement. *The South African Mercantile Law Journal, 241*.

Phora, J. S. (2017). *Developing a legal framework for e-commerce in South Africa*. University of Pretoria.

Pretorius, L. S. (2016). *Rural consumers' consciousness and use of the Consumer Protection Act in the Valspan community within the Phokwane Municipality*. University of the North West.

Rahman M.S. (2017) The Advantages and Disadvantages of Using Qualitative and Quantitative Approach and Methods in Language Testing and Assessment Research: A literature Review. *Journal of Education and Learning, 6*(1). Canadian Center of Science and Education.

Saleem, A., Ghafar, A., Ibrahim, M., Yousuf, M., & Ahmed, N. (2015). *Product Perceived Quality and Purchase Intention with Consumer Satisfaction:* Global Journals Inc. USA. *Global Journal of Management and Business Research, 15*(1).

Saunders, M., Lewis, P., & Thornhill, A. (2016). *Research Methods for Business Students* (7th ed.). Pearson Education India.

Sharrock, R. (2016). The Law of Banking and Payment in South Africa. Juta and Company Ltd.

Terblanche, B., Corbishley, B., Nel, F., & Venter, P. (2016). *Retail Management SA Perspective* (2nd ed.). Oxford University Press.

Usman, D.J., Yaacob, N. and Ralman, A. (2015). *Lack of Awareness: A major challenge for electricity consumers in Nigeria: Canadian Center of Science and Education.* Asian Social Science. doi:10.5539/ass.v11n24p240

Van Der Linde, S. (2017). *Product liability: The common law and the consumer protection act 68 of 2008*. University of Pretoria.

Van der Oordt, C. (2015). *Consumers' knowledge and attitudes towards consumerism and subsequent complaint behavior concerning consumer electronics*. University of Pretoria.

Van Schalkwyk P. J., Beven-Dye A. and Akpojivi U. (2015). South African independent retailers' knowledge of the Consumer Protection Act. *The Retail and Marketing Review 11* (2).

Weijo, H. A., Martin, D. M., & Arnould, E. J. (2018). Consumer Movement and Collective Creativity: The Case of Restaurant Day. *Journal of Consumer Research*. https://academic.oup.com doi:10.1093/jcr/ucy003

Wirtz, J., & Lovelock, C. (2016). *Service Marketing* (8th ed.). World Scientific Publishing Co. Inc. doi:10.1142/y0001

Woker T. (2016). *Consumer protection and alternative dispute resolution. South African Mercantile Law Journal, 21*.

Zeithaml, V. A., Wilson, A., Jo Betner, M., & Gremler, D. D. (2016). *Services marketing* (3rd European ed.). McGraw Hill Education.

Chapter 5
COVID-19 and Cognitive vs. Emotional Consumer Variations on Decision Making:
COVID-19's Impact on Consumers

Saraju Prasad
Siksha 'O' Anusandhan, India

ABSTRACT

The Covid-19 crisis has propelled no small extent of changes in the attitude and behavior of people all over the world. This has created a challenge for the consumers' consumption on different categories of products. Consumers' behavior on the basis of their personalities, like emotional and cognitive, is the key area to study during the pandemic. Affect and cognition have profound impacts on behavioral pattern of consumers in all times. The pandemic changed purchase behavior and made consumers behave with cognition and emotion. The study has verified a deviation in consumer behavior on consumption of essential goods. The result is based on the brand consciousness and price sensitivity of both cognitive and emotional consumers during the purchase of essential commodities. Structural equation modeling utilized to study the extent of deviations in behavior during the purchases.

INTRODUCTION

Pandemics are always changing in behavior of customers towards long term decisions. Customers focused mostly quality based to quantity based when uncertainty is longer in economic condition of the country and at the same time customers in hygienic products focused more on quality than quantity. Fear is more towards the sustainability of human life in terms of day-to-day consumption and quality hygienic product for safety purpose. The study is based on the length of the pandemic and its psychological impact on consumer during purchase decision. The focus of consumer more towards the priority of the essential commodities in their life with the minimum expenses they will enhance the level of consumption and skip the requirement which has less importance to them for life. Today consumer is categorizing the

DOI: 10.4018/978-1-6684-5853-2.ch005

product consumption according to his priority or requirement. Importance of purchase is based on the minimum necessity for life. The product can be categorized on the basis of two categories physiological and safety need but not considering the other needs of Maslow need hierarchy theory.

Covid-19 is one among all pandemic where the pattern of shift in consumer sentiment and behavior is quite visible through their purchases. Consumers are the final shareholders of all the product and service sectors. When the fear of the pandemic has gone down finally consumers has preferred to start their normal lives. But the usual life will be something different for the consumer so companies must try to be proactive and behave accordingly to address the normalcy that will be after the situation. Experience from the previous situations also prevail that, after every unprecedented crisis with a heavy emotional change and shift in consumer taste & preferences happens at least for a time toward different products and services. This leads a greater attention of government to classic or region-based products and services like craftsmanship and heritage and less to essential commodities (Novemsky, 2020).

The expectation for a comfortable shopping environment has collapsed because of the fear of pandemic. Unless the spreading speed of the pandemic reduced there is no chance to attract customers into the store and keeps them for longer duration. Shopping malls are designed to keep the customers for longer time inside the store increase the spending. Pandemic is a strong psychological force to keep the customers away from shopping. First one is scarcity it means stores found to be running out of certain items. Pandemic is giving a sense of discomfort about the storage of essential commodities which is in turn increases the storage of more things to combat with the situations. There is a high level of insecurity and uncertainty about the life and customers are worrying to regret about not buying something what they require in day-to-day life. This anticipation of customers leads to buy fewer things compared to the actual required commodities for their house. The purchases are mostly based on the requirement of the family members they concern more and for safety. The other ways of panic buying by consumers like purchasing of more quantity to suffice their additional requirement in the near future. This is a modern pattern of thinking which is very often coming to mind naturally to consumers to think significantly less about the additive effects and keep more stuff for their own family. During the pandemic emotions are very high where both positive steps and negative steps are likely to be remembered more than company actions and have a disproportionately varied effect on people's attitudes toward those companies. Here consumers have to be careful about actions to be taken in the situation rather than to wait after the crisis because of emotions that are less potent and less likely to ride over the actions (Achille & Zipser 2020).

LITERATURE REVIEW

The artificial scarcity created by the major business establishments during Covid-19 created a great panic in the market and became an advantage for sellers to raise price on the basic commodities. The government initiatives through the 'Department of Trade and Industry' (DTI) to control the price and avail sufficient quantity mitigate the country demand for essential commodities. It is very often the creativity of capitalists those take always advantage over the situation to offer products online with a high price. The overpricing on essential commodities is an unfair sales practice by taking advantages during the need of consumers which violates the Consumer Act (Rivas, 2020). 'Moral panic is an extreme sense of concern about a threat that is perceived as destruction to physical safety or culture of the society' (Goode, 2017). If expert's opinion related to pandemic should not be publicized more to spread over community at the right time, then unnecessarily panic will be created (Greco, 2005). During the times of any pandemic, social responses will come accordingly with the aggression of the epidemic along with the public awareness. This became the urge of community to get advantage of rationality over the pandemic (Panter-Brick & Fuentes, 2009). Some of the behavioral change among the consumers like panic buying, keeping more capital for future uncertainty and more believing in news available in various on the social sites are very common during the pandemic situation (Alalykin-Izvekov, 2017). The fear created in the community results in spreading of some unexpected behavior among consumers in social media news like panic buying, xenophobia etc. (Alalykin-Izvekov, 2017). This creates artificial shortages in the market and the remained people are left with shortages of essential commodities which subjects to a panic. These kinds of response very much reasonable on the market are called as psychological egoism (Burks, 1966). During this period a fake belief of public health crises arises due to misinformation communicated everywhere in the society. The heavy news coverage about the new corona variant which has not thoroughly analyzed but the repercussion of two past epidemics which gave new reports about Covid-19 continued to support the negative rumors about a health crisis among the community (Stix, 2020). During the pandemic few behaviors of consumers change during their purchases. The changing behaviors in purchases are based on their personalities.

COVID-19 AND CONSUMERS BEHAVIOR

Consumer behavior encompasses through the interaction among human emotions and thinking, behavior and around the society. However, the adverse thinking and distractions are due to various information create anxiety from the present situation can finally lead to an apathetic outlook to a particular crisis (Abraham, 2018).

Health Consciousness personality persons **a**re thinking dominantly about individual habits about the person with the diet to the lifestyle and the types of sleeping and exercises. Everybody is trying to maintain or regain health (Nuriddin, 2018). Day by day each individual is trying to be health conscious to enhance the immune system in a way to protect self from being infected by the virus. This can be done by continuous checking of health status by measuring body temperature (Ferreira et al., 2017). *Optimism* personality persons are primarily focusing on the most expectable aspects of any situation. Despite the increase in intensity of pandemic, the country still expects the solution to overcome this by trusting the scientists Ingledew and Brunning (1999), (Boldor, Bar-Dayan, Rosenbloom, Shemer, & Bar-Dayan, 2012). *Cautiousness* personalities person are cautious on the sanitation of the surroundings. *Protection* oriented personalities are compliant with the protection oriented individuals calculates to avoid acquiring pandemic through using face mask and more use of alcohol (Department of Health & Human Services, 2020). Persons with *Compliance* personality have behavior similar with the health advice (Davey, Sterling, Field, Sterling, & Albery, 2014). *Composure* oriented personalities remain with their sanity and calmness during the period of pandemic. They have trust on the scientists and the present development on science (Nguyen, Yan, Thai, & Eidenbenz, 2012). *Information Dissemination* personalities entrap by misinformation or fake news and mostly with the limitation to verify the challenging environment (Noyes, Reich, Clancy, & O'Gorman, 2018).

Worry on self and family personality persons are worried on contamination the pandemic for themselves, their families and other members (Thompson, Garfin, Holman, & Silver, 2017). '*Relating to Past Pandemics*' personalities person always relates the pandemic to previous pandemics and plague.

Anxiety oriented persons mainly concerns on the more danger related to the further spreading of pandemic to self (Bults et al., 2011). *Transmission of Virus* personality persons always see the crisis is not similar to other contagious diseases, people are quite curious about the way of spreading (Wheaton, Abramowitz, Berman, Fabricant, & Olatunji, 2012). *Fear* oriented personalities are expected to see panic in society like previous pandemics. The scarcity of local govt. help is one of the sources of fear (Walsh, 2020). *Sadness* is a personality where the people feel the end of the pandemic within a very short duration (Chew & Eysenbach, 2010). Govt. started taking action like suspension of work and work from home during the number of infected people touched hundred. *Paranoia* is a type of personality where people feel unsecured because of scientists unable to trace the behavior of the virus.

'*Nihilism* is a kind of personality where a person experiences little meaning, dimensionality, depth, or transcendent bearing in the world, and feels empty or soulless (Fisher & Abram, 2013; Eckersley, 2008). *Annihilation* kind of personalities nullifies all things and makes people feel like nothing in life (Landau, 2017). Indifferent kind of personalities does not give cease care and not willing to take action on anything happened around him/her.

The discussed several personalities are very much associated with two broad categories of personalities which they have shown during the shopping behavior. Two broad categories discussed here are cognitive and emotional in their consumption behavior.

Cognitive Consumers

A cognitive consumer is an individual who believes on himself and behaves by observing the external environment day to day basis. Cognitive consumers always in a process of learning try to have knowledge about interior and exterior reality and involve knowing it better and acting accordingly. Cognitive consumer encompasses through the different components of psychological field like perception, imagination, discovering, thinking, learning and making judgements for final decision. The way the decision takes place based on cognitive theory which is based through the learning and developing and finally comprehending. The principles of consumer cognitive behavior are through the process of understanding, thinking, experiencing and getting knowledge for decision-making and finally buying a particular product. In all situations taking in account of the alternative availability by use of logic, functionality, price-quality relationship and finally select goods/services are all examples of dominating characteristics of cognitive behavior.

Emotional Consumers

In affective or emotional consumer behavior the emotional aspects are seen through a visible change in one's behavior during shopping. As comparing to cognitive/rational mind, the emotional mind has quicker response in market place which does not include analytical thinking just like the cognitive mind. Being emotional is type of a psychological phenomenon and having uniqueness for sub-conscious experience with feelings and mood. Consumers' emotional responses to the various products of different companies may be positive and negative. The emotional aspects of the consumer show to a certain behavior without previously formed attitude. Impulsive purchase is one of such phenomena where the response of the stimuli is describing a situation where customer's emotion dominates the other factors to select the product/service. These key features of impulsive or affective behavior differentiate the cognitive or rational behavior of the consumers in marketplace. In Howard Sheth model economic situation, time pressure, social status of consumers can influence a lot in buying products and services by reducing the probability of impulsive shopping. Emotions are mostly deep and uncontrollable feelings which have direct effect on behavior (Bagozzi, Gopinath & Nyer, 1999). Emotion plays a major role in the selection of products with a reputed brand and finally consumer get satisfied and became brand loyal. Consumers are anxious to take role in consumption behaviors to enlighten the mood during the experience of negative emotions (Cohen, Tuan, & Andrade, 2008).

Prevention Behavior

The variables under the prevention behaviors are maintain social distancing, hand cleaning, avoid contact with persons having fever, stay alone at home during sick, cover cough or sneeze with tissue papers or cottons, throw used tissue papers in dust bean, cover face with mask to protect from others, cover face with mask to protect others if infected and finally clean and sterilize frequent touched surfaces.

Consumer Type

Different approaches adopted for better decision making by observing the different psychology of the consumers. As per the different studies numbers of typological classifications occur and five major approaches emerged. All of those five approaches describes the different models of man, and gave emphasis to examine the different variables (Foxall, 1993). In this study two types of consumers purchasing behavior has observed and analyzed. These two are cognitive and emotional customers and theirs purchase behavior. *Cognitive consumer* plays a vital role in processing information (Ribeaux & Poppleton, 1978). For internal decision-making consumers mostly require and receive environmental and social stimuli as inputs for information processing (Stewart, 1994). *Emotional consumers* need to balance between the rational, cognitive side of marketing of products or services and make research on the emotional aspects of the marketing behavior' (Nataraajan, 1999).

Behavioral Biases of Individuals

Research has demonstrated that when people face complex decisions, they often rely on basic judgments and preferences to simplify the situation rather than acting completely rationally. Although such approaches are quick and intuitively appealing, they may lead to suboptimal outcomes. In contrast to this body of research, traditional economic and financial theory generally assumes that individuals act rationally by considering all available information in the decision-making process, leading them to optimal outcomes and supporting the efficiency of markets. Behavioral finance challenges these assumptions by incorporating research on how individuals and markets actually behave. In this reading, we explore a foundational concept of behavioral finance: behavioral biases. Investment professionals may be able to improve economic outcomes by understanding these biases, recognizing them in themselves and others, and learning strategies to mitigate them.

The reading proceeds as follows. Section 2 describes and broadly characterizes behavioral biases. Sections 3 and 4 discuss specific behavioral biases within two broad categories: cognitive errors and emotional biases. The discussion includes a description of each bias, potential consequences, and guidance on detecting and mitigating the effects of the bias. Section 5 discusses market anomalies, which are essentially aggregate expressions of individual biases among financial market participants. A summary and practice problems conclude the reading.

Behavioral biases potentially affect the behaviors and decisions of financial market participants. By understanding these biases, financial market participants may be able to moderate or adapt to them and, as a result, improve upon economic outcomes. Behavioral biases may be categorized as either cognitive errors or emotional biases. The type of bias influences whether its impact may be moderated or adapted to.

Among the points made in this reading are the following:

- Individuals do not necessarily act rationally and consider all available information in the decision-making process because they may be influenced by behavioral biases.
- Biases may lead to suboptimal decisions.
- Behavioral biases may be categorized as either cognitive errors or emotional biases. A single bias may have aspects of both, however, with one type of bias dominating.
- Cognitive errors stem from basic statistical, information-processing, or memory errors; cognitive errors typically result from faulty reasoning.
- Emotional biases stem from impulse or intuition and tend to result from reasoning influenced by feelings.
- Cognitive errors are more easily corrected for because they stem from faulty reasoning rather than an emotional predisposition.
- Emotional biases are harder to correct for because they are based on feelings, which can be difficult to change.
- To adapt to a bias is to recognize and accept the bias and to adjust for the bias rather than to attempt to moderate the bias.
- To moderate a bias is to recognize the bias and to attempt to reduce or even eliminate the bias within the individual.
- Cognitive errors can be further classified into two categories: belief perseverance biases and information-processing biases.
- Belief perseverance errors reflect an inclination to maintain beliefs. The belief is maintained by committing statistical, information-processing, or memory errors. Belief perseverance biases are closely related to the psychological concept of cognitive dissonance.
- Belief perseverance biases include conservatism, confirmation, representativeness, illusion of control, and hindsight.
- Information-processing biases result in information being processed and used illogically or irrationally.
- Information-processing biases include anchoring and adjustment, mental accounting, framing, and availability.
- Emotional biases include loss aversion, overconfidence, self-control, status quo, endowment, and regret aversion.
- Understanding and detecting biases is the first step in overcoming the effect of biases on financial decisions. By understanding behavioral biases, financial market participants may be able to moderate or adapt to the biases and, as a result, improve upon economic outcomes.
- Behavioral finance has the potential to explain some apparent deviations from market efficiency (market anomalies).

COGNITIVE AND EMOTIONAL BIASES

Every day of our lives is filled with decisions we take, some may be important, and some are effortless as a result of habit. Unfortunately, these decisions are influenced by the observations we make, the experiences we've had, how we've been conditioned to reach, etc.

Even when we are grocery shopping, we favor some products over the others simply because we like the celebrity that advertised them. Investors suffer from these biases too. His may not come as a surprise as investors often experience a roller coaster of emotions while investing or trading.

Today we take a look at common investment biases that exist. Here, we'll be covering Cognitive vs Emotional Biases while investing. We do this with the aim of studying what leads to wrong decisions as this would assist us in avoiding huge future losses.

The economic and financial theory is based on the assumption that individuals will act rationally and consider all available information in their decision-making process, and that markets are efficient. But this is rarely the case. Studies have shown that 80% of individual investors and 30% of institutional investors are not always logical.

This brings us to Behavioral finance. Behavioral finance is a branch of economics that explains the irrational decisions of an investor. These irrational decisions are a result of strongly ingrained biases that exist deep in our psyche. These biases have been classified as cognitive and emotional.

Cognitive Biases

Cognitive biases are generally related to the way a person is wired to think. These biases are said to arise from statistical, information procession, or memory errors that cause the decision to deviate from a rational decision. Because of this, they are also easy to correct with better information, education, and advice.

Here are a few common types of cognitive biases in behavioral finance while investing:

Confirmation Bias

Confirmation bias takes further as people with confirmation bias only seek out evidence that confirms their beliefs and ignore evidence that contradicts them. In order to support this, you only look for confirmation from studies, research in order to support your argument without even considering any opposing argument. Your decisions are now blurred due to confirmation bias. The easiest way to counter this would be to consciously gather the information that is contrary to your opinion.

Gamblers Fallacy

Humans make an effort to ensure that everything makes sense to them. This often leads them to look for patterns in areas where they are nonexistent. This happens in investing as well; people tend to invest in funds simply because they have performed well for the last 5 years. Investors may perceive this as a trend that may carry into the future as well. If a study is done statistically, it may make sense but past events don't connect to future events. If the market has been rising for the last 1 month continuously it is not necessary, that it will fall tomorrow. Shorting the market only based on this information is flawed.

Status Quo Bias

People are more comfortable when things remain the same and are generally averse to changes. In investing this may be seen as investing only in industries that you seem to understand. Although a deeper understanding is necessary in investing it becomes a hindrance when people do not further their appetite to educate themselves further. This would limit their profit potential only to certain opportunities.

Negativity Bias

This occurs when investors give more weight to bad news over good news. When corona broke out in the country in Feb-March the markets began their bearish trends. After a few months, however, the markets resumed with bullish trends. Many investors missed this rally due to negative news. This bias can diminish the possibility of rewards.

Over Confidence Bias

A person who possesses this bias believes that his cognitive abilities and skills in the investment field are better than that of others. They also may not necessarily be in investing as a whole. A person working in the steel industry may believe that he has a better ability to trade in steel companies because he is from the same background. These investors overestimate their ability and the control they have over the markets. They also reduce the time required to assess risks.

When investors are overconfident in markets it generally leads to excessive trading. This leads to bubbles in financial markets. Securities here are bought at high prices and later sold at low prices. These traders/ investors underperform in the markets as they overlook various factors that affect their performance.

Bandwagon Effect

One of the greatest investors in the world, Warren Buffet attributes much of his success to resisting the bandwagon effect. Here investors feel better when they invest along with the crowd, this also adds to their confirmation bias.

Emotional Biases

Emotional biases stem from feelings, perceptions, beliefs about elements. Unfortunately, mixing emotions and investing often leads to bad decisions. Here basically the investor's brain is distracted due to his emotions. These biases are generally tougher to fix in comparison to cognitive biases.

Here are a few common types of emotional biases in behavioral finance while investing:

Loss Aversion Bias

One of our aims in investing is to avoid losses. But this has become such a big part of our nature that we try to avoid losses even when we know that by doing so we are causing more harm. The disposition effect is the tendency of investors to sell winning positions and hold onto losing positions.

Investors here are so averse to losses they cannot sell a security to avoid further losses. The rational thing to do here would be to sell the security and redirect the investment into quality stocks.

Self-Attribution bias

When investors attribute the success of outcomes to their own actions and bad outcomes to external factors they are said to possess self-attribution bias. When their investments increase in value the investors claim that it is self-attributed ignoring other factors that may have been in play. But when the stocks decrease in value it is due to external factors.

Endowment Bias

Investors who possess this bias assume that the asset they own is more valuable than what they do not own. This may lead him to hold onto securities even when there are brighter opportunities elsewhere.

HYPOTHESES

The consumption behavior of both the customers' type (cognitive and emotional) has any relationship with the Covid-19 pandemic situation. As government guidelines restrict the customers to purchase the different brands of essential commodities during a specific time period. So, the customers having those personalities may behave differently in the market space. The hypothesis designed to study their shopping behavioral change during the impact of pandemic. Two hypotheses formulated on the basis of their shopping behavior.

Hypothesis-I

H0 = Emotional consumers are not price sensitive but brand conscious

Hypothesis-II

H0 = Cognitive consumers are not brand conscious but price sensitive

OBJECTIVES

Covid-19 pandemic changed the consumers' life in different way. Today's consumers are being forced to change their purchase behavior with the influence of environmental change with lots of uncertainty related to various aspects of life. In this situation it is very much vital to understand the consumer response at the various types of stimuli from internal and external environments. This study focused in the area of changing life style of consumers in terms of consumption of products. The study also considers the influential parameters during the pandemic of Covid-19 on consumers' personalities during the decision-making process. Finally, the consumer behavior is cognitive or emotional and the behavioral change during purchases of various kinds of products.

METHOD

The research conducted on the purchase behavior of cognitive and emotional consumer during the pandemic situation in India. It is a descriptive study conducted through a survey by using questionnaire during the covid-19. The sampling method used in this study is convenient which is non-probability and studied in Bhubaneswar city (capital of Odisha, an eastern State of India). During the pandemic an easy and cost effective method of sampling (convenient sampling method) implemented and having high response rate (Eze, Manyeki, Yaw, & Har, 2011; Ritchie, Lewis, Nicholls, McNaughton, & Ormiston, 2014).

The study conducted on 300 respondents of different age-group, categories of occupation with various experience in online shopping for a personal interview and 90% of respondents participated which is around 270 respondents. The data collected at various places like convenient stores, milk parlors, small retail stores, and banks etc. which are opened during the lockdown period of the government. Out of total 250 valid responses are considered for the final analysis. The tabulated data analyzed by using statistical software SPSS 21.

Table 1.

Demographic Profile			
Type	**Particulars**	**Frequency**	**Percentage**
Gender			
	Male	174	70.4
	Female	76	29.6
Age			
	Less than 25	0	0
	25-35	120	48
	35-45	88	35.2
	Above 45	42	16.8
Educational Qualification			
	Non-Tech Graduation	37	14.8
	Tech Graduation	58	23.2
	Non-Tech Post Graduation	95	38
	Tech Post Graduation	60	24
Occupation			
	Salaried Employees	95	38
	Businessmen	51	20.4
	Professionals	48	19.2
	Other Profession	56	22.4
Family Income per month			
	Less than 40K	58	23.2
	40K-80K	144	57.6
	Above 80K	48	19.2

Demographic Profile

The data through questionnaire are analyzed on the basis of statistical tools to quantify the results and inferences. The result is based on the involvement of young and middle-aged executives, businessmen and professionals in purchases of essential commodities during Covid-19 in Bhubaneswar. Mostly the respondents are selected those having the income more than Rs. 40,000 per month and their deviations in shopping behavior due to cognitive or emotional character are observed. Out of the valid responses 39.3% are salaried employees in various government, public or private sector companies, 29% are businessmen and 20.6% professionals and 11% are others. The respondents' age profile is as 54% are of 25-35 yr and 31.3% are of 35-45 yr and 14.6% are above 45yrs.

RESULT

Emotional Consumer

Emotional and Cognitive consumer observed value and expected values for brand consciousness purchases are shown in the table 2. The table shows the emotional or cognitive consumers Brand consciousness vs Brand Non-Conscious scores.

Table 2. Cross tabulation of personality with brand consciousness

Personality * Brand Conscious Cross tabulation					
			Brand Conscious		Total
			Brand Conscious	Brand Non-Conscious	
Personality	Emotional	Count	80	49	129
		Expected Count	69.0	60.0	129.0
		% within Personality	62.0%	38.0%	100.0%
	Cognitive	Count	43	58	101
		Expected Count	54.0	47.0	101.0
		% within Personality	42.6%	57.4%	100.0%
Total		Count	123	107	230
		Expected Count	123.0	107.0	230.0
		% within Personality	53.5%	46.5%	100.0%

In the table 3 the Person chi-square test value is significant with the p-value of 0.003 (Less than 0.05). Hence the NULL hypothesis is accepted which explains as:

Hypothesis-I

H0 = Emotional consumers are not price sensitive but brand conscious

Table 3. Chi-square test of personality with brand consciousness

Chi-Square Tests					
	Value	**df**	**Asymp. Sig. (2-sided)**	**Exact Sig. (2-sided)**	**Exact Sig. (1-sided)**
Pearson Chi-Square	8.606[a]	1	.003		
Continuity Correction[b]	7.842	1	.005		
Likelihood Ratio	8.645	1	.003		
Fisher's Exact Test				.004	.003
Linear-by-Linear Association	8.569	1	.003		
N of Valid Cases	230				
a. 0 cells (0.0%) have expected count less than 5. The minimum expected count is 46.99.					
b. Computed only for a 2x2 table					

Cognitive Consumers

Emotional and Cognitive consumer observed value and expected values for price sensitive purchases are reflected in the table 4. The table explains the emotional or cognitive consumers Price Sensitive vs Non-Price Sensitive scores.

Table 4. Cross tabulation of personality with price sensitive

Personality * Price Sensitive Cross tabulation					
			Price Sensitive		Total
			Price Sensitive	**Non-Price Sensitive**	
Personality	Emotional	Count	43	86	129
		Expected Count	60.6	68.4	129.0
		% within Personality	33.3%	66.7%	100.0%
	Cognitive	Count	65	36	101
		Expected Count	47.4	53.6	101.0
		% within Personality	64.4%	35.6%	100.0%
Total		Count	108	122	230
		Expected Count	108.0	122.0	230.0
		% within Personality	47.0%	53.0%	100.0%

In the table 5 as the p-value is 0.000 (Less than 0.05) so the Pearson chi-square test value is significant. Hence the NULL hypothesis is accepted as:

Hypothesis-II

H0 = Cognitive consumers are not brand conscious but price sensitive

Table 5. Chi-square test of personality with price sensitive

Chi-Square Tests					
	Value	**df**	**Asymp. Sig. (2-sided)**	**Exact Sig. (2-sided)**	**Exact Sig. (1-sided)**
Pearson Chi-Square	21.889[a]	1	.000		
Continuity Correction[b]	20.661	1	.000		
Likelihood Ratio	22.204	1	.000		
Fisher's Exact Test				.000	.000
Linear-by-Linear Association	21.794	1	.000		
N of Valid Cases	230				
a. 0 cells (0.0%) have expected count less than 5. The minimum expected count is 47.43.					
b. Computed only for a 2x2 table					

SUMMARY OF THE RESEARCH

The study has given a picture of a consumers' attitude towards different companies' products during the pandemic like Covid-19. As there was a continuous bombardment of information related to pandemic from national and international news agencies majority of consumers' decisions are being controlled by the uncertainty in country's financial positions. Cognitive consumers are less affected than the emotional consumers during purchases of commodities. It was found from the regression analysis that the independent variables have positive impact on emotional consumers by which they are still brand loyal during the crisis or pandemic. The emotional consumers remain brand conscious during the crisis and they searched the various retail outlet to select their preferred brands. But in case of cognitive consumers the effect of pandemic has negative impact which forced them to give higher priority to quantity or price-based decisions. Cognitive consumers more focused to products than the brand and they try to maximize the quantity of products to fight against the pandemic rather their preferred brand of limited quantity.

Theoretical Implications

The pandemic has created an environment to create a challenge for consumer in decision making process. The government guidelines created a platform to restrict the behavior of consumer top select the preferred brand for consumption. This environmental change pressurizes the consumers to behave differently with the changing time and government regulations. The shopping behavior for essential commodities shown by the consumers during the crisis can be differentiated on the basis of cognitive and emotional behavior. That behavior leads them to take decision for price or brand sensitive decisions. Finally, the brand choices for rationality or recognition were based on cognitive or emotional consumer.

Practical Implications

Consumers show mixed behavior during pandemic because of the lock down and social distancing guidelines of government. Although uncertainty in environment still consumer have shown both cognitive and emotional behavior during the purchases of essential commodities. Reputed companies should think to bring optimism and positivity among consumers to motivate among themselves to purchase more preferred brands. This research will help the consumer to think about their preferred brand before purchase on the basis of cognitive or emotional behavior.

CONCLUSION

Limitations and Directions for Future Research

The research passes through a phase where everybody was in the fear of spreading of Covid-19. Instead of the strict guidelines of government the number of respondents' availability and their gathering in front of the retail store became the great challenge for the researcher to get response. The model of cognitive and emotional consumers' behavior may behave in a different way after the pandemic. The unpredictable behavior of pandemic may change the situation faster than the companies could have ever imagined (ET Brand Equity, April 25, 2020). Further research can be made by considering the new challenges Covid-19 will give to the different countries in the world. New research dimension can be to find the way for marketers to enhance sales in the market for all category products during the pandemic.

REFERENCES

Abraham, M. (2018) *Apathy: Anxiety's Unusual Symptom*. CalmClinic. https://www.calmclinic.com/anxiety/apathy

Achille, A., & Zipser, D. (2020), *A perspective for the luxury-goods industry during and after coronavirus*. McKinsey & Company, https://www.mckinsey.com/ industries/retail/our-insights/a-perspective-for-the-luxury-goods-industry-during-and-after-coronavirus

Alalykin-Izvekov, V. (2017). The anatomy of a sociocultural crisis: calamities in Pitirim A. Sorokin's philosophy of history. *Biocosmology —neo-Aristotelism, 7*(2), 204-228.

Arbuckle, J. L. (2012). *IBM SPSS Amos 21*. Amos Development Corporation.

Bagozzi, R. P., Gopinath, M., and Nyer, P., U. (1999), The Role of Emotions in Marketing. *Journal of the Academy of Marketing Science, 27*(2), 184-206.

Boldor, N., Bar-Dayan, Y., Rosenbloom, T., Shemer, J., & Bar-Dayan, Y. (2012). Optimism of health care workers during a disaster: A review of the literature. *Emerging Health Threats Journal, 5*(1), 7270. doi:10.3402/ehtj.v5i0.7270 PMID:22461847

Browne, M. W., & Cudeck, R. (1989). Single sample cross-validation indices for covariance structures. *Multivariate Behavioral Research, 24*(4), 445–455. doi:10.120715327906mbr2404_4 PMID:26753509

Bruning, R., Schraw, G., & Ronning, R. (1999). *Cognitive psychology and instruction*. Prentice Hall.

Bults, M., Beaujean, D. J. M. A., de Zwart, O., Kok, G., van Empelen, P., van Steenbergen, J. E., & Voeten, H. A. C. M. (2011). Perceived risk, anxiety, and behavioural responses of the general public during the early phase of the Influenza A (H1N1) pandemic in the Netherlands: Results of three consecutive online surveys. *BMC Public Health*, *11*(1), 2. doi:10.1186/1471-2458-11-2 PMID:21199571

Burks, D. M. (1966). Psychological egoism and the rhetorical tradition. *Speech Monographs*, *33*(4), 400–418. doi:10.1080/03637756609375507

Chew, C., & Eysenbach, G. (2010). Pandemics in the age of Twitter: Content analysis of Tweets during the 2009 H1N1 outbreak. *PLoS One*, *5*(11), e14118. doi:10.1371/journal.pone.0014118 PMID:21124761

Cohen, J. B., Pham, M. T., & Andrade, E. B. (2007). The nature and role of affect in consumer behavior. In C. P. Haugtvedt, P. M. Herr, & F. R. Kardes (Eds.), *Handbook of consumer psychology* (pp. 297–348). Erlbaum.

Davey, G., Sterling, C., Field, A., Sterling, C., & Albery, I. (2014). *Complete Psychology*. Taylor & Francis. doi:10.4324/9780203783979

Department of Health & Human Services. (2020). *Guidance on Preparing Workplaces for COVID-19*. OSHA 3990-03 2020. https://www.osha.gov/Publications/OSHA3990.pdf

Eckersley, R. (2008). Nihilism, fundamentalism, or activism: Three responses to fears of the apocalypse. *The Futurist*, *42*(1), 35.

Eze, U. C., Manyeki, J. K., Yaw, L. H., & Har, L. C. (2011). Factors affecting internet banking adoption among young adults: Evidence from Malaysia. In *International Conference on Social Science and Humanity, IPEDR* (*Vol. 11*, pp. 377–381).

Ferreira, J. N. A. R., Fricton, J., & Rhodus, N. (2017). *Orofacial Disorders: Current Therapies in Orofacial Pain and Oral Medicine*. Springer International Publishing. doi:10.1007/978-3-319-51508-3

Fisher, A., & Abram, D. (2013). Radical Ecopsychology. Psychology in the Service of Life (2nd ed.). State University of New York Press.

Foxall, G. (1993). Situated Consumer Behaviour: A behavioral interpretation of purchase and consumption. *Research in Consumer Behaviour*, *6*, 113–152.

Goode, E. (2017). Moral Panic. The Encyclopedia of Juvenile Delinquency and Justice, pp. 1-3.

Greco, P. (2005). Pandemic: How to Avoid Panic? *Journal of Science Communication*, *04*. doi:10.22323/2.04040501

Ingledew, D. K., & Brunning, S. (1999). Personality, preventive health behaviour and comparative optimism about health problems. *Journal of Health Psychology*, *4*(2), 193–208. doi:10.1177/135910539900400213 PMID:22021479

Landau, I. (2017). *Finding Meaning in an Imperfect World*. Oxford University Press. doi:10.1093/acpr of:oso/9780190657666.001.0001

March, J. (1995). Cognitive-behavioral psychotherapy for children and adolescents with OCD: A review and recommendations for treatment. *Journal of the American Academy of Child and Adolescent Psychiatry*, *34*(1), 7–18. doi:10.1097/00004583-199501000-00008 PMID:7860461

Mathew, J. (2020). Post COVID-19. Will consumer behaviour patterns mutate? *BrandEquity*. https://brandequity.economictimes.indiatimes.com/news/marketing/post-Covid-19-will-consumer-behaviour-patterns-mutate/75369733

Nataraajan, R., & Bagozzi, R. P. (1999). The Year 2000: Looking Back. *Psychology and Marketing*, *16*(8), 631–642. doi:10.1002/(SICI)1520-6793(199912)16:8<631::AID-MAR1>3.0.CO;2-N

Nguyen, N. P., Yan, G., Thai, M. T., & Eidenbenz, S. (2012). *Containment of misinformation spread in online social networks*. Paper presented at The 4th Annual ACM Web Science Conference, Evanston, Illinois. 10.1145/2380718.2380746

Novemsky, N. (2020), *Why a Pandemic Leads to Panic Buying*. Yale Insights. https://insights.som.yale.edu/insights/why-pandemic-leads-to-panic-buying

Noyes, R., Reich, J., Clancy, J., & O'Gorman, T. W. (2018). Reduction in Hypochondriasis with Treatment of Panic Disorder. *The British Journal of Psychiatry*, *149*(5), 631–635. doi:10.1192/bjp.149.5.631 PMID:3814956

Nunnally, J. C., & Bernstein, I. H. (1994). *Psychometric theory* (3rd ed.). McGraw-Hill.

Nuriddin, A. J. (2018). Help Yourself to Ultimate Health: Know the Causes, Symptoms, and Solutions to Optimal Health. *iUniverse*.

Panter-Brick, C., & Fuentes, A. (2009). Health, Risk, and Adversity. *Recommendations for the Management of the Coronavirus Disease 2019 (COVID-19)*. Berghahn Books.

Ribeaux, P. (1978). *Psychology and Work*. Macmillan Education.

Ritchie, J., Lewis, J., Nicholls, C., McNaughton, J., & Ormiston, R. (2014). *Qualitative research practice: A guide for social science students and researchers*. SAGE Publications. doi:10.4135/9781452230108

Rivas, R. (2020). Hoarding, overpricing would lead to criminal charges, warns DTI. *Rappler*. https://www.rappler.com/business/254286-dti-warning-hoarding-overpricing-would-lead-criminal-charges

Stewart, J. (1994). The psychology of decision making. In D. Jennings & S. Wattam (Eds.), *Decision Making: an Integrated Approach*. Pitman.

Stix, G. (2020). Attempts at Debunking "Fake News" about Epidemics Might Do More Harm Than Good. *Scientific American*.

Thompson, R. R., Garfin, D. R., Holman, E. A., & Silver, R. C. (2017). Distress, Worry, and Functioning Following a Global Health Crisis: A National Study of Americans' Responses to Ebola. *Clinical Psychological Science*, *5*(3), 513–521. doi:10.1177/2167702617692030

Walsh, K. (2020). *Should we use fear in our public health messages about pandemics?* MDPI.

Walter, C. G., & Paul, G. W. (1970). Consumer Behaviour: An Integrated Framework. In *Home Wood, ILL* (p. 7). Richard D Irwin.

Wang, L., Fan, X., & Willson, V. (1996). Effects of non-normal data on parameter estimates and fit indices for a model with latent and manifest variables: An empirical study. *Structural Equation Modeling, 3*(3), 228–247. doi:10.1080/10705519609540042

Wheaton, M. G., Abramowitz, J. S., Berman, N. C., Fabricant, L. E., & Olatunji, B. O. (2012). Psychological Predictors of Anxiety in Response to the H1N1 (Swine Flu) Pandemic. *Cognitive Therapy and Research, 36*(3), 210–218. doi:10.100710608-011-9353-3

APPENDIX

Cognitive Consumer Regression Model Fit Summary

(Exhibit-1)

Test of normality of data through Kurtosis and Skewness for Cognitive Customer Regression Analysis

Descriptive Statistics										
	N	Minimum	Maximum	Mean	Std. Deviation	Variance	Skewness		Kurtosis	
	Statistic	Statistic	Statistic	Statistic	Statistic	Statistic	Statistic	Std. Error	Statistic	Std. Error
CONSUMPTION	250	2.00	38.00	18.6543	8.60306	74.013	.203	.154	-.786	.307
c1	250	3.00	5.00	4.1040	.52754	.278	.113	.154	.457	.307
c2	250	3.00	5.00	4.1600	.68136	.464	-.211	.154	-.848	.307
c3	250	3.00	5.00	4.2680	.62429	.390	-.263	.154	-.630	.307
c4	250	3.00	5.00	4.2800	.68372	.467	-.421	.154	-.835	.307
c5	250	3.00	5.00	4.2840	.56268	.317	-.043	.154	-.518	.307
c6	250	3.00	5.00	4.3240	.63612	.405	-.400	.154	-.681	.307
c7	250	2.00	5.00	4.0360	.69616	.485	-.193	.154	-.473	.307
c8	250	2.00	5.00	4.1400	.56717	.322	-.118	.154	.560	.307
c9	250	3.00	5.00	4.2440	.55289	.306	.040	.154	-.337	.307
Valid N (listwise)	250									

Exhibit-2 (CMIN)

Model	NPAR	CMIN	DF	P	CMIN/DF
Default model	27	329.037	28	.000	11.751
Saturated model	55	.000	0		
Independence model	10	931.970	45	.000	20.710

Exhibit-3 (RMR, GFI)

Model	RMR	GFI	AGFI	PGFI
Default model	.553	.848	.702	.432
Saturated model	.000	1.000		
Independence model	.519	.615	.530	.504

Exhibit-4 (Baseline Comparisons)

Model	NFI Delta1	RFI rho1	IFI Delta2	TLI rho2	CFI
Default model	.647	.433	.667	.455	.661
Saturated model	1.000		1.000		1.000
Independence model	.000	.000	.000	.000	.000

Exhibit-5 (RMSEA)

Model	RMSEA	LO 90	HI 90	PCLOSE
Default model	.055	.041	.071	.000
Independence model	.090	.099	.122	.000

Emotional Consumer Regression Analysis Model Fit Summary
Exhibit-6
Test of normality of data through Kurtosis and Skewness for Emotional Customer Regression Analysis

Descriptive Statistics										
	N	Minimum	Maximum	Mean	Std. Deviation	Variance	Skewness		Kurtosis	
	Statistic	Statistic	Statistic	Statistic	Statistic	Statistic	Statistic	Std. Error	Statistic	Std. Error
CONSUMPTION	250	2.00	38.00	18.6543	8.60306	74.013	.203	.154	-.786	.307
e1	250	3.00	5.00	4.1920	.52559	.276	.184	.154	.056	.307
e2	250	3.00	5.00	4.3280	.52681	.278	.143	.154	-.809	.307
e3	250	3.00	5.00	4.2520	.62454	.390	-.240	.154	-.616	.307
e4	250	3.00	5.00	3.9200	.58906	.347	.017	.154	-.134	.307
e5	250	3.00	5.00	3.8280	.53625	.288	-.125	.154	.087	.307
e6	250	3.00	5.00	3.9240	.51311	.263	-.118	.154	.734	.307
e7	250	3.00	5.00	3.7080	.60015	.360	.221	.154	-.592	.307
e8	277	2.00	5.00	4.1191	.56808	.323	-.106	.146	.519	.292
e9	250	3.00	5.00	4.1360	.70959	.504	-.201	.154	-.997	.307
Valid N (listwise)	250									

Exhibit-7

CMIN

Model	NPAR	CMIN	DF	P	CMIN/DF
Saraju model	31	477.625	24	.000	19.901
Model Number 2	31	477.625	24	.000	19.901
Saturated model	55	.000	0		
Independence model	10	1273.504	45	.000	28.300

Exhibit-8
RMR, GFI

Model	RMR	GFI	AGFI	PGFI
Saraju model	1.432	.838	.629	.366
Model Number 2	1.432	.838	.629	.366
Saturated model	.000	1.000		
Independence model	.585	.547	.446	.448

Exhibit-9
Baseline Comparisons

Model	NFI Delta1	RFI rho1	IFI Delta2	TLI rho2	CFI
Saraju model	.625	.297	.637	.308	.631
Model Number 2	.625	.297	.637	.308	.631
Saturated model	1.000		1.000		1.000
Independence model	.000	.000	.000	.000	.000

Exhibit-10
RMSEA

Model	RMSEA	LO 90	HI 90	PCLOSE
Saraju model	.026	.090	.122	.000
Model Number 2	.026	.090	.122	.000
Independence model	.048	.136	.160	.000

Chapter 6
Customer Empowerment, Customer Retention, and Performance of Firms:
Role of Innovation and Customer Delight as Mediators Through Satisfaction

Manoj Kumar Mishra
O.P. Jindal University, India

Leena Singh
Indira Gandhi National Open University, India

ABSTRACT

This study looked into how customer empowerment affects a company's performance (i.e., a bank). The relationship between customer empowerment and the firm's performance of banks in India's Delhi and NCR region has been studied, and innovation and customer satisfaction have been found to mediate this relationship. 439 bank employees, both male and female, were chosen for this study. Confirmatory factor analysis was used to analyze the data, and it was discovered that the variables met the requirements of path analysis. Customer empowerment has been found to have a significant impact on firm performance (i.e., a bank) as well as a negligible impact on customer satisfaction and customer retention. Therefore, this research differs from earlier studies that demonstrate that customer empowerment has a significant impact. It suggests a comprehensive framework that explains the connections between customer empowerment, innovation, customer satisfaction, customer retention, and business performance.

DOI: 10.4018/978-1-6684-5853-2.ch006

INTRODUCTION

In the current competitive and dynamic business environment customers seek the value product and services, where innovations may be considered as an important element for customer satisfaction. Innovation is all about offering product and services in such a way that it may fulfil the expected need want and desire of the customers, but at the same time, it may also provide pleasure and satisfaction through astounding and attractive features in the product and services (Potra et al., 2018) Customer satisfaction is considered and verified as a source of mediator between service quality and firm's performance (Otto et al., 2020). Whereas innovative products or services are all about offering unique products & services or techniques to customers which makes the use of product and services more convenient and easier (Mahmoud et al., 2017; Michel et al., 2008). Innovation plays a vital role in the banking industries across the globe. Innovation is not only contributing towards the customer's satisfaction, but it helps in value addition to the corporate reputation of the banking institutions as well as reduces the cost and makes them stronger in the competitive position of the bank (Berraies & Hamouda, 2018).

It has noticed that the industrial revolution brought changes for the producers as well as digital revolution and innovation has changed the lifestyle of customers. In the current business scenario relationships between companies and consumers are changing, i.e., it has changed the trends of traditional marketing concepts in favour of the empowerment of consumers (Berraies & Hamouda, 2018; Chatterjee & Kamesh, 2020). In today's business world, the customer's power is enhanced and it is expected that if the customer is happy, he will only continue to use the company and its products. By making the product more innovative and more focused on the ongoing performance of the business, companies today are shifting their strategic focus from gaining new customers to retaining existing ones (Yin et al., 2019). Nowadays customer satisfaction is one of the basic requirements of the services industry in developing countries. It has also observed that there is an integrated perspective on customer satisfaction and innovation that leads to customer retention and financial performance of the business. Customer satisfaction and innovation both directly and indirectly affect the financial performance of the firm because customer's satisfaction & innovation are key factors that strongly connected to the customer retention and it leads to improving the financial performance of the firm (Shin et al., 2018).

Innovation is important for gaining a competitive edge, and customer satisfaction and innovation affect a firm's financial performance. Innovation can affect product and service quality, boosting firm performance (Ngo & O'cass, 2013). To gain a competitive advantage, companies must understand how to create, communicate, and deliver value products to customers (Ulaga, 2011).

According to the findings of previous studies, it is clear that the empowerment of customers has a significant impact on the level of satisfaction experienced by customers (Castillo, 2017; O'Cass & Ngo, 2011). According to the findings of this study, the empowerment of customers does not have a significant impact on the degree to which customers are satisfied or how long they remain customers. Comparative research between India's public sector banks and the country's private sector banks has been conducted, and the findings of that research indicate that customers favor private banks over public sector banks (Ahmed et al., 2020; Kant & Jaiswal, 2017; Virk & Mahal, 2012). It is evident from people perceptions also that customer satisfaction in pirate banks is very low because of bad behaviour of employees in these banks. It is accepted by the employees of the bank that though; they are making lots of efforts to enhance customer satisfaction in public sector banks but accepted that it is hard to achieve. While it is found that customer empowerment has significant impact on Firm's performance and the results are aligned with the findings of previous researches (Berraies & Hamouda, 2018; Sharanya & Kumari, 2019). This research is unique in nature to highlight the harsh reality of Indian public sector banks.

BACKGROUND AND LITERATURE REVIEW

Customer Empowerment (CE)

In the past, customer empowerment (CE) was associated with the perspective of the company, according to which the delegation of activities to customers could result in increased management efficiency (Auh et al., 2019; Fuchs & Schreier, 2011). The empowerment of customers has recently led to a shift away from the perspective of the company and toward that of the customer (Berraies & Hamouda, 2018). The term "customer empowerment," or CE, has become increasingly prevalent in recent years as an essential component of various marketing strategies, most notably in-service marketing. CE plays a significant part in ensuring that customers are happy, which in turn increases a company's profitability. In this context (Aldaihani & Ali, 2018; Fuchs & Schreier, 2011; Khenfer et al., 2020) has studied that most of the business organizations are now focusing on consumer empowerment to enhance customer satisfaction by delivering better products at a minimum price. Whereas, Pranic & Roehl (Pranic & Roehl, 2012) said that customer empowerment (CE) helps to develop a more positive brand attitude (Fuchs & Schreier, 2011) with a brand perceived as more innovative (Chaney et al., 2021; Poetz & Schreier, 2012).

In addition, customers express a high demand for the product, if he gets then only, he is ready to participate in the positive word of mouth (Fuchs et al., 2010; Meißner et al., 2017). These benefits, however, appear to depend on the nature of the sector and the circumstances. If they work effectively for consumer goods (Acar & Puntoni, 2016; Fuchs et al., 2010; Lee et al., 2021) or the context of service delivery (Pranic & Roehl, 2012).

Customer Empowerment and Customer Satisfaction

Customer empowerment is a vital component of the advanced marketing framework. It has observed in the latest years that, in the banking industry, the practice of customer empowerment has increased, and it is directly related to the services quality and customer satisfaction. Customer satisfaction can be increased by fulfilling the buyer's expectation that comprises exploring and giving what consumer needs and wants. (Acar & Puntoni, 2016; Aldaihani & Ali, 2018; Al-Omari et al., 2020; Chebat & Kollias, 2000; Han et al., 2019) defined customer empowerment as engagement strategies that give customers a say in the company's offerings. Customer empowerment can also be used to involve customers in the development of the products and services that the company offers (Aldaihani & Ali, 2018; Auh et al., 2019; Berraies & Hamouda, 2018; Lubis et al., 2020; Mohammad, 2020). For the operational definition of customer empowerment, it is necessary to consider three aspects: customer awareness of their rights, customer engagement, and customer skills. This is what (Gazzola et al., 2017) found. According to Fuchs and Schreir (2011), customers are empowered in the context of novel product design, and they are empowered to choose these designs (Agolla et al., 2018).

H 1: Customer Empowerment (CE) is significantly related with Customer satisfaction.

Customer Empowerment and Innovation

In the past few years, innovation has captured a very pertinent role in the business environment, as producers and service providers accepted its important role for economic growth and progress. Companies who are adopting innovation have become the building blocks of better economies in various regions in the world (Tanniru & Sandhu, 2019) Companies with innovative new skills are among the organizations, which are considered as the main sources of new ideas, products, and processes that are essential for finding and maintaining economic competitiveness especially in technology (Berraies & Hamouda, 2018; Dodgson et al., 2008; Zhang & Xiao, 2020). Consumers are becoming increasingly empowered with new technologies, rich resources and a wide selection of products and demand digitalization for businesses as a result. Empowered customers expected to demand more effectively in contrast to those who are underpowered. It has also found that the increasing use of ICT and innovation is shifting his power from suppliers to consumers (YuSheng & Ibrahim, 2019).

H2: Customer Empowerment is significantly related with innovation practices in organisations.

Customer Satisfaction and Customer Retention

Customer satisfaction is defined by Verma and Chaudhuri (2009) as the emotional reaction of the customer to the firm's products or services (Darzi & Bhat, 2018; Gichuru & Limiri, 2017). Customer repurchase rates rise when products and services meet or exceed customer expectations, according to the operational definition of customer satisfaction (Chen & Liu, 2019; Schwarz & Clore, 1983). You can compare how satisfied customers are with a product or service by looking at previous purchases they've made (Agolla et al., 2018; Alketbi et al., 2020). The trust between the company and the customer is another dimension that can be assumed from the same study for customer satisfaction. According to customer satisfaction, a company's performance is defined as its ability to meet or exceed customer expectations in terms of the value they provide.

H3: Customer Satisfaction is significantly related with the Customer retention.

Innovation and Customer Retention

A great economist Schumpeter (2013) defined that innovation is a process of encompassing the idea that contributes and helps the marketer to increase the demand for the product and services. According to the Oslo Manual (OECD, 2005), a product, design, or marketing process that significantly improves the firm's products, processes or methods qualifies as an innovation. Customers' wants and needs guide the development of new products, which the companies aim to make as convenient and comfortable as possible for them. Because innovation is a continuous process, it can be used as a catalyst for business growth and customer retention by providing consumers with innovative products and services, as has been shown in previous studies (Diaw & Asare, 2018; Fatima et al., 2021).; Ganesan & Sridhar, 2016; Gengeswari et al., 2013; Jansen et al., 2006; Kyei & Bayoh, 2017; Lochab et al., 2018). It is also evident that innovations are one of the important elements for the firm to remain in business and retain the customers, as well as Innovation in Product and service, is the key to satisfying and retaining customers (Aldaihani & Ali, 2018).

H4: An innovative practice is significantly related with Customer retention.

Customer Retention and Firm Performance

Customer retention can be considered, as a strategic step for improving a firm's performance. In most cases, Customer retention may be considered as an element for growth & firm's performance (Ho et al., 2020; Otto et al., 2020) has analysed the role of customer retention (CR) and found that CR acts as a mediating agent in the performance of service and also found that satisfaction of customer and performance of Firm's have positive association with each other. Customer retention, according to Al-Hawari (2006), can be viewed as an asset and resource for the business that can improve performance (Beckers et al., 2017; Kumar & Awasthi, 2018; Lochab & Kumar, 2019; Lochab et al., 2020; Rubera & Kirca, 2017). These factors, along with profitability and product innovation, all contribute to the growth of a firm's financial performance. Some researchers looked at customer retention in terms of accounting metrics, such as the company's financial performance, growth, and profit. Customer retention, lower marketing costs, and an increase in the market share of its customers are all associated favourably with customer satisfaction, word-of-mouth advertising, and consumer loyalty (Diaw & Asare, 2018; Madhani, 2020; Ullah & Narain, 2020).

H 5: Customer retention is significantly related with the firm performance.

Customer Empowerment and Firm Performance

Some empirical studies show that positive orientation and focus towards customers are directly related to firm's performance (Kirca et al., 2005). In many research areas, it has been shown that there are positive and direct impacts of Customer empowerment on financial performance of the firm. Consumer's satisfaction, innovations directly empower the customers and acts as a mediating agent between Customer empowerment and financial performance of the firm (Aldaihani & Ali, 2018; Aldaihani & Ali, 2018; Berraies & Hamouda, 2018; Kumar et al., 2020; MacCallum et al., 1996; Meißner et al., 2017). It has been discovered that a number of service providers are attempting to connect with customers by utilizing a variety of modes and channels of communication in order to give their customers more agency and to co-create relationship value with the company. These activities have been beneficial to the company and have a direct impact on the performance of the company. It has a tendency to hold the belief that CE is overly associated with customers and market orientation and that it is also considered to be a predictor of firm performance (Auh et al., 2019; Berraies & Hamouda, 2018; Chernikov et al., 2015).

H6: Customer Empowerment is significantly related with the Firm Performance.

Mediating Effect of Customer Satisfaction and Innovation Between Customer Empowerment and Firm Performance

Nowadays, customer satisfaction is considered as important tools for consumer's empowerment and improving firm's performance. Customer satisfaction is based on pre and post expectation and reaction of consumer's purchase behaviours. Generally, pre-purchase expectations are related to the product and service compared to the actual purchase experience (Berraies & Hamouda, 2018; Mohammad, 2020) resulting in satisfaction, discontentedness or indifference. Alternative studies view satisfaction as an emotional response to a consumption experience in contrast to the current interpretation of satisfaction as a psychological feature (Aldaihani & Ali, 2018) It also tends to follow the cognitive-affective approach and outline satisfaction, although few literatures have defined customer satisfaction in terms of supporting emotional and psychological feature processes. On the other hand, the majority of the findings from the research indicated that a significant association exists between satisfied customers and financial performance. Researchers have found that there is a positive relationship between customer satisfaction and financial performance. These findings have been applied to all measures of profitability, including earnings, return on assets, and net revenues. Ittner and Larcker (Ittner & Larcker, 1998) also stated that there is a high positive correlation between customer satisfaction and the financial performance of the company, and they demonstrated this correlation with evidence by demonstrating that the publication of customer satisfaction measures will yield incremental information on the stock market.

H 7: Customer satisfaction mediate between customer empowerment and firm performance

H8: Innovation mediate between customer empowerment and firm performance

Figure 1. Hypothesised Model
Source: (Adapted from Berraies, & Hamouda, (2018)

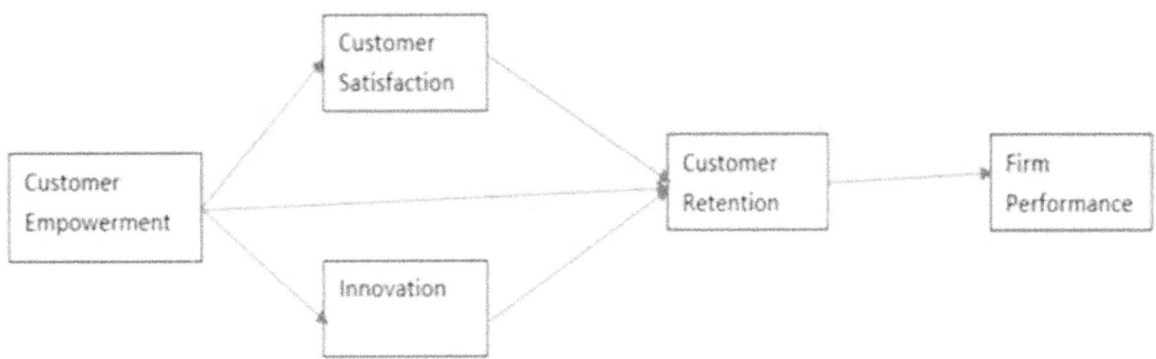

It is evident from the previous research that none of the studies have explored the relationship between customer empowerment and customer satisfaction w.r.t. Indian public sector banks. This is an important gap which has been identified in case of Indian public sector banks and customer empowerment.

RESEARCH METHOD

The relationship between the various variables that were considered for this study is depicted in figure 1, which can be found above. The figure also indicates the direction of the relationship between the various variables. Within the scope of this research, five aspects of business were investigated: customer empowerment; customer satisfaction; innovation; customer retention; and firm performance. The research was carried out with the intention of accomplishing a number of goals, the first of which was to determine the nature of the connection that exists between customer empowerment and both innovation and customer satisfaction. Second, the relationship between satisfied customers and new innovations and continued customer retention. Third, the correlation between customer retention and company performance. The final and mediating role played by customer satisfaction and innovation between the empowerment of customers and the performance of businesses. In order to accomplish the goals of this investigation, a comprehensive questionnaire in its original form was modified. The questionnaire comprises 32 items. There are six statements in the customer empowerment category, while there are seven statements in the customer satisfaction category. Innovation comprises six statements. The retention of customers is covered by six statements, and the performance of the company is covered by seven statements. After putting these items through a test to determine the reliability of the variables, it was discovered that the variables meet the criteria for reliability (i.e., alpha=0.951) (Nunnally, 1970). It was determined through the use of AMOS software version 22 and confirmatory factor analysis that the variables in question meet the requirements for path analysis. AMOS Software was also utilized in order to test the hypothesized model that was used in the study. The study's sample was collected from a wide variety of public sector banks located in the Delhi and National Capital Region (NCR) area. For the purpose of this study, participants were chosen from among bank employees. In the sample that was taken for this research, there are both male and female workers included, and they span several age brackets. Data was collected from the Delhi and National Capital Region (NCR) region through Google (online). A total of more than 1,350 employees working for various public sector banks were given questionnaires to fill out. There were a total of 536 responses received, but only 439 of those responses were considered appropriate for the purpose of this study. Only 39% of people responded to the survey. The researcher also used SPSS to calculate the mediating effect of customer satisfaction and innovation Andrew F. Hayes **(Fuchs & Schreier, 2011),** which he then applied to the PROCESS macro to examine the relationship between customer empowerment and firm performance.

Table.1 Demographic detail of respondents (N=439)

	Groups	**Frequency**	**Percentage**
Age	25-35	139	33.94
	36-45	209	45.33
	46-55	63	12.98
	Above 55	34	7.7
Gender	Male	321	73.12
	Female	118	26.87
Profile/Job categories	Low	47	10.70
	Medium	323	73.57
	High	69	15.71
Education	UG	81	18.45
	PG	272	61.95
	Any other	86	15.58
Experience	0-10	137	31.20
	11-20	346	78.81
	More than 20	26	5.92

Source: Researcher's Own

The data relating to the respondents' demographic characteristics are presented in Table 1. It is clear from the table that the ages of the respondents have been divided into four distinct categories; these range from 22 to 35 years old, 36 to 45 years old, 46 to 55 years old, and over 55 years old. These age groups have respective percentages of 33.9%, 45.3%, 12.9%, and 7.7% of the total population. Only males and females are classified according to their gender among the respondents. Males make up 73.1 percent of the total, while females account for 26.8 percent. The jobs of the respondents are divided into one of three categories: low, medium, or high. These three groups each account for 10.7, 73.5, and 15.7 percent of the total, respectively. The educational backgrounds were divided into three categories: elementary school, secondary school, and any other. The percentages of these three components are as follows: 18.4, 61.9, and 15.5% respectively. The respondents' years of experience were divided into three distinct groups: 0-10 years, 11-20 years, and more than 20 years. These three categories each have a percentage that is as follows: 31.2%, 78.8%, and 5.9% respectively.

Measures

- **Customer Empowerment:** It is measured with the help of six statements that were provided by Hunter and Garnefeld (2008); Gazzola et al. (2017), holding a Cronbach value of 0.88; CR=0.886 and AVE=0.565. It has been determined that each measure is appropriate for the objectives of this study. In table No. 2, you'll also find the means, standard deviations, factor loadings, and standardized regression weights for each of the statements that were utilized for the purpose of this study.

- **Customer retention**: It has been measured using a Likert five scale, with 1 representing strong disagreement and 5 representing strong agreement. It is evaluated using six statements that were provided by Gangeswari et al. (2013), each of which had a Cronbach alpha value of 0.91; CR = 0.91 and AVE = 0.645. It has been determined that each measure is appropriate for the objectives of this study. In table No. 2, you'll also find the means, standard deviations, factor loadings, and standardized regression weights for each of the statements that were utilized for the purpose of this study.

- **Customer Satisfaction**: It is determined based on seven statements provided by Galbreath (2010) and its Cronbach alpha value is 0.90; CR=0.90 and AVE=0.576. It has been determined that each measure is appropriate for the objectives of this study. In table No. 2, you'll also find the means, standard deviations, factor loadings, and standardized regression weights for each of the statements that were utilized for the purpose of this study. On the Likert scale, where 1 indicates strong disagreement and 5 indicates strong agreement, the scale was used.

Table 2. Statistics of construct item

Construct/variable	Measurement Items	Mean Score	SD	Factor Loading	SRW	Model Type
Customer Empowerment (alpha= 0.88; CR=0.886; AVE=0.565); Hunter and Garnefeld (37); Gazzola et al. (28)	CE1	4.19	1.016	0.541	0.745	Reflective
	CE2	4.21	0.993	0.628	0.774	
	CE3	4.05	1.027	0.656	0.708	
	CE4	4.24	0.923	0.524	0.731	
	CE5	4.13	1.010	0.539	0.769	
	CE6	4.28	0.925	0.722	0.779	
Customer Retention (alpha=0.91; CR=0.916; AVE=0.645) Gangeswari et. al (27)	CR1	4.20	1.029	0.764	0.746	Reflective
	CR2	4.25	0.925	0.741	0.837	
	CR3	4.25	0.925	0.705	0.842	
	CR4	4.24	0.929	0.734	0.814	
	CR5	4.11	1.019	0.695	0.806	
	CR6	4.28	0.945	0.560	0.771	
Customer Satisfaction (alpha=0.90; CR= 0.905; AVE=0.576) Galbreath (26)	CS1	4.26	0.682	0.804	0.774	Reflective
	CS2	4.22	0.678	0.803	0.779	
	CS3	4.23	0.660	0.806	0.782	
	CS4	4.47	0.761	0.798	0.763	
	CS5	4.54	0.733	0.816	0.785	
	CS6	4.49	0.743	0.754	0.706	
	CS7	4.50	0.734	0.768	0.72	
Innovation (alpha=0.85; CR=0.904; AVE=0.613) Jasen et. al. (35)	IN1	3.89	1.107	0.743	0.685	Reflective
	IN2	4.12	1.000	0.621	0.816	
	IN3	4.06	1.018	0.546	0.763	
	IN4	4.18	0.989	0.604	0.841	
	IN5	4.27	0.930	0.655	0.82	
	IN6	4.18	0.993	0.638	0.763	
Firm Performance (alpha=0.92; CR=0.920; AVE=0.623) Kalpan and Norton (42)	FP1	4.29	0.915	0.543	0.824	Reflective
	FP2	4.31	0.913	0.587	0.859	
	FP3	4.19	0.968	0.576	0.838	
	FP4	4.24	0.951	0.725	0.731	
	FP5	4.32	0.936	0.745	0.757	
	FP6	4.34	0.887	0.728	0.783	
	FP7	4.10	0.980	0.547	0.723	

Source: Research Output

Note: SD= Standard Deviation; SRW=Standardized Regression Weight

Innovation

It is evaluated using six statements that were provided by Jasen et al. (2006), with a Cronbach value of

0.85, CR equal to 0.90, and AVE equal to 0.613. It has been determined that each measure is appropriate for the objectives of this study. In table No. 2, you'll also find the means, standard deviations, factor loadings, and standardized regression weights for each of the statements that were utilized for the purpose of this study. On the Likert scale, where 1 indicates strong disagreement and 5 indicates strong agreement, the scale was used.

Performance of Firm

It is evaluated based on seven statements provided by Kalpan and Norton (2005), each of which has a Cronbach alpha value of 0.92; CR = 0.92 and AVE = 0.623. It has been determined that each measure is appropriate for the objectives of this study. In table No. 2, you'll also find the means, standard deviations, factor loadings, and standardized regression weights for each of the statements that were utilized for the purpose of this study. We used the Likert five-point scale, where "1" means "strongly disagree" and "5" means "strongly agree."

RESULTS

Table 3. Correlation table

	CE	CR	FP	IN	CS
CE	1				
CR	**0.966****	1			
FP	0.945**	**0.949****	1		
IN	0.930**	0.893**	**0.951****	1	
CS	-0.049	-0.046	-0.021	**-0.024**	1

Source: Research Output

The correlation values among the variables are represented in table 3. It also gives the value of r, which is the correlation between the variables. The results show that there is a link between customer loyalty and customer empowerment (0.966), between customer loyalty and firm performance (0.949), between innovation and firm performance (0.951), and between customer satisfaction and innovation (0.966). (-0.024).

Figure 2. Structural Model showing various causal Relationships
Source: Research Output

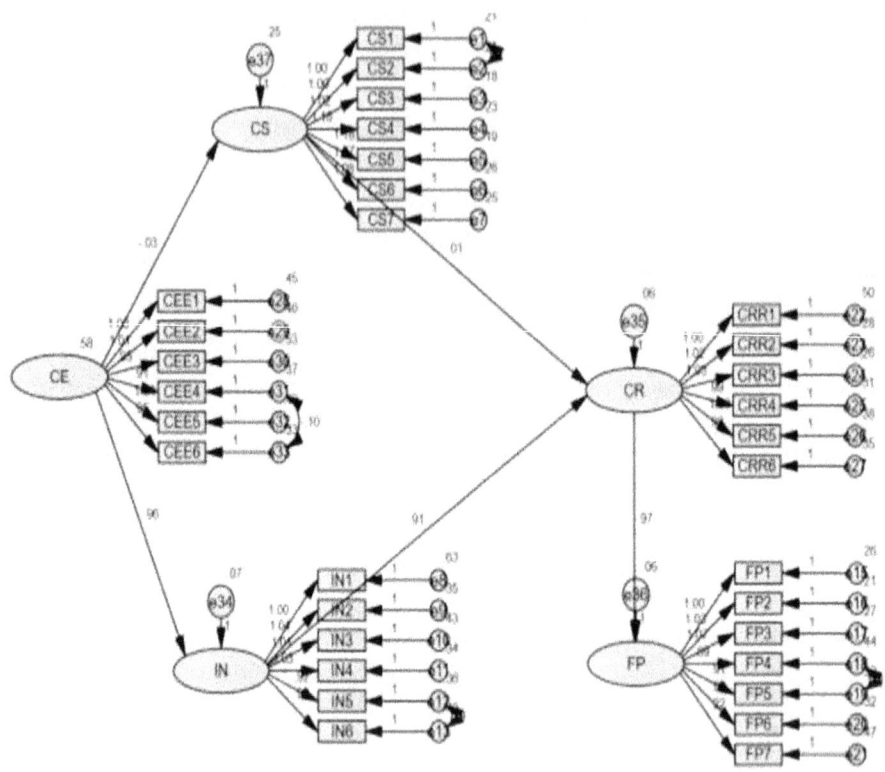

Table 4. Fit indices for customer empowerment, customer satisfaction, innovation, customer retention and firm performance

Sample Details (N=439)	CMIN	DF	CFI	TLI	GFI	AIC	RMSEA
Model 1	28.79	8	0.984	0.970	0.978	54.79	0.077
Model 2	181.48	52	0.964	0.954	0.934	233.48	0.075
Model 3	527.06	147	0.941	0.931	0.886	613.06	0.077
Model 4	862.01	266	0.932	0.923	0.862	980.01	0.072
Model 5	1124.30	450	0.936	0.929	0.861	1280.30	0.058

Source: Research Output

The primary conclusion drawn from the CFA method is the degree to which individual factors in the model represent the data. This is something that can be investigated with the aid of model fit indices. If it is determined that the parameters of the model fit well, then the model will be validated. With a CMIN/DF value of 2.78 (ranging from as high as 5.0 to as low as 0.0), it was determined that the structural model provided a satisfactory fit. Hu and Bentler (1999), GFI = 0.936 (>0.90, Kline (1998), TLI = 0.929 (>0.90, Hooper et al. (2008) RMSEA = 0.058 (0.07, according to MacCallum, Brown, and Sugawara, (1996) and between 0.08 and.10, according to Mac Callum et al., (1996); AIC = 1280.30. According to the structured model of the study that was proposed, all of the paths are statistically significant, and the p-values of all of the paths are lower than 0.05.

Table 5. Results of regression analysis

Path Analysis	Beta	t	Sig	Hypothesis
Customer Empowerment - Customer Satisfaction (R² =0.002)	-0.034	-1.032	0.303	Not Supported
Customer Empowerment - Innovation (R² =0.865)	0.933	52.917	0.000	Supported
Customer Satisfaction - Customer Retention (R² =0.002)	-0.068	-0.046	0.338	Not Supported
Innovation - Customer Retention (R² =0.798)	0.909	41.556	.000	Supported
Customer Retention - Firm Performance (R² =0.901)	0.936	63.051	.000	Supported
Customer Empowerment - Firm Performance (R² =0.894)	0.951	60.577	.000	Supported

Source: Research Output

To begin, it is clear from looking at table 5 that the level of customer empowerment (CE) has no significant bearing on the level of customer satisfaction (CS). Since p is greater than 0.05 and b is less than 0.034, we can conclude that the first hypothesis, H1, is not supported.

Second, it is clear from looking at table 5 that customer empowerment (CE) has a significant impact on the innovative process (IN). Since b (0.933), t (52.917), and p (less than 0.05), we can conclude that the second hypothesis (H2) is correct.

Third, looking at table 5 makes it abundantly clear that the level of customer satisfaction (CS) has a negligible effect on the percentage of retained customers (CR). Since b (0.933), t (52.917), and p (less than 0.05), we can conclude that the second hypothesis (H2) is correct.

Figure 3. SEM Model
Source: Research Output

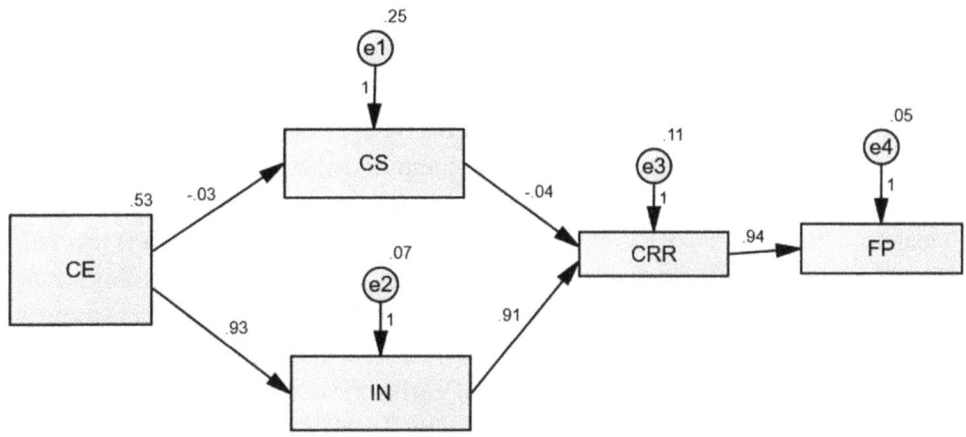

Table 6. Results of mediation through PROCESS macro-analysis

Bootstrapping	Direct effect	Indirect	BootSE	95% confidence interval		Mediation
				LLCI	ULCI	
CE →CS→FP	.9507	-.0001	0.0011	-.0024	.0024	No Mediation
CE →IN→FP	.4535	0.4970	0.0590	.3752	.6075	Full Mediation

Source: Research Output

The mediation analysis makes it abundantly clear that there is no mediating effect that customer satisfaction has on the relationship between customer empowerment (CE) and firm performance. The correlation between CE and CS is not significant, whereas the correlation between CE and FP is significant (as shown in Table 5). In addition, the values of the intervals between the lower confidence interval CI and the upper confidence level CI for indirect effect found zero (as demonstrated in Table 6), which indicates that there is no indirect effect (Zhao et al., 2010). When compared to the effect that is visible in Table 6, it is clear that the indirect effect has no impact at all. This conclusion can be drawn from the data presented. As a result, the study revealed that there was both a direct effect as well as a non-significant indirect effect. From this, we can draw the conclusion that there was no mediation (Jacoby & Jaccard, 2010) in the study. As a result, the seventh hypothesis cannot be maintained.

The mediation analysis makes it abundantly clear that innovation has a moderating effect on the relationship that exists between customer empowerment (CE) and firm performance. Both the connection between CE and innovation and the connection between CE and FP were significant (as shown in Table 5). Additionally, the interval values between the lower confidence interval CI and the upper confidence level CI for indirect effect did not find zero (as shown in Table 6), which indicates that there was an indirect effect (Zhao et al., 2010). In light of the findings presented in Table 6, it is clear that the indirect effect has a magnitude that is significantly greater than that of the direct effect. As a result, not only did the study reveal a significant indirect effect, but it also revealed a direct effect. From this, we can draw the conclusion that the study involved some form of partial mediation (Jacoby & Jaccard, 2010). Therefore, the validity of hypothesis 8 was established.

DISCUSSION

The study has investigated how all of the conceptual model's constructs relate to one another in terms of their relationships. The results of the study indicate, based on the samples that were drawn from it, that CE has a significant influence on the performance of firms (i.e. bank). Numerous researchers, including (Berraies & Hamouda, 2018; Chernikov et al., 2015) themselves, have come to the same conclusions. The findings of the most recent study were consistent with the findings of the studies that came before it.

It is also clear from the analysis of the data that CE has a negligible impact on the level of satisfaction experienced by the customer. Which goes against the conventional wisdom regarding it? In spite of the fact that customers are given more agency within the banking system in India, customers are consistently unhappy with the behavior of bank employees. This is one thing that is abundantly clear about the banking system in India. According to the findings of earlier research, the quality of service provided in terms of the human elements has a greater impact on the level of customer satisfaction (Lenka et al.,

2009) than do the technical and tangible elements. Because of this, empowering customers is not the goal here; rather, providing customers with relevant information in a humane manner is significantly more prominent and important than simply sharing relevant information with customers.

The findings of the study also make it abundantly clear that customer engagement (CE) plays a significant role in retaining existing customers. Previous research (Aldaihani & Ali, 2018) has also revealed findings that are consistent with this one.

The idea that CE has a significant impact on the factors that motivate innovation in business practices is investigated further. What is the result of the study, which demonstrates that CE has a significant influence on innovation? Previous research has shown that providing customers with more agency over their purchasing decisions leads to creative new product designs and makes it easier for businesses to adopt innovative business practices (Agolla et al., 2018; Berraies & Hamouda, 2018).

This study highlights the fact that customer satisfaction (CS) does not act as a mediator between customer engagement (CE) and financial performance (FP) in regard to the mediating role of innovation and customer satisfaction. whereas innovation acts as a bridge between CE and FP, creating a win-win situation for both. The CS does not serve as a mediator because, in the case of public sector banks, it has been discovered that customers are not satisfied despite the various efforts that have been made by the banks. Because of this, the results of this study indicate that CS does not have a mediating effect between CE and FP, which is an important finding in the case of Indian public sector banks. (Chatterjee & Kamesh, 2020)

In addition, the findings of this research make a contribution to the existing body of literature by highlighting the role that CS and innovation play as mediators between CE and firm performance. It is clear that CE has no influence whatsoever on CS, but it does have a significant influence on innovations, which in turn lead to the retention of customers and improved firm performance.

According to the findings of the research, the level of empowerment felt by customers is unrelated to their level of satisfaction. The harsh reality of the situation is that very few customers are satisfied with the services provided by Indian public sector banks. Despite the fact that people have no control over their circumstances, a growing number of them are opening bank accounts in the public sector. On the other hand, it is clear from the findings of the study that customers of public sector banks are dissatisfied with the behavior of those institutions.

CONCLUSION

Implications, Limitations, and the Scope for Future Research in this Area

The purpose of this research was to investigate the connection that exists between the empowerment of customers and the performance of businesses. According to the findings of the study, it has a significant effect on the overall performance of the company. In addition, it is investigated whether or not customer satisfaction and innovation do have mediating effects. It was discovered that CS does not have mediating effects between CE and FP, whereas innovation does have mediating effects. This research stands out from other studies because it proposes an integrated model that produces the relations between customer empowerment, innovation, customer satisfaction, customer retention, and firm performance. This model is what distinguishes this research from other studies. As a result, the most important contribution made by this study is that it sheds light on the role that mediating variables, specifically innovation and CS, play in the relationship. The finding that CS does not have a mediating effect is perhaps even more important. The circumstances surrounding this study are very different from those of other studies that have been conducted in the past. The Indian public sector banks have been the primary focus of this study. Practices in India's public sector banks are very different from those in the country's private sector banks in almost every respect.

It is possible to say that giving customers more control will improve the performance of banks, and that this improvement will allow customers to be retained for a longer period of time. The findings of the study point in the same direction.

The implication of this study is that it can encourage managers and bankers to comprehend how critical it is to give customers more control over their financial transactions. When the manager understands the significance of this procedure, they will begin to provide individualized service to the clients of the company. Customers will have the opportunity to voice their concerns regarding various types of requirements. Customers will remain loyal to the bank and contribute to the institution's overall performance if it is determined that their concerns will be addressed by bank employees. One insightful observation that can be made to managers working in the banking industry is that it is not only the empowerment of customers that plays an important role, but also how nicely all staff members behave with them. This is something that can be suggested as an important observation. Therefore, in order to improve the customers' overall satisfaction, it is recommended to the managers that they kindly practice customer-friendly ways. CE is beneficial for innovation, customer retention, and financial performance, but in order to achieve CS, more was required of it than just CE.

Nevertheless, the existing literature has been significantly advanced by the contributions that this paper has made. Nevertheless, there are some restrictions that come with this study. The areas surrounding India's national capitals were the only ones included in the sample for the public sector banks in India. This research can easily be expanded to include findings from other regions of the country. Data that is comparable can also be obtained from private banks, and then the results can be compared. It's possible that there are other significant factors that can act as a mediator in the connection between CE and FP. The variables may include things like customer engagement and customer relations management, among other things. In subsequent studies, it is conceivable that not one but both quantitative and qualitative approaches to data collection will be utilized. In conclusion, research of this kind can also be conducted in various other fields.

REFERENCES

Acar, O. A., & Puntoni, S. (2016). Customer empowerment in the digital age. *Journal of Advertising Research*, *56*(1), 4–8. doi:10.2501/JAR-2016-007

Agolla, J. E., Makara, T., & Monametsi, G. (2018). Impact of banking innovations on customer attraction, satisfaction and retention: The case of commercial banks in Botswana. *International Journal of Electronic Banking*, *1*(2), 150–170. doi:10.1504/IJEBANK.2018.095598

Ahmed, R. R., Romeika, G., Kauliene, R., Streimikis, J., & Dapkus, R. (2020). ES-QUAL model and customer satisfaction in online banking: Evidence from multivariate analysis techniques. *Oeconomia Copernicana*, *11*(1), 59–93. doi:10.24136/oc.2020.003

Al-Hawari, M. (2006). The effect of automated service quality on bank financial performance and the mediating role of customer retention. *Journal of Financial Services Marketing*, *10*(3), 228–243. doi:10.1057/palgrave.fsm.4770189

Al-Omari, Z., Alomari, K., & Aljawarneh, N. (2020). The role of empowerment in improving internal process, customer satisfaction, learning and growth. *Management Science Letters*, *10*(4), 841–848. doi:10.5267/j.msl.2019.10.013

Aldaihani, F. M. F., & Ali, N. A. B. (2018). Impact of social customer relationship management on customer satisfaction through customer empowerment: A study of Islamic Banks in Kuwait. International Research Journal of Finance and Economics, 170(170), 41-53. [.

Aldaihani, F. M. F., & Ali, N. A. B. (2018). The mediating role of customer empowerment in the effect of relationship marketing on customer retention: an empirical demonstration from Islamic banks in Kuwait. *European journal of economics, finance and administrative sciences, 99*, 42-52.

Alketbi, S., Alshurideh, M., & Al Kurdi, B. (2020). the influence of service quality on customers' retention and loyalty in the uae hotel sector with respect to the impact of customer' satisfaction, trust, and commitment: a qualitative study. *PalArch's Journal of Archaeology of Egypt/Egyptology, 17*(4), 541-561.

Almohaimmeed, B. (2019). Pillars of customer retention: An empirical study on the influence of customer satisfaction, customer loyalty, customer profitability on customer retention. *Serbian Journal of Management, 14*(2), 421–435. doi:10.5937jm14-15517

Alolayyan, M. N., Al-Hawary, S. I. S., Mohammad, A. A. S., & Al-Nady, B. A. H. A. (2018). Banking service quality provided by commercial banks and customer satisfaction. A structural equation modelling approaches. *International Journal of Productivity and Quality Management*, *24*(4), 543–565. doi:10.1504/IJPQM.2018.093454

Auh, S., Menguc, B., Katsikeas, C. S., & Jung, Y. S. (2019). When does customer participation matter? An empirical investigation of the role of customer empowerment in the customer participation–performance link. *JMR, Journal of Marketing Research*, *56*(6), 1012–1033. doi:10.1177/0022243719866408

Beckers, S. F., van Doorn, J., & Verhoef, P. C. (2017). Good, better, engaged? The effect of company-initiated customer engagement behavior on shareholder value. *Journal of the Academy of Marketing Science*, *45*(3), 1–18.

Berraies, S., & Hamouda, M. (2018). Customer empowerment and firms' performance: The mediating effects of innovation and customer satisfaction. *International Journal of Bank Marketing*, *36*(2), 336–356. doi:10.1108/IJBM-10-2016-0150

Castillo, J. (2017). The relationship between big five personality traits, customer empowerment and customer satisfaction in the retail industry. *The Journal of Business and Retail Management Research, 11*(2).

Chaney, D., Gardan, J., & De Freyman, J. (2021). A framework for the relationship implications of additive manufacturing (3D printing) for industrial marketing: Servitization, sustainability and customer empowerment. *Journal of Business and Industrial Marketing*.

Chatterjee, D., & Kamesh, A. V. S. (2020). Significance of Relationship marketing in banks in terms of Customer Empowerment and satisfaction. *European Journal of Molecular & Clinical Medicine*, 7(4), 999–1009.

Chebat, J. C., & Kollias, P. (2000). The impact of empowerment on customer contact employees' roles in service organizations. *Journal of Service Research*, 3(1), 66–81. doi:10.1177/109467050031005

Chen, C. M., & Liu, H. M. (2019). The moderating effect of competitive status on the relationship between customer satisfaction and retention. *Total Quality Management & Business Excellence*, 30(7-8), 721–744. doi:10.1080/14783363.2017.1333413

Chernikov, V., Kushch, S., & Tikkanen, H. (2015). Customer empowerment and firm performance: Benefits and potential harm. In *Ideas in marketing: Finding the New and polishing the old* (pp. 138–138). Springer. doi:10.1007/978-3-319-10951-0_48

Darzi, M. A., & Bhat, S. A. (2018). Personnel capability and customer satisfaction as predictors of customer retention in the banking sector: A mediated-moderation study. *International Journal of Bank Marketing*, 36(4), 663–679. doi:10.1108/IJBM-04-2017-0074

Diaw, B., & Asare, G. (2018). Effect of innovation on customer satisfaction and customer retention in the telecommunication industry in Ghana: Customers' Perspectives. *European Journal of Research and Reflection in Management Sciences*, 6(4), 15–26.

Dodgson, M., Gann, D. M., & Salter, A. (2008). *The management of technological innovation: strategy and practice*. Oxford University Press on Demand.

Fatima, T., Awan, T. M., & Kamran, M. (2021). Impact of Interactive and supportive service innovation in customer retention: an interplay of value creation and participation. *Foundation University Journal of Business & Economics,* 6(1).

Fuchs, C., Prandelli, E., & Schreier, M. (2010). The psychological effects of empowerment strategies on consumers' product demand. *Journal of Marketing*, 74(1), 65–79. doi:10.1509/jmkg.74.1.65

Fuchs, C., & Schreier, M. (2011). Customer empowerment in new product development. *Journal of Product Innovation Management*, 28(1), 17–32. doi:10.1111/j.1540-5885.2010.00778.x

Fuchs, C., & Schreier, M. (2011). Customer empowerment in new product development. *Journal of Product Innovation Management*, 28(1), 17–32. doi:10.1111/j.1540-5885.2010.00778.x

Galbreath, J. (2010). How does corporate social responsibility benefit firms? Evidence from Australia. European Business Review.

Ganesan, P., & Sridhar, M. (2016). Service innovation and customer performance of telecommunication service provider: A study on mediation effect of corporate reputation. *Corporate Reputation Review*, 19(1), 77–101. doi:10.1057/crr.2015.29

Gazzola, P., Colombo, G., Pezzetti, R., & Nicolescu, L. (2017). Consumer empowerment in the digital economy: Availing sustainable purchasing decisions. *Sustainability*, 9(5), 693. doi:10.3390u9050693

Gengeswari, K., Padmashantini, P., & Sharmeela-Banu, S. A. (2013). Impact of customer retention practices on firm performance. *International Journal of Academic Research in Business & Social Sciences*, *3*(7), 68.

Gichuru, M. J., & Limiri, E. K. (2017). Market segmentation as a strategy for customer satisfaction and retention. International Journal of Economics. *Commerce and Management. United Kingdom*, *V*(12), 544–553.

Han, X., Fang, S., Xie, L., & Yang, J. (2019). Service fairness and customer satisfaction: Mediating role of customer psychological empowerment. Journal of Contemporary Marketing Science.

Ho, M. H. W., Chung, H. F., Kingshott, R., & Chiu, C. C. (2020). Customer engagement, consumption and firm performance in a multi-actor service eco-system: The moderating role of resource integration. *Journal of Business Research*, *121*, 557–566. doi:10.1016/j.jbusres.2020.02.008

Hooper, D., Coughlan, J., & Mullen, M. (2008, September). Evaluating model fit: a synthesis of the structural equation modelling literature. In *7th European Conference on research methodology for business and management studies* (pp. 195-200). Academic Press.

Hooper, D., Coughlan, J., & Mullen, M. R. (2008). Structural equation modelling: Guidelines for determining model fit. *Electronic Journal of Business Research Methods*, *6*(1), 53–60.

Hu, L. T., & Bentler, P. M. (1999). Cutoff criteria for fit indexes in covariance structure analysis: Conventional criteria versus new alternatives. *Structural Equation Modeling*, *6*(1), 1–55. doi:10.1080/10705519909540118

Hunter, G., & Garnefeld, I. (2008). When does consumer empowerment lead to satisfied customers? Some mediating and moderating effects of the empowerment-satisfaction link. *Journal of Research for Consumers*, *15*, 1–14.

Ittner, C. D., & Larcker, D. F. (1998). Are nonfinancial measures leading indicators of financial performance? An analysis of customer satisfaction. *Journal of Accounting Research*, *36*, 1–35. doi:10.2307/2491304

Jacoby, L., & Jaccard, J. (2010). Perceived support among families deciding about organ donation for their loved ones: Donor vs nondonor next of kin. *American Journal of Critical Care*, *19*(5), e52–e61. doi:10.4037/ajcc2010396 PMID:20810408

Jansen, J. J., Van Den Bosch, F. A., & Volberda, H. W. (2006). Exploratory innovation, exploitative innovation, and performance: Effects of organizational antecedents and environmental moderators. *Management Science*, *52*(11), 1661–1674. doi:10.1287/mnsc.1060.0576

Kant, R., & Jaiswal, D. (2017). The impact of perceived service quality dimensions on customer satisfaction: An empirical study on public sector banks in India. *International Journal of Bank Marketing*, *35*(3), 411–430. doi:10.1108/IJBM-04-2016-0051

Kaplan, R. S., & Norton, D. P. (2005). The balanced scorecard: Measures that drive performance. *Harvard Business Review*, *83*(7), 172. PMID:10119714

Keränen, J., & Jalkala, A. (2014). Three strategies for customer value assessment in business markets. *Management Decision*, *52*(1), 79–100. doi:10.1108/MD-04-2013-0230

Khenfer, J., Shepherd, S., & Trendel, O. (2020). Customer empowerment in the face of perceived Incompetence: Effect on preference for anthropomorphized brands. *Journal of Business Research, 118,* 1–11. doi:10.1016/j.jbusres.2020.06.010

Kirca, A. H., Jayachandran, S., & Bearden, W. O. (2005). Market orientation: A meta-analytic review and assessment of its antecedents and impact on performance. *Journal of Marketing, 69*(2), 24–41. doi:10.1509/jmkg.69.2.24.60761

Kline, R. B. (1998). Software review: Software programs for structural equation modeling: Amos, EQS, and LISREL. *Journal of Psychoeducational Assessment, 16*(4), 343–364. doi:10.1177/073428299801600407

Kumar, S., & Awasthi, P. (2018). Human resource accounting and organizational performance. *Indian Journal of Accounting, 50,* 1.

Kumar, S., Gupta, A., & Mishra, M. K. (2020). Human Resource Practice and Patient Empowerment: Mediating Role of Quality of Patient Care. *Test Engineering and Management, 83,* 22755–22764.

Kyei, D. A., & Bayoh, A. T. M. (2017). Innovation and customer retention in the Ghanaian telecommunication industry. *International Journal of Innovation, 5*(2), 171–183. doi:10.5585/iji.v5i2.154

Lee, S., Han, H., Radic, A., & Tariq, B. (2020). Corporate social responsibility (CSR) as a customer satisfaction and retention strategy in the chain restaurant sector. *Journal of Hospitality and Tourism Management, 45,* 348–358. doi:10.1016/j.jhtm.2020.09.002

Lee, T., Liu, C. H. S., & Li, P. H. (2021). The influences of cooperative climate, competitive climate and customer empowerment on service creativity. *Journal of Retailing and Consumer Services, 63,* 102726. doi:10.1016/j.jretconser.2021.102726

Lenka, U., Suar, D., & Mohapatra, P. K. (2009). Service quality, customer satisfaction, and customer loyalty in Indian commercial banks. *The Journal of Entrepreneurship, 18*(1), 47–64. doi:10.1177/097135570801800103

Lochab A., & Kumar S. (2019). "HR Analytics: The Winding Path Ahead," Journal of the Gujarat research society, 21(11), 1215-1261.

Lochab, A., Kumar, S., & Himanshi. (2020). Dilemma to decision: Human resource analytics for organizational performance-an empirical analysis. *Asian Journal of Multidimensional Research, 9*(2), 143–151. doi:10.5958/2278-4853.2020.00028.2

Lochab, A., Kumar, S., & Tomar, H. (2018). Impact of Human Resource Analytics on Organizational Performance: A Review of Literature Using R-Software. International Journal of Management. *Technology And Engineering, 8,* 1252–1261.

Lubis, A., Dalimunthe, R., Absah, Y., &Fawzeea, B. K. (2020). "The Influence of Customer Relationship Management (CRM) Indicators on Customer Loyalty of Sharia Based Banking System," Lubis, A, 84-92.

MacCallum, R. C., Browne, M. W., & Sugawara, H. M. (1996). Power analysis and determination of sample size for covariance structure modelling. *Psychological Methods, 1*(2), 130–149. doi:10.1037/1082-989X.1.2.130

Madhani, P. M. (2020). Effective rewards and recognition strategy: Enhancing employee engagement, customer retention and company performance. *The Journal of Total Rewards*, *29*(2), 39–48.

Mahmoud, M. A., Hinson, R. E., & Anim, P. A. (2017). Service innovation and customer satisfaction: The role of customer value creation. *European Journal of Innovation Management*.

Meißner, M., Haurand, M. D., & Stummer, C. (2017). With a little help from my customers: The influence of customer empowerment on consumers'perceptions of well-established brands. *International Journal of Innovation Management*, *21*(06), 1750048. doi:10.1142/S1363919617500487

Michel, S., Brown, S. W., & Gallan, A. S. (2008). An expanded and strategic view of discontinuous innovations: Deploying a service-dominant logic. *Journal of the Academy of Marketing Science*, *36*(1), 54–66. doi:10.100711747-007-0066-9

Mohammad, A. A. (2020). "The effect of customer empowerment and customer engagement on marketing performance: the mediating effect of brand community membership," Verslas: teorijair praktika, 21(1), 30-38.

Ngo, L. V., & O'cass, A. (2013). Innovation and business success: The mediating role of customer participation. *Journal of Business Research*, *66*(8), 1134–1142. doi:10.1016/j.jbusres.2012.03.009

Nunnally Jr, J. C. (1970). Introduction to psychological measurement.

O'Cass, A., & Ngo, L. V. (2011). Achieving customer satisfaction in services firms via branding capability and customer empowerment. *Journal of Services Marketing*, *25*(7), 489–496. doi:10.1108/08876041111173615

OECD. (2005). Enhancing the performance of the services sector. Paris: OECD.

Otto, A. S., Szymanski, D. M., & Varadarajan, R. (2020). Customer satisfaction and firm performance: Insights from over a quarter century of empirical research. *Journal of the Academy of Marketing Science*, *48*(3), 543–564. doi:10.100711747-019-00657-7

Pham, M. T. (1998). Representativeness, relevance, and the use of feelings in decision making. *The Journal of Consumer Research*, *25*(2), 144–159. doi:10.1086/209532

Poetz, M. K., & Schreier, M. (2012). The value of crowdsourcing: Can users really compete with professionals in generating new product ideas? *Journal of Product Innovation Management*, *29*(2), 245–256. doi:10.1111/j.1540-5885.2011.00893.x

Potra, S., Pugna, A., Negrea, R., & Izvercian, M. (2018). Customer perspective of value for innovative products and services. *Procedia: Social and Behavioral Sciences*, *238*, 207–213. doi:10.1016/j.sbspro.2018.03.025

Pranic, L., & Roehl, W. S. (2012). Rethinking service recovery: A customer empowerment (CE) perspective. *Journal of Business Economics and Management*, *13*(2), 242–260. doi:10.3846/16111699.2011.620137

Rubera, G., & Kirca, A. H. (2017). You gotta serve somebody: The effects of firm innovation on customer satisfaction and firm value. *Journal of the Academy of Marketing Science*, *45*(5), 741–761. doi:10.100711747-016-0512-7

Schumpeter, J. A. (2013). Capitalism, socialism and democracy. Routledge.

Schwarz, N., & Clore, G. L. (1983). Mood, misattribution, and judgments of well-being: Informative and directive functions of affective states. *Journal of Personality and Social Psychology*, *45*(3), 513–523. doi:10.1037/0022-3514.45.3.513

Sharanya, E., & Kumari, K. V. (2019). Structural Relationship between Dimensions of Psychological Empowerment, Customer Oriented Behaviour and Job Satisfaction of Employees in Public Sector Banks. *Indian Journal of Public Health Research & Development*, *10*(11), 101. doi:10.5958/0976-5506.2019.03432.6

Shin, K., Kim, E., & Jeong, E. (2018). Structural relationship and influence between open innovation capacities and performances. *Sustainability*, *10*(8), 2787. doi:10.3390u10082787

Tanniru, M., & Sandhu, K. (2019). Engagement leading to empowerment-digital innovation strategies for patient care continuity. *Journal of Hospital Management and Health Policy*, *3*, 28. doi:10.21037/jhmhp.2019.09.01

Ulaga, W. (2011). Investigating customer value in global business markets: Commentary essay. *Journal of Business Research*, *64*(8), 928–930. doi:10.1016/j.jbusres.2011.04.005

Ullah, I., & Narain, R. (2020). The impact of customer relationship management and organizational culture on mass customization capability and firm performance. *International Journal of Customer Relationship Marketing and Management*, *11*(3), 60–81. doi:10.4018/IJCRMM.2020070104

Verma, S., & Chaudhuri, R. (2009). Effect of CRM on Customer Satisfaction in Service Sector in India. *Journal of Marketing Communications*, *5*(2).

Virk, N., & Mahal, P. K. (2012). Customer satisfaction: A comparative analysis of public and private sector banks in India. In Information and Knowledge Management (Vol. 2, No. 3, pp. 01-07).

Yin, Y., Wang, Y., & Lu, Y. (2019). Why firms adopt empowerment practices and how such practices affect firm performance? A transaction cost-exchange perspective. *Human Resource Management Review*, *29*(1), 111–124. doi:10.1016/j.hrmr.2018.01.002

YuSheng, KIbrahim, M. (2019). Service innovation, service delivery and customer satisfaction and loyalty in the banking sector of Ghana. *International Journal of Bank Marketing*.

Zhang, H., & Xiao, Y. (2020). Customer involvement in big data analytics and its impact on B2B innovation. *Industrial Marketing Management*, *86*, 99–108. doi:10.1016/j.indmarman.2019.02.020

Zhao, X., Lynch, J. G. Jr, & Chen, Q. (2010). Reconsidering Baron and Kenny: Myths and truths about mediation analysis. *The Journal of Consumer Research*, *37*(2), 197–206. doi:10.1086/651257

Chapter 7
Customer Experience and Delight in the Metaverse

Sai Shrinivas Sundaram
Aptitude Global, India

Deepika Sachdev
Nokia, Singapore

Shailendra Pokhriyal
Himalayiya University, India

ABSTRACT

Customer delight is defined as exceeding client expectations through an experience that is truly differentiated. Customer delight is not limited to delivering service quality, but it is also about how the service is delivered and customer experience of the service provided. Customer experience will traverse seamlessly across the virtual and physical worlds with the evolution of the metaverse resulting in 'innovative disruption'. As the new playing field for corporates and engagement with consumers, it will transform customer experience. This will be augmented by turning historical notifications and transactions into real-time personalized communications. In this chapter the authors look at key pillars of how the metaverse will impact customer experience and delight. Through a literature survey, this chapter identifies the key pillars of the metaverse that will impact customer experience. The study then further drills into how customer experience is likely to be shaped in the metaverse for key sectors including retail, technology, and banking.

INTRODUCTION: IMPACT OF METAVERSE ON CUSTOMER EXPERIENCE

Customer Delight

In addition to existing dimensions such as reliability and responsiveness, in the Digital World Customer delight is augmented by the multi-channel interactions that take place for e.g., the customer first interacts with the brand on the website and their views of the brand are shaped by the ease of use, informa-

DOI: 10.4018/978-1-6684-5853-2.ch007

tion access and knowledge. This is often followed by interactions that might take place through social media tools (experience shared by friends and family) and the broader network, influencers who shape the thinking of a brand. This is then followed by physical interaction at the store with the expectation that store personnel offer greater insights than what has already been gained by the Customer from the previous steps. It is expected that each of the above interactions drive exceeding expectations for the Customer to be delighted.

Technology is at an interesting inflection point where we are moving from a multi-channel experience to a possible immersive experience in the metaverse where real-life is mirrored in the metaverse.

Metaverse

The origins of the name "metaverse" is in the early 1990's from a science fiction novel Snow Crash. It is a combination of "meta" and "universe". metaverse creates an immersive and three-dimensional experience in the virtual world for Consumers by using advanced virtual reality technology (Sheridan et al., 2021).

As explained by Bloomberg Intelligence (Wheatley & Bakthavatchalam, n.d.) the metaverse revenue globally could grow to somewhere between $800B and more than a trillion dollars, making it the next big tech platform. Sensing this potential, all industry verticals are exploring metaverse and cryptocurrencies/NFTs with blockchain technology to make their mark in the virtual world. The metaverse is currently growing through the hype cycle of maturity as explained below in Figure 1; Evolution cycle of the metaverse:

Figure 1. Evolution cycle of the metaverse

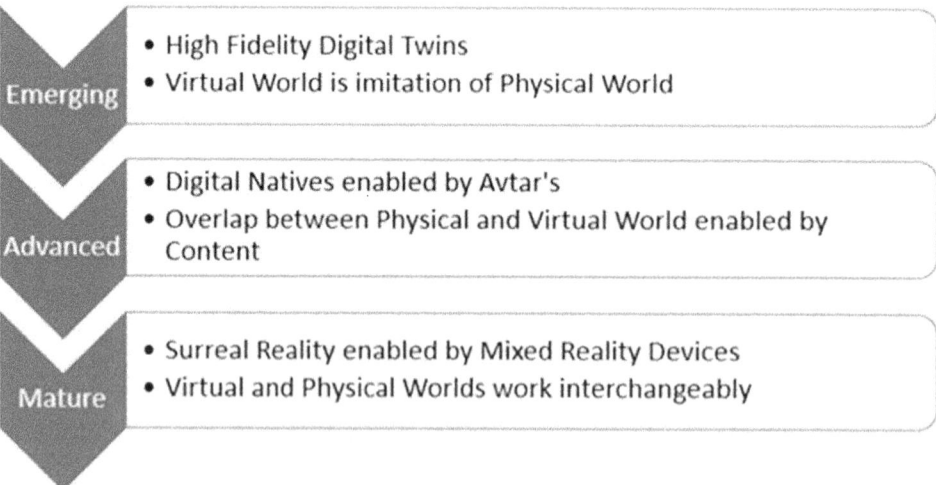

Gartner report states that the metaverse is a virtual digital ecosystem that is immersive but siloed. There is ongoing development to create communication protocols that will make the siloed metaverses as interoperable. The metaverse is powered by content which can seamlessly intersect and co-exist with the physical world. The content is created in a collective, persistent, interoperable, and decentralized mode so that it can merge into the spatially indexed and organized content of the real world.

By 2026, approximately 25% of the consumers will spend approximately sixty minutes in a day in the metaverse for all their online activities related to retail purchasing, gaming, banking, social interactions, and entertainment. BCG, JPMorgan, and McKinsey estimate the market size for metaverse to be between $500bn to $1Tn+ by 2030. As per the study "For Meta or Worse" 66% of consumers are looking forward to the convergence of real and virtual world for their day-to-day interactions to enrich their lives as explained in the "Promise and perils of the metaverse"

Since metaverse is focused on the virtual world it often requires VR and AR headsets to engage. It is envisaged that in the foreseeable future metaverse becomes another channel in the omni channel experience route for the Customer. Several brands have already started engaging in the metaverse using NFTs, virtual events and selling and buying of virtual real estate.

RESEARCH METHODOLOGY

This book chapter uses Grounded Theory and Framework Analysis Technique for verifying the impact of metaverse on Customer Experience and Delight. Grounded Theory helps to generate a theory from the qualitative data collected which has been analyzed systematically. As the name suggests, the theory is grounded in the data collected by the researcher. Grounded Theory can help to analyses the patterns of relationships hidden in the data and transcripts. Framework Analysis is a Qualitative Technique which is used to get feedback from the Users who implement the metaverse as well as use it. Framework Analysis provides a "Systematic Approach" for qualitative data analysis of Consumer experience in the metaverse. It scientifically helps to analyze interview transcripts to a easy and analyzable format as explained in Figure 2: Research Methodology

Figure 2. Research Methodology

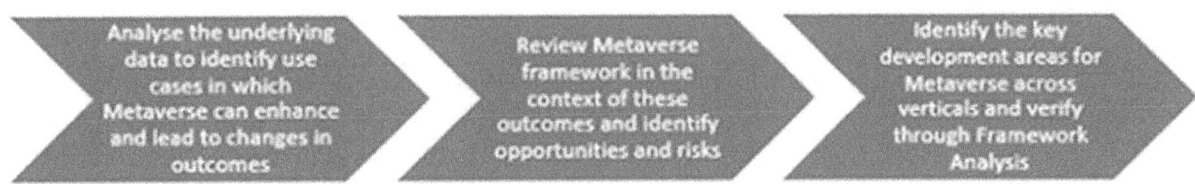

Key Pillars of metaverse for Customer Experience

Hyper Personalization

Recent McKinsey research (*The value of getting personalization right—or wrong—is multiplying*, 2021) shows that 71% of customers expect companies to provide personalized experiences. Personalization drives enhanced outcomes, responses, and success rate. Companies that show growth drive more than 40 percent more of their value from personalization as compared to their slower-growing competition.

While the consumer's expectations for a more personalized online experience are increasing, the regulatory framework is making it increasingly difficult to track personalized data for online portals. Online applications use third party cookies to collect personalized information such as locations, demographics, and personal information. However, due to privacy concerns most browsers have stopped using third party cookies. The dominant browser using cookies currently is Google, however as explained by end of 2022 this will also be phased out. Hence personalization experience will be impacted.

metaverse will take personalization experience to the next level for consumers with the AR/VR headsets bridging the gap between virtual and physical worlds. For example, if Nike launches new shoe brand, the consumer can first try and demonstrate it online. Based on the feedback received on social media he or she can then decide to make the physical purchase. The important driving factor for the success of the metaverse is enriched content which could possibly be shared across online applications using headless commerce. However, it is important to decentralize Content Creation through enablement tools and technology as it is everyone's right in the metaverse (Chen & Zhang, 2022). As explained by Wang et al. (2022) the metaverse will be enriched when participants actively contribute content which creates a blended cyberspace between the physical and virtual worlds.

Phygital

As explained by Sui and Shaw (2022) there is a strong dependence and correlation between the physical and virtual worlds with each influencing the other. Both the physical as well as virtual worlds interact closely to create the immersive experience resulting in the term "Phygital". To take a real-world case, when a consumer places an order in the online world, in the backend it triggers a transaction to the inventory in the physical world to initiate the delivery to the consumer. Hence the bridge between the physical and virtual worlds is constantly reduced to give the consumer a seamless experience. The consumer gets an immediate, interactive, and immersive experience.

Interoperability

Interoperability suggests a possibility for no single metaverse provider but there is a chance consumers prefer a hybrid and converged metaverse platform. As explained by Frank Palermo in current ecosystem of metaverse does not support Interoperability due to an ongoing balance between Gatekeepers and Decentralization. The metaverse Standards Forum is accelerating development of interoperable APIs across varied organizations by evolving a set of protocols and standards that will help securely exchange content as well we personalized experiences across the organizations. As of September 2022, approximately 1800 organizations globally have joined the metaverse forum to accelerate the development of Standards. As explained by Outlier Ventures (*Overview of Community Token Economics*, 2017) the important phrase is open, which can be interpreted as:

- harmonization to enable free markets across all verticals
- existence of the sovereign individual
- Collective fluidity across various organizations

The important thing is that interoperability across metaverses is not limited by open-source software and API's but also by a culture of interaction and data exchange embraced by the organizations. The important aspect is whether they allow the transfer of content and value beyond their ecosystem. It is also critical how that interacts with fiat-based systems. The ability to decentralize content, value, and currency across varied metaverses will create the evolution path as defined by the metaverse Standards.

Decentralization

Web 3 / Decentralization is the use of technologies like DLT to avoid one or more organizations controlling the ecosystem. Through a decentralized mechanism it is possible to use digital currencies to facilitate transactions within the metaverse. As explained by Wang et. al NFTs will be relevant only to some virtual worlds in the metaverse. Non-fungible: A non-fungible item is unique and not interchangeable with another item, like the Mona Lisa. A closed, centralized platform (like the video game Fortnite) can define its own system of ownership of in-world goods. Representing ownership of in-world goods in an open and verifiable manner, using NFTs, is useful when individuals want to port their goods across worlds, and when virtual worlds are designed to make that easy.

Technology (Augmented/Virtual/Mixed Reality)

As explained in The Corporate Hitchhiker's Guide to the metaverse (Bobier et al., 2022) the metaverse is underpinned by various technologies like XR, VR and AR supplemented by 6G technologies that allow sufficient bandwidth, Identity technologies to engage in a deeply immersive experience.

However, explained by Chang et al. (2022) the metaverse is still in an emerging phase of evolution due to which the Customer Experience is limited in immersive and real world feel. This is because the underlying devices, peripherals and computers are still evolving. The hepatic devices are still in an early stage of development. The underlying access technologies i.e., virtual reality (VR), augmented reality (AR) and mixed reality (MR) are fundamental to metaverse. In addition, there is evolution ongoing for Customer Identity and Authentication, interactive content which makes the virtual and physical experience seamless and infrastructure including data connectivity empowered by 5G and 6G technology as explained by Ingraham and Clair (2020). The customer experience in the metaverse will significantly evolve as we see an evolution of the underlying technologies as explained in Figure 3: metaverse Categories

Figure 3. metaverse Categories

Augmented Reality (AR)	Virtual Reality (VR)	Mixed Reality (MR)
• Offers Enhanced and contextual learning experience through immersive learning in real world • Combining physical and virtual to achieve learning outcomes for e.g. looking at a tree identification of the tree, its various parts and how they interact with each other • Real world cases included Pokemon and Realistic Content	• Interaction is through the virtual world and requirement of headsets etc for interaction • Virtual reality can be imagined so for e.g. a world millions of years ago and being in that world and interacting virtually is possible • Real world cases include Roblox, Second Life, Minecraft and Zepeto	• These have a two way interaction between the physical and digital and the technology needs to enhance further to achieve this • Mixed reality can drive significant leadership, collaboration and problem solving use cases as actions in the virtual world have a physical consequence and vice versa • Real world scenarios include Map based applications such as Google Maps, AirBnB and Google Earth

As explained by Lee et al. (2021) "Simultaneous Localization and Mapping" (SLAM) is a technology that enables the metaverse to see and interpret content in real time. It overcomes the challenge of unknown user, space, and movement to create a virtual environment which is like the current real world. This will be quite effective in entertainment vertical, e.g., Disney Theme Park where the customer feels that he is embedded in the virtual environment.

Semiconductor Shortage

As explained by Chandar and Ferraioli (2021) while many of the hardware components involved in VR/AR rely on semiconductor, an industry that has been experiencing shortages since the onset of the pandemic. We feel the impact to adoption has been minimal at this point. The companies involved in VR/AR currently derive small portions of their revenue directly from VR/AR offerings. Longer term, we expect semiconductor shortages to diminish, as new fabrication facilities come online and supply chain issues from COVID-19 fade. Hence no negative impact of semiconductor shortage is envisaged on the metaverse.

Social Interaction

As outlined by Bobier et al. (2022) with the metaverse it is critical that there is a cross disciplinary research on the appropriate engagement. Especially when analyzing the metaverse for children it is important to factor various touchpoints including education, gaming, and entertainment. As explained by Hanlon (2022) the metaverse makes the universe to be "together-alone". While the metaverse can help to bring together people during times of pandemic, it can also isolate people due to Digital exhaustion. Hence the following factors need to be kept in mind:

- Guard rails that are needed to ensure that demarcation between physical and digital is understood and these boundaries are maintained to avoid addictive behavior
- It is important to ensure that metaverse is an age inclusive technology. With increased longevity the senior generation contributes more to Digital innovation and interaction. For increasing access to the senior citizens, it is important to make the metaverse an easy-to-use technology with limited technology barriers. This will result in improved health care as well as financial services for senior citizens.
- Optimal time that can be spent in the metaverse especially with respect to education and other engagement with the metaverse (namely gaming, entertainment) based on psychological impact. physiological impact namely with respect to wearing of VR/XR headsets until community devices are available.
- Regulatory framework that monitors the controls within the metaverse to protect children and their rights as one would have done in physical schools. This regulatory framework can cover all types of use cases with the metaverse.
- Especially for the education use case in the metaverse how we can collectively ensure that access is available to all children of various socio-economic categories thus allowing the benefits of metaverse to be truly transformational.

Metaverse Applications for Customer Experience in Industry Verticals

Figure 4. Key Use Cases per Sector

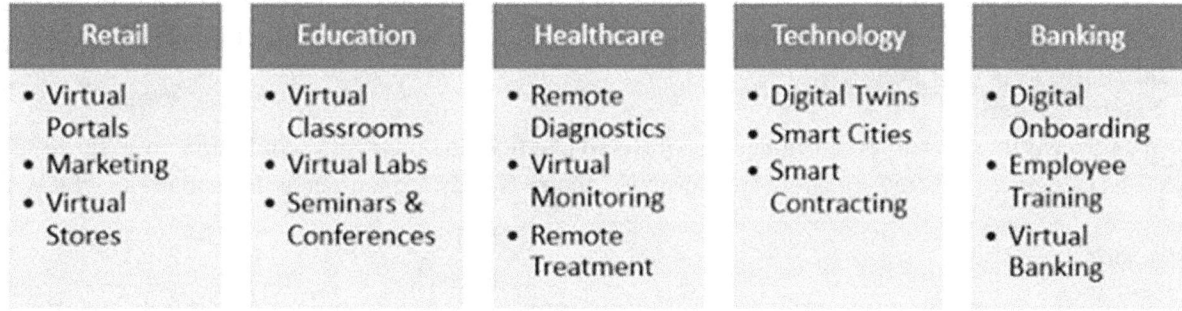

As explained in Figure 4: Key Use Cases per Sector metaverse has key applications across various sectors.

Retail Sector

In the retail sector, with the immersive experience possible in the metaverse, the physical retail experience is likely to be replaced with the virtual experience. This will be enabled using latest technologies like virtual try-on technologies. Customer experience will be shaped by the virtual interactions within the metaverse and the ability to complete a transaction virtually without re-engaging in the physical world. Chiu (n.d.) reports that in 2021 it has been reported that more than 100 million customers have experienced online browsing and shopping through an Augmented Reality enabled website. As part of a survey done by Deloitte Digital in 2021 including approximately 15000 global customers the majority felt that even though the metaverse experience is currently like a "toy-like" experience, more than 70% also expressed the desire to move to an evolution stage where it seamlessly becomes a part of their everyday lives, like the Internet and Mobile phone evolution. Probably the "toy-like" experience was due to an initial stage where most AR enabled applications such as Snapchat Filters and Pokémon Go where initially designed to give a friendly interface to the consumers.

Is it likely that the Retail shops of today would be replaced fully by virtual shops in the metaverse? We envisage that it is unlikely though similar trends to online commerce, there is likely to be shift to shopping in the metaverse with physical touchpoints continuing to remain for certain categories of products.

As explained by Robinson, Whyte, and Segura (2022) through an open platform enabled by headless commerce, very rapidly the metaverse will evolve into an aggregated service where the consumer can easily interact, visualize, and experience the products before the actual purchase. The purchase experience will be simplified by 3D enabled content which the consumer. In case of purchase of clothes and shoes the consumer can try on the products before making the final decision. This will reduce the overhead of purchase and returns which adds significant cost to e-commerce sites currently.

Retail metaverse for clothes and shoes is already a reality and we see a plethora of leading brands who have already invested in Augmented reality enabled stores where the customer can try the product before the purchase. Nike has launched Nikeland which is enabled on the Roblox platform. It is modelled on the Nike headquarters and customers can get real immersive experience before the final purchase. Zepeto is a similar platform which was launched approximately three years. It has in Asia nearly a .25 billion Subscribers. Luxury brands including Dior and Gucci have released their products virtually on Zepeto to enhance the customer experience. Facebook which recently for rebranded as Meta has also launched an online retail platform where the customer gets immersive experience through Augmented Reality. In March 2022, the world witnessed the first metaverse enabled Fashion Week where luxury brands showcased their products.

Enterprise/work

We now explore certain broad categories of Retail and how the metaverse could transform these sectors. The categories covered are Grocery, Clothing, Luxury Goods, Consumer goods and Interior Design.

Grocery

In countries like India, the arrival of online commerce has transformed the sector with delivery times in the 10 minutes range to procure certain products. As explained by Chatterjee et al. (2021), grocery channels in the US have witnessed a significant increase in SKU's in the last seven years with the advent of online marketing.

With the digital twin of one's home in the metaverse, it would be possible to mirror the availability of various grocery items in the digital twin in the metaverse with the ability to trigger replenishments directly from the metaverse to the relevant e-commerce players. As explained in "Framing the Future of Web3.0" (Sheridan et al., 2021). Roblox has been approached by various retail stores for extending the metaverse experience.

In order to enable digital twinning at such scale, newer devices that are IoT enabled to capture current quantity for various products would need to be refined and these need to be fully wi-fi enabled and connected thus providing a huge market opportunity in future homes.

Consumer Goods

Like grocery, digital twinning will allow consumer goods within the home to be monitored in the metaverse for proactive maintenance that could be triggered. Buying of new products can be explored in the metaverse through interactive usage and immersive experience. Customer experience of a product is likely to be shaped by their usage and availability of information in the virtual world. As explained in the "Hitchhikers guide to the metaverse" Bobier et al. (2022) have demonstrated the strong emotional power of the new medium, which can offer the consumer tailored experiences which give a real world feeling.

Clothing

Virtual try-on technologies are already being tested out in retail stores. These can be further extended to the virtual world where one could visit the shop in the metaverse and try out new clothing and obtain instant feedback from friends and family who can also be part of the visit to the virtual store irrespective of physical location within the metaverse. Companies already operating in this space are Meta and Reactive Reality. Indirect benefits of virtual try-on could be numerous including reduced carbon footprint for shopping, reduced operational costs and increased footfall. Stefan Hauswiesner, co-founder, and CEO of Reactive Reality mentioned that "Mixed reality (MR) solves one of the biggest problems of online shopping, which is the ability to try out and try on products before we buy them. This in turn will reduce the problem of return of goods.

Going further as explained in "All one needs to Know About the metaverse" (Lee et al., 2021) digital textile is enhanced with new material and special threads which enable conductivity in the fabric so that when the customer interacts with these fabrics the User Interface is enabled for Virtual reality.

Luxury Goods

As explained by research by Anat, Sandrine, and Silvia (2016) we witness that less than ten percent of sales for luxury brands is done online. Even though these brands have spent significant amount in enabling online channels, the Consumer still wants to make a physical visit before making the decision. Even though purchase is not done online there is evidence that more than 50 percent of purchasing decisions are made after online reviews and browsing. This leads to a trend that Multi Channel and Multi Brand online retailers have a significant advantage over offline or single brand retailers. Another factor influencing sale of luxury goods is price and scarcity of commodity. There are cases where the value of the article is very expensive, so it is jointly purchased by multiple owners through Non-Fungible Tokens (NFT's). NFT will be embedded in the metaverse framework and hence will boost purchases.

Interior Design

Home builders are likely to provide a digital twin of one's home in the metaverse allowing interior design to be carried out on the digital twin and design to be done of the virtual home prior to the actual design in the physical world. Those who can bridge the virtual and real world would provide exceptional customer experience that would be truly differentiated.

Financial Services

In Banking, customers could open a bank account in the metaverse with their Know Your Customer (KYC) requirements being completed through how they engage with the metaverse and subsequently identity information securely transferred to the Bank through web 3 or decentralized infrastructure and digital wallets.

Customers would be able to gain insight on new products through an immersive experience with the ability to try out the products virtually and understand the risks, returns and suitability for them far more intuitively than the current experience. For e.g., virtual markets mirroring the real-world markets can be created in the metaverse in which customers would be able to simulate and understand financial products like mutual funds and experience both the ups and downs of the market without real world impact. This can lead to deeper insights on the product / services leading to thorough understanding of the products / services.

The regulatory environment within financial services requires that products are sold according to the knowledge level of the consumer. Through the metaverse the knowledge level of the consumer can be enhanced with potential real-life simulation undertaken within the metaverse. Even though these are at early stages of implementation within the metaverse due to access constraints, these possibilities open up a marketplace that can lead to increased revenues and better alignment between the consumer and their product requirements.

As explained by Wheatley et. al. (Wheatley & Bakthavatchalam, n.d.), American Express plans to provide issuing and processing payments of virtual cards, banking services, fraud detection, marketplace for NFTs and cryptocurrency services. Meanwhile, Mastercard plans to extend its payment processing and marketplace for downloadable digital goods, events and more in the new virtual economy. Many of the Tier 1 banks now have a presence in the metaverse though it is limited to creating engagement in the metaverse, onboarding of customers and product knowledge sharing.

Insurance

metaverse has stated making active progress in customer Experience in the Insurance vertical. With Microsoft, GE and other large players replicating cities within the metaverse it would be possible using AI and advanced analytics to provide an immersive experience of what the future might be based on historical and projected risks to consumers. This would bring to life the value proposition for insurance and broaden adoption for insurance products across the marketplace. As explained by CB Insights IMA Financial Group, an insurance company, has launched a metaverse insurance R&D lab called Web3Labs in Decentraland. The project will first look at the risk associated with NFTs.

Education

The current generation utilizes video-based learning using videos and other visuals to learn a theory or concept or understand a challenging process as explained by Seemiller & Grace (2017). As explained in Journal of Educational Evaluation for Health Profession (Kye et al., 2021), the metaverse will provide a high degree of freedom unlimited by space and time to the students of the future. As explained by Hirsh-Pasek et al. (2022) active learning as compared to passive ensures children thrive and acquire knowledge best in such environments It also means that immersive experiences rather than simple swiping or working through non-interactive content cannot be considered as interactive learning as explained by Wright (2019). As explained in "A whole new world: Education meets the metaverse February 2022 Policy brief" by Hirsh-Pasek et al. (2022) explains how metaverse will help bridge the gap from passive to active learning for students.

Due to acceleration by the pandemic, the metaverse is not limited to paper-based research but has entered the current education system actively as explained by Kye et al. (2021)]. Based on a study on 338 elementary schools in Korea on average approximately 98% of school students from primary classes had metaverse experiences and about 96% of them related it to their everyday life as explained by Hanlon (2022). Going ahead, based on a study conducted on Greek teachers Mystakidis and Christopolous (2022), it is observed that teachers up to K-12 are open to use interactive social media for students. In

- Invat Metaveristy will be built on the convergence of Web 3.0 and education. It will provide employability focussed training to help the workforce realign with digital world.
- Alyx which is a famous VR game Half-Life is used to teach science lessons by teachers in Poland.
- Health and safety training is being conducted using virtual reality by companies e.g., Skanska. Education in the future using metaverse will enable the learning on sustainability and climate change.
- As explained in 6G Edge enabled AI for the metaverse (Bobier et al., 2022), a learning English platform like Hoodoo Labs transposed more than 300 characters and 4,300 English conversation scenarios into virtual reality scenarios allowing users to improve their English skills through immersion Without the need to travel to another continent or city.
- On similar lines "Virbela" which is a virtual platform is used for increased collaboration is remote learning courses. While the Covid-19 platform was ongoing Davenport University used it to create a customized virtual campus called "Davenport Global". Like a physical campus it had tutorial rooms, auditoriums with interactive media, presentation screens. Students got a collaborative environment where they could interact with other peers akin to the real world.

As explained by Collins (2008) these private "walled gardens" are internally consistent, though the content created within that environment cannot be exported and imported into other worlds. Hence the interoperability of content across various educational institutes is still an area of concern.

Technology

In Technology, new product development could be a crowd sourcing initiative conducted through the metaverse where future features can be road tested well before even a single line of code is written. User groups can have more immersive experiences on the usage and learning experience of using the product that can help them to adopt these within their organizations.

As explained by Robinson, Whyte, and Segura (2022) globally the first city to develop a metaverse platform for facilitating public services and events for culture is Seoul. It is expected that by the year 2026 this platform will be fully operational. The platform will not only be limited by administration functions to be done by the government such as filing complaints or historical tours using VR technology. It will also be extended in addition with AI and digital tools to improve for citizens healthcare, economy and central infrastructure. In addition, it has created an alliance of more than 500 firms for the metaverse. This has a state backing of 26 million$.

Across all verticals metaverse enables digital twinning. This involves linking a real-world asset to a virtual asset and can be used to link real world supply chain ecosystem to the virtual ecosystem providing deeper insights into customer touch points and interactions. Big companies like GE, IBM have digital twin technology solutions for industrial products while Microsoft is building these for real world objects and people. Customers could have virtual factories mirroring their physical factories in the metaverse that provide a real-time dashboard on areas that require their immediate attention and focus. Multiple stakeholder insights can be visualized and engaged with in their corresponding metaverse.

Health Care

As explained by Thomason (2021) it is possible to create a sustainable and affordable paradigm in health care using the metaverse, and technology leaders in health care need to be part of its creation. Further as detailed by Chandar and Ferraioli (2021), in the health care industry, VR/AR has been used to help treat soldiers with post-traumatic stress disorder also known as PTSD. The New York Times reported recently that Weill Cornell Medical Center used VR/AR headsets in intensive care units during the pandemic to bring additional expertise into the room without risks to the doctors or experts. As explained by Chen and Zhang (2022) the metaverse provides valuable inputs for education and remote surgeries in healthcare.

As explained in "Exploring Health Trends for metaverse" by Chen and Zhang (2022) the metaverse is currently used for a variety of medical and health services like remote monitoring of seriously ill patients, analysis of patient data for clinical symptoms, heart rate and blood glucose monitoring. In addition, this can be used for tracking physical fitness records such as walking and running. and other medical and health services, etc. in a three-dimensional immersive way. Remote assistance in Orthopedic surgery has been possible using Oculus headsets, Meta took over Oculus recently.

FRAMEWORK BASED ANALYSIS

A survey was conducted to get initial response of applications of metaverse across various verticals. It was distributed from age group of 16 to 60. The background varied from college students to experienced professionals with varied degree and exposure to the metaverse. Attached below is the Interview Protocol and Survey Analysis as explained below in Table 1: Interview Protocol

Table 1. Interview Protocol

Survey Theme/ Question	Significance	Observation
What is the profile of the respondents	Characterizing based on Profile Information we try to understand the distribution of expertise and seniority in the Organization. There is a common concept that Information Sharing is dominated by younger respondents who are open to newer ideas. Hence Research Questions were focused on Age, Demographics, Profession, and region.	• Most of the respondents were less than 30 years old. • Majority of responses were from Asia. • Significant portion of the respondents were from IT. Above signifies the fact that metaverse is still understood by early adopters and those who are closely tied to Technology
What are respondents view on metaverse Usage	To understand views on potential metaverse usage and associated use cases	• 83% of respondents felt that personalization will be accelerated by metaverse. • Approx. 60% of respondents were not familiar with NFTs and digital currencies and its uses in the metaverse • 63% felt that metaverse was not advisable for children.
Which industry sectors are more likely to be benefited from metaverse?	Research questions were focused to understand which sectors have the most applicable use cases for metaverse for Discovery and Purchase	• 67% of respondents felt that they would use the metaverse to learn about new products and services but would prefer to buy from a physical venue • 54% of respondents felt that Education (including financial awareness and literacy) and Retail were the most relevant use cases for metaverse.
Accessories required to engage with the metaverse	Research queries were directed to understand the investment and attributes associated with metaverse engagement by users	• 50% of respondents were willing to spend up to $300 on a VR/AR headset • Vision Clarity and Price (83%), followed by portability and comfort (75%) were the key attributes in a VR/AR headset
Interoperability in metaverse	Research questions were targeted to understand data and profile that respondents would like to be interoperable across varied metaverses	• 50% of respondents wanted to have the ability to share their digital identity across metaverses • Avatars and purchase patterns were other attributes that respondents were keen to be transferable across metaverses
Type of metaverse: What type of metaverse would respondents be comfortable to engage with	Research questions were targeted to understand whether public, private or hybrid metaverses were preferred	• 33% preferred public metaverses that were not owned by a centralized entity • 41% did not have a preference on whether it was public or private metaverse. • 17% considered both to be fit for purpose.
Customer Experience: Attributes that will drive exceptional customer service in the metaverse	Understand the key attributes that will drive exceptional customer services in the metaverse	Reimagined customer journey and engagement were key attributes for 67% of respondents that drive customer experience.

SOLUTIONS AND RECOMMENDATIONS

The summary of analysis from the above survey has been further shared with Industry experts including Managing Director, Fintech (Hongkong), Senior Director of Learning ASB (Malaysia) and Director Philips Innovation Campus (Bangalore). Following is known benefits and limitations of the metaverse across Industry Verticals which influence Customer Experience:

Content Personalization

For experienced customers who have witnessed virtual reality using an AR/VR device in recent past the experience has been enriching, insightful and personalized. However, there is scarcity of good quality content, devices as well as fast speed network connectivity.

Participatory design, a co-design process that encourages all stakeholders to participate and collaborate to create the digital world together will be essential to create an inclusive metaverse. Understanding motivations and aligning incentives like any real-world exercise would accelerate content creation in the metaverse. For developing a creator economy, it will be essential to embrace cultural diversity, cross generational content creation and to preserve legacy content (i.e., digital heritage). NFTs and newer economic models will be essential to drive this creator economy where social influence and peer recognition are important along with monetary benefits.

Tools for content creation needs to be accessible to a broad set of creators in order to allow diverse demographics and groups to create content and share it in the metaverse. Inbuilt controls need to be available based on the student population it is targeted at metaverses that are meeting the education use case should follow a standard code of conduct, guidelines and rules that are jointly agreed through a multi-disciplinary panel of experts comprising of educators, parents, child psychologists, behavioral scientists, legal and government officials.

Identical to the challenges that are being faced in the online world where it has become difficult to know the truth, it is an obligation on the metaverse infrastructure providers, content creators to ensure there are guardrails present to ensure students are provided facts and unbiased views.

Network and Infrastructure Scalability

metaverse is far from achieving its full potential of immersive experiences, real life virtual mirrors and scalability because of computing power, sensory devices, and resources. Mobile communication platforms with very-low latency, high bandwidth and extremely high reliability combined with automated services will be key to making the metaverse widely available and accessible like how free data in India created the explosion of Internet usage and digital services across India.

Security and Privacy

VR/AR headsets are dependent on software, memory, and integrated circuits. They can also be targets for malicious actors who can through location spoofing, device manipulation takes over user identities and perpetuate fraud or illegal activities after entering the metaverse. Privacy laws need to be considered as content will explode in the metaverse, how will GDPR requirements be met in the metaverse? How can a person be forgotten in the metaverse? Improper augmentation of content in the metaverse can lead to copyright infringement. In case of healthcare scenarios in the metaverse, granular level access to data, patient privacy and safety raise wider questions and concerns.

The need to provide security and privacy for students in the metaverse will be essential due to the immersive nature of the experience. It will be imperative that like the real world, checks and balances are created in the metaverse where content creation or engagement takes place between students and other actors in the metaverse. The learnings from the current Internet needs to be taken as we embark on the metaverse to avoid creating similar risks and concerns for students without losing sight of the decentralized nature of the metaverse and the creator economy that it could support.

Hypothesis One: Based on the above we can conclude that metaverse has the potential to have a significant impact on Customer Satisfaction for experienced clients in Retail and Banking sector. This is impacted by personalization of information, Phygital experience as well as enhanced Customer interaction experience. Customer satisfaction is measured in terms of an increase in brand value as well as additional customer revenues (upsell / cross sell and referrals).

Hypothesis Two: Customer experience will be enhanced by the metaverse, however there are significant challenges registered based on feedback from survey and interviews including interoperability with other systems and latency in current network. Hence, we conclude that metaverse is currently in the Emerging state across all verticals and hence will need significant improvement in Content, Connectivity, Privacy, and Interoperability before it reaches the mature stage.

FUTURE RESEARCH DIRECTIONS

Balance Between Virtual and Real World

Based on survey and interview feedback we realize that users who are constantly immersed in the metaverse for a majority of there time find it hard to distinguish between the virtual and the

physical world. It will have a serious impact on their work, life and study. This is a multi-disciplinary future research topic involving psychologists, User experience designers, doctors and technologists to achieve an optimal balance across the two realms of physical and virtual worlds. It is important to ensure that while the experience remains high quality in the Virtual world it does not become addictive and impact normal human interaction. Since children are more susceptible to exposure this can be done by age and usage limiting of metaverse access. In addition, there needs to be a governance to constantly monitor the impact of external influence on all age groups and regulation mechanisms.

Metaverse Inclusivity

The Internet revolution created huge opportunities across the world, but this growth was not equitable across various strata of society or across income groups or demographics. There is a need to ensure that the metaverse which is considered a multi-trillion opportunity is an inclusive opportunity whose growth does not create another version of "have" and "have-nots". It can be achieved through equitable access to virtual worlds, access to creator economy tools, community devices for access rather than highly priced individual devices, data network connectivity that is reasonably priced. These challenges are not unique to emerging economies but to also well-developed economies where some of these differences are already stark. With changing demographics globally, having the elderly being able to access the metaverse and ease of use needs to be considered.

User Interface

An immersive user experience is a critical characteristic of the metaverse. Accessing the metaverse will need to be considered. It can be through an application, browser, games console or all the above. A critical factor to access and improved user experience is the presence of a high-speed network connection with ultra-low latency. Due to low network bandwidth, even in advanced countries the metaverse experience is accompanied with delay and visual jitter. These negatively impact the Customer experience in the metaverse. Optimal 5G Telco Edge Cloud standards development work has already commenced to resolve some of these challenges. An important research topic for the future is continuous innovation in improving network connectivity as well as device optimization.

Standards and Interoperability

Based on decentralized trends seen in Blockchain and cryptocurrency it is evident that there will not be one dominant metaverse. Hence there is need for interoperability to allow users to retain their avatars and possessions as they traverse across multiple metaverses. There is a need to allow users to traverse multiple and diverse online spaces.

The seamless functioning of the metaverse requires interoperability across various virtual worlds to provide an enriched customer experience. Additional challenges with respect to interoperability include the integration of avatars, importing of digital assets and content from one metaverse into others and ensuring their value and purpose is retained across these digital worlds, similar to real life assets and content. Like the battle to capture user eyeballs by large technology players, a similar battle is emerging in the metaverse with large technology companies like Microsoft, Meta, Google working to create their own versions of the metaverse while there are numerous startups that are working actively to create a digital world that is decentralized. The formation of the metaverse standard forum should enable more collaboration across the metaverse creators allowing eventually for seamless movement of digital identities, assets, and interoperability across the digital universe.

CONCLUSION

The emergence of metaverse has the potential to drive significant benefits for consumer Experience in the Retail, Education and Banking sector. However, there are concerns on interoperability, ease of Use and Security concerns that inhibit its growth in the current environment. The current ecosystem of metaverse does not support Interoperability due to an ongoing balance between Gatekeepers and Decentralization. The walled gardens benefit the traditional owners but add to the overheads of the consumers. In addition, due to limited network speeds as well as Graphic Content the Interface needs to be evolved to reach the masses. Customer satisfaction and customer delight in a new virtual environment will require reimagining satisfaction and delight in a virtual world with many interdependencies on access, network, content, and the immersive experience. Brands that are already in the metaverse will have a lead in understanding these aspects as first movers in a new environment like how online shopping, recommendation engines that drive the shopping experience were differentiated and drove additional revenues and customer experience. For each of the use cases across verticals in the metaverse, new ways of engagement with the customer needs to be imagined and these can be explored only through early experimentation in the metaverse. More research is needed to allow the metaverse to truly support an immersive experience that adds to human experience rather than increased indulgence and escapism from reality.

REFERENCES

Anat, K., Sandrine, C., & Silvia, B. (2016). *Online Luxury Retailing: Leveraging Digital Opportunities Research*. Industry Practice, and Open Questions.

Bobier, J. F., Merey, T., Robnett, S., Grebe, M., Feng, J., Rehberg, B., & Hazan, J. (2022). *The Corporate Hitchhiker's guide to the metaverse*. Boston Consulting Group.

Chandar, V., & Ferraioli, J. (2021). *Virtual Reality, Augmented Reality and the Metaverse—Opportunities in Digital Worlds*. Morgan Stanley. https://advisor.morganstanley.com/the-irvin-and-bevack-group /documents/field/i/ir/irvin-and-bevack-group/Vr%20ar%20metav erse%20alphacurrents.pdf

Chang, L., Zhang, Z., Li, P., Xi, S., Guo, W., Shen, Y., & Wu, Y. (2022). *6G-enabled Edge AI for metaverse: Challenges, Methods, and Future Research Directions*. arXiv:2204.06192.

Chatterjee, B. I., Küpper, J., Mariager, C., Moore, P., & Reis, S. (2011). The decade ahead : Trends that will shape the consumer goods industry, Consum. Shopp. Insights. McKinsey Co.

ChenD.ZhangR. (2022). Exploring Research Trends of Emerging Technologies in Health metaverse: A Bibliometric Analysis. Available at SSRN 3998068. doi:10.2139/ssrn.3998068

Chiu, E. (n.d.). New realities Into the Metaverse and beyond. *INTO THE METAVERSE, 2*.

Collins, C. (2008). Looking to the future: Higher education in the Metaverse. *EDUCAUSE Review*, *43*(5), 50–52.

Hanlon, A. (2022). *Metaverse–together alone?* LSE Business Review.

Hirsh-Pasek, K., Zosh, J., Hadani, H. S., Golinkoff, R. M., Clark, K., Donohue, C., & Wartella, E. (2022). *A whole new world: Education meets the metaverse*. Policy.

Ingraham, A., & Clair, J. S. (2020). The fourth industrial revolution of healthcare information technology: key business components to unlock the value of a blockchain-enabled solution. *Blockchain*.

Kye, B., Han, N., Kim, E., Park, Y., & Jo, S. (2021). Educational applications of metaverse: Possibilities and limitations. *Journal of Educational Evaluation for Health Professions*, 18.

Lee, L. H., Braud, T., Zhou, P., Wang, L., Xu, D., Lin, Z., & Hui, P. (2021). *All one needs to know about metaverse: A complete survey on technological singularity, virtual ecosystem, and research agenda*. arXiv:2110.05352.

Mystakidis, S., & Christopoulos, A. (2022). Teacher Perceptions on Virtual Reality Escape Rooms for STEM. *Education for Information*, *13*(3), 136.

Overview of Community Token Economies. (n.d.). Outlier Ventures. https://outlierventures.io/research/ overview-of-ctes/

Robinson, J., Whyte, J., & Segura, C. (2022). Exploring the metaverse and the digital future. *Groupe Special Mobile Association Intelligence (GSMA)*, 1-27.

Seemiller, C., & Grace, M. (2017). Generation Z: Educating and engaging the next generation of students. *About Campus: Enriching the Student Learning Experience*, 22(3), 21–26.

Shamash, D., & Nordnes, R. A. (2022). *The Open Metaverse 2021/22*. Outlier Ventures.

Sheridan, E., Ng, M., Czura, L., Steiger, A., Vegliante, A., & Campagna, K. (2021). *Framing the Future of Web 3.0–Metaverse Edition*. Goldman Sachs.

Sui, D., & Shaw, S. L. (2022). New Human Dynamics in the Emerging Metaverse: Towards a Quantum Phygital Approach by Integrating Space and Place (Vision Paper). In *15th International Conference on Spatial Information Theory (COSIT 2022)*. Schloss Dagstuhl-Leibniz-Zentrum für Informatik.

The value of getting personalization right—or wrong—is multiplying. (2021). McKinsey. https://www.mckinsey.com/capabilities/growth-marketing-and-sales/our-insights/the-value-of-getting-personalization-right-or-wrong-is-multiplying

Thomason, J. (2021). MetaHealth-How will the Metaverse Change Health Care? *Journal of Metaverse*, *1*(1), 13–16.

Wang, Y., Su, Z., Zhang, N., Xing, R., Liu, D., Luan, T. H., & Shen, X. (2022). A survey on metaverse: Fundamentals, security, and privacy. *IEEE Communications Surveys and Tutorials*.

Wheatley, O., & Bakthavatchalam, S. (n.d.). *What Does the Metaverse Mean for the Banking and Financial Services Industry?* ISG. https://isg-one.com/articles/what-does-the-metaverse-mean-for-the-banking-and-financial-services-industry

Wright, D. B. (2019, December). Research methods for education with technology: Four concerns, examples, and recommendations. In Frontiers in Education (Vol. 4, p. 147). Frontiers Media SA.

KEY TERMS AND DEFINITIONS

Blockchain: A decentralized and immutable record of Transactions
Decentralization: Control of data and information by a consortium instead of individual ownership
Digital Twin: Representing a physical entity in Virtual environment
DLT: Digital Ledger Technology
Metaverse: Is an immersive digital environment of independent, yet interconnected networks
NFT: Non-Fungible Tokens
Phygital: Phygital is the concept of using technology to bridge the digital world with the physical world with the purpose of providing a unique interactive experience for the user.
Web 3: An iteration of the World Wide Web which is decentralized

Chapter 8
Enhancing Employee Productivity Through Human Capital Analytics

Devesh Bathla

iD https://orcid.org/0000-0003-3990-5934

Chitkara Business School, Chitkara University, Punjab, India

Raina Ahuja

Kurukshetra University, India

ABSTRACT

Human capital analytics transforms this information into significant understanding which reveals deeper insights. HR analytics is the utilization of systematic procedure to determine the HR issues. Starting from discovering best fit candidate until his retention, businesses are taking a stab at a lot of keen choices. The choice of selection in HR for the majority depends on trust and dislike in other verticals in the organisations. In the author's analytical view, human resource is an abundantly disregarded field by and large when contrasted with different business verticals, however the right fit candidates are required for each business unit for better outcomes. Be that as it may, after the recession time frame of later half of first decade of the 20th century, the majority of the associations perceived the need of evidence based human resource management. To come up with better decision making in the field of HR, evidence based HRM driven by information and data should rehearse with analysis, making choices, and critical thinking.

INTRODUCTION

Human capital analytics transforms this information into significant understanding which reveals deeper insights. HR analytics is the utilization of systematic procedure to determine the HR issues. Starting from discovering best fit candidate till his retention, businesses are taking a stab at a lot of keen choices. The choice of selection in HR for the majority depends on trust and dislike how in other verticals in the organisations. In my analytical view, human resource is abundantly disregarded field by and large when

DOI: 10.4018/978-1-6684-5853-2.ch008

contrasted with different business verticals however the right fit candidates are required for each business unit for better outcomes. Be that as it may, after the recession time frame of later half of first decade of the 20th century, the majority of the associations perceived the need of evidence based human resource management. To come up with better decision making in the field of HR, evidence based HRM driven by information and data should rehearse with analysis, making choices and critical thinking. Along these lines, the idea of evidence based HRM with its successful HR analytics techniques fortifying the precise dynamic intensity of HRM. This research work raises significance of HR analytics, appropriateness, and practices in various apprehensions. Human resource management by this 2020 has evolved as being the most efficient while leveraging the optimum benefits from the technological advancements and innovations. Purposely driven via dynamic and lightening paced technologically-empowered improvements in the very field of human resource management (HRM), human resource analytics (HRA) is penetrating the research and business plan. HR analytics is tied in with gathering, sorting out, and approving the information identified with HR tasks like manpower acquisition, learning and development, benefits to the employees, relationship among employees, and till the last level of employee retention to assist them for taking the best decision spreading over all these spheres. HR verticals are utilizing various sorts of new technology software and innovative techniques in technology to make the majority of information consistently.

An evidence- based mechanism utilizing an integrative combination of peer-reviewed literature on HR Analytics was carried out. The pursuit of a few published databases reviewed 64 articles on this subject, anyway just 16 articles shortlisted in evaluated in quality peer-reviewed journals. While five these articles were reviewed, a need to address the following five questions that comprise **4Ws** and **1H** emerged: (1) **W**hat best defines Human Resource Analytics (2) **W**ho all are responsible for Human Resource Analytics to succeed? (3) **W**hy Human Resource Analytics operates? (4) **W**here can the impact of Human Resource Analytics be seen?(5) **H**ow does Human Resource Analytics work? It is reasoned that regardless of proof connecting the selection of Human Resource Analytics to hierarchical execution that reception of Human Resource Analytics is abysmally less, also scholastic research, thus, evidence on this subject is meagre. Potential clarifications for this contradiction simultaneously recommend paths for future research.

Purpose

This purpose of this paper is to explore (or may be termed as pre-empt in the analytics terminology) the relevance of human resource (also popular as HR) analytics on willingness of employees to enhance the effectiveness and efficiency of their performance. In this attempt, this paper studies the issues pertaining to the PA or performance appraisal system. This also illustrates that factors that impact the willingness of employees to enhance performance and also tends to decide that how analytics of Human Resource may prove a proposed recommendation to handle similar matters.

Methodology and Design: This work builds up a feasible system alongside recommendations by incorporating the set of scholastic, as well as professionally, written works, in the very sphere of analytics pertinent to human resource.

Finding and Observations

This work recommends that the utilization of HR investigation will be adversely identified with detailed inclination in the PA framework, in this manner emphatically influencing representatives' apparent reasonableness and tends to come up with exactness. This further decidedly influences representatives' fulfilment with the Performance Appraisal framework, which along these lines builds workers' eagerness to improve execution.

Research Constraints and Implications

The paper gives suggestions to the analysts as well as the professionals in the exhibition the executives region for improving workers' presentation by the application of Human Resource analytics as a key instrument in the PA framework. It likewise gives suggestions to future analysts to experimentally test the applied structure in various hierarchical settings. Innovation/esteem: The paper offers bits of knowledge into the process of the unveiling the utilization of HR analytics can manage subjective manners with predisposition in the PA framework and decidedly influences representatives' ability to improve execution.

As comprehended that Analytics in human asset the executives has been around for a considerable length of time. Here the question arises that does it really foresee the future achievement of the association as the statement above proposes HR experts need to accept? A parallel reason for this research work is to start to answer these inquisitive and in doing so make a couple of commitments to the human asset writing on HR Analytics. Initial, a proof-based audit of existing excellent research and logical information about the estimation of HR Analytics is given. Second, new research areas will be distinguished.

Utilizing HR analytics assists with improving hierarchical execution, pick up and keep up an upper hand. It furnishes associations with a system for dynamic, take care of complex business HR issues, drive maintainable development through advancement, envision and plan for change while overseeing and adjusting dangers. At the end of the day HR analytics is the measurable procedures for knowledge and assessing the causal connection between HR rehearses and hierarchical execution results. Institutionalization of such HR rehearses has helped organizations to accomplish significant objectives like consistency, productivity and decency to increase a worldwide perspective on their workforce. In this way the HR capacities currently has two significant orders i.e., to perceive the one-of-a-kind ability of every representative and send these gifts in a way that boosts the workers vitality to drive business results. To re-engineer the ability framework and create HR capacities for personalization, customisation of HR rehearses are required in workers and their associations. HR professionals basic to build up the sort of abilities that advertisers used to exceed expectations at customization, for example, co-creation, division, getting information, becoming acclimated to seeing innovation to help this customization. They should discover better approaches to join representatives behind the association even as representatives have progressively differentiated, customized encounters in the work environment. For all these HR needs to have devoted examination bunches for their capacities. From the purpose of enrolment to the point of whittling down, huge scope association are utilizing information and programming's to make portions inside the association as far as workers with the goal that they can give better help and concentrate better outcomes from those representatives. The accomplishment of the association relies upon its workforce. HR analytics help to adapt and make do amidst quickly developing and quick changing socio – financial condition by misusing business opportunity with the base hazard and difficulties. Thus, HR analytics is essentially significant and gives a vital preferred position in the savage serious market.

Explicitly for this work, proof-based survey rules are intended to improve choices by tending to the way that administration experts utilize numerous sorts of proof in their choices, yet normally give little consideration to nature of proof (Barends, Briner, & Rousseau, 2014). Barends et al. (2014) characterizes HRM based upon evidence as settling on choices via the faithful, express and wise utilization of one of the supreme accessible proof from various sources by making an interpretation of a down to earth issue into a liable inquiry, methodically looking for and recovering proof, fundamentally making a decision about the proof, arranging the proof, consolidating the proof into the dynamic procedure, and afterward assessing the result of the choice taken.

Right now, questions are encircled, deliberately scan for, and recover an especially great wellspring of proof (peer-explored and distributed articles), and basically analyse the sanity and ramifications of the discoveries and furthermore the example and degree of proof. Utilization of an integrative blend that tends to be an acknowledged proof-based approach so as to give the best accessible proof from various sources to respond to key inquiries. Integrative amalgamation is suitable for human resource analytics, in light of the fact that it includes three-dimensional proof from both qualitative as well as quantitative distributed research works (Rousseau et al., 2008) and along these lines boosts utilization of all wellsprings of distributed proof. It explores designs across essential research considers, making up for single-study shortcomings in look into configuration to enhance the interior and outside legitimacy of different works of research. Integrated union isn't meta-investigation, which includes outlining quantitative experimental outcomes over numerous examinations (Rousseau et al., 2008).

As a sign of integral combination is utilizing foreordained inquiries and determination criteria. (Rogers, 2003) proposed a DOI abbreviated as Diffusion of innovation theory was shortlisted as key reason for determining the foreordained inquiries that control this proof based integral combination. With just 16% of associations detailing selection (Cedar Crestone's seventeenth Annual HR Systems), human resource analytics impact the different advancement, keeping the fact in mind that the selection has been made, post the distillation for a long time. In this manner, nurturing Human Resource Analytics as a diffusing advancement appears to be fitting. Rogers (2003) considers the choice to embrace a development (for example something new or another thought) as a five advance procedure: (i) information, (ii) influence, (iii) choice, (iv) usage, and (v) affirmation. Since Human Resource Analytics appears generally latest, early adopters organize (for example under 20% of associations), focus will be around questions identifying with the initial two phases: picking up information about Human Resource Analytics and being convinced about the fact whether to receive H Human Resource Analytics or not.

The choice to inspect HR analytics through the viewpoint of development reception is likewise reliable with ongoing advances in hypotheses in regard to why organizations receive rehearses. As Paauwe and Boselie (2005, p. 989) mentioned, new institutionalisation analyses why associations inside a populace show comparable attributes to clarify similarity of associations (DiMaggio and Powell, 1983). Similarity is the point at which one unit in a populace takes after different units that face a similar arrangement of natural conditions. Paauwe and Boselie (2005) observed that similarity in initial adopters is governed by 'serious' factors, for example, monetary as well as some serious judiciousness, administrative soundness and assessed chance bring tradeoffs back. They noted that later phases of appropriation may see expanding impact from 'institutional' powers, with an inclusion of 'coercive' (worker's organizations, enactment), 'mimetic' (replicating best acts of others), and 'standardizing' (standards advanced by regarded establishments, for example, colleges, proficient affiliations, informal organizations, and so forth.). Since HR analytics is recognized at the early adopter organize, this survey is surrounded as far as the 'serious' powers, including judiciousness, and assessed chance bring trade-offs back. Positively 'institutional' isomorphism powers influence progressively develop HR rehearses and may even now here and there influence the reception of fundamental Analytics related to Human Resource (for example at the point when guidelines require detailing certain segment insights and drive the reception of investigation techniques to create those reports). Be that as it may, centre around what seems, by all accounts, to be the experimentally progressively normal circumstance that same Analytics related to Human Resource is an advancement in the stage of initial adoption, and therefore 'institutional' isomorphism has not been inspected here. Purposely driven via dynamic and lightening paced technologically empowered improvements in the very field of human resource management, human resource analytics is penetrating the research and business plan. HR analytics is tied in with gathering, sorting out, and approving the information identified with HR tasks like manpower acquisition, learning and development, benefits to the employees, relationship among employees, and till the last level of employee retention to assist them for taking the best decision spreading over all these spheres. HR verticals are utilizing various sorts of new technology software and innovative techniques in technology to make the majority of information consistently.

Rogers (2003) noticed that the incremental choice procedure is a data chasing and handling activity wherein an individual gets data so as to step by step decline vulnerability about the advancement. In this particular phase, an individual must realize what development is, and why does it exists and must emphasise to learn about how it works. Steady with this first stage of data gathering, while the integrative blend tends to the data collecting inquiries regarding Human Resource Analytics:

- Question Number 1 - What best defines Human Resource Analytics?
- Question Number 2 - How Human Resource Analytics operates?
- Question Number 3 - Why Human Resource Analytics operates?

The primary question identifies with creating develop legitimacy. The subsequent inquiry is about reason impact connections and inner legitimacy, and the third inquiry is to fundamental hypothetical structure helping the rationale of the reason-impact relationship.

At the subsequent phase of the choice procedure, the chief looks for data concerning the normal results of embracing the development so as to conclude whether to receive an advancement. Inquiries being posed at this stage identify with understanding the outcomes of reception and what relevant elements may direct or intervene the general reason impact relationship. Thus, the integrative blend consequently is likewise guided by these two incremental queries:

Question Number 4 - Where can the impact of Human Resource Analytics be seen?

Question Number 5 - Who all are responsible for Human Resource Analytics to be successful?

What Best Defines Human Resource Analytics?

Of the different, most describe HR Analytics, all the more for the most part, as either an investigation procedure or dynamic procedure. Human Resource Analytics is a moderately contemporary term; initially showing up in the literatures related to HR in 2003–2004 as per this examination of significant databases. HR analytics are proportions of key HRM results, delegated proficiency, viability or effect.

Bassi (2011) contends that HR Analytics can be viewed as both as 'methodically giving an account of a variety of HR indices or progressively complex arrangements, in light of 'pre-emption models'. What's more, Bassi's definition incorporates the idea of taking a 'proof based way to deal with' settling on choices on the 'individuals side of the business'. She finishes up HR analytics 'is an evidence-based methodology for settling on better choices on the individuals side of the business; it comprises of a variety of devices and advancements, starting from basic update of HR indices as far as possible up to pre-emption. At long last, concentrating on the connection with vital HRM, Mondare, Douthitt, and Carson (2011) characterize HR analytics as showing the immediate effect of individuals on significant business results.

These definitions and marks share a few things for all intents and purpose. To start with, HR analytics isn't HR metrics. It includes increasingly modern examination of HR-related information. Second, HR analytics doesn't concentrate solely on HR utilitarian information, and includes coordinating information from various inside capacities and information outer to the firm. Third, HR analytics includes utilizing data innovation to gather, control, and report information. Next, HR analytics is tied in with supporting individuals related choices. At last, HR analytics is tied in with connecting HR choices to business results and hierarchical execution. This fifth part of the meaning of HR analytics catches the most convincing part of this build and connections it to the key HRM writing. HR analytics offers augmented than HR Metrics by virtue of its capability to interface HR procedures and choices with hierarchical execution, which is a road to hoisting HRM of possessing an increasingly key job and joining different business capacities at the methodology table.

Together all these different definitions brought, HR analytics may be defined as:

A HR activity empowered by data innovation that utilizes enlightening, visual, and factual examinations of information identified with HR forms, human capital, authoritative execution, and outer monetary benchmarks to build up business affect and empower information driven dynamic.

Prima-facie it appears soon to evaluate whether HR analytics is seemingly perpetual development that in the end spreads across organizations to turn into a regulated HRM practice or a brief trend. The appropriate response might be enlightened by responding to the rest of the inquiries presented underneath.

How Human Resource Analytics Operates?

First presented in the book by Boudreau and Ramstad (2007) titled *Beyond HR: The New Science of Human Capital,* and hence drawing a cohort with a significant number of the articles, LAMP model is hereby endorsed. The alphabets used the in LAMP represent logic, analytics, measures, and processes, contend are the 4 basic segments of an estimation framework essential both to reveal proof-based connections and furthermore to inspire improved choices dependent on those examinations. They additionally recommend that these 4 components might be critical to understanding the reason impact connection between HRM forms and key HRM and results of business. Notwithstanding the abovesaid model, the various steps form depicted in a few of these articles additionally perceive to operationalise various parts of the human resource scorecard, a different model connecting human resource management procedures and individuals to business results, which is itemized in *The Human Resource Scorecard: Connecting Strategy with People and their Performance.*

There would seem, by all accounts, to be incredible prospect to summon speculations of development, social impact and discernment to aide direct and clarify reason impact connections between HR analytics forerunners, results and arbitrators. Mechanical brain research has some history tending to this inquiry with respect to the appropriation of 'utility examination's during the decade of 1970 and also the decade of 1980 (Cascio & Boudreau, 2010). It has also been likewise proposed that choices of pioneers outside the HR order might be affected by evaluating their prevailing models, and revamping HR analytics and revealing utilizing analogies to systems from other administration teaches, for example, activities, funds, and advertising (Rousseau & Boudreau, 2011).

Why Human Resource Analytics Operates?

Not very many of the research works checked on alluded to an express hypothetical system. This isn't startling; provided most of the articles were fundamentally qualitative exact research. Predictable with the vital HR hypothetical structure basic the LAMP model and the Human Resource Scorecard, four articles were coded (Coco, Jamison, & Black, 2011; Mondare et al., 2011; Douthitt & Mondore, 2014; Rasmussen & Ulrich, 2015) has having inferred hypothetical systems got from vital administration speculations and specifically, the resource-based view, which centers around creating inward worth delivering and one of a kind abilities and assets. The ramifications of this hypothetical point of view is that human resource analytics is related with improved execution and upper hand when it is one of a kind and worth creating.

Strangely, the one examination that exactly tried explicit theories (Aral, Brynjolfsson, & Wu, 2012), receives office hypothesis as the essential hypothetical focal point. Aral and partners contend that organizations which utilize a blend of pay for execution remuneration, HCM abbreviated as human capital management programming, and human resource analytics are increasingly beneficial in light of the fact that this mix permits chiefs to both adjust impetuses and screen representative conduct. Utilizing a board test of 189 firm-level information gathered more than 5 years from 1995 to 2006, they show that organizations with this mix of capacities and assets were fundamentally progressively profitable. Especially particular about this examination, the creators misused the longitudinal idea of their information to build up a circumstances and logical results relationship with the end goal that having each of the three elements delivered ensuing a better profitability at firm-level. Besides, it was likewise found that HR analytics didn't upgrade profitability. Once comprehended with HCM programming and pay for execution does HR analytics foresee efficiency. Despite the fact that Aral et al. (2012) use office hypothesis as their illustrative structure, their outcomes are likewise predictable with vital HRM hypothesis of opportunity and ability motivation (Jiang et al., 2012). Better chanced of perform than their opponents who don't have this mix are here for the organizations, which enlist people that have capacity, and give inspiration and chance to play out their employments well. Their outcomes may likewise be deciphered as reliable with LAMP model, which has proven to be doing well in conjunction of "investigation" with a "procedure" (pay for execution) and "measures" (from HCM programming) which appeared to create superlative impact.

Where can the Impact of HR Analytics be Seen?

As noted over, the one investigation of my 16-article study that observationally tried theories gave solid proof to a reason impact connection between Human Resource Analytics and monetary execution (Aral et al., 2012). Be that as it may, Harris, et al. (2011) likewise note that effectiveness results (for example cost investment funds on human resource forms) are probably not going to bring about business sway in light of the fact that authoritative expenses regularly just speak to 3% of an organization's capital, operational and managerial costs, so no measure of reserve funds wrung from diminishing HR regulatory costs is probably going to have any effect on business execution.

Giving triangulated proof to a connection between business effect and utilization of Human Resource Analytics set up observationally by Aral et al. (2012), 8 un-imperial research works give support to contextual investigations which the author contended to have recorded a proportional relationship. For instance, Contextual analysis on how the retail chain grown from basic was given by Coco et al. (2011), Lowes, utilized HR Analytics for setting up a connection between HR forms, worker commitment, and store execution. Through utilization of human resource management, Lowes had the option to build up that profoundly drawn in workers lead to 5% higher normal client ticket deals per outlet. A reference to Harris et al. (2011) gives significant level contextual investigation guides to delineate the 8 articles they contend include Human Resource Analytics and connection these to business sway. For instance, they portray how the most popular search engine utilizes Human Resource Analytics to foresee representative execution utilizing their candidate database.

At long last, a few examinations archive the low degree of human resource analytics dispersion across organizations, which is astounding given the early, yet inadequate, proof in reference to a causal connection between Human Resource Analytics and results obtained by the business. Falletta (2014) directed a review to decide utilization of human resource analytics among Top 1000 firms. With an example of 219 firms, Falletta (2014) suggested that merely 16% of participants guaranteed HR analytics assumed a focal job in deciding or actualizing HR system. Unmistakably there gives off an impression of being a detachment between enticing proof of impactful business effect and choices to embrace and actualize powerful HR Analytics. Outcomes tending to the next inquiry may recommend potential clarifications.

Who all are Responsible for HR Analytics to be Successful?

The most as often as possible referred to reason that HR analytics isn't all the more generally embraced is the lack of systematically gifted HR experts. Bassi (2011) predicts that without fundamental IT insight (how to utilize scientific programming instruments) and budgetary aptitudes (access and use proportions of business outcomes), HR capacities will unavoidably surrender duty regarding examination to both the informational technology and account capacities. Angrave et al. (2016) reverberated the concern and rose another query.

On the off chance that HR isn't completely engaged with the displaying procedure, there is altogether more noteworthy extension for models to be built in a manner which on a very basic level misconstrues the idea of human capital contributions to the procedures of creation and administration convey. Rather than perceiving the adaptability of work; that efficiency and execution change with abilities, inspiration and structure of human procedures associations, work is displayed as a non-recurring cost that should be capped. Except if investigation is implanted in a complete and extensive expository outcome, the more restricted data accessible in the MIS organizations might be misjudged by execution excellence and money related administrators with constrained tolerance for or comprehension of HR. Utilizing HR analytics assists with improving hierarchical execution, pick up and keep up an upper hand. It furnishes associations with a system for dynamic, take care of complex business HR issues, drive maintainable development through advancement, envision and plan for change while overseeing and adjusting dangers. At the end of the day HR analytics is the measurable procedures for knowledge and assessing the causal connection between HR rehearses and hierarchical execution results. Institutionalization of such HR rehearses has helped organizations to accomplish significant objectives like consistency, productivity and decency to increase a worldwide perspective on their workforce. In this way the HR capacities currently has two significant orders i.e., to perceive the one-of-a-kind ability of every representative and send these gifts in a way that boosts the workers vitality to drive business results. To re-engineer the ability framework and create HR capacities for personalization, customisation of HR rehearses are required in workers and their associations. HR professionals basic to build up the sort of abilities that advertisers used to exceed expectations at customization, for example, co-creation, division, getting information, becoming acclimated to seeing innovation to help this customization. They should discover better approaches to join representatives behind the association even as representatives have progressively differentiated, customized encounters in the work environment.

Hence, not exclusively does the absence of explanatory aptitude have all the earmarks of being blocking the take-up of HR Analytics inside organizations, earmarks worry for HR Analytics when received won't be constrained by HR experts however by other people who may misjudge or not explain the observations. Angrave (2016) suggests is that not exclusively will HR experts pass up on a chance to build up a competency that improves their key dynamic and effect on authoritative execution yet in addition it might be hazardous for society in that workers and business openings might be contrarily affected. Conversely, Boudreau (2010, 2012) and associates (Cascio & Boudreau, 2010) have contended that a proper joint effort between HR pioneers and useful specialists in controls, for example, account, activities, showcasing, and building might be critical to building up the legitimate structures for HR analytics which can draw in important leaders and interface all the more plainly to hierarchical results.

Levenson (2011) distinguishes the particular expository abilities required for HR experts to perform HRA viably. These are essential information examinations, moderate information investigations, fundamental multivariate models, progressed multivariate models, information planning, main driver investigation, look into configuration, overview structure, and quantitative information assortment and examination. As indicated by the study of HR analytics experts he and his associates gathered (Levenson, Lawler, & Boudreau, 2005), be that as it may, the more elevated level measurable abilities expected to build up business sway are not sought after. The terrible news is that even at this low degree of interest there is an insufficient stockpile. Short of what one-third of HR analytics experts announced to possess competency in cutting edge multivariate measurements and when just considering HR experts not explicitly procured for HR Analytics, that extent drops to just 3% .

The subsequent prerequisite for HR analytics is politically based, to be more effective All together aimed at HR experts to access the cross useful information expected to play out their investigations, chiefs from different capacities are happy to give access and furthermore to be associated with the procedure. Moreover, HR experts must form believability among ranking directors who may not accept information driven outcomes. Rasmussen and Ulrich (2015) see that there is an inclination to dismiss information that compromises the ongoing convictions. So as to conquer such obstruction, those engaged with HR Analytics must include key partners in front of directing the examinations. Coco et al. (2011) portrays how the HR group at Lowes, a popular grown retailer, put forth an admirable attempt so as to manufacture trust and purchase in for their HR Analytics venture from ranking directors and the ones beyond the HR work.

Different examinations demonstrate, be that as it may, that data innovation (IT) can be both a gigantic empowering agent and a noteworthy obstruction to HR Analytics. Empowering the influence, thoughtfully e-HRM should catch, capture, and make available information from across organization capacities and produce reports, scorecards, and dashboards. The truth of persistent e-HRM capacities, be that as it may, doesn't coordinate the guarantee. Those organizations performing HR analytics have all the earmarks of being directing these investigations in spite of HRM IT instead of as a result of it. This circumstance is probably going to change as innovation merchants see HR Analytics as an approach to push more items and put resources into improved usefulness and capacity to coordinate different information. In any case, for the time being, apparently guarantees of 'press button' natural HR analytics by means of e-HRM innovation, for example, HCM programming or incorporated talent management cloud-based arrangements ought to be inspected cautiously and fundamentally (Angrave et al., 2016). He suggests that not exclusively will HR experts pass up on a chance to build up a competency that improves their key dynamic and effect on authoritative execution yet in addition it might be hazardous for society in that workers and business openings might be contrarily affected. Conversely, Boudreau (2010, 2012) and associates (Cascio & Boudreau, 2010) have contended that a proper joint effort between HR pioneers and useful specialists in controls, for example, account, activities, showcasing, and building might be critical to building up the legitimate structures for HR analytics which can draw in important leaders and interface all the more plainly to hierarchical results.

INTERPRETATION OF THESE FIVE QUESTIONS

An important observation was the lack of insightful articles concentrating fundamentally on human resource analytics or the comparative pursuit terms that were utilized, and the much more modest number of experimental investigations among that gathering. Proof about human resource analytics is certainly in its earliest stages. There have been some striking occasions that appear to have generated uncommon diary challenges on HR analytics (Davenport et al., 2010; Bryant, 2011; Garvin, 2013). This hunt on peer-inspected articles showing up in regarded academic administration inquire about diaries and observed that out of these sixty-four reviewed diary articles, about thirty-two of them were in peer-assessed articles and among these, sixteen showed up in the Quality List Journal frequently depended upon by colleges to assess productions for residency. Point with this centre was to disconnect the kind of proof frequently accentuated by proof-based administration advocates. Without a doubt, there are a lot more online journals, white papers, counselling reports and tributes accessible to leaders, yet it shows up reasonable for state that a chief planning to draw upon top notch peer-looked into insightful work will discover not many investigations accessible. Apparently, the subject of 'human resource analytics' has not gotten the enthusiasm of most of the administration insightful network, not at all like other Human Resource issues, for example, determination approval, representative turnover, objective setting, and execution dependent prizes. The modest number of articles recommends that research is still at a beginning period of consideration from the administration proficient network. The significantly more modest number of articles showing up in insightful distributions recommends that administration researchers have demonstrated even less enthusiasm for inspecting the forerunners and results of human resource analytics. This is appalling, considering the noteworthy key ramifications in the field of HR Analytics that possess for the job HRM plays in associations and for the HR calling, considering some proof of a cohesive connection with HR analytics and association viability and effect as nitty gritty right now. Extensively, there are two eminent queries. First is that notwithstanding the fame of HR Analytics there is restricted great logical proof put together research with respect to this theme. The subsequent contradiction, maybe identified with the principal oddity, is the obviously constrained appropriation of HR analytics when the accessible research appears to be as often as possible to propose that it is related with positive hierarchical results.

The work will progress with a model around HR Analytics and move towards the conclusion.

HR ANALYTICS MATURITY MODEL

HR analytics encourages individuals' administrators and groups to see increasingly about the challenges of the workers factor in their association how they are performing and making an incentive for the association. With the help of HR analytics, HR professionals are empowered to take progressively educated choices, and are additionally ready to take a gander at the workforce quality, information, abilities, and experience of people and groups. For this reason the HR office in an association has (big data) immense number of individuals related information (eg., abilities, execution rating, age, instructive foundation, and so forth., which could be utilized to increase better comprehension of the associations current creation, execution, and hazard. There are many new devices and methods for examining Big Data, yet associations experience four phases of advancement as they come up with Big Data in HR procedures. This four-arrange development model clarifies how associations advance from profoundly versatile detailing framework to cutting edge investigation, hazard relief, and models (figure 1).

Figure 1. Four Level Model Illustration. Source: Talent Analytics Maturity Model: Bersin by Deloitte

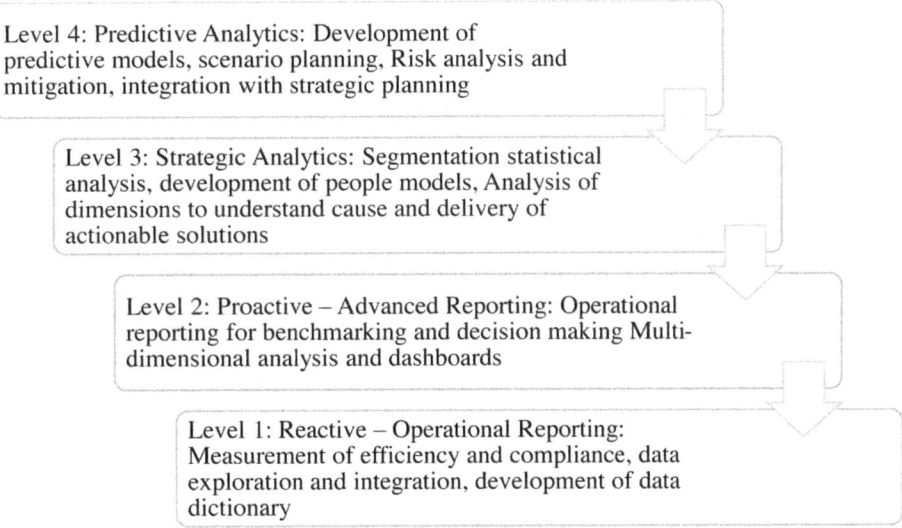

Level 4: Predictive Analytics: Development of predictive models, scenario planning, Risk analysis and mitigation, integration with strategic planning

Level 3: Strategic Analytics: Segmentation statistical analysis, development of people models, Analysis of dimensions to understand cause and delivery of actionable solutions

Level 2: Proactive – Advanced Reporting: Operational reporting for benchmarking and decision making Multi-dimensional analysis and dashboards

Level 1: Reactive – Operational Reporting: Measurement of efficiency and compliance, data exploration and integration, development of data dictionary

Evidence-based human resource is a group of works on, joining research proof with logical data and individual judgment of HR experts. In spite of the fact that HR look into is now very much created right now, with groups of proof identified with the principle HR areas, there are still very a few holes. This makes HR professionals are needing new proof-based discoveries. Current test in the earth of associations builds this need considerably more. In addition, HR specialists require a general system, a general methodology or perspective to help the HR choices. The foundation for selection of HR's evidence-based model, Talent, can be viewed as a significant initial phase right now. All partners can have an influence in further structure ability. Proof based administration gives apparatuses and a typical language that helps both the investigation individuals and human individuals utilize information in dynamic.

As indicated by the *HR Matters* blog, the primary advantages of proof based human asset practice are:

1. Firms can foresee progressively educated and successful dynamic;
2. Improved capacity to adjust human asset practice bearing a set of objectives of the association;
3. Human Resource strategy and theories can be founded on what works, instead of what is estimated to be effective;
4. Enhanced validity for the control of human asset practice and pertaining to professionals;
5. A increasingly scientific analogy depending upon existing data, information, investigation and deep insights liable to be held inside the group or division;
6. There will be progressively predictable dynamic and intercessions; and powerful administration of hazard.

These standards can be seen as industry guidelines to legitimize for what reason would it be advisable for them to change their HR towards analytics?

CONCLUSION

During the conduct of literature review, on HR Analytics and in spite of proof of a developing enthusiasm for this advancement, it was discovered next to no and restricted logical proof to help dynamic concern of embracing HR Analytics. Of the 16-research works chosen dependent on meeting logical quality benchmarking from an underlying populace of 64 research works, at last just 6 included observational examinations of HR Analytics. Of these 6, just one tended to observationally prove connecting HR Analytics to organization execution. The staying 10 investigations independently gave almost no proof supporting inside legitimacy, end legitimacy, and generalizability. There were no hypothesis-based expectations of connections and no information gathered to assess hypothetical forecasts. Subsequently, the example articles gave restricted logical proof. Then again, they provided some data concerning significant logical mediators and a reason for some triangulation with the couple of observational examinations to get some level of generalizability.

It can likewise be drawn from this work Human Resource examination enables associations to use the information so as to address difficulties confronted by Human Resource, yet additionally the centre business. It gives associations the capacity to create and actualize a people methodology in accordance with its business technique, along these lines improving execution across expansive scope of measurements. It helps the associations to utilize the information adequately to distinguish HR issues so as to discover an answer. And furthermore by utilizing analytics tools and systems in the HR fraternity, associations can see how these individuals related variables identify with business results.

At last, it is intriguing that the accessible proof recommends that HR Analytics has constructive outcomes, yet appropriation shows up extremely moderate. Once more, it is hazy whether this is on the grounds that all developments must depend on a little arrangement of early adopters, or on the off chance that it proposes that leaders don't accept or don't know about the current proof. It can be presumed that these inquiries are interesting and deserving of top-notch research, and expectation our audit will add to the development of such research.

Future of HR Analytics

HR Analytics is turning into a proof-based procedure for improving the presentation of both individual and association for settling on better choices. Human Resource Analytics would now be able to make a believability of all the capacity and occupations in the association by improving the viability of Human Resource rules and practices. So as to accomplish upper hand to associations, HR capacities and experts need to grow new aptitudes and abilities, so they can adequately collaborate with promoting and fund individuals on HR analytics activities and hazard surrendering. Be that as it may, the HR experts should address related moral predicaments like when HR analytics will and won't be utilized. Indeed, HR analytics can diminish the present difficulties confronting numerous associations. Be that as it may, it can likewise bring about a headway of the status of the business and its specialists by supporting them to support their originations to decide the association between progressively gainful and increasingly edified management and employee development.

Scope for Future Research

Further research may derive and grow the investigation of Angrave et al. (2016). This research work is commendable, yet it is additionally eminent for its irregularity. It gives an intriguing model to further research; in that it moves toward a very much acknowledged issue in the Human Resource field – the job of execution and pay in rousing execution – and inspects the extra impacts of Human Resource Management data innovation and Human Resource Analytics. Different issues can be envisioned, for example, candidate's decision to opt for a role, validity of the selection procedure, development of the employee, effectiveness of the trainings, and performance assessments, and so on that are likewise the subject of many years of research, and that may fill in as stages for looking at the incremental impacts of Human Resource Analytics.

REFERENCES

Angrave, D., Charlwood, A., Kirkpatrick, I., Lawrence, M., & Stuart, M. (2016). HR and analytics: Why HR is set to fail the big data challenge. *Human Resource Management Journal, 26*, 1–11. http://scholar.google.com/scholar_lookup?hl=en&publication_year=2016&pages=1-11&author=D.+Angrave&author=A.+Charlwood&author=I.+Kirkpatrick&author=M.+Lawrence&author=M.+Stuart&title=HR+and+analytics%3A+Why+HR+is+set+to+fail+the+big+data+challenge

Aral, S., Brynjolfsson, E., & Wu, L. (2012). Three-way complementarities: Performance Pay, human resource analytics, and information technology. *Management Science, 58*(5), 913–931. doi:10.1287/mnsc.1110.1460

Barends, E., Rousseau, D. M., & Briner, R. B. (2014). *Evidence-based management: The basic principles.* Amsterdam: Center for Evidence-Based Management. http://scholar.google.com/scholar_lookup?hl=en&publication_year=2014&author=E.+Barends& author=D.+M.+Rousseau&author=R.+B.+Briner& title=Evidence-based+management%3A+The+basic+principles

Bassi, L. (2011). Raging debates in HR Analytics. *People & Strategy, 34*, 14–18. https://scholar.google.com/scholar_lookup?hl=en&publication_year=2011&pages= 14-18&author=L.+Bassi&title=Raging +debates +in+HR+Analytics

Boudreau, J. W. (2010). *Retooling HR.* Harvard Business Publishing. https://scholar.google.com/scholar_lookup?hl=en&publication_year=2010&author=J.+W.+Boudreau&title=Retooling+HR

Boudreau, J. W. (2012). Decision logic in evidence-based management: Can logical models from other disciplines improve evidence-based human resource decisions? In D. Rousseau (Ed.), *The Oxford handbook of evidence-based management* (pp. 223–248). Oxford University Press. https://scholar.google.com/scholar_lookup?hl=en&publication_year=2012&pages=223-248&author=J.+W.+Boudreau&title=Decision+logic+in+evidence-based+management%3A+Can+logical+models+from+other+disciplines+improve+evidence-based+human+resource+decisions%3Fdoi:10.1093/oxfordhb/9780199763986.013.0013

Boudreau, J. W., & Ramstad, P. M. (2007). *Beyond HR: The new science of human capital.* Harvard Business School Pub. http://scholar.google.com/scholar_lookup?hl=en&publication_year=2007&author=J.+W.+Boudreau&author=P.+M.+Ramstad&title=Beyond+HR%3A+The+new+science+of+human+capital

Bryant, A. (2011, March 12). Google's 8-point plan to help managers improve. *The New York Times.* https://www.nytimes.com/2011/03/13/business/13hire.html https://scholar.google.com/scholar_lookup?hl=en&publication_year=2011&author=A.+Bryant&title=Google %E2%80%99s+8-point+plan+to+help+managers+improve

Cascio, W., & Boudreau, J. (2010). *Investing in people: Financial impact of human resource initiatives.* Ft Press. http://scholar.google.com/scholar_lookup?hl=en&publication_year=2010&author=W.+Cascio&author=J.+Boudreau&title=Investing+in+people %3A+Financial+impact+of+human+resource+initiatives

Coco, C. T., Jamison, F., & Black, H. (2011). Connecting people investments and business outcomes at Lowe's: Using value linkage analytics to link employee engagement to business performance. *People & Strategy, 34*, 28–33. http://scholar.google.com/scholar_lookup?hl=en&publication_year=2011&pages=28-33&author=C.+T.+Coco&author=F.+Jamison&author=H.+Black& title=Connecting+people+investments+ and+business+outcomes+at+Lowe%E2%80%99s%3A+Using+value+linkage+ analytics+to+ link+employee+ engagement+to+business+performance

Davenport, T. H., Harris, J., & Shapiro, J. (2010). Competing on talent analytics. *Harvard Business Review, 88*, 52–58. http://scholar.google.com/scholar_lookup?hl=en&publication_year=2010&pages=52-58&author =T.+H.+Davenport&author=J.+ Harris&author= J.+Shapiro&title=Competing+on+talent+analytics

DiMaggio, P., & Powell, W. W. (1983). The iron cage revisited: Collective rationality and institutional isomorphism and collective rationality in organizational fields. *American Sociological Review, 48*, 147–160. http://scholar.google.com/scholar_lookup?hl=en&publication_year=1983&pages=147-160&author= P.+DiMaggio&author=W.+W.+Powell&title=The+iron +cage+revisited%3A+Collective+rationality+ and+institutional+isomorphism+and+collective+ rationality+in+organizational+fields

Douthitt, S., & Mondore, S. (2014). Creating a business-focused HR function with analytics and integrated talent management. *People & Strategy, 36*, 16–21. http://scholar.google.com/scholar_lookup?hl=en&publication_year=2014&pages=16-21&author=S.+Douthitt&author=S.+Mondore&title=Creating+a+business-focused+HR+function+with+analytics+and+integrated+talent+management

Falletta, S. (2014). In search of HR intelligence: Evidence-based HR Analytics practices in high performing companies. *People & Strategy, 36*, 28–37. https://scholar.google.com/scholar_lookup?hl=en&publication_year=2014&pages=28-37&author=S.+Falletta&title=In+search+of+HR+intelligence%3A+Evidence-based+HR+Analytics+practices+in+high+ performing+companies

Garvin, D. A. (2013). How google sold its engineers on management. *Harvard Business Review, 91*, 74–82. [PubMed], https://scholar.google.com/scholar_lookup?hl=en&publication_year=2013&pages=74-82&author=D.+A.+Garvin&title=How+google+sold+its+engineers+on+management

Harris, J. G., Craig, E., & Light, D. A. (2011). Talent and analytics: New approaches, higher ROI. *The Journal of Business Strategy, 32*(6), 4–13. http://scholar.google.com/scholar_lookup?hl=en&publication_year=2011&pages=4-13&author=J.+G+Harris&author=E+Craig&author=D.+A+Light&title=Talent+and+analytics%3A+New+approaches%2C+higher+ROI. doi:10.1108/02756661111180087

Jiang, K., Lepak, D. P., Hu, J., & Baer, J. C. (2012). How does human resource management influence organizational outcomes? A meta-analytic investigation of mediating mechanisms. *Academy of Management Journal, 55*, 1264–1294http://scholar.google.com/scholar_lookup?hl=en&publication_year=2012&pages=1264-1294&author=K.+Jiang&author= D.+P.+Lepak&author=J.+Hu&author=J.+C.+Baer&title=How+does+human+resource+ management+influence+ organizational+outcomes%3F+A+meta-analytic +investigation+of+mediating+mechanisms

Levenson, A. (2011). Using targeted analytics to improve talent decisions. *People & Strategy, 34*, 34–43. https://scholar.google.com/scholar_lookup?hl=en&publication_year=2011&pages=34-43&author=A.+Levenson&title=Using+targeted+analytics+to+improve+talent+decisions

Levenson, A., Lawler, E. E. III, & Boudreau, J. W. (2005). *Survey on HR Analytics and HR transformation: Feedback report*. Center for Effective Organizations, University of Southern California., http://scholar.google.com/scholar_lookup?hl=en&publication_year=2005&author=A.+Levenson&author=E.+E.+Lawler&author=J.+W.+Boudreau&title=Survey+on+HR+Analytics+and+HR+transformation%3A+Feedback+report

Mondare, S., Douthitt, S., & Carson, M. (2011). Maximizing the impact and effectiveness of HR Analytics to drive business outcomes. *People & Strategy, 34*, 20–27. http://scholar.google.com/scholar_lookup?hl=en&publication_year=2011&pages=20-27&author=S.+Mondare&author=S.+Douthitt&author=M.+Carson&title=Maximizing+the+impact+and+effectiveness+of+HR+Analytics+to+drive+business+outcomes

Paauwe, J., & Boselie, P. (2005). 'Best practices … in spite of performance': Just a matter of imitation? *The International Journal of Human Resource Management., 16*, 987–1003. http://scholar.google.com/scholar_lookup?hl=en&publication_year=2005&pages=987-1003&author=J.+Paauwe&author=P.+Boselie&title=%E2%80%98Best+practices+%E2%80%A6+in+spite+of+performance%E2%80%99%3A+Just+a+matter+of+imitation%3F

Rasmussen, T., & Ulrich, D. (2015). Learning from practice: How HR Analytics avoids being a management fad. *Organizational Dynamics, 44*, 236–242. http://scholar.google.com/scholar_lookup?hl=en&publication_year=2015&pages=236-242&author=T.+Rasmussen&author=D.+Ulrich&title=Learning+from+practice%3A+How+HR+Analytics+avoids+being+a+management+fad

Rogers, E. M. (2003). *Diffusion of Innovations* (5th ed.). Simon and Schuster. https://scholar.google.com/scholar_lookup?hl=en&publication_year=2003&author=E.+M+Rogers&title=Diffusion+of+Innovations

Rousseau, D. M., & Boudreau, J. W. (2011). Sticky findings: Research evidence practitioners find useful. In S. A. Mohrman & E. E. Lawler III, (Eds.), *Useful research: Advancing theory and practice*. Berrett-Koehler. https://scholar.google.com/scholar?hl=en&q=Rousseau%2C+D.+M.%2C+%26+Boudreau%2C+J.+W.+%282011%29.+Sticky+findings%3A+Research+evidence+practitioners+find+useful.+In+S.+A.+Mohrman%2C+%26+E.+E.+Lawler+%2C+III+%28Eds.%29%2C+Useful+research%3A+Advancing+theory+and+practice+%28ch.+14%29.+Berrett-Koehler

Rousseau, D. M., Manning, J., & Denyer, D. (2008). 11 Evidence in management and organizational science: Assembling the field's full weight of scientific knowledge through syntheses. *The Academy of Management Annals, 2*, 475–515. http://scholar.google.com/scholar_lookup?hl=en&publication_year=2008&pages=475-515&author=D.+M.+Rousseau&author=J.+Manning&author=D.+Denyer&title=11+Evidence+in+management+and+organizational+science%3A+Assembling+the+field+%E2%80%99s+full+weight+of+scientific+knowledge+through+syntheses

Chapter 9
Envisioning Delight in School Education Service:
Observations From Implementation of Global Citizenship Education (GCED) in Indian Schools

Shilpa Arora Narang

Institute of Innovation in Technology and Management, GGSIP University, New Delhi, India

Sarmistha Sarma

iD https://orcid.org/0000-0001-8747-8012

Institute of Innovation in Technology and Management, GGSIP University, New Delhi, India

Ashita Raveendran

National Council of Educational Research and Training, New Delhi, India

P. D. Subhash

National Council of Educational Research and Training, New Delhi, India

ABSTRACT

Global citizen education (GCED) is a strategic area of UNESCO's education sector program and builds on the work of peace and human rights education. It may prove to be a key area of focus for school education services around the world. India has always been a key stakeholder in implementing the SDGs in its policies. The education sector plays a pivotal role in realizing the SDG targets, and GCED curriculum implementation plays are strategic roles in realizing this target of achieving SDG in education. India has played an active role in making efforts to implement GCED in school education. This chapter focuses on GCED practices, traces its origin, its prospective arrival in the Indian education scenario, and the state of affairs at present in terms of its implementation in prominent states around the country. Therefore, the chapter describes GCED implementation in Indian school system and its contribution to making the school education system a delightful and sustainable practice.

DOI: 10.4018/978-1-6684-5853-2.ch009

INTRODUCTION

Regardless of how chaotic the world may be becoming more connected, human rights violations, inequality, and poverty continue to pose a threat. The solution proposed by UNESCO to address these issues is global citizenship education (GCED). It functions by enabling students of all ages to see that these are global concerns rather than local ones and to take an active role in promoting more harmonious, tolerant, inclusive, secure, and sustainable communities.

The work of peace and human rights education is built upon by GCED, a strategic component of UNESCO's Education Sector Program. Creativity, innovation, and a commitment to peace, human rights, and sustainable development are among the principles, attitudes, and behaviours it strives to instill in students.

The Universal Declaration of Human Rights and the *Education 2030 Agenda and Framework for Action*, specifically Target 4.7 of the *Sustainable Development Agenda, the Recommendation concerning Education for International Understanding, Co-operation and Peace and Education relating to Human Rights and Fundamental Freedoms* (1974), and *the World Programme for Human Rights* serve as the foundation for UNESCO's work in this area.

UNESCO has a number of unique themes under the GCED banner, including: educating people to stop violent extremism, providing information on genocide and the Holocaust, the use of foreign languages in the classroom and the promotion of international law

The UNESCO Mahatma Gandhi Institute of Education for Peace and Sustainable Development (MGIEP), the International Institute for Capacity Building in Africa (IICBA), the UNESCO Institute for Statistics (UIS), the Asia-Pacific Centre of Education for International Cooperation, and other regional organisations are among the many intergovernmental and regional organisations that UNESCO works with to spread GCED.

The goal of global citizenship education (GCED) is to equip students of all ages to actively contribute to the creation of societies that are more serene, tolerant, inclusive, and secure on a local and global scale.

The three learning domains of cognitive, socio-emotional, and behavioural are the foundation of GCED:

- **Cognitive:** the knowledge and reasoning abilities required to comprehend the world and all of its complexities.
- **Socio-emotional:** Beliefs, attitudes, and social abilities that support students' emotional, psychosocial, and physical growth as well as their ability to coexist peacefully and respectfully with others.
- **Behavioral**: include involvement, performance, behaviour, and performance.

The three learning domains listed above serve as the foundation for the key learning outcomes, key learner traits, subjects, and learning objectives indicated in GCED. They are connected and included in the educational process.

Prospective Curriculum for Global Citizenship Curriculum (GCC)

The following list identifies information and understanding, skills, values, and attitudes as the essential components for fostering engaged and responsible global citizenship. As a result, a learner's education should focus on helping them continue to develop early skills like cooperation and communication. The curriculum framework should act as a catalyst for additional reflection, discussion, and preparation; it is not an exhaustive or prescriptive manual.

A wide range of interactive teaching and learning strategies are used in education for global citizenship, including discussion and debate, role playing, ranking tasks, cause and effect activities, and communities of inquiry. Although these approaches are not exclusive to learning for global citizenship, they can increase awareness of the world while cultivating abilities like critical thinking, questioning, communication and cooperation when used in tandem with a global perspective.

Additionally, they give students the opportunity to discover, articulate and express their own ideas and opinions while respectfully considering those of others.

This is a crucial step in helping students make educated decisions about their involvement in global concerns. The case studies that follow demonstrate how educators have effectively included an emphasis on global citizenship into their curriculum development. They shed light on how global citizenship might improve several facets of the curriculum for all age groups.

Prominent Initiatives by different states to implement Global Citizenship Education (GCED) in Indian Schools

To adopt a global citizenship schools approach in education, different states have taken initiatives to bring global citizenship education (GECD) to limelight By embracing and upholding the proposals like GCED school code and encouraging the GCED Innovative Mindset, one can fully realise the transformative potential of global citizenship education. GECD accreditation can make that school, one of the top most school in promoting global citizenship in a nation, hence, by utilising the certification course for students, capacity-building, and a community.

MAHARASHTRA

About

Maharashtra is the second most populated State of India and third largest by area. The capital of Maharashtra, Mumbai, is the most populated urban area. Mumbai is also financial or commercial capital of India in a heavily industrialized State. According to 2011 census, Maharashtra has112.37 million of population, wherein the male population was 58.24 million and female population was 54.13 million. The literacy rate of Maharashtra was 82.34%, where the male literacy rate is 88.38% and female literacy rate is 69.87%. The sex ratio of Maharashtra was 929 females per 1000 males, which is slightly below the national average of 940.

In the field of education, Maharashtra has been an efficient State. In 2010-11, there were 97,256 number of Elementary schools out of which 49,085 were Primary schools, 48,171 were Upper Primary schools and 5,595 were Secondary and Higher Secondary schools. Of the total number of Elementary schools, 67,241 were Government managed schools and 30, 015 schools were privately managed schools.

In the 2022 budget of Maharashtra government presented in March for financial year 2022-23, Rs. 3370.24 crore has been allocated as the budget for the education sector. In the previous year, the budget was Rs. 2945.78 crores. 5% of this amount would be utilised in renovation of schools. Another provision of 3 crore has been allocated to build study centers in various educational institutions that will assist youth to gain knowledge about historical icons and figures. A sum of Rs 1 crore has been given to enhance the facilities and conditions of schools in some specific villages like Sane Guruji, Savitribai Phule, Maharishi Karve, Rashtrasant Tukadoji Maharaj, Krantisinha Nana Patil, and Gadgebaba Maharaj.

During the pandemic, in a report published by National Achievement Survey(NAS), there was a regular decline in understanding levels of students of higher education. Whereas amongst government schools, students' performance in 3rd standard was observed at 66.33%. In private schools, similar was observed at 55.44%. In the same report of NAS, students (up to class 5th) experienced less difficulty in accessing education as compared to students of higher education. Approximately 70% of students of primary level, indulged in hobbies like singing, dancing, and played outdoor games and forhigher education, this percentage was 35%.

In the context of sustainable development goals, NITI Aayog has published the SDG Index report: Baseline report. As per the Index of 2018, Maharashtra ranks 4th in whole country with a score of 64.

The SDG 4 features access, equity and inclusion, gender equality, quality of education and lifelong learning. It calls every country of the world to improve its education system. It plays a fundamental role in building sustainable, inclusive, and resilient societies. SDG 4.7 which is a subpart of SDG 4 embraces two important and emerging concepts of including education for sustainable development (ESD) and global citizenship education (GCED). These concepts embrace every key dimensions of educational transmission like curriculum, pedagogy and evaluation, principles and practices as well as teaching and learning.

This report intends to highlight status of Maharashtra in context of SDG 4.7 based on a structured questionnaire which was sent to the States to collect information regarding the key elements of GCED and ESD existing in their policies, curricula, teachers' education, students' assessment and other school practices.

Sustainable Development

For Sustainable Development Maharashtra had taken following initiatives –

Maharashtra Green Army: Green army is a platform given by the state to its citizens so that they can participate in the preservation of wildlife and forests. The State Government of Maharashtra aims to increase the forest cover in the state from 20%(currently) to the nationally mandated 33% of Maharashtra's land area. The lack of manpower with the Forest Department call for this program of Green Army. It gives social platform to citizens to interact in the activities. Citizens such as students from schools, from colleges/Universities, Women and Government Employee/ Officers, etc. are encouraged to participate.

There are several activities which are organized under this initiative such as Plantation, Group patrolling for conservation of forest, Volunteering for Wild-life census, Volunteering to prevent Forest fires, Celebration of commemorative days/ international observance/international days by Maharashtra Forest Department for propagating awareness regarding Forest, Wildlife and Environment, Active participation in Forest festivals like (Forest week & Wildlife week), proctive contribution in organizing knowledge drives like cycle rally, road shows, road site dramas, prabhat pheri,etc.

Paryavarn Seva Yojana (14 Jan. 2011): Under this scheme, A workshop on making Ganesh idols from clay was organized on 08-09-2021 at Karma veer Bhaurao Patil Vidyalaya, Askheda, Tal. Baglan, Nashik. Beautiful Ganesh idols were made with the participation of 60 students. This initiative created interest not only in art among the students but encouraged them to become great artists. It is commendable that this initiative is being implemented in the school in terms of environmental protection.

Another activity conducted in 2021 is Bird Restaurant and Panpoi in Nashik Division. During the period of Covid-19, the students have carried out all the activities at home level. According to this, the students have been assigned weekly activities. The students have provided food and water for the birds around the house.

At the same time, birds were observed and recorded on the water poi.

For this, students were sent e-books (PDF) books and brochures about bird restaurants and water poi for birds.

1. Photo of Bird Restaurant for birds.
2. Photo of drinking pot kept for birds
3. Bird Observed Register Photo Full name of the student, name of the school, district and students have been updated on WhatsApp group of Paryavaran Seva Yojana.

Paryavaran Mitra Programme

Paryavaran Mitra (Friend of Environment) demonstrates environmental citizenship qualities through positive change in behavior and action at individual, school, family and community levels.

A national programme is underway to develop a network of young leaders from schools all around the nation who are capable of addressing the issues of environmental sustainability in their individual domains of influence. Students, as Paryavaran Mitra, show commitment to make a difference by taking handprint action. The action could be towards resolving a local issue, or to improve the condition within the school premises, and at home, or in the community in five thematic areas;

In the educational process of project based learning the student would develop understanding in environmental sustainability, inculcate the required attitude, values and behaviour towards environmental sustainability, and build skills through hands-on experience in the immediate environment.

Schools have to involve students in class rooms, in eco-clubs, and in the whole school in action-oriented activities and carry out projects under five themes: Water, Waste Management, Energy, Biodiversity, Culture and Heritage. A Paryavaran Mitra school is one that provides support, time, and space for students and teachers to be actively engaged in learning by doing. In other words, it is a school that promotes exploration, discovery, thinking, and action.

A uniquely designed, and curriculum linked "Teacher's Handbook" (free download for registered schools) provides the basic resource facilitating the implementation of Paryavaran Mitra activities and projects within and beyond the classroom. It is equipped with a lot of background information, class activities from the 5 themes, beyond classroom projects and ideas.

Balrakshak Movement (2017): The State has initiated Bal Rakshak movement for the mainstreaming of out of school children and to put an end to children migration in order to provide good quality education to the children. Out of 78501 out of school children 66958 (85%) out of school children are admitted in age-appropriate class in regular schools and provided special training.

In 2020, to ensure that students do not face difficulties due to the coronavirus pandemic and lockdown, the State Council of Educational Research and Training (SCERT) has updated its bal rakshak policy at a village level.

Scholarships for deprived students and female students (1996)

Human Rights

Getting Education is one of the fundamental human rights as per Indian constitution. For protecting human rights and creating awareness among students and parents following initiatives are taken by Maharashtra.

. The protection of Human rights Act (1993)
· Scholarships for deprived students and female students(1996)
· NHRC (Procedure) Amendment regulations (1997)
· Maharashtra, Right to Education 2011
· Curriculum of primary education (2012)
· Right to Education - Duty of Local Bodies 2014 (20 Aug. 2014)
· Balrakshak Movement (2017)
· SIOS (state institution of Open school) (2018)
· Along with this effective implementation of inclusive education, Age Appropriate class enrollment is emphasized in schools of Maharashtra.
· SCERT, Maharashtra conducted teacher training on Child rights and security.

PEACE AND NON-VIOLENCE

For peace and non- violence Maharashtra had taken following initiatives

· Juvenile justice (2006)
· The sexual harassment of women at workplace (2012) Along with this Following activities are taken in schools of Maharashtra
· Anapan and Meditation activities are taken during the assembly in schools.
· Students from primary school level are oriented about Good Touch and Bad Touch with various stories and videos along with awareness programme.

GLOBAL CITIZENSHIP

For global citizenship Maharashtra had taken following initiatives –

· International quality cell in SCERT(2016) GLOBAL CITIZENSHIP
· International level Schools development (2017)
· Maharashtra International school board (2018
· International level school curriculum development (2018)
· Model Schools development (2021)

Along with this Maharashtra state introduced Theme based textbooks for primary grades (2021) of Model schools of Maharashtra.

· SCERT, Maharashtra conduct the Workshops on PISA to attempt International level.

GENDER EQUALITY

For creating awareness among the students regarding gender equality Maharashtra State take following initiatives.

· Scholarships for women's (1996)
· SAMATA Cell establishment (2016)
· Audit of textbooks as per gender equity component.

Mostly Co- education is given in the schools of Maharashtra to enhance gender equality.

Boys from secondary school also oriented about Menstrual Hygiene for getting aware about girls health.

To promote Gender Equality, the Maharashtra government launched the Menstrual Hygiene Management program. Awareness talks are conducted in schools and in aganwaadis twice a month. Most importantly, more than 100 schools introduced safe waste management approaches. They included sustainable practices to properly and safely dispose the menstrual waste. (Example, making an incinerator out of earthen pot and dry leaves).

DIVERSITY

For creating unity in diversity the Maharashtra state undertaken following initiatives:

· CWSN Act (2016 and 2018)
· Dialect Books for students (2019)
· Maze Samvidhan Maza Abhiman (2021) (My constitution, my prestige)

The following details highlight curricular activities conducted in the Maharashtra State.

SCERT, Maharashtra and Shantilal Muttha Foundation were together undertaken Mulyavardhan (programme) for inculcating values in primary level students.

Maharashtra's Mulyavardhan program enables students to develop values, competencies, and critical thinking to become caring, responsible, and democratic citizens who abide by constitutional values. This program trains the school teachers for the successful implementation of this program. It focuses on a child-centric and activity-based approach. Many good practices are demonstrated to children by teachers, classes take place outside of the classrooms, best out of waste activities, conducting sanitation drives, distributing paper bags, feeding animals, watering plants, and other activities that promote love for nature, etc.

Textbooks follow gender equality norms.

Dialect books for students in 2019. Introduction of bilingual books for children to grasp concepts better.

With the help of "Teacher's Handbook", at least five activities in each of these five themes are to be undertaken. Most of the activities can be conducted within the premises of the school but at least one has to reach out being executed in the student's family or community. Eco-Clubs can take a leading role in project implementation.

· SCF (2010), SAMATA Cell establishment in SCERT (2016)

· Along with this there is special subject as an Environmental Education at higher secondary level.
· School education department introduce 'Aapla Pani' (Our Water) supplementary book for grade Ist to 8th for creating awareness about Jal Saksharta
· Following activities are conducted in schools e.g. Parasbag, plantation of trees, Vruksh Mitra (Trees friend), Ghan van (Dense Forest), Vruksh dindi, Vanrai Bandhara, Jangle Safari, Vanbhojan, Street play, Science exhibition, like these programs are always taken in schools along with allocation, debate, essays, drawing competition for environmental education and spreading awareness about ecology among students and parents.
· There are various activities based on democracy are conducted in schools e.g. Balsabha, Proxy Voting, School Cabinet, Preamble reading in school assembly.
· 'Saturday story' this program is undertaken by SCERT for students from grade 1st to 8th.
· School arranges various awareness programme about peace and justice with the help of NGOs.
· Maharashtra is having combined class of normal children and CWSN children.
· CWSN children are given equal opportunity for their development
. Students of different caste and religions learn together in the school of Maharashtra
· Different types of cultural programs are organized to portray the diversity of our country.
· Various programs of different religions are taken in the school to create unity among diversity.
· Programs like Sahbhojan are organized to eliminate the difference between religion, caste, and creed.
· The content of the school syllabus gives equal justice to the people of different religious, and castes and portrays the greatness of leaders of different communities.
· Social science and languages cover the topic from local to global as well as culture of different communities.
· Bold size books, brail language books, and different helpful apparatus and instruments were provided to CWSN children.
· SCERT, Maharashtra conducted teacher training on teaching-learning pedagogy for CWSN according to their learning style.
· Inclusive Education section is developed in each district and section in DIET.
· Separate Mobile teachers are appointed to help in learning of CWSN.
· Various health checking camps are conducted for CWSN.
· Writer or half hour is given extra to the CWSN.
· Obstacle free infrastructure and CWSN friendly environment is created in schools.

In the section A of Maharashtra's questionnaire, it can be observed that ESD and GCED themes are covered considerably with the exception of Global Citizenship which is incorporated only slightly. When it comes to mainstreaming of ESD and GCED themes in the school education (A.3), global citizenship is covered moderately and rest of the themes are covered considerably or extensively. In A.5, there is mention of incorporation of new trends in syllabus, curriculum but no specific nature of details have been provided.

In the section B, themes are majorly covered in upper primary, secondary levels and vocational/adult education in schools. At primary level, global citizenship is scantily covered. Human Rights and Peace & non-Violence are completely covered at all school levels as well as in vocational/adult education.

In B.2, one can see, sub-themes of sustainable development are majorly covered subject areas if languages, social sciences, science and roughly covered in mathematics. Human Rights are only covered at languages and social sciences.

Peace and non-violence in majorly covered in languages and social sciences whereas only two (out of four) sub-themes are covered in science and one in mathematics.

All sub-themes of Global Citizenship, Gender equality, and Diversity are covered in subject areas of languages and social sciences. In mathematics and science, they are scantily covered.

At the primary level, integrated, cross-curriculum, and whole school approaches are applied. At upper primary and secondary levels, integrated and whole school approaches are followed.

Section C deals with teacher education. In the pre-service curriculum, all themes are incorporated considerably. All themes are covered in languages, social sciences, and science. Only sustainable development and diversity are covered in mathematics.

In the in-service training programmes, all themes are incorporated considerably as well. They are incorporated in languages, social sciences, science, and mathematics.

In C.6, one can observe teachers are trained to teach all learning dimensions on the theme of human rights. In themes like peace & non-violence, global citizenship, and gender equality, teachers are trained to teach knowledge, values, and attitudes/behaviors. In sustainable development, they are trained to teach knowledge, skills, and attitudes/behaviors. Within diversity, they are trained to impart knowledge, and attitudes/behaviors.

Section D deals with student assessment. Sustainable development, global citizenship, and diversity are extensively assessed whereas remaining themes are examined partially.

All learning dimensions are reflected considerably in the student assessments/examinations with the exception of skills & competencies which is reflected moderately.

Knowledge is assessed through methods like written examinations, debates, and quizzes.

Skills and competencies are assessed through projects.

Values are not assessed through any method.

Lastly, attitudes/behaviors are assessed through projects, debates, and quiz Knowledge and attitudes/behaviors are the most assessed learning dimensions.

An instrumentalist view of the curriculum's GCED GCED does not now have a common definition or conceptualization. In a 2013 assessment of the literature, Oxley and Morris established eight dimensions of global citizenship: political, moral, economic, cultural, social, critical, environmental, and spiritual. These categories were then further subdivided into subcategories. The theories and approaches of articulating what constitutes global citizenship are varied for each category.

GCED curricula come in a variety of forms, but they all have the goal of articulating and teaching the moral, economic, and civic imperatives for a changing and interconnected world (OECD 2018). For instance, it is asserted that GCED can assist in preparing future citizens to live amicably in a globalised society made up of "multicultural communities" with regard to the moral imperative (OECD 2018, p. 2). GCED promotes principles like "respect for variety, solidarity, and a shared sense of humanity" in this way (UNESCO 2018, p. 2). In terms of the ecological necessity, GCED equips future citizens to prosper in a shifting labour market (OCED 2018).

In this light, "effective communication and appropriate behaviours" stemming from intercultural understanding, along with critical reflections on the set of technologies, become important aspects of global competence (OECD 2018, p. 5). Finally, concerning the civic imperative, GCED prepares future citizens to "participate in and contribute to the community at a range of levels from the local to global" (Giles 2019, p. 15).

Accordingly, "successful communication and acceptable behaviour" resulting from international awareness, as well as critical reflections on the range of technology, become crucial components of global competence (OECD 2018, p. 5). GCED trains future citizens to "participate in and contribute to the community at a range of levels from the local to global" with regard to the civic imperative (Giles 2019, p. 15).

GCED encourages "understanding and acting on local concerns in a global context, coupled with global drivers for responsibility such as the Universal Declaration of Human Rights and the Sustainable Development Goals (SDGs)" in this regard (p. 15).

According to current GCED curricula and frameworks, education should be centred on global interconnectedness and the rapidly changing global environment. The goal of GCED is to support each learner's development of multidimensional capacity and global competence domains. (OECD, 2018)

In this, the focus is prominently on two documents developed by international organizations:

- OECD's (2018) Preparing Our Youth for an Inclusive and Sustainable World: The OCED PISA Global Competence Framework
- UNESCO's (2015) Global Citizenship Education: Topics and Learning Objectives.

According to PISA, global competence is "a multifaceted capacity" that includes cognitive, socio-emotional, and behavioural knowledge and abilities (OECD 2018, p. 3). The worldwide competence of the OECD is divided into four areas:

1.examine local, global, and intercultural issues

2.understand and appreciate the perspectives and worldview of others

3.engage in open, appropriate, and effective interactions

4.take action for collective well-being and sustainable development. (p. 26)

In turn, as a global assessment tool, the PISA Cognitive Test for Global Understanding was created based on these four dimensions.

The concept of global competence as a multidimensional capacity is reflected in UNE SCO's document as well. The topics and learning objectives for GCED were built based on "three domains of learning": cognitive (i.e., knowledge and thinking skills), socio-emotional (i.e ., values, attitudes, and social skills), and behavioral (i.e ., conduct, performance, practical application, and engagement) (UNESCO 2015, p. 19). Based on these three domains of learning, GCED learning outcomes, key learner attributes, topics, and specific learning objectives are listed in categories. Two popular views of GCED portrayed in these two documents are global competence as instrumental action and a binary view of global-local relations.

First, the PISA Cognitive Test for Global Understanding and UNESCO's learning objectives by ages show us that global competence is viewed as instrumental action for learners to show and prove their knowledge, skills, and attributes related to GCED. Such a conceptualization is driven by a Tylerian-instrumental view of curriculum, what Ted Aoki (2004) refers to as "ends-means (technical) evaluation orientation". The ends-means evaluation orientation views knowledge as objective and a form of empirical data; it emphasizes "efficiency effectiveness, predictability and certainty [of knowledge in curriculum] ... in the service of control" (Aoki, 2004, as cited in Pinar and Irwin2005, p. 9). Ralph Tyler (1949) stated that curriculum should be based upon authority found in subject matter, social needs, and the needs of learners as individuals. Learning objectives are an important aspect for Tyler because they provide the educational goals that are sought and reflect the values of a society. As such, curriculum focuses on specifying goals and experiences for education in support of societal goals.

Following the Tylerian approach for GCED, stakeholders in multi-lateral organizations participate in imagining "the global" as "a utopic site of transgressive intermixture, hybridity and multiplicity" (Ang, 1998, p. 14). Attempting to reach the vision of the global community, curriculum producers select specific societal goals, followed by learning topics and objectives. Teachers then select pedagogical approaches and a series of experiences for learners to develop global competence as conceptualized in GCED curricula. Such an instrumental view of GCED faces what Scott (2014) referred to as the external fallacy: knowledge and the future of the state are considered as "provisional, contingent and arbitrary ... [but] curricular knowledge is identified exclusively in terms of specific social goals" (p. 6).

As pedagogical guidance, UNESCO's (2015) topics and learning objectives are to be contextualized at the "national level ... with support from other partners and stakeholders" (p. 8). The document provides various examples of different countries' approaches to GCED linking with GCED objectives put forth by UNESCO. In a way, UNESCO seems to be promoting a glocalized approach of GCED. Here, I wonder how teachers and students conceptualize "the global": Is there a single, homogenized world of the global? In a way, the glocalized approach of GCED connects diverse locals under the name of GCED but considers global-local relations as an incommensurable binary whereby the global is always located outside the local.

Indeed, structured in the Tylerian-instrumentalist view of curriculum, GCED is viewed as something that can be delivered in a closed system, wherein global-local interactions are bounded by geographical borders in a causal manner. Curriculum offers pedagogy and activities that examine global-local issues as cause-and-effect transactions (e.g ., How would local action impact global issues? Or global issues impact local action?). Through a linear, instrumentalist approach to competence-based curriculum, GCED operates with an abstract and decontextualized understanding of what the global community entails. In turn, teachers and students are confined in their own classrooms to offer actions that can be feasibly executed in their local surroundings. As such, popular slogans, including "think globally and act locally", are perpetuated within GCED curricula.

I see a global paradox in these GCED curricula and frameworks because "while it encourages all of us to think what unites us, it simultaneously fragments us by its incitation to focus our political practice on each of our immediate local surroundings" (Ang, 1998, p. 26). Indeed, many GCED-related activities focus on action toward immediate local surroundings, while thinking of the impacts of their action globally or examining the issues critically in their classrooms. These activities do not necessarily require actual encounters with other communities. For these reasons, GCED has been criticized as being an empty term and a superficial gesture that is used by stakeholders for local agendas rather than fostering globally oriented citizens (Pais and Costa, 2020).

These current GCED discourses assume the global economy is a knowledge-based economy. A knowledge-based economy is driven by neoliberalism, whereby individual competence is evaluated as a commodity for success. Exploring the influence of neoliberalism on curriculum is beyond my focus here. Here, I would like to focus on our current era conceived of as a learning economy. In 1994, economist Anne Carter already predicted that "the main function of most non-production workers is to introduce or cope with change" (Lundvall, 2008, p. 5). Focused on the rate of accelerated changes in our current reality, Lundvall suggested that we are no longer in a knowledge-based economy. We are in the era of a learning economy, wherein "the success of individuals, firms, regions and countries reflect [emphasis added], more than anything else, their ability to learn [emphasis added]" (p. 2). To better distinguish a learning economy from a knowledge-based economy, I turn to my family story.

KERALA

About

gained first position in the NITI Aayog SDG Index of 2020-21.

This figure shows that Kerala State has units/cells/centers designated to SDGs, there are mapped department and schemes, and consultations/trainings/orientations related to SDGs.

It is a combination of competitiveness or high-quality growth, an equitable society and sustainable environment that creates the ideal conditions for life. Kerala wishes to be one such society by 2030.

Thiruvananthapuram and Kochi have found their place among the top five in the urban sustainable development goal index released by NITI Aayog. The quality of life is better in these cities compared to others.

They were assessed through indicators, including poverty reduction, health, education, women empowerment, water and sanitation, clean energy, economic growth, industry, urban development, climate action and governance.

Kochi stood first in gender equality and second in quality education; clean water and sanitation; and peace, justice and strong institutions. Kochi had its lowest scores (Aspirant) in industry, innovation and infrastructure (19); decent work and economic growth (39) and sustainable production and consumption patterns (48).

Sustainable Development

Diversity Parks: They are part of school policies. Kerala government asked to convert school campus to biodiversity parks. In many government aided schools, this policy was implemented. The objective is to provide fresh learning environment and students are asked to collect information for learning as well.

Venal Pacha: This is an activity book which covers many environments related activities (like protection of environment). These activities are performed at home and school both.

Mannezhuthu diary & Entemaram: The focus of this program is to develop child's relationship with soil/mud. There are many activities conducted under it and they have to write reports of the same in their diary.

Under Entemaram program, every child is required to plant their own tree.

Nature clubs: This has been started in association with forest department of Kerala. Several activities such as nature education camps, nature study projects, tree planting, nature games, pond ecosystem study, etc., are conducted. It aims to generate social awareness towards environmental degradation and generate ecological sensitivity.

Peace and Non-Violence Student police cadet: This program is school based initiative of Kerala police along with various ministry departments. It inculcates in students respect towards law, discipline, civic sense a democratic value. It nourishes within them dedication towards their family, the community, and the environment.

Diversity

Ullasaparavakal

This is handbook developed by SCERT Kerala. The aims is to provide children with disabilities for 'adaptive and positive behavior' in order to deal constructively with the demands and challenges of day to day life and to develop healthy habits and responsible behavior, including gender sensitivity, through imparting of participatory Life Skill Education Programme.

These infographics represent which sub-themes of ESD and GCED themes are followed at each level of schools.

From Section A, we obtained details of some programs in Kerala which do promote the values of ESD and GCED themes. Many activities, curricular programs and schemes do take effort to promote the conscience towards our environment, surroundings and people as well as holistic development of students. For Teacher education, no specific activity has been pointed out.

In Section B, which studies curricula, except peace and non-violence and global citizenship, every sub-theme of ESD and GCED themes is covered in all three levels of schools. However, within this, some sub-themes from each section are not incorporated. For example, economic sustainability and education for sustainable development are not covered at the primary level. Education for sustainable development is not covered at any level. In the same manner, amongst the sub-themes of Human Rights, Human Rights education is not covered at the primary and secondary levels both. In peace and non-violence, peace education is not covered at the secondary level whereas no themes are covered at the primary level. Within the global citizenship theme, none of the sub-themes are covered at primary. Additionally, multiculturalism and global citizen are not covered in secondary, it is however, incorporated in upper primary level. Global local-thinking is not covered in upper primary level and it is incorporated at secondary level. Most sub-of Gender equality are covered in primary level of school within which gender equality subject is covered at all three levels. Diversity is as a theme is the most covered theme with the exception of disability which is not covered at secondary level. None of the themes are imparted as a part of vocational/adult education.

Most themes are covered in the subject area of social sciences, followed by languages and science. Diversity is only covered in the subject area of social science.

At both primary and upper primary levels, integrated approach is followed. At secondary level, few themes like sustainable development, human rights and diversity are taught as a separate subject. For the rest of the themes, integrated approach is applied.

In teacher education, with the exception of global citizenship every theme is incorporated in the pre-service training considerably. Themes like sustainable development, gender equality and diversity are covered in languages, social sciences and science whereas the remaining themes are incorporated only in languages and social sciences.

In the in-service training programs, most themes are reflected extensively. All themes of ESD and GCED are covered in subject areas of languages, social sciences, science and math.

In C.6, we observe that teachers are trained to impart sustainable development, gender equality and diversity in all learning dimensions. Amongst human rights and global citizenship, teachers are able to teach in knowledge, values and attitudes/behaviors. In peace and non-violence, teachers are trained to teach only knowledge.

Section D deals with student assessment. With the exception of peace and non- violence and global citizenship, the remaining themes are incorporated extensively in student assessments or examinations. The former two are assessed partially.

All learning dimensions are included moderately in the student examinations. Knowledge is the most assessed learning dimension which is examined through written examination, debates and quiz. Attitudes and behaviors are examined by written examination and debates. Skills & competencies and values are only assessed by written examination plus, they are the least assessed dimensions.

Sustainable Development Goal 4.7: Policies and
Practices in School Education

GUJARAT

About

Gujarat is a state along the western coast of India and its capital city is Gandhinagar. The state's official language is Gujarati. Gujarat is the fifth largest state in India by area and the ninth populous state, with a population of 60.4 million. The economy of Gujarat is the fourth largest in India.

Gujarat ranks 21st among Indian states and union territories in human development index. As per the report titled "SDG India Index and Dashboard 2020-21: Partnerships in the Decade of Action" published by NITI Aayog, overall Gujarat ranks 10th in composite SDG score at 69, taking into account all 16 goals on 115 quantitative indicators, against an India average of composite SDG score of 66 and thus figures in the top bracket of 'front runner'. As far as Target SDG 4 is concerned, Gujarat ranks 17th among states with the SDG score at 52 which put Gujarat in the performer category.

Below are few of the following initiatives, policies, legislations, programs and activities with respect to SDG 4.7:

1.   Paryavaran Prayogshala:

Environment Laboratory (Paryavaran Prayogshala) has been introduced into the curriculum by the Government of Gujarat under Samagra Shiksha. It is the annual course with the planning of various activities including different fields like environment, water, soil, nursery, biological fertilizers, energy, animal husbandry, organic farming, plastic, etc. in the Environmental Laboratory.

In 6123 government schools (primary and secondary) in the state, focus activities were conducted to create environmental awareness and increase participation through environmental project work at the school level. These activities resulted in an awareness of the importance of creating a single- use plastic-free society and the side effects of the overuse of chemical fertilizers. The initiative succeeds in bringing awareness of environmental conservation into the daily life of students.

2.   Green School:

Sarva Shiksha (SS) is a flagship programme of the central government for achievements of Universalization of Elementary Education (UEE) in a time bound manner as mandated by 86th Amendment of the constitution of India making free and compulsory education to the children of 6- 14 years age group which a fundamental right.

To attain the aims of SS- access, enrolment, retention and quality education to all children, Govt. of Gujarat has initiated Green & Sustainable School Programme. Green & Sustainable School Programme is about not only sustainable development but maintaining Green in the context of ecological balance through active participation of students, teachers and the community. 'Green' is about the present generation's responsibility to improve the future generation's life by restoring the previous ecosystem and resisting contributing to future ecosystem damage.

The objectives are to learn importance and benefit of green schools, to develop creativity and better understanding among the children, to learn the concepts of science, mathematics, social science and language in the world around the children, to create innovative ideas for the society.

The goal is to sensitize and mobilize schools to become sustainable ecosystems and let children be the torch-bearer of the movement.

3.   Youth and Eco Club:

The objectives are to instil Environment friendliness among students by developing awareness and education on judicious use of Natural resources, Sustainability and conservation, to empower students to participate and take up meaningful environmental activities and projects for experiential activities to promote sound environmental behavioural, to develop life skills, build self-esteem & self- confidence and resilience and counter negative emotions of stress, shame and fear which will enhance child's capability to combat the challenges in their future life, to strengthen physical, mental, emotional and social skills of students by providing opportunities to think critically and solve problems logically through participatory, and process-oriented activities.

Under SS, all government Elementary and Secondary Schools in the State has Youth and Eco Club. As part of Youth and Eco club initiative, Schools conducted curricular and co-curricular activities to bring awareness about the Public Campaigns such as 'Jal Shakti Abhiyan', Swachh Bharat Abhiyan and 'Fit India movement'. YEC activities included activities like plantation, cleanliness, beautification and conservation of the school campus area or any other innovative practice. Debates, music, arts, sports, reading, physical activities conducted as part of YEC initiative. These activities help in utilising the idle school infrastructure like play-ground, sports equipment, libraries, in-school garden area, musical instruments etc. which helps the students to develop hobbies, skills and interest they might not otherwise be able to explore.

Under YEC, schools organised various activities such as Book reading, Storytelling and moral- sharing etc ., to encourage use of Libraries and improve the reading habits of students.

4, Periodic Assessment Test:

Periodic Assessment Tests (PAT) are conducted every Saturday in all the government schools of Gujarat for Std 3 to 9. PAT supports a lot in bringing quality in teaching learning processes in the classroom. Annual PAT calendar was shared with the schools which help the teachers to complete the syllabus timely. These periodic assessments help to track the performance of the students regularly. Teachers find out the gaps in learning of the students and provide necessary support and adjust their lesson plan accordingly. A separate PAT booklet is provided to all the students for this assessment. GCERT prepares the learning outcome-based assessments for these tests. PAT isconducted on every Saturday between 8.30 am to 9.30 am in the schools and teachers evaluate the booklet within a week and sent it to the parents for their signature on it. This creates awareness among parents on the learning level and progress of their children. After getting the signature from the parents, children bring the booklet back to the school so that they can write their next test on the same booklet.

More than 40 lakh students studying at Elementary and Secondary level in All the Government Schools of Gujarat. Initially PAT was introduced only for Std 3 to 8. Later based on positive feedback the same was also implemented with Secondary level students. PAT is appreciated by all the stakeholders of the education system. It helps to improve the attendance of the students in the school. Teachers are completing the syllabus timely and parents are also observing their kids regularly. Regular assessment helps the students to cope out from examination phobia.

5.   Right of Children to Free and Compulsory Education act 2009:

As per Right of Children to Free and Compulsory Education Act-2009 Government of Gujarat has pass the bill of Gujarat Educational Act (Amendment) Bill- 2010 in Legislative Assembly and State has implemented Right to Education Act since Dt. 01/04/2010. Every child between the ages of 6 to 14 years has the right to free and compulsory education. This is stated as per the 86th Constitution Amendment Act via Article 21A. The Right to Education Act seeks to give effect to this amendmen. The government schools shall provide free education to all the children and the schools will be managed by School Management Committees (SMC). Private schools shall admit at least 25% of the children in their schools without any fee. The National Commission for Elementary Education shall be constituted to monitor all aspects of elementary education including quality. The Right to Education Act 2009 prohibits all kinds of physical punishment and mental harassment discrimination based on gender, caste, class, and religion, screening procedures for admission ofchildren capitation fee, private tuition centres, and functioning of unrecognized schools.

8.   Celebration of Gyansapath:

Gujarat government has celebrated 'Gyan Saptah' for Teacher's Day from September 1 to 5 during which several activities included cleanliness drive in villages, competitions for students, felicitation of teachers as well as approval to build infrastructure facilities for schools were organised. On September 1, a cleanliness drive called 'Swatchh-Gaam', for each village had been conducted. On September 2, the government approved different infrastructural works for schools and also gave approval to build toilets, compound walls, extra class rooms or any other work related to infrastructure facility for schools. On the remaining three days, school students were involved in different activities, such as mock-teaching rounds, one-act plays, drawing competitions as well as meeting with parents.

9. Police Mitra:

Police Mitra, or Friends of Police, is an initiative of the State police. Civilian citizens having 'good social record' like ex-army men, students, advocates, and housewives are responsible in tying up with the police beat staff to look after the law and order, traffic and crowd management, safety of women prevention of crime and informing about suspected elements around their area.

10. Computer Aided Learning Project in Primary School:

The Government of India leads Sarva Shiksha program to make and compulsory education to the children of 6-14 years age group, a fundamental right. Gujarat Council of Elementary Education implemented this project in Gujarat State. Computer aided learning program (CAL) is created for the rural children to enrich the education by making "learning play", "assessment fun" and "equivalent knowledge for all". The computer learning program (CAL) creates an environment, where learning and assessment is fun and the opportunities to learn is equitable among the rural and urban children. The CAL is primarily introduced in rural government elementary schools covering the classes 1 to 8 to attract and retain children and also in the process, enhance the quality of learning by making "learning play", "assessment fun" and "equal knowledge for all. "

The main objective of the CAL programme is to attract the children, retain them in the schools andto improve the quality of the education through animated multimedia based educational content. CAL objective is to sought to be achieved through story based, animated cartoon, interactive games and riddles with the use of multimedia features. Spontaneous, self initiated and self regulated, the three critical aspects that make an activity play are integerated in CAL to make Learning Play and use of cartoons, story line and music is intended to make CAL as self intiated and engaged in learning.

This program has improved the IT literacy in the rural areas particularly and is going well in removing the digital divide in the state. It had improved the interests of students in school studies and thus increase school attendance and better performance in examinations. I t had also improved the teaching process with the integration of the IT in the class which lead to the improvement in the student and reacher learning and productivity. Moreover, the CAL program had made the children better prepared for getting into secondary education and continue with Computer Education at a higher level.

11 GSEB and director of primary to all schools:

The Gujarat Secondary and Higher Secondary Education Board or GSEB is a government of Gujarat body responsible for determining the policy-related, administrative, cognitive, and intellectual direction the state's secondary and higher secondary educational system takes. The main responsibilities of the Board includes academics, conducting examinations and research and development. The board is responsible for registration and administration of higher secondary and secondary schools in the state of Gujarat.

12. Twining school:

Twinning of schools is known as 'Partnership among schools' under which two schools come together for greater exposure. The aim is to promote shared learning among students and teachers with focus to encourage learning inside and outside the classroom. This results in increased interaction amongst students and teachers, sharing of experiences, ideas and best practices.

The Objectives are sharing of best practices on academic and co-curricular activities between partner schools, capacity building of Teachers and Students through knowledge sharing, enablingstudents to have hands-on learning with Peer-to-Peer and group learning, enable both the partner schools to adopt best practices from each other, get an exposure to the strength and weakness of self and others and learn jointly, provide opportunities to the teaching fraternity to adopt better and more effective practices.

As the current status, all in total 12,988 government schools spread across 33 Districts of Gujarat participated in Twinning of Schools program The effectiveness of the program can be witnessed in Gujarat as participating schools had the opportunity to exchange work within academic and co-curricular activities, enhance the capacity of teachers and students through knowledge sharing, synchronization of each other's abilities provided an opportunity to learn jointly by complementing each other's weaknesses, the Twinning of Schoolprogram has been instrumental in strengthening the learning process by providing students with an environment for peer learning and group learning, this program provided teachers with the opportunity to adopt better and effective teaching methods.

13. Gujarat Kanya Kelavani Nidhi:

Kanya Kelavani Nidhi was launched by Ministry of Women and Child Development, Government of Gujarat (GoG Resolution 2003). It bought women into the mainstream of development in the rural areas of Gujarat. Kanya Kelavani Nidhi intensively focuses to endorse girl education in the state. Under this scheme, Gujarat government bears expenses of girl's education in state. The government bear balance fifty percent fee from Kanya Kelavani Nidhi in self-financed colleges which made medical education for girl almost free. Kanya Kelavani Nidhi has provided fund to foster women education. This scheme had increased the female participation in education field and also reduced the dropout ration of females in education. Donation received and money generated through auction of gifts goes to the Kanya Kelavani Nidhi Fund.

CONCLUSION

A universally acknowledged "blueprint," the SDGs state that "sustainability for all" is one of their main goals (UN, 2015). The SDGs are described by Sterling (2019) as "a essential and timely reaction to the world problematique," but he also raises a critical question: "What circumstances have led to planetary system conditions—here in the early 21st century—such that a set of remedial UN SDGs are necessitated?"

The SDGs do not specify a recommended educational approach; rather, they simply recommend that ESD, GCED, and CCE be integrated in national curricula. In their 2016 Global Education Monitoring Report, UNESCO—who has been designated as the "custodian agency" for Target 4.7 (UNESCO, 2019—admits that a pedagogical reorientation is required (GEM). While the GEM Report is easily criticised as "an extension of hegemonic globalising thought," Wals (2016) notes that it also includes "a possible shift," signifying a change in "mainstream UN-speak." Given how firmly ingrained the "education as usual" concept has been in teacher preparation, classroom materials, and educational institutions, this presents a number of difficulties. How can we start to change?

Students can start by looking into the SDGs using Inquiry-Based Learning (IBL) and the associated "cluster of teaching and learning methodologies" (Blessinger & Carfora, 2015, p. 5). IBL is a student-centered approach based on issue situations that encourages students to critically examine themselves, their communities, and the nature of the problems they are researching. It is also known as real-world, problem-, project-, and place-based learning (Herman & Pinard, 2015). The IBL style of teaching, which is "a means of building self-knowledge through intensive inquiry," predates Socrates (Jones, 2015, p. 277). By allowing students to "build their own knowledge rather than just having that knowledge being spoon-fed to them by others," the inquiry method was further refined by constructivist thinkers including Dewey, Vygotsky, Piaget, and Bruner. (Blessinger & Carfora, 2015, p. 5). The active involvement played by students in creating the questions, goal, and course of discovery is a crucial aspect of IBL. The customary partnership between a teacher and the student is disrupted, which can be a challenging transition as participants form new perspectives about their responsibilities in the classroom, the goal of education, and the nature of learning (ibid.). An IBL environment that has been expertly created and facilitated is collaborative, cross-disciplinary, empowering, and intentionally unpredictable.

In a nutshell, a place to start when reimagining how all of this might play out in the classroom is by changing the way we think about subjects and implementing systematic educational change. Learning opportunities are increased when interdisciplinary themes replace the segregated disciplines that are traditionally the emphasis of classroom instruction and encourage siloed thinking.

Hence, any modification to the current educational systems looks onerous given how deeply ingrained global learning patterns are in efforts to standardise. Our "capacity and ability to learn and evolve" will, however, determine the quality of our shared future (Sterling, 2014, p. 90). Students are not waiting for top-down reforms to take place, as evidenced by the numerous recent youth-led civic events, therefore educators must implement change beginning in their own classrooms. It is time to fundamentally change the goals and organisation of schools, beginning a process of unlearning that goes beyond "reframing or reconstructing our current thinking but moving away from our existing mental structures towards a position which enables a fundamentally different way of seeing the world." (Sterling, 2017; Laininen, 2019). The SDGs may contribute to a "living tradition of inquiry" rather than being viewed as a "technical toolbox" and act as a standard, universally acknowledged reference point for educators. While the SDGs are being discussed, the globe is becoming warmer and inequalities are getting worse. If we define global citizenship education pragmatically using the SDGs, then pedagogical strategies like inquiry- and problem-based learning come to life with a clear and pressing goal.

"Whatever education a university or institutes of higher education imparts, it must achieve the global level of benchmarking given the vastness and diversity of global village we live in today."

-Narendra Modi, Prime Minister of India (2019)

REFERENCES

2015). UNESCO- United Nations Educational, Scientific and Cultural Organization. https://en.unesco.org/gem-report/taxonomy/term/199

Ang, I. (1998). Doing cultural studies at the crossroads: Local/global negotiations. *European Journal of Cultural Studies*, *1*(1), 13–31. doi:10.1177/136754949800100102

Aoki, T. (2004). Teaching as indwelling between two curriculum worlds (1986/1991). In W. Pinar & R. L. Irwin (Eds.), *Curriculum in a new key: The collected works of Ted Aoki* (pp. 159–165). Peter Lang. doi:10.4324/9781410611390

Blessinger, P., & Carfora, J. M. (2015). Innovative approaches in teaching and learning: An introduction to inquiry-based learning for multidisciplinary programs. In P. Blessinger & J. M. Carfora (Eds.), *Inquiry-Based Learning for Multidisciplinary Programs: A Conceptual and Practical Resource for Educators* (pp. 3–22). Emerald Group Publishing Limited. doi:10.1108/S2055-364120150000003001

Giles, L. (2019). Learning to live together and a life worth living. In *APCEIU reconciliation, peace and global citizenship education: Pedagogy and practice* (pp. 12–19). Incheon: UNESCO Asia-Pacifc Centre of Education for International Understanding (APCEIU). https://www.gcedclearinghouse.org/sites/default/fles/resources/190516eng.pdf

GoG Resolution. (2003). https://govinfo.me/kanya-kelavni-nidhi-gujarat/

Herman, W. E., & Pinard, M. R. (2015). Critically examining inquiry-based learning: John Dewey in theory, history, and practice. In P. Blessinger & J. M. Carfora (Eds.), *InquiryBased Learning for Multidisciplinary Programs: A Conceptual and Practical Resource for Educators* (pp. 43–62). Emerald Group Publishing Limited., doi:10.1108/S2055-364120150000003016

Jones, D. E. (2015). The life arts project: Application of an inquiry-based learning model for adult learners. In P. Blessinger & J. M. Carfora (Eds.), *Inquiry-Based Learning for Multidisciplinary Programs: A Conceptual and Practical Resource for Educators* (pp. 275–288). Emerald Group Publishing Limited., doi:10.1108/S2055-364120150000003031

Laininen, E. (2019). Transforming our worldview towards a sustainable future. In J. W. Cook (Ed.), *Sustainability, human well-being, and the future of education* (pp. 161–200). Palgrave Macmillan., doi:10.1007/978-3-319-78580-6_5

Lundvall, B. Å., Rasmussen, P., & Lorenz, E. (2008). Education in the Learning Economy: A European Perspective. *Policy Futures in Education*, *6*(6), 681–700. doi:10.2304/pfie.2008.6.6.681

Modi, N. (2019). *Aboout NFSU*. National Forensic Sciences University. https://www.nfsu.ac.in/about

Pais, A., & Costa, M. (2020). An ideology critique of global citizenship education. *Critical Studies in Education*, *61*(1), 1–16. doi:10.1080/17508487.2017.1318772

Schleicher, A. (2018). Insights and Interpretations. *PICA*. https://www.oecd.org/pisa/PISA%202018%20Insights%20and%20Interpretations%20FINAL%20PDF.pdf

Scott, D. (2014). Knowledge and the curriculum. *Curriculum Journal, 25*(1), 14–28. doi:10.1080/095 85176.2013.876367

Sterling, S. (2014). Separate tracks or real synergy? Achieving a closer relationship between education and SD, post-2015. *Journal of Education for Sustainable Development, 8*(2), 89–112. doi:10.1177/0973408214548360

Sterling, S. (2017). Assuming the future: Repurposing education in a volatile age. In B. Jickling & S. Sterling (Eds.), *Post-Sustainability and Environmental Education* (pp. 31–45). Palgrave Macmillan., doi:10.1007/978-3-319-51322-5_3

Sterling, S. (2019). Planetary primacy and the necessity of positive dis-illusion. *Sustainability, 12*(2), 60–66. doi:10.1089us.2019.29157

Tyler, R. (1949). Curriculum Development: The Tyler Model. *Educational Research Techniques.* https:// educationalresearchtechniques.com/2014/07/01/curriculum-development-the-tyler-model/

UN. (2015). *Sustainable Development Goals knowledge platform.* UN. https://www.un.org/sustainabledevelopment/sustainable-develo pment-goals/

UNESCO – United Nations Educational, Scientific and Cultural Organization. (2019). *A stepping stone towards monitoring progress towards measuring progress towards SDG 4.7.* UNESCO. https://en.unesco.org/news/stepping-stone-towards-measuring-progresstowards-sdg-47

Wals, A. (2016). Does the GEM 2016 report signify a change from the dominant neo-liberal agenda that sees education as an extension and a driver of the globalizing economy and its push for infinite growth, innovation and expansion? *Learning for sustainability in times of accelerating change.* https://transformativelearning.nl/2016/09/14/does-the-gem-20 16-report-signify-achange-from-the-dominant-neo-libeal-agenda-that-sees-education-as-an-extension-and-a-driver-of-the-globalizing-economy-and-the-its-push-for-infinite-growth-innovat/

Chapter 10
Factors for Customer Satisfaction for OTT Subscription Using Service Quality Framework:
Impact of Quality of Content and Monetary Value on Customer Satisfaction and Willingness to Pay

Ritika Sharma
KIIT University, India

Pallabi Mishra
Utkal University, India

ABSTRACT

Over the last few years, the digital technologies have grown at a rapid pace and have become a part of the daily lives of billions of people across the world. The advancements in the field of telecommunications and the availability of devices with enhanced capabilities have a major role to play in this growth. Numerous studies have also addressed and explained about this emerging trend in the entertainment and media industry in many parts of the world. Over-the-top services, commonly known as OTT, are delivered directly through a stable internet connection. Consumers are spending more time on the internet than ever before. The internet has become an essential part of their lives, and so is the usage of OTT. There has been a shift in the habits of consumers, particularly young consumers, between the age group of 16-34 years. For OTT players to continue and succeed further, a combination of ad-based models and subscription-based models seem viable. Here the authors have tried to understand the major factors responsible for the adoption OTT services among Indian consumers.

DOI: 10.4018/978-1-6684-5853-2.ch010

INTRODUCTION

Over the last few years, the internet and the subsequent digital technologies have grown at a rapid pace and have become a part of the daily lives of billions of people across the world. The advancements in the field of telecommunications and the availability of devices with enhanced capabilities have a major role to play in this growth. Numerous studies have also addressed and explained about this emerging trend in the entertainment and media industry in many parts of the world. Over-the-top services, commonly known as OTT, are delivered directly through a stable internet connection. As per reports, India's internet penetration rate is at 47% of the total population. This is mainly because of the affordable data plans and smartphones availability. It has contributed immensely in the consumption of video content offered by OTT platforms. As per the definition provided by U.S. Federal Communications Commission (FCC, 2013), "an OTT is defined as an online video distributor that delivers video programming content to consumers over the Internet". Companies like Netflix, Amazon Prime, Hotstar, and many others have revolutionized the way digital entertainment is consumed by Indian audience. An important contributing factor to their popularity in India is the locally oriented content, customizable subscription plans and the widespread use of 4G internet speed. There are increased expectations from consumer for personalized content along with convenience to access anytime and anywhere. This shift from conventional media services to streaming media services is further accentuated, especially during the lockdown period when people were at home due to COVID – 19 pandemic. Consumers are spending more time on internet than ever before. The internet has become an essential part of their lives, and so is the usage of OTT. There has been a shift in the habits of consumers, particularly young consumers, between the age group of 16-34 years. They are now consuming more of at-home media, be it the traditional Television, online games or the use of OTT for entertainment or educational purposes. Because of COVID induced work from home culture, marketers witnessed a decrease in demand for consumer goods, which in turn caused a significant reduction in advertisement spending by the companies. For OTT players to continue and succeed further, a combination of ad-based models and subscription based models seem viable.

This increase in usage of OTT services is very encouraging for the new service providers in the market to launch their platforms. Also, many foreign OTT players (like Hulu and HBO max) are also looking to launch their services in India, looking at the favourable trend. There is an increasing demand for such services in India. Now, the bigger challenge for OTT service providers is to attract as well to retain their subscriber base and to understand the reasons behind the consumer preferences and to formulate effective ways in order to make it easy and convenient for consumers to adopt this format and to consume the content in an effective way. This research paper is a novel approach where the authors have tried to understand the consumption patterns and the major factors responsible to adopt OTT services among Indian consumers. It explores the relationship between the factors mainly quality of content, monetary value and customer satisfaction which lead a customer to intend to pay or subscribe for these services. This research uses a quantitative approach with respondents who are currently using any OTT services and also former users who have used one or more services provided by the OTT platforms in India. The OTT service providers need to match the delivery standards based on these parameters to ensure continuous revenues from the customers. It is also examined in this paper whether different factors such as gender, education & age affect the customer satisfaction and the intention to pay for OTT subscription. The data has been collected through primary research. This study helps to understand the primary factors to enhance customer satisfaction towards preferring an OTT subscription service. This study expands on the existing research on OTT subscription by investigating the effect of consumer satisfaction and engagement on the purchase intention of consumers in the context of India. The findings contributed in this paper have practical managerial implications for application and further research into OTT. The findings suggested that the quality of content and monetary value is significantly related to consumer subscription intention. A user's search process for watching videos in OTT platforms can be compared to a similar process that a shopper goes through while he/she searches for an appropriate material in the context of e-commerce. Generally, an online shopper would identify the need himself/herself for purchasing a particular item. Then they go for information search for the product, and after considering multiple factors, they end up purchasing. The OTT service subscribers also go through a similar process of deriving information to find the video content as per their suitability, that should fulfil their taste and preferences. Therefore, marketers seeking to enhance the satisfaction of their consumers and to better engage with them are suggested to foster a culture of Intention to use the OTT services reinforced through better quality of content and a better monetary value extracted from the subscription price offered to ensure continuous consumer participation in value chain activities. The authors have also covered some of the managerial implications, limitations, and scope of future research in this study. Future studies in this domain should consider implementing a qualitative approach, namely in-depth interviews to gain a better understanding of consumer insights and experiences which might influence their purchase intentions. Additionally, the influence of other factors of self- concept and lifestyle such as identity salience and social value can be added for further literature review. Keeping all the factors in mind, there is an underlying need to explore the long term impact of change in viewership pattern in the future and the newer strategies to be adopted for the businesses to adjust to the changes. With the world slowly emerging out of the impact caused by the pandemic, the implications derived from this study would present immense opportunities for the OTT services so that they can capitalize on the trends and the perceived change in consumer behaviour to the best of their advantage.

The outbreak of Covid-19 has affected the behaviour of humans and businesses alike. The preventive measures and the restrictions imposed by the governments around the world during Pandemic has impacted many industries, including the entertainment industry. (Mohammed et al., 2021; Bagchi et al., 2020; Ozili and Arun, 2020). The producers in the entertainment businesses halted the production. There was a shortage of labour and cash flows were disrupted during the pandemic times. Consumers started finding entertainment options from home, which led to the rise of over the top (OTT) media services, in addition to the presence of television and online games, particularly in the age group of 16-34 years. (Menon, 2020). Watching content on OTT gathered more popularity as compared to other entertainment options mainly due to its quality of content, price affordability, and also convenience and accessibility. (Dutta and Sardar, 2021; Madnani et al., 2020). Most OTT platforms work on a subscription-based model. This helps them in maintaining resilience and to maintain steady cash flows. The preference and usage for OTT services by the consumers has continued post pandemic also. It has been discussed by some authors (Sheth, 2020) that the pandemic has led to formation of new habits in the consumers over a period of time, which in turn will increase their willingness to pay for subscription for these services. Recent studies have reported that Indian OTT consumers will become habitual and willing to continue with OTT subscriptions after the pandemic appears high (Devaki and Babu, 2021; Gupta and Singharia, 2021). Consumers preferences and behaviours are ever evolving. Therefore, it becomes imperative to study the long-term impact of this phenomenon in viewership by consumer as well as for businesses to adjust their strategies accordingly. Considering its nature and the spread of COVID -19, it becomes important to understand whether the strategies adopted by the OTT players are sustainable or not.

Growth of over the top platforms in India

The digital entertainment industry thrives on internet which makes the need for a set top box irrelevant. The unique feature of OTT services is that the customers can watch content anytime, anywhere, and on any device (Moyler & Hooper, 2009). Consumers are looking for good content for entertainment and as well as educational purposes. As per the latest reports, Indian viewers watch television for 3 hour 44 minutes every day, on an average. Television watching is considered more of a community experience and a ritual as most of the households in India are single TV households. Segmenting the users according based on their viewing choices and designing programs accordingly has always been a daunting task for TV broadcasters. With the increasing trend of exclusive watching and cheaper data/handsets at the customer's perusal, the switching rates of viewers have increased (Kim, 2012). Also, the overall time spent on media consumption is even more. Many scholars have also investigated the user motivations for adopting OTT services. (e.g. Lim & Lee,2013).

As per Neilsen's Indian Readership Survey 2019, 75% of households have a color Television whereas 91% have mobile phone. It is interesting to note that while there is one Television in a household on an average, mobile phones are often more than one in a single household. Each member of the family has their own phone (smartphone in 50% of the cases). Also, almost 60% of the internet users in India are young people, followed by housewives and elder people. Out of all mediums used to access internet, smartphone is the primary medium (as per BCG Consumer Insight survey). This phenomenon is leading to increased demand for a single person viewing experience and has opened many new avenues for content providers to curate specific content keeping in mind the demography of a single individual accordingly.

There is an emergence of an umbrella model widely known as "TV Everywhere (TVE)". In this model, the aggregation of television programming is provided by a cable operator or MVPD at no cost to the consumer. The only authentication required here is that the online user needs to be an MVPD subscriber also. Also, viewers are segmented basis the content that the program provides. Headen et al. (1979), Rust & Alpert (1984) have mentioned about ten program types in their research. These are serial drama, action drama, psychological drama, game show, talk or variety, movies, news, comedy, sports, and other.

Over the Top, also called OTT refers to streaming services delivered directly for consumer's usage, over the internet. There are no intermediaries such as distributors, cable operators or broadcasting companies between the consumer and the service provider. The content provided by OTT platforms can be accessed by any device, at any time. (Shin et al., 2016). OTT is one of the fastest growing sectors in India with 26% growth in 2020 and a CAGR of 32% for 2016-20 in the media and entertainment industry (KPMG in India's Media and Entertainment Report, 2020). A report in Business Standard estimates that the OTT market in India would reach $7 billion by 2027. India recorded 97 million OTT subscribers, by the end of March this year. The standard business models for OTT players are: a la carte rentals and purchases, video-on-demand (VOD) (e.g. iTunes), subscriptions: advertiser supported (e.g. Hulu) or authentication dependent (e.g. Netflix) and offline/online bundled content. A detailed description of revenue models of OTT players is as follows:

1. **SVOD** – It means Subscription Video on Demand. In this model, the OTT applications earn through the subscription money that is paid by the users to view the content. The subscription value changes from platform to platform. This model is adopted by online streaming giants like Netflix, Amazon Prime, and Sony Liv.

2. **AVOD** –It means Advertising Video on Demand. This model allows the subscribers or users to view the content for free. These platforms earn through the Ad revenue model, where they charge brands and companies for posting ads on their platform. This model is adopted by Youtube, Voot & MX Player.

3. **Hybrid** – This model is a combination of both SVOD and AVOD. In this model, the OTT platform offers both free and paid subscriptions to its users and generates revenue through both models. This pattern is followed by service providers like Hotstar plus, and Zee5.

4. **TVOD** – It means Transaction Video on demand. This model comprises two steaming options that can be chosen by the subscriber as per their needs. This kind of revenue model is followed by Sky Box Office, Apple's iTunes, and Amazon Video Store.

In order to understand all the revenue streams better, here is a compilation of revenue streams of major OTT service providers and their subscription cost.

Table 1.

S.No.	OTT Platform	Revenue streams	Subscription cost
1	Netflix	SVoD	Rs 199 – Rs 799 per month
2	Amazon Prime	SVoD, TVOD and Hybrid	Rs 999 per year
3	Hotstar	Hybrid	Rs 199 per month – Rs 999 per annum
4	Voot	AVoD	Rs 299 per year
5	Youtube	Majorly AVoD	Rs 199 per month, Rs 399 for 3 months
6	Eros Now	Majorly AVoD	Rs 99 per month, Rs 399 per year
7	ZEE5	Majorly AVoD	Rs 499 per year
8	ALTBalaji	SVoD	Rs 43 per month, Rs 300 per year
9	SonyLiv	AVoD & SVoD	Rs 299 per month, Rs 999 per year

The subscription based models have historically been a successful and a popular model. A subscribed user tends to become a loyal customer and it increases the chances for continuation to pay for the service. Thus, the businesses which are subscription based have a higher probability of generating increased revenues and capitalize on the compounding value of customer relationships (Campbell, 2020). This model enables companies to collect relevant customer data, understand their needs and wants better and provide them the services in the form of content and price in a customized manner. (Warrillow, 2016). The automatic repeat customers form a critical resilience element of the subscription model, mainly when customers are fickle, the market environment changes, competition is cut-throat or during a crisis like the COVID-19 pandemic (Warrillow, 2016).

Situational Factors and Consumer Behaviour

Situational factors are external factors which have an influence on the consumer behaviour. It originates from situationism theory in psychology which states that the one can witness the change in consumer behaviour, based on the situational factors rather than the personal or intrinsic traits of the consumer. The extent of influence of situational factors on the consumer's buying behaviour is beyond the control of the marketer. (Upton, 2009). Situational factors include product environment such as music, light, sound and aroma in a physical store setup, social aspects of shopping (decision making roles in family), the purpose of shopping (e.g. anniversary), state of mind of the consumer and place and timing of purchase. Some situational factors are more permanent whereas some others are more transitory. In marketing research, most of the situational factors being investigated are transient in nature. The impact of these factors is short lived with low predictability and control of marketers. It also affects the marketing communication and the stages of buying decision. The magnitude of their impact/length of effect is short-lived, predictability of its impact on behaviour is low, control by marketers is very difficult, and it affects communication and stages of buying decision (Hand et al., 2009). COVID-19 can be considered a situational phenomenon which has played an important role in increased consumption of digital entertainment through OTT platforms. However, the consumers' usage of OTT content continues over time. Now the onus is upon the service providers to keep the interest of the consumers growing. Although the situational theories indicate that they have an established role in consumer behaviour, however, there is still not enough literature paying attention to the long-term impact on consumer behaviour in the context of enduring situations like COVID-19.

LITERATURE REVIEW

Over-the-top (OTT) industry is still considered to be a growing industry. There are multiple definitions of OTT being used in academic literature as well as among experts. As per ITU, 2019, OTT platforms are those services which compete with traditional Pay-TV providers as an alternate and conveniently available internet content delivery mechanism for TV programming. Most of the definitions do not include other streaming services like music, games, or VoIP. Hence the players like Spotify, Gaana etc are not considered as OTT channels as per the current literature available.

Impact on Consumer Behavior

Indian market is both price sensitive as well as value sensitive. Netflix started with providing international content and targeted urban population, hence it kept its subscription charges higher as compared to other players. This helped them gained popularity initially with exclusive shows like Narcos, The Queen's Gambit, Stranger Things, Game of Thrones, and House of Cards. However, their subscriber base started declining after a certain period of time. OTT service providers such as Zee5 and SonyLiv became popular at this phase because of the regional content catering mainly to Tier 2 and Tier 3 cities. Affordability was also one of the reasons for consumers' preferring these services instead of Netflix. This also leads to cord cutting behaviour by the consumers. (Fuduri´c et al., 2018).

Factors Driving the Adoption of OTT Streaming Services

Digitization has impacted every industry, not just the entertainment industry. The fact that the digital media is accessible on all devices at all times makes it even more preferred choice. There are multiple factors that that lead a consumer to opt for OTT streaming services, the two most important ones being price and content. We shall discuss about both the factors here.

Price

The price plans for most of the OTT players are flexible and slab wise. Some streaming services are totally free, some services offer some content as free and rest chargeable. Some other OTT players need a consumer to subscribe (monthly or annually) before being able to watch any content. For Indian audience, price plays an important role in adoption rates and engagement levels with the OTT services. (Bhullar and Chaudhary, 2020). The price dynamics in mature markets such as US, Canada, and the UK is different than in India. Consumers have choice to watch only that much content as they desire, and they pay only for what they watch. This is also referred to cord cutting behaviour by consumers. Some OTT service providers like Hotstar also provide sample content for free, which helps a consumer to make subscription decision. Consumers also have a choice to add or cancel the services keeping the best value for their time and money (Gupta and Singharia, 2021). An economical subscription plan encourages customers to opt for OTT services even if they don't watch 100% of the content being offered. Another factor which works in OTT's favour is that the content is streamed on the internet and there is no added installation cost such as set top boxes etc. Heavy smartphone penetration with cheap internet charges adds up to the effect. Although theory suggests that a subscribed customer generates consistent income for the company, however, there still exists a fear of subscription cancellation amongst OTT players. This might be because of various reasons such as subscription fatigue, repetitive content, price increases, availability of pirated content etc.

Content

There are so many entertainment options in front of the consumer in today's times. The phrase "content is king" coined by Bill Gates in an iconic speech way back in 1996 becomes totally relevant here. He said "Content is where I expect much of the real money will be made on the internet, just as it was in broadcasting". The times have become more interesting with enormous amount of content available to the audience to choose from. The viewers as well as the content providers have evolved in their choice of preferences. The nature of the content and the means through which it gets delivered has also witnessed a dramatic shift. The most exclusive and the most engaging content provider will be the one with the top preference of the viewer. Since the majority of the earlier posted content on the OTT platforms is in English, the viewers who know English have already accepted and are active users of OTT. However, the next step for these OTT platforms is to capture the rural audience which constitutes to about 60% of the Indian population. The content offered in English language to such audience has a low probability of garnering more subscriber base. Hence, the demand for content in regional languages has increased. The availability of handsets at a much cheaper cost and also the internet plans being affordable has played an important role in increasing the demand for regional content. The regional language speaking user base in India has grown at a CAGR of 41% in a five-year time span between 2011 and 2016. Now this user base has reached 234 million. It is also expected to grow at a CAGR of 18% to reach 536 million by 2021 versus English speaking user base which is expected to grow at only 3% CAGR so that it reaches upto 199 million by 2021. According to some other industry reports, by the end of the year 2021, the regional language speaking user base will account for 75% of the total internet users in the country. The OTT provider firms have understood this behavior of consumers. Although most OTT platforms have now started offering good content in Hindi, which is considered to be India's unofficial official language, some platforms like Voot, ALTBalaji and Koimoi have content offered in many other regional languages such as Kannada, Marathi, Tamil, Bangla and Gujarati also.

The content offered by any entertainment provider is the major deciding factor to choose a particular service over another by a consumer. Streaming services with their sophisticated search algorithms have become more popular as they provide customized suggestions to each subscriber based on their interests. They have a large repository of new, interesting and original content to choose from that the consumers would not find anywhere else. The rise in popularity of social media apps also has led to the preference of video content across all platforms. Interactive shows like Ranveer Vs Wild with Bear Grylls enable users to decide the course of the show which increases the engagement levels and hence customer satisfaction. There is more probability for such consumer to continue their subscription plan. The landscape of entertainment has become more dynamic with the advent of digital media. There are specific preferences developed by consumer for different platforms based on the content that they offer. Previous research has identified seven content formats or genres, namely comedy shows, dramas, reality shows, news, documentaries, educational content, and entertainment magazine formats. (Cha, 2013). Even further research shall be required to understand other facets of content as well which would have an impact on customer satisfaction as well as adoption. Traditional TV channels do not offer the freedom to the customer to choose the time and the type of the content to be watched. The consumer has to search through channels to identify and watch their preferred show and sometimes wait for the show to start. Watching content on OTT gives that advantage that the content is available at all times with an interactive interface. (Kim, 2018). Consumers are inclined to prefer OTT streaming services when they can view a wide range of content. The impact of Covid-19 can be seen first with the increase in subscriber base. This can be attributed to the consumers looking for entertainment options from home. After some time, there was a decrease in new content, mainly because the productions were stalled because of Covid outbreak, making it difficult for the OTT platforms to keep the consumers continually engaged. A study done in Taiwan (Chen, 2019) suggested that sports programs are positively correlated with customer satisfaction whereas movies or dramas did not show a strong correlation. The results for a different sample size or a different demography may be different from the results mentioned here.

Barriers for OTT Video Consumption

No doubt OTT is a new technology which has gained acceptance and popularity very quickly. However, whenever a big change happens in any industry, there are bound to be both positive and negative repercussions. Previously, there have been researches where independent influence of each barrier to new technology has been discussed. (Ram, 1987; Mani & Chouk, 2017; Laukkanen, 2016; Heidenreich and Handrich, 2015). Ram and Sheth's model (1989) have been considered by most of the researches in this area. According to the authors, the barriers can be classified in two major types, practical barriers, and risk and psychological barriers. Practical barriers include value and use whereas risk barriers and psychological barriers include image and tradition. For the youth in India who are yet not earning and who constitute the primary consumer base for OTT content, there is a growing trend of accessing freely available and downloadable pirated content. This practice acts as a barrier for subscription to OTT streaming services. Also, the phenomenon of shared passwords is also very common among Indian youth which leads to lesser revenue generation for these OTT players. The reasons for the supply of such pirated content can be many other factors, other than making money. (Thomson et al, 2017). Many users rely on the downloadable pirated content, often ignoring the attached privacy issues. Since there is a lot of exclusive content which would not be accessible on any other platform and there is a need to subscribe to be able to view or watch the exclusive content, many viewers tend to incline towards watching content in a pirated form (Agrawal, 2019). Another factor for resorting to pirated content could be affordability (Subscription plans being too high) and inflexibility in the price offerings (Lu et al., 2021).

RESEARCH GAP

Most of the research done on OTT subscription intentions of the consumer have been done in other countries and very few have been conducted in Indian context. Also, with the increase in demand of regional content on the rise and research focussing on the impact of regional content as a major quality parameter for OTT service providers becomes all the more important. The existing research has largely focused on the factors that affect their level of satisfaction with the OTT services. However, there has been no significant research which has gone beyond the understanding of "subscription intention" by examining the specific impact of the two most important factors, namely quality of content and monetary value with respect to customer satisfaction which leads to willingness to pay or subscribe.

THEORETICAL FRAMEWORK

Customer satisfaction is defined as a measure to understand the process of meeting a consumers' expectations of a product or a service, as per the Management Guide. Customer satisfaction is considered to be a high return-low risk economic asset to any company. In order to measure service quality by comparing user expectations, perceptions and satisfaction levels, we user SERVQUAL as a popular framework. Based on this framework, there are various frameworks developed by authors. There are specific frameworks being developed in specific electronic fields. In this study also, the authors have applied SERVQUAL framework to enhance the relationship between the components in the digital entertainment industry. An emerging framework, ESSQUAL is now widely used to assess electronic subscription service quality. It has majorly three components, quality of content, quality of accessibility, and quality of experience. However, this framework has its limitations in the terms of only assessing internally from the service provider's perspective and it does not take into account other factors such as user perceived factors that can affect customer satisfaction. In this study, the authors have combined ESSQUAL framework with perceived values of monetary value, which is an important determinant in making a decision to subscribe by a user. When a user is willing to pay a sum of money to purchase a product or a service, that phenomenon is called willingness to pay. (J. Ström and K. B. Martinez, 2013). Knowing the willingness to pay is very important for companies, so that they can determine their offered price. Price is directly related to the demand for a product or a service. This study will analyse whether a combination of ESSQUAL and a perceived value of monetary value can affect willingness to pay for a consumer.

CONCEPTUAL FRAMEWORK

With the support of existing literature, we have taken a conceptual model which indicates that quality of content and monetary value impact customer satisfaction, which in turn affects the willingness to pay or subscribe for OTT services. Here the dependent variables are customer satisfaction and the willingness to pay and the predictors or the independent variables are quality of content and the monetary value. This model has been tested and the results are shown in analysis part. Data has been collected through primary research.

Figure 1.

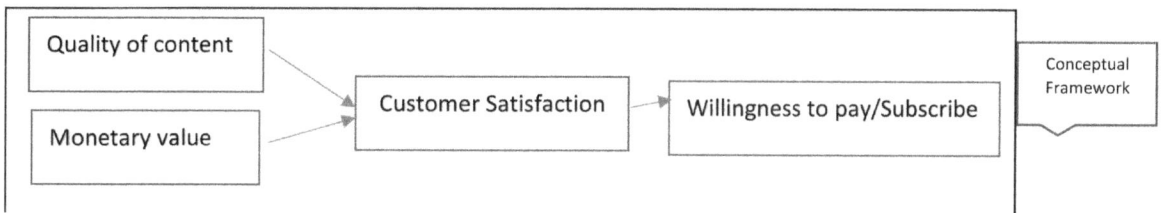

RESEARCH OBJECTIVES AND METHODOLOGY

We have narrowed down to the two critical factors that impact customer satisfaction, namely quality of content and monetary value. Quality of content comprises of the attributes like the quantity of content, the exclusiveness, the frequency of updating the content as per the likeliness and preference of the viewers. The Monetary value includes value of money with respect to the content shown and the duration of the subscription and flexibility in subscription fee plans.

Research Objectives

Based on the factors identified above as well as the gaps identified from the literature review, the research objectives were formulated as below:

1. To examine the perception towards OTT subscription intention factors such as quality of content and monetary value.
2. To explore the relationship of these factors with customer satisfaction and willingness to pay.
3. To identify the major factors influencing customer's willingness to pay for OTT services.

Research Hypotheses

We have formed the following hypotheses for this study:

1. H1: Quality of content has an impact on customer satisfaction.
2. H2: Monetary value has an impact on customer satisfaction.
3. H3: Customer satisfaction has an impact on willingness to pay.

Based on the above formulated hypotheses, a questionnaire was framed, and the data has been collected through primary research. Further analysis was done on the primary data collected.

Research Methodology

The data has been collected through convenience sampling method. An online questionnaire was circulated among the prospective users of OTT services. Simultaneously, some data was collected physically as well. The survey was conducted over a period of 6 months.

The total number of responses collected for this research is 230. Further data collection will enhance the validity and reliability of the instruments used in the research. Once the data was collected and screened, a structured analysis of data was conducted using SPSS software with primary data. The data analysis tools such as descriptive statistics, graphs, charts, bi-variate analysis and regression analysis have been conducted.

DATA ANALYSIS

The data for this research was collected using a structured questionnaire. Post data collection, a proper compilation and sorting was done so as to ensure smooth and meaningful comparison, computation and analysis. The primary data was coded with the help of Microsoft Excel and further transported to SPSS software for a proper statistical analysis.

The first part of primary data analysis comprised of interpretation of various demographic variables. After that, certain basic aspects of OTT viewership were explored such as usage of OTT services, average monthly spent, the duration of viewing and the time of association with the service provider.

A multiple regression was conducted for multi-variate analysis. The results helped the authors to have a thorough understanding of various factors responsible for customer satisfaction and willingness to pay for an OTT service.

In conjunction with the sequence of questions in the questionnaire, some basic variables are depicted in the form of appropriate diagrams and charts followed by a brief narration for each variable.

Figure 2.

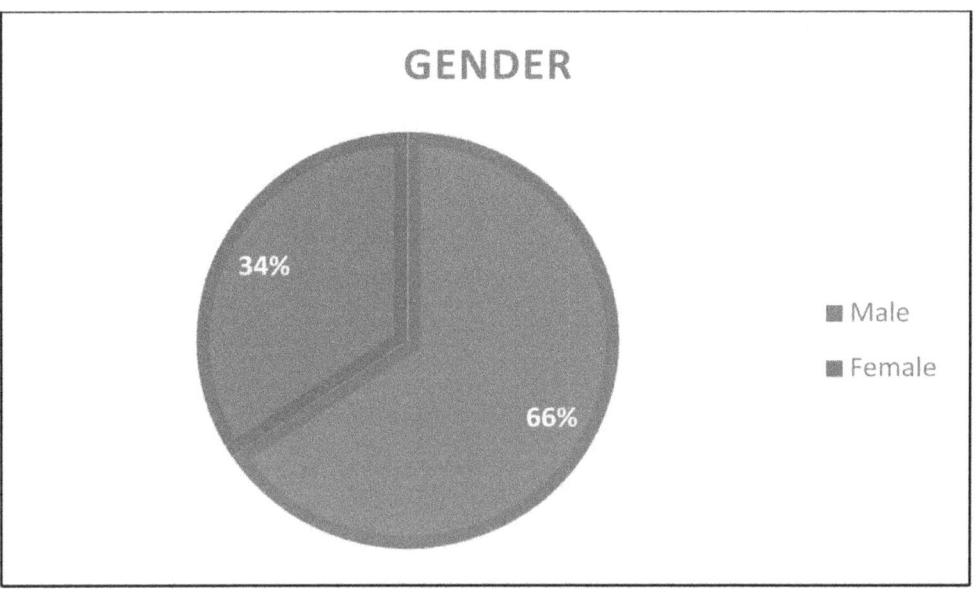

Figure 3.

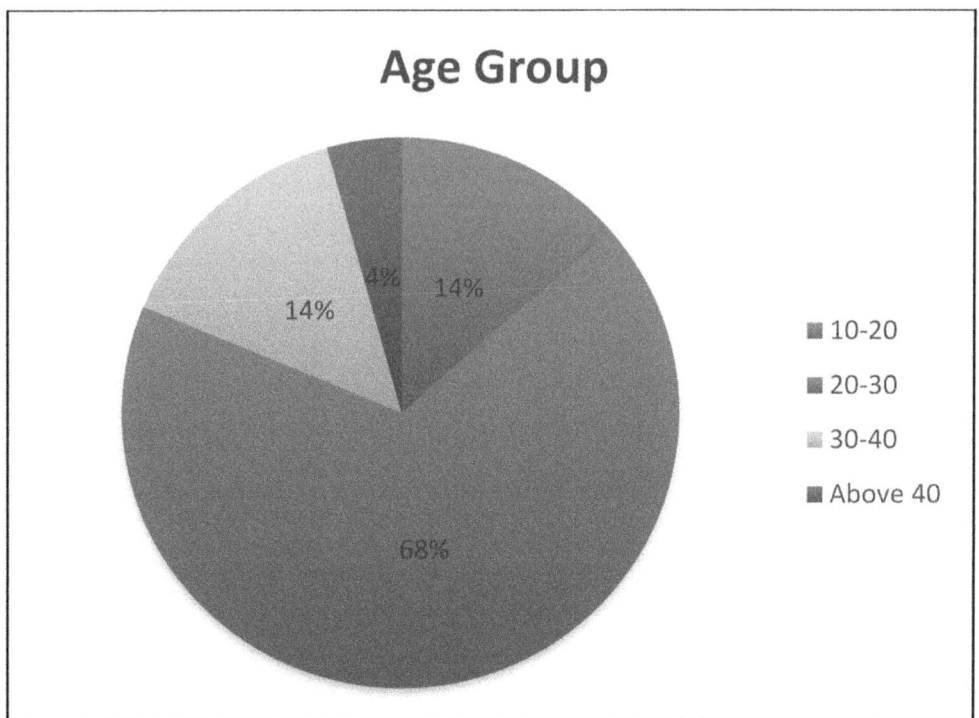

In the questionnaire, the respondents were given an option of choosing their gender, wither male, female, or others. This was done in order to enable them to be free and without bias in their responses. As can be seen in Figure 1, 66% of the respondents are male and 34% of the respondents are female.

As can also be seen in Figure 2, 68% of the respondents are in the age group of 20-30 years, both 10-20 years age bracket and 30-40 years age bracket have 14% of the respondents. 4% of the respondents are from the age group of Above 40 years. This gives us representation from young, middle aged as well as a little aged group of respondents for this research.

Figure 4.

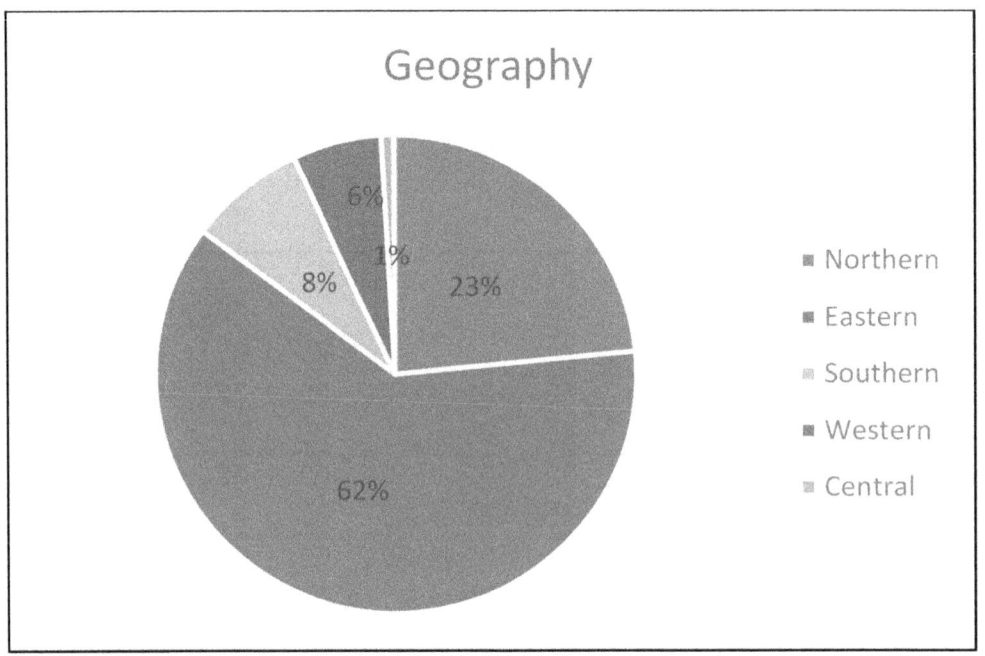

Figure 5.

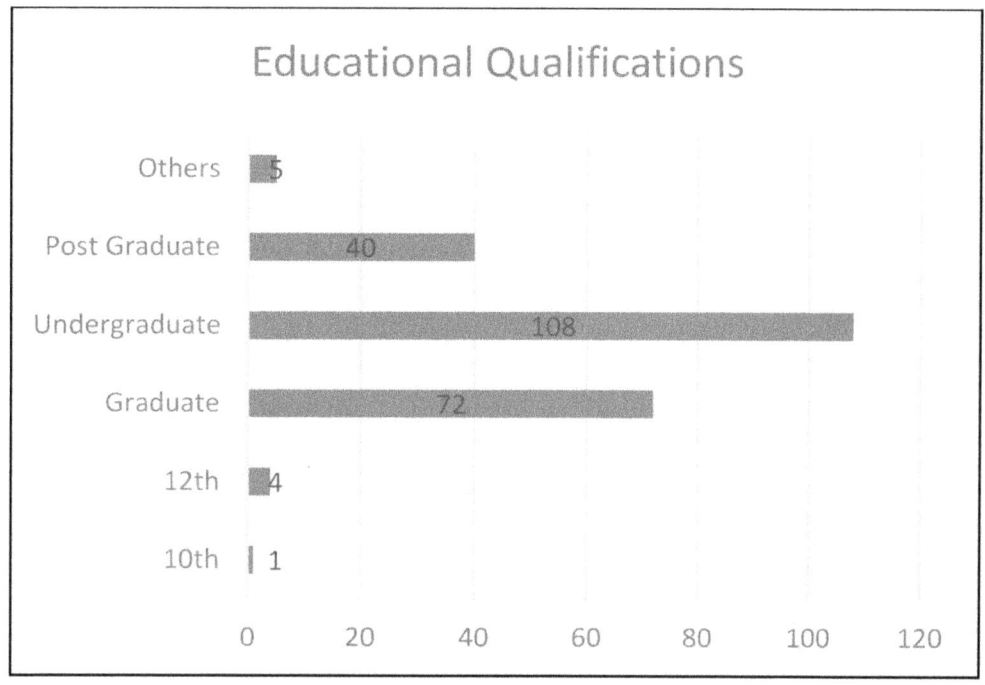

In our questionnaire, the respondents had to choose the region where they are currently residing in India. This will help us to know the role of region in understanding the difference in perception arising due to geographical differences regarding the subscription price and content provided by OTT streaming services. The respondents were given 5 options to choose from – Northern, Western, Central, Eastern and Southern. From the figure, it can be deduced that more than half (62%) of the respondents belonged to Eastern India, followed by Northern (23%), Southern (8%), And subsequently Western and Central Region (6% & 1% respectively). Regarding educational qualifications, 47% of the respondents are undergraduate i.e. currently pursuing graduation, followed by Graduate respondents (31%). The number of respondents with post-graduation is 40 i.e. 17%. The intended target viewers here belong to youth and are wither pursuing graduation or have completed graduation. This constitutes maximum viewers for OTT in general. Hence our dataset is representative of the Indian consumers belonging to different regions who are concerned about content and cost as important factors to decide to subscribe for any particular OTT service.

Figure 6.

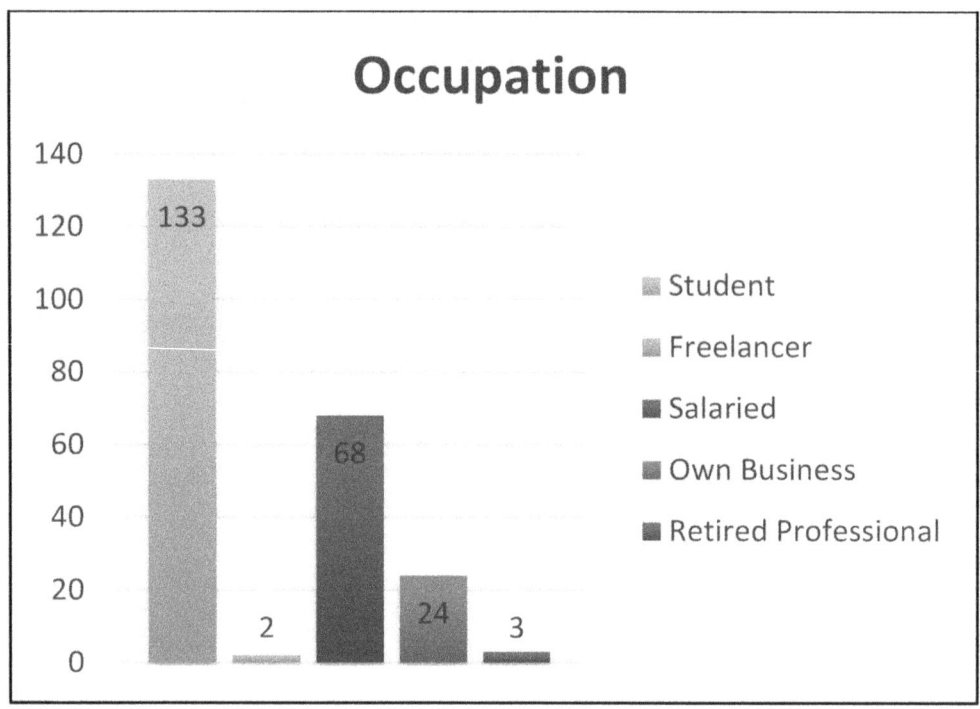

Figure 7.

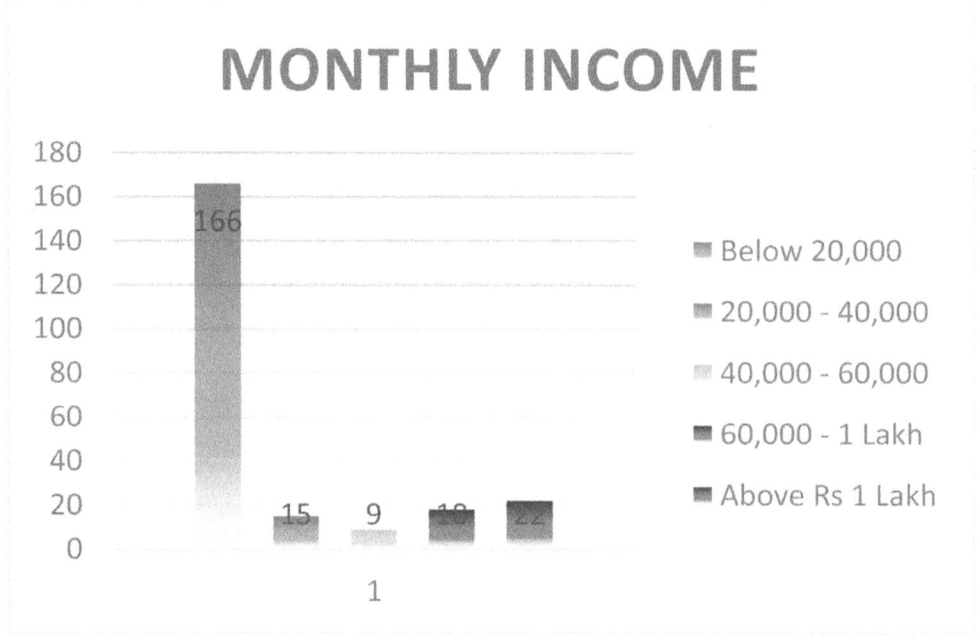

As per Figure 5, 58% of the respondents are students, followed by salaried (30%), Entrepreneurs or own business owners contribute 10% of the respondents. Freelancers and Retired professionals are 1% each.

It can be found in Figure 6 that 72% respondents have selected the option of income below 20,000. It could be inferred that many respondents in this segment may not have started earning yet and would be still pursuing their studies. 10% of the respondents have a monthly income of above Rs 1 Lakh. Respondents earning between 20,000 per month to 1 Lakh per month are 7%, 4% and 8% respectively, based on the income slabs given in the questionnaire.

Figure 8.

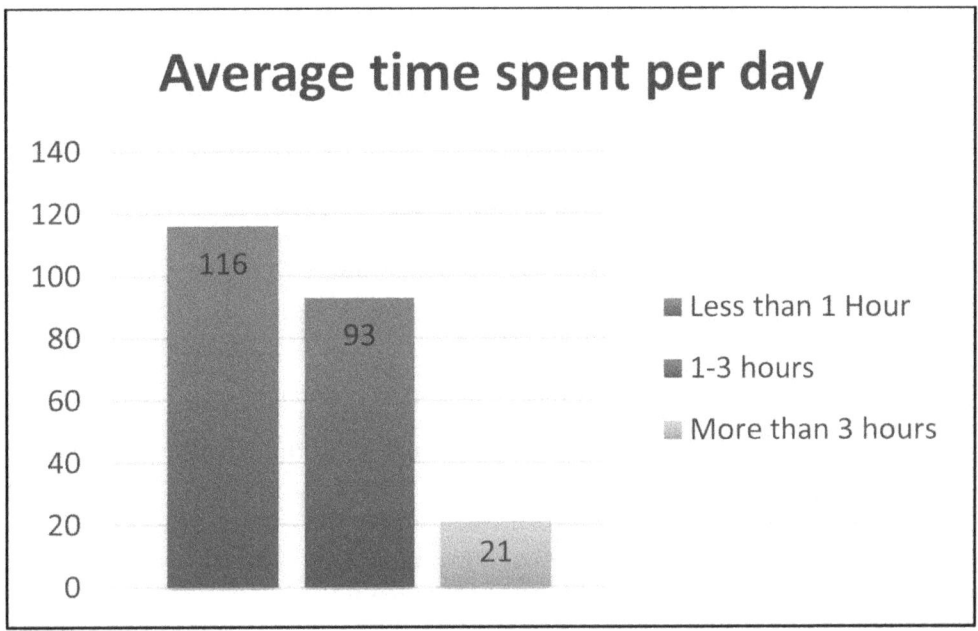

The time spent per day watching OTT differs from person to person. Here, we have taken the average time spent per day per user and presented it in a readable and decipherable manner.

Figure 9.

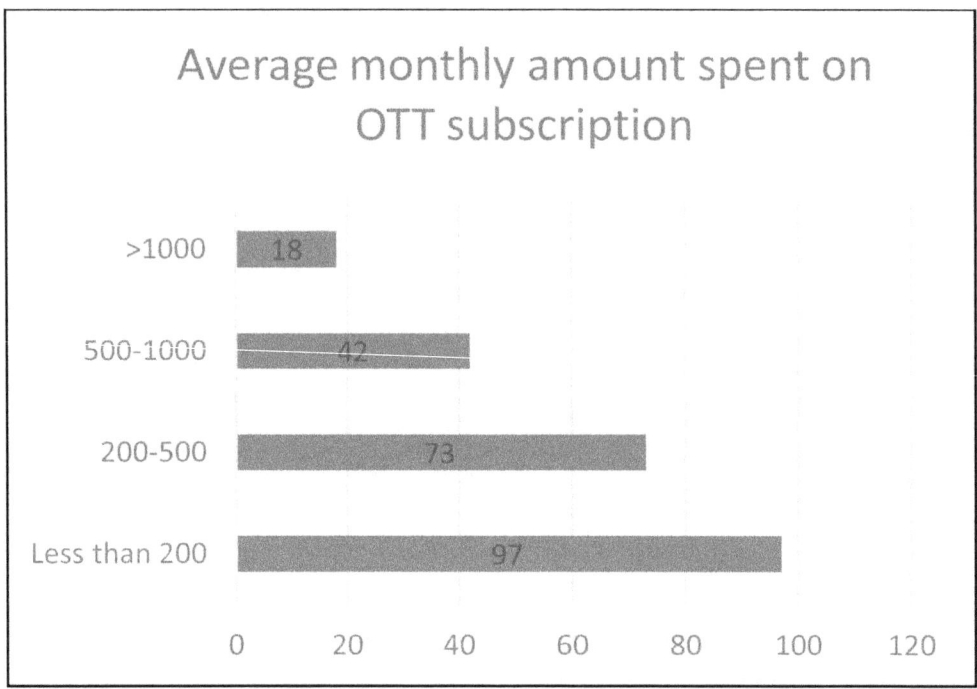

As per Figure 8, out of the 230 respondents, 97 respondents spend less than Rs 200 on an average per month for subscribing to OTT services. 73 respondents spend anywhere between Rs 200 – Rs 500 average monthly for the same. 42 respondents spend between Rs 500 – Rs 1000 as OTT subscription fees per month, and only 18 respondents i.e. 8% spend more than Rs 1000 for subscribing to OTT services. These kind of respondents have generally subscribed to more than 1 OTT service on a monthly basis. Since a majority of respondents are students and are not earning yet, they do not like to spend much for OTT subscription. There is a trend of sharing user credentials and OTT passwords in this age group, therefore we do not see per person spent to be on the higher side.

Hypothesis to be Tested

H1: Quality of content has an impact on customer satisfaction.

Table 2.

Model Summary										
Model	R	R Square	Adjusted R Square	Std. Error of the Estimate	Change Statistics					
					R Square Change	F Change	df1	df2	Sig. F Change	
1	.639ᵃ	.408	.406	.67001	.408	157.390	1	228	.000	
a. Predictors: (Constant), QC										

The influence of independent variable i.e. quality of content comprising of predictors namely quantity of content, exclusivity of content, frequency of updating new content on the OTT platform, and creation of content as per the likeliness of the audience was analysed on the dependent variable i.e. customer satisfaction by using regression analysis with the help of SPSS. The output is presented in the table below:

Output Table: Linear Regression

Table 3.

ANOVAᵃ						
Model		**Sum of Squares**	**df**	**Mean Square**	**F**	**Sig.**
1	Regression	70.654	1	70.654	157.390	.000ᵇ
	Residual	102.351	228	.449		
	Total	173.005	229			
a. Dependent Variable: CS						
b. Predictors: (Constant), QC						

We find after the regression analysis that the values are significant. That means there is significant relationship between the dependent variable and the independent variable. In other words, quality of content does have an impact on customer satisfaction.

H2: Monetary value has an impact on customer satisfaction.

The independent variable "Monetary Value" comprises of predictors namely value for money with respect to the content shown, the duration of the subscription and flexibility in subscription fee offerings. The influence of this independent variable was explored through regression analysis using SPSS. The output is presented in the table below:

Table 4.

Model Summary									
Model	**R**	**R Square**	**Adjusted R Square**	**Std. Error of the Estimate**	**Change Statistics**				
					R Square Change	**F Change**	**df1**	**df2**	**Sig. F Change**
1	.647ᵃ	.419	.416	.66425	.419	164.103	1	228	.000
a. Predictors: (Constant), MV									

Table 5.

	Model	Sum of Squares	df	Mean Square	F	Sig.
	ANOVA[a]					
1	Regression	72.406	1	72.406	164.103	.000[b]
	Residual	100.599	228	.441		
	Total	173.005	229			
a. Dependent Variable: CS						
b. Predictors: (Constant), MV						

The output of the regression shows that it is significant. In other words, there is a significant relationship between monetary value and customer satisfaction. Monetary value thus has an impact on customer satisfaction.

H3: Customer satisfaction has an impact on willingness to pay.

The relationship between the dependent variable i.e. willingness to pay and the dependent variable i.e. customer satisfaction is explored through regression analysis using SPSS. The willingness to pay comprises of predictors namely value for money, continuation of services in general, and in with the increase or decrease in subscription cost and the intention to continue with the service. The customer service variable comprises of enjoyment, satisfaction with the service, meeting the set expectations and complying to the ideal standards of an OTT service.

The output of regression analysis is presented in the following table:

Table 6.

					Change Statistics				
Model	R	R Square	Adjusted R Square	Std. Error of the Estimate	R Square Change	F Change	df1	df2	Sig. F Change
1	.634[a]	.402	.400	.62516	.402	153.367	1	228	.000
a. Predictors: (Constant), CS									

Model Summary

Table 7.

	Model	Sum of Squares	df	Mean Square	F	Sig.
	ANOVA[a]					
1	Regression	59.940	1	59.940	153.367	.000[b]
	Residual	89.108	228	.391		
	Total	149.048	229			
a. Dependent Variable: WTP						
b. Predictors: (Constant), CS						

The relationship has been found to be significant between the dependent variable i.e. willingness to pay and the independent variable i.e. customer satisfaction. So we can say that customer satisfaction does have an impact on willingness to pay for an OTT customer.

FINDINGS AND CONCLUSION

Demographics

- 68% of the OTT viewers are aged between 20-30 years of age. This indicates the popularity and maximum consumption of OTT amongst the youth in India.
- Talking about gender, almost two third (66%) of the respondents are male and 33% are female respondents. This gives an indication that the males have transitioned more and earlier towards the entertainment options provided by OTT, whereas their female counterparts are catching the OTT wave slowly.
- Out of the total participants in this research, around 78% are graduates or are pursuing graduation. This age is heavily influenced by peers. The choice of shows and other content on OTT is largely influenced by their peer group.
- Since most of the respondents are young and are still studying, more than 50% of the respondents are not earning yet and are still dependent. Although they are the consumers for OTT services, but they are not the customers i.e. these respondents would not be able to pay for the services, even if willingness is there. Here another important phenomenon of shared passwords and the increasing rate of piracy needs to be studied. Companies like Netflix are taking measures to stop or mitigate password sharing among multiple users [20].

Preference for OTT Platforms

- Netflix and Amazon Prime are among the most preferred OTT platforms for the almost two third of the respondents. Netflix has gained popularity across the world before entering the Indian market with suitable content. Amazon Prime, with its features like Trivia etc and the repository of Indian cinema makes it a preferred choice for Indian viewers. 22% of the respondents had selected Disney Hotstar as their preferred OTT platform in the survey.
- 42% of the respondents spend less than 200 per month for subscription to OTT services. This again indicates to the phenomenon of shared passwords, mentioned above. Netflix had a subscription fees of about Rs 599 per month earlier, which was not accepted well by the Indian audience. Now the company has reduced it to Rs 199 per month with limited services. This move has helped them increase their subscriber base. Disney Hotstar, on the other hand, offers some content for free, without any charges. Since it is managed by Start TV network, the advantage here is that all the programs on regular channels of Star TV can be streamed anytime through Hotstar. There are some seasonal preferred OTT platforms for the viewers. For example, during IPL season, the

viewership of Hotstar increases. Similarly, during the telecast of Big Boss on Colors Tv, the viewership of Voot also increases for few months.

- 50% of the respondents spend less than 1 hour on OTT during a day, on an average. Since most of the content is not live streamed or time bound, it can be watched on any day. Also, most of the web series available on OTT have the episodes of almost 1-hour duration. Binge watching behaviour has not been captured through the questionnaire.

Findings from Regression Analysis

Through the regression analysis, a strong equation was found between the independent variables, namely "Quality of Content" and the independent variable of "Customer Satisfaction". The independent variable comprised of parameters such as quantity, newness, frequency of update, content creation as per likeliness of audience and exclusivity of the content on the platform. The dependent variable comprised of parameters such as enjoyment, satisfaction, meeting expectations and conforming to ideal standards. (R-square = 41%)

There was also significant relationship found between the dependent variable "Customer Satisfaction" and the independent variable "Monetary Value". The independent variable comprised of parameters like value for money, flexibility in duration and amount of subscription plans. (R-square = 42%).

The dependent variable "Customer Satisfaction" acts as a dependent variable for the first two hypotheses and the independent variable for the third hypothesis. The relationship between customer satisfaction and willingness to Pay has also been found significant in this study. (R-square = 41%).

CONCLUSION

Taking into consideration all the findings that have emerged from this research as well as the existing literature, some conclusions can be drawn with respect to the hypothesis being formulated for the purpose of this research. As elaborated above, the findings of this research indicate a relationship between the selected independent variables i.e. quality of content and the monetary value with the dependent variables customer satisfaction (for the first two hypotheses) and willingness to pay (for the third hypothesis).

There were also a few conclusions drawn from the analysis of demographic variable like income, age, and gender with the preference of OTT platforms and their viewership patterns. It was found that the variables of income, age and gender have an impact on the OTT usage in general and also plays a role in selecting their preferred OTT platform.

We have witnessed a tremendous growth in the digital entertainment industry all across the world over the past few years. The outbreak of Covid-19 has played a major role in accelerating the growth of OTT platforms for all economies. With the help of technology, the OTT service providers are becoming smarter by the day, by providing personalized nad customized content for each viewer. However, the real battle is with respect to provide a good user experience. Since this industry is heavily internet dependent, problems of not streaming the content properly or breakdown and shut down might occur. Companies like Netflix and Spotify are already ahead of the game by providing personalized recommendations for their viewers using sophisticated data analytics algorithms. Seamless transition between devices i.e. Mobile to Laptop or TV and vice versa would also be an important factor for a consumer to take a decision to subscribe for a particular service. With the lockdown now lifted in many counties of the world and in India, people are now looking for out-of-home entertainment options as well. The OTT service providers need to devise effective strategies to retain their subscriber base. A suitable content and price offering combination would be helpful in ensuring substantial revenues for these companies.

Implications and Future Scope

Through its various findings, this research aims to contribute useful insights for academicians, researchers as well as other industry stakeholders. Talking about academic viewpoint, this research may act as a useful tool for ideating on the different aspects of OTT viewers behaviour and also pave the way for further research in this area.

This research can also be of use to business firms who can make use of the findings from this study in order to gain a better understanding of an OTT viewer's behaviour. The OTT service providers ideating on useful recommendations and finding ways to retain their existing user base and who aim at increasing their subscriber base may benefit from the insights of this research. Also, OTT platforms who are yet to launch their services in India, specifically Eastern region may also keep these findings in consideration while designing their strategies. Digital entertainment providers may design their offerings of content and subscription price using these findings. Efficient marketing strategies can also be planned keeping in mind the findings and insights from this research, so as to provide a better viewing experience to the existing as well as new OTT subscriber base.

Moreover, the results of multiple regression analysis may prove as a useful base for marketing organizations and other businesses in order to design more effective online campaigns which can attract more subscribers and can translate into a better online presence. Overall, this research would be added as a useful piece to the existing knowledge base of OTT viewer behaviour while also, at the same time, providing scope for more meaningful research in this direction.

Limitations

- As the entire OTT industry is internet based and has no geographical boundaries, this study, however, has been limited to India, with most of the respondents belonging to the Eastern region. There is definitely a scope for expanding this research to other states across India for much better and balanced insights.
- This study focusses on only two aspects, Quality of Content and Monetary Value, based on Service Quality Framework. However, other factors based on this framework, such as Identity Salience, Social Value, Perceived Enjoyment and Perceived Usefulness can also be explored.

REFERENCES

Agrawal, S. (2019). *Effect of Governance, Piracy, and Investment on OTT Subscription Numbers* [Doctoral dissertation]. The Ohio State University.

Bagchi, B., Chatterjee, S., Ghosh, R., & Dandapat, D. (2020). Impact of COVID-19 on global economy. In *Coronavirus Outbreak and the Great Lockdown. Springer Briefs in Economics.* Springer. doi:10.1007/978-981-15-7782-6_3

Bhullar, A., & Chaudhary, R. (2020). Key factors influencing users' adoption towards OTT media platform: An empirical analysis. *Int. J. Adv. Sci. Technol., 29*(11), 942–956.

Campbell, P. (2020). *Guide to subscription business models for 2019.* Available at: www. priceintelligently.com/subscription-business-model

Cha, J. (2013). Predictors of television and online video platform use: A coexistence model of old and new video platforms. *Telematics and Informatics, 30*(4), 296–310.

Chen, Y. N. K. (2019). Competitions between OTT TV platforms and traditional television in Taiwan: A Niche analysis. *Telecommunications Policy, 43*(9), 1–10. doi:10.1016/j.telpol.2018.10.006

Devaki, R. P. C., & Babu, S. D. (2021). The future of over-the-Top platforms after covid-19 pandemic. *Annals of the Romanian Society for Cell Biology, 25*(6), 11307–11313. doi:10.1177/0972262921989118

Dutta, M., & Sardar, S. (2021). Impact of covid-19 on the rise of OTT platforms in India. In Interdisciplinary Research in Technology and Management. CRC Press. doi:10.1201/9781003202240-99

FCC. (2013). *Annual assessment of the status of competition in the market for the delivery of video programming.* MB Docket No. 12-203. FCC 13-99.

Fuduri'c, M., Malthouse, E. C., & Viswanathan, V. (2018). Keep it, shave it, cut it: A closer look into consumers' video viewing behavior. *Business Horizons, 61*(1), 85–93. doi:10.1016/j.bushor.2017.09.008

Gupta, G. M., & Singharia, K. (2021). Consumption of OTT media streaming in COVID-19 lockdown: Insights from PLS analysis. *Vision. The Journal of Business Perspective, 25*(1), 36–46. doi:10.1177/0972262921989118

Hand, C., Dall'Olmo Riley, F., Harris, P., Singh, J., & Rettie, R. (2009). Online grocery shopping: The influence of situational factors. *European Journal of Marketing, 43*(9/10), 1205–1219. doi:10.1108/03090560910976447

Headen, R. S., Klompmaker, J. E., & Rust, R. T. (1979). The duplication of viewing law and television media schedule evaluation. *JMR, Journal of Marketing Research, 16*(3), 333–340. doi:10.1177/002224377901600305

Heidenreich, S., & Handrich, M. (2015). What about passive innovation resistance? Investigating adoption-related behavior from a resistance perspective. *Journal of Product Innovation Management, 32*(6), 878–903.

ITU. (2019). *OTT and related on-line services in Arab Region.* Retrieved 24 May 2021 from International Telecommunication Union: https://www.itu.int/en/ITU-D/ Regional-Presence/ArabStates/Documents/events/2015/EFF/OTT%20services%20in%20the%20Arab%20Region%2

Kim, J. (2018). A Study on the Displacement of Mobile OTT Video Services on Home TV. *J. Korea Contents Assoc., 18*(8), 434–445. doi:10.5392/JKCA.2018.18.08.434

Laukkanen, T. (2016). Consumer adoption versus rejection decisions in seemingly similar service innovations: The case of the Internet and mobile banking. *Journal of Business Research*, *69*(7), 2432–2439.

Lee, H. W., Oh, H. G., & Choi, M. H. (2012). The formation process of public broadcasting audience's willingness to pay: Analysis through structural equation modeling (SEM). *Korean Journal of Journalism & Communication Studies*, *56*(6), 101–126.

Lim, S., & Lee, Y. J. (2013). N screen service users' motivations for use and dissatisfying factors. *Journal of Korea Contents Association*, *13*(3), 99–108. doi:10.5392/JKCA.2013.13.03.099

Lu, S., Rajavi, K., & Dinner, I. (2021). The effect of over-the-top media services on piracy search: Evidence from a natural experiment. *Marketing Science*, *40*(3), 548–568.

Madnani, D., Fernandes, S., & Madnani, N. (2020). Analysing the impact of COVID-19 on over-the-top media platforms in India. *International Journal of Pervasive Computing and Communications*, *16*(5), 457–475. doi:10.1108/IJPCC-07-2020-0083

Mani, Z., & Chouk, I. (2017). Drivers of consumers' resistance to smart products. *Journal of Marketing Management*, *33*(1-2), 76–97.

Menon, G. (2020). *KPMG India- Media and entertainment post-COVID: The best of times, the worst of times*. Available at: https://home.kpmg/in/en/home/insights/

Mohammed, T., Mustapha, K. B. J., Godsell, Z., Adamu, K. A., Babatunde, D. D., Akintade, A., Acquaye, H., Fujii Ndiaye, M. M., & Yamoah, F. A. (2021). A critical analysis of the impacts of COVID-19 on the global economy and ecosystems and opportunities for circular economy strategies. *Resources, Conservation and Recycling*, *164*, 105169. Advance online publication. doi:10.1016/j.resconrec.2020.105169 PMID:32982059

Moyler, A., & Hooper, M. (2009). *Over the Top TV (OTT TV) Platform Technologies*. BCi Ltd. and Endurance Technology Ltd.

OziliP. K.ArunT. (2020). Spillover of COVID-19: impact on the global economy. doi:10.2139/ssrn.3562570

Ram, S. (1987). *A model of innovation resistance*. ACR North American Advances.

Ram, S., & Sheth, J. N. (1989). Consumer resistance to innovations: The marketing problem and its solutions. *Journal of Consumer Marketing*, *6*(2), 5–14.

Rust, R. T., & Alpert, M. I. (1984). An audience flow model of television viewing choice. *Marketing Science*, *3*(2), 113–124. doi:10.1287/mksc.3.2.113

Sheth, J. (2020). Impact of covid-19 on consumer behaviour: Will the old habits return or die? *Journal of Business Research*, *117*, 280–283. doi:10.1016/j.jbusres.2020.05.059

Shin, J., Park, Y., & Lee, D. (2016). Strategic management of over-the-top services: Focusing on Korean consumer adoption behaviour. *Technological Forecasting and Social Change*, *112*, 329–337. doi:10.1016/j.techfore.2016.08.004

Ström & Martinez. (2013). *The determinants of customer satisfaction, loyalty and willingness to pay in subscription based streaming services*. Stockholm School of Economics.

Thomson, W., Mahanti, A., & Gong, M. (2017, October). Understanding uploader motivations and sharing dynamics in the one-click hosting ecosystem. In *2017 IEEE 42nd Conference on Local Computer Networks (LCN)* (pp. 520-522). IEEE.

Upton, C. L. (2009). Virtue ethics and moral psychology: The situationism debate. *The Journal of Ethics*, *13*(2/3), 103–115. doi:10.100710892-009-9054-2

Warrillow, J. (2016). *The Automatic Customer; Creating a Subscription Business in Any Industry*. Penguin.

Chapter 11
Factors Influencing Ease of Access to Banks:
A Case Study of the State Bank of India

Priyabrata Panda
Gangadhar Meher University, India

Manisha Satapathy
Gangadhar Meher University, India

Satyabrata Acharya
Gangadhar Meher University, India

ABSTRACT

Customers prefer a bank that can be easily accessed from the point of view of the location, staff co-ordination, service delivery, etc. In this context, the present study tries the factors stimulating ease of access to banks by customers. The study also focuses to assess the relationship of personal interest of staff, coordinated approach of staff, and customer support approach with prompt service delivery to customers. Data has been collected through scheduled questionnaires from SBI customers. The study is confined to the western part of Odisha, India. Exploratory factor analysis, multiple linear regression, and canonical correlation have been applied for data analysis. It is found that service quality, staff behaviour, and gender have a significant impact on the ease of access to the bank. It is also revealed that the personal interest of staff and coordinated approach of staff have a significant relationship with prompt service to customers. The findings of this research work will be helpful to banks to revamp their strategy for long-term endurance.

DOI: 10.4018/978-1-6684-5853-2.ch011

INTRODUCTION

The economic and societal developments of countries all over the world largely depend on the contribution of their service sector (Yalley and Agyapong, 2017). At present, the service sector is considered the most important growth engine as it creates and enlarges the wealth of a nation. As a service sector, banks play a vital and active role in this context. In the Indian context, the bank is the focal point in the cycle of the economy. The presence of such intermediaries leveraged the system and policymakers as well. Thus, the economic growth of a country is positively influenced by its effective banking system (Ayadi *et al.*, 2015) because of several reasons. However, Indian banks have been witnessing several emerging issues in the recent past, and mitigating competition and sustainable performance are one of them. The rise of foreign banks and private sector banks transformed the industry and on the other hand intensified the competition. In order to soak it, banks started innovating a variety of products along with changing the way of delivering it. In the process, customer retention and attracting new customers have been emphasised. Hence, customer satisfaction is an important ingredient in this industry which is closely related to service quality (Silvestri *et al.*, 2017) and it is a crucial determinant of success for a bank (Özkan et al., 2020). On the other hand, better customer satisfaction results in several behavioural outcomes such as commitment, customer retention, building bonds, increasing customer tolerance for service failures, and positive word of mouth (Oh and Kim, 2017).

The convenience of location also plays an important role in satisfying customers. Customers with higher knowledge about a service are more likely to use self-service channels like ATMs and internet banking. But convenience is a key driver of channel choice for the majority of consumers (Berry *et al.*, 2002). The ease of access to banks creates confidence among the customers in bank selection. The present study attempts to explore ways in which SBI can implement effective ease of access to the Bank. The process can be devised by understanding the relationship between the customer's perceptions of the bank's service quality and the bank's effort to acquire new customers, evaluating the customer value, staff behaviour, bank ambiance, processing time, and building customer knowledge, eventually leading to satisfied customers. The relationship reveals the intermediary effect of customer knowledge between service quality perception and customer value evaluation and then acquiring the customer. SBI is the major commercial bank in India and is providing high-quality services to its valued customer to maximize profits. SBI is the largest commercial bank in terms of deposits, branches, employees, and many others (Subalakshmi *et. al.,* 2018), thus such a bank has been chosen for the study purpose. The observations of the paper are based on an empirical survey conducted by the authors on the customers of the State bank of India in the select districts of the western part of Odisha. The introductory part of the paper replicated the relevance of the study, problem statement, research questions, literature review, objectives and methodology. The data is analysed in the central part of the paper. The concluding part narrated the implications and further scope of the research work.

REVIEW OF LITERATURE

Literature is traced from science direct and google scholar database. Keywords like "service quality and bank performance", "ease of access", and "employee behaviour", etc are applied for the selection of literature. A total of ninety five literature are reviewed which included literature for both subject support and methodology support.

A greater number of researchers worked on customer satisfaction and preference through service quality like Li *et al.* (2021) have revealed that cloud services, security, e-learning, and service quality are four significant factors influencing customer satisfaction and attitude towards different banking services. Chitra and Ramasethu (2021) inferred that service as per customers' needs can satisfy the majority of customers to a large extent. Kaur *et al.* (2021) identified customer-centric efforts at bank branches as an important stimulus for customers' overall attraction toward banks whereas Bhatt (2020) established the impact of service fairness on service quality on customer satisfaction. Zephaniah *et al.* (2020) concluded that advertising has the strongest effect on customer loyalty followed by personal selling, public relations, and sales promotion. These studies tinctured several factors for customer satisfaction like service quality, service fairness, identification of need, and demand of customers' demand. Ramachandran and Chidambaram (2012) summarized customer satisfaction towards the service of a bank from five different perspectives namely service encounter, waiting time of the customer to get the service, the role of intermediaries, quality of service provided, and customer complaints toward the bank. Attraction, retention, and enhancement of the customer relationship are essential to maintain delighted and committed customers for the sustainable competitive position of the bank.

Hue *et al.* (2020) worked on factors affecting the access to bank credit of SMEs and found that commercial enterprises' access to credit is better than industrial enterprises and agricultural enterprises. Do *et al.* (2019) worked on factors affecting access to finance of SMEs and concluded that managerial experience, the owner-managers financial literacy, business plan, financial management regulations, owner-managers education, and business size are affecting factors. Saraswathy and Suganya (2018) hinted that customers can be satisfied through innovative schemes in the banking sector. Erdogan (2018) worked on factors affecting SME access to bank financing and revealed that the commitment of an SME to its credit obligations, combined with its financial data, affects its access to bank loans. Agolla *et al.*, (2018) investigated those innovative banks are likely to attract and satisfy their customers. Calabrese and Girardone (2017) worked on Access to Bank Credit: for UK SMEs and found that financial literacy is an important factor in this regard. Mohan (2017) deduced that competitive advantage through high-quality service is an important weapon for customer satisfaction in the banking sector. Rabbani *et al.* (2017) indicated about the link among service quality, customer satisfaction, and loyalty programs which are important factors that can increase the loyalty of customers towards its banks. Thus, service quality and loyalty can improve customers' confidence. These group of authors accentuated financial literacy, business strategy, financial management regulations, innovation schemes of banks, etc. can largely influence banks and eased the path of access for the customers.

On the other hand, Gupta *et al.* (2017) stressed about the facilitating conditions and social influencing factors which are the direct determinants of the behavioural intention of bank customers. Similarly, Ozatac *et al.* (2016) revealed that customer satisfaction in the banking sector depends on firm relations, building trust between customers and bank employees. Rod *et al.*, (2016) traced a distinct factor that relational service delivery only significantly impacts customer satisfaction. Chocholáková *et al.* (2015) opined about satisfied and loyal customers that satisfied customers were significantly more likely to recommend their bank to their friends and loyal customers who are more interested in the services of their banks. Gamage (2013) found that access to bank finance is largely determined by the location of the firm, availability of audited financial statements, and the owner-managers perception of access to finance. Amoah-Mensah (2010) concluded that reliability, convenience, tangibles, and empathy are 4 dimensions of customer satisfaction in the banking industry. The set of findings in the above review underlined a few noteworthy recommendations for a better customer friendly approach. Determinants like location of the firm, relational service delivery, convenience, social factors, and facilitating conditions are accented.

Bena (2010) found that long-term relationship is the basis for customer satisfaction. Amin and Isa (2008) detected those customers highly preferred a smooth transaction system, friendly behaviour of staff, efficiency of services, and confidentiality matters. Manrai and Manrai (2007) concluded that the nature of competitive offerings for different types of banking services available from other banks is an important factor in switching the customer from one bank to another. Levesque and McDougall (1996) replicated about the service problems and banks' service recovery ability which have a major impact on customer satisfaction in the retail banking sector. Joseph *et.al*, (1999) indicated that consumers have perpetual problems with some aspects of electronic banking.

A significant number of literatures detected and focused the grandness of factors stimulating customers' attitudes and satisfaction. Moreover, easy access to bank credit is also analysed by some researchers. Several factors which affect customer were empirically detected. However, little effort was made to assess the impact of factors influencing ease of access to banks.

Based on the literature review, the research work is intended to measure the impact of service quality, the coordinated approach of bank staff in solving customer grievances, and employee behaviour in toto on ease access to a bank. In addition, the research work attempts to trace the correlation between Personal interests of Staff, Coordinated Approach of Staff, and Customer Support Approach with prompt service delivery to customers.

DATA AND METHODOLOGY

The study is based on primary data which are collected through a scheduled questionnaire. The questionnaire was distributed both in google forms and hard copies. The collected data has been encoded to statistical software for further processing. The study is exploratory in nature. An attempt is made to assess the ensuing process without putting any treatment to the experimental group. Thus, the research design is bound to be rigid and specific in terms of scale development to data analysis. A detailed analysis of the methodology is mentioned in the following segments.

Scale Development and Justification of Variables

This research work aims to investigate the factors influencing Ease of Access to the State Bank of India in the western part of Odisha. Data are collected with a structured questionnaire. The first part of the questionnaire elicited personal details of the respondents which are age, gender, educational qualification, monthly income, types of accounts, and years of banking experience. On the other hand, the second part had statements using a 5- point Likert scale from strongly agree to strongly disagree. Primary data are measured on ordinal and nominal scales. However, different factors are traced by applying factor analysis which is measured on a continuous scale.

Variables are selected from different literature. It is tried to trace core activities of the bank for the formation of variables like the personal interest of staff, processing time of each transaction, and coordination among bank staff in delivering services. The guidance of staff, bank ambiance, and placing of electronic equipment in suitable places have been considered and used as variables. The convenient location of banks and ATMs for ease of access of customers is also focalised. A total of six demographic and eleven core variables are processed for exploratory factor analysis and are shown in table 2.

Sampling Methods and Selection of Sample Units

Data have been collected from 383 respondents and after removing the unengaged responses and missing values, 362 responses are finally processed for further analysis. Data has been collected during the month of January and February of 2020 and again survey process has started after the unlocking process during the month of November and December of 2020. Random sampling method has been used for such purpose. Sample units are selected as per Kline (2011) who advocated that a multiple of 10 to 20 numbers as against per estimator should be preferable. Kaiser-Meyer-Olkin (KMO) test is also conducted to check sampling adequacy. SPSS 23 is used for such analysis. The study is confined to the customers of the State Bank of India (SBI) of select districts in the western part of Odisha like Sambalpur, Balangir, Bargarh, and Jharsuguda as per the convenience of the researcher. As SBI is the leading bank and the majority of customers belong to such bank, SBI is taken as a case study.

Table 1. Demographic profile of respondents

Variable	Categories	Number of Respondents (%)
Age	Below 21	39(10.8)
	21-30	232(64.1)
	Above 30	91(25.1)
Gender	Male	168(46.4)
	Female	194(53.6)
Educational Qualifications	Matriculate	29(8)
	Intermediate	18(5)
	Graduate	218(60.2)
	Post Graduate	88(24.3)
	Other	9(2.4)
Monthly Income	Less than 10000	72 (19.9)
	10000-30000	41(11.3)
	30000-50000	29(8)
	More than 50000	200(55.2)
Type of Account	Saving Account	164(45.2)
	Current Account	112 (30.9)
	Fixed Account	52(14.3)
	Multiple Accounts	34(9.6)
Years of Banking	Less than 1	48(13.26)
	1-5	77(21.27)
	5-10	75(20.71)
	More than 10	162(44.75)

Source: Author's own Compilation

Table 1 above explains the demographic factors. It is interesting to infer that a greater number of female respondents have participated in the survey. About 54 percentage of female participants have responded as compare to 46 percentage of male respondents. As expected, large number of youth population have been engaged in the survey. 232 respondents belong to the age group of 21-30. A major number of participants have graduation degrees. It can be said that respondents are educated and sensible. It is also observed that a greater number of participants belong to highest income category. 200 participants have income more than Rs 50,000. Among the participants, the number of saving account holder is more as compare to current and fixed account holders. About 45 percentage of respondents have saving accounts. Similarly, a greater number of respondents have more than ten years of banking experience.

It is inferred that greater numbers of respondents have the graduate level of qualification, highest monthly income, and maximum years of banking service. The demographic nature of respondents resembles an unbiased opinion.

Reliability Analysis

Primary data sent is processed further but subject to reliability analysis. Reliability measures the internal consistency of scale as a whole (Singh and Sharma, 2010). It ensures same results under same conditions and methods. It is the coefficient at which stable and consistent results are expected. The reliability of the variables is measured with Cronbach's Alpha (1951). Such value should be more than .7 (Nunnally, 1978, 1988). Such statistics in this study is .713 which is corresponding to the recommended criteria.

Exploratory Factor Analysis

In factor analysis, observed variables are tailored to adequate latent variables (Yong and Pearce, 2013). There are two types of factor analysis such as Exploratory factor Analysis (EFA) and Confirmatory Factor Analysis (CFA). The later one makes path analysis and confirms a hypothesized model while EFA is applied for variable grouping and factor generation. It aims to trace number of factors and its pattern of influence on the surface variables (Tucker and MacCallum, 1997). It is applied for building scales (Yong and Pearce, 2013) and predictions (Child, 2006). Factor extraction can be carried on by applying the Scree test (Catell, 1996), Parallel Analysis (Horn, 1965), and Principal Component Analysis (PCA) (Pallant, 2013). PCA is popular and widely used (Mishra *et* al., 2017) which is applied in the present study. Before applying such technique, outliers are checked (Field, 2009) along with correlations (Gorsuch, 1983) and (Tabachnick and Fidell, 2007), factor loadings (Harman, 1976) are also emphasized. Missing value analysis also has been conducted for such purpose (Watkins, 2018). In addition, the findings of Hair et al. (2010) and Zainuddin (2012) are referred for robust results. Such technique was first advocated by Spearman (1904) and later on well adopted by (Haig, 2014; Olea and Abad, 2014).

Kaiser-Meyer-Olkin (KMO) Measure of Sampling Adequacy

A large sample size yield better results EFA (Watkins, 2018). Kaiser-Meyer-Olkin (KMO) statistics measures sampling adequacy (Kaiser, 1970; Hadi, *et al.*, 2016). Different opinions are observed regarding its recommended value. Its value ranges from .00 to 1. Kaiser (1970) and Field (2000) inferred that its value must be more than .5 while Pallant (2013) and Shree *et al.* (2017) deduced that its value must be more than .6. Hoelzle and Meyer, 2013 and Lloret et al., 2017 stated that its preferred value should be more than .7.

In the study, such value is more than .7 which denotes no issue with sampling criteria. According to (Comrey and Lee, 1992), in factor analysis, variables should consist of 5 to 10 observations. In addition, Guadagnoli and Velicer (1988) deduced a different approach to sampling adequacy for such analysis and opined that the data set with higher loadings can work with a smaller sample size which may be 150.

Bartlett Test of Sphericity

Bartlett's Test of Sphericity measures the relatedness of variables for factor analysis (Bartlett, 1950,1951). Here, the null hypothesis i.e., variables are uncorrelated, is rejected at a 1% level of significance as the p-value is .00 by denoting the relatedness of variables.

Out of many methods available for factor extraction, principal component analysis is popular and widely applied to trace and categorize inter-correlated variables (Sehgal *et.al.*, 2014; Mishra *et al.*, 2017). Such a method is adopted in this research work for factor extraction.

Communalities

Communalities are the squared factor loadings of variables (Panda et al., 2021). Watkins (2018) inferred in a different way and opined that communalities can be interpreted as R square in regression. It is the variability as explained by the factors.

Table 2. Communalities

Sl No	Variables	Initial	Extraction
1.	V1	1.000	.586
2.	V2	1.000	.461
3.	V3	1.000	.617
4.	V4	1.000	.461
5.	V5	1.000	.485
6.	V6	1.000	.502
7.	V7	1.000	.691
8.	V8	1.000	.596
9.	V9	1.000	.425

Source: Authors' own Compilation
Note: V- Variables

The value of communalities lies between 0 to 1. Such value must be more than 4 (Osborne, 2014) and anything less than .2 can be removed. (Child, 2006). All such values in the table are more than .4.

Total Variance Explained

The table below contains three columns like Initial Eigenvalues, sum of squared loadings and rotation loadings. The initial eigen value explains the variance a factor or component. It is written in percentage in the next column. Eigen value more than can be referred for selecting the number of factors in the model. Such value is more than 1 in four factors. Thus, factors are proceeded further for analysis.

Table 3. Total Variance Explained

Components	Initial Eigenvalues			Extraction Sums of Squared Loadings			Rotation Sums of Squared Loadings		
	Total	% of Variance	Cumulative %	Total	% of Variance	Cumulative %	Total	% of Variance	Cumulative %
1	3.1	25.950	25.950	3.11	25.950	25.95	1.9	16.608	16.608
2	1.3	10.867	36.816	1.30	10.867	36.81	1.6	13.647	30.255
3	1.06	8.791	45.607	1.0	8.791	45.60	1.5	12.580	42.835
4	1.03	8.427	54.034	1.01	8.427	54.03	1.3	11.199	54.034
5	.84	7.054	61.088						
6	.793	6.610	67.698						
7	.777	6.475	74.173						
8	.754	6.287	80.460						
9	.643	5.360	85.819						
10	.619	5.160	90.979						
11	.573	4.771	95.750						
12	.510	4.250	100.000						
Extraction Method: Principal Component Analysis.									

Source: Author's own compilation

The variance of these four factors is more than 50%. Thus, the data can be proceeded for further analysis.

Table 4. Rotated component matrix

Variables	Factor Loading	Factors
The personal interest was taken by staff in giving service and in solving problems	.679	Service Quality
Bank takes minimum time for processing of the loan	.645	
Prompt service provided by staff at the counters	.528	
Good and Harmonious relations between customers and bank employees	.746	Coordinated Approach
Coordination among staff in the bank in delivering service	.670	
Availability Electronic equipment like passbook printing machine, swipe machine, etc.	.815	Easy Access to Bank
The convenient location of bank and ATM	.749	
Overall customer support services of the Bank	.832	Employee Behaviour
The guidance provided by the staff to the customers, especially to the less educated people	.601	

Source: Factor Extraction results from SPSS 23.

The rotated component matrix explains the factor loadings which is the correlation between the variable and the factors or components (Panda *et al.,* 2021). Four components or factors are extracted with a certain number of variables. After a rigorous literature review and after analysing the nature of variables, such factors are suitably titled. Easy access to the bank describes the location of the bank and its ATM along with the internal ambiance of the bank. Employee behaviour suggests the support and guidance of bank staff, whereas Service Quality is based on transaction processing time and personal involvement of bank staff in addressing customer grievances.

Easy access to the bank has been taken as a dependent factor as per the objective of the study and other variables are treated as independent factors. The following regression equation is formulated accordingly.

Easy Access to Bank = α + Service Quality + Coordinated Approach + Employee Behaviour+ Age + Gender + Є

Table 5. Regression parameters

R Square	Adjusted R Square	Durbin-Watson	F Stat. (P-value)	Std. Residual Mean	Std. Residual Std. Deviation
.20	.19	1.719	16.702 (0.00)	.000	.996

Source: Source: Authors' Own Compilation

Different regression assumptions like R square, Durbin-Watson Stat for auto-correlation, F-Stat, variance, and normality of residuals (Chan, 2004) should be measured before drawing conclusions on its estimates. R square measures explain the extent of variation in the dependent variables by the independent variables. A low R square and adjusted R square value are witnessed in the regression model. The model can be further processed even with this low R square value as such measure is termed as a biased estimator (Akossou and Palm, 2013) and substantiative inference cannot be drawn by these statistics (Filho *et al.,* 2011). Thus, a low R square value cannot affect this regression model. However, other regression assumptions should be verified. The Durbin-Watson (1950) statistic measures that there is no autocorrelation at lag 1 when it ranges from 1.5 to 2.5 (Maxwell and David, 1995; White, 1992). In the above model, such value lies within the required criteria. F statistics is rejected at a 1% level of significance which concludes that the processed model is a fit model for regression analysis.

Normality of residuals and constant variance of residuals are two important prerequisites of linear regression. The residuals will be normal when the mean and standard deviation of standardized residuals must be zero and 1. The above table satisfies the said criteria.

MODEL AND DISCUSSION

Table 6. Regression coefficients

Variables	B	Std. Error	t	Sig.	Tolerance	VIF
(Constant)	1.512	.232	6.478	.000		
Service Quality	.263	.081	3.260	.000	.572	1.751
Coordinated Approach	.097	.067	1.450	.148	.583	1.716
Employee Behaviour	.142	.053	2.659	.000	.883	1.132
Gender- Male or otherwise	.525	.117	4.480	.000	.527	1.896
Age above thirty or otherwise	-.173	.130	-1.327	.185	.567	1.764

Source: Author's own compilation

Note: B: Unstandardised beta coefficient; Std. Error: Standard Error; t: T Statistics; Sig: Significant Value or P Value; VIF: Variance Inflation Factor

Service quality, employee behaviour, and gender-male or otherwise have a significant impact at a 1% level as the sig. value is 0.00 on easy access to the bank. When there is one unit acceleration in ease of access to bank, service quality, employee behaviour and gender contribute .263, .142, and .525 respectively. Service quality has a greater influence on easy access to the bank than the other two variables. Age of customers has no significant impact on accessing the bank. In the above table, constant is also significant which has less relevance here as other dependent variables are also significant. Tolerance and VIF measure the multicollinearity of variables that are within the limit and reveal no such collinearity in the model.

Table 7. Canonical correlation test statistics

Variable 1	Variable 2	Canonical Correlation
Personal Interest of Staff	Prompt Service to Customers	.28***
Coordinated Approach of Staff	Prompt Service to Customers	.19**
Customer Support Approach	Prompt Service to Customers	09

Source: Author's own compilation

*** Significant at 1% level; **Significant at 5% level

The correlation between the personal interest of staff with prompt service is significant at a 1% level and the coordinated approach of staff is correlated with prompt service at 5% level of significance. But there is no correlation of the customer support approach with prompt delivery of services.

MANAGERIAL APPLICATION

Every entrepreneur or manager wants that their business should be easily accessed by customers. No barrier is expected between business and customer. Wong *et.al* (2008) concluded that large discrepancies were found between customer expectations and their perceived performance of traditional banking services.

This study reveals that customers do prefer quick transaction processing time for overall transactions in general and loan processing time in particular. Zhang *et al.,* (2014) substantiated that work culture has immense importance for the stability of an organisation. On the other side, service quality in all respect largely matters. Researchers like Pakurár *et al.,* (2019) and George and Kumar (2014) also emphasized service quality to retain and satisfy customers. Time of service delivery and personal interest of staff will be a key stimulus for customer attraction, retention, and satisfaction. Chair et.al (2016) concluded that bank performance is influenced by service quality, innovation, technology, and employee commitment. Various authors have confirmed that service quality is a strong parameter for performance management.

In addition, a coordinated customer service approach makes it more convenient in delivering services by the bank. Bellou and Andronikidis (2008) substantiated those employees are more likely to improve their general performance by showing a cooperative attitude. Al-hawari and Ward (2006) confirmed that customer satisfaction act as a mediator in the relationship between automated service quality and financial performance. Al- Hawari (2005) mentioned the role of customer retention as a mediator in the effect of automated service quality on financial performance. Zhou (2004) examines specific dimensions of the performance-only measurement of service quality as a determinant of customer satisfaction and subsequent behavioral intentions associated with banking services in mainland China. Akroush (2009) indicated that marketing capabilities exerted the strongest mediation effect on the relationships between technical service quality and bank performance.

Staff or employee behaviour is a key to customer attraction and retention. Butt *et al.,* (2018) also stressed the factors like convenience, service quality, and employee behaviour for better productivity and efficiency. Thus, managers should focus that employee should show personal interest than official interest while dealing with customers. The employees must provide proper guidance to the less educated people who believe that banking activities are too difficult to perform. The staff should personally help them in filling up different forms, the process of applying for loans, submission of KYC requirements, Aadhar and PAN link, etc. In addition, it is observed that a coordinated approach to the customer with a personal interest in the delivery of services reduces the processing time which can ensure prompt service to customers.

CONCLUSION

After extracting factors, a regression technique is applied to assess the impact of different factors on ease of access to the bank when the use of smart mobile phones is hiked and virtual banking has been geared up. Thus, banks with the use of fintech tools have been imparting e-banking apart from traditional banking. The present pandemic also fostered more e-access than physical access. But with less financial and technological literacy levels with low penetration of network created hurdles in e-access to the bank. On the contrary, when the situation will be normal, customers will rush to the bank for complying with their pending requirements. In this context, the findings of this study can help SBI, in particular, and other Indian banks in general, to build better business strategies for the easy delivery of services. It is revealed in the study that service quality, employee behaviour, and coordinated approach can make it convenient for customers to access the bank. In this context, <u>Butt</u> *et al.,* (2018) also stressed on the factors like convenience, service quality, and employee behaviour for better productivity and efficiency. Similarly, Lassar *et.al.,* (2000) and Angur *et.al.,* (1999) examined the effect of service quality on customer satisfaction and on firm performance. In addition, Mukherjee *et.al* (2003) concluded that the optimal level of service quality can be generated using existing resources and the opportunity cost for sub-optimal service delivery.

Limitations and Directions for Future Research

There is always the issue of generalizability in research of consumer behaviour. The present study is confined to the select districts of western part of Odisha. Its geographical scope could be expanded. Further, it was very difficult to collect data from customers by visiting the branch during the pandemic. Thus, the sample size is limited to 362. The number of variables is also limited which could have been increased to get more robust results. A low R square value has been witnessed which can be improved by adding more variables in a better model. The minimum level of education in the study has been taken as matriculation ignoring fewer literate customers. The study results can be socially more relevant if such respondents would have been included.

REFERENCES

Abhijith, M., & Remya Vivek, M. (2018). Study on Customer Satisfaction in Indian Banking Sector. *International Journal of Pure and Applied Mathematics, 118*(20), 4297–1302. http://www.ijpam.eu

Agolla, J. E., & College, S. (2018). Impact of banking innovations on customer attraction, satisfaction, and retention: The case of commercial banks in Botswana Tshepiso Makara Gladness Monametsi. *Int. J. Electronic Banking, 1*(2), 150–170. doi:10.1504/IJEBANK.2018.095598

Ahmed, S. M., Ahmad, K., & Jan, M. T. (2017). The impact of service quality on customer satisfaction and customer loyalty: An empirical study on Islamic banks in Bahrain. *VFAST Transaction of Education and Social Science, 5*(1), 39–47.

Akossou, A. Y. J., & Palm, R. (2013). Impact Data Structure on the Estimators R-Square and Adjusted R-square in Linear Regression. *International Journal of Mathematics and Computation, 20*(3), 84–93.

Akroush, M. N. (2009). Does service quality implementation mediate the relationship between technical service quality and performance : An empirical examination of banks in Jordan. *Int. J. Services. Economics and Management, 1*(3), 209–232.

Al-hawari, M. (2005). The effect of automated service quality on bank financial performance and the mediating role of customer retention. *Journal of Financial Services Marketing, 10*(3), 228–243. doi:10.1057/palgrave.fsm.4770189

Al-hawari, M., & Ward, T. (2006). The effect of automated service quality on Australian banks ' financial performance and the mediating role of customer satisfaction. *Marketing Intelligence & Planning, 24*(2), 127–147. doi:10.1108/02634500610653991

Amin, M., & Isa, Z. (2008). An examination of the relationship between service quality perception and customer satisfaction: A SEM approach towards Malaysian Islamic banking. *International Journal of Islamic and Middle Eastern Finance and Management, 1*(3), 191–209. doi:10.1108/17538390810901131

Amoah-Mensah, A. (2010). Customer Satisfaction in the Banking Industry: a Comparative Study of Ghana and Spain. *Girona.* http://hdl.handle.net/10803/22657%0AADVERTIMENT

Angur, M. G., Nataraajan, R., & Jr, J. S. J. (1999). Service quality in the banking industry : An assessment in a developing economy. *International Journal of Bank Marketing, 17*(3), 116–125. doi:10.1108/02652329910269211

Ayadi, R., Arbak, E., Naceur, S. B., & De Groen, W. P. (2015). Financial development, bank efficiency, and economic growth across the Mediterranean. In Economic and Social Development of the Southern and Eastern Mediterranean Countries. Springer International Publishing.

Bartlett, M. S. (1950). Tests of significance in factor analysis. *British Journal of Psychology, 3*(2), 77–85.

Bartlett, M. S. (1951). The effect of standardization on a Chi-square approximation in factor analysis. *Biometrika, 38*(3/4), 337–344. doi:10.2307/2332580

Bellou, V., & Andronikidis, A. (2008). The impact of internal service quality on customer service behaviour: Evidence from the banking sector. *International Journal of Quality & Reliability Management, 25*(9), 943–954. doi:10.1108/02656710810908098

Berry, L. L., Seiders, K., & Grewal, D. (2002). Understanding Service Convenience / 1 Understanding Service Convenience. *Journal of Marketing, 66*(3), 1–17. doi:10.1509/jmkg.66.3.1.18505

Bhatt, K. (2020). Measuring service fairness and its impact on service quality and satisfaction: A study of Indian Banking Services. *Journal of Financial Services Marketing, 25*(1-2), 35–44. doi:10.105741264-020-00069-7

Bose, S., & Gupta, N. (2013). Customer Perception of Services Based on the SERVQUAL Dimensions: A Study of Indian Commercial Banks. *Services Marketing Quarterly, 34*(1), 49–66. doi:10.1080/1533 2969.2013.739941

Butt, I., Ahmad, N., Naveed, A., & Ahmed, Z. (2018). Determinants of low adoption of Islamic banking in Pakistan. *Journal of Islamic Marketing, 9*(3), 655–672. doi:10.1108/JIMA-01-2017-0002

Calabrese, R., Girardone, C., & Sun, M. (2017). Access to Bank Credit: The Role of Awareness of Government Initiatives for UK SMEs. *Financial Markets, SME Financing, and Emerging Economies,* (January), 5–20. Advance online publication. doi:10.1007/978-3-319-54891-3_2

Catell, R. R. (1966). The screen test for a number of factors. *Multivariate Behavioral Research, 1*(2), 245–276. doi:10.120715327906mbr0102_10 PMID:26828106

Chaia, B. B., See, P., & Shong, T. (2016). Banking Services that Influence the Bank Performance. *Procedia - Social and Behavioral Sciences, 224*(August), 401–407. doi:10.1016/j.sbspro.2016.05.405

Chan, Y. H. (2004). Biostatistics 201: Linear Regression Analysis. *Singapore Medical Journal, 45*(2), 55–61. PMID:14985842

Child, D. (2006). *The essentials of factor analysis* (3rd ed.). Continuum International Publishing Group.

Chitra, S., & Ramasethu, A. (2021). A Study on Customer Satisfaction towards Banking Services Provided by SBI in Reference with Coimbatore City. *The International Journal of Analytical and Experimental Modal Analysis*, *12*(11), 306–315.

Chochoľáková, A., Gabčová, L., Belás, J., & Sipko, J. (2015). Bank customers' satisfaction, customers loyalty, and additional purchases of banking products and services. A case study from the Czech Republic. *Economia e Sociologia*, *8*(3), 82–94. doi:10.14254/2071-789X.2015/8-3/6

Comrey, L. A., & Lee, H. B. (1992). *A first course in factor analysis* (2nd ed.). Lawrence Erlbaum Associates.

Cong Do, P., Tan Phong, V., Van Thuong, P., Hoang Tien, N., Van Dung, H., & Author, C. (2019). Factors Affecting Access to Finance By Small and Medium Enterprises In Vietnam. *American International Journal of Business Management*, *2*(10), 69–79.

Cronbach, L. J. (1951). Coefficient Alpha and the Internal Structure of Tests. *Psychometrika, 16*(3) 297–334. doi:10.1007/BF02310555

Durbin, J., & Watson, G. S. (1950). Testing for Serial Correlation in Least Squares Regression, I. *Biometrika*, *37*(3–4), 409–428. PMID:14801065

Erdogan, A. I. (2018). Factors affecting SME access to bank financing: An interview study with Turkish bankers. *Small Enterprise Research*, *25*(1), 23–35. doi:10.1080/13215906.2018.1428911

Field, A. (2000). *Discovering Statistics using SPSS for Windows*. Sage publications.

Field, A. (2009). *Discovering Statistics Using SPSS: Introducing Statistical Method* (3rd ed.). Sage Publications.

Filho, D., B., F., Silva, J., A., & Rocha, E. (2011). What is R^2 all About? *Leviathan – Cadernos de Pesquisa Política*, *3*, 60-68.

Gamage, P. (2013). Determinants of access to bank finance for small and medium-sized enterprises: The case of Sri Lanka. *Corporate Ownership and Control*, *10*(3), 314–321. doi:10.22495/cocv10i3c3art6

George, A., & Kumar, G. S. (2014). Impact of service quality dimensions in internet banking on customer satisfaction. *Decision (Washington, D.C.)*, *41*(1), 73–85. doi:10.100740622-014-0028-2

Gorsuch, R. L. (1983). *Factor analysis* (2nd ed.). Lawrence Erlbaum Associates.

Guadagnoli, E., & Velicer, W. F. (1988). Relation to sample size to the stability of component patterns. *Psychological Bulletin*, *103*(2), 265–275. doi:10.1037/0033-2909.103.2.265 PMID:3363047

Gupta, K. P., Manrai, R., & Goel, U. (2017). Factors influencing adoption of payments banks by Indian customers: Extending UTAUT with perceived credibility. *Journal of Asia Business Studies*, 2–29.

Hadi, N. U., Abdullah, N., & Ilham, S. (2016). An Easy Approach to Exploratory Factor Analysis: Marketing Perspective. *Journal of Educational and Social Research*, *6*(1), 215–223.

Haig, B. D. (2014). *Investigating the psychological world: Scientific method in the behavioral sciences*. MIT Press. doi:10.7551/mitpress/9780262027366.001.0001

Hair, J. F., Black, W. C., Babin, B. J., & Anderson, R. E. (2010). *Multivariate Data Analysis* (7th ed.). Pearson.

Harman, H. H. (1976). *Modern factor analysis* (3rd ed. revised). University of Chicago Press.

Hoelzle, J. B., & Meyer, G. J. (2013). Exploratory factor analysis: Basics and beyond. In I. B. Weiner, J. A. Schinka, & W. F. Velicer (Eds.), *Research methods in psychology, 2* (2nd ed., pp. 164–188). Wiley.

Horn, J. L. (1965). A rationale and test for the number of factors in factor analysis. *Psychometrika, 30*(2), 179–185. doi:10.1007/BF02289447 PMID:14306381

Hue, L. T., Thuy, N. T., Huy, D. T. N., Nuong, L. N., Binh, N. V., Huyen, D. T. T., & Thao, N. T. M. (2020). Factors affecting the access to bank credit of SMEs in northeastern region, Vietnam. *International Journal of Entrepreneurship, 24*(2), 1–12.

Irina, B. E. N. A. (2010). Evaluating customer satisfaction in banking services. *Management & Marketing, 5*(2), 143–150.

Izquierdo, I., Olea, J., & Abad, F. J. (2014). Exploratory factor analysis in validation studies: Uses and recommendations. *Psicothema, 26*, 395–400. doi:10.7334/psicothema2013.349 PMID:25069561

Jit, S., Liaqat, K., Kabir, A. M., & Al, H. (2021). Adoption of digital banking channels in an emerging economy: Exploring the role of in - branch efforts. *Journal of Financial Services Marketing, 26*(2), 107–121. doi:10.105741264-020-00082-w

Joseph, M., Mcclure, C., & Joseph, B. (1999). Service quality in the banking sector : The impact of technology on service delivery. *International Journal of Bank Marketing, 17*(4), 182–191. doi:10.1108/02652329910278879

Kaiser, H. (1970). A Second-Generation Little Jiffy. *Psychometrika, 35*(4), 401–415. doi:10.1007/BF02291817

Kaur, S. J., Ali, L., Hassan, M. K., & Al-Emran, M. (2021). Adoption of digital banking channels in an emerging economy: Exploring the role of in - branch efforts. *Journal of Financial Services Marketing, 26*(2), 107–121. doi:10.105741264-020-00082-w

Kaura, V., Prasad, C. S. D., & Sharma, S. (2013). Customer Perception of Service Convenience: A Comparison between Public and New Private Sector Banks. *Global Business Review, 14*(3), 529–547. doi:10.1177/0972150913496884

Kline, R. B. (2011). *Principles and Practice of Structural Equation Modeling*. Guilford Press.

Lassar, W. M., Manolis, C., & Winsor, R. D. (2000). Service quality perspectives and satisfaction in private banking. *Journal of Services Marketing, 14*(3), 244–271. doi:10.1108/08876040010327248

Li, F., Lu, H., Hou, M., Cui, K., & Darbandi, M. (2021). Customer satisfaction with bank services: The role of cloud services, security, e-learning and service quality. *Technology in Society, 64*, 1–11. doi:10.1016/j.techsoc.2020.101487

Lin, H. (2011). An empirical investigation of mobile banking adoption : The effect of innovation attributes and knowledge-based trust. *International Journal of Information Management, 31*(3), 252–260. doi:10.1016/j.ijinfomgt.2010.07.006

Lloret, S., Ferreres, A., Hernandez, A., & Tomas, I. (2017). The exploratory factor analysis of items: Guided analysis based on empirical data and software. *Anales de Psicología, 33*, 417–432. doi:10.6018/analesps.33.2.270211

Manrai, L. A., & Manrai, A. K. (2007). A field study of customers' switching behavior for bank services. *Journal of Retailing and Consumer Services, 14*(3), 208–215. doi:10.1016/j.jretconser.2006.09.005

Maxwell, L. K., & David, C. H. (1995). The Application of the Durbin-Watson Test to the Dynamic Regression Model Under Normal and Non-Normal Errors. *Econometric Reviews, 14*(4), 487–510. doi:10.1080/07474939508800333

Mercier, C. R. (1996). Sufficiency Ratings for Secondary Roads: Model Development. *International Journal of Bank Marketing, 14*(7), 12–20.

Mishra, S., Sarkar, U., Taraphder, S., & Datta, S. (2017). Principal Component Analysis. *International Journal of Livestock Research, 7*(5), 60–78.

Mohan, D. (2017). A Study on Customer Satisfaction Towards Services Provided by State Bank Of India-With Special Reference To Nagappattinam District. *Aarhat Multidisciplinary International Education Research Journal, 6*(5), 180–190.

Mukherjee, A., Nath, P., & Pal, M. (2003). Resource, service quality and performance triad : A framework for measuring efficiency of banking services. *The Journal of the Operational Research Society, 54*(7), 723–735. doi:10.1057/palgrave.jors.2601573

Nambiar, B. K., Ramanathan, H. N., Rana, S., & Prashar, S. (2019). Perceived Service Quality and Customer Satisfaction: A Missing Link in Indian Banking Sector. *Vision: The Journal of Business Perspective, 23*(1), 44–55. doi:10.1177/0972262918821228

Nippatlapalli, A. R. (2013). A Study On Customer Satisfaction Of Commercial Banks:Case Study On State Bank Of India. *IOSR Journal of Business and Management, 15*(1), 60–86. doi:10.9790/487X-1516086

Nunnally, J. C. (1978). *Psychometric Theory*. McGraw-Hill Publishing.

Nunnally, J. C. (1988). *Psychometric Theory*. McGraw-Hill, Englewood Cliffs.

Oh, H., & Kim, K. (2017). Customer satisfaction, service quality, and customer value: Years 2000-2015. *International Journal of Contemporary Hospitality Management, 29*(1), 2–29. doi:10.1108/IJCHM-10-2015-0594

Osborne, J. W. (2014). *Best Practices in Exploratory Factor Analysis*. Scotts Valley, CA. *CreateSpace Independent Publishing., ISBN-13*, 978–1500594343.

Ozatac, N., Saner, T., & Sen, Z. S. (2016). Customer Satisfaction in the Banking Sector: The Case of North Cyprus. *Procedia Economics and Finance, 39*(November), 870–878. doi:10.1016/S2212-5671(16)30247-7

Özkan, P., Süer, S., Keser, İ. K., & Kocakoç, İ. D. (2020). The effect of service quality and customer satisfaction on customer loyalty: The mediation of perceived value of services, corporate image, and corporate reputation. *International Journal of Bank Marketing, 38*(2), 384–405. doi:10.1108/IJBM-03-2019-0096

Pakurár, M., Haddad, H., Nagy, J., Popp, J., & Oláh, J. (2019). The Service Quality Dimensions that Affect Customer Satisfaction in the Jordanian Banking Sector. *Sustainability, 11*(4), 1113. doi:10.3390u11041113

Pallant, J. (2013). *SPSS Survival Manual. A step-by-step guide to data analysis using SPSS* (4th ed.). Allen & Unwin. www.allenandunwin.com/spss

Panda, P., Mishra, S., & Behera, B. (2021). Developing a Research Methodology with the Application of Explorative Factor Analysis and Regression. *IOSR Journal of Business and Management, 23*(4), 23-34.

Rabbani, M. A., Qadri, F. A., & Ishfaq, M. (2017). Service Quality, Customer Satisfaction and Customer Loyalty: An Empirical Study On Banks In India. *VFAST Transaction of Education and Social Science, 5*(1), 39–47.

Ramachandran, A., & Chidambaram, V. (2012). A review of customer satisfaction towards service quality of banking sector. *Periodica Polytechnica Social and Management Sciences, 20*(2), 71–79. doi:10.3311/pp.so.2012-2.02

Rod, M., Ashill, N. J., & Gibbs, T. (2016). Customer perceptions of frontline employee service delivery: A study of Russian bank customer satisfaction and behavioural intentions. *Journal of Retailing and Consumer Services, 30*, 212–221. doi:10.1016/j.jretconser.2016.02.005

Saraswathy, C., & Suganya, R. V. (2018). A Study on Customer's Satisfaction Of Banking Services In Pudukkottai District. *International Journal of Pure and Applied Mathematics, 119*(7), 1027–1038.

Sehgal, S., Singh, H., Agarwal, M., & Shantanu, V. B. (2014). Data Analysis Using Principal Component Analysis. *International Conference on Medical Imaging, m-Health and Emerging Communication Systems*, 45–48.

Sharma, S. (2014). Internet banking adoption in India Structural equation modeling approach. *Journal of Indian Business Research, 6*(2), 155–169. doi:10.1108/JIBR-02-2013-0013

Shree, S. V., Pugazhenthi, R., & Chandrasekaran, M. (2017). Statistical Investigation of the Performance Evaluation in Manufacturing Environment. *International Journal of Pure and Applied Mathematics, 114*(12), 225–235.

Silvestri, C., Aquilani, B., & Ruggieri, A. (2017). Service quality and customer satisfaction in thermal tourism. *The TQM Journal, 29*(1), 55–81. doi:10.1108/TQM-06-2015-0089

Singh, S., & Arora, R. (2011). A Comparative Study of Banking Services and Customer Satisfaction in Public, Private and Foreign Banks. *Journal of Economics, 2*(1), 45–56. doi:10.1080/09765239.201 1.11884936

Spearman, C. E. (1904). "General intelligence," objectively determined and measured. *The American Journal of Psychiatry, 15*, 201–293.

Subalakshmi, S., Grahalakshmi, S., & Manikandan, M. (2018). Financial Ratio Analysis of SBI. *ICTACT Journal on Management Studies, 4*(1).

Tucker, L. R., & MacCallum, R. C. (1997). *Exploratory factor analysis*. Retrieved from https://www.unc.edu/~rcm/book/factor.pdf

Watkins, M. W. (2018). Exploratory Factor Analysis: A Guide to Best Practice. *The Journal of Black Psychology, 44*(3), 219–246. doi:10.1177/0095798418771807

White, K. (1992). The Durbin-Watson Test for Autocorrelation in Nonlinear Models. *The Review of Economics and Statistics, 74*(2), 370–373. doi:10.2307/2109675

Wong, D. H., Rexha, N., & Phau, I. (2008). Re-examining traditional service quality in an e-banking era. *International Journal of Bank Marketing, 26*(7), 526–545. doi:10.1108/02652320810913873

Yalley, A. A., & Agyapong, G. K. Q. (2017). Measuring service quality in Ghana: A Crossvergence cultural perspective. *Journal of Financial Services Marketing, 22*(2), 43–53. doi:10.105741264-017-0021-x

Yong, A. G., & Pearce, S. (2013). A Beginner's Guide to Factor Analysis: Focusing on Exploratory Factor Analysis. *Tutorials in Quantitative Methods for Psychology, 9*(2), 79–94. doi:10.20982/tqmp.09.2.p079

Zainuddin, A. (2012). *Research Methodology and Data Analysis* (2nd ed.). Selangor: UiTM Press.

Zephaniah, C. O., Ogba, I. E., & Izogo, E. E. (2020). Examining the effect of customers' perception of bank marketing communication on customer loyalty. *Scientific American, 8*, 1–22. doi:10.1016/j.sciaf.2020.e00383

Zhang, M., Di Fan, D., & Zhu, C. J. (2014). High-Performance Work Systems, Corporate Social Performance, and Employee Outcomes: Exploring the Missing Links. *Journal of Business Ethics, 120*(3), 423–435. doi:10.100710551-013-1672-8

Zhou, L. (2004). A dimension-specific analysis of performance- only measurement of service quality and satisfaction in China's retail banking. *Journal of Services Marketing, 18*(7), 534–546. doi:10.1108/08876040410561866

Chapter 12
Importance of Motivators for Crowds to Participate in an Online Crowdsourcing Activity:
A Tool for Perceived Value, Customer Delight, and Customer Satisfaction

Parul Singh
Indian Institute of Foreign Trade, India

Areej Aftab Siddiqui
Dubai Business School, University of Dubai, UAE

ABSTRACT

Online crowdsourcing is a concept which is gaining momentum among business organizations for various reasons. It is a modern age digital marketing tool. It may be considered as a tool for gathering information, views, opinions, work, assigned task, ideas, solution to problems generally from crowds (a group of people) via the internet. This has enabled organizations to save resources such as time and money by utilizing different skills and expertise of people globally. Realizing the numerous benefits that crowdsourcing offers to organizations, they are adopting online crowdsourcing models not only to engage customers for co-creation, co-engagement, and collaboration but also for brand building and creating customer satisfaction. Organizations in a crowdsourcing model throws a contest, task, or a problem in hand to the crowd. The interest lies in understanding what motivates crowd to participate in such contests, which offers them delight, perceived value, and satisfaction.

DOI: 10.4018/978-1-6684-5853-2.ch012

INTRODUCTION

The term 'Crowdsourcing' is relatively new, but the concept has its historical roots. There have been various other examples from the past where various new ideas and projects have been made possible because of crowdsourcing. The drilling down of history gives various crowd sourced concepts even before the term existed. The Longitude Prize, the Oxford English Dictionary, Canned Food, Toyota Logo Contest, the Sydney Opera House are some of the results of the wisdom of the crowd. Businesses also have a rich history of trying to tap into crowds, using consumer surveys, focus groups, and experiential marketing to provoke customer engagement. Product R&D, in particular, has seen significant activity, with open innovation campaigns launched by many large companies, including 3M, BMW, General Mills, and Stanley Black & Decker. Later certain websites were also results of the crowds' contribution such as Wikipedia, and YouTube. Later in 2006 the term 'crowdsourcing' was coined by Jeff Howe and the web exploded the concept and made its execution easy. In conceptualizing the term, Howe suggested that "crowdsourcing represents the act of a company or institution taking a function once performed by employees and outsourcing it to an undefined (and generally large) network of people in the form of an open call. This can take the form of peer production (when the job is performed collaboratively) but is also often undertaken by sole individuals. Crowdsourcing competitions like the $30million Google Lunar XPRIZE, the $25 million Michelson Prize or the £10 million 2014 Longitude Prize are challenging – and incentivizing – professional scientists, engineers, entrepreneurs, and innovators from all over the planet, amateur and professional alike, to develop novel solutions to the world's 'wicked' problems. Crowdsourcing is a concept where crowd present globally is accessed. The purpose is to bring the pool of talent on board so that their talent and creativity can be channelized for some benefit. Organizations especially start-ups or SMEs who may not have access to expert domains or have limited resources can highly use the potential of crowdsourcing.

The rise of the new kind of consumers has changed the traditional role of consumer from that of a passive participant to an active and engaged participant (Hanna et al., 2011). This has changed the situation by transferring the power to the consumer from that of the business organizations (Pires et al., 2006; Wind, 2008). Accordingly, organizations have started looking for the solution to their problems to look beyond their own departments and employees for finding out solutions to their problems (Tapscott and Williams, 2006). Organizations such as P&G, CocaCola, Nestle, Samsung among others are all adopting crowdsourcing (eYeka, 2014). According to eYeka, a global market leader in creative crowdsourcing for marketers and creatives, 85% of the top global brands have used crowdsourcing in the last ten years. Gartner, Inc. anticipates that by 2018, 75% of the world's high performing enterprises will be using crowdsourcing. That's leading crowdsourcing companies, such as eYeka, InnoCentive, Kaggle and Top-Coder, to 'industrialise' approaches to finding optimum solutions, and they now manage many aspects of the innovation process to help businesses tackle problem solving with a minimum of effort. And if it's not the aggregate 'wisdom of the crowd' being sought but simply the best person to fulfil a specific task, then companies like Gigwalk, Upwork, 99Designs, Streetbees, DesignCrowd and Writology help businesses connect with and manage talented experts right across the world.

Crowdsourcing has the ability to generate value for most of the activities related to the marketing and hence can be used in various tasks such as product development and testing, creating innovative ideas, communications and others (Gatautis & Vitauskaite, 2014).

Crowdsourcing is a way of creating value for both organizations and consumers Djelassi and Decoopman, 2013). For creating ideas for advertisements, crowdsourcing can substitute traditional advertisement agencies (Pétavy et al., 2012). In a study conducted by Marsden (2009), it has been mentioned that in a crowdsourcing initiative conducted by an organization, 90% of the audience is passive and only 10% is active. This is a very small number for an organization. The passive audience is too large to be neglected. Hence, the present study explores the motivating factors for the same. The objective of the study is to analyse and assess the motivational factors for encouraging participation in crowdsourcing activities which results in customer delight, and customer satisfaction. Accordingly, different motivational factors are then ranked as they appeal to the crowd to participate in online crowdsourcing activities.

LITERATURE STUDY

Though the concept of crowdsourcing is not new but the literature on digitally enabled crowdsourcing or social media crowdsourcing is limited. The concept is evolving fast because of the advent of digital and internet-based technologies. The rapid rise in crowdsourcing has been fuelled by the development in Web 2.0 and social media (Zhao and Zhu, 2014). The topic is gaining attention no among the researchers and organizations. The literature has been studied as depicted in the figure 1 below.

Figure 1. Literature study

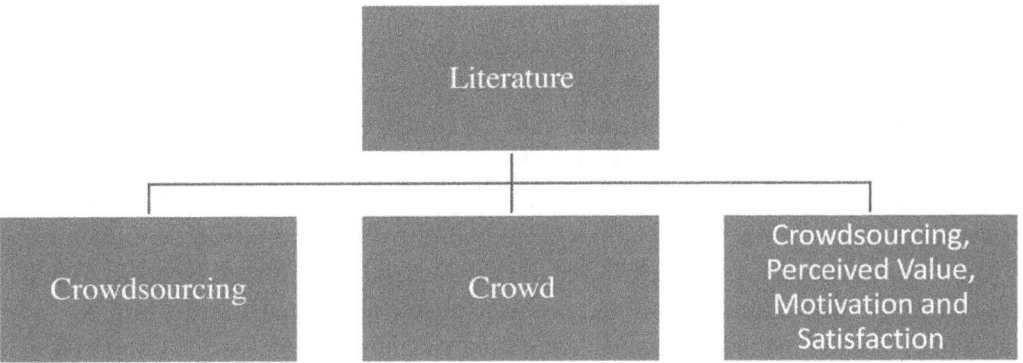

Crowdsourcing

The term 'Crowdsourcing' can be seen as combination of two words: 'Crowd' + 'Sourcing' simply indicating sourcing or seeking something from the crowd. As discussed above, the sourcing could be of new ideas, content creation, problem solving, and task completion among others.

As defined by defined by Merriam-Webster, crowdsourcing is the practice of obtaining needed services, ideas, or content by soliciting contributions from a large group of people and especially from the online community rather than from traditional employees or suppliers.

The term 'crowdsourcing' was first published in 2006 by Jeff Howe in "The Rise of Crowdsourcing" in Wired. He defined the term as "the act of taking a job traditionally performed by a designated agent (usually an employee) and outsourcing it to an undefined, generally large group of people in the form of an open call". Since then, the concept has gained more popularity and momentum, also because of the progression in the digital technologies and digital marketing. Crowdsourcing is one an important tool that can be used by organizations to allow customers to answer queries of other customers.

Brabham (2008) defined the term as "a strategic model to attract an interested, motivated crowd of individuals capable of providing solutions superior in quality and quantity to those that even traditional forms of business can." It is a web-based model that enables to assign the task of the employees of the organization to communities or network of that helps the organization to solve its problems in an efficient way (Chwiałkowska, 2012). Organizations invite for valuable contributors via an open call for participating in crowdsourcing activity (Steils and Hanine, 2019). The idea of crowdsourcing is to enable deliberate mobilization for commercial exploitation of creative ideas and other types of work accomplished by customer (Kleeman, Voss, and Rieder, 2008).

Crowdsourcing enables to connect with individual of the global crowd with the help of digital technologies and allows organizations to achieve benefits of the innovative talent of the crowd which may also be without offering remuneration. The crowdsourcing enabled by the Internet has allowed the access to the global labour market, removing the transportation costs and cost of facilities. The organization are moving from outsourcing towards crowdsourcing. This is especially for the organizations that do not follow formal heterarchical form, it is difficult for them to reach out to external expertise or intellectual property. Organizations adopted the use of the internet to reach to the global crowd for innovations. Organizations looking for innovative content via crowdsourcing, crowdsource it in an open electronic call format or crowdsource it in a form of a competition. Crowdsourcing has become a new system of hiring and work practices (Ettlinger, 2017).

Estellés-Arolas and González Ladrón-de-Guevara (2012), defined the term in a way that covers any type of crowdsourcing initiative. "Crowdsourcing is a type of participative online activity in which an individual, an institution, a non-profit organization, or company proposes to a group of individuals of varying knowledge, heterogeneity, and number, via a flexible open call, the voluntary undertaking of a task. The undertaking of the task, of variable complexity and modularity, and in which the crowd should participate bringing their work, money, knowledge and/or experience, always entails mutual benefit. The user perceives value, feels delighted and receive the satisfaction of a given type of need, be it economic, social recognition, self-esteem, or the development of individual skills, while the crowdsourcer will obtain and utilize to their advantage that what the user has brought to the venture, whose form will depend on the type of activity undertaken."

Hammon and Hippner (2012) deduced the following general definition of crowdsourcing-Crowdsourcing is defined as the act of outsourcing tasks originally performed inside an organization, or assigned externally in form of a business relationship, to an undefinably large, heterogeneous mass of potential actors. This happens by means of an open call via the Internet for the purpose of free, value creative use. The incentive to participate can be monetary and/or non-monetary in nature.

Crowdsourcing can be classified on the basis of the form of the crowdsourced task and on the basis of the initiator of crowdsourcing. The classified on the basis of the form of the crowdsourced task could be such as crowdsourcing idea game, problem solving or prediction markets. The crowdsourcing classification by initiator are the ones initiated and supported by intermediary platforms, User initiated crowdsourcing, company-initiated platforms, idea marketplaces and public crowdsourcing initiatives (Stanoevska-Slabeva, 2011). Crowdsourcing which is generally done in a contest or competition form results in winners. The expectations of these winners are met which results in creating perceived value and hence satisfaction from their participation and engagement (Piyathasanan et al, 2007). Literature shows that the success of a crowdsourcing contests mainly depends on mass participation (Boons et al., 2015; Zhao and Zhu, 2014; Frey et al., 2011). In a crowdsourcing contest, the more the number of participants, greater the probability of receiving high-quality solutions (Yin et al, 2022). If the contest fails to incite intense sufficient crowd interest, this may impact the quality of ideas as there will be no adequate alternative solutions (Martinez, 2015). Crowdsourcing helps solvers in earning rewards via digital platforms, show their talent and at the same time fulfill their psychological, emotional, or social demands (Alam and Campbell, 2017; Pee et al, 2018; Feng et al, 2018). Organization adopts crowdsourcing for business solution and decision making (Zhao and Zhu, 2014). By adopting crowdsourcing, organizations can enhance customer relationships and visibility of their brands (Djelassi and Decoopman, 2013; Ye and Kankanhalli, 2015).

Crowd

For individual workers, the crowd creates opportunities for a different kind of employment, greater freedom of choice and sometimes bigger rewards, too. The idea of open-source talent via crowdsourcing is itself growing in scale, sophistication and importance as an alternative staffing model. According to influential innovation academics Kevin Boudreau and Karim Lakhani (2013) "Crowds are energized by intrinsic motivations, such as the desire to learn or to burnish one's reputation in a community of peers." Reputation aside, the earnings of the most successful crowdsourcing challenge participants can now also easily exceed $500,000 per annum. Brabham (2010) defined crowd in a crowdsourcing application as 'the collective of Web-users who participate in the problem-solving process by posting solutions. The crowd's strength lies in its composite or aggregate of ideas, rather than in a collaboration of ideas'

Classification of Crowdsourcing/Crowd

- Smith et al. (2013), distinguished between three different types of crowds - a task-based public crowd, an information-exchange public crowd, and an employee-based crowd. Task-based public crowd is enrolled to perform some tasks. An information-exchange public crowd consist of participants seeking technical information as well as participants providing technical information. These two roles are interchangeable. Employee-based crowd consists of employee-based crowd which are employed by the host company. Accordingly, differing motivational drivers were identified for each crowd type.
- Nicholas Carr in his blog 'Rough Type' classified crowd on the basis of labour performed by the crowd. He discussed four forms of online crowd - Social-production crowds, Averaging crowds, Data-mine crowds, and Networking crowds. Clay Shirky suggested a fifth crowd type that is Transactional crowds. Tom Lord suggested a sixth category that is Event crowd. Each of this crowd type has its own distinctive features, strengths and weaknesses.
- Eric Martineau (2012) gave four categories of typology of participants as Communals, Utilizers, Aspirers and Lurkers. This classification was based on two measures: level of engagement and actions posed as part of crowdsourcing

Crowdsourcing, Perceived Value, Motivation and Satisfaction

Value creation is deemed an important indicator of customer engagement behaviour (Kumar et al., 2010). It is stated that organizations should co-create values with their customers via marketing activities

(Venkatesan, 2017). One of the studies highlights that creative process engagement of a customer in a crowdsourcing task enable the creation of other kinds of values for organizations as well as for participants. These are customer loyalty which is a firm value and epistemic value which is a customer value. Hence, creative process engagement creates value which is beyond the creative submission (Piyathasanan et al., 2013; Djelassi and Decoopman, 2013). Customer engagement leads to creation of customer value which is important. In this new linkage between organization and customers, perceptions of satisfaction and associated value are high ((Piyathasanan et al., 2017). Feedback from others and social appreciation leads to highly engaged participants and value perceptions (Sawhney et al., 2005). Customer value perceptions are prime predictors of subsequent customer behaviour such as satisfaction, loyalty, recommendation, and re-purchase (Cronin et al., 2000; Sirdeshmukh et al., 2002). The perceived value generates high customer loyalty leading to less brand switching (McDougall and Levesque, 2000). The link between participant's creative process engagement and value creation is moderated by the recognition need and disconfirmation of expectations (Piyathasanan, 2017).

Motivation leading to satisfaction is of prime importance for a crowd to participate in crowdsourcing activities. Hence, to understand what motivates crowd for a success of a crowdsourced activity is of paramount importance to business organizations going ahead with this concept.

Motivation can be considered as a desire of an actor for incentives, or goals, both consciously and unconsciously (Winter et al., 1998). A concern that organizations must face while adopting crowdsourcing is how to motivate contributors (Kohler et al., 2011; Suhada et al., 2021), to contribute meaningfully for free or for certain important tasks such as customer co-creation etc. The problem aggravates when the organization is not paying for their ideas. This leads to an important question to answer as to how to motivate individuals to engage in such crowdsourcing activities (Suhada et al, 2021). The co-creation of products leads to consumer empowerment and are considered to be in the customers' zone of individual preferences (Füller, 2010; Van Dijk et al., 2014). This results in increase in delighted and loyal customers as the customers participate with the brand through activities initiated by the organizations (Hollebeek, 2011; Nysveen and Pedersen, 2014).

There are multiple theories on motivation in the literature. Self-determination theory discusses how individuals are motivated and their development and wellbeing is affected by this motivation. The theory focusses primarily on the outcome of intrinsic and extrinsic types of motivation. Intrinsic motivation is attached to the actor whereas the extrinsic motivation is attributed by external events. Enjoyment, self-esteem, and the need for achievement are some of the examples of intrinsic motivation. It is challenging to manage intrinsic motivation as organizations cannot influence them directly. The organizations can enable an environment so that intrinsic motivation can grow organically. On the contrary, extrinsic motivation is easier to be managed by the organizations as individuals who meet goals can be rewarded. However, extrinsic motivation has a tendency of short-term reinforcing effects as individuals motivated by extrinsically prefers to have growing rewards over time to sustain performance levels. In case these rewards do not keep pace, the engagement or performance of individuals drops (Suhada et al., 2021). An individual's motivation can be pecuniary and/ or non-pecuniary in nature. Enjoyment, reputation building, personal development, career development, altruism, utilitarianism, ideology, sense of community, reciprocity, self-efficacy are the ones categorized as non-pecuniary motivators. Financial motivator is pecuniary in nature (Suhada et al, 2021).

The classification of the motivational factors leading to customer satisfaction has done on the basis of intrinsic and extrinsic factors is discussed in the lierture. Intrinsic motivation is when an individual engages because of his behaviour and not because of any external incentives. External motivation is driven by incentives such as some form of monetary return (direct/ indirect) or any other form of recognition. (Leimeister et al., 2009; Hossain, 2012). Individuals with intrinsic motivation are more likely to contribute creative answers to problems (Amabile 1988). Intrinsic motivation and extrinsic incentives affect task effort in crowdsourcing contests as they both increase solver's task effort. Extrinsic incentives reinforce the impact of engagement on task effort. When the extrinsic incentive is high, intrinsic motivation's force is weak on task effort (Liang et al, 2018).

Brabham (2010) conducted interviews with members of the crowd at Threadless to identify motivations for participation in crowdsourcing. He identified four primary motivators - the opportunity to make money, the opportunity to develop one's creative skills, the potential to take up freelance work, and the love of community at Threadless. A fifth theme of 'addiction' as mentioned by the interviewees to describe their activity was also discussed.

Finzen and Kintz (2012), in their survey studied remuneration/ motivation of users for contribution to a crowdsourcing project and identified that most crowdsourcing platforms offer a predominantly monetary compensation. In some of the cases users are also motivated by their expectation of future knowledge. The other motivators identified were altruism, hedonism, and self-expression. Clearly, in their survey they found extrinsic motivators to be dominating over intrinsic motivators.

Smith et al. (2013), identified motivational drivers for different crowd classifications they gave. For task-based public crowds, the motivational drivers identified were financial payment, skills improvement, enjoyment and fun, and community-related motivations. For employee-based crowds motivational drivers include immediate payment of rewards, such as peer recognition, career advancement, and professional development. For information-exchange public crowds motivational drivers consists of access to technical experts to solve problems, learning, fun, and being part of a community.

Roth et al. studied different motivational categories to participate in crowdsourcing. They used the following three categories to study individuals' reactions to different ad copy in the context of crowdsourcing:

1. Intrinsic Motivators: consisting of tasks that are intrinsically playful
2. Internalized Extrinsic Motivators: consisting of self-efficacy, status development and the desire for recognition or visibility, the opportunity to make friends, self-efficacy, information seeking, and skill development
3. Extrinsic Motivators: consisting of personal need and dissatisfaction as well as the opportunity for monetary compensation

Alexander Hars (2002), studied the reasons that why developers participate in open-source projects, and classified motivations into two categories as internal factors and external rewards. Examples of internal factors are intrinsic motivation, altruism, and community identification. Examples of external factors are expected future returns, personal needs. This study to identify motivations for participating in open-source projects was conducted before the existence of the term crowdsourcing.

Because participation in these external groups is typically voluntary and often uncompensated, it makes sense that most of the research on motivations has focused on those that are intrinsic. That said, there are extrinsic motivations provided by communities and crowds. The most unambiguous is monetary payment, whether for those who are paid by their employer to work in a community (Hertel et al., 2003; Fleming and Waguespack, 2007) or for user entrepreneurs forming their own companies (Hienerth, 2006). Similarly, for crowd participants, the motive to win a prize can be compelling. Others extrinsic motivations include career signalling, the desire to access other contributions, and the related expectation of reciprocity (Franke and Shah, 2003; Lakhani and von Hippel, 2003; O'Mahony, 2003).

It has also been observed that individuals' motivations change over time. This suggests that organizations need to adopt strategies to engage individuals depending on their motivational state. Also, how these different motivational stages can be leveraged to reap the maximize benefits by the organization (Suhada et al, 2021).

Customer satisfaction is the most important component of marketing. Variables such as information quality, system quality, and service quality play a significant role. Customer satisfaction can be considered as an attitude. It is an evaluative judgment. Customer delight, however, is a positive emotional state. (Torres and Kline, 2013). Crowdsourcing model brings in increased human-to-human engagement along with improved customer understanding leading o better knowledge curation. Crowdsourcing supports customer satisfaction in various ways. It encourages human to human interaction. Th fans of the brand connects with the customers to help them understanding them and their needs. This can lead to a positive environment around a brand / organization. The crowd can also answer the numerous queries of the customers. This can further be incorporated to the knowledge management systems of the company. This can be tool to keep customers delight and happy.

After going through the literature on crowdsourcing motivators, clearly the factors can be divided into two i.e., intrinsic and extrinsic. Intrinsic motivational factors are the ones which provided internal satisfaction to the participating crowd. This internal satisfaction could be challenge completion, fun or entertainment, identification by community etc. Extrinsic motivation factors are external rewards provided. The external rewards could be such as monetary compensation, self-marketing etc.

After discussing the literature, an individual's motivator to participate could be compiled as placed below:

- Intrinsic / Internal / Intangible / Non-pecuniary: enjoyment, self-esteem, self-determination, altruism, personal fulfilment, own behaviour, hobby, fun, source of entertainment, identification by the community, for own's sake, reputation building, personal development, career development, altruism, utilitarianism, ideology, sense of community, reciprocity, self-efficacy (Singh, 2014)
- Extrinsic / External / Tangible / Pecuniary: monetary return (direct/ indirect), payments, prestige, status, self-marketing, recognition in the society, any kind of immediate compensation, self-advertisement, other form of recognition (Singh, 2014).

METHODOLOGY AND DATA COLLECTION

In order to analyse and assess motivational factors for crowdsourcing, cluster analysis along with correlation has been applied. Cluster analysis is a statistical method which is applied in order to group similar items into specific categories. It is a way of segmentation analysis. Cluster analysis groups items with respect to their degree of association. If the degree of association is high, then they are categorised in the same while in separate groups if the association is low. Cluster analysis is preferred and differs from other statistical methods. It is primarily applied when there are no assumptions for the research. It is an analysis technique applied in exploratory research and is used to identify structures in data. Though a limitation of this method is that it does not provide a distinction between dependent and independent variables and does not provide interpretations.

In the field of marketing, cluster analysis is used to develop segments, position products and to explore new markets and develop new products which are found relevant. This method also assists in effective decision making.

Cluster Analysis

In cluster analysis, similar customers are grouped based on certain specific parameters. The main aim of cluster analysis is to personalise customer marketing techniques. This helps in targeting customers and offering incentives for personalised needs and wants. Clustering is not based on pre-defined rules but on the pattern of customer data that inherently exists in the population. In case thresholds are created, the results may be misleading and may have large variances in each customer segment. The main advantages of analytical segmentation of cluster analysis are:

- The analytical approach is more practical as using predetermined rules may not segment customers based on dimensions.
- Analytical clustering leads to homogeneity and reducing variances between groups which predict better results.
- It is more dynamic and insightful.

The process of clustering as follows:

1. Check the data is metric: For clustering and application of statistical tools, data has to be metric i.e. measurable and in numbers. If the data is not metric, best practices for segmentation have to be adopted and converted into numbers.
2. Scaling: The data from the survey has to be scaled on the same magnitude as other collected variables. Variables with different scales/ranges may lead to problems and it is important to standardise data.
3. Selecting variables for segmentation: the decision of variable selection for undertaking segmentation has to be taken wisely and should be such that it profiles clusters based on attitude, behaviour and demography of customers.
4. Similarity measure: The goal of clustering is based on similarity of observations and thus understanding of similarity between selected variables is important. There are a number of statistical tools for assessing the similarity too like Manhattan distance metric and Euclidean distance. This step has to be carried out carefully and may even be carried out multiple times to achieve viable segmentation.
5. Visualisation: The next step is to visualise data and check pairwise distances between variables.
6. Method of segmentation: there are many methods of segmentation and statically robust methods should be used for the same. The two widely used methods are K-means and Hierarchical Clustering. In these methods, similarity between observations has to be measured. The prime difference between the two is that in K means the user has to create segments while it is not so in hierarchical clustering. The segments created should be independent of the method adopted for clustering. In case there are large deviations in cluster formation due to methods adopted, the segments formed are not viable.

7. Descriptive statistics: Once the clusters are formulated, profiling and interpretation of the segments is important. Values like means can be taken for profiling of attributes.
8. Robustness: It is important to statistically test the viability and robustness of the clusters.

Cluster Analysis and Customer Value and Satisfaction

Customer satisfaction is of utmost importance to companies these days as it ensures that customers will return, buy more, share their experiences and increase customer base along with retention. To enhance the experience of customers and serve them in a better way, clustering is important for the following reasons:

1. Customer retention: It is one of the most crucial aspect of an organisation's strategy and the surety of returning customers is based on customer service. As an organisation may have a large number of customers, serving them poses a tedious task without clustering. Analysing data will assist the organisation in selecting actions and moves for marketing.
2. Strategies: Clustering customers based on purchasing habits, leisure behaviour and occasions helps organisations to decide modifications in strategies and thsu making feel customers valued.
3. Offers and discounts: detection of clusters of customers who might discontinue purchases may lead organisations to offer discounts and promotions and thus retaining customers.
4. Personalised transactions: Through clustering, identification of trends and thus offering personalised experience to customers becomes easier.

Thus, in today's world, customer satisfaction is of utmost importance as same offering may not be suitable to all and mat lead to failure of strategies. The companies have to develop smarter methods and thus clustering helps in customer retention as well as satisfaction.

Primary Survey

To assess customer value and satisfaction through primary survey, important parameters which should be measured are:

1. Customers to be interviewed: the right target audience has to be identified to assess the trends in customer demand and satisfaction. There needs to be an assessment of multiple views of customers as various departments of the organisation need inputs for serving customers. Thus, an adequate and apt sample is required for assessing customer satisfaction.
2. Measurement parameter: The parameters required to be measured should be well and pre-defined. These variables may range from satisfaction level to frequency of buying to recommendations to the organisation or to further contacts. Hygiene factors and importance level of each parameter should be assessed too.
3. Assessment of survey: Apart from survey, there are a few factors like sales volume, profitability, customer complaints, feedback which can also be assessed. Focus group interviews can also be undertaken.
4. Measuring Satisfaction: Satisfaction can be measured in a number of ways. No complaints may be an indication of satisfaction and not returning as a customer may be dissatisfied. It is better to use numeric or verbal scales which may indicate measuring attitude.

The present study employs the primary and most common method of clustering which is hierarchical cluster. This method is similar to factor analysis and creates a series of models with cluster solutions. This method can also handle data which maybe ordinal, nominal or scale. This form of cluster analysis suits our data set which not too large and thus helps in giving significant results.

The proposed clustering method was applied to 306 responses received for the questionnaire designed. In the study, a small sample was targeted. The questionnaire comprised questions pertaining to attributes of stakeholders. The attributes addressed were mainly gender, age, employment status and education. The clustering algorithm along with correlation was applied to the set.

ANALYSIS AND INTERPRETATIONS

On empirically assessing the data and carrying out cluster analysis, it is seen that out of the total 306 respondents, two clusters are generated. Cluster 1 has 99 (32.4%) respondents and Cluster 2 has 207(67.6%). These clusters have the attributes as enlisted in table 1.

Table 1. Cluster profile

Attributes	Cluster-1	Cluster-2
Males	72	126
Females	27	81
Age <20 years	72	168
20-30 years	25	35
30-40 years	0	4
40-50 years	1	0
< 50 years	1	0
Employed unemployed	54	171
0-5 years	36	18
5-10 years	9	0
10-15 years	0	9
<15 years	0	9
Education Class V- IX	0	9
Class X-XII	54	171
Graduate	18	27
Post-Graduation	18	0
Doctorate	9	0

From Table-1 it can be inferred that out of the total respondents, the share of males is higher than females with an age of less than 20 years. The respondents are either unemployed or with an employment status of less than 5 years usually from Class X to graduates.

Table 2. Results of cluster analysis

Motivational factors	Cluster-I	Cluster-II
Planning And Developing Goals	3.64	3.83
Giving Directions	3.45	3.87
Select Tasks	3.36	3.83
Help Others	2.73	4.00
Freedom To Decide	3.09	3.52
Be Yourself	2.91	3.65
Good At Solving Crowdsourcing Problems	2.55	3.09
Values Of the Crowdsourcing Project	2.82	3.57
Challenge	2.55	3.83
Financial Rewards	3.36	3.00
Build Social Network	2.27	4.04
Positive Feeling Towards A Crowdsourcing Project	2.64	3.65
Cause of the Project	2.55	3.70
Communicate	2.55	3.70
Enjoyment	2.64	3.57
Curiosity	2.64	3.52
Confidence	2.55	3.52
Competency	2.55	3.52
Develop Contacts	2.64	3.43
Skills	2.27	3.78
Career Promotion	2.82	3.22
Give Up Attempt to solve problems with trivial sequence of steps	2.91	3.13
Delegate Work	2.64	3.39
Showcase Talent	2.36	3.61
Ability To Personalise Interface	2.55	3.39
Time Pass	2.36	3.57
Recognition	2.64	3.22
Exert	2.45	3.35
Continue Participation	2.18	3.61
Income Goals	2.73	3.05
Belongingness	2.36	3.30
Solve Problems	2.55	3.91
Doing Better Than Others	2.36	3.22
Overcome Obstacles	2.18	3.39
Give Up Attempt to solve complex problems	2.82	2.74
Obligation Towards A Crowdsourcing Project	2.36	3.04
Number Of Hours	1.82	2.39
Time	1.91	2.09

From the mean scores of the two clusters, it can be said that cluster-I is more inclined towards planning, freedom to decide in participating in crowdsourcing projects and its values. While for cluster-II the emphasis is on building social networks, helping others, solving problems and planning. This also correspond to the population of respondents in Cluster-I and Cluster-II. In Cluster-I, the proportion of respondents is lower than Cluster-II of unemployed and in Class X-XII.

Figure-2 gives an overview of the mean construct scores after standardisation. The main constructs which emerge in order to determine motivators for crowd to participate in online crowdsourcing activities are financial rewards, income goals, career promotion, recognition, good at solving crowdsourcing problems, doing better than others, positive feeling towards a crowdsourcing project, obligation towards a crowdsourcing project, values of the crowdsourcing project, belongingness, curiosity, enjoyment, challenge, time pass, help others, freedom to decide, be yourself, ability to personalise interface, confidence, competency, showcase talent, develop contacts, communicate, build social network, delegate work, planning and developing goals, giving directions, select tasks, solve problems, give up attempt, exert, number of hours, skills, time, overcome obstacles, continue participation.

Figure 2. Mean Construct Scores

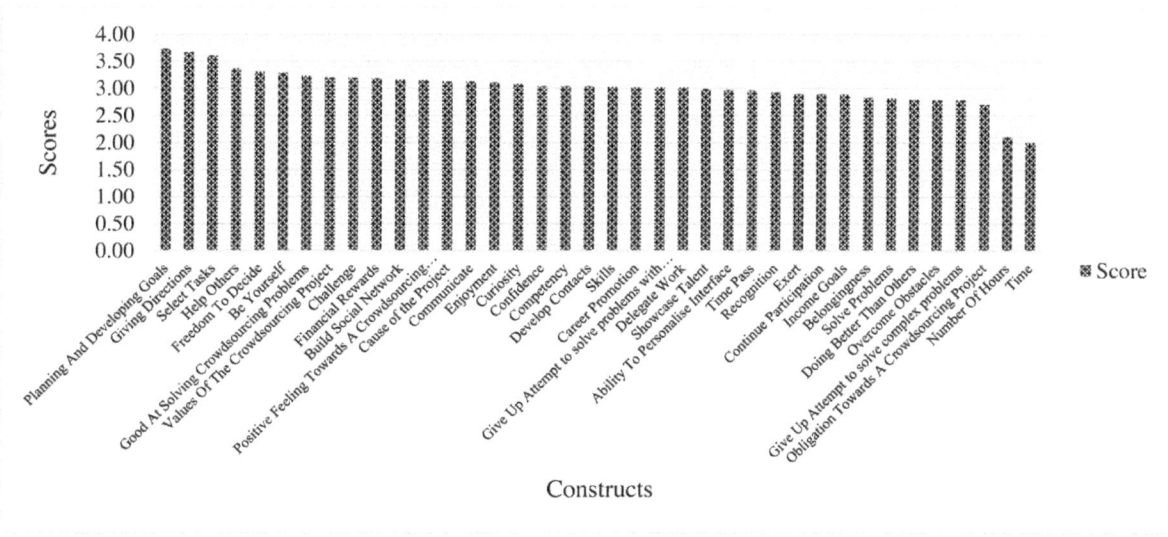

The construct with highest score is Planning and Developing Goals followed by giving directions, selecting tasks, helping others and freedom to decide as depicted in figure 2. Time construct is least important as depicted in figure 2.

On the whole it is seen that motivators which are intrinsic in nature rank higher than extrinsic counterparts.

For further analysing the demographics and the constructs, correlation analysis is used. The significance levels are two tailed and asymptotic and based on 5% level of significance. It is seen that gender specific motivators are mainly financial rewards, positive feeling towards a crowdsourcing project, values of the crowdsourcing project, belongingness, time pass, help others, freedom to decide, ability to personalise interface, competency, giving directions, select tasks, solve problems, give up attempt, exert, number of hours, time and continue participation.

Table 3. Correlation results

Parameters	Gender	Age	Employment status	Education
Financial Rewards	-.154**	.021	-.159**	.407**
Income Goals	-.085	-.038	.427**	-.120*
Career Promotion	-.069	-.031	.226**	-.357**
Recognition	-.082	-.032	.303**	-.078
Solve Problems	.088	-.082	.168**	-.059
Doing better than others	.095	-.015	.171**	-.009
Positive feeling towards this crowdsourcing project	.157**	-.070	.006	-.280**
Strong obligation	.070	-.101	.152**	-.065
Values	-.058	.046	.040	-.105
Cause of the Project	-.184**	.109	-.096	.039
Belongingness	-.120*	-.073	.000	.033
Curiosity	.074	-.056	.247**	.006
Enjoyment	-.013	-.030	.159**	-.007
Challenge	.004	-.044	.108	-.198**
Time Pass	.158**	-.119*	.153**	-.334**
Help others	.206**	-.072	.226**	-.156**
Be yourself	.005	-.064	.243**	-.173**
Freedom to decide	-.134*	-.023	-.077	.158**
Ability To Personalise Interface	.118*	.016	-.223**	-.017
Competency	.131*	-.074	-.138*	-.022
Confidence	.109	-.105	.108	-.135*
Showcase Talent	-.036	-.075	-.125*	-.147**
Develop Contacts	-.010	-.056	.016	-.149**
Communicate	-.129*	-.030	-.031	-.146*
Build Social Network	.020	-.114*	.028	-.243**
Delegate Work	-.050	-.140*	.061	-.171**
Planning and developing goals	.060	-.115*	-.247**	-.127*
Giving directions	.422**	-.208**	.104	-.157**
Select Tasks	.153**	-.197**	.079	-.095
Solve Problems	.221**	-.084	.201**	-.117*
Give Up Attempt to solve complex problems	.060	-.107	.211**	-.168**
Give Up Attempt to solve problems with trivial sequence of steps	-.274**	-.068	.187**	-.151**
Exert	-.184**	.046	.111	.011
Number of hours	.167**	-.070	.170**	-.053
Skills	-.035	-.096	-.014	-.202**
Time	.143*	-.037	.071	-.017
Overcoming Obstacles	.073	-.052	.038	-.201**
Continue participation	.130*	-.048	.085	-.247**
**. Correlation is significant at the 0.01 level (2-tailed).				
*. Correlation is significant at the 0.05 level (2-tailed).				

While in case of age, the main motivators for crowdsourcing are time pass, build social network, delegate work, planning and developing goals, giving directions and select tasks with higher control.

While employment status signifies motivators to be mainly income goals, career promotion, recognition, good at solving crowdsourcing problems, doing better than others, obligation towards a crowdsourcing project, curiosity, enjoyment, time pass, help others, be yourself, ability to personalise interface, competency, showcase talent, planning and developing goals, solve problems, give up attempt and number of hours.

In terms of education levels, the motivators which emerge significant are income goals, career promotion, positive feeling towards a crowdsourcing project, challenge, time pass, help others, freedom to decide, be yourself, confidence, showcase talent, develop contacts, communicate, build social network, delegate work, planning and developing goals, giving directions, solve problems, number of hours, skills and time.

Thus, crowdsourcing motivators for participation in crowdsourcing activities are mainly for financial rewards, building a social network, communication, delegating tasks and spending time.

THEORETICAL AND MANAGERIAL CONTRIBUTION

Researchers in the past have linked crowdsourcing and market activities like advertising, brand development, promotion, and distribution (Howe, 2008; Roth & Kimani, 2014; Zadeh & Sharda, 2014). However, adoption of crowdsourcing activities is accompanied by a number of challenges for organisations. The present study indicates that crowdsourcing can be used for understanding the positioning and dynamic capabilities of firms. By using crowdsourcing, managers gain specialised knowledge and assist in taking strategic decisions and access new business opportunities (Priem, Li, & Carr, 2012). Crowdsourcing is also an important tool of market research which can be used by both researchers and practitioners (Poynter, 2013; Zadeh & Sharda, 2014) and is also reliable (Fawcett and Waller, 2014).

Crowdsourcing can be used by entrepreneurs of startups and managers of established firms too based on the vision and mission of their organisation. To ensure customer satisfaction, managers can access content pertaining to customer preferences quickly and access information which is useful and effective. In terms of managerial implication, the managers of firms develop customer specific products and consider their preferences while undertaking marketing promotions and giving offers and discounts. Adoption of crowdsourcing will also result in enhancing skill sets of managers and employees to keep up to date with latest technological advances to adopt IT related infrastructure.

LIMITATIONS AND SCOPE OF FUTURE RESEARCH

In the present study customers were interviewed and it is being presumed that the data is accurate. The dataset was analysed by dividing into clusters, which could have generated reliable results had it been clustered using logical methods. A major limitation of the study is adoption of qualitative methods rather than scientific measures for analysis through which robustness can be checked of the results.

The paper opens up avenues for future research as the questions are inclined in assessing the inter-relationship between crowdsourcing and customer satisfaction. Further research can be undertaken to incorporate the recommendations of this paper by targeting new customers, retaining old customers and introducing new markets. In this era of heavy reliance on social media, technology related to artificial intelligence can aid managers in developing insights and making efficient decisions. The present research can be extended to the impact of crowdsourcing on all marketing activities and strategies like idea generation, customer preferences, customer engagement, motivation, service quality and customer delight. This concept of crowdsourcing can also be applied to a number of marketing activities especially for online sales considering the current practices of doing business globally.

CONCLUSION

Crowdsourcing is relatively new domain to research and study. This paper is an outcome of comprehensive study on crowdsourcing, crowd and its motivators and derived customer satisfaction, delight, and perceived value. Of interest here in the study is the motivators for the crowd in India. The paper helps to understand the concept of crowdsourcing and tries to define and classify various kinds of crowds. The study considers how firms leverage the external collaborations (with crowd) to support their open innovation strategies, and how these strategies are similar and different based on these three attributes – the form of collaboration, the degree of community innovativeness and the degree of firm involvement. In particular, because motivation is essential assuring a supply of ideas (external innovations) (West & Gallagher, 2006), it focuses on what motivates the participants in these collaborations and what firms can do to increase that motivation. As can be inferred from the empirical analysis carried out in the paper, for individuals to participate in crowdsourcing activities the main motivators are financial rewards, building a social network, communication, delegating tasks and spending time.

Despite the massive advantages, crowdsourcing has its own set of unconventional issues, related to intellectual property, management, performance guarantees, costs and integration. Today's workers are also frustrated with the directions their careers are taking. They want to work on a greater diversity of projects and concentrate their time on those activities that drive both reward and social worth. Thus, crowdsourcing presents huge potential gains for both firms as well as individuals through proper understanding and management, allowing firms to save on time and cost, as well as allowing individuals to break the monotony and often receive better compensation.

Firms face challenges of motivating external community and crowd participants to achieve their own objectives. The first is the necessity of understanding the community or crowd in question – namely its governance system and social norms. One potentially useful perspective is the idea that communities and crowds may represent "loosely coupled" organizational systems (Weick, 1976) which firms must both understand and adapt to if they hope to profit from interaction. An organization must encourage crowd to participate and should not only restrict to seeking help. For the success of crowdsourcing, it is important to have right kind of motivation factor to drive the crowd to participate. Firms must understand the nature of individual participation, and how to leverage it. Participation is driven by a combination of co-existing extrinsic and intrinsic motives (e.g., Alexander Hars, 2002, Dahlander and Magnusson, 2005; Lakhani and Wolf, 2005; West and Gallagher, 2006; Markus, 2007). If mangers wish to harness the benefits of these external groups, they must both understand the motivations of such individual participate, and the various ways their firm might be able to capitalize upon it.

The nexus between crowdsourcing and marketing is questionable especially when it comes to using crowdsourcing as a marketing tool. Each of the variables selected in the present study contribute a new dimension to customer value and satisfaction. Based on literature and definition of crowdsourcing, it is a process by which firms can increase their resources and thus generating marketing activity and fulfilling customer needs (Ballantyne & Varey, 2006; Kelley, 2017). Having access to resources by organisations whether less or more irrespective of firm size and age, crowdsourcing requires outside resources. Though crowdsourcing even from the present study indicates that it leads to motivation, new product development, customer satisfaction, accessing new markets and thus generating continuous business, there are a few negative aspects to crowdsourcing too. Crowdsourcing affects consumer privacy and public policy making. It also involves financial involvement as advanced technologies have to be adopted by firms and application of Artificial intelligence and Big Data. There is a continuous need for compliance and maintaining standards as per rules. Crowdsourcing above all helps in creating competitive advantage and customer profiling for better revenue generation (Vargo & Lusch, 2004). Utilising crowds helps organisations to solve problems by tapping resources and thus finding innovative ways for customer satisfaction. Hence, crowdsourcing can be used as a tool for enhancing marketing activities like promotion, advertising, product development, and marketing research.

With the ongoing creation and diffusion of Internet collaboration technologies by firms and individuals, the external forms of networked collaborations will become even more important going forward. Researchers on crowdsourcing and communities will continue to benefit by collaborating with each other and drawing insights from their respective scientific and managerial research.

REFERENCES

Alam, S. L., & Campbell, J. (2017). Temporal motivations of volunteers to participate in cultural crowdsourcing work. *Information Systems Research, 28*(4), 744–759.

Alexander Hars, S. O. (2002). Working for free? Motivations for participating in open-source projects. *International Journal of Electronic Commerce, 6*(3), 25–39.

Amabile, T. M. (1988). A model of creativity and innovation in organizations. *Research in Organizational Behavior, 10*(1), 123–167.

Ballantyne, D., & Varey, R. J. (2006). Creating value-in-use through marketing interaction: The exchange logic of relating, communicating and knowing. *Marketing Theory, 6*(3), 335–348.

Boons, M., Stam, D., & Barkema, H. G. (2015). Feelings of pride and respect as drivers of ongoing member activity on crowdsourcing platforms. *Journal of Management Studies, 52*(6), 717–741.

Boudreau, K. J., & Lakhani, K. R. (2013). Using the crowd as an innovation partner. *Harvard Business Review, 91*(4), 60–69.

Brabham, D. C. (2008). Crowdsourcing as a model for problem solving: An introduction and cases. *Convergence, 14*(1), 75–90.

Brabham, D. C. (2010). Moving the crowd at Threadless: Motivations for participation in a crowdsourcing application. *Information Communication and Society, 13*(8), 1122–1145.

Carr, N. (2010). *A typology of crowds.* http://www.roughtype.com/?p=1346

Chwiałkowska, A. (2012). Crowdsourcing as a customer relationship building tool. *Journal of Positive Management, 3*(1). Advance online publication. doi:10.12775/JPM.2012.002

Cronin, J. J. Jr, Brady, M. K., & Hult, G. T. M. (2000). Assessing the effects of quality, value, and customer satisfaction on consumer behavioral intentions in service environments. *Journal of Retailing, 76*(2), 193–218.

Dahlander, L., & Magnusson, M. G. (2005). Relationships between open source software companies and communities: Observations from Nordic firms. *Research Policy, 34*(4), 481–493.

Djelassi, S., & Decoopman, I. (2013). Customers' participation in product development through crowdsourcing: Issues and implications. *Industrial Marketing Management, 42*(5), 683–692.

Estellés-Arolas, E., & González-Ladrón-De-Guevara, F. (2012). Towards an integrated crowdsourcing definition. *Journal of Information Science, 38*(2), 189–200.

Ettlinger, N. (2017). Open innovation and its discontents. *Geoforum, 80*, 61–71.

Fawcett, S. E., & Waller, M. A. (2014). Can we stay ahead of the obsolescence curve? On inflection points, proactive preemption, and the future of supply chain management. *Journal of Business Logistics, 35*(1), 17–22.

Feng, Y., Ye, H. J., Yu, Y., Yang, C., & Cui, T. (2018). Gamification artifacts and crowdsourcing participation: Examining the mediating role of intrinsic motivations. *Computers in Human Behavior, 81*, 124–136.

Finzen, J., & Kintz, M. (2012, January). A Comparative Study of Innovation-Related Crowdsourcing Projects in Germany. In *ISPIM Conference Proceedings* (p. 1). The International Society for Professional Innovation Management (ISPIM).

Fleming, L., & Waguespack, D. M. (2007). Brokerage, boundary spanning, and leadership in open innovation communities. *Organization Science, 18*(2), 165–180.

Frey, K., Lüthje, C., & Haag, S. (2011). Whom should firms attract to open innovation platforms? The role of knowledge diversity and motivation. *Long Range Planning, 44*(5-6), 397–420.

Füller, J. (2010). Virtual co-creation of new products and its impact on consumers' product and brand relationships. *Academy of Management Annual Meeting Proceedings, 1*, 1–6.

Gatautis, R., & Vitauskaite, E. (2014). Crowdsourcing application in marketing activities. *Procedia: Social and Behavioral Sciences, 110*, 1243–1250.

Hanna, R., Rohm, A., & Crittenden, V. L. (2011). We're all connected: The power of the social media ecosystem. *Business Horizons, 54*(3), 265–273.

Hienerth, C. (2006). The commercialization of user innovations: The development of the rodeo kayak industry. *Research Management, 36*(3), 273–294.

Hollebeek, L. (2011). Demystifying customer brand engagement: Exploring the loyalty nexus. *Journal of Marketing Management, 27*(8), 785–807.

Hossain, M. (2012, May). Users' motivation to participate in online crowdsourcing platforms. In *2012 International Conference on Innovation Management and Technology Research* (pp. 310-315). IEEE.

Howe, J. (2006). The rise of crowdsourcing. *Wired*. Retrieved from https://www.wired.com/wired/archive/14.06/crowds_pr.html

Howe, J. (2008). *Crowdsourcing: How the power of the crowd is driving the future of business*. Random House.

Kleeman, F., Voss, G. G., & Rieder, K. (2008). Un(der)paid innovators: The commercial utilization of consumer work through crowdsourcing. *Science. Technology and Innovation Studies, 4*(1), 5–26.

Kohler, T., Fueller, J., Stieger, D., & Matzler, K. (2011). Avatar-based innovation: Consequences of the virtual co-creation experience. *Computers in Human Behavior, 27*(1), 160–168.

Kumar, V., Aksoy, L., Donkers, B., Venkatesan, R., Wiesel, T., & Tillmanns, S. (2010). Undervalued or overvalued customers: Capturing total customer engagement value. *Journal of Service Research, 13*(3), 297–310.

Lakhani, K. R., & Von Hippel, E. (2004). How open source software works:"free" user-to-user assistance. In *Produktentwicklung mit virtuellen Communities* (pp. 303–339). Gabler Verlag.

Lakhani, K. R., & Wolf, R. G. (2005). Why Hackers Do What They Do: Understanding Motivation and Effort in Free/Open Source Software Projects. Academic Press.

Leimeister, J. M., Huber, M., Bretschneider, U., & Krcmar, H. (2009). Leveraging crowdsourcing: Activation-supporting components for IT-based ideas competition. *Journal of Management Information Systems, 26*(1), 197–224.

Liang, H., Wang, M. M., Wang, J. J., & Xue, Y. (2018). How intrinsic motivation and extrinsic incentives affect task effort in crowdsourcing contests: A mediated moderation model. *Computers in Human Behavior, 81*, 168–176.

Markus, M. L. (2007). The governance of free/open source software projects: Monolithic, multidimensional, or configurational? *The Journal of Management and Governance, 11*(2), 151–163.

Marsden, P. (2009). Crowdsourcing: Your recession—Proof marketing strategy? *Contagious Magazine, 18*, 24–28.

Martineau, E. (2012). *A typology of crowdsourcing participation styles* [Doctoral dissertation]. Concordia University.

Martinez, M. G. (2015). Solver engagement in knowledge sharing in crowdsourcing communities: Exploring the link to creativity. *Research Policy, 44*(8), 1419–1430.

McDougall, G. H., & Levesque, T. (2000). Customer satisfaction with services: Putting perceived value into the equation. *Journal of Services Marketing*.

Nysveen, H., & Pedersen, P. E. (2014). Influences of cocreation on brand experience. *International Journal of Market Research, 56*(6), 807–832.

O'Mahony, S. (2003). Guarding the commons: How community managed software projects protect their work. *Research Policy, 32*(7), 1179–1198.

Pee, L. G., Koh, E., & Goh, M. (2018). Trait motivations of crowdsourcing and task choice: A distal-proximal perspective. *International Journal of Information Management, 40*, 28–41.

Pétavy, F., Céré, J., Tan, C., & Roth, Y. (2012). *Online co-creation to accelerate marketing and innovation*, Academic Press.

Pires, G. D., Stanton, J., & Rita, P. (2006). The internet, consumer empowerment and marketing strategies. *European Journal of Marketing*.

Piyathasanan, B., Mathies, C., Patterson, P., & de Ruyter, K. (2013). The Value of Crowdsourcing: Antecedents and Value Creation of Creative Process Engagement. *ANZMAC 2013*.

Piyathasanan, B., Mathies, C., Patterson, P. G., & de Ruyter, K. (2017). Continued value creation in crowdsourcing from creative process engagement. *Journal of Services Marketing*.

Poynter, R. (2013). *Crowdsourcing lessons for market research*. Academic Press.

Priem, R. L., Li, S., & Carr, J. C. (2012). Insights and new directions from demand-side approaches to technology innovation, entrepreneurship, and strategic management research. *Journal of Management, 38*(1), 346–374.

Roth, Y., Brabham, D. C., & Lemoine, J. F. (2015). Recruiting individuals to a crowdsourcing community: Applying motivational categories to an ad copy test. In *Advances in crowdsourcing* (pp. 15–31). Springer.

Roth, Y., & Kimani, R. (2014). Crowdsourcing in the production of video advertising: The emerging roles of crowdsourcing platforms. In *International perspectives on business innovation and disruption in the creative industries*. Edward Elgar Publishing.

Sawhney, M., Verona, G., & Prandelli, E. (2005). Collaborating to create: The Internet as a platform for customer engagement in product innovation. *Journal of Interactive Marketing, 19*(4), 4–17.

Singh, P. (2014). Social media crowdsourcing: Supporting user-driven innovation by generating ideas. *International Journal of Online Marketing, 4*(2), 1–14.

Sirdeshmukh, D., Singh, J., & Sabol, B. (2002). Consumer trust, value, and loyalty in relational exchanges. *Journal of Marketing, 66*(1), 15–37.

Smith, D., Manesh, M. M. G., & Alshaikh, A. (2013). How can entrepreneurs motivate crowdsourcing participants? *Technology Innovation Management Review, 3*(2).

Stanoevska-Slabeva, K. (2011). *Enabled innovation: Instruments and methods of internet-based collaborative innovation*. Conference Draft, 1st Berlin Symposium in Internet and Society.

Steils, N., & Hanine, S. (2019). Recruiting valuable participants in online IDEA generation: The role of brief instructions. *Journal of Business Research, 96*, 14–25.

Suhada, T. A., Ford, J. A., Verreynne, M. L., & Indulska, M. (2021). Motivating individuals to contribute to firms' non-pecuniary open innovation goals. *Technovation, 102*, 102233.

Tapscott, D., & Williams, A. D. (2006). Wikinomics, how mass collaboration changes everything. Penguin Group.

The State of Crowdsourcing in 2015: How the world's biggest brands and companies are opening up to consumer creativity. (n.d.). *eYeka*. https://en.eyeka.com/resources/analyst-reports#CSreport2015? utm_campaign=csr&utm_content=1&utm_medium=act&utm_source=prc &utm_term=en

Torres, E. N., & Kline, S. (2013). From customer satisfaction to customer delight: Creating a new standard of service for the hotel industry. *International Journal of Contemporary Hospitality Management*.

Van Dijk, J. (2011). *Co-creation in practice: Exploring practitioner views on co-creation*. Retrieved from http://issuu.com/joycediscovers/docs/article_interviews

Vargo, S. L., & Lusch, R. F. (2004). The four service marketing myths: Remnants of a goods-based, manufacturing model. *Journal of Service Research*, *6*(4), 324–335.

Venkatesan, R. (2017). Executing on a customer engagement strategy. *Journal of the Academy of Marketing Science*, *45*(3), 289–293.

Weick, K. E. (1976). Educational organizations as loosely coupled systems. *Administrative Science Quarterly*, 1–19.

West, J., & Gallagher, S. (2006). Challenges of open innovation: The paradox of firm investment in open-source software. *Research Management*, *36*(3), 319–331.

Wind, Y. (2008). A plan to invent the marketing we need today. *MIT Sloan Management Review*, *49*(4), 21–28.

Winter, D. G., John, O. P., Stewart, A. J., Klohnen, E. C., & Duncan, L. E. (1998). Traits and motives: Toward an integration of two traditions in personality research. *Psychological Review*, *105*(2), 230.

Ye, H. J., & Kankanhalli, A. (2015). Investigating the antecedents of organizational task crowdsourcing. *Information & Management*, *52*(1), 98–110.

Yin, X., Zhu, K., Wang, H., Zhang, J., Wang, W., & Zhang, H. (2022). Motivating participation in crowdsourcing contests: The role of instruction-writing strategy. *Information & Management*, *59*(3), 103616.

Zadeh, A. H., & Sharda, R. (2014). Modeling brand post popularity dynamics in online social networks. *Decision Support Systems*, *65*, 59–68.

Zhao, Y. C., & Zhu, Q. (2014). Effects of extrinsic and intrinsic motivation on participation in crowdsourcing contest: A perspective of self-determination theory. *Online Information Review*.

Chapter 13
Journey of FinTechs in India From Evolution to Revolution

Neha Gupta
IBCS, SOA University (Deemed), India

Ankita Agarwal
🔟 https://orcid.org/0000-0001-5017-367X
Biju Patnaik Institute of Information Technology and Management Studies, India

Varun Agarwal
Biju Patnaik Institute of Information Technology and Management Studies, India

ABSTRACT

FinTech refers to the introduction of technology into the financial sector as a result of the development of digital technology. FinTech uses technology-savvy financial innovations to create business models that are advanced, operations, or new products/services. This has led to the development of new types of services, improved financial markets, and better financial institutions. India is moving towards a powerful environment that provides a platform for FinTech startups to become billion-dollar unicorns. FinTech in India has several goals, from opening new divisions to exploring overseas markets. India's economy, typically money-driven, has seen tremendous growth in FinTech by capitalising on the opportunities presented as a result of growth in e-commerce and greater smartphone penetration rates. Hence, based on a thorough literature review by using exploratory research method, this chapter seeks to study the growth and evolution of FinTech in India, with special reference to the COVID-19 pandemic.

INTRODUCTION

FinTech, also known as financial technology, essentially refers to the use of technology for providing various financial services. It is mostly implemented through technology start-ups that are on the route to competing with banks and other financial institutions to gain a strong foothold in the financial markets. According to Kukreja et al. (2021) customers today are spoilt for choice with the array of services being provided by FinTechs, right from money transfer to payment solutions, to online portfolio management,

DOI: 10.4018/978-1-6684-5853-2.ch013

among many others. Entrepreneurs as well as established financial institutions are realizing the tremendous scope that FinTech offers and are working towards leveraging the same for building enhanced service quality and customer satisfaction by developing many breakthrough products and solutions. Some of the prominent technologies that are driving the growth of FinTechs are Artificial Intelligence (AI), big data, Machine Learning and Robotic Process Automation.

The word FinTech originated in the 21st century and initially referred to the use of technology in the back-end systems of prominent financial organizations. But today, FinTech covers a broad array of industries such as banking, education, retail and investment management to name a few. Emerging payment methods such as crypto currencies are also now considered within the purview of FinTech. There has also been a rapid shift from providing mere industry-oriented services to a more focused and demanding consumer oriented approach.

India has been emerging as one of the largest FinTech markets globally over the past decade. According to Findexable's Global FinTech Ranking Report, 2021, India has been ranked 23 in the FinTech Country Rankings. Three Indian cities – New Delhi, Bangalore and Mumbai also found a place among the top 50 of the city rankings. Many factors such as wider internet penetration rate, affordable internet, growth in the number of startups and increasing investments in technology have all contributed to the growth of FinTech in India, Muthukannan et al..(2020). Customers are looking for simple, reliable and safe financial services and FinTechs have been able to provide just that. A recent report by Boston Consulting Group and FICCI has mentions that India is in a good position to achieve a financial sector valuation of USD 150-160 billion by 2025. This indicates an incremental value creation potential of USD 100 billion. To achieve this, over the next five years, India's FinTech sector will need USD 20-25 billion worth of investments. It is just an indicator of the enormous scope that FinTech has in India. The government has also been supporting the FinTech landscape by coming up with initiatives such as Jan Dhan Yojana, Start-up India, Digital India, Make in India, etc. Digital infrastructure has also seen major updates in the form of technologies such as Aadhaar, UPI, GST, etc. Along with this, the role of regulators such as RBI, SEBI and IRDAI has been vital in ensuring the provision of safe and affordable digital financial systems. At the 2nd Global FinTech Fest 2021, the Union Minister of Commerce & Industry, Consumer Affairs and Food & Public Distribution and Textiles, Shri Piyush Goyal, mentioned that against the global average of 64%, India has the highest FinTech adoption rate in the world at 87%. He also highlighted the role that the Indian FinTech industry played during the Covid-19 pandemic saying that it enabled people to carry out critical activities from the safety of their homes, especially during the lockdown periods. He further mentioned that FinTech does have the scope to bring investments for many digital infrastructures including mobile apps, e-commerce, etc.

The Indian FinTech industry mainly offers the products/services such as payments (which comprises of payment banks, mobile wallets, payment gateways and payment infrastructure) and online financial products (lending, insurance, e-NPS and mutual funds/broking) as depicted in the figure given below.

Figure 1.
Source: www.rbi.org.in

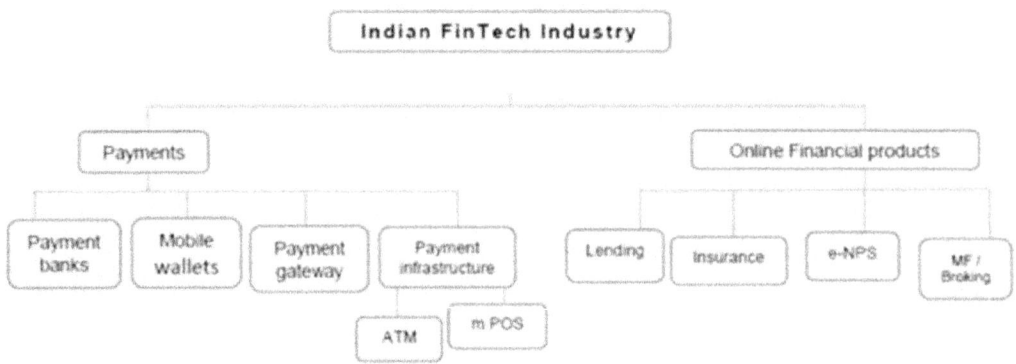

Looking at the presence of FinTechs from a geographical viewpoint, though FinTechs earlier were concentrated mostly in the major metropolitan cities of India such as Mumbai, Delhi, Bengaluru and Hyderabad, over the years FinTechs have been establishing their base in smaller cities as well such as Jaipur, Ahmedabad, Pune, etc.

Figure 2.
Source: *RBI Bulletin November 2020*

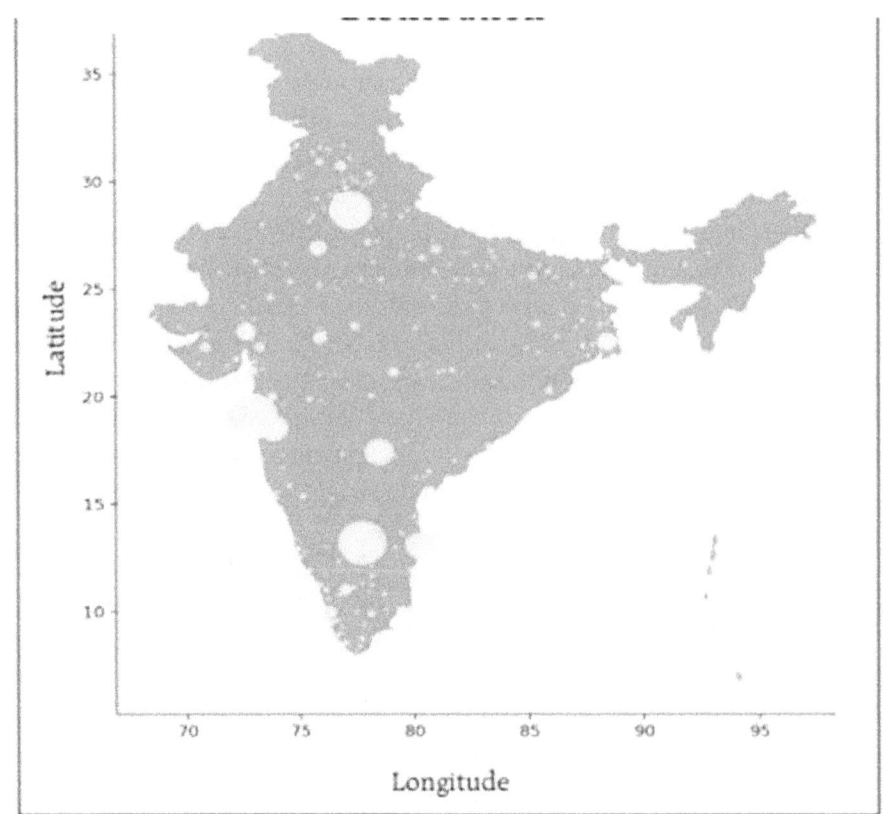

The enormous demand for digital services has led to creation of the world's third largest tech unicorn ecosystem in India. Unicorns are basically companies with a valuation of than $1 billion. As per Le (2021) the recent Covid-19 pandemic also brought about many changes in Indian consumer behaviour. The pandemic led to a major increase in the adoption of digital payments thus leading to a boom in FinTech operations in the country. Given in the table below, is the details of FinTechs that achieved unicorn status year wise.

Figure 3.

Year	Unicorn event by year (16)							
2021 (YTD, 8)	Cred	Chargebee	Digit	Groww	Zeta	BharatPe	CoinDCX	OfBusiness
2020 (3)	Razorpay	Zerodha	Pine Labs					
2019 (3)	Razorpay	Billdesk	Zoho					
Upto 2018 (2)	Paytm	Policy Bazaar						

Source: Tracxn, Sept 2021

Some of the major FinTech companies in India are listed below:

- Paytm
- Razorpay
- Pine Labs
- Groww
- Bharat Pe
- Policybazaar
- CRED
- Digit Insurance
- CoinSwitch
- Zeta

LITERATURE REVIEW

Rani (2021) conducted a study to understand the purpose, challenges faced and latest developments in FinTech by considering certain variables such as perception, customer satisfaction, behaviour, adoption and security. The results of the study showed that perceived ease of use, perceived risk, perceived usefulness, trust, compatibility and performance were the variables that were the most examined in FinTech literature. The author highlighted that security concerns act as a huge barrier in terms of customer satisfaction in FinTech. Hence, there needs to be more focus on taking better measures to enhance security and ensure the safety of customers of FinTech.

Baber (2019) carried out a study to measure the service quality of FinTech that was being offered by the Islamic banks of UAE and Malaysia and its impact on customer satisfaction. The study also included the dimension of Shariah compliance in order to make it more relevant to Islamic banks. It was found from the results that the major determinants for customer satisfaction in these banks were transaction and promise fulfilment, efficient and reliable services, aesthetics of the site and information in accordance with Shariah. The study made use of an e-SERVQUAL model in order to measure the service quality of FinTech in Islamic banks.

Alwi et al. (2019) studied the level of customer satisfaction on mobile payment services offered by FinTechs in Malaysia. The study made use of both primary as well as secondary data and the data collection was done by conducting a survey among 300 people in Malaysia who were aged 17 and above and also had experience with regard to usage of FinTech mobile payment services. The results of the study found a strong correlation between the dependent variables i.e., customer satisfaction and the independent variables i.e. convenience, ease of use, service, quality, information presentation and security and privacy. It was also found that security and privacy was a very strong influencing factor in case of FinTech mobile payment services, followed by ease of use, service quality and presentation of information. The authors suggested various measures to enhance the service quality of mobile payment services offered by FinTechs.

Pant (2020) conducted a study to understand the trends adopted by various FinTechs globally. The results of the study indicated that there have been major transformations in the world of finance as a result of newer technologies being adopted by FinTechs. It was found that India and China have been leading the world in terms of awareness stage and adoption rate of digital payments. The Indian government especially has been very encouraging towards digital payments and has been focussing on eliminating corruption while also ensuring cost reduction of transactions, Sharma (2021). It was also found that central banks and regulatory bodies have been playing a major role in setting up the right environment and policies for development of FinTech. The study further highlighted that latest technology such as block chain, AI, cloud computing, big data, drones, etc. are being leveraged by FinTech firms. The author posits that future research can focus on examining the development of FinTech by exploring areas such as digital invoicing, digital leasing, crowd investing, cryptocurrencies, etc.

Sharma et al. (2022) carried out a study to explore the elements influencing consumer use of Fin-Tech in India. Empirical research method was used for carrying out the study. Data was collected using structured questionnaires handed out to a selected group of clients of a bank. The results of the study indicated that consumers' preferences with regard to FinTech changes depending upon various internal elements such as living standards, location, adaptability of people, etc. The authors posit that factors such as growth in innovation, breakthroughs in technology, changing expectations of clients, changes with respect to financial background have all contributed towards the growth of FinTech in India. Further, FinTech was also found to have the scope for improving financial inclusion as the poorer sections of the society which are still unbanked can be considered.

Evolution of FinTechs in India

FinTech is one of the fastest growing financial services industries in the world. For the past decade, Fin-Tech has been at the heart of customer-centric innovation (Anifa et al., 2022). The steady and efficient provision of wages, credit, insurance, wealth management and intermediaries disrupted the industry and led to the rebranding of financial services. In line with international trends, FinTech's ecosystem in India has shown tremendous growth over the last 5 years.

Vibrant FinTech Ecosystem on a High-Growth Trajectory:

- Not only has FinTech been integrated by Indian consumers across all industries, but the acceptance of FinTech products by financial institutions has also increased dramatically. As a result, the number of FinTechs in India is on the rise. 67% of the more than 2,100 FinTechs currently operating in India have been established in the past five years. The FinTech investment is also significant: Indian FinTechs have raised over $ 10 billion since 2016. To date, eight FinTechs have reached a value of "$ 1 billion" and there are 44 FinTechs. It is estimated to exceed $ 100 million.
- The total value of India's FinTech industry is estimated at $ 50-60 billion, making it a large and dynamic FinTech ecosystem. (See Exhibit 1).
- While FinTech revenues to India declined sharply in 2020 (see Figure 2), India remains among the top 5 FinTech companies. In addition, COVID-19 raised digital levels in groups. While some segments of Fin¬Tech (such as loans) may experience a decline in the near future, there is a significant shift in tightening the digital offer of financial services. Between March 2020 and January 2021, UPI payments (in value) tripled the value of the initial blow, while the proportion of alternative payment methods declined. A similar increase was observed in online broadcasting, where the proportion of clients working with the FinTech discount broker (Zeroda, Upstox, 5paisa) increased from 43% to 57% (see Appendix 3). Unsurprisingly, FinTech's rating in India has grown significantly over the past 14 months: 3 new Unicorns (Pine Labs, Razorpay and Digit Insurance) and five new Soonicorns were launched in January 2020.
- The robustness of the Indian business environment is also reflected in the diversity of the FinTech base. Although payments and other forms of financing accounted for over 90% of India's investments in 2015, there has been a change in the distribution of investments between sectors. In 2020, FinTech and InsurTechs to reflect 4-5 times increase and recorded a total investment of $ 145 million and $ 215 million, respectively.

Figure 4.

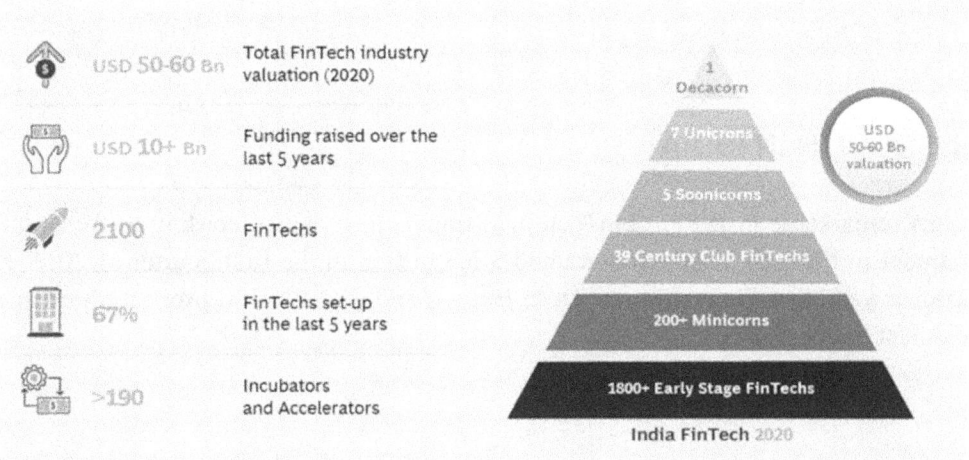

USD 50-60 Bn	Total FinTech industry valuation (2020)	1 Decacorn
USD 10+ Bn	Funding raised over the last 5 years	7 Unicorns / USD 50-60 Bn valuation
2100	FinTechs	5 Soonicorns
67%	FinTechs set-up in the last 5 years	39 Century Club FinTechs / 200+ Minicorns
>190	Incubators and Accelerators	1800+ Early Stage FinTechs

India FinTech 2020

Figure 5.

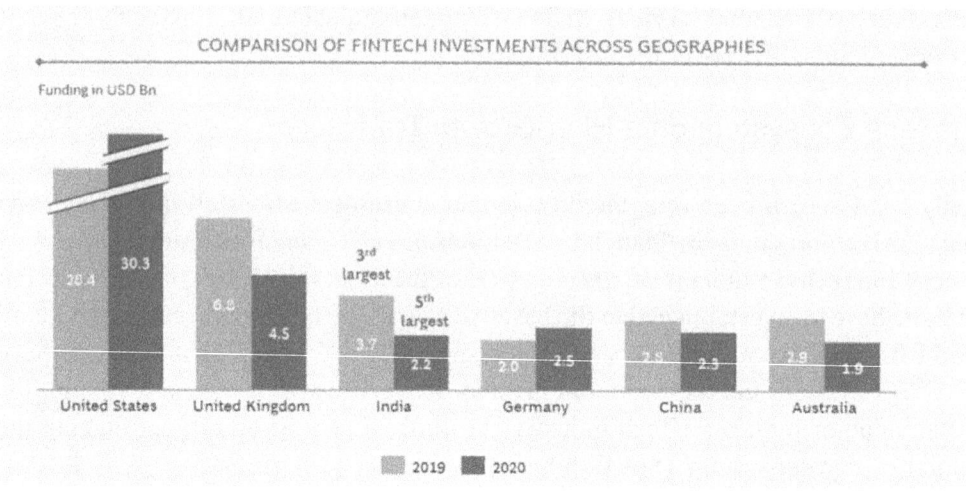

Figure 6.

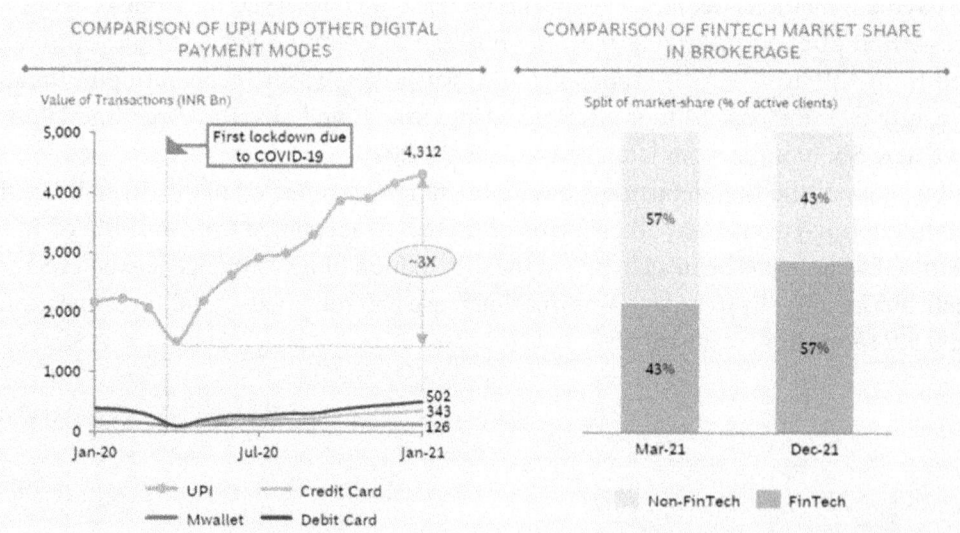

FINTECH GROWTH IN INDIA

There has been remarkable growth in FinTech investments in India. According to Accenture (2016a), global investment in FinTech businesses reached $ 5.3 billion in the first quarter of 2016, an increase of 67% year-over-year, and FinTech's growth in Europe and Asia-Pacific proportion of investment in companies almost doubled to 62%.

With one of the largest markets in the world, India has become one of the largest FinTech industries in recent years. In India, unsecured loans, mobile phone transactions, secure payment gateways, wallets, and other strategies have already been adopted.

Two years ago, the introduction of digital payments in India facilitated the exchange of key financial services on the go. The growth and expansion of the FinTech environment in India have led to several factors including the development of smartphones, the development of the internet, and a high level of connectivity Ernst & Young. (2021).

Indeed, according to reports by the Boston Consulting Group (BCG) and Federation of Indian Chambers of Commerce and Industry (FICCI), India is in a well-off position to achieve growth in FinTech. By 2025, the industry will be worth 150-160 billion dollars, with a potential value-added of 100 billion dollars. According to the report "India FinTech: $100 Billion Opportunity", the FinTech sector in India will need investments to the tune of 20-25 billion dollars in the next few years in order to achieve this.

As far as India is concerned, it has always been seen that payment services are usually carried out through the medium of banks. But, as technology grows, this situation no longer holds true, as the earlier situation of banks holding a monopoly position in the area of payment services has now been disrupted.

The payments infrastructure in India has seen extremely wonderful growth in the last few years, especially after new ways of payments as well as interventions were introduced. Some of the popular ones include IMPS (Instant Payment Service), UPI (Unified Payments Interface), BHIM (Bharat Interface for Money), etc. The government of India has also introduced various initiatives such as "Make in India" and "Digital India". These initiatives have contributed immensely to the profitability of FinTechs in India. It has also been seen that the RBI (Reserve Bank of India) has of late been encouraging more usage of electronic payment systems in order to build a cash community.

In addition, the government introduction of new schemes like GST rebates has also created positive growth for FinTech services. While access to foreign currency has provoked much controversy and outrage, especially among the general public, it has ultimately been a factor in the transition of the currency-based economy to digital, electronic technology community support conference. FinTech conversion is now available. It is reasonable to assume that COVID-19 has led to the fast spread of digitally enabled financial transactions among all forums to promote uninterrupted support to cashless and touchless payments Kandpal et al. (2019).

Digital payments have become a way of life in India and 10-15 million new customers have joined the digital platform in the past 12 months. Two factors have contributed to the change: the size of the unit and the distribution of Covid-19. There is a very complicated backend ecosystem for these platforms but it has given a massive convenience to the end-user and has made it more popular with consumers, which has led to its widespread use, "said Hemant Gala, India's head of payment and digital finance services at PhonePe. Further, he also emphasized the fact that out of more than 2100 FinTechs operating in the country, 67% of them have been established within the last five years.

With the development of convenient and highly competitive payment mediums such as PayTM, Mobikwik, Google Pay, Phone Pe, etc., the Indian FinTech market's standards are no longer restricted just to digital payments. Further, the international partnership between two popular firms – Reliance Jio and Facebook, is also expected to give an additional boost to the digital payments system in India, as the focus here would be on digital businesses spanning two and three cities in the region.

Considering that India is now one of the key players in the Asian financial market, this chapter aims to explore the challenges associated with FinTech in India and discuss their future outlook. This chapter makes use of an exploratory research method using secondary data.

Contribution of FinTechs towards Financial Inclusion in India

Financial inclusion is being actively promoted in India through initiatives such as Jan Dhan Yojana, Aadhaar enrolment, licensing of Payment Banks/Small Finance Banks, etc. by the Govt. of India along with Reserve Bank of India (2018). This has been an opportunity for FinTech companies in India to leverage technology and take advantage of these initiatives by growing financial inclusion.

Figure 7.
Source: *Report of the Working Group on FinTech and Digital Banking, Reserve Bank of India (2018)*

S. No.	Area of Financial Inclusion	Use of FinTech
1	Augment the government social cash transfer in order to increase the personal disposable income of the poor. It would put the economy on a medium-term sustainable inclusion path.	Easy cash transfer App
2	Banks should make special efforts to step up account opening for females belonging to lower income group under this scheme for social cash transfer as a welfare measure (Sukanya Shiksha Scheme).	Modification to existing Bank FinTech App.
3	Aadhaar should be linked to each individual credit account as a unique biometric identifier which can be shared with Credit information bureau to enhance the stability of the credit system and improve access.	Integration of Aadhaar Infrastructure
4	Bank's traditional business model should be changed with greater reliance on mobile technology to improve 'last mile' service delivery.	Enhanced Mobile Banking
5	Increase the formal credit supply to all agrarian segments through Aadhaar-linked mechanism for Credit Eligibility Certificates (CEC).	Digitisation of land records
6	Corporates should be encouraged to nurture Self Help Groups (SHGs) as part of Corporate Social Responsibility (CSR) initiative	Loan / Payment App
7	Replacement of Government's current agricultural input subsidies on fertilizers, irrigation and power by a direct income transfer scheme as a part of second generation reforms.	Direct Account Transfer App with the help of Aadhaar Infrastructure
8	Introducing universal crop insurance scheme by Government covering all crops starting with small and marginal farmers with monetary ceiling of Rs. 2 lakhs	Crop Insurance App
9	To provide credit guarantees in niche areas for micro and small enterprises (MSEs). It would also explore possibilities for counter guarantee and re-insurance.	Multiple Guarantee App for agencies
10	Introduction of UID for all MSME borrowers and information from it should be shared with credit bureaus	UID for MSME App

Services Provided by FinTechs in India

Fintechs in India Revolve Around 5 Core Aspects, Namely:

1. FinTech companies (comprising of capital markets, wealth management firms, payments firms, crowd-funding, etc.)
2. Financial Institutions (comprising of venture capitalists, banks, brokerage firms, insurance companies, etc.)
3. Customers (comprising of organizations as well as individuals)
4. Technology Developers (comprising of firms involved in development of social media, technologies such as big data, crypto-currencies, cloud computing, etc.)
5. Government

All the above components together, boost economy, encourage collaboration and competition in the financial sector, and ultimately create a win-win situation for customers.

The companies mentioned above are very focused on entrepreneurship and have introduced many new methods in lending, wealth management, payments, community finance, capital markets and insurance, reduction of operating costs, focusing on various niche markets and services, offering services that are more unique and customized than the traditional ones. These are the ones that trigger the occurrence of unbundling of financial services, that seriously disrupts the banking business (Walchek, 2015). The ability to separate services is one of the main drivers of growth in the FinTech sector, as traditional financial institutions are at a disadvantage in this regard.

Instead of relying on a financial institution to meet their needs, consumers are beginning to choose the service they need from different FinTech companies. Venture capitalization and private equity investment help FinTech start-ups grow, and the amount of investment has risen significantly over time. The government has provided a favorable regulatory environment for FinTech since the 2008 financial crisis (Holland FinTech, 2015). Depending on national economic development plans and policies, different governments offer different levels of regulation (e.g., financial services licensing, capital exemptions, and tax cuts) to FinTech start-ups to stimulate FinTech innovation and increase global financial competitiveness.

For example, Singapore has changed its online payment rules to make it easier for payment service providers to use the rules and to stimulate the development of payment technology (Reuters, 2016). On the other hand, traditional financial institutions in 2008 have been subject to stricter government regulations, capital requirements and reporting obligations. Stricter regulatory requirements for FinTech start-ups will allow them to provide more personalized, cheaper and more affordable consumer financial services than traditional institutions.

Although some regulations are favorable to FinTech start-ups, they still need to understand how these regulations can affect their services. LintUp, a FinTech company, has been fined $ 3.63 million for violating consumer financial protection laws, including Truth in Foreign Law and the Dodd-Frank Wall Street Consumer Reform and Reform Bureau. Financial customers are one of the sources of income for FinTech firms. Though large institutions are considered to be some of the major sources of income, private clients and small and medium-sized enterprises (SMEs) are the main sources of income for FinTech companies. A survey showed that younger and richer customers use mainly FinTech services (Holland FinTech, 2015). FinTech users are generally the first to understand technology, younger people in urban areas and with higher incomes. Today, millennials (people between the ages of 18 and 34) make up a significant portion of FinTech consumption.

The future demographic position will simplify FinTech companies in the coming years; Millennial knowledge of technology will represent the majority of the population and will be a driving force for the growth of FinTech service in India. Traditional financial institutions are also one of the pillars of the FinTech ecosystem, Rajeswari & Vijai (2021).

Innovation in FinTechs is now being supported by plans developed by financial institutions by making re-assessments of their current business models. The impact of FinTech on the market is very well recognized by these financial institutions and they are working on minimizing its potential impact. As compared to start-ups in FinTech, financial institutions are considered to be more aggressive and competitive with respect to capital investment and size. However, these financial institutions mostly provide general products and services to customers without any kind of personalisation or specialization. These specialized services are rather offered by FinTechs.

- Even though the FinTech industry that has been on a high growth trajectory has always been treated as a threat by the financial industry, it is also emphasized that partnerships with FinTech start-ups does give a wide range of financial options. Rather than capital, this kind of understanding can be undertaken for staying in technology.

Adoption of FinTech Among Digitally Active Consumers

Table 1.

	Money transfer and paymen ts	Financial Plannin g	Savings And Investme nts	Borrowi ng	Insura nce
India	72%	20%	39%	20%	47%
Glob al	50%	10%	20%	10%	24%

Source: EY FinTech Adoption Index 2017 Country Dashboard.

Motivating Factors For Adoption of FinTechs Are:

1. Simplicity of setting up an account
2. Greater access to a wide range of products and services
3. Highly effective quality of service
4. Pleasant online experience as well as proper functionality
5. Fees and rates that are attractive enough
6. Round the clock accessibility in terms of services
7. Innovation in products as compared to the traditional financial institutions

Obstacles for Adoption of FinTechs Are:

1. Inadequate awareness
2. Insufficient awareness regarding the usage and functions of FinTechs
3. Belief that providers of traditional financial services are more reliable
4. Inability to trust financial technologies

Creating Superior Customer Experiences for Added Advantage

Though customers are said to be the primary beneficiaries of any business; being able to establish superior customer experiences may prove to be a highly beneficial situation for all, including existing firms. In fact if financial institutions think of redesigning customer experiences effectively, then it can lead to customers believing that financial institutions are indeed experts who they can approach for advice and also to access better and wider range of services.

Some factors can have a positive impact on customer experience. Firms can help to improve customer experiences by focusing on certain critical elements such as the ones mentioned below.

Figure 8.
Source: Created by the author

- **More personalization:** As per the tastes and preferences of customers, personalized services and offerings may be provided to them effectively if huge customer data can be accessed easily.
- **Enhanced service delivery:** Customers today want things done quickly and digitally. Delays in service deliveries lead to customers being turned off. Hence there is a need for the speed of service delivery to be increased.
- **Providing convenience:** Round the clock access to services through any channels or devices is necessary for improving service quality and customer experiences.
- **Ease of interaction:** Better customer experiences can be created by implementation of design based user interfaces. In addition, firms can also make use of AR or VR technologies to engage customers in a better manner.
- **Improved functionality:** By bridging gaps and providing innovative solutions to customer needs and requirements, firms can improve themselves and reach new heights.
- **Driven insights:** Customer experiences can be enhanced by making use of predictive analytics which help in identifying and understanding the needs of customers well in advance and enable

firms to provide services accordingly. This also helps customers to protect themselves from frauds and leads to opportunities for saving money. Sometimes, this is what ultimately leads to customer delight.

FinTech Industry Segments

Figure 9.

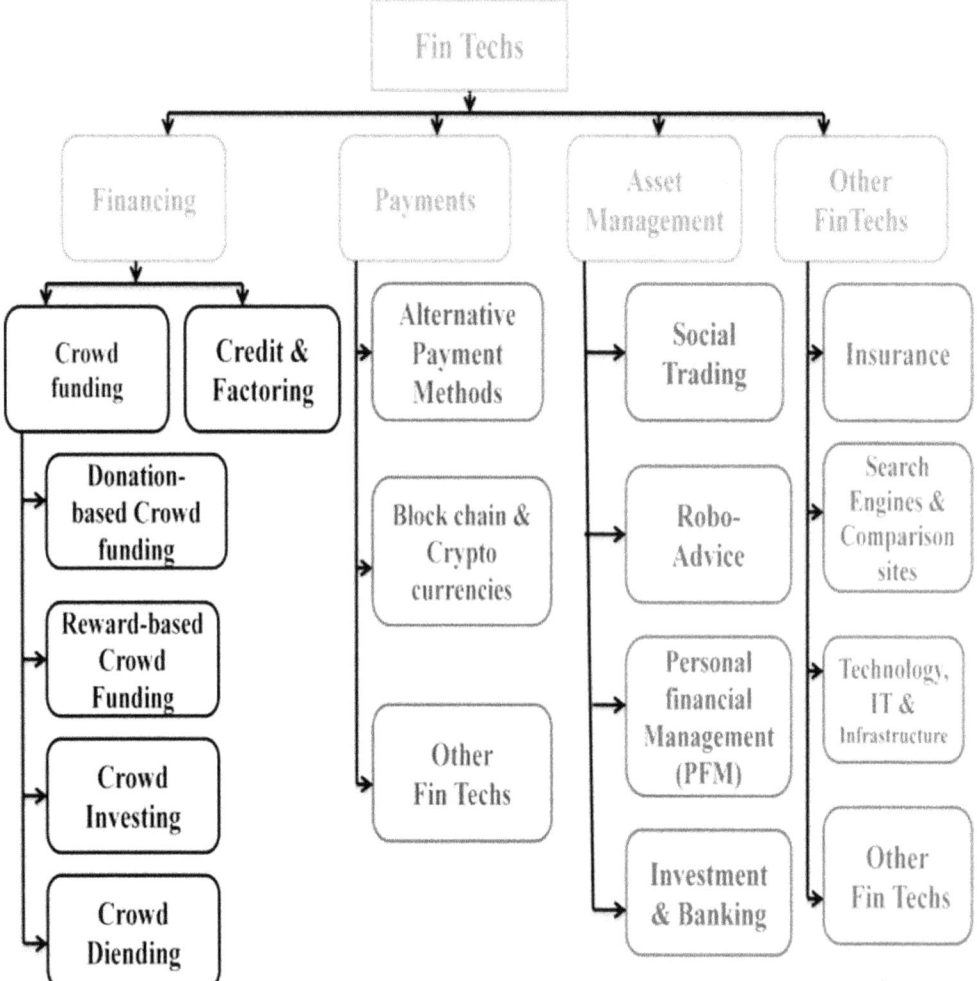

Financing

FinTechs are playing a huge role in development of financing and lending processes as customers now need not depend only on banks for loans. FinTechs aid customers by directly providing loans. The application and approval process of loans through FinTechs is also simpler and quicker as compared to banks. Borrowers' creditworthiness is assessed and the underwriting process is automated.

The two main ways of financing are Crowd funding and Credit & Factoring.

Crowd Financing

Various methods of crowd finance are available to customers today. Each such option has its own set of benefits for both investors and businesses. Customers can go for them as per their needs. The various options are described below:

Crowd Financing based on Donations

This type of crowd finance is meant mainly for the purpose of charity or a certain cause. No returns are expected from such donations. It is done purely to gain satisfaction.

Reward based Crowd Financing

In this type of crowd financing, investors look at funding a venture in order to gain non-financial benefits. It is a very unique source and also works similar to a tiered system. The higher the investor donates, the greater is the reward (in the form of free gifts, coupons, event tickets, etc.). Such type of rewards given do not sink a hole in the pockets of the business and are hence beneficial.

Crowd Investing

This method of crowd funding is mostly based online. Typically, a huge number of people (the crowd), co-invest into businesses or people over the internet. This comprises of both debt as well as equity firms. Returns are in the form of shares or interest. It is not necessary for those investing to know each other beforehand.

Crowd Lending

This type of crowd funding is like an alternative to bank functions. Crowd lending gives an opportunity to both businesses as well as individuals to raise debt from the public. It is a very powerful and methodical system which connects investors and borrowers. Returns are gained in the form of a certain percentage of money lent as interest.

Credit and Factoring

Just like lending, factoring is also now online. Many FinTechs are providing an opportunity to small business entrepreneurs to gain access to working capital through online applications. It has become simpler and easier for businesses to get money into their accounts in a short period of time with a just a click. Seller can get loans on their receivables through factoring.

Payments

Payments is a popular category of the FinTech market. This actually reduces the dependence on banks by allowing people to send money to each other directly. Usually customers make payments through banks, they have to pay a huge amount of money as fees for making even simple payments like peer-to-peer transfer.

FinTechs provide an opportunity to consumers to make payments quickly and effectively. The use of certain technologies such as block chain for example, are making it possible for quicker processing of payments by firms and also more cost effectively as compared to banks.

Alternative Payment Methods

Another huge benefit that FinTechs are offering is the option of multiple payment methods. Usually customers who are dependent on banks have to log in to their bank account and then make a payment from there. But the arrival of FinTech has changed that. Customers can now conveniently make payments through various options as and when they want to without going through the hassle of logging into their bank account. A few companies also give an option to customers to pay using social media platforms such as Whatsapp, Facebook and Twitter.

Blockchain Technology and Cryptocurrency

Block chain has been a breakthrough technology in the banking and finance industry. It enables people to track their asset movement more efficiently and also keep a record of transactions. It is also a safer option as it is not possible for theft of information because the information has been stored in personal devices that form a network. Block chain is faster, simpler and more affordable and does not comprise of any intermediaries.

Asset Management

As a part of asset management, FinTechs provide high-net worth individuals with services such as financial and investment advisory. Wealth managers help people to plan out their financial needs such as retirement planning, insurance, portfolio handling, etc. There is no requirement of many people or companies being involved.

Social Trading

This is a somewhat new concept and is based on the belief that the collective wisdom of thousands of traders is far superior as compared to the wisdom of one. Social trading hubs provide a platform for traders all over the globe to connect. A network is thus created which encourages sharing of viewpoints and trades of various people. An investor can easily use such information for making important social decisions instead of having to depend on recommendations, company fundamentals or quantitative data.

Robo-advice

Sometimes customers are in a situation where they do not wish to take the help of a financial advisor as they cannot afford to pay for the same. For dealing with such situations, a new type of software has been developed through which Robo advisors help customers in managing their investments and build a diversified portfolio. These Robo advisors use an algorithm to provide automated investment advice.

Personal Financial Management (PFM)

The recent years have also seen the development of software that enables budgeting through the use of technology. Individuals can manage their investments and spending and stick to a budget, thus avoiding debt. Such software helps by letting customers add accounts from multiple financial institutions and keeping track.

Investment and Banking

The world of finance has seen a lot of automation in the recent years. Traditional investment banking models are being replaced with FinTechs that offer the same services at lower costs Painoli et al. (2021). FinTechs have also begun to target and invade the business models of big investment banks. They have started offering services such as wealth management, loans and private investment.

Other FinTechs

The category of other FinTechs refers to those FinTech businesses that are giving services other than that of traditional banking functions such as asset management, financing and payments. This includes search engines, insurance, websites enabling comparisons, technology, information technology and infrastructure.

Insurance

The insurance business has also entered into the domain of FinTechs. Almost all the companies are putting their focus on distribution of insurance. Various apps are being used to reach out to customers. As compared to traditional insurers, FinTechs are more flexible. As the market for insurance is also heavily regulated, FinTechs are hence entering into partnerships with traditional insurance service providers. This category of FinTechs are referred to as InsurTechs.

Search Engines and Comparison Sites

Another category of FinTechs consists of search engines that enable customers to compare different financial products and services provided by various players in the market.

Technology, IT, and Infrastructure

This sub segment comprises of FinTechs that offer the required technical solutions to various financial services providers.

CHALLENGES FACED BY FINTECH IN INDIA

Despite having great opportunities, FinTech does face a rough path ahead. Given below, is a list of possible hurdles that FinTechs may face.

1. Entering into the Indian market itself is not easy because of the strict legal framework that is made to steer clear of fraud Baporikar, N. (2021). A new entrant has to go through a lot of formalities before starting operations. This poses as a big barrier.

2. Low literacy level, poor internet infrastructure and a largely unbanked population are some hurdles faced by FinTechs. Though a bank account is a must for conducting online transactions, a large chunk of Indians still do not have accounts with banks. As per a study by Priya & Anusha, (2019) people also have the issue of low connectivity to the internet, which leads to more processing time for completing transactions. Also, many Indians do not have adequate financial literacy to understand various processes associated with online transactions. So they still prefer cash transactions.

3. Another challenge is to change the mindset of Indian customers, especially sellers and users who are dealing with cash transactions on a daily basis. Most of the old aged persons find it difficult to let go of their old habits of dealing with cash and adopting online transactions instead.

4. Lot of work is also required on the part of FinTechs to make the whole system safer and more trustable by bringing about improvements in technology, infrastructure and consumer friendliness. Online frauds are a common irritant for customers.

5. The growth of FinTech in India also requires more support from the government and incentives for protecting their interests. This is usually a point of loss of morale amongst entrepreneurs. The right guidance and support will certainly ensure the betterment of India's economy on the whole.

6. Gaining the trust of investors is again a very difficult task for FinTechs just like any other industry. Getting on-time investments are the needed seed capital is becoming very tough and may reflect negatively on the functioning and operations.

Future Trends in FinTech

As per the report published by World Bank, more than 1.7 billion people worldwide do not or cannot access the financial system. Because of shortage of funds we don't have a savings account because there aren't enough (over 60 percent), unnecessary (30 percent) and too expensive (26 percent), the survey reveals. The report also found that only two percent of India's population has at least some form of insurance, with FinTech leading the way. Here are some of the upcoming FinTech trends that will revolutionize the financial services industry:

- **Digital banking**: Visiting a bank branch today for your financial needs has become a part of past thing now, people these days demand FinTech services so that they can use and avail all financial transactions by sitting at home at a click on their computer or mobile phones and this defines the future of FinTech's. According to the company's expectations, the number of digital solutions will continue, and by 2024 more than 71% of population will start using internet banking and other FinTech platforms. The main factors driving the trend are the widespread use of mobile phones in financial services, convenience and wide access, and low operating costs. Mobile Payments The biggest "thing" in FinTech is the rise of the mobile payments industry, Potey & Soni (2019). Customers want instant, anonymous and free payments (IIF). Mobile payment technology could do away with our traditional wallets as global consumers become less reliant on cash. Google, Apple, Tencent and Alibaba have their own payment systems and are starting to use new technologies such as biometric access control, fingerprint activation and facial recognition.

- **Blockchain**: Blockchain will make the financial services industry more efficient. Since fraud and identity theft cost financial companies trillions of dollars a year, blockchain has the ability to prevent such severe losses for businesses. By 2023 it is expected that FinTech market will cross $6700 million. FinTech's can use Blockchain technology for building smart contracts, making automatic transfers, privacy and stock exchanges regulation. It is also estimated that in near future software-as-a-service cloud infrastructure will become a standard practice among FinTech companies across the world. At present also companies make use of, shared data infrastructure systems, CRM systems and human resources administration.

- **Artificial Intelligence and Big Data:** With the help of Artificial intelligence and Big Data companies will be able to collect, store and mine data knowledge, can achieve personalization at an unmatched level. FinTech firms can also have all data on their clients about past and present financial actions and social habits. Because of AI real-time omnichannel system can be accessible real time experiences to provide their clients a individualized attention. Many well-established companies like Kotak, Paytm, Bharti Airtel and DBS have already made the first step for the Indian market to launch digital-only banking services.

- **Robotics Process Automation**: Due to huge cost involved in developing AI systems many FinTech companies do not have ample resources to develop independent AI technologies, they are looking for other solutions - the best option is to outsource to a technology provider. In coming years, AI will be a strategic part of long-term operations, to carve a competitive position in market. According to the Accenture report, bank customers get digital support systems because they offer personalized services according to their needs. 71 percent of users can provide computer support. We have seen an increase in the use of FinTech so far and it will only increase in the future. New businesses will gain exposure to FinTech-based products and services. Subsidiaries can merge and introduce innovative products and services in this area. The potential of FinTech can be seen in emerging economies and in developing economies like India, where most of the population falls under the age of 35. This clearly shows the need for innovative and strong products and services for successful entrepreneurs.

CONCLUSION

FinTech technologies has brought a sea change in traditional ways of providing in financial services and thus has put a question mark on companies to evaluate their old ways of doing business. Over the years, the huge impact FinTech have created on the financial sector was not only destructive for old businesses, but also alarming. Initially there was slow growth of pace for FinTech but in the recent years this front has seen a surprisingly very high accelerated growth thanks to the Indian government's digitization initiatives.it is also predicted that in coming two decades, this growth will continue to rise at an fast pace reason being constant growth in the population & growing technical know-how among people of India. India, being hugely populated country with around 1.3 billion people, managing levels of demand and supply will still pose a challenge in front of business.

Businesses with FinTech technologies should work more on creating mobile-friendly approach of buying goods as Indians spend more time on their mobile phones as compared to any other offline and online platform. Using mobile data will also be cheaper as compared to other digital platforms. Major changes in technologies like switch from 4 G to 5 G, concessions on corporate taxes, startup friendly policies, and reasonable handholding by government in this field would improve pace and ease the way for FinTech's in the future. As India has the lowest price for one giga byte of data around the globe, mobile first solution would be simpler to accomplish. FinTech firms can also focus upon localization of content in different regional languages this will remove language barrier, and will lead to adoption of FinTech technology by more number of people.

Looking at the bigger picture, it is very evident that there is a plethora of FinTechs emerging in India. Observing their pace of development, it cannot be denied that India does have tremendous potential in terms of entrepreneurship. There are more than 1500 FinTech startups operating in the country. Out of these, almost half were started in the past two years. FinTech firms need to be groomed well both financially and technically. Most of the successful startups are in the payments space and the same is expected from other financial segments also. There is a need for introduction of various initiatives by the government of India as well as other regulatory bodies in order to encourage the future growth of FinTechs.

The role of regulators as far as FinTech is concerned is quite complex, but also an extremely important one as they could have direct impact over the level of competition amongst existing FinTechs and new entrants. Eventually they have to ensure that there is a level playing field, while also encouraging a secure, innovative and competitive financial market. Additionally, collaborations between banks and FinTechs need to be encouraged in order to ensure better operational excellence and a smoother customer experience. FinTechs can also be encouraged to collaborate with start-ups and Insurtech companies to enable a smoother customer experience and in a cost-effective way. The government can also consider providing tax subsidies to merchants that accept a part of their business revenues through the use of digital payment services instead of cash.

Consumers today are growing more tech savvy by the day and are hence expecting greater levels of personalization and enhanced digital experiences. Market regulators may focus on these aspects in order to increase the level of education/awareness among customers.

REFERENCES

Accenture. (2016a). *Global Fintech investment growth continues in 2016 driven by Europe and Asia, Accenture study finds.* Available at https://newsroom.accenture.com/news/ global-Fintech-investme nt growth-continues-in-2016- drivenby- europe-and-asia-accen ture-study-finds.htm

Alwi, S. (2021). Fintech as financial inclusion: Factors affecting behavioral intention to accept mobile e-wallet during Covid-19 outbreak. *Turkish Journal of Computer and Mathematics Education, 12*(7), 2130–2141.

Anifa, M., Ramakrishnan, S., Joghee, S., Kabiraj, S., & Bishnoi, M. M. (2022). Fintech Innovations in the Financial Service Industry. *Journal of Risk and Financial Management, 15*(7), 287. doi:10.3390/ jrfm15070287

Baber, H. (2019). *Financial inclusion and FinTech: A comparative study of countries following Islamic finance and conventional finance.* Qualitative Research in Financial Markets. doi:10.1108/QRFM-12-2018-0131

Baporikar, N. (2021). FinTech Challenges and Outlook in India. In Innovative Strategies for Implementing FinTech in Banking (pp. 136-153). IGI Global. doi:10.4018/978-1-7998-3257-7.ch008

Ernst & Young. (2021). *The winds of change Trends shaping India's FinTech sector.* Author.

Holland FinTech. (2015). *The future of finance: The socialization of finance.* Author.

Kandpal, V., & Mehrotra, R. (2019). Financial inclusion: The role of FinTech and digital financial services in India. *Indian Journal of Economics & Business, 19*(1), 85–93.

Kukreja, G., Bahl, D., & Gupta, R. (2021). The Impact of FinTech on Financial Services in India: Past, Present, and Future Trends. IGI Global. doi:10.4018/978-1-7998-3257-7.ch012

Le, M. T. (2021). Examining Factors That Boost Intention and Loyalty to Use FinTech Post Covid-19 Lockdown As a New Normal Behaviour. *Heliyon, 7*(8), 1–9. doi:10.1016/j.heliyon.2021.e07821

Muthukannan, P., Tan, B., Gozman, D., & Johnson, L. (2020). The emergence of a FinTech ecosystem: A case study of the Vizag FinTech Valley in India. *Information & Management, 57*(8), 103385. doi:10.1016/j.im.2020.103385

Painoli, G., Dhinakaran, D., & Vijai, C. (2021, June). Impact of FinTech on the Profitability of Public and Private Banks in India. *Annals of the Romanian Society for Cell Biology, 25*(6), 5419–5431.

Pant, S. (2020, September). FinTech: Emerging Trends. *Telecom Business Review, 13*(1), 47–52.

Potey, D., & Soni, J. (2019). A Study on How Digital Payments have Revolutionized the Customer Experience. *The Management Quest, 2*(1).

Priya, P., & Anusha, K. (2019, September). FinTech Issues and Challenges in India. *International Journal of Recent Technology and Engineering, 8*(3), 904–908.

Rajeswari, P., & Vijai, C. (2021). FinTech Industry In India: The Revolutionized Finance Sector. *European Journal of Molecular & Clinical Medicine, 8*(11), 4300–4306.

Rani, M. S. B. A. (2021). Study on customer satisfaction, adoption, perception, behaviour, and Security on financial technology (fintech) services. In *International Conference on Multidisciplinary Innovation and Economics* (*Vol. 8*). Academic Press.

Reserve Bank of India. (2018). *Report of the Working Group on FinTech and Digital Banking.* Retrieved from https://www.rbi.org.in/Scripts/PublicationReportDetails.aspx?UrlPage=&ID=892

Sharma, S., Srivastav, S., Gupta, A., & Manglick, A. (2022). Application of Technology and Innovation in FinTech and it's Adaptability in India. In *2nd International Conference on Innovative Practices in Technology and Management (ICIPTM)* (pp. 305-311). 10.1109/ICIPTM54933.2022.9753933

Sharma, V. (2021). Examination of Service Quality of Digital Payments among Working Professionals. *Turkish Journal of Computer and Mathematics Education, 12*(2), 777–783.

Walchek, S. (2015). *The unbundling of finance.* TechCrunch.

Chapter 14
Microfinancing Global Observation on the Interplay Between Service Quality and Customer Delight

Demissie Admasu
KIIT University, India

Sasmita Samanta
KIIT University, India

Shikta Singh
KIIT University, India

ABSTRACT

This chapter discusses theories that explain how microfinance interacts with service quality and customer delight globally. It also identifies moderating elements between satisfaction and service quality. Microfinance provides services to low-income, self-employed, and financially disadvantaged people who don't have access to formal banking. The concept of "service" is the provision of an intangible act or performance by one party to another without ownership. Microfinance services are categorized into financial and non-financial services. And the service quality parameters are reliability, tangibility, responsiveness, assurance, and empathy. Customer delight means customers are happy with a product or service if it exceeds their expectations. Moreover, institutional affiliations (religious or secular), adaptability of new technologies, and geographical (regional) concerns moderate the relationship between service quality and customer satisfaction level.

DOI: 10.4018/978-1-6684-5853-2.ch014

INTRODUCTION

Background of the Study

Microfinance is a collection of financial activities oriented at people who do not have access to regular banking, and it has been providing services to people with low incomes, self-employed, and financially disadvantaged ones. In this context, "microfinance" refers to a broad spectrum of financial services that includes lending, savings, payment, and insurance choices, which are intended to help unbanked people to achieve economic growth and independence. The beginning of microfinance can be traced back to the nineteenth-century cooperative movement, the rural finance experience following World War II, and the establishment of the micro-enterprise development sector in the 1970s. Muhammad Yunus established Bangladesh's first microfinance institution in 1983 in order to reduce world poverty, he established the Grameen bank in Bangladesh, which provides small loans to the poorest section of the society. He started with an initial loan provision to 42 women in the community with only $27 from his own income.

The establishment of microfinance as an industry was a goal in the 1990s. The information revolution facilitated the distribution of information about the size of microfinance markets and the profitability of microfinance institutions, resulting in the exponential rise of commercial microfinance at the millennium's turn. Following that, the formal microfinance organisation began with a small number of underprivileged women and a meagre amount of money, but millions of poor people have benefited from the service, which has grown globally over the last thirty to forty years. MFIs have been utilised by both industrialised and developing countries to combat poverty and generate revenue. This is to ensure that institutions can continue to function. The institutions have been serving their customers with the delivery of different financial and non-financial services. In this regard, a measure of how well an organisation meets its customers' needs with its services is a primary concern. Customers purchase services because they have specific requirements. They are either aware or unaware that they have standards and expectations regarding how a company should meet their needs. A company that provides high-quality service goes above and beyond what its customers expect. Therefore, in the traditional and modern marketing ages, customer feedback is explained in different states of expression. The first step to customer satisfaction is meeting of customer's expectations. Customer delight is the process of going above and beyond customer's expectations to give them a long-term, positive experience with a product or service and a brand.

In the previous years, there has been significant growth in the scope and depth of research conducted in the fields of microfinance performance, outreach, service quality and customer behaviour. Moreover, the majority of studies conducted in Asian regions were emphasizing more on satisfaction studies. To analyse the aspects that can influence one's level of happiness, researchers have devised a variety of models. However, research conducted over the course of the past few years has demonstrated that merely satisfying a client's needs is not enough to make an indelible impression on that consumer. A number of research papers have demonstrated that providing exceptional customer service is essential to maintaining existing clientele. In recent years, the financial service sector has placed a significant emphasis on ensuring high levels of service quality and customer satisfaction. An acceptable level of service provides the consumer with the reassurance that his choice was appropriate and, as a result, has the potential to bring about happiness, which is the end goal of all businesses operating in modern times.

Hence, the purpose of this chapter is to identify, examine, and report theories and findings that will assist the readers in understanding how microfinancing around the world in a cross-cultural setting deal with service quality and customer delight, and specifically, how it operates in different regions.

Hence the following objectives have been sketched out:

Objectives

- To identify different regional specific study constructs for service quality (SQ), customer satisfaction (CS), and customer delight (CD).
- To comprehend the gaps and limitations in the current microfinancing research.
- To develop a conceptual map of microfinancing research modelling themes based on previous studies eliminating the gaps.

WHAT ARE MICROFINANCING SERVICES?

Service is the provision of a basically intangible act or performance by one party to another that does not give rise to the ownership of something (Kottler and Keller, 2009). The intangibility, inseparability, variability, and perishability of services are their defining features. Services are intangible and cannot be previewed via the five senses viz. (taste, touch, hearing, feel and smell). The micro finance institutions have been delivering different services for their customers. The services in microfinance have been classified in two main categories, such as financial service and non-financial services. Financial services are loan, housing loan, leasing, saving, micro insurance, payment, and transfer, and the non-financial services are social services, business service and technical assistance. The utilization of anticipated income for current investment or consumption is made possible by credit services. Chatterjee (2004), Customers can choose between two types of credit facilities offered by microfinances. As a result, working capital finance is extended to satisfy day-to-day short-term operating requirements such as commodity sales and purchases, raw material purchases that are processed and finished before being sold, and so on. The customers are offered the second type of finance in the form of short- and medium-term loans to meet his/her long-term capital requirements for the establishment of a new product, for expansion, and diversification of an existing project.

Leasing is a way of financing the acquisition of equipment and machinery. It is a legal agreement in which the 'lessor' grants the 'lessee' the right to use an asset in exchange for regular lease rental payments. There are two types of leases; Operating or services leases and financial leases. Under Operating lease, the lessor is responsible for resorting to repair and maintenance, insurance, and taxes, which is a short-term lease and that can be terminated at any point of time. Assets leased under an operating lease include computers, air conditioners, and vehicles (Deodhar and Aditi, 2012). A financial lease is a medium- term to long-term, non-cancellable agreement that is primarily defined by its duration with 3–5–8 years as in case for, machines, aircraft, land, and building (Deodhar and Aditi, 2012). Housing is one of the most basic human needs, and as a result, there is an ever-increasing need for home. However, the procedures for supplying funding for housing construction operations, particularly for the economically disadvantaged, have not been sufficiently developed (Deodhar and Aditi, 2012). The other service type is saving and there are two types of micro savings deposits: compulsory and voluntary. The standard "hidden collateral" of microcredit is mandatory savings. Voluntary saving products, on the other hand, are driven by demand.

According to the recent studies, marginalized households save actively having an access to a savings account which has a significant positive influence to save. Compulsory savings can be viewed as a loan product rather than a savings product; once accumulated, it serves as collateral for the loan received. It is frequently utilized to provide tangible collateral to back up a group guarantee (Teshome, 2020). Individuals or organizations willingly deposit money in this account. The main difference is that they can be withdrawn and are not required as part of the credit application procedure; MFIs provide these services to both borrowers and non-borrowers. The three categories of deposits are demand deposits, contractual products, and time deposits. Savings services give customers the ability to earn returns on their investments and retain extra liquidity for use in the future. Overall, low-income groups can benefit from microfinance services by lowering risk, improving management, increasing productivity, obtaining higher returns on investments, raising incomes which will result in improving their standard of living and the lives of those on whom they are depended on. The Figure 1 clearly depicts the various types of microfinance services under provision.

Figure 1. Classification of Microfinance services
Source: Hudon, Labie, and Szafarz (2019)

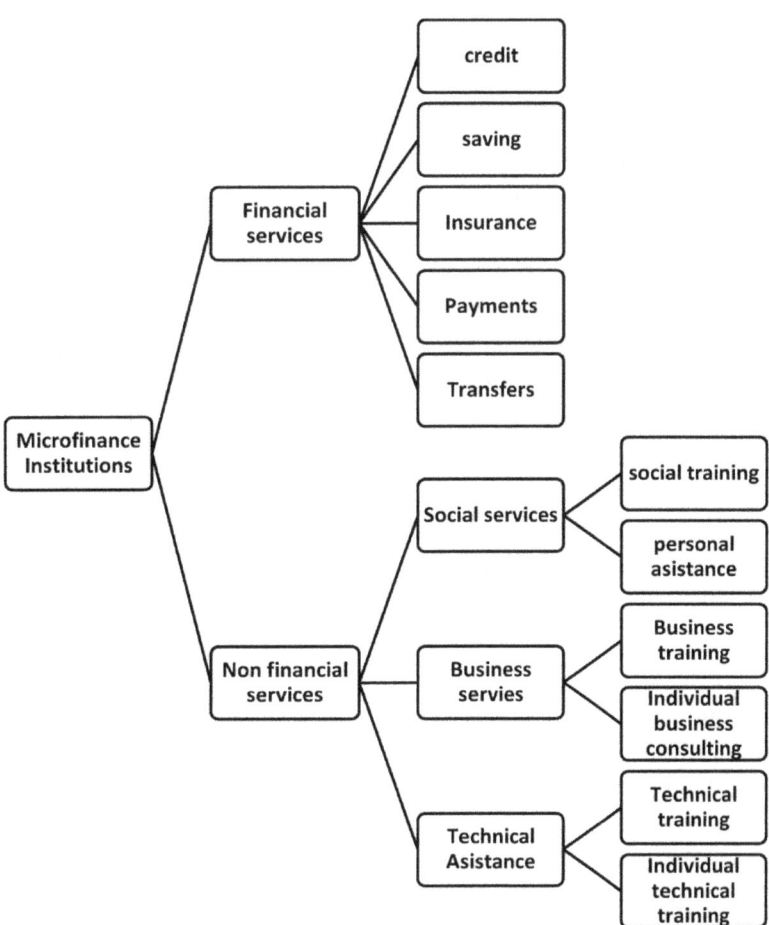

SERVICE QUALITY IN MICROFINANCE

Quality is an important service concept because it is an important indicator of customer satisfaction, which can be linked to an organization's success, efficiency, and productivity. Service quality is the explanation of the service extent between expectations and actual delivered services. The perceived service quality from customer's point of view is different from expected service quality. There is quality assurance when the satisfaction on service quality is greater than the customers' expectations, on the contrary, lower quality mean that the lesser services quality compromising on customer expectations. Still there is ongoing discussion over the service quality and its numerous facets. In the published literature, there is no consensus among researchers regarding the universal characteristics that characterizes service quality. It could be due to differences in population, cultural standards, religious practices, geographical conditions, illiteracy level, or any number of other causes. Regarding this, the microfinancing service quality dimension is also not far from this global truth. Parasuraman et al. (1988, 1991) and Gronroos, (1988) developed the six criteria of good perceived service quality tool to measure service quality parameter such as reliability, tangibility, responsiveness, assurance, and empathy.

Reliability and Trustworthiness

The capacity to carry out tasks in a dependable, accurate, and consistent manner is what we mean when we talk about reliability. It uses these five components to evaluate the correctness and legitimacy of the services provided by microfinance institutions. This aspect of service quality analyses how well the institutions keep their commitments and how well they carry out their operations from the perspective of the consumer. In addition to these strong personal services, the attitude, expertise, and skills of staff members, reliability is a key factor in determining product quality. It has been discovered that service reliability is the "core" aspect of the service for the majority of customers, and managers so as to take advantage of every opportunity to cultivate a "do-it-right-first" mind-set with their employees. Moreover, service marketing emphasizes the role of staff members, particularly customer service contact, in providing high-quality service and contributing to customer happiness(Bahman, S. P., Nazari, 2013). Peter Drucker made the following observation regarding people: "your people" can be referred to either your employees or your clients, or both. These two should be taken together. To put it another way, if you take care of your people (that is, your employees), they will typically devote greater attention to taking care of "your customers". This has been and will always be the most important principle of marketing (Cohen, 2013). The ability of service provider employees and systems to keep promises and perform in the best interests of customers is a well-proven process-related criterion.

Tangibility

It depicts the physical characteristics of the services such as physical facilities, the appearances of workers, and the tools utilised to provide services. It is more concerned with the aesthetic aspects of institutions. MFIs should build-up client relationships by providing additional tangible and intangible features to their primary goods. The tangibility components of microfinance institutions that supports execution or communication of the services, as well as the environment in which the service is supplied and where the company and client interacts. Letterhead, report formats, equipment, and branch facilities are just a few examples (Zeithaml, Bitner, and Gremler, 2013). To ensure and justify quality, it considers the aesthetic and physical environment. The physical environment and other visible indicators can heavily influence customers' perceptions of the quality of service they receive (Bitner, 2010). Customers frequently rely on tangible cues, or physical evidence, to evaluate the service before purchasing it, as well as to assess their satisfaction with the service during and after consumption (Zeithaml, Bitner, and Gremler, 2013). Tangibility elements include general physical facilities (services scape) and other forms of tangible communication (such as business cards, stationary, billing statements, reports, employee dress, brochures, web pages, virtual service scape). Customers are affected by the physical service scape, which includes both exterior attributes (such as signage, parking, and the landscape) and interior attributes (such as design, layout, equipment, temperature, sound/music/lighting) (Zeithaml, Bitner, and Gremler, 2013).

Responsiveness

Dimension shows employees' eagerness or readiness to provide clients with immediate services. Customers are particularly sensitive to the working circumstances of service staff. A correct match between employee competencies and customer expectations resulted in higher customer service quality. Service recovery and problem resolution are recognised as key components of service quality. Consumers are satisfied with microfinance services overall due to the effective communication, service delivery, and conflict resolution.

Assurance

Along with dependability and responsiveness to customer needs, is a crucial component of service quality. Assurance has the greatest influence on client satisfaction, which results in positive word-of-mouth. Customer satisfaction can be created by institutions ensuring trustworthy behaviour and reflecting on true commitments to service offering. It has been discovered that trust and dedication are critical variables in bringing consumer happiness.

Empathy

It demonstrates the level of care and special attention that is given to each and every customer. There is evidence to imply that workers are committed to providing high-quality services and deftly managing customer complaints with practice of empathy.

MICROFINANCING GLOBAL PERSPECTIVES AND SERVICE QUALITY

Microfinance institutions are financial service delivery systems for economically disadvantaged groups.

In this regard, there are several elements that moderate the relationship between service quality and client happiness. Some of the elements influencing customer satisfaction levels are institutional connections (religious or conventional), new technology adaptability, and geographical (regional) considerations, which cause variations in the degree of customer satisfaction around the world.

Religious Affiliated and Conventional Microfinancing and Service Quality

The service quality dimensions also have to be measured in the religious and conventional contexts. Microfinance institutions that follow the traditional model have not been successful in alleviating poverty, particularly within the Muslim community. Conventional microfinance institutions still use an interest system, which is forbidden in Islamic teachings because it is considered to be a form of usury. This is one of the reasons why this problem exists. In addition, there are still practices that are prohibited in the dealings that take place within microfinance institutions, such as the use of maysir and gharar. For this reason, the existence of Islamic microfinance institutions is anticipated to be a solution for the Muslim community, a significant portion of which is still living below the federal poverty line. Microfinance institutions based on Islam conduct their business by adhering to the principles outlined in Islamic teachings.

Some of the values in this category include monotheism, the application of Shariah maqashid, the ban on usury, the upholding of justice, the eradication of injustice, and the abolition of elements of gambling in financial transactions. Islamic microfinance institutions have contracts in place that cover buying and selling (bai' al-murabahah), business cooperation (al-musharakah and al-mudharabah), leasing (al-ijarah), and interest-free loans (al-mudharabah) (qardh-hasan).

Table 1. The diffrence between conventional and Islamic MFIs

Items	Conventional MFI	Islamic MFI
Fund Source	external financing, client savings,	External funds, saving of customers, Islamic generous sources
Asset (financing mode)	Interest based	Islamic financial instrument
Providing for the poorest	The poorest are excluded	provides for the most vulnerable by combining zakat with microfinance
Transfer of funds	Cash given	In-kind transfer
Deduction at contract's initiation	A portion of the funds is deducted at the start.	no initial deduction
Target group	women	family
Purpose of the targeting women	Empowerment of women	Easy of accessibility
The obligation of the loan (given to women)	recipient	Recipient and spouse
Employee incentive schemes	monetary	Monetary and spiritual
Managing Defaults	Group center pressure and threat	Group/center/spouse guarantee and Islamic ethics
Program for Social Development	Nonspiritual, behavioural, ethical, and social development	Religious (includes behaviour, ethics and social)

Source: Ahmed (2002)

The service quality extent is also different, and some literature confirms the fact that Islamic microfinance and conventional microfinance have different treatment for their customers regarding the five dimensions. In order to meet customer needs, Islamic microfinance has been providing better customer service than traditional microfinance service delivery. An Islamic microfinance institution should introduce new products (services) like interest-free products, risk-sharing activities, and strong ties with Shariah principles in order to compete with conventional microfinance for long-term benefits. So, according to some literature, Islamic microfinance institutions is working in ways that are efficient and focused on quality to keep customers happy and satisfied in the long run.

New Technology Adaptability and Microfinance Service Quality

Technology is evolving at a rapid rate and corporate needs are diverse. Microfinance institutions must heavily invest in the newest technologies to keep up with the constantly shifting demands, focusing on IT and innovation to show what technological advancements are currently available on the market that microfinance institutions can use. The vast majority of these resources are freely and easily accessible to everybody without the need for substantial investments. Improving outreach is a crucial element in the pursuit of sustainability. Outreach and sustainability have a significant relationship. The greater the number of clients that microfinance institutions can serve, the greater is their chances for long-term survival. Innovations in technology can assist microfinance institutions in expanding their client base and establishing their long-term viability.

There are numerous forms of technology that have been implemented in a variety of different countries, including developing countries as well as industrialized countries, such as social media and electronic banking. As a result, the institution is able to improve the customer experience, which in turn helps to attract new customers and keep existing customers as a whole. This is accomplished by generating customer delight through the supply of high-quality services. Microfinance institutions are able to reach customers through a variety of channels, one of which is social media. Facebook, LinkedIn and Twitter are the most common forms of social media utilized by financial organizations, such as banks and microfinance institutions, for the goal of connecting with their consumers. In this context, making effective use of social media can increase the amount of positive customer feedback as well as levels of consumer loyalty and involvement. In order to improve customer satisfaction, increase the degree of differentiation from the competition, and ultimately involve the entire organization in customer satisfaction in the current competitive world, financial institutions have been forced to raise the level of services offered. This is a result of the recent economic crisis, globalization, and the increased homogeneity of financial products and services. On the other side, the microfinancing sector has seen the introduction of new technology solutions through the use of the internet, which has led to the development of electronic banking. The term "electronic banking" refers to the practice of combining traditional online banking with customer relationship management (relational marketing) via the internet. E-banking makes it possible to deliver services at a lower cost by removing the need for intermediaries and making them freely available. Additionally, the internet offers an additional marketing channel that a bank may utilize to attract and keep new customers.

GEOGRAPHICAL (REGIONAL) CONSIDERATIONS

According to convergency report (2018) the microfinance global trends summarized as follow; Over the past ten years, microfinance institutions have made hundreds of billions of dollars in loans, with an average annual growth rate of 11.5% over the previous five years. In 2018, 139.9 million borrowers benefited from microfinance institutions' (MFIs') services, up from just 98 million in 2009. Despite the rise in the total number of borrowers over the past ten years, the proportion of female borrowers (80%)

and rural borrowers (65%) has remained constant at 139.9 million. This is the case even though the total number of borrowers has increased. MFIs continued their expansion in 2018, posting a growth rate of 8.5% compared to the previous year, reaching a total estimated credit portfolio of $124.1 billion. With the most borrowers (85.6 million in 2018) and the fastest population growth (+13.8% between 2017 and 2018), South Asia continues to rule the world of microfinance. It also has Vietnam, Bangladesh, and India as its top three creditors.

The majority of borrowers in the area (89% in 2018) are female, which is a notable characteristic. South Asia comes in second in terms of credit portfolio despite making up nearly two-thirds of all global borrowers, with an estimated $36.8 billion in outstanding debt in 2018. Latin America and the Caribbean make up 44% of the global microfinance sector portfolio, with $48.3 billion in outstanding loans (+5% annually on average since 2012). This region is the second largest in terms of the number of borrowers in 2018, with 22.2 million customers, a slightly lower number (-0.3%) after years of growth. Low rural penetration rates are another characteristic of the Latin American and Caribbean region. Only 23% of clients at MFIs in the region are from rural areas, making them the least rurally focused institutions.

In contrast to these top regions, Eastern Europe, Central Asia, and the MENA region are smaller markets. Their customer base and credit portfolio are both growing, though. In Eastern Europe and Central Asia, the number of borrowers has increased by more than 30% since 2012, reaching 2.5 million in 2018. The number of borrowers in the MENA region is equal to that worldwide. Female borrowers made up 49% of MFIs' total borrowers in Eastern Europe and Central Asia and 60% in the MENA region in 2018, respectively. At the same time, credit portfolios in these two areas expanded. Eastern Europe and Central Asia saw a 5% increase, reversing the declines of 2015 and 2016, while the MENA region only saw a 1% increase between 2017 and 2018. African MFIs' total outstanding balance has grown by 56% since 2012, while the number of borrowers has grown by 46%, reaching 6.3 million in 2018. MFIs in East Asia and the Pacific continue to grow, with a portfolio of $21.5 billion in 2018, an increase of 13.1% from the previous year, and total clients that are 73% female and 79% rural borrowers. 20.8 million beneficiaries in this region took out MFI loans in the same year (+10.2%). Since 2012, the region's total outstanding MFIs have grown by 16% annually on average, while the number of clients has increased steadily but more slowly (+6%/year).

Various regions of microfinance services benefitted a large number of the world's poor population, and their service coverage can be measured by a county's economic status, like developed and developing countries, urban and rural setups, and levels of adult illiteracy, all of which have contributed to differences in the quality of services provided and the degree to which customers are delighted. for example: Microfinance institutions in Africa, for instance, have started providing digital finance services to their customers. In Kenya, 82% of the population has an official bank account, 35% of the population in Ethiopia has one, 50% of the population in Rwanda has erroneous account, and 35% of the population in Kenya has an official bank account. Despite of this, the institutions only offer a restricted digital service to its clientele. They are working with fundamental services such as point-of-sale terminals, automated teller machines, internet banking, mobile wallets, and so on. The various method of provide clients with access to financing, even in rural locations, by allowing them to submit loan applications online and upload the required papers without having to travel great distances. Internet-based technology is a valuable resource for MFIs since it can be utilized for a variety of purposes. Some MFIs in developed countries uses the Internet to engage in active dialogue with their clients, donors, staff, and volunteers, as well as to facilitate business-to-business collaboration, as demonstrated in the following examples. There are further MFIs that provide financial and non-financial services, as well as those that use technology for monitoring and coaching or to meet group lending demands.

On the contrary the developing countries MFIs has at infant stage for using technology to facilitate their works to reach customers. Some of the reasons are; a high rate of illiteracy in few parts of world for instance in Sub-Saharan Africa, the illiteracy rate among adults aged 15 and older was 34.7 percent in 2019. The illiteracy rate in South Asia was 27.1 percent.

Adult illiteracy is defined as the percentage of people aged 15 and above who are unable to read or write. Another reason is geographical setup which means that the people who are residing in rural area i.e., Africa 56% and Asia 48%, which has a serious barrier to the adoption of electronic banking and hinders the accessibility of banking services due to a lack of basic ICT literacy. There is a low level of internet penetration and poorly developed telecommunication infrastructure; there are no internet facilities available in rural areas. These are some of the major challenges that African and other developing countries face in regards to the use of new technology for providing quality customer service. Threatening characteristics that are not provided include political instability in the country, frequent power interruptions, resistance to changes in technology among customers and staff due to a lack of awareness and fear of risk, and people may be resistant to new payment mechanisms. In addition, frequent power interruptions are also not provided.

CUSTOMER SATISFACTION

Customer satisfaction is defined differently and from multiple perspectives by various academics. These are some of the definitions: Gronroos and Voima (2013) defined Customer satisfaction is the customer's assessment, both cognitively and emotionally, of all service episodes throughout the relationship. According to Lovelock and Wirtz (2007), is a term that has drawn a lot of interest and attention from academics and practitioners. This may be because of its importance as a crucial component of business strategy and a goal for all business activities, particularly in today's competitive market. Kotler and Keller (2006) defined a person's satisfaction is determined by how well a product performs (or produces a result) in comparison to his or her expectations. Satisfaction is a "psychological concept involving the feeling of well-being and pleasure that results from obtaining what one hopes for and anticipates from an alluring product or service" Kotler and Keller (2006).

We define customer satisfaction as a judgment that follows a purchase act or a series of consumer product interactions, in contrast to Lovelock and Wirtz's (2007) definition of customer satisfaction as an attitude-like evaluation. Customer satisfaction was defined by Oliver (1992) as the consumer's post-purchase assessment and emotional response to the overall product or service experience. When nothing goes wrong, the needs and desires of the consumer are satisfied. According to Saha and Zhao (2005), customer satisfaction is a grouping of perceptions, assessments, and psychological reactions to the use of a product or service. As a result of a cognitive and affective evaluation in which the actual perceived performance is measured against a reference standard, Saha and Zhao defined customer satisfaction as the end result.

So, Customer satisfaction is described as customers' feelings or attitudes about a product or service after using it. Customer happiness was defined in terms of customer feedback, customer knowledge, service recurrence, and customer loyalty towards a particular brand. Some of the services that contribute to customer satisfaction are local bank convenience, account opening/closing procedures, ATM machine accessibility, usefulness of net banking services, security of online transactions, transaction alerts (messages from banks to mobile), neatness and organization, simplicity of net banking, ease of getting a debit or credit card, enough staff to assist customers, check collection, and appropriate responses to inquiries from customers.

Customer Satisfaction Levels

Customers are more likely to be pleasantly surprised when their experience with a product or service exceeds their expectations. Customers' happiness can be gauged in a variety of ways, the majority of which use a scale that can be roughly categorized into three groups:

- Above average (much better than expected): Customers are likely to be completely happy with a product or service if they evaluate its worth to be higher than their expectations. They will be dedicated customers who will not only come back to the store again and again, but will also spread the word about the brand to their friends and family. The customer in microfinance institutions are economical poor and medium income people so the service providers should monitor their activities regarding the service expectation of their customer.
- At par (As Expected): When customers get what they expected under the terms that were already agreed upon, they are usually happy. These customers are not in a rush to switch, but they might if they find a better offer.
- Below average (worse/different than anticipated): the likelihood of customers returning is slim when the level of service anticipated by customers is significantly higher than what is delivered or perceived.

They might even start to criticize and offer constructive criticism. Numerous untrained employees, the use of outdated equipment, including slow and unreliable computers, the absence of a customer feedback desk where clients could view their needs and suggestions for the services offered, and other factors contribute to dissatisfied clients. Moreover, the scarcity of ATMs in areas where the number of customers is high, the lack of tellers and the inability of some staff to provide customers with the information they need, requiring them to go elsewhere. There are always broken ATMs, long lines, and inadequate internal and external communication.

All employees and management contribute to customer satisfaction. Collaboration can maintain a high level of consumer satisfaction. Keeping this in mind that a corporation should not overreach in its pursuit of client satisfaction. Free products, refunds, and free services increases brand loyalty somewhat and aims to delight to the customers, but avoid being exploited in the process.

The following Figure 2 depicts the customer's satisfaction level of MFIs

Figure 2.
Source: Authors own, 2022

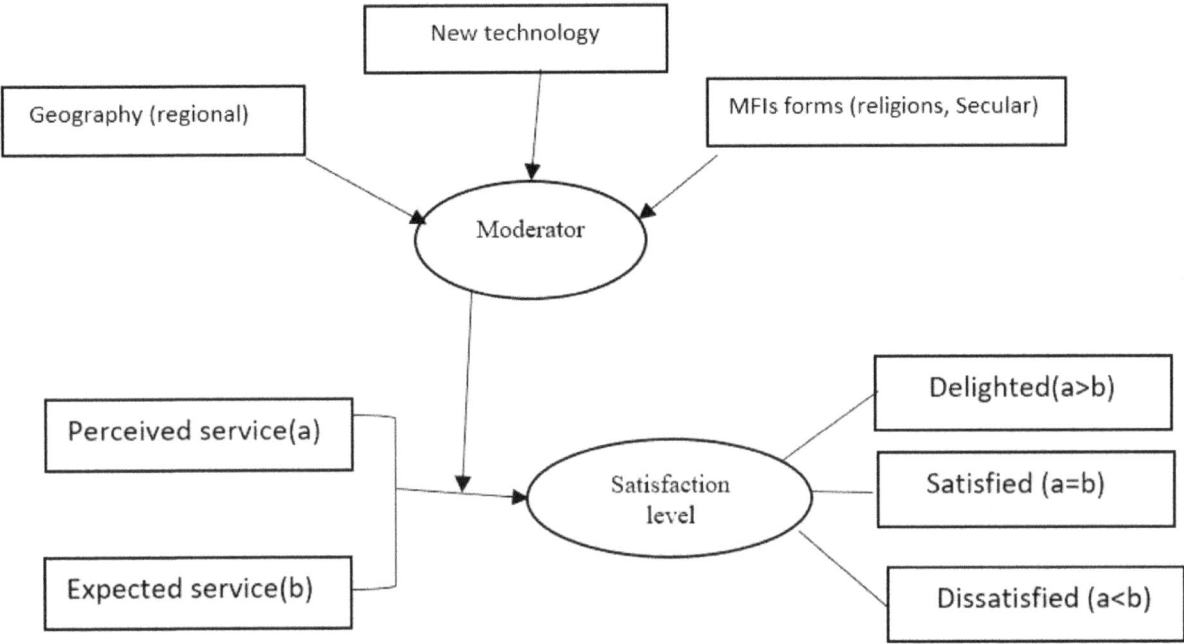

CUSTOMER DELIGHT

Businesses often spend five times as much money acquiring new clients as they do retain current ones. However, there is a rising awareness that customer retention is both easier and more profitable. A satisfied customer tells 3-5 other people about his or her experience. A delighted customer is one who receives more than what was promised or expected (Seth & Seth, 2005). Customer delight is the process of exceeding a customer's expectations in order to provide them with a positive, lengthy experience with a product or service and a brand.

Indicators of Customer Delight Performance

It should come as no surprise that client satisfaction is a reliable indicator of a company's future. This is where KPIs (Key Performance Indicators) come into play. One can track the customer's delight with these simple indicators and make progress toward your objective.

Turnover Rate

The churn rate is the overall percentage of consumers who stop using a product during a specified period of time. One can minimize this metric as much as feasible. A high churn rate is an indicator that a company may soon run out of earnings and that it is time to focus on the specifics. It follows from the formula:

Number of Clients Lost During a Period of Time ÷
Number of Clients at the Start of the Period

Rate of Retention

Simply said, the retention rate is the antithesis of the churn rate. To quantify customer satisfaction, one must have a high client retention rate. To accomplish this, one must compare the number of clients they had at the beginning of the year or quarter to the number of clients at the end. It follows from the formula:

Existing Clients at the End of the Year ÷ Existing
Clients at the Beginning of the Year

Customer Lifetime Value

Client Lifetime Value is the value that each customer gives to a business over the course of their respective relationship, be it a year or a quarter. In addition, it forecasts the net profit over the course of the relationship with a customer, from the first interaction to the last. It is computed from the following formula:

Average Sale Value x Retention Period x Profit Margin x Transaction Volume

The Basic Principles of Customer Delight

There is different principle of customer delight such as; knowing the difference between customer delight and customer satisfaction, create a knowledgeable customer service team, dazzle customers with unexpected actions, Let Maya Angelou serve as your mentor, Obtain customer satisfaction survey feedback, provide timely solutions to your customers' problems both now and in the future.

The Distinction Between Customer Contentment and
Customer Delight must be Understood

Customers are satisfied when they receive what they expect. When you give someone something they did not anticipate, you delight them. A famous example is an auto repair shop that washes your vehicle after repairing it. When you pick up your automobile, not only does it perform better, but it also looks fantastic. You can change the fact that most people do not leave your auto repair shop with a grin on their face.

Another example concerns a customer who complains about a faulty product. Customer satisfaction is achieved when you promptly offer to have the customer return the defective product and replace it for no cost, including return shipping costs. The buyer is delighted when you include a $25 gift certificate toward the purchase of another one of your goods. According to Steve Curtan, author of Delight Your Customers, eighty percent of businesses believe they offer exceptional customer service, while just eight percent of customers agree. You want your clients to have no question, regardless of what else occurs, that you went above and beyond to care for them.

Develop an Informed Customer Service Team

Customers should be pleasantly surprised with the following by customer service representatives who are sufficiently skilled to deliver some "wow factor": speed of response; lack of holding the customer while they wait for a representative to answer; immediate problem identification and prompt resolution; demonstration of technical and professional knowledge that shows the representative clearly understanding what to do and how to do it; ability to quickly and effectively get caught up in the details of the situation

Surprise your Consumers, Do the Unthinkable

It should come as no surprise that if you are late with your payment, you will receive a reminder. But wouldn't you be thrilled if you unintentionally got a letter or email thanking you for always making your payments on time (along with a coupon for 10% off your subsequent order)? Using surprise and delight marketing, which entails finding ways to surpass clients' expectations without asking for anything in return, you can transform a routine into an unforgettable experience. Research speaks 90% of consumers have a more favorable perception of a brand when it implements this marketing tactic.

Let Maya Angelou be Your Guide

Maya Angelou was a poet, not a businessperson, but businesspeople love to quote her: "People will forget what you said and what you did, but they will never forget how you made them feel." Every connection we have at work, no matter how brief, leaves a lasting impact and an emotional imprint. To put it another way, each and every one of those exchanges leaves a mark, either strengthening or weakening relationships, empowering or depriving people of their rights, or bringing us closer together or further apart. The sum of these contacts has a significant impact on our self-perception, how others see us, and how satisfied we are in our jobs. It demonstrates that rather than the subject matter or the actual content of the work, the issues that give leaders and supervisors the most anxiety are those involving interpersonal relationships. Conflicts at work, communication, stress management, and regular contacts among coworkers can make or break the launch of a new product, a new business, or the beginning of a new initiative. That is why the field of team building is so large and important.

Collect Feedback on the Consumer Satisfaction of your Business

Using a customer joy index is an excellent method for gauging client satisfaction with your products and services. You can measure your success using a variety of comment tools, including through focus groups, surveys, and interviews. Regardless of the tools you use, you must ask customers for feedback on the value, friendliness, and customer service of your product or service. You'll be able to grow your company going forward and improve customer satisfaction thanks to this.

Solve the Problems of your Clients, Both Now and in the Future

One should offer new and present client's solutions to their difficulties or assistance in achieving their objectives. Ensure that your solutions are tailored to their specific needs and preferences. While rapid and effective customer solutions are helpful in the near term, it is crucial to provide customers with knowledge, techniques to help them handle their difficulties, and if possible, can be taught as to how to do. This can also help in resolving future difficulties for your consumers. By authoring instructional blog entries, offering social media ideas, and developing a self-service knowledge base, one may offer the clients with educational materials, recommendations, and success tools.

Be Prompt in your Replies

A significant component of customer satisfaction is ensuring prompt responses to the client inquiries. This demonstrates that you care and that addressing their inquiries or concerns is a top priority. Even if you are unable to resolve the issue immediately, letting your clients know that you are working on it will demonstrate that you value their satisfaction.

THE DIFFERENCE BETWEEN CUSTOMER DELIGHT AND CUSTOMER SATISFACTION

How customers feel depends on the service they expect. The goal of customer satisfaction, which is to give customers what they were promised, seems to be reasonable. Why change a model that works? But the most important thing right now is to find ways to set yourself apart. Customer satisfaction can be the "wow" factor that tips the scales in your favour.

Multiple Levels Versus Pinnacle

Different types of customer satisfaction can be broken down into steps that can be taken to improve them. Peak customer satisfaction, on the other hand, would be delight, which is when a customer is so happy with the product or service that they buy it again.

Action Versus Emotion

Using different metrics, one can figure out how happy your customers are. Especially for customer support teams, it becomes more important to solve problems quickly. Tools like Screen jar, which lets customers quickly share screen recordings to help solve problems faster, can turn a normal, satisfactory experience into a delightful one.

Referral Versus Influence

Customers who are happy will say nice things about a business if asked, which can help them get a few new customers (or at least a foot in). Customers who have had a good experience usually tell their friends and family about it and share their positive experiences through different channels. The brand gets more credibility from the good results.

Return Purchases Versus Loyalty

Customers who are happy with your product or service can go to a competitor if they think there isn't much difference in quality or function. They might think about leaving if the competitor helped them in some way, like with new feature ads, better pricing, or quick problem-solving. These things make customers happy, and a happy customer wouldn't even think about going to a competitor.

These ways of making customers happy are important for Software as a Service i.e. SaaS businesses, because giving customers extra value makes them feel valued, increases their loyalty, and makes the relationship stronger.

CONCLUSION

Microfinance provides services to low-income, self-employed, and financially disadvantaged people who don't have access to normal banking. The concept Service is the supply of a basically intangible act or performance by one party to another, which does not give rise to the ownership of something. The services in microfinance are classified into two primary categories, such as financial services like loans, housing loans, leasing, saving, micro insurance, payment, and transfer, and non-financial services like social services, business services, and technical assistance. The two categories of service in microfinance have the parameters to measure the service quality, such as reliability, tangibility, responsiveness, assurance, and empathy. Subsequently, customer delight means that customers are likely to be completely happy with a product or service if they evaluate its worth to be higher than their expectations. The key performance indicators for customer delight are the turnover rate, the retention rate, and the client lifetime value. On the other hand, there are a number of factors that act as moderators in the link between the quality of service and the contentment of the customer are institutional affiliations (religious or secular): Islamic microfinance institutions are one of the religious affiliated, and they have increased awareness about their products (services) to compete with conventional microfinance for long-term benefits. They should introduce new products (services), such as interest-free products, risk-sharing activities, and strong ties with Shariah principle. Next, consider the adaptability of new technology: Microfinance institutions are required to make significant investments in the most recent technologies, including information technology (IT) and innovation, in order to keep up with the ever-shifting demands. These investments should demonstrate what kinds of technological advances are currently available on the market that microfinance institutions can take advantage of, and geographical (regional) considerations such as developed and developing countries, urban and rural settings, and degrees of illiteracy, all of which have contributed to disparities in service quality and customer satisfaction. Consider the following: Several MFIs in developed nations use the Internet to participate in active interaction with their clients, donors, staff, and volunteers, as well as to enable business-to-business collaboration, and there are further MFIs that offer financial and non-financial services, as well as those that use technology for monitoring and coaching or to meet group lending needs. On the contrary, developing-country MFIs are still in the early stages of employing technology to help them reach customers because of a high rate of illiteracy in a few places in the world.

Overall aspects of the discussion states that the micro financing global observation act as an Interplay between Service Quality and Customer Delight and new looks into a conceptual framework proposed for the further studies. In addition, it will be helping to ensure that service quality for customer delight in microfinance has been developed systematically with scientific validation principles. Moreover, the chapter provided future perspectives and benefits to regional countries and global institutions on service quality and customer delight in microfinance.

REFERENCES

Ahmed, H. (2002). Financing Microenterprises : An Analytical Study of Islamic Microfinance Institutions. *Islamic Economic Studies, 9*(2), 27–64. http://www.isdb.org/irj/go/km/docs/documents/IDBDevelopments /Internet/English/IRTI/CM/downloads/IES_Articles/Vol 9-2.Hab ib Ahmed.Financing Microenterprises.dp.pdf

Bahman, S. P., Nazari, K. & M. E. (2013). The effect of marketing mix in attracting customers: Case study of Saderat Bank in Kermanshah Province. *AJBM, 7*(34), 3272-3280,.

Bitner, M. J. (2010). Service scapes: The impact of physical surroundings on customers and employees. *Journal of Marketing*, 57–71.

Chatterjee, A. (2004). *Credit Management: Practical Aprroach*. SKYLARK.

Cohen, W. A. (2013). *Fowarded by Philip Kottler, Drucker on Marketing lessons from world's most influencial business thinker*. Book, Tata McGra.

Deodhar, S. B., & Aditi, A. A. (2012). Indian financial system. Himalaya Publishing House.

Gronroos, C. (1988). Service quality: The six criteria of good perceived service. *Review of Business, 9*(3), 10.

Gronroos, C., & Voima, F. P. (2013). Critical Service Logic: Making Sense of Value Creation and Co-Creation. *Journal of the Academy of Marketing Science, 41*(2), 133–150. doi:10.100711747-012-0308-3

Hudon, M., Labie, M., & Szafarz, A. (Eds.). (2019). *A research agenda for financial inclusion and microfinance*.

Kotler, P., & Keller, K. (2006). Marketing Management (12th ed.). Prentice Hall.

Kottler, P., & Keller, K. L. (2009). *Marketing management*. Erlangga.

Lovelock, C., & Wirtz, J. (2007). *Services Marketing: People, Technology, Strategy*. Prentice Hall.

Oliver, M. (1992). Changing the Social Relations of Research Production? *Disability, Handicap & Society, 7*(2), 101–114.

Parasuraman, A., Berry, L. L., & Zeithaml, V. A. (1991). Understanding customer expectations of service. *Sloan Management Review, 32*(3), 39–48.

Parasuraman, A., Zeithaml, V. A., & Berry, L. (1988). *SERVQUAL: A multiple-item scale for measuring consumer perceptions of service quality*. Academic Press.

Saha, P., & Zhao, Y. (2005). *Relationship between online service quality and customer satisfaction: a study in internet banking*. Academic Press.

Seth, R., & Seth, K. (2005). *Creating Customer Delight: The How and Why of Customer Relationship Management*. SAGE Publications. https://books.google.co.in/books?id=cwAKAQAAMAAJ

Teshome K., A. K. (2020). *Ethiopian MicroFinance Institutions Performance Analysis Report*. Academic Press.

Zeithaml, V. A., Bitner, M. J., & Gremler, D. D. (2013). *Services Marketing: Integrating customer focus Across the firm*. Sixth.

Chapter 15
Performance and Science Mapping Analysis on Service Quality in the Healthcare Sector:
A Bibliometric Analysis Using Scopus Database

Jyotisankar Mishra
KIIT University, India

Pruthiranjan Dwibedi
ⓘD https://orcid.org/0000-0001-6049-2199
KIIT University, India

ABSTRACT

The authors conducted a bibliometric study of the aforesaid area of interest since healthcare service quality is becoming more important in the literature. Its goal is to look at the trends and patterns that have been observed in the literature on healthcare service quality. R Software is used for analysis. Performance analysis and science mapping programs of the software have been used for the study. Using the Scopus database, the publication pattern from 1996 to 2022 was examined. Two thousand one hundred seventeen articles in the subject area were found, retrieved, and used in the study. The most successful and well-known authors were recognised. Analysis of co-authorship and co-occurrence was done. The leading nations publishing of papers relating to healthcare service quality according to the results of co-authorship and co-occurrence have been analysed. The bibilometric study was carried out to find trends in the healthcare sector's service quality. The study's findings revealed a publication tendency that was perhaps growing and would continue to grow.

DOI: 10.4018/978-1-6684-5853-2.ch015

INTRODUCTION

It is necessary to understand and examine the contributions made to the body of knowledge that every scientific discipline develops over time in order to grasp and appreciate the present discipline level and knowledge level, which is inherited by the empirical work and theoretical work of researchers (Li Ma & Qu, 2017). Out of all the tools available for the purpose, tool that may be used to scientifically look at the matter is bibliometric analysis.

According to Evren and Kozak (2014) and Munoz-Leiva, Porcu, and Barrio-Garca (2015), analysis through bibliometric technique is a quantitative approach that aids in identifying and analysing data in relation to keywords used and those are searched in the literature, relationship among chosen keywords, the number of research articles produced over a specific period of time, and their citation analysis. It is used in a variety of contexts and disciplines, such as management (Hughes. Et al., 2019; Kumar. Et al., 2019; Odriozola-fernández & Berbegal-mirabent, 2019; Ramos-Rodríguez & Ruiz-Navarro, 2004), tourism and hospitality (Koc & Boz., 2014; Kwateng et al., 2017; Marimon et al., 2017) and concern related to environmental (Id. Estoque. Et al.,2019; Liu. Et al., 2019). The study we presently undertake, however, is concentrated on the bibliometric investigation in the area of Quality of Service in medical sector.

Like other services, healthcare-services includes a wide range of intricate and sophisticated actions. Patients, who are also consumers of healthcare services, expect the service rendered by service providers in healthcare sector including physicians, mid-wives, and other support personnel to produce the intended results (McCain, 1990; Meleddu et al., 2019). The healthcare industry has received a lot of attention recently due to its significance and impact on the economy and population of nations, the reduction of health inequities, and the provision of providing important information to policy makers (Muir. Et al., 2010; Swain, 2018; Ng. & Luk., 2018; Mohammadi & Salehi, 2019). Additionally, the availability of both commercial and public healthcare has strengthened business rivalry, forcing healthcare providers to improve their services and address any flaws (Kalaja, Myshketa, & Scalera, 2016).

Nobody can envision a nation without access to healthcare (Javed & Nawaz, 2019). It is one of the sectors on which a nation's economy and other sectors, including its Social, economic, political, and moral ideas depend upon. In addition to its tremendous importance, the global healthcare industry is among the fastest-growing and most fiercely competitive (Islam, Ahmed, & Tarique, 2016). In this aspect, healthcare services are providing higher service quality compared to their rivals due to their quick expansion and severe rivalry.

Service quality is a special, and complex in nature (Abbasi-moghaddam et al., 2019; Brady & Robertson, 2001; Reeves & Bednar, 1994; Shieh, Huang, & Wu, 2019 and Tuzkaya et al. 2019). However, a few well-known academics have developed a definition of service quality that is the foundation for the majority of research in the literature (Amankwah, et al., 2019; Badiwan, 2016). Parasuraman, Zeithaml, and Berry (1985, 1988) among others, defined service quality as the discrepancy between consumers' perceptions and expectations in 1988 and 1985, respectively. Chien and Tsai (2000) described service quality as the consistency between customers' expectations and perceptions of service providers, which is similar to the description given above.

Therefore, 'Service Quality' has received considerable attention from researchers, academics, and practitioners, despite the fact that it has been examined in a number of studies. So, the current study's objective is to undertake a bibliometric analysis of healthcare service quality from 1996 to 2022. It aims to determine the pattern of papers published in the relevant field, identify important contributions to the quality of healthcare services, examine the co-authorship of authors from various nations, and examine the co-occurrence of author keywords.

This chapter aims to provide information on the following issues:

1. The total number of articles published in the field of service quality in healthcare sector
2. The themes which have been largely used in the field of service quality in healthcare sector
3. Information regarding the most productive authors, universities, and countries in the area of service quality in healthcare sector
4. The authors having highest number of collaborations in the field of service quality in healthcare sector
5. Information regarding the core articles in the area of service quality in healthcare sector

The current work is based on two bibliometric methodologies, performance analysis and scientific mapping analysis, to accomplish these goals. The performance analysis comprises the overall number of citations per year, the number of scientific publications produced, the most productive writers, the most widely referenced documents, the most cited nations, the most relevant affiliations, keywords, and authors. The scientific mapping analysis is done using R software, which comprises the theme mapping, author and country collaboration networks, coupling maps, and keyword co-occurrence maps. The remainder of the essay is structured as follows. The introduction is covered in the first section, and the methodology is covered in the second. The performance analysis and science mapping study highlighted in the third segment. The discussion, consequences, limits, future research, and conclusion are included in the last part.

BRIEF BACKGROUND: HEALTHCARE RESEARCH AND BIBLIOMETRIC ANALYSIS

Numerous studies that concentrate on various facets of healthcare service quality are accessible in the literature. First, several studies have focused on evaluating the concept of "Service Quality" in the healthcare sector (Abbasi-moghaddam et al., 2019; Ampah, Ali, Ampah, & Ali, 2019; Anabila, Kumi, & Anome, 2018; Fatima et al., 2018; Fauziah, Surachman, & Muhtadi, 2019; Jahantigh, 2019). Second, literature has concentrated on service quality measuring models (Behdioğlu, Acar, & Burhan, 2019; Chang et al., 2019; Gupta & Singh, 2017; Ibrahim & Ahmed, 2019; Jahantigh, 2019; Jebraeily et al., 2018; Materla & Cudney, 2017; Shafiq & Naeem, 2017; Shieh et al., 2019; Singh & Prasher, 2019; Srivastava & Goel, n.d.; Tuzkaya et al., 2019). Thirdly, certain studies have examined patients' satisfaction and literature on service quality in healthcare included analysed patients' loyalty (Meesala & Paul, 2018; Koseoglu et al., 2016; Sarkodie & Strezov, 2019). The goal of the current bibliometric analysis is to rate these facets of the research. Because the bulk of the literature has studied them together, additional threads and ties of satisfaction, loyalty, and assessment models like SERVQUAL have been discovered to be connected with service quality. The present study's findings also revealed the streams and their relative strengths in relation to those concepts and service quality in the "Authors' Keywords" session.

The word "bibliometrics," first used by Pritchard in 1969, denoted the application of mathematical and statistical methods to various media of communication. Among these items is bibliographic content that may be quantitatively evaluated using a technique called bibliometric analysis (Broadus, 1987). It aids in explaining the entirety of the body of knowledge that is currently available in a particular field with regard to its citations, keyword and concept mapping, graphic structuring of scientific research, and its evolution in various literary spheres (Montero-Diaz et al., 2018). According to Odriozola-fernández and Berbegal-mirabent (2019), bibliometric analysis is used to examine not only this body of literature but also to identify the specific authors and organisations directing toward a specific target. This information helps the new researchers to develop new ideas and strategies which will contribute to the synthesis of a particular field.

3. REVIEW OF LITERATURE

3.1 On Bibliometrics

A proactive effort is to identify the recurring patterns in an area in order to better comprehend them and encourage additional research. Research scholars can able to spot possible research gaps and possibilities for further study by mapping and reviewing the body of literature (Tranfield et al., 2003; Brown, et al., 2020; Ellegaard & Wallin, 2015). Researchers have used a variety of strategies while performing these literature evaluations. "Popularity-based approach" technique was developed to look at the titles and keywords of different articles which was published in various academic domains. Because bibliometric analysis provides additional information on authors, affiliations, Key words and phrases and frequency of usage, it can specifically offer insights that other reviews cannot capture or analyse. However, despite the popularity-based approach's ability to reveal the significance of the titles and keywords in a particular researched field by examining how often they are used in papers, important data can only be gained after publication (Choi. et al., 2011). Bibliometrics is a branch of study that uses the statistical & mathematical methods to examine the publication patterns in the dissemination of related information. It is a set of techniques that academics can use to analyse the published dataset (McCain, 1996). These methods include bibliometric mapping, citation and co-citation analysis, and impact indicators. Citation analysis works under the assumption that authors will only cite sources they believe to be crucial to their research. As a result, the frequency with which certain papers are quoted may be correlated with their perceived influence on the subject (Culnan, 1987). Co-citation analysis examines the articles that make use of a specific set of references, gathering information from databases and utilising analytical and visual display methods (McCain, 1996). This method of citation may highlight content similarities and aid in the identification of groups of subjects and writers as well as possible relationships between them (Ruiz-Navarro, 2004; Pilkington & Liston-Heyes, 1999; Ramos-Rodriguez, 2004). Since years, there has been an increase in the use of bibliometric approaches to map and analyse the body of information published in many domains. These techniques have already been used to investigate several management-related topics like finance, supply chain management, human resource management, innovation and operation management (Tahai & Meyer, 1999). Studies on corporate social responsibility are among the areas or subfields within the management discipline for which bibliometric analysis has been used (De Bakker, Groenewegen, & Den Hond, 2005). A key difficulty for business academics who want to learn more about the bibliometric approach and its use for business research in a comprehensive yet understandable way is the absence of an authorised guidance to bibliometric study in business research. Despite the fact that there are reliable guides for doing comprehensive literature reviews (Snyder, 2019; Palmatier, et al. 2018)

3.2 On Healthcare Quality

Established the HEALTHQUAL model utilising structural equation modelling to evaluate the quality of healthcare services. It discovered empathy, palpable safety, efficiency, and care service improvements and shed fresh light on their relative weight. In order to increase the quality of hospital services and operational effectiveness, they compared the various patient treatment options (inpatients, outpatients, and emergency rooms) among patients as well as members of the general public (Lee and Kim, 2017; Lee D, 2017). By using a qualitative method to add fresh perspectives to the literature on service quality. They discovered receptivity, worth, technical, accessibility, interpersonal, tangibles, and result. It is necessary to empirically validate these dimensions (Fatima et al., 2019, Gronroos, 2001; Haddad, 2019; Park, 2019). Sumaedi et al. (2016) have identified three key dimensions. These dimensions were identified by in their hypothesis in Jakarta for a multilevel healthcare service quality model. This model was steady when compared to the respondents' gender, age, and income. hospital service quality was measured in terms of expected waiting time, access to service, physical environment, consultation with doctors, patient related information, and expected services cost to customer (Pouragha & Zarei, 2016; Pekkaya et al., 2017; Pilkington & Meredith, 2019). The "Modified Hierarchical Approach model" that includes three broad areas: interaction quality, Outcome Quality, physical environment quality. Patient happiness, waiting time, loyalty of patient, and image of service provider are four service performance variables that the authors noted had a significant link with them. High levels of content validity, convergent validity and discriminant validity were shown by the model. The approach cannot be generalised to hospitals in the private sector because it is limited to a government hospital exclusively. This study must be experimentally evaluated in developed countries as well because it was conceptualised in a developing country (Chahal and Kumari, 2010). The SERVQUAL conception proposed a four-factor solution to assess the quality of hospital services in poor nations. 'Ultra-Modern facilities,' 'trust on doctors,' 'workers getting appropriate assistance from the hospital,' 'willing to asist patients,' and 'dependable' are some of the key contributing variables to service quality evaluation. Scale's dependability is proof of the components' stability. Due to SERVQUAL's lack of contextual stability, the author critiqued it and called for it to also undergo empirical testing in industrialised nations (Lee, J, 2006). According to reports, strongly collectivist and politically remote nations have poor standards for the quality of their services. They said that cultures that prioritise short-term goals demand lower service quality than counterparts that prioritise long-term goals and cultural practices in developing countries like India, where quality of service emphasises on cost as a distinguishing tactic (Donthu and Yoo, 1998; Rodriguez et al., 2019; Shankar et al., 2019; Upadhyai & Roy, 2019).

4. RESEARCH METHODOLOGY

4.1 Choice of Database

For doing specific sorts of analysis, including bibliometric analysis, well-known databases are accessible. These include Google Scholar, Scopus, and Web of Science (WoS). The Scopus database is the foundation for the analysis of the present study. Because it is thought to be the biggest abstract and citation repository of peer-reviewed articles and literature and because it covers such a broad range of topics, Scopus database was chosen (Khudzari, Kurian, Tartakovsky, & Raghavan, 2018). Scopus is the most popular tool for this type of study since it is the best data management tool and complies with other criteria, such as accessibility and the fact that the articles it indexes are among the most referenced (Hall, 2011). Bibliometric analysis quantifies the examination of bibliographical components. Since publications published in journals are regarded as "certified knowledge" and come from an evaluation procedure, which gives the results credibility, so we opted to use them (Callon et al.,1993 & Ramos-Rodríguez, 2004). Therefore, we only considered articles for the current study and exclude review papers, book chapter, conference proceedings, news and other documents found in Scopus documents.

Both co-occurrence analysis and citation analysis were employed. Citation evaluation is based on how highly academics regard a work when citing it as a source. Therefore, it can be deduced that an article's influence on the academic researchers in advancing a certain field would increase with its frequency of citation (Ramos Rodriguez & Ruiz Navarro, 2008).

4.2 Strategy for Data Retrieving

Major focus was placed on Service Quality and Quality of Service in Healthcare in the search string of Scopus. As on 09.12.2022 at 11.22 a.m. data extraction process was done from Scopus database. The period of search included in the research is from 1996 to 2022. Initially the extraction process was made by searching," TITLE-ABS-KEY ("Quality of Service") OR TITLE-ABS-KEY ("Service Quality") and TITLE-ABS-KEY (Health*)" in the search bar of Scopus database. The above search extracted 10,133 documents. Out of these documents, we exclude the documents related to the year 2023 and the search was limited to Business, Management & Accounting and Economics, Econometrics & Finance and Social Science in subject area, articles in document type and English in language. After the above search 2121 articles was left, out of which 5 articles are excluded due to non-availability of author details. So finally, 2117 articles are considered for bibliometric analysis. The search string in Scopus is "(TITLE-ABS-KEY ("Quality of Service") OR TITLE-ABS-KEY ("Service Quality") AND TITLE-ABS-KEY (Health*)) AND (EXCLUDE (PUBYEAR, 2023)) AND (LIMIT-TO (SUBAREA, "BUSI") OR (LIMIT-TO (SUBAREA, "SOCI") OR (LIMIT-TO (SUBAREA, "ECON")) AND ((LIMIT-TO (DOCTYPE, "ar")) AND (LIMIT-TO (LANGUAGE, "English"))."

4.3 Choice of Bibliographic Technique

Earlier manual exertion was used for both data gathering and bibliometric analysis (Garfield, 1955). However, the development of multiple approaches, such as bibliometrics and scientometrics approach, has made it quite simple to synthesise knowledge in recent years (Pritchard, 1969). An enormous amount of data can be organised and analysed with the support of bibliometrics.

4.4 Data Analysis Tool

Performance analysis and science mapping are used in the study to analyse the data. Performance analysis has made use of a variety of scientific players, such as the most referenced nations, most pertinent affiliated institute, most pertinent authors, and most pertinent keywords used in the literature (Gaviria-Marin et al., 2018). The science mapping analysis and performance analysis of service quality in healthcare sector was performed by R software. R software package offers a set of tools for quantitative bibliometric and scientometric research, in contrast to existing bibliometric tools like Vosviewer and CitNet Explorer.

It is written in the open-source language R. The library (Bibliometrix) and Biblioshiny() procedures were designed to carry out the bibliometric analysis. The bibliometrix tool aids in data extraction from Elsevier's database and Clarivate Analytics' database, the two most popular bibliographic databases (Aria and Cucurullo, 2017).

5. DATA ANALYSIS

5.1 Performance Analysis

Main Information about the Data

Table 1 provides the details regarding the data that were included in the bibliometrics analysis. It includes the time period of the study from 1996 to 2022, 2117 articles with 13.59% of annual growth rate, average citation per document is 17.11 and having 87,654 references. Data also includes 4262 keywords plus and 4928 authors keyword along with 5629 authors details. Out of 2117 articles under study, 277 articles are sole authored articles.

Table 1. Most crucial information about data

Sl. No.	Details	Outcome
A	**DETAILS ABOUT DATA ANALYSIS**	
1	Time Period Under Study	1996:2022
2	Source of Data	781
3	No. of Articles	2117
4	Per Year Growth Rate %	13.59
5	Average Age of Article	7.47
6	Average citations per article	17.11
7	Reference included	87654
B	**CONTENTS OF DOCUMENT**	
1	Keywords Plus	4262
2	Author's Keywords	4928
C	**AUTHORS**	
1	Total No. of Author	5629
2	Authors of single-authored docs	277
D	**COLLABORATION OF AUTHORS**	
1	Sole authored Articles	292
2	Co-authors per Articles	3.12
3	International co-authorships %	21.9
E	**TYPE OF DOCUMENT**	
1	articles	2117

Annual Document Production

The documents we have analysed in Table 2 and Fig 1 were published in between 1996 to 2022, which indicated number of documents produced over the periods, total citation, and average citation per year. Though research papers related to service quality in healthcare were published since 1969, but publication related to business, management, economics, finance, and social science were first published in the year 1996. Initially the production was very less. Only 8 documents were published in the year 1996 and 19 documents were published in 1997 in the concerned area of research. From 1998 production of documents were increased at a slow pace and it was triggered from 2016. In 2022, number of documents produced rose to 220. The increase in the number of articles being published implies that the subject is moving into a more advanced level. Different study routes may be pursued as a result, such as investigating new related topics, looking more closely at regions that have received much less attention, or even attempting to address "classic challenges" using novel frameworks. Expanding the scope of the investigation might also benefit from investigating new international collaboration.

Figure 1. Annual Article Production

Table 2. Annual article production

Sl. No.	Year	Number of Documents	Average Citation Per Article	TC
1	1996	8	13.13	105
2	1997	19	40.95	778
3	1998	32	33.16	1061
4	1999	31	18.39	570
5	2000	20	51.90	1038
6	2001	28	43.61	1221
7	2002	31	42.03	1303
8	2003	30	29.60	888
9	2004	28	50.18	1405
10	2005	24	37.83	908
11	2006	32	31.94	1022
12	2007	48	43.27	2077
13	2008	45	35.93	1617
14	2009	55	26.44	1454
15	2010	65	32.37	2104
16	2011	72	22.33	1608
17	2012	65	20.72	1347
18	2013	90	23.80	2142
19	2014	87	16.95	1475
20	2015	78	18.71	1459
21	2016	98	13.56	1329
22	2017	110	14.26	1569
23	2018	156	11.53	1799
24	2019	156	10.07	1571
25	2020	194	6.84	1327
26	2021	178	6.12	1090
27	2022	220	5.00	1102

(TC: Total Citation)

Most Productive Country

The result of biblioshiny indicates that USA is the most productive and most cited country in the world with respect to service quality in healthcare sector in business, management, economics, finance, and social science area. Table 3 depicts a clear picture about the most productive counties in the world. USA has 902 documents to his credit with 10,143 citations followed by Unite Kingdom having 407 documents and 2850 citations, China with 291 documents, India having 288 documents and so on. The average article citation of USA is 11.25 where as UK is 7, China is 7.88 and India is 6.98. out of the 20 listed countries in the study Greece stood last in the table with 41 documents and Saudi Arabia with

46 documents holds second last position. But surprisingly the average citation of Greece is the highest among all, that is 21.85. USA is almost producing double of documents than UK.

Table 3. Productive country

Sl. No.	Country	No of Documents	TC	Average Article Citations
1	USA	902	10143	11.25
2	UNITED KINGDOM	407	2850	7.00
3	CHINA	291	2294	7.88
4	INDIA	288	2010	6.98
5	AUSTRALIA	209	1413	6.76
6	IRAN	195	940	4.82
7	CANADA	145	1247	8.60
8	MALAYSIA	131	775	5.92
9	ITALY	105	420	4.00
10	KOREA	85	512	6.02
11	TURKEY	78	470	6.03
12	BRAZIL	67	229	3.42
13	PORTUGAL	66	433	6.56
14	PAKISTAN	60	423	7.05
15	SWEDEN	56	440	7.86
16	NETHERLANDS	56	328	5.86
17	GERMANY	52	171	3.29
18	SPAIN	48	356	16.95
19	SAUDI ARABIA	46	164	10.25
20	GREECE	41	437	21.85

Worldwide Most Cited Documents

The bibliometrics analysis in the Table 4 (Supplementary Materials Page) in the present researched area indicates the most cited articles in the world in the subject area of management, business, economics, finance, and social science derived from Scopus database. The paper title "A hierarchical model of health service quality: Scale development and investigation of an integrated model" authored by Shieh, Wu and Huang (2010) published by Journal of Service Research is considered as the highly cited documents with 474 citations in Scopus. "A DEMATEL method in identifying key success factors of hospital service quality", published in "Knowledge-Based Systems" secured the second place with 421 citations and so on. Article titled "Customer positivity and participation in services: An empirical test in a health care context" by Gallan, A.S. et al. in 2013, which is published in "Journal of the Academy of Marketing Science" stood last in the table with 181 citations. The following table indicates the most impactful document related to healthcare sector.

Table 7: Most Cited Document, Worldwide

*Can be found at the supplementary documents after references

Most High-Yielding Journals

Table 4 depicts the list of most yielded journal in the present researched area relating to business, management, economics, finance, and social science subject area. Journal of Marketing holds the first position with 1633 production of documents in the above specified area, followed by Int. Jour. of Health Care Qlt. Assurance with 1281 documents, Journal of Retailing with 956 documents, Jour. of Business Research with 578 articles and so on. Health Service Research holds the twentieth position in the list having 251 documents to its credit.

Table 4. Most high-yielding journals

Sl. No.	Sources	Articles
1	JOURNAL OF MARKETING	1633
2	INTERNATIONAL JOURNAL OF HEALTH CARE QUALITY ASSURANCE	1281
3	JOURNAL OF RETAILING	956
4	JOURNAL OF BUSINESS RESEARCH	578
5	JOURNAL OF SERVICES MARKETING	529
6	JOURNAL OF MAKT. RES.	502
7	JOUR. OF THE ACAD. OF MAKT SC.	469
8	JOUR. OF SERVICE RESEARCH	454
9	MANAGING SERVICE QUALITY	444
10	EUROPEAN JOURNAL OF MARKETING	417
11	JOURNAL OF HEALTH CARE MARKETING	397
12	SOCIAL SCIENCE & MEDICINE	346
13	JOURNAL OF APPLIED PSYCHOLOGY	340
14	INTERNATIONAL JOURNAL OF SERVICE INDUSTRY MANAGEMENT	334
15	SOCIAL SCIENCE AND MEDICINE	328
16	TOURISM MANAGEMENT	318
17	INTERNATIONAL JOURNAL FOR QUALITY IN HEALTH CARE	299
18	BENCHMARKING: AN INTERNATIONAL JOURNAL	266
19	JOURNAL OF CONSUMER RESEARCH	257
20	HEALTH SERVICES RESEARCH	251

Most Pertinent Author List

Table 5 explains the most pertinent and impactful author list of in the current field of research relating to business, management, economics, finance, and social science subject area. The table provides the details regarding the name of the author with number of relevant publications, total citation, and average citation per document. Kumar, S. holds the first position with 9 documents to his credit followed by Chahal, H. having 7 documents, Malik, S.A. having 7 documents and so on. Shieh secured the last position in the table with 4 documents to his name. but surprisingly when we analysed the citation of these authors, Shieh becomes the highest cited author with only 4 publications to his credit and Lee, H. having 539 citations, in this subject area. Even if Kumar, S. has the highest publication, but the citation is very less as 93.

Table 5. Most pertinent author

Sl. No.	Author	Total Documents	Total Citation	Average Citation Per Document
1	KUMAR S	9	93	10.33
2	CHAHAL H	7	220	31.43
3	MALIK SA	7	310	44.29
4	RAVANGARD R	7	57	8.14
5	AKTER S	6	514	85.67
6	JR	6	96	16.00
7	LI L	6	26	4.33
8	QIN H	6	64	10.67
9	BAHADORI M	5	49	9.80
10	D'AMBRA J	5	512	102.40
11	LEE H	5	539	107.80
12	LEE S	5	490	98.00
13	O'CONNOR SJ	5	210	42.00
14	RAJENDRAN C	5	402	80.40
15	SHEWCHUK RM	5	215	43.00
16	WANG J	5	12	2.40
17	WANG Y	5	88	17.60
18	WHITE L	5	13	2.60
19	ZHANG L	5	53	10.60
20	SHIEH JI	4	801	200.25

Most Pertinent Affiliation

Following table 6 describes the most relevant affiliated institutions in quality service in healthcare sector research. R software is unable to reveal the name of the top institute due to non-availability of data which has been published 52 documents. Then University of Jammu becomes the second affiliated institute with 13 documents followed by University of Manchester, University of Sains Malaysia and so on. Arizona State University, Curtin University, IIT Madras and University of new South Wales individually produced 7 documents each and holds the last position in the reported table.

Table 6. Most pertinent affiliation

Sl. No.	Affiliated Institute	Articles
1	NOT REPORTED	52
2	UNIVERSITY OF JAMMU	13
3	UNIVERSITY OF MANCHESTER	13
4	UNIVERSITI SAINS MALAYSIA	12
5	UNIVERSITY OF CALIFORNIA	12
6	UNIVERSITY OF KENT	12
7	JOHNS HOPKINS BLOOMBERG SCHOOL OF PUBLIC HEALTH	11
8	UNIVERSITY OF SURREY	11
9	MULTIMEDIA UNIVERSITY	10
10	UNIVERSITY OF QUEENSLAND	10
11	GRIFFITH UNIVERSITY	9
12	SCHOOL OF BUSINESS	9
13	SCHOOL OF MANAGEMENT	9
14	WORLD BANK	9
15	UNIVERSITY OF SYDNEY	8
16	ARIZONA STATE UNIVERSITY	7
17	CURTIN UNIVERSITY	7
18	INDIAN INSTITUTE OF TECHNOLOGY MADRAS	7
20	UNIVERSITY OF NEW SOUTH WALES	7

5.2 Science Mapping Analysis

Keyword Analysis

Figure 2 and Figure 3 depicts the most prominent keyword used in this field of research. Human word is used for 643 times whereas female word is 585 times, human word is for 524 times and so on. Hospitals and health care delivery word is used for 145 and 140 times.

Figure 2. Keyword Analysis

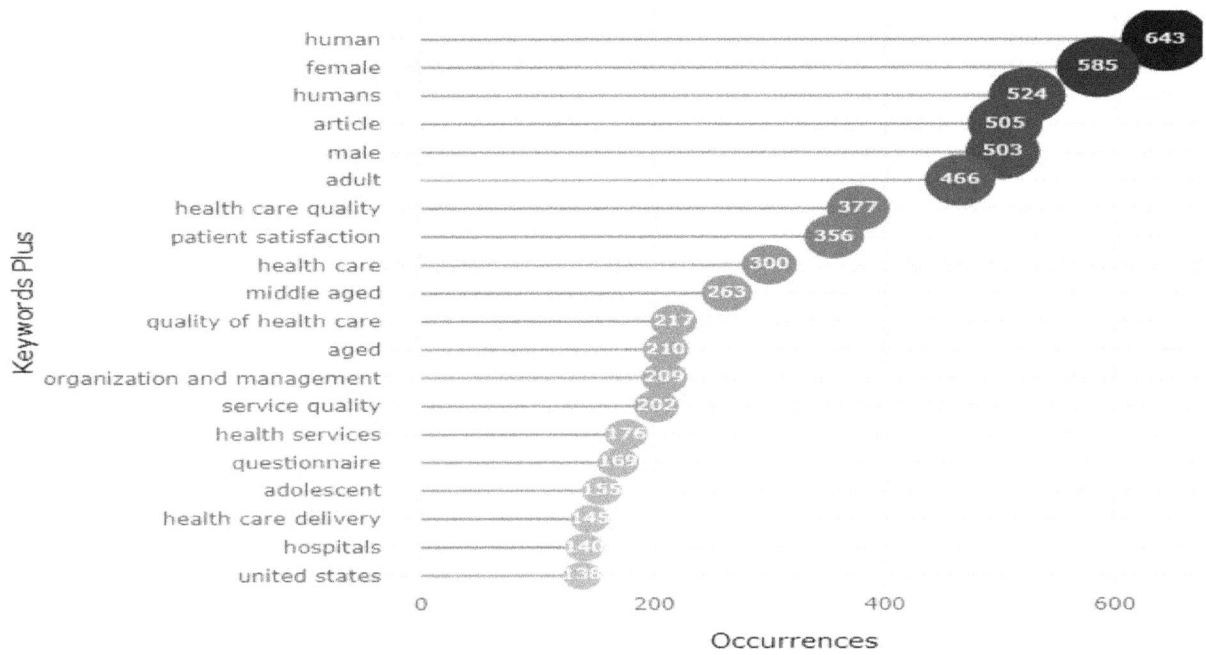

Figure 3. Word Cloud

Co-occurrence Network

In figure 3 co-occurrence network reflects the linkage between keywords. In the below figure the highlighted network is build among the word human, article, human, health care quality, human, male and female.

Figure 4. Co-occurrence Network

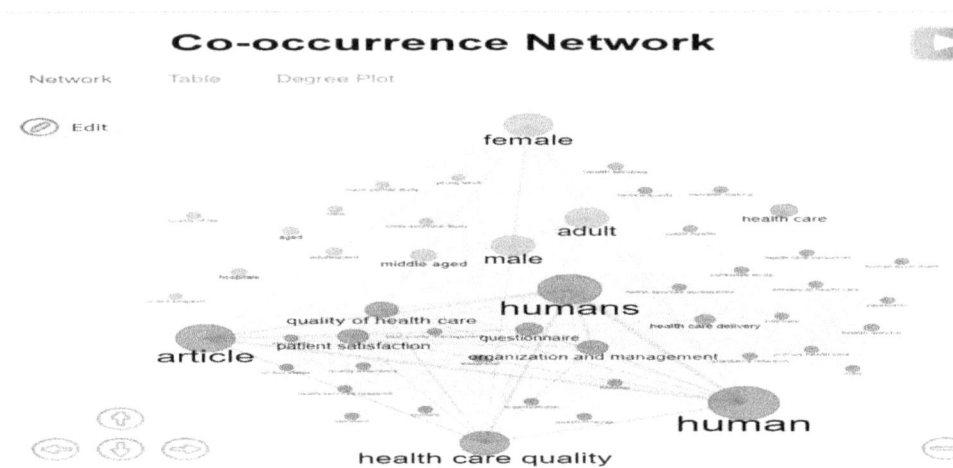

Collaboration Network

Fig. 4 indicates the collaborative network among different authors of various independent institutions across globe. The strongest network is identified among D'ambraj, Akter, S. and Ray, P.

Figure 5. Collaboration Network

Co-Citation Network

Figure 5 depicts the frequency at which two or more documents are cited by a different documents. The figure shows Parsuraman A is having the highest co-citation network amongst all.

Figure 6. Co-citation Network

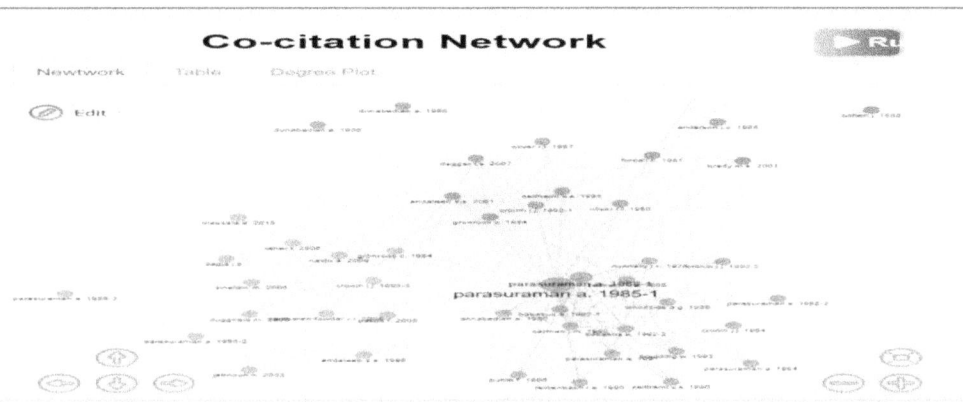

CONCLUSION

The current chapter's goal was to perform a bibliometric examination of healthcare service quality. As a result, 4689 documents from 1996 to 2022 were examined using the Scopus database. The number of papers in the field of service quality research was rising each year. The highest number of publication and significant authors of service quality in healthcare were identified in the current study. Co-authorship analysis of writers and nations was carried out to look into the relationships between authors and nations where documents on healthcare service quality were authored. Additionally, a co-citation analysis of the author's keywords was carried out to find, examine, and correlate the keywords related to the study of service quality in healthcare industry across the globe in the subject area of business, management, economics, finance, and social science.

The current study was not without its flaws. The analysis might have included other settings and their service quality, such as education of employee, transportation facility, hospitality provided by industry, superstores, and other services, however it was only focused on the context of healthcare. The analysis was also restricted to the Scopus database; further analysis may be carried out using other databases like Clarivate's Web of Science or MedLine, or a combination of these. Finally, VOSviewer was only used for co-authorship and co-occurrence analysis; additional techniques like co-citation and bibliographic coupling may also be used with the same programme.

Research on the quality of healthcare services has seen an increase in the usage of models like Fuzzy (Kano, 1984). It is recommended that these models be used to assess service quality in healthcare settings. The majority of research on healthcare service quality has focused on measurable results like satisfaction and loyalty. As a result, it is advised to include a few new outcome variables in connection to healthcare service quality. Studying the connection between service quality and patient or customer welfare in healthcare is also necessary. Considering that the review did not contain any keyword streams that connected patient welfare to service excellence.

REFERENCES

Abbasi-Moghaddam, M. A., Zarei, E., Bagherzadeh, R., Dargahi, H., & Farrokhi, P. (2019). *Evaluation of service quality from patients' viewpoint.* Academic Press.

Amankwah, O., Choong, W., & Mohammed, A. H. (2019). *Modelling the influence of healthcare facilities management service quality on patients satisfaction.* doi:10.1108/JFM-08-2018-0053

Ampah, I. T., Ali, R. S., Ampah, I. T., & Ali, R. S. (2019). Measuring Patients (Customers) *Perceptions and Expectations of Service Quality in Public Healthcare Institutions: Servqual Model.* Academic Press.

. Anabila, P., Kumi, D. K., & Anome, J. (2018). *Patients' perceptions of healthcare quality in Ghana A review of public and private hospitals.* doi:10.1108/IJHCQA-10-2017-0200

Aria, M., & Cuccurullo, C. (2017). Bibliometrix: An R-tool for comprehensive science mapping analysis. *Journal of Informetrics, 11*(4), 959–975. doi:10.1016/j.joi.2017.08.007

Bahadori, M., Teymourzadeh, E., Faizy Bagejan, F., Ravangard, R., Raadabadi, M., & Hosseini, S. M. (2018). Factors affecting the effectiveness of quality control circles in a hospital using a combination of fuzzy VIKOR and Grey Relational Analysis. *Proceedings of Singapore Healthcare, 27*(3), 180–186. doi:10.1177/2010105818758088

Behdioğlu, S., Acar, E., & Burhan, H. A. (2019). Evaluating service quality by fuzzy SERVQUAL: A case study in a physiotherapy and rehabilitation hospital. *Total Quality Management & Business Excellence, 30*(3–4), 301–319. doi:10.1080/14783363.2017.1302796

Brady, M. K., & Robertson, C. J. (2001). Searching for a consensus on the antecedent role of service quality and satisfaction: An exploratory cross-national study. *Journal of Business Research, 51*(1), 53–60. doi:10.1016/S0148-2963(99)00041-7

Broadus, R. (1987). Toward a definition of "bibliometrics.". *Scientometrics, 12*(5–6), 373–379. doi:10.1007/BF02016680

Brown, T., Park, A., & Pitt, L. (2020). A 60-year bibliographic review of the Journal of Advertising Research: Perspectives on trends in authorship, influences, and research impact. *Journal of Advertising Research, 60*(4), 353–360. doi:10.2501/JAR-2020-028

Budiwan, V., & Efendi. (2016). The understanding of Indonesian Patients of Hospital Service Quality in Singapore. *Procedia: Social and Behavioral Sciences, 224*, 176–183. doi:10.1016/j.sbspro.2016.05.436

Callon, M., Courtial, J.-P., & Penan, H. (1993). *La scientométrie* (Vol. 2727). Presses Universitaires de France.

Chahal, H., & Kumari, N. (2010). Development of multidimensional scale for healthcare service quality (HCSQ) in Indian context. *Journal of Indian Business Research*, *2*(4), 230–255. doi:10.1108/17554191011084157

Chang, B., Kao, H., Lin, S., Yang, S., Kuo, Y., & Jerng, J. (2019). ScienceDirect Quality gaps and priorities for improvement of healthcare service for patients with prolonged mechanical ventilation in the view of family. *Journal of the Formosan Medical Association*, *118*(5), 922–931. doi:10.1016/j.jfma.2018.09.019 PMID:30301580

Chien, C.-J., & Tsai, H.-H. (2000). Using fuzzy numbers to evaluate perceived service quality. *Fuzzy Sets and Systems*, *116*(2), 289–300. doi:10.1016/S0165-0114(98)00239-5

Choi, J., Yi, S., & Lee, K. C. (2011). Analysis of keyword networks in MIS research and implications for predicting knowledge evolution. *Information & Management*, *48*(8), 371–381. doi:10.1016/j.im.2011.09.004

Culnan, M. J. (1987). Mapping the intellectual structure of MIS, 1980-1985: A co-citation analysis. *Management Information Systems Quarterly*, *11*(3), 341–353. doi:10.2307/248680

De Bakker, F. G., Groenewegen, P., & Den Hond, F. (2005). A bibliometric analysis of 30 years of research and theory on corporate social responsibility and corporate social performance. *Business & Society*, *44*(3), 283–317. doi:10.1177/0007650305278086

Donthu, N., & Yoo, B. (1998). Cultural influences on service quality expectations. *Journal of Service Research*, *1*(2), 178–186. doi:10.1177/109467059800100207

El Haddad, R. (2019). Exploring Service Quality of Low Cost Airlines Exploring Service Quality of Low Cost Airlines. *Services Marketing Quarterly*, *0*(0), 1–15. doi:10.1080/15332969.2019.1665901

Ellegaard, O., & Wallin, J. A. (2015). The bibliometric analysis of scholarly production: How great is the impact. *Scientometrics*, *105*(3), 1809–1831. doi:10.100711192-015-1645-z PMID:26594073

Evren, S., & Kozak, N. (2014). Bibliometric analysis of tourism and hospitality related articles published in Turkey. *Anatolia*, *25*(1), 61–80. doi:10.1080/13032917.2013.824906

Fatima, I., Humayun, A., Iqbal, U., & Shafiq, M. (2018). *Dimensions of service quality in healthcare: A systematic review of literature.* doi:10.1093/intqhc/mzy125

Fatima, I., Humayun, A., Iqbal, U., & Shafiq, M. (2019). Dimensions of service quality in healthcare: A systematic review of literature. *International Journal for Quality in Health Care*, *31*(1), 11–29. doi:10.1093/intqhc/mzy125 PMID:29901718

Fauziah, F., Surachman, E., & Muhtadi, A. (2019). Integration of service quality and quality function deployment as an effort of pharmaceutical service improvement on outpatient in a referral hospital. Academic Press.

Garfield, E. (1955). Citation analysis as a tool in journal evaluation. *Science*, *122*(3159), 108–111. doi:10.1126cience.122.3159.108 PMID:14385826

Gaviria-Marin, M., Merigo, J. M., & Popa, S. (2018). Twenty years of the Journal of Knowledge Management: A bibliometric analysis. *Journal of Knowledge Management*, *22*(8), 1655–1687. doi:10.1108/JKM-10-2017-0497

Grönroos, C. (2001). The perceived service quality concept–a mistake? *Managing Service Quality*, *11*(3), 150–152. doi:10.1108/09604520110393386

Gupta, T. K., & Singh, V. (2017). Measurement of service quality of automobile organisation by artificial neural network. *International Journal of Management Concepts and Philosophy*, *10*(1), 32–53. doi:10.1504/IJMCP.2017.081989

Hall, C. M. (2011). Publish and perish? Bibliometric analysis, journal ranking and the assessment of research quality in tourism. *Tourism Management*, *32*(1), 16–27. doi:10.1016/j.tourman.2010.07.001

Hughes, D., Hughes, A., Powell, A., & Al-Sarireh, B. (2019). *Hepatocellular carcinoma's 100 most influential manuscripts: A bibliometric analysis*. doi:10.5348/100083Z04DH2019OA

Ibrahim, M. S., & Ahmed, M. S. (2019). SERVQUAL Reliability and Validity A Pilot Study to Evaluate Patients '. *Satisfaction in the Jordanian Hospitals.*, *15*(1), 56–67.

Id, X. Z., Estoque, R. C., Xie, H., Murayama, Y., & Id, M. R. (2019). *Bibliometric analysis of highly cited articles on ecosystem services*. Academic Press.

Islam, R., Ahmed, S., & Tarique, K. M. (2016). Prioritisation of service quality dimensions for healthcare sector. *International Journal of Medical Engineering and Informatics*, *8*(2), 108–123. doi:10.1504/IJMEI.2016.075751

Jahantigh, F. F. (2019). Evaluation of healthcare service quality management in an Iranian hospital by using fuzzy logic. *International Journal of Productivity and Quality Management*, *26*(2), 160. doi:10.1504/IJPQM.2019.097764

Javed, S. A., & Nawaz, M. (2019). *Patients ' satisfaction and public and private sectors' health care service quality in Pakistan: Application of grey decision analysis approaches*. doi:10.1002/hpm.2629

Jebraeily, M., Safdari, R., Rahimi, B., Makhdoomi, K., & Ghazisaeidi, M. (2018). The application of intelligent information systems in hemodialysis adequacy promotion. *Journal of Renal Injury Prevention*, *7*(2), 64–68. doi:10.15171/jrip.2018.16

Kalaja, R., Myshketa, R., & Scalera, F. (2016). Service quality assessment in health care sector: The case of Durres public hospital. *Procedia: Social and Behavioral Sciences*, *235*, 557–565. doi:10.1016/j.sbspro.2016.11.082

Kano, N. (1984). Attractive quality and must-be quality. *Hinshitsu (Quality, The Journal of Japanese Society for Quality Control)*, *14*, 39–48.

Khudzari, J. M., Kurian, J., Tartakovsky, B., & Raghavan, G. S. V. (2018). Bibliometric analysis of global research trends on microbial fuel cells using Scopus database. *Biochemical Engineering Journal*, *136*, 51–60. doi:10.1016/j.bej.2018.05.002

Koc, E., & Boz, H. (2014). Triangulation in tourism research: A bibliometric study of top three tourism journals. *Tourism Management Perspectives, 12,* 9–14. doi:10.1016/j.tmp.2014.06.003

Köseoglu, M. A., Sehitoglu, Y., Ross, G., & Parnell, J. A. (2016). The evolution of business ethics research in the realm of tourism and hospitality: A bibliometric analysis. *International Journal of Contemporary Hospitality Management, 28*(8), 1598–1621. doi:10.1108/IJCHM-04-2015-0188

Kumar, P., Sharma, A., & Salo, J. (2019). A bibliometric analysis of extended key account management literature. *Industrial Marketing Management, 82*(January), 276–292. doi:10.1016/j.indmarman.2019.01.006

Kwateng, K. O., Lumor, R., & Acheampong, F. O. (2017). Service quality in public and private hospitals: A comparative study on patient satisfaction. *International Journal of Healthcare Management, 0*(0), 1–8. doi:10.1080/20479700.2017.1390183

Lee, D. (2017). HEALTHQUAL: A multi-item scale for assessing healthcare service quality. *Service Business, 11*(3), 491–516. doi:10.100711628-016-0317-2

Lee, D., & Kim, K. K. (2017). Assessing healthcare service quality: A comparative study of patient treatment types. *Int J Qual Innov, 3*(1), 1. doi:10.118640887-016-0010-5

Lee, J. (2006). Measuring service quality in a medical setting in a developing country: The applicability of SERVQUAL. *Services Marketing Quarterly, 27*(2), 1–4. doi:10.1300/J396v27n02_01

Li, X., Ma, E., & Qu, H. (2017). Knowledge mapping of hospitality research– A visual analysis using CiteSpace. *International Journal of Hospitality Management, 60,* 77–93. doi:10.1016/j.ijhm.2016.10.006

Liu, W., Wang, J., Li, C., Chen, B., & Sun, Y. (2019). Using Bibliometric Analysis to Understand the Recent Progress in Agroecosystem Services Research. *Ecological Economics, 156*(October), 293–305. doi:10.1016/j.ecolecon.2018.09.001

Marimon, F., Gil-doménech, D., & Bastida, R. (2017). *Total Quality Management & Business Excellence Fulfilment of expectations mediating quality and satisfaction: the case of hospital service.* doi:1 0.1080/14783363.2017.1401458

Materla, T., & Cudney, E. A. (2017). *Identifying Factors Affecting Patient Satisfaction using the Kano Model.* Academic Press.

McCain, K. W. (1990). Mapping authors in intellectual space: A technical overview. *Journal of the American Society for Information Science, 41*(6), 433.

McCain, K. W. (1996). *Dictionary of bibliometrics.* Academic Press.

Meesala, A., & Paul, J. (2018). Service quality, consumer satisfaction and loyalty in hospitals: Thinking for the future. *Journal of Retailing and Consumer Services, 40*(November), 261–269. doi:10.1016/j. jretconser.2016.10.011

Meleddu, M., Pulina, M., & Scuderi, R. (2019). Socio-Economic Planning Sciences Public and private healthcare services: What drives the choice? *Socio-Economic Planning Sciences, 100739*(October). doi:10.1016/j.seps.2019.100739

Mohammadi-Sardo, M., & Salehi, S. (2019). Emergency Department Patient Satisfaction Assessment using Modified Servqual Model; a Cross-sectional Study. *Advanced Journal of Emergency Medicine*, *3*(1), e3–e3. doi:10.22114/ajem.v0i0.107 PMID:31388652

Montero-Díaz, J., Cobo, M.-J., Gutiérrez-Salcedo, M., Segado-Boj, F., & Herrera-Viedma, E. (2018). Mapeo científico de la Categoría «Comunicación» en WoS (1980-2013). *Comunicar*, *26*(55), 81–91.

Muir, K. W., Bosworth, H. B., & Lee, P. P. (2010). Health Services Research and How It Can Inform the Current State of Ophthalmology. *American Journal of Ophthalmology*, *150*(6), 761–763. doi:10.1016/j.ajo.2010.07.006 PMID:21094708

Muñoz-Leiva, F., Porcu, L., & del Barrio-García, S. (2015). Discovering prominent themes in integrated marketing communication research from 1991 to 2012: A co-word analytic approach. *International Journal of Advertising*, *34*(4), 678–701. doi:10.1080/02650487.2015.1009348

Ng, J. H. Y., & Luk, B. H. K. (2018). Patient satisfaction: Concept analysis in the healthcare context. *Patient Education and Counseling*, *102*(4), 790–796. doi:10.1016/j.pec.2018.11.013 PMID:30477906

Odriozola-fernández, I., & Berbegal-mirabent, J. (2019). *Open innovation in small and medium enterprises: A bibliometric analysis.* doi:10.1108/JOCM-12-2017-0491

Palmatier, R. W., Houston, M. B., & Hulland, J. (2018). Review articles: Purpose, process, and structure. *Journal of the Academy of Marketing Science*, *46*(1), 1–5. doi:10.100711747-017-0563-4

Parasuraman, A., Zeithaml, V. A., & Berry, L. (1988). *SERVQUAL: A multiple-item scale for measuring consumer perceptions of service quality.* Academic Press.

Parasuraman, A., Zeithaml, V. A., & Berry, L. L. (1985). A conceptual model of service quality and its implications for future research. *Journal of Marketing*, *49*(4), 41–50. doi:10.1177/002224298504900403

Park, J. (2019). *Service Quality in Tourism: A Systematic Literature Review and Keyword Network Analysis.* Academic Press.

Pekkaya, M., İmamoğlu, Ö. P., & Koca, H. (2017). *Evaluation of healthcare service quality via Servqual scale: An application on a hospital.* doi:10.1080/20479700.2017.1389474

Pilkington, A., & Liston-Heyes, C. (1999). Is production and operations management a discipline? A citation/co-citation study. *International Journal of Operations & Production Management*, *19*(1), 7–20. doi:10.1108/01443579910244188

Pilkington, A., & Meredith, J. (2009). The evolution of the intellectual structure of operations management—1980–2006: A citation/co-citation analysis. *Journal of Operations Management*, *27*(3), 185–202. doi:10.1016/j.jom.2008.08.001

Pouragha, B., & Zarei, E. (2016). The effect of outpatient service quality on patient satisfaction in teaching hospitals in Iran. *Materia Socio-Medica*, *28*(1), 21. doi:10.5455/msm.2016.28.21-25 PMID:27047262

Pritchard, A. (1969). Statistical bibliography or bibliometrics. *The Journal of Documentation*, *25*(4), 348–349.

Ramos-Rodríguez, A., & Ruíz-Navarro, J. (2004). Changes in the intellectual structure of strategic management research: A bibliometric study of the Strategic Management Journal, 1980–2000. *Strategic Management Journal, 25*(10), 981–1004. doi:10.1002mj.397

Ramos Rodríguez, A. R., & Ruiz Navarro, J. (2008). Base intelectual de la investigación en creación de empresas: Un estudio biométrico. *Revista europea de dirección y economía de la empresa, 17*(1), 13-38.

Reeves, C. A., & Bednar, D. A. (1994). Defining quality: Alternatives and implications. *Academy of Management Review, 19*(3), 419–445. doi:10.2307/258934

Rodríguez-lópez, M. E., Alcántara-pilar, J. M., Del Barrio-garcía, S., & Muñoz-leiva, F. (2019). International Journal of Hospitality Management A review of restaurant research in the last two decades: A bibliometric analysis. *International Journal of Hospitality Management, 102387*(September). doi:10.1016/j.ijhm.2019.102387

Sarkodie, S. A., & Strezov, V. (2019). Science of the Total Environment A review on Environmental Kuznets Curve hypothesis using bibliometric and meta-analysis. *The Science of the Total Environment, 649*, 128–145. doi:10.1016/j.scitotenv.2018.08.276 PMID:30172133

Shafiq, M., & Naeem, M. A. (2017). *Service Quality Assessment of Hospitals in Asian Context: An Empirical Evidence From Pakistan.* doi:10.1177/0046958017714664

Shankar, A., Datta, B., & Jebarajakirthy, C. (2019). Are the Generic Scales Enough to Measure Service Quality of Mobile Banking? A Comparative Analysis of Generic Service Quality Measurement Scales to Mobile Banking Context. *Services Marketing Quarterly, 40*(3), 224–244. doi:10.1080/15332969.2019.1630176

Shieh, J., Huang, K., & Wu, H. (2019). *Service quality evaluation of a geriatric long-term care: A combination of SERVQUAL model and importance-performance analysis.* doi:10.1080/09720510.2018.1555080

Shieh, J. I., Wu, H. H., & Huang, K. K. (2010). A DEMATEL method in identifying key success factors of hospital service quality. *Knowledge-Based Systems, 23*(3), 277–282. doi:10.1016/j.knosys.2010.01.013

Singh, A., & Prasher, A. (2019). Measuring healthcare service quality from patients" perspective: Using Fuzzy AHP application. *Total Quality Management & Business Excellence, 30*(3–4), 284–300. doi:10.1080/14783363.2017.1302794

Snyder, H. (2019). Literature review as a research methodology: An overview and guidelines. *Journal of Business Research, 104*, 333–339. doi:10.1016/j.jbusres.2019.07.039

Srivastava, N., & Goel, S. (n.d.). *A Study of Patient Satisfaction Level in Inpatient Spine Department of a Tertiary Care Multispecialty Hospital.* doi:10.15419/jmri.147

Sumaedi, S., Yarmen, M., & Yuda Bakti, I. G. (2016). Healthcare service quality model: A multi-level approach with empirical evidence from a developing country. *International Journal of Productivity and Performance Management, 65*(8), 1007–1024. doi:10.1108/IJPPM-08-2014-0126

Swain, S. (2018). *Do patients really perceive better quality of service in private hospitals than public hospitals in India?* doi:10.1108/BIJ-03-2018-0055

Tahai, A., & Meyer, M. J. (1999). A revealed preference study of management journals' direct influences. *Strategic Management Journal, 20*(3), 279–296. doi:10.1002/(SICI)1097-0266(199903)20:3<279::AID-SMJ33>3.0.CO;2-2

Tranfield, D., Denyer, D., & Smart, P. (2003). Towards a methodology for developing evidence-informed management knowledge by means of systematic review. *British Journal of Management, 14*(3), 207–222. doi:10.1111/1467-8551.00375

Tuzkaya, G., Sennaroglu, B., Kalender, Z. T., & Mutlu, M. (2019). Socio-Economic Planning Sciences Hospital service quality evaluation with IVIF-PROMETHEE and a case study. *Socio-Economic Planning Sciences*, (September), 100705. doi:10.1016/j.seps.2019.04.002

Upadhyai, R., & Roy, H. (2019). A Review of Healthcare Service Quality Dimensions and their. *Measurement, 21*(1), 102–127. Advance online publication. doi:10.1177/0972063418822583

APPENDIX

Table 7. Worldwide most cited documents

Sl. No.	Title	Journal	Year of Publication	Total Citations
1	A hierarchical model of health service quality: Scale development and investigation of an integrated model	Journal of Service Research	2007	474
2	A DEMATEL method in identifying key success factors of hospital service quality	Knowledge-Based Systems	2010	421
3	Health sector reform and public sector health worker motivation: A conceptual framework	Social Science and Medicine	2002	416
4	Health care: A fertile field for service research	Journal of Service Research	2007	396
5	Service quality perceptions and patient satisfaction: A study of hospitals in a developing country	Social Science and Medicine	2001	391
6	Why do customers switch? The dynamics of satisfaction versus loyalty	Journal of Services Marketing	1998	373
7	The relationships among quality, value, satisfaction and behavioural intention in health care provider choice: A South Korean study	Journal of Business Research	2004	328
8	Judging the quality of care at the end of life: Can proxies provide reliable information?	Social Science and Medicine	2003	287
9	The organizational context of children's mental health services	Clinical Child and Family Psychology Review	2002	281
10	Factors affecting patient satisfaction and healthcare quality	International Journal of Health Care Quality Assurance	2009	262
11	Customer loyalty to content-based Web sites: The case of an online health-care service	Journal of Services Marketing	2004	262
12	Factors influencing healthcare service quality	International Journal of Health Policy and Management	2014	239
13	Service quality, consumer satisfaction and loyalty in hospitals: Thinking for the future	Journal of Retailing and Consumer Services	2018	223
14	SERVQUAL: A tool for measuring patients' opinions of hospital service quality in Hong Kong	Total Quality Management	1997	213
15	Integration of standardization and customization: Impact on service quality, customer satisfaction, and loyalty	Journal of Retailing and Consumer Services	2017	204
16	The impact of operational failures on hospital nurses and their patients	Journal of Operations Management	2004	196
17	Increasing community health worker productivity and effectiveness: A review of the influence of the work environment	Human Resources for Health	2012	194
18	A study of patients' expectations and satisfaction in Singapore hospitals	International Journal of Health Care Quality Assurance	2000	186
19	Customer positivity and participation in services: An empirical test in a health care context	Journal of the Academy of Marketing Science	2013	181

Chapter 16
Retailing Narrative:
A Systematic Literature Review and Outlook for Further Research

Lingam Naveen

Biju Patnaik Institute of Information Technology and Management Studies (BIITM), India

Rabi N. Subudhi

KIIT School of Management, KIIT University, India

ABSTRACT

The world of retail is very dynamic and interesting. The evolution of retail as an industry withholds immense richness in terms of research literature. This study has adopted a review research design to study the retailing literature of last two decades. The bibliometric database Scopus was used to extract the list of studies. The central constructs considered for the study are service quality (SQ), customer satisfaction (CS), and customer delight (CD). A systematic literature review approach was undertaken along with PRISMA framework. Multiple rounds of screening were done to finalize a total of 92 documents for the review. To identify, evaluate, and study various themes and variables related to the central constructs, several research tools were used like network analysis, temporal analysis, citation analysis, and mind maps. The findings of the study would help both retail researchers and practitioners to understand consumer behavior concerning retail sector and devise the future course of action to develop higher levels of customer loyalty and retention.

INTRODUCTION AND BACKGROUND OF THE STUDY

Retailing has seen multiple facets in the past 2 decades. Retail landscape has evolved from traditional mom and pop stores to modern retail where one-place-get-all, convenience and better prices catalyzed the growth (Knezevic, 2011). Last decade witnessed a big revolution in retail, progressing to e-retail and online shopping. Though different drivers played key roles at different stages of the development. Customer satisfaction and customer retention has always been the center piece of the extent research. Customer expectations have been totally changed from just buying items to acquiring consistent and

DOI: 10.4018/978-1-6684-5853-2.ch016

seamless shopping experiences (Morschett et al., 2005). Recent literature suggests a shifting behavior amongst customers to different retail formats and avenues based on the satisfaction they receive from them (Sivadas and Baker-Prewitt, 2000). In continuation, needless to say retailers around the world are working out ways to enhance customer satisfaction and in turn improve customer retention (Kirkup et al., 2004). Along with various retail enablers, retailers are more focused to provide better service quality to increase customer loyalty towards the retail outlet (Hegner-Kakar et al., 2018). Literature suggests that consumption and purchase of goods and services is guided by the attitude of customer towards retailers and their offerings (Carrel and Li, 2019). A satisfied customer tends to be more loyal and show up more often to a retail store than a dissatisfied customer (Petzer and van Tonder, 2019). Thus, customer satisfaction is definitely one of the key factors considering customer loyalty and retention (Hare, 2003). A greater mind share and higher share of wallet can be expected from them. And whenever customer satisfaction is discussed, service quality is not very far behind in any context. Moreover, satisfaction-loyalty linkage is one of the most discussed (Makanyeza and Chikazhe, 2017) and researched topics in marketing literature.

Customers being the center of modern value chain paradigm (Huber et al., 2001). The delicate yet gradual shift has differentiated the way retailing has been practiced and perceived. In the super competitive efforts to go over and beyond one's expectation to create and maintain satisfied and loyal customers, retail practitioners elevated to something called 'customer delight' which a notch higher than mere satisfaction. For some organizations, ''doing more'' recommends the creation of more uplifted levels of feeling and emotions than those related with mere customer satisfaction. And the developing conviction among numerous leaders is that customers presented to pleasant, unexpected encounters - those encounters which are delightful – have a better chance of becoming a loyal patron. Thus, creating delightful experiences obviously requires new ways to deal with customers and their physical, psychological and emotional needs. In line with these retail marketplace developments, recent attention of service quality and satisfaction researchers has begun to concentrate on these ''higher levels'' of satisfaction that may generate extraordinary results in the form of unflappable customer loyalty (Rokonuzzaman et al., 2020). This dimension of customer emotion is relatively new and not been researched enough in context of retail. However, few marketing researchers have attempted to study customer delight in recent past. In relation to the constructs of customer satisfaction and customer delight, there exists a few negating concepts like unfavorable/dissatisfying experiences, customer dissatisfaction and "terrible" shopping experience (Arnold et al., 2005). These topics are scarcely researched in retail setting, but their presence cannot be overlooked.

With this backdrop, this review study aims to identify, analyze and report the findings in a systematic way which would help the readers to have a clear and vivid understanding of service quality, customer satisfaction, customer delight and customer loyalty in context of retailing.

Given this setup for the study, the following are the research objectives:

- To identify various research constructs related to service quality (SQ), customer satisfaction (CS) and customer delight (CD) in context of retailing
- To study various research themes related to retailing in the past 2 decades
- To develop a timeline temporal view of retail studies involving SQ, CS and CD
- To understand the gaps and limitations in the present research of retailing
- To analyze the distributions of models and theories flourished around SQ, CS and CD in retailing context

.

- To develop a mind-map of retail research topics, themes and methodologies used in existing literature

METHODOLOGY

The study adopts a systematic review approach. A successful review can create a strong base for promoting knowledge, facilitate development of theory and uncovers areas where research is needed. As defined by Kitchenham & Charters (2007), systematic review is a process of identifying, evaluating, and interpreting all available research relevant to research objectives, area of study, or rising phenomenon of interest. A systematic review of literature is strategically implemented to collect evidence both empirical and theoretical, concerned to retailing which map to the research objective.

To make the research design more robust and the methodology more transparent, accurate and reliable PRISMA framework is used. PRISMA stands for Preferred Reporting Items for Systematic Reviews and Meta-Analyses. This framework enables the authors to collect the required empirical evidence to fit the qualification criteria to fulfill the research objective. PRISMA methodology is known for minimizing bias and providing structure to reporting.

Post screening the selected studies were further analyzed. The identified documents are thoroughly investigated to study the research areas, themes, models and theories used by researchers in retailing with respect to SQ, CS and CD. The findings will be reported in a systematic manner through nomological networks, keyword networks, temporal timeline views, descriptive graphics & images, interpretative mind-map and other forms of illustrative representations to make it detailed and effective for the readers.

Data Collection

For collecting relevant studies (research articles and book chapters), one of the largest online indexed and bibliometric databases i.e. Scopus was used. It is a renowned database amongst the management fraternity. Additionally, this database has shown consistent increase for publications and citations throughout the areas of humanities, economics and social sciences including management (Harzing and Alakangas, 2016). Hence, Scopus is selected as the database to be used for search due to the sheer size of the database and indexing provisions.

Due to the vastness of the area of study i.e. retail in combination with SQ, CS and CD, the period for the search was restricted. The timeline selected for the study was year 2000 onwards, which effectively covers more than 22 years of retailing literature. In total 4 keywords were used to search the relevant studies. 'Retail' keyword was used in conjunction with 'AND' operator along with 'service quality', 'customer satisfaction' and 'customer delight' in three separate searches. Further, to keep the articles' relevancy under the scope of the study the subject areas were limited to 'social sciences', 'business, management and accounting', 'economics, econometrics and finance', 'decision sciences', 'arts and humanities' and 'multidisciplinary'. The document type was also restricted to peer reviewed journal articles and book chapters. The language of the documents was kept to English. Thus, after applying the abovementioned search criteria, a total of 1708 records were obtained as search result for the given keywords.

Exclusion and Inclusion Criteria

The result of the initial search was then scrutinized to four rounds of screening to obtain the final consideration set of publications. In the first round of screening, the duplicate entries (n = 266) based on title were identified and removed. Subsequently, in the second round of screening, articles' title and abstract were looked through. Documents focusing on offline physical retail were taken into consideration and those pertaining to online, e-tail, internet shopping, mobile shopping and other internet related buying processes were dropped. Also, studies related to pure retailing were chosen for further analysis. The articles focusing on other study areas like banking, supply chain management, inventory management, B2B, hospitality industries and other service sectors not considered. Thus, after second round of screening a total of 402 articles were chosen for subsequent screening.

In round three, the documents selected from second screening were put to citation test. Higher citation represents better credibility of a study (Frandsen, 2017). Documents with 10 and higher citation as per Scopus database were moved to fourth round of screening. 207 documents rejected for not having the required number of citations. In the fourth round full text of the selected studies were accessed and reviewed. Based on the constructs and context used by the studies, screening was administered. The co-relation and inter-construct linkage was matched with the objectives of the study and themes pertaining to SQ, CS, CD, customer delight and other relative themes was observed. After the filtration in round four, a total of 86 studies were narrowed down for final analysis. Further, to not miss out on important and relevant literature, forward and backward snowballing was performed which yielded six more paper which were added to the consideration set. Hence, the grand total of documents considered for doing the systematic literature review was 92. The diagrammatic representation of the search process is shown with the help of PRISMA in figure 1.

Figure 1. PRISMA flowchart based on Moher et al. (2009)
Source: Authors' estimate

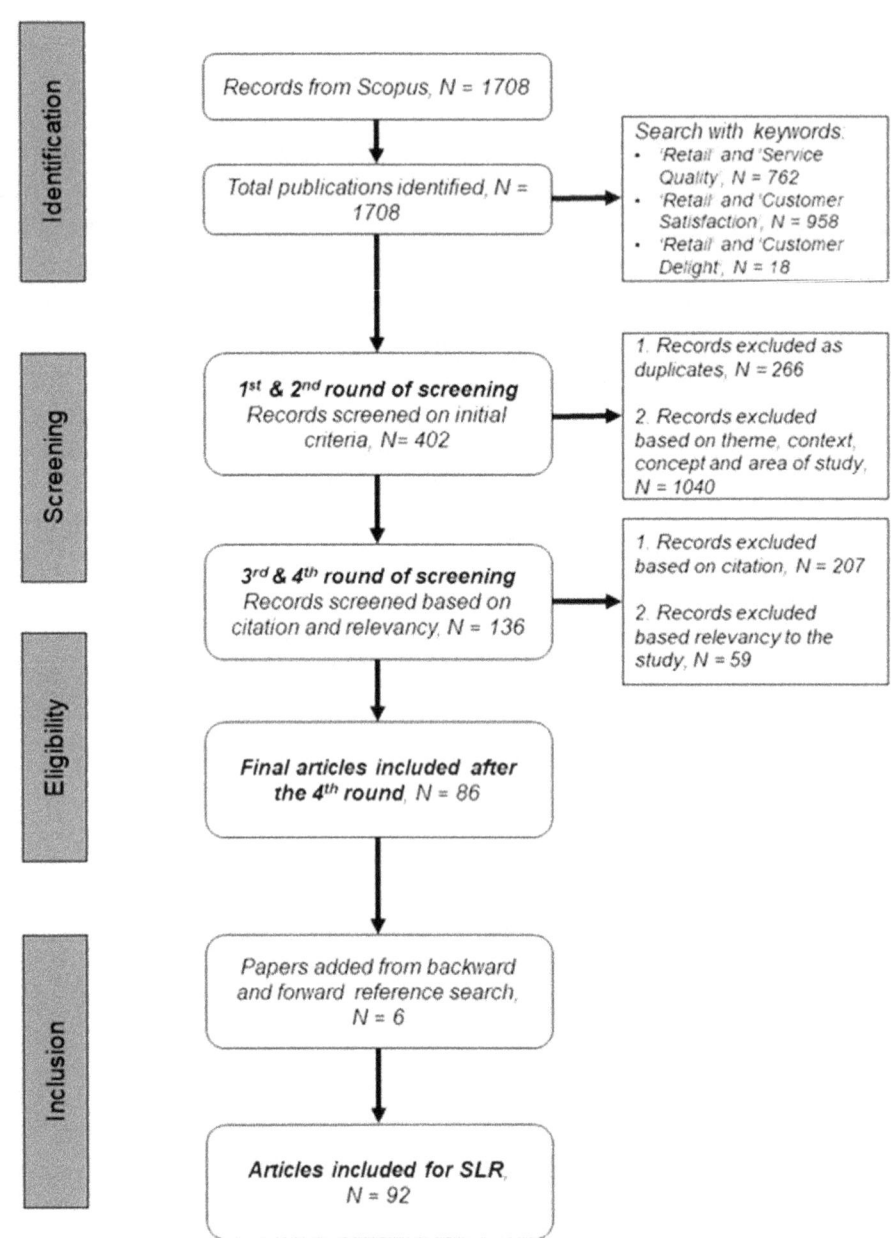

FINDINGS AND ANALYSIS

Methodologies Used by the Publication

Majority of the studies adopted a quantitative research design wherein data was collected from the respondents through a structured questionnaire or survey prior to statistical analysis.

A few studies had taken on a more rigorous methodology like experimental research design. Pornpitakpan and Han (2013) conducted a cross-culture experiment to study the moderating effect of SQ on the relationship of culture on impulse buying. Burns and Neisner (2006) investigated how cognition and emotion interact to create CS in a retail environment through their experimental research design. There are also studies like Chen and Quester (2006), which implemented a mixed method research approach, where first qualitative method was used to develop a measurement scale and then it was empirically tested by using a survey questionnaire. Also, the study by Chen and Quester (2006) had undertaken a dyadic data collection approach, where the data was collected from both the retailer and the customer and analysed simultaneously.

Evolution of Retail Formats and its Customers

From 1980s, researchers have been constantly contributing to the literature of the construct 'customer satisfaction'. Although the focus towards retailing context shifted during 1990s and it grew substantially in this century with the bloom of retail and its new formats (Sathish and VenkatramaRaju, 2010). A key trend due to increasing competition in retail is retail format diversification (Amorim and Saghezchi, 2014). To match the variety of customers, their shopping needs and situations, various formats of retail has emerged (Reynolds et al., 2002) like convenience stores, departmental stores, specialty stores, supermarkets, hypermarkets etc. These plethora of options offer different store attributes and cater to individual customers' preferences and characteristics (Carpenter and Moore, 2006). Additionally, Gijsbrechts et al. (2008) in their study indicated that shoppers allocate their visitation and shopping budget across various store categories to explore the offerings of various retail settings. However, early retail literature of the present century suggested a concept of 'main store' (Rhee and Bell, 2002) or 'first choice' store (Knox and Denison, 2000), to showcase loyalty and preference, where customers visited more often than other store and reported spent a higher amount on their purchases.

Network Analysis

Figure 2. Network analysis output using VOSviewer
Source: Scopus database search

Network analysis was performed using VOSviewer tool which yielded 10 nodes or cluster based on the popularity of the themes and constructs used by the retailing studies within the designated time frame. The different clusters are highlighted in figure 2 using different colors. Cluster 1 had seven items namely customer service, customer value, retail industry, retail service quality scale, service quality, SERVQUAL and structural equation modelling. Cluster 2 contains seven items i.e. consumer behavior, consumer delight, consumer loyalty, consumer retention, consumer satisfaction, shopping and shopping experience. In cluster 3, the network analysis produced 5 items. Those were consumer behavior, customer service quality, perceived service quality, retail environment and service convenience. Again in cluster 4 there were 5 items obtained namely behavioral intentions, consumer satisfaction, customer experience, retail and retailer. 4 items were obtained in cluster 5 i.e. behavioral intentions, brand loyalty, corporate image and retail stores. In cluster 6 the items generated by network analysis were 4. Those were retail patronage, retailing, self-service technology and supermarket. Cluster 7 yielded 4 items namely loyalty, shopping behavior, trust and value. In 8th cluster 2 items were obtained i.e. customer relations and retail trade. In the 9th cluster again 2 items got highlighted namely personal interactions and retail service quality. Lastly in cluster 10, 2 items were obtained namely. Those were retail store and store image.

Citation Analysis

Table 1. Citation analysis obtained using VOSviewer

Country	Citations	Documents	Total link strength
United Kingdom	345	23	19
Saudi Arabia	321	12	17
India	278	62	25
China	167	11	14
United States	153	14	9
Spain	132	10	2
Indonesia	114	22	4
Pakistan	108	10	8
Malaysia	95	19	14
Germany	64	8	5
South Korea	45	7	6
Vietnam	32	14	8
South Africa	27	9	5
Greece	15	3	2

Source: Scopus database search

The citation and link strength analysis was performed by using VOSviewer in addition to network analysis. The analysis results showed that the citations are almost uniformly spread across the globe. With UK leading the citation dynamics followed by Saudi Arabia and India. The analysis also pointed out that the link strength of Indian studied were the highest as compared to other nations. Asian countries seemed to dominate the citations with countries like India, China, Indonesia, Pakistan, Malaysia, South Korea and Vietnam contributing significantly to retailing literature. Refer to table 1.

Temporal Analysis

Figure 3. Temporal analysis of research publication pertaining to retail
Source: Scopus database search and authors' estimate

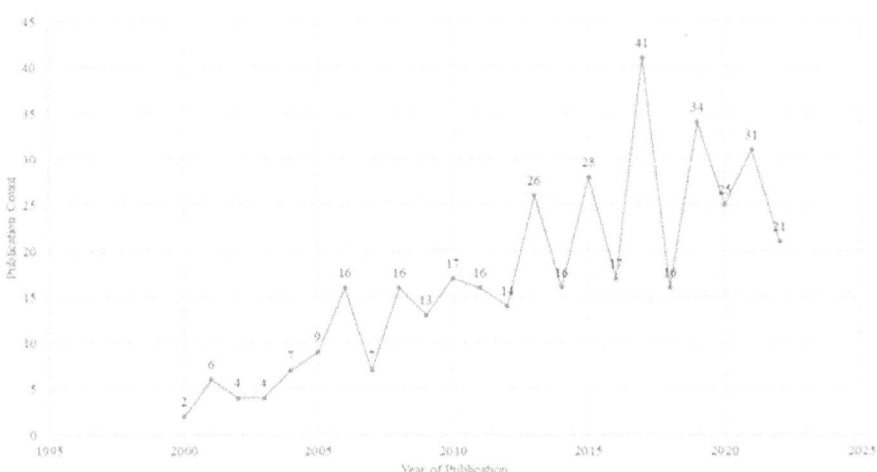

A temporal analysis (represented in figure 3) was done on the research publication filtered out after third round of screening. The analysis showed an overall upward trend in the number of publications from 2000 to 2022. However, in the year 2017, highest number of studies (41) got published and it was not matched in the subsequent years. It is very interesting and encouraging to see the gaining interest among the researchers in the field of retailing. With upcoming avenues and different retail format clubbed with modern technology, the publications might see an upsurge breaking the temporary stagnation in customer satisfaction, service quality and customer delight studies.

Mind Mapping

Figure 4. Mind map of retail research themes, topics and the methodologies uses
Source: Authors' estimate

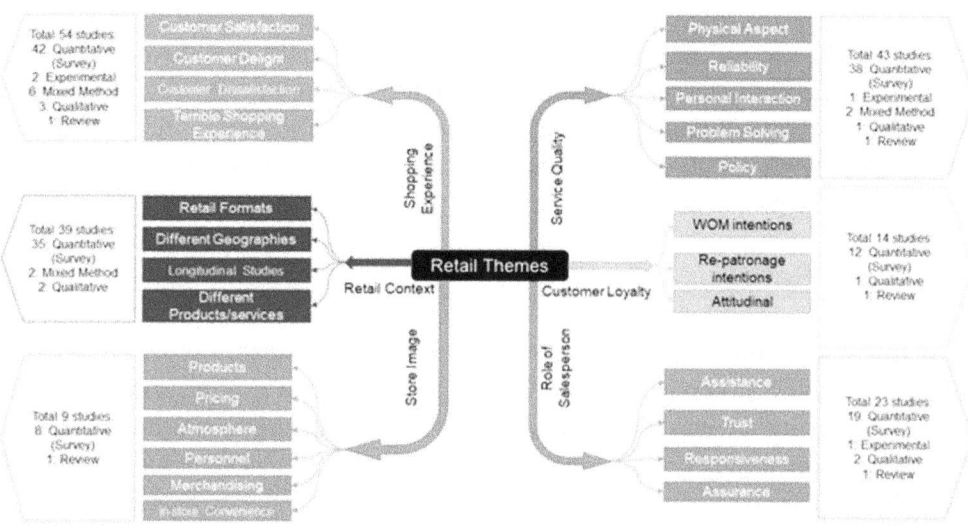

Table 2. Description of retail research themes

Study Theme	Description
Service Quality	Includes study which revolve around various types of services in a retail setting and the associated quality of services provided by the retailers
Role of salesperson	Includes the articles which focus on the importance and dependence of retailers and customers on the salespersons.
Customer Loyalty	Includes the study which had focus on appreciative attitude and repeated purchase intention towards a retailer
Store Image Attributes	Includes study which considered various store related attributes and their linkage to the study variables
Retail Context	Includes various retail settings in terms of product/service, retail format, geographies and timeline
Shopping Experience	Includes the physical and emotional experiences felt by customers after being exposed to a retail setting

A mind map was created using the retail research themes and the topics conveyed under them. Figure 4 depicts six retail themes and the research methodologies undertaken. The description of the retail research themes is presented in table 2. As depicted for all themes, quantitative method was the most used approach. In service quality theme, there were 43 studies. Out of them 38 studies which adopted questionnaire method, 2 of them used mixed method and 1 study each adopted experimental, qualitative and review methodology. Similarly, under shopping experience theme, most of the studies (42) used a quantitative approach followed by 6 mixed method studies. Few themes used experimental research design like shopping experience (2) and role of salesperson (1). Finally, review technique was used by various studies under the given themes like customer loyalty (1), role of salesperson (1), store image (1) and shopping experience (1).

DISCUSSION

This section caters to the various study constructs namely SQ, CS and CD, their usage in various studies and the interlinking themes and variables developed around these central themes like customer loyalty, store image and role of salesperson in a retail setting. There has been also discussion related to the models and theories used and developed by various retailing studies. The evolution of study constructs' scales and measures are also the part of the discussion.

Service Quality in Retail

One of the most researched constructs in retailing literature is service quality. It has been popularly linked with various other constructs in context of retail. But a significant amount of research work has been done linking service quality and customer satisfaction in retailing. The linkage has been explored vehemently and empirically tested in various geographies and retail formats. A few such instances are sportswear retail (Saricam, 2022), Vietnamese supermarkets (Nguyen, 2020), marketing haat (Attri, 2014), specialty store (Prakash et al., 2018), Indian organized (Samantaray et al., 2017) and unorganized retail sector (Thenmozhi and Dhanapal, 2011), Pakistani small & medium retail stores (Irfan et al., 2019), emerging markets (Greenland et al., 2006), Malaysian large-scale retail (Saeidi et al., 2017), convenience store (Sharma, 2014), hypermarkets and supermarkets (Amorim and Saghezchi, 2014). Some studies tried to compare the customers' perception of SQ in various settings and contexts e.g. Amorim and Saghezchi (2014) assessed SQ across supermarkets and hypermarkets in Portugal.

It is universally acknowledged that perception of SQ amongst customers is a source of CS, customer loyalty, and, subsequently, competitive advantage (Martinelli and Balboni, 2012). More recent research work also suggest that SQ invariably leads to customer loyalty. A study undertaken by Alam and Noor (2020) explained the SQ – loyalty linkage in young Gen-Y cohorts in Bangladesh's superstores retail setting. Other important constructs which has been extensively linked to SQ is store image (Bao et al., 2011). The American Advertising Affiliation (2019) characterized store image according to two particular viewpoints — one is from retailing view point addressed by store attributes i.e. "store mage" and other is from comprehensive point of view addressed by the general impression of customers toward the store known as "corporate picture" (CI). The differentiation of the image pictured in retailing lies in a definitive discrepancies of focus given.

However, the issue of SQ is very distinguished in different areas of business management, this issue is more significant in retailing industry because of the presence of prominent competition (Bhat, 2016; Hsiao, 2018). Hence, guaranteeing the conveyance of SQ at the best is viewed as by the retailers as one of the fundamental and essential strategic matter (Ihtiyar and Ahmad, 2015). Regardless of the rising interest among the academicians and experts, an agreement on the conceptualization and operationalization of SQ is as yet sparse as various researchers characterized this build with different qualities clubbing into various dimensions (Lopes et al., 2019).

Customer Satisfaction

Traditionally, CS was seen as an objective result of the extent and direction of the discrepancy between expectations and the actual level of performance received (Burns and Neisner, 2006). Hence, it was believed to be based on emotions. Later, it was gradually realized that CS in a retail setting doesn't only depend on the physical product, but the retailer or the service provider also plays a key role in enticing the required satisfaction. Sailing through the timeline it was also realized that the store environment too has an important contribution to play in creating customer satisfaction. A store's setting/environment/atmosphere may be able to draw consumers, encourage purchases, and entice them to make repeat purchases (Sharma and Stafford, 2000). In fact, Summers and Hebert (2001) stated in their study that store atmosphere can be more compelling in favor of CS than the tangible product itself in context of purchase decision. It also has the ability to influence the level of CS endured by the retailer. The store image attribute to CS linkage is also a popular area of retailing research (Hackl et al., 2000; Thang and Tan, 2003). Another study by Theodoridis, P. K., & Chatzipanagiotou (2009) conducted in Greece, empirically tested the functional linkage between image attributes of store and CS in supermarket setting in Greece. The study also identified 4 specific types of buyers i.e. occasional, social, typical and unstable.

Customer satisfaction although an independently studied construct in various contexts. It has been pointed out in the extent literature that CS is highly format contextual. The factors important for CS in a particular retail format may not be equally relevant in other retail format (Hui et al., 2013).

CS predictors in context of a shopping mall or shopping center can be somewhat different from that of a stand-alone grocery store. CS with a shopping mall can be regarded as an individual's emotional response to personal assessment of the overall set of experiences which are encountered while visiting the shopping mall (Anselmsson, 2006).

It is more keenly studied for its mediating roles. Retailing literature suggest that customer loyalty can be developed through improving CS which in turn improves the customer retention and patronage through high quality service (Hurst et al. 2009; To et al., 2013; Wong and Sohal 2003).

Customer Delight in Retail

It was not very late when researchers realized that customers need a top up and simple satisfaction was not going to work for either customer or practitioners (Oliver, 1997). The reasons attributable for the same are growing competition, expansive product assortment, retail location convenience, round the clock shopping options and internet penetration (Arnold et al., 2005).

Although the concept on customer delight was first proposed by Oliver (1980), re-assessed by Schlossberg (1990), the initial work related to customer delight in retail context was done by Arnold et al. (2005). They implemented a qualitative method (conducted in US) to identify the factors which lead to delightful and terrible shopping experiences in retail context. Additionally, Reichheld (1996) in his study pointed out that mere customer satisfaction is not enough to keep a company profitable. His study was supported by Berman (2005), who suggested that satisfaction is perception based and cognitive, whereas, delight is affective. As compared to a satisfied customer a delighted customer provides advantage to the retail house by engaging in more repeat purchase. Delighted customers are proven to be more loyal (Barnes et al., 2010), committed, have higher willingness to pay (Barnes et al., 2010) and repurchase intention (Chitturi et al., 2008; Meyer et al., 2017).

Delight as per traditional literary view is related to an experience of surprise and positive affect when exposed to a product or service (Loureiro and Kastenholz, 2011). On the contrary, some studies indicated that it is very difficult to achieve the desired levels of customer delight in a setting where regular transactions are involved (Crotts and Magnini, 2011; Dixon et al., 2010; Kumar et al., 2001) like daily grocery purchase. Loureiro et al. (2014) in their study extended the argument stating perceived value, trust, and customer satisfaction could have a greater impact on customers' behavioral outcomes than customer delight in frequent-use retail setting.

Customer retention has been a pressing problem in retail sector (Kamran-Disfani et al., 2017), especially in developing countries (Grosso et al., 2018). And as suggested by literature, CD can be a solution to this daunting issue.

Customer Loyalty (CL)

CL is one of the highly researched outcome in retailing literature (Eryandra et al., 2018). But, over years this concept has developed a split view point (Ali et al., 2016). One of them is a behavioral view point where loyalty develops action. The actions may be positive word-of-mouth (Lai, 2019), rebuy and repurchase intention (Ngobo, 2017). The other perspective is an attitudinal one which is more of a conative dimension which can be perceived as a customer's incomprehensible personal commitment to buy a specific item or product (Almeida-Santana and Moreno-Gil, 2018; Le Chi, 2016). By characterizing CL exclusively from either behavioral or attitudinal point of view isn't sufficient to measure the genuine picture of CL (Suhartanto et al., 2020), thus it is advised to address both the features of CL (Bapat, 2017). Indeed, even this incorporation is more fundamental for retailing because of particular attributes connected to it (Sivapalan and Jebarajakirthy, 2017).

Importance of Retail Employees in Creating Customer Satisfaction and Customer Delight

Employees working in a retail store and providing firsthand experience to the customer have been considered very crucial in delivering customer satisfaction and customer delight (Meyer et al., 2017). The presence and assistance of the salesperson in a retail setting adds value to the purchase process and reduces the perceived purchase risks associated (Kumar et al., 2008). It has been proved that informative communication (Agnihotri et al., 2009) and interaction (Paswan and Ganesh, 2005) between customer and salesperson induce higher levels of comfort and satisfaction among customers. The expertise of the salesperson was found to positively impact customer satisfaction (Liu and Leach, 2001) and customer delight (Arnold et al., 2005). There has been argument to train the salespersons to render experiences which lead to customer delight (Arnold et al., 2005; Barnes et al., 2011). Pinto et al. (2020) in their study indicated that store associates and the resulting personal interaction significantly influence female shoppers.

However, it has been evidently pointed out in retailing literature that salespersons or retail employees have a very important and significant role to play in CS and CD. But, it attrition is one of the biggest challenge in retail (Reddy, 2019). Store managers and retailers are worried about the same and figuring out ways to retain the best talents for generating CS and store loyalty.

Evolution of Scales Related to the Study Constructs

The most fundamental and early scale for measuring service quality was developed by Parasuraman et al. (1988) and it is popularly known as SERVQUAL scale. The five dimensions of the scale are: tangibles, reliability, responsiveness, assurance and empathy. Although, researchers in the subsequent years tried and modified the scale fitting to particular contexts. Similarly, for retailing context a highly used, reliable and validated scale was developed by Dabholkar et al. (1996). This scale also known as RSQS or ReServQual is widely tested and accepted to measure the customer perception of retail service quality. The modified dimensions of this scale are: physical aspects, reliability, personal interaction, problem solving and policy. Out of the 5 dimensions of RSQS, two dimensions are second order constructs having 2 sub-dimensions each. Over the last two decades, the SERVQUAL and RSQS scales have been tested on numerous occasions and modified time and again to fit the research context pertaining to retail. Few such instances are Hong Kong multinational departmental store chain (Siu and Cheung, 2001), urban retail setting (Vazquez et al., 2001), discount stores in US and Korea (Kim and Jin, 2002), Indian organised relate (Parikh, 2006), Italian grocery retail (Martinelli and Balboni, 2012) and large retail formats like hypermarkets and supermarkets (Amorim and Saghezchi, 2014). A few other studies adopted items from both the scales i.e. SERVQUAL and RSQS. One such example is the study by Sum and Hui (2009) in which a combination of items was taken from both scales to measure salespersons' SQ in Hong Kong fashion retail setting. To measure customer loyalty, different approaches were adopted. One of the most popular and most used approach is a multiple item measure in which items were related to word-of-mouth intentions, re-patronage intentions and satisfaction (Söderlund, 2006; Sum and Hui, 2009).

In some rare occasions it was also observed that researchers tried a contextual combination of both SERVQUAL and RSQS. Even more surprising is that on few instances data didn't fit either of the scale's dimensions and authors had to define new dimensions (To et al., 2013). The reason for the same has been dedicated to the assumption that perception of SQ might differ across cultures and geographies (Ueltschy, and Krampf, 2001).

Models and Theories Around the Selected Study Variables

The analysis of the selected documents indicated the development of new models and modification of existing models revolving around the chosen constructs i.e. SQ, CS and CD. Wong and Sohal (2006) developed and empirically tested a customer relationship strength (RS) model. Their study examined the impact of SQ, commitment and trust on RS. And then the effect of RS on attitudinal and behavioural outcomes were tested. Anselmsson (2006) in his study conducted on shopping centers in Sweden successfully captured eight new factors (selection, convenience, promotional activities, performance of sales people, refreshments, atmosphere, location and merchandising policy) which contribute to customer satisfaction, supporting the study of Severin et al. (2001). To add to the list or new models, a qualitative study done in Taiwan proposed a customer store loyalty model based on CS, staff performance and a value-based market orientation practice (Chen and Quester, 2006).

Among the existing frameworks, S-O-R framework had been used by a few studies (Alam and Noor, 2020; Chang et al., 2011). The model was proposed by Mehrabian and Russell (1974), where S-O-R stand for stimulus, organism and behavioural response respectively. The model has been modified to accommodate retailing setup by absorbing variables that motivate consumers' decision making (Chang et al., 2015).

Mediating and Moderating Roles of the Study Variables

CS has been studied in plenty as the mediator (Martinelli and Balboni, 2012) and in some case as the researchers identified few moderators between the SQ and customer loyalty linkage. Owing to the stagnation and saturation demonstrating CS as intervening variable, retailing literature keeps experimenting with new constructs (Baumann et al., 2017). Researchers in the retailing literature have studied CS in linkage several different outcomes e.g. CL, customer retention and sales performance (Martenson, 2007). CS has been also studied in mediation to retail brand trust and brand social responsibility image (Umar and Bahrun, 2017). In other context, SQ was also found to be moderating the effects of culture on impulse buying behaviour in retail in a bi-cultural study conducted in Singapore and America (Pornpitakpan and Han, 2013).

In retailing context, the interaction between salespersons and customers nurture an important and unique aspect of sales performance (Sum and Hui, 2009). Such type of interactions develops a positive effect on retail CL (Darian et al., 2001). According to Gomez et al. (2004), there is an asymmetric relationship between CS and sales SQ. For instance, improvements in sales service quality may not greatly boost CS, but declines in sales service quality will sharply lower it.

IMPLICATIONS

It has been studied extensively and researched heavily that how the predictors controlled by retail management impact the attitudinal (relationship quality) and behavioral (customer loyalty) outcomes (Hennig-Thurau et al., 2002).

Change is a very commonly used term in consumer behavior. And customer satisfaction and customer delight studies have helped and will continue to help retail firms to stay vigilant (Miranda, 2005) and mend their strategies according to their customers. This review chapter might shed light on the existing literature gaps in retailing context and help researchers and practitioners better understand their customers and service them accordingly. For researchers, there seems to be a scope in exploring the structural linkage between retail store SQ and customer loyalty (Nguyen et al., 2016).

This review chapter would help the stakeholders and readers understand the effective dimensions of the offline (physical) retail customers' expectations in terms of retail service quality, customer satisfaction linked to retail shopping and customer delight drivers with respect to retailing experience. The themes identified through the exhaustive literature review would help researchers and practitioners to implement relevant factors transcending to retailer loyalty. The findings on the study will pave path to new and futuristic retail avenues in both organized and unorganized retailing context.

LIMITATIONS AND SCOPE FOR FURTHER STUDY

The study attempted to cater to the research publication done in last 22 years pertaining to few selected research constructs namely service quality, customer satisfaction and customer delight. However, the authors tried to incorporate, assimilate, analyze and report as much a possible within the limited scope of the study. But the retailing literature is huge and there has been constant contribution from all the parts of the world. The Scopus database yields more than thirty thousand results on searching by the keyword 'retail'. This study didn't take into account the internet shopping or e-commerce dimension, which can be explored in further research. Also, the timeline chosen of the study was year 2000 onwards. The timeline can be extended by subsequent studies to capture all the aspects of retailing since the very inception. Finally, other databases and publication sources could be explored to make the study more comprehensive, detailed and effective. The field of retail has unlimited possibilities in terms of models, methods, research designs, formats and analyses, which are yet to be fully explored.

REFERENCES

Agnihotri, R., Rapp, A., & Trainor, K. (2009). Understanding the role of information communication in the buyer-seller exchange process: Antecedents and outcomes. *Journal of Business and Industrial Marketing*, *24*(7), 474–486. doi:10.1108/08858620910986712

Alam, M. M. D., & Noor, N. A. M. (2020). The relationship between service quality, corporate image, and customer loyalty of Generation Y: An application of SOR paradigm in the context of superstores in Bangladesh. *SAGE Open*, *10*(2). doi:10.1177/2158244020924405

Ali, F., Ryu, K., & Hussain, K. (2016). Influence of experiences on memories, satisfaction and behavioral intentions: A study of creative tourism. *Journal of Travel & Tourism Marketing*, *33*(1), 85–100. doi:10.1080/10548408.2015.1038418

Almeida-Santana, A., & Moreno-Gil, S. (2018). Understanding tourism loyalty: Horizontal vs. destination loyalty. *Tourism Management*, *65*, 245–255. doi:10.1016/j.tourman.2017.10.011

American Marketing Association. (2019). *Resource library dictionary: Store image*. Author.

Amorim, M., & Saghezchi, F. B. (2014). An investigation of service quality assessments across retail formats. *International Journal of Quality and Service Sciences*, *6*(2/3), 221–236. doi:10.1108/IJQSS-02-2014-0015

Anselmsson, J. (2006). Sources of customer satisfaction with shopping malls: A comparative study of different customer segments. *International Review of Retail, Distribution and Consumer Research*, *16*(1), 115–138. doi:10.1080/09593960500453641

Arnold, M. J., Reynolds, K. E., Ponder, N., & Lueg, J. E. (2005). Customer delight in a retail context: Investigating delightful and terrible shopping experiences. *Journal of Business Research*, *58*(8), 1132–1145. doi:10.1016/j.jbusres.2004.01.006

Attri, M. (2014). An empirical study on levels of customer satisfaction with retail service quality in a marketing haat. *FIIB Business Review*, *3*(2), 46–56. doi:10.1177/2455265820140209

Bao, Y., Bao, Y., & Sheng, S. (2011). Motivating purchase of private brands: Effects of store image, product signatureness, and quality variation. *Journal of Business Research*, *64*(2), 220–226. doi:10.1016/j.jbusres.2010.02.007

Bapat, D. (2017). Exploring the antecedents of loyalty in the context of multi-channel banking. *International Journal of Bank Marketing*, *35*(2), 174–186. doi:10.1108/IJBM-10-2015-0155

Barnes, D. C., Beauchamp, M. B., & Webster, C. (2010). To delight, or not to delight? This is the question service firms must address. *Journal of Marketing Theory and Practice, 18*(3), 275–284. doi:10.2753/MTP1069-6679180305

Barnes, D. C., Ponder, N., & Dugar, K. (2011). Investigating the key routes to customer delight. *Journal of Marketing Theory and Practice, 19*(4), 359–376. doi:10.2753/MTP1069-6679190401

Baumann, C., Hoadley, S., Hamin, H., & Nugraha, A. (2017). Competitiveness vis-à-vis service quality as drivers of customer loyalty mediated by perceptions of regulation and stability in steady and volatile markets. *Journal of Retailing and Consumer Services, 36*, 62–74. doi:10.1016/j.jretconser.2016.12.005

Berman, B. (2005). How to delight your customers. *California Management Review, 48*(1), 129–151. doi:10.2307/41166331

Bhat, I. H. (2016). Validating a retail service quality instrument in grocery specialty stores. *International Journal of Information, Business and Management, 8*(2), 205.

Burns, D. J., & Neisner, L. (2006). Customer satisfaction in a retail setting: The contribution of emotion. *International Journal of Retail & Distribution Management, 34*(1), 49–66. doi:10.1108/09590550610642819

Carpenter, J. M., & Moore, M. (2006). Consumer demographics, store attributes, and retail format choice in the US grocery market. *International Journal of Retail & Distribution Management, 34*(6), 434–452. doi:10.1108/09590550610667038

Carrel, A. L., & Li, M. (2019). Survey-based measurement of transit customer loyalty: Evaluation of measures and systematic biases. *Travel Behaviour & Society, 15*, 102–112. doi:10.1016/j.tbs.2019.01.003

Chang, H. J., Cho, H. J., Turner, T., Gupta, M., & Watchravesringkan, K. (2015). Effects of store attributes on retail patronage behaviors: Evidence from activewear specialty stores. *Journal of Fashion Marketing and Management, 19*(2), 136–153. doi:10.1108/JFMM-03-2014-0019

Chang, H. J., Eckman, M., & Yan, R. N. (2011). Application of the Stimulus-Organism-Response model to the retail environment: The role of hedonic motivation in impulse buying behavior. *International Review of Retail, Distribution and Consumer Research, 21*(3), 233–249. doi:10.1080/09593969.2011.578798

Chen, S. C., & Quester, P. G. (2006). Modeling store loyalty: Perceived value in market orientation practice. *Journal of Services Marketing, 20*(3), 188–198. doi:10.1108/08876040610665643

Chitturi, R., Raghunathan, R., & Mahajan, V. (2008). Delight by design: The role of hedonic versus utilitarian benefits. *Journal of Marketing, 72*(3), 48–63. doi:10.1509/JMKG.72.3.048

Crotts, J. C., & Magnini, V. P. (2011). Is Surprise Essential? *Annals of Tourism Research, 38*(2), 719–722. doi:10.1016/j.annals.2010.03.004

Dabholkar, P. A., Thorpe, D. I., & Rentz, J. O. (1996). A measure of service quality for retail stores: Scale development and validation. *Journal of the Academy of Marketing Science, 24*(1), 3–16. doi:10.1007/BF02893933

Darian, J. C., Tucci, L. A., & Wiman, A. R. (2001). Perceived salesperson service attributes and retail patronage intentions. *International Journal of Retail & Distribution Management, 29*(5), 205–213. doi:10.1108/09590550110390986

Dixon, M., Freeman, K., & Toman, N. (2010). Stop trying to delight your customers. *Harvard Business Review, 88*(7/8), 116–122.

Eryandra, A., Sjabadhyni, B., & Mustika, M. D. (2018). How older consumers' perceived ethicality influences brand loyalty. *SAGE Open, 8*(2). doi:10.1177/2158244018778105

Frandsen, T. F. (2017). Are predatory journals undermining the credibility of science? A bibliometric analysis of citers. *Scientometrics, 113*(3), 1513–1528. doi:10.100711192-017-2520-x

Gijsbrechts, E., Campo, K., & Nisol, P. (2008). Beyond promotion-based store switching: Antecedents and patterns of systematic multiple-store shopping. *International Journal of Research in Marketing, 25*(1), 5-21.

Gomez, M. I., McLaughlin, E. W., & Wittink, D. R. (2004). Customer satisfaction and retail sales performance: An empirical investigation. *Journal of Retailing, 80*(4), 265–278. doi:10.1016/j.jretai.2004.10.003

Greenland, S., Coshall, J., & Combe, I. (2006). Evaluating service quality and consumer satisfaction in emerging markets. *International Journal of Consumer Studies, 30*(6), 582–590. doi:10.1111/j.1470-6431.2005.00484.x

Grosso, M., Castaldo, S., & Grewal, A. (2018). How store attributes impact shoppers' loyalty in emerging countries: An investigation in the Indian retail sector. *Journal of Retailing and Consumer Services, 40*, 117–124. doi:10.1016/j.jretconser.2017.08.024

Hackl, P., Scharitzer, D., & Zuba, R. (2000). Customer satisfaction in the Austrian food retail market. *Total Quality Management, 11*(7), 999–1006. doi:10.1080/09544120050135524

Hare, C. (2003). The food-shopping experience: A satisfaction survey of older Scottish consumers. *International Journal of Retail & Distribution Management, 31*(5), 244–255. doi:10.1108/09590550310472415

Harzing, A. W., & Alakangas, S. (2016). Google Scholar, Scopus and the Web of Science: A longitudinal and cross-disciplinary comparison. *Scientometrics, 106*(2), 787–804. doi:10.100711192-015-1798-9

Hegner-Kakar, A. K., Richter, N. F., & Ringle, C. M. (2018). The customer loyalty cascade and its impact on profitability in financial services. In *Partial least squares structural equation modeling* (pp. 53–75). Springer. doi:10.1007/978-3-319-71691-6_3

Hennig-Thurau, T., Gwinner, K. P., & Gremler, D. D. (2002). Understanding relationship marketing outcomes: An integration of relational benefits and relationship quality. *Journal of Service Research, 4*(3), 230–247. doi:10.1177/1094670502004003006

Hsiao, C. H. (2018). The effects of post-adoption beliefs on the expectation–confirmation model in an electronics retail setting. *Total Quality Management & Business Excellence, 29*(7-8), 866–880. doi:10.1080/14783363.2016.1250621

Huber, F., Herrmann, A., & Wricke, M. (2001). Customer satisfaction as an antecedent of price acceptance: Results of an empirical study. *Journal of Product and Brand Management, 10*(3), 160–169. doi:10.1108/10610420110395403

Hui, E. C., Zhang, P. H., & Zheng, X. (2013). *Facilities management service and customer satisfaction in shopping mall sector*. Facilities. doi:10.1108/02632771311307070

Hurst, J. L., Niehm, L. S., & Littrell, M. A. (2009). Retail service dynamics in a rural tourism community: Implications for customer relationship management. *Managing Service Quality, 19*(5), 511–540. doi:10.1108/09604520910984355

Ihtiyar, A., & Ahmad, F. S. (2015). The impact of intercultural communication competence on service quality and customer satisfaction. *Services Marketing Quarterly, 36*(2), 136–152. doi:10.1080/153329 69.2015.1014238

Irfan, W., Siddiqui, D. A., & Ahmed, W. (2019). Creating and retaining customers: Perspective from Pakistani small and medium retail stores. *International Journal of Retail & Distribution Management, 47*(4), 350–367. doi:10.1108/IJRDM-03-2018-0045

Kamran-Disfani, O., Mantrala, M. K., Izquierdo-Yusta, A., & Martínez-Ruiz, M. P. (2017). The impact of retail store format on the satisfaction-loyalty link: An empirical investigation. *Journal of Business Research, 77*, 14–22. doi:10.1016/j.jbusres.2017.04.004

Kim, S., & Jin, B. (2002). Validating the retail service quality scale for US and Korean customers of discount stores: An exploratory study. *Journal of Services Marketing, 16*(3), 223–237. doi:10.1108/08876040210427218

Kirkup, M., De Kervenoael, R., Hallsworth, A., Clarke, I., Jackson, P., & Del Aguila, R. P. (2004). Inequalities in retail choice: Exploring consumer experiences in suburban neighbourhoods. *International Journal of Retail & Distribution Management, 32*(11), 511–522. doi:10.1108/09590550410564746

Kitchenham, B., & Charters, S. (2007). *Guidelines for performing systematic literature reviews in software engineering*. Academic Press.

Knezevic, B., Renko, S., & Knego, N. (2011). Changes in Retail Industry in the EU. *Business. Management in Education, 9*, 34–39.

Knox, S., & Walker, D. (2001). Measuring and managing brand loyalty. *Journal of Strategic Marketing, 9*(2), 111–128. doi:10.1080/713775733

Kumar, A., Olshavsky, R., & King, M. (2001). Exploring alternative antecedents of customer delight. *Journal of Consumer Satisfaction, Dissatisfaction & Complaining Behavior, 14*.

Kumar, V., George, M., & Pancras, J. (2008). Cross-buying in retailing: Drivers and consequences. *Journal of Retailing, 84*(1), 15–27. doi:10.1016/j.jretai.2008.01.007

Lai, I. K. W. (2019). Hotel image and reputation on building customer loyalty: An empirical study in Macau. *Journal of Hospitality and Tourism Management, 38*, 111–121. doi:10.1016/j.jhtm.2019.01.003

Le Chi, C. (2016). A formative model of the relationship between destination quality, tourist satisfaction and intentional loyalty: An empirical test in Vietnam. *Journal of Hospitality and Tourism Management*, *26*, 50–62. doi:10.1016/j.jhtm.2015.12.002

Liu, A. H., & Leach, M. P. (2001). Developing loyal customers with a value-adding sales force: Examining customer satisfaction and the perceived credibility of consultative salespeople. *Journal of Personal Selling & Sales Management*, *21*(2), 147–156.

Lopes, E. L., de Lamônica Freire, O. B., & Lopes, E. H. (2019). Competing scales for measuring perceived quality in the electronic retail industry: A comparison between ES-Qual and E-TailQ. *Electronic Commerce Research and Applications*, *34*, 100824. doi:10.1016/j.elerap.2019.100824

Loureiro, S. M. C., & Kastenholz, E. (2011). Corporate reputation, satisfaction, delight, and loyalty towards rural lodging units in Portugal. *International Journal of Hospitality Management*, *30*(3), 575–583. doi:10.1016/j.ijhm.2010.10.007

Loureiro, S. M. C., Miranda, F. J., & Breazeale, M. (2014). Who needs delight? The greater impact of value, trust and satisfaction in utilitarian, frequent-use retail. *Journal of Service Management*.

Makanyeza, C., & Chikazhe, L. (2017). Mediators of the relationship between service quality and customer loyalty: Evidence from the banking sector in Zimbabwe. *International Journal of Bank Marketing*, *35*(3), 540–556. doi:10.1108/IJBM-11-2016-0164

Martenson, R. (2007). Corporate brand image, satisfaction and store loyalty: A study of the store as a brand, store brands and manufacturer brands. *International Journal of Retail & Distribution Management*, *35*(7), 544–555. doi:10.1108/09590550710755921

Martinelli, E., & Balboni, B. (2012). Retail service quality as a key activator of grocery store loyalty. *Service Industries Journal*, *32*(14), 2233–2247. doi:10.1080/02642069.2011.582499

Meyer, T., Barnes, D. C., & Friend, S. B. (2017). The role of delight in driving repurchase intentions. *Journal of Personal Selling & Sales Management*, *37*(1), 61–71. doi:10.1080/08853134.2016.1272052

Miranda, M. J., Kónya, L., & Havrila, I. (2005). Shoppers' satisfaction levels are not the only key to store loyalty. *Marketing Intelligence & Planning*, *23*(2), 220–232. doi:10.1108/02634500510589958

Moher, D., Liberati, A., Tetzlaff, J., & Altman, D. G. (2009). Preferred reporting items for systematic reviews and meta-analyses: The PRISMA statement. *Annals of Internal Medicine*, *151*(4), 264–269. doi:10.7326/0003-4819-151-4-200908180-00135 PMID:19622511

Morschett, D., Swoboda, B., & Foscht, T. (2005). Perception of store attributes and overall attitude towards grocery retailers: The role of shopping motives. *International Review of Retail, Distribution and Consumer Research*, *15*(4), 423–447. doi:10.1080/09593960500197552

Ngobo, P. V. (2017). The trajectory of customer loyalty: An empirical test of Dick and Basu's loyalty framework. *Journal of the Academy of Marketing Science*, *45*(2), 229–250. doi:10.100711747-016-0493-6

Nguyen, H. L., Cao, T. K., & Phan, T. T. H. (2016). The Influence of service quality on customer loyalty intentions: A study in the Vietnam retail sector. *Asian Social Science*, *12*(2), 112–112. doi:10.5539/ass.v12n2p112

Nguyen, H. T. (2020). An application of the Kano model and retail service quality scale to Vietnamese supermarkets. *International Journal of Productivity and Quality Management, 31*(2), 189–206. doi:10.1504/IJPQM.2020.110025

Oliver, R. L. (1980). A cognitive model of the antecedents and consequences of satisfaction decisions. *JMR, Journal of Marketing Research, 17*(4), 460–469. doi:10.1177/002224378001700405

Oliver Richard, L. (1997). *Satisfaction: A behavioral perspective on the consumer.* Irwin-McGraw-Hill.

Parasuraman, A., Zeithaml, V. A., & Berry, L. (1988). *SERVQUAL: A multiple-item scale for measuring consumer perceptions of service quality.* Academic Press.

Parikh, D. (2006). Measuring retail service quality: An empirical assessment of the instrument. *Vikalpa, 31*(2), 45–56. doi:10.1177/0256090920060203

Paswan, A. K., & Ganesh, G. (2005). Cross-cultural interaction comfort and service evaluation. *Journal of International Consumer Marketing, 18*(1-2), 93–115. doi:10.1300/J046v18n01_05

Petzer, D. J., & Van Tonder, E. (2019). Loyalty intentions and selected relationship quality constructs: The mediating effect of customer engagement. *International Journal of Quality & Reliability Management, 36*(4), 601–619. doi:10.1108/IJQRM-06-2018-0146

Pinto, P., Hawaldar, I. T., & Pinto, S. (2020). *Impulse buying behavior among female shoppers: Exploring the effects of selected store environment elements.* Academic Press.

Pornpitakpan, C., & Han, J. H. (2013). The effect of culture and salespersons' retail service quality on impulse buying. *Australasian Marketing Journal, 21*(2), 85–93. doi:10.1016/j.ausmj.2013.02.005

Prakash, N., Somasundaram, R., & Krishnamoorthy, V. (2018). An empirical study on apparel retail service quality and its impact on customer loyalty in specialty store. *International Journal of Services and Operations Management, 30*(4), 505–519. doi:10.1504/IJSOM.2018.10014628

Reddy, N. S. (2019). The profitability interlinkage model of retail store management. *International Journal of Mechanical Engineering and Technology, 10*(2).

Reinchheld, F. F. (1996). The loyalty effect: The hidden force behind growth, profits, and lasting value. *Long Range Planning, 29*(6), 909–909. doi:10.1016/S0024-6301(97)82843-9

Reynolds, K. E., Ganesh, J., & Luckett, M. (2002). Traditional malls vs. factory outlets: Comparing shopper typologies and implications for retail strategy. *Journal of Business Research, 55*(9), 687–696. doi:10.1016/S0148-2963(00)00213-7

Rhee, H., & Bell, D. R. (2002). The inter-store mobility of supermarket shoppers. *Journal of Retailing, 78*(4), 225–237. doi:10.1016/S0022-4359(02)00099-4

Rokonuzzaman, M. D., Harun, A., Al-Emran, M. D., & Prybutok, V. R. (2020). An investigation into the link between consumer's product involvement and store loyalty: The roles of shopping value goals and information search as the mediating factors. *Journal of Retailing and Consumer Services, 52*, 101933. doi:10.1016/j.jretconser.2019.101933

Saeidi, S. P., Rasli, A. B. M., Saeidi, P., Saaeidi, S. A., & Saeidi, S. P. (2017). How service quality results in customer satisfaction of large-scale retailers in Malaysia. *Advanced Science Letters*, *23*(9), 9050–9054. doi:10.1166/asl.2017.10021

Samantaray, A., Mishra, U. S., Das, J. R., & Mahapatra, J. (2017). Analysing the mediating effect of customer satisfaction on the relationship between service quality and customer loyalty in indian organized retail sector. *International Journal of Applied Business and Economic Research*, *15*(25), 243–251.

Saricam, C. (2022). Analysing Service Quality and Its Relation to Customer Satisfaction and Loyalty in Sportswear Retail Market. *AUTEX Research Journal*, *22*(2), 184–193. doi:10.2478/aut-2021-0014

Sathish, D., & VenkatramaRaju, D. (2010). The growth of Indian retail industry. *Advances in Management*.

Schlossberg, H. (1990). Satisfying customers is a minimum; you really have to 'delight'them. *Marketing News*, *24*(11), 10–11.

Severin, V., Louviere, J. J., & Finn, A. (2001). The stability of retail shopping choices over time and across countries. *Journal of Retailing*, *77*(2), 185–202. doi:10.1016/S0022-4359(01)00043-4

Sharma, A., & Stafford, T. F. (2000). The effect of retail atmospherics on customers' perceptions of salespeople and customer persuasion: An empirical investigation. *Journal of Business Research*, *49*(2), 183–191. doi:10.1016/S0148-2963(99)00004-1

Sharma, D. (2014). *Examining the influence of service quality on customer satisfaction and patronage intentions in convenience store industry*. Academic Press.

Siu, N. Y., & Cheung, J. T. H. (2001). A measure of retail service quality. *Marketing Intelligence & Planning*, *19*(2), 88–96. doi:10.1108/02634500110385327

Sivadas, E., & Baker-Prewitt, J. L. (2000). An examination of the relationship between service quality, customer satisfaction, and store loyalty. *International Journal of Retail & Distribution Management*, *28*(2), 73–82. doi:10.1108/09590550010315223

Sivapalan, A., & Jebarajakirthy, C. (2017). An application of retailing service quality practices influencing customer loyalty toward retailers. *Marketing Intelligence & Planning*, *35*(7), 842–857. doi:10.1108/MIP-09-2016-0178

Söderlund, M. (2006). Measuring customer loyalty with multi-item scales: A case for caution. *International Journal of Service Industry Management*, *17*(1), 76–98. doi:10.1108/09564230610651598

Suhartanto, D., Brien, A., Primiana, I., Wibisono, N., & Triyuni, N. N. (2020). Tourist loyalty in creative tourism: The role of experience quality, value, satisfaction, and motivation. *Current Issues in Tourism*, *23*(7), 867–879. doi:10.1080/13683500.2019.1568400

Sum, C. Y., & Hui, C. L. (2009). Salespersons' service quality and customer loyalty in fashion chain stores: A study in Hong Kong retail stores. *Journal of Fashion Marketing and Management*.

Summers, T. A., & Hebert, P. R. (2001). Shedding some light on store atmospherics: Influence of illumination on consumer behavior. *Journal of Business Research*, *54*(2), 145–150. doi:10.1016/S0148-2963(99)00082-X

Thang, D. C. L., & Tan, B. L. B. (2003). Linking consumer perception to preference of retail stores: An empirical assessment of the multi-attributes of store image. *Journal of Retailing and Consumer Services*, *10*(4), 193–200. doi:10.1016/S0969-6989(02)00006-1

Thenmozhi, S. P., & Dhanapal, D. (2011). Unorganised retailing in India–A study on retail service quality. *European Journal of Social Sciences, 23*(1), 71-78.

Theodoridis, P. K., & Chatzipanagiotou, K. C. (2009). Store image attributes and customer satisfaction across different customer profiles within the supermarket sector in Greece. *European Journal of Marketing*, *43*(5/6), 708–734. doi:10.1108/03090560910947016

To, W. M., Tam, J. F., & Cheung, M. F. (2013). Explore how Chinese consumers evaluate retail service quality and satisfaction. *Service Business*, *7*(1), 121–142. doi:10.100711628-012-0149-7

Ueltschy, L. C., & Krampf, R. F. (2001). Cultural sensitivity to satisfaction and service quality measures. *Journal of Marketing Theory and Practice*, *9*(3), 14–31. doi:10.1080/10696679.2001.11501894

Umar, A., & Bahrun, R. (2017). The mediating relationship of customer satisfaction between brand trust, brand social responsibility image with moderating role of switching cost. *Advanced Science Letters*, *23*(9), 9020–9025. doi:10.1166/asl.2017.10015

Vazquez, R., Rodríguez-Del Bosque, I. A., Díaz, A. M., & Ruiz, A. V. (2001). Service quality in supermarket retailing: Identifying critical service experiences. *Journal of Retailing and Consumer Services*, *8*(1), 1–14. doi:10.1016/S0969-6989(99)00018-1

Wong, A., & Sohal, A. (2003). Service quality and customer loyalty perspectives on two levels of retail relationships. *Journal of Services Marketing*, *17*(5), 495–513. doi:10.1108/08876040310486285

Wong, A., & Sohal, A. S. (2006). Understanding the quality of relationships in consumer services: A study in a retail environment. *International Journal of Quality & Reliability Management, 23*(3), 244–264. doi:10.1108/02656710610648215

Chapter 17
To Study the Service Gap Between Customer Perceptions and Expectations in Services Provided by Cab Aggregators

Amandeep Singh
 https://orcid.org/0000-0002-0970-5467
Chitkara Business School, Chitkara University, Punjab, India

Devesh Bathla
 https://orcid.org/0000-0003-3990-5934
Chitkara Business School, Chitkara University, Punjab, India

Amrinder Singh
 https://orcid.org/0000-0003-0830-7245
Jain University (Deemed), India

ABSTRACT

The most important objective of service quality is the retention of the customer to provide repeatability of services through customer satisfaction. Since customer perceptions and expectations affect the service quality, this study helps to understand and identify the service quality gaps in services provided by cab aggregators to customers in India using SERVQUAL Gap Analysis between perception and expectation. The main objective of this chapter is to understand, study, and compare the customer perception and expectations from customers using services of the cab aggregators within India to identify the areas of service quality gaps. Primary data was collected from 495 respondents from various cities across different demographic variables such as gender, age, income, education, and occupation. The responses were taken using Google Forms, which is consolidated in an Excel sheet. It is suggested to also create a service quality framework for cab aggregators on the basis of service quality gaps identified in the current study.

DOI: 10.4018/978-1-6684-5853-2.ch017

INTRODUCTION

Transportation services are the activities designed to help a person to travel or making goods move from one place to another. The movement of people or goods could be through land, water, or air. Transportation enables people to move from one place to another and is therefore an important need of people on daily basis through numerous civilizations. It helps in translating human needs in different parts of the world through commercial, agricultural, and industrial evolution. In ancient times, people used to walk, ropes were used to transport goods. However, things started changing slowly and animals were used as means of transport to carry people and goods from one place to another followed by invention of a wooden cart used for transportation on land. And then one day, people were able to freely sail, sail through boats, and then came a remarkable invention of horse-drawn vehicle. Without doubt, modern transportation has developed over a period. Other progressive means of development in the field of transportation has been the invention of steam engine, the steam trains. Discovery of natural gas and oil have contributed immensely to humankind in fulfilling their needs by inventing different modes of transport including bus, truck, car, two wheelers that run on petrol, diesel or gas followed by air transport. With the advent of technology advancement, life has become smooth with transportation available through different kind of cars and aircrafts, trains, submarines, and space conveyance.

Trade seemed to be simpler, secure, well timed, prompt, dependable and advantageous that enhanced standard of living globally. Different objects were sent across the world in exchange for other products. With technological development in transportation every time, world started getting closer resulting in 50% reduction in flight times. Thus, different places in the world can be reached in shorter period. Cab Industry globally has a very crucial role to play in our society in fulfilling the basic need of traveling from one place to another. Cabs are extremely important means of transport for people who either don't have their own car or are not keen on using public means of transport due to their choice especially in cities and urban areas. Cabs are considered an easy, accessible, and dependable source of transport thereby becoming a preferred medium of transport globally in a short span of time. With the increase in living standard of people, development in Technology and Telecom facilities, change in people's preferences have led to the immense growth of app-based cab services globally. Thus, it can be concluded that Cab Industry really helps in simplifying our life by achieving our transportation goals and needs at the click of a button on our smart phone.

(Basu, 2019) mentioned in his study about Indian taxi market. This consists of markets which are either organized or unorganized. Estimated value of unorganized taxi market is $8.5 billion dollar while value of organized market is appx $500 million. The growth forecast of Indian taxi market is 13.7% from 2017-22 (Khade and Patil, 2018). Transport development in a city is closely related to its development index, it's social, economic, and technological level. With the changing scenario as per the global landscape, customer expectations, smart phone usage increasing and considering the evolution in technology, the traditional taxi services have transformed to app-based cab services working on technology. It has been observed as per the findings of this study that maximum number of travellers were happy with factors like ease of availability and booking, convenience, dependability, safety, driver behavior, option to pay apart from cash, overall pricing provided by the app-based cab services to its customers.

Cab aggregator is a marketplace that can be used by customers to connect with a driver for moving from one place to another. In other words, as per cab aggregator Model definition, it is a business and network model whereby the concerned firm collects information about a service provider, thus collaborating and forming their partners, thereby selling services of the service providers under its brand name. Some of the Cab aggregators providing services are currently available in India are Ola Cabs, Uber, Meru Cabs, Carzonrent, Savaari, Fasttrack Taxi Mega Cabs, Tab Cab, BlaBla car and so on. The reason for success of Uber and other cab aggregator service providers can be attributed to its business model as compared to the traditional taxi services.

Responsiveness and willingness to help customers by providing quick services are important dimensions that impact customer satisfaction. Delivering quick services, following timeliness, providing 24 by 7 services are considered important parameters for cab service providers. The major areas of customer expectations are User Friendly Interface, well updated GPS tracking and Monitoring devices, instant query supporting system, round the clock operating hours, drivers to be courteous, sensitive, and helpful and having multiple platform support. On the customer perception front, the different type of service quality problems experienced by different type of customers when their services are used with issues pertaining to app, surge pricing, cab availability, price, reliability, timeliness, safety, bad behavior of cab drivers and poor Customer Service. These insights could be used for improving the satisfaction of the customer thereby bridging the variance of customer perception and expectations to offer better service quality.

The cab aggregator business has been growing enormously in last 10 years. Indian cab aggregator market is expected to further expand by 17 to 20 per cent on yearly basis with an estimated $6 to $9 billion dollars. Over $400 million have been invested by venture capitalists in last 6 years. Indian radio taxi market has undergone changes after app-based cab companies like Ola and Uber have started their services which are easily accessible on the smart phone. App based cab service providers have been very popular with advertisements seen on television, newspaper blogs, articles that appear daily aiming at eliminating the gap prevailing between existing demand and supply thereby consistently focusing on improving their services. SERVQUAL concept in app-based cab services helps in identifying the difference between perception and expectations of the customers.

With the introduction of Meru cab services in 2004, Indian market has witnessed organized rental cabs for the first time. However, the app-based cab services pioneered in 2010 and was the actual turn around with Uber launching its India operations in 2013. This launch has completely changed the market dynamics along with increasing customer expectations. And this has actually led to cab companies making an effort to implement various strategies by creating customer demand, retaining old customers thereby building customer loyalty during the process.

The term e-commerce means a customer can buy or sell his products or services be it electronically or through internet. Higher penetration in internet services, increase in people shopping on-line, changing lifestyle, increase in disposable income and tremendous usage of smart phones has resulted in rise in e- commerce market. There are different types of e-commerce activities depending upon the business dynamics. It could be B2B, B2C, C2C, C2B, B2A or C2A. Example of B2C transaction could be Pantaloons selling a dress to a lady consumer. Example of C2C transaction could be Selling my car to another customer through a broker. E-commerce thus helps in covering a large base of customers (geographically catering to different age groups with diversity). It helps in deriving customer insights through constant tracking and analytics thereby making the business processes faster and dynamic with lesser paperwork. It is thus an efficient response to any change in consumer trend and market demand which lowers costs and provides more opportunities to "Sell" through the online sales channel. It also helps in sharing personalized messaging to advertise products and services to consumers, prospects therefore increasing the sales.

Service quality establishes the relation between services delivered versus the customer expectations (Lewis and Booms, 1983). As per service quality perceived is the difference between customer expectations versus the perceptions related to the services delivered to customers. Also, perceived service quality results in providing competitive advantage. Service quality is measured as customer's perception of services offered to him– customer expectations from the firm offering services to a customer (Parasuraman, Zeithaml, and Berry 1988).

Service quality can be evaluated and measured as per different service quality parameters of SERVQUAL Model: tangibility, reliability, responsiveness, assurance, and empathy. There is an important relation between service quality and customer satisfaction. Customer satisfaction plays an important role in services provided to a customer. Customer satisfaction is a pleasure or disappointment derived when an outcome arising from the perceived performance of a product with respect to the customer's expectations. In short, a buyer transacts with a seller by way of satisfying the customer needs and providing value to the customer as per his expectations.

The assessment model to measure customer satisfaction to improve the services as per the customer expectations is called SERVQUAL. Numerous interactions that a customer has with the service provider over a period actually determines experience of the customer from the product or its services.

App-based taxi services have decreased the demand of traditional taxi services by about 50% and at the same time replaced other modes of transport as well. This is simply due to customer's preference, perspective of having more comfort, convenience, and lesser wait time without any hassle of finding a parking space while opting for online taxi services.

The word Taxi emerged in early 20th century. The name "taxi" has been shortened from the original word "taxicab", which has been derived from two words: "taximeter" and "cabriolet". The name "taxi-meter" has been taken from the Mid-Latin "taxa", meaning "tax or charge". Meter has been derived from the French noun 'mètre'; an instrument used for measurement. The first documented use of the word "taxicab" was in March, 1907 in London.

As per data shared from Ride Hailing - India | Statista Market Forecast, 2019, Ola and Uber are ahead of competitors in the Indian market and along with Uber contributes to these numbers. In 2018, the total rides grew to 3.5 million on daily basis. In 2017, the total rides grew by 57% to 2.8 million a day. In 2016, the total rides grew by 90% to 1.9 million a day. In 2015, the total rides grew by 100% to 1 million a day. 40% of smart phone users in India have downloaded at least one cab service app on their phone. Cab hailing services are presently available in 125 Indian cities. Some of the app-based Cab services currently available in India: Ola Cabs, Uber, Meru Cabs, Carzonrent, Savaari, Fasttrack Taxi App, Mega Cabs, Tab Cab, BlaBla car.

OBJECTIVE THE STUDY

The main objective of this research paper is to understand, study and compare the customer perception and expectations from customers using services of the cab aggregators within India to identify the areas of service quality gaps. Since customer perceptions and expectations affect the service quality, so this study helps to understand and identify the service quality gaps in services provided by cab aggregators to customers in India using SERVQUAL Gap Analysis between perception and expectation. The most important objective of service quality is retention of the customer to provide repeatability of services through customer satisfaction.

ADVANTAGES OF APP-BASED CAB SERVICES

Convenient and Cashless

A customer through app on his smart phone can easily book the nearest cab from his current location to his destination and have his preferred cab arrived within minutes of booking the cab. Customer's credit and debit card can be linked to the taxi app account (as an option, if he wishes to choose it), so he does not even have to carry the cash. Once, the ride gets over, a payment receipt of the customer's ride is sent on his email account along with an acknowledgement on his mobile phone. Therefore, app-based Companies as per the customer's preference should keep working on providing convenient options to the customers regularly (Furunes and Mkono, 2019).

Simple to Use and Time Saving

Simplicity and time savings are the top two reason for customers using Uber or other cab services provider over traditional taxi service. Customers and drivers get connected through technology platform. The nearest driver gets an alert on his mobile app to accept the new booking. Basis that notification, he picks up the customer. The customer on the other hand gets information about the cab and the driver details to pick him up from his selected location on app. Therefore, website or the platform design should enable the user to have a quick and easy access to book the ride experience (Farooq et al., 2019).

Safer and More Flexible for Drivers

One of the most important features for drivers is safety and security of their work. Uber and other app-based cab service providers offers employment opportunities to its drivers to become entrepreneurs with flexible working hours and better incomes than the traditional taxi drivers. Due to freedom and flexibility being available in their work hours, they work as independent contractors since they log-in and log-out of the app platform (for accepting bookings) as per their discretion (Bonchek and France, 2016). A driver doesn't have to worry about returning change to the customer since transactions are cashless. Further, Uber or app-based cab service providers might deactivate a customer's account on account of the repeatedly low ratings by drivers or due to their rude or aggressive behavior as per the feedback or complaint received from the customers.

RESEARCH METHODOLOGY

Primary Data was collected from 495 respondents from various cities across different demographic variables such as gender, age, income, education and occupation. The responses were taken using Google Forms, which consolidated in an excel sheet. After initial scrutiny to check missing data, outliers and consistency, the responses were coded using numeric numbers. These responses were then analysed in SPSS 21.0. Differences in the level of Expectation & Perception of Service have been assessed with respect to the demographic variables and analysed using non-parametric tests including the Gap analysis. Also, secondary data was referred to search related to service quality, service quality related issues, factors impacting customer satisfaction related articles and research papers. The search showed articles and Papers from different industries and of various countries. The keywords were made more specific for search pertaining to services of cab aggregators within India. Each article was carefully reviewed for its relevance to the present study.

REVIEW OF LITERATURE

The current study was done basis customers who have been facing service quality issues for numerous service-related companies apart from cab industry like retail, restaurants, on-line food apps, hotels, airlines, social media, e-banking, and e-commerce with respect to the literature review done for cab service providers. The aim of this study is to understand the service-related problems experienced by customers who use services of cab aggregators in India. The service quality has an impact on customer satisfaction, customer experience and customer loyalty. Research papers related to service-related problems, service quality issues, factors impacting customer satisfaction were explored from the databases such as Emerald, EBESCO and Google Scholar. Further, the keywords were made more specific for search pertaining to cab aggregators and customer expectations, perceptions and service quality issues faced while using services of service industry including restaurants, retail stores, social media platform, e-commerce sites, e-banking and so on. The search resulted in over 100 research papers with app-based cab service providers data across the globe.

India has witnessed immense growth in travel in last few years (Parasuraman et al., 1985). It is important to understand the relation between service quality and customer satisfaction and study the various dimensions of service quality. In the context of online cab services, it is the tangibles or the appearance of physical facilities, equipment, people are important from customer satisfaction point of view.

Measuring, analysing, and comparing the service quality of Kuala Lumpur, Malaysia's online cab companies. The latest and the most often used service in urban areas of Malaysia are mobile app-based taxi services. On-line cab services have numerous benefits over traditional taxi service that mainly includes convenience and security. This study has found four quality parameters: design of the website, the accuracy of information provided, following the practices to keep customer's data secure, and the services imparted. Practitioners of on-line cab industry will also find it quite relevant to further improve the most significant service quality parameters as per the user expectations. Following are the variables and research design.

- **Website Design:** Quick and easy to book the ride. App has good sections. App has a good level of personalization. The app does not waste time while booking a ride.
- **Reliability:** One got what one had ordered. The car comes on time as promised. The same Car comes which is shown on the app.
- **Privacy Security:** The safe transaction with the site. My privacy is protected. Adequate safety procedures.
- **Overall Service Quality:** Sincere interest in customer's issues. The company is willing to respond. Adequate safety procedures.

As per the study done on the customers of Indore city, it was observed that customers were not satisfied with the high cancellation charges and expected better condition of cabs along with commuter safety and availability of women drivers. These gaps, if plugged could improve the service quality of the cab aggregators resulting in higher customer satisfaction which will translate to increase in number of customers. For customers, the highlight of using services of online cab aggregators is the convenience of booking a cab from their doorsteps, ease of cab availability. Also, customers are concerned about their safety during the ride, which needs to be taken seriously by the cab aggregators especially with numerous women related incidents that have taken place during the travel. Cab aggregators must ensure consistent focus on improving their services by building better relationship with the customers and the drivers to face the increase in competition (Devda et at., 2019).

The word Taxi emerged in early 20th century. The name "taxi" has been shortened from the original word "taxicab", which has been derived from two words: "taximeter" and "cabriolet". The name "taximeter" has been taken from the Mid-Latin "taxa", meaning "tax or charge". Meter has been derived from the French noun 'mètre'; an instrument used for measurement. The first documented use of the word "taxicab" was in March, 1907 in London.

Customer satisfaction level of using app-based cabs is impacted by the service quality in the city of Ernakulam in India. Since the perceived reliability has high impact on Customer Satisfaction level, so Uber should make sure about the various parameters of reliability, especially the overall availability of cabs. It should therefore take required steps to ensure that the cabs always arrived on time. Company should also ensure and provide correct information to the people. Secondly, Comfort has a significant role in Customer Satisfaction and the company should take necessary steps to ensure a smooth ride of its customer. The air condition facility of cabs also needs to improve. Thirdly, Driver Behavior has a significant role. Thus, company should try to improve the drivers" knowledge about different routes. The next important factor as shown by this study is the Safety. Uber should at the same time try to improve the safety measures for its customers. Company can reduce the concentration on Price, Discount and Promotional activities because these dimensions have lesser impact on Customer Satisfaction.

Trust based on Institution has been identified as a crucial factor in promoting online sales in the e-commerce research arena. This research applies to institution related trust in view of ridesharing and conducting an empirical study to evaluate the significant institutional mechanisms that might be useful in creating customer's confidence and trust in the cab hailing of DiDi, China. The empirical study results thus highlight the effectiveness of payment security, driver certification, feedback and surge pricing being perceived to be enhancing customers' trust in the ridesharing platform. This in turn reduces customers' perceived risk and promote their continuance intention. This is mainly market-driven, and these legally binding factors are based on the institutional environment of ridesharing.

Five attributes were found to be of high importance related to price, driver's professional behavior, ease of booking the cab, quality of cab hired, and responsiveness of cab hired. Professional behavior of drivers and convenience were two attributes that had highest impact on the overall satisfaction of the customers (Khan et al., 2016). With the changing scenario, the traditional taxi services have transformed to app-based cab services working on technology to be able to meet the expected and actual service delivery. It was found that most of the travelers were satisfied with availability, reliability, pricing, safety, cashless option, driver behavior, comfort, transparency, and surge pricing. The drivers were happy because of higher earnings but were not too happy with the long working hours and were uncertain about cut in their incentives regularly. So, these companies need to strike a balance between the driver expectations and handling customer perception. Further accepting different payment options including e-banking, wallets, cash. Rating mechanism with positive feedback is encouraged. So, the future of mobility-based transport system in Kolkata is quite competitive with a bright future provided companies look at the option of optimum resource utilization (Basu, 2019).

Services having several inherent issues such as difficulty in attaining uniformity apart from designing service and the delivery processes. Effective supply chain management could result in reducing the overall resources needed to align with the service requirements of the customer. Therefore, improvement in services offered to the customers by enhancing the availability of the product and reducing the processing time along with the decreased costs. The significant performance measures for taxi aggregator service supply chain could be described as: delivering the service pertaining to customer processing time – how fast can a ride be booked using the app. including determining the wait time for customers – The services to be available at benchmark time as per the experiential data. This parameter can actually be called "Service Order Lead Time".

In a study about Uber and Ola particularly in India have promoted entrepreneurship by committing about sustainable livelihood, decent earning opportunities, along with entrepreneurial opportunities through vehicle ownership, flexibility in terms of work and freedom to have a large base of drivers. Initially, these companies paid very high incentives to keep the drivers on board. But when the pressure to turn profitable was raised, these incentives were considerably reduced, thus resulting in steep reduction in income of all these drivers. As the total number of cars attached to Uber and Ola started increasing, the incentives and the number of rides per cab started reducing and so did the driver's income. Further, Uber and Ola's entrepreneurship drive seemed comparatively better in India as it highlighted the pride of owning a car, owning a vehicle being associated with a high social and economic status in India.

Balachandran and Hamzah (2017) has referred several variables having a considerable impact on the service quality front of cab services influencing the customer satisfaction in some way or the other, either completely or partially. The parameters or variables that impact the customer satisfaction are tangibility, reliability, price, comfort, coupon redemption behavior and promotion. While all these variables are considered to be independent variables that influence customer satisfaction, a dependent variable. All these independent variables thus impact the service quality in a positive way. As part of this study, comfort has been considered as an extremely significant variable impacting satisfaction of customer the highest in context to the app-based cab services in Malaysia.

Dillon (2016) highlighted about Uber building its competitive advantage by resolving its customer's problems, by offering nice cars to its customers to travel from one place to another, allowing the riders to know the location of the driver and the time when the cab will arrive, sharing the customer's location with the driver and customers having to travel without the hassle of physically carrying cash with them. Considering transportation sector is one of the largest employers globally, it becomes imperative for Uber or app-based cab service providers to work towards improving their services continuously keeping pace with the innovation in technology. This will ensure app-based cab service providers are able to cater to changing customer demands keeping in mind the dynamics of this industry. The merging mobile app technology has brought opportunities for several new entrants to offer their cab services to the customers to fulfil the ever-changing demands of customers. Thus, Uber and Grab have in a way completely revamped this sector and increased competition with the traditional taxi services and the public transport facility.

Boateng et al., (2019) have shared as part of their research study about people in a developing economy like Ghana using Uber or app-based cab services on account of economic and social-economic reasons. In other words, people of Ghana feel using Uber's cab services helps them to improve their self-esteem and social connections. They will be introduced to new people that could blossom to new friendships thus strengthening their support network, a benefit of participating in sharing economy. This could further benefit them socially and economically. In short, those using traditional taxi services or public mode of transport add to their social connections while those using Uber rides could create new friendships apart from building social relations. Both traditional taxi services as well as app-based cab services provide opportunity to people of Ghana to interact with the driver and other passengers during the ride.

Traditional taxi service has been totally transformed by introducing a booking app on smart phone. With the help of technology, a cab could be booked anytime and from anywhere as per the customer's demand, thus converting an idle car and driver into an asset through an on-demand cab service available as per customer's requirement. Further, it is expected to have an on-demand cab availability where all the required services are accessible to the customers all the time thus changing the dominant and traditional business into a service business model. The driver incomes are neither driven by fixed incomes nor by wages but are much more than what a traditional taxi driver used to earn. Flexibility in working hours along with other incomes complimented is the most interesting part which attracts the drivers towards Uber's services. The driver incomes are neither driven by fixed incomes nor by wages but are much more than what a traditional taxi driver used to earn.

In a research study about the importance to identify different innovative business models that could disrupt long established traditional industries. It has been seen that industry specific regulation slows down the innovative processes or innovations completely. Sharing of ride, competitive analysis apart from competition policy, regulations driving the market and different government policies. An important requirement of the sharing economy is the deeper understanding of business model of Uber cabs or other app-based cab service providers. Further, it is important to understand and relate to the analysis between regulation and Uber's innovative business model.

Surie and Sharma (2019) have shared as per their research that Uber and Ola in India have created additional employment opportunities those of the digital labor market for the taxi drivers by using the mobility app-based cab services. The digital labor market is attracting the migrant workers around and outside Bengaluru to be part of the mobility platforms. This transition seems simple as well as rewarding for the migrant workers since it is an alternative working opportunity not depending upon relationships or social status or any other thing. This rather seems to be a great opportunity for them to flourish considering it is not impacted by any climatic changes or is dependent on relationships, not involving any agriculture related risk or any social debt. This is based on the ample benefits being offered, the cab service opportunities are an adaptive strategy to improve their livelihood which was otherwise quite often impacted by climatic changes in the urban labor markets.

This study is primarily to assess the customer perception vis-a-viz the improvements required in services offered by Ola cabs. Without doubt, Ola cabs remain a provider offering robust transportation related technology platform offering flexible option for its customers to book and pay their cabs. Drivers to be trained on using mobile applications properly, proper management of time, communicate to the customer in case of any changes in the cab number, calls made to the drivers should not be charged, no change in tariff rates even during the peak hours of the day, proper maintenance of the cab to be done regular, cabs to have logo and sticker of Ola and it should also be visible, payments through card should be available, increase the number of vehicles and their availability, special offers and discounts to be provided during festival season.

The objective is to understand customer expectations from cab service providers like Ola especially in the region of Delhi NCR and to improve its services which affect customer's satisfaction. Customer's willingness to use services will be through the perceived value leading to repeating the services thus suggesting a proposed solution of high-quality services with lower price to the customers thereby providing customers value for their money. Service quality is completely based on perceived quality which results from service-related expectations of the customers and their perception of actual service performance.

FINDINGS AND DISCUSSION

The GAP analysis mentioned as per the research study helps to identify the service quality gaps in services provided by cab aggregators as per each dimension of SERVQUAL model: tangibility (app), tangibility (in car), reliability, responsiveness, empathy and assurance. Most importantly, this study aims at mapping the end-to-end customer experience with customer satisfaction while taking ride with any of the cab aggregators in India.

It could help cab aggregators in consolidating information related to service-related issues faced by customers to improve the services provided and work towards plugging the identified gaps in service quality of the app-based cab service providers in India. This section analyses the gap between expectation and perception along with relevant inferences. The gap analysis has been done between expectation and perception along with relevant inferences. The statistical significance of each of attribute of 5 dimensions (including tangibility, reliability, responsiveness, empathy, and assurance) is also assessed to provide insights.

Tangibility (app):
- Booking app is easy to use.
- Available on multiple platforms.

Tangibility (in-car):
- First aid kit available inside the cab.
- Fire extinguisher available inside the cab
- Emergency button in the cab.

Reliability:
- My preferred cab type is easily available from my location.
- My preferred cab type is easily available as per the preferred timings.
- Ease of cab availability at the time of bad weather.

Responsiveness:
- Prompt search of different options on their app.
- The wait time is less than expected.

Assurance:
- Driver is always willing to help.

Table 1. Gap analysis of expectation and perception

Dimensions	Expectation (Mean Score)	Perception (Mean Score)	Gap (P-E)	% Gap	Inference
Tangibility	4.51	3.71	-0.8	-21.56%	Service providers perform 21.56% less than the expected level w.r.t. Tangibility
Reliability	4.42	3.69	-0.73	-19.78%	Service providers perform 19.78% less than the expected level w.r.t. Reliability
Responsiveness	4.46	3.65	-0.81	-22.19%	Service providers perform 22.19% less than the expected level w.r.t. Responsiveness
Empathy	4.45	3.73	-0.72	-19.30%	Service providers perform 19.30% less than the expected level w.r.t. Empathy
Assurance	4.54	3.81	-0.73	-19.16%	Service providers perform 19.16% less than the expected level w.r.t. Assurance
Overall	4.48	3.72	-0.76	-20.43%	Overall, Service providers perform 20.43% less than the expected level

The table 1 shows the percentage difference between expectation & perception and its inferences. Overall perception is 20.43% lesser than expected level of service. Likewise, on other dimensions viz., the perception is lesser than expected level Tangibility by 21.56%, Reliability by 19.78%, Responsiveness by 22.19%, Empathy by 19.30%, Assurance by 19.16%. Also, statistical significance of Expectation and Perception of each attribute has been studied and analysed. The app-based service providers need to focus on the above-mentioned gaps since the percentage differences (between customer perception and expectations) are higher. Since the average of the difference between perception and expectation in the above-mentioned table is 0.73, so attributes with 0.73 or above value have been considered as the major gap areas that app-based service providers need to focus upon.

Table 2. Statistical significance of Expectation & Perception of each attribute

Attributes	Expectation	Perception	Gap (P- E)	%Difference	t- value	Sig(p-value)
Tangibility						
Booking app is easy to use	4.75	3.87	-0.88	**-22.74%**	15.560	**.000**
Available on multiple platforms.	4.62	3.88	-0.74	-19.07%	13.456	**.000**
Multiple modes to make payment	4.58	3.87	-0.71	-18.35%	12.540	**.000**
Cab is in good condition	4.6	3.83	-0.77	-20.10%	13.938	**.000**
Cab is clean.	4.57	3.84	-0.73	-19.01%	12.938	**.000**
Air conditioner is working properly.	4.58	3.84	-0.74	-19.27%	13.556	**.000**
wi-fi available in the cab	4.39	3.61	-0.78	-21.61%	12.887	**.000**
First aid kit available inside the cab.	4.42	3.45	-0.97	**-28.12%**	16.081	**.000**
Fire extinguisher available inside the cab.	4.39	3.4	-0.99	**-29.12%**	15.979	**.000**
Emergency button in the cab.	4.23	3.36	-0.87	**-25.89%**	15.940	**.000**
Live tracking of cab movement	4.56	3.88	-0.68	-17.53%	12.323	**.000**
Driver is dressed properly.	4.43	3.58	-0.85	**-23.74%**	14.149	**.000**
Driver follows traffic rules.	4.51	3.81	-0.7	-18.37%	12.458	**.000**
Reliability						
My preferred cab type is easily available from my location.	4.61	3.79	-0.82	-21.64%	14.874	**.000**
My preferred cab type is easily available as per the preferred timings	4.52	3.74	-0.78	-20.86%	13.997	**.000**
Shared cab / carpooling option is available in their app	4.42	3.71	-0.71	-19.14%	12.775	**.000**
Enables customers to redeem coupon while making the payment to book the cab.	4.34	3.47	-0.87	**-25.07%**	14.028	**.000**
Makes sure none of the rides gets cancelled.	4.36	3.64	-0.72	-19.78%	11.575	**.000**
Cab pricing fare are regulated.	4.4	3.65	-0.75	-20.55%	12.727	**.000**
Customer is not over charged because of more time taken during the ride	4.39	3.68	-0.71	-19.29%	11.878	**.000**
Driver does not charge the customer anything apart from the billed amount	4.39	3.82	-0.57	-14.92%	9.585	**.000**
Driver willingness even for a short distance ride	4.45	3.74	-0.71	-18.98%	12.373	**.000**
Proper information is provided about the ride related details.	4.41	3.79	-0.62	-16.36%	11.233	**.000**
Billing accuracy for the ride.	4.46	3.75	-0.71	-18.93%	12.168	**.000**
Doorstep pick-up is provided.	4.38	3.36	-1.02	**-30.36%**	17.799	**.000**
Wi-fi works properly in the cab.	4.31	3.66	-0.65	-17.76%	11.350	**.000**
Ease of cab availability even during any time of my emergency.	4.39	3.67	-0.72	-19.62%	11.621	**.000**
Ease of cab availability at the time of bad weather.	4.42	3.64	-0.78	-21.43%	12.683	**.000**
Maintains privacy about customer's ride.	4.41	3.77	-0.64	-16.98%	10.662	**.000**
Delivers quality services to its customers.	4.46	3.82	-0.64	-16.75%	11.015	**.000**
Responsiveness						
Prompt search of different options on their app.	4.56	3.67	-0.89	**-24.25%**	15.423	**.000**
Their app is updated with cab status on timely basis.	4.52	3.78	-0.74	-19.58%	13.233	**.000**
Customer is always dropped at the right location.	4.49	3.81	-0.68	-17.85%	11.605	**.000**
The wait time is less than expected.	4.43	3.43	-1	**-29.15%**	16.869	**.000**

Continued on following page

Table 2. Continued

Attributes	Expectation	Perception	Gap (P- E)	%Difference	t- value	Sig(p-value)
Communicates different discount offers regularly.	4.33	3.51	-0.82	**-23.36%**	14.653	**.000**
The support team responds promptly to any feedback shared by the customer.	4.45	3.69	-0.76	-20.60%	13.019	**.000**
Empathy						
Personalized attention to the customer during the ride.	4.23	3.39	-0.84	**-24.78%**	14.872	**.000**
The ride experience makes the customer happy.	4.49	3.84	-0.65	-16.93%	12.478	**.000**
Cab ride is comfortable.	4.51	3.81	-0.7	-18.37%	12.688	**.000**
Will have different languages for booking on app.	4.45	3.75	-0.7	-18.67%	12.478	**.000**
Rating option is available on their booking app.	4.47	3.84	-0.63	-16.41%	10.551	**.000**
An action is taken basis my rating provided on their app.	4.51	3.75	-0.76	-20.27%	12.996	**.000**
Their helpline is available for the customers whenever required.	4.45	3.69	-0.76	-20.60%	12.408	**.000**
Customer queries are addressed immediately.	4.45	3.76	-0.69	-18.35%	11.688	**.000**
Customer support team completely resolves every customer problem.	4.44	3.72	-0.72	-19.35%	12.810	**.000**
Assurance						
Build customer's trust through their services provided.	4.72	3.84	-0.88	**-22.92%**	16.079	**.000**
Build customer's confidence through their services provided.	4.69	3.89	-0.8	-20.57%	15.157	**.000**
Driver is courteous.	4.58	3.83	-0.75	-19.58%	13.823	**.000**
Driver is always willing to help.	4.53	3.77	-0.76	-20.16%	13.895	**.000**
Customer safety throughout the ride.	4.51	3.87	-0.64	-16.54%	11.981	**.000**
The driver's documents are displayed in the cab.	4.43	3.72	-0.71	-19.09%	12.508	**.000**
Driver always acts in a professional way.	4.48	3.6	-0.88	**-24.44%**	15.136	**.000**
Trains its driver to improve his navigation skills of different routes.	4.45	3.73	-0.72	-19.30%	13.196	**.000**
Never insists for cash payment only.	4.49	3.83	-0.66	-17.23%	10.860	**.000**
Payments made on their portal are secured.	4.51	3.97	-0.54	-13.60%	9.815	**.000**

Table 2 shows the comparison of expectation & perception on all attributes of the scales.

As all p-values are <0.05, all items have statistically significant differences. The app-based service provider must focus on highlighted factors as the percentage differences are higher.

Following are the possible areas where app-based providers need to focus –

- Booking app to be easy to use.
- First aid kit to be available inside the cab.
- Fire extinguisher to be available inside the cab
- Emergency button to be there in the cab.
- Driver to be dressed properly.
- Enable customers to redeem coupon while making the payment to book the cab.
- Doorstep pick-up to be provided.
- Prompt search to be there for different options on their app.

- The wait time to be less than expected.
- Communicate different discount offers regularly.
- Personalized attention to be provided to the customers during the ride.
- Building customer's trust through their services provided.
- Driver to always act in a professional way.

CONCLUSION

Implications and Areas of Future Research

The current study helps to understand the differences in terms of expectations and perceptions of services provided by the app-based cab service providers across different demographic variables: gender, age, marital status, occupation, and income levels of customers with regards to the demographic characteristics. It also helps to understand the differences between customer expectations and perceptions as per all the dimensions of extended SERVQUAL (tangibility_in-car, tangibility app, reliability, responsiveness, empathy, assurance). This study helps to identify the dependent and independent variables, their relation, statistical significance, and their overall impact. Thus, 06 dimensions of Service Quality have been derived from the analysis with regards to customer perception and expectation: tangibility_app (app related statements), tangibility in-car (statements related to in-cab facilities), reliability, responsiveness, empathy, and assurance. So, there are in total 6 dimensions of Service Quality as per the extended SERVQUAL model.

The research study further helps in understanding the perception of all six factors pertaining to Service Quality namely Tangibility_app, Tangibility_in-car, reliability, responsiveness, empathy, and assurance that affect the customer satisfaction apart from the overall perception of service. Further, the study helps in identifying the service quality gaps in services provided by cab aggregators in India by studying the respondents' data and applying appropriate statistical tools. This study also helps in proposing service quality framework with recommendations for cab aggregators to plug the identified service quality gaps.

The current study helps to understand and identify the areas of service quality gaps in services provided by cab aggregators to customers in India by understanding, analysing, and studying the differences in terms of expectations and perceptions of services provided by the app-based cab service providers. Since Service quality is an attribute that affects customer satisfaction, customer retention and repeatability of services. It is therefore important to understand the relationship between service quality and customer satisfaction by mapping the five dimensions (Tangibility, Reliability, Assurance, Empathy and Responsiveness) of Service Quality with customer perceptions and expectations leading to satisfaction model. Further, it is suggested to also create a service quality framework for cab aggregators on the basis of service quality gaps identified from the current study.

Customer satisfaction is an attribute that has the highest impact on loyalty of the customer towards the service provider. Therefore, it becomes imperative to study and analyse service quality and customer satisfaction along with their relation and their significance to determine the customer experience and build the customer loyalty. How can these cab aggregators plug the service quality gaps to build the long-term relationship, customer commitment and customer loyalty? It is therefore important to map the end-to-end customer experience with customer satisfaction while a customer is taking ride with a cab aggregator thereby understanding customer concerns, challenges, and problems. With intense competition and changing customer preferences, cab aggregators need to formulate strategies to be able to provide customer satisfaction and retain the existing customers, consistently working towards improving customer experience and the quality of services thus help in creating customer loyalty along with repeatability and long-standing relation with customers. This study is based on identifying the service quality gaps as per the different dimensions of SERVQUAL and how service quality affects the customer satisfaction.

The current study, however, does not consider the service quality gaps with respect to shared ride or cab pooling services. It should also identify the service-related issues and identify the service quality gaps with respect to shared cab services offered by cab aggregators.

REFERENCES

Balachandran, I., & Hamzah, I. B. (2017). The influence of customer satisfaction on ride-sharing services in Malaysia. *International Journal of Accounting and Business Management*, 5(2), 184–196. https://ftms.edu.my/journals/pdf/IJABM/Nov2017/184-196.pdf

Basu, A. (2019). Viability assessment of emerging smart urban para-transit solutions: Case of cab aggregators in Kolkata city, India. *Journal of Urban Management*, 8(3), 364–376. doi:10.1016/j.jum.2019.01.002

Boateng, H., Kosiba, J. P. B., & Okoe, A. F. (2019). Determinants of consumers' participation in the sharing economy. *International Journal of Contemporary Hospitality Management*, 31(2), 718–733. doi:10.1108/IJCHM-11-2017-0731

Bonchek, M., & France, C. (2016). Build your brand as a relationship. *Harvard Business Review*, 5, 1–6. https://hbr.org/2016/05/build-your-brand-as-a-relationship

Devda, S. S., Attri, A., & Attri, R. (2019). *Need Gap Analysis of Online Taxi Aggregation Business.* https://www.semanticscholar.org/paper/Need-Gap-Analysis-of-Online-Taxi-Aggregation-Devda/cae2b71c64e329f2efcd227f8040bc9 26a265587

Dillon, K. (2016). *What Airbnb understands about Customer "Jobs to be done".* Harvard Business Review. https://hbr.org/2016/08/what-airbnb-understands-about-customers-jobs-to-be-done

Farooq, M., Ali, W., Younas, W., Khalil-ur-Rehman, F., & Qurashi, Q. A. (2019). The era of Transformative Marketing: Service Quality of Mobile App Based Taxi Services in Kuala Lumpur. *Proceedings on Engineering Sciences*, 1(2), 49–58. doi:10.24874/PES01.02.006

Furunes, T., & Mkono, M. (2019). Service-delivery success and failure under the sharing economy. *International Journal of Contemporary Hospitality Management*, 31(8), 3352–3370. doi:10.1108/IJCHM-06-2018-0532

India, M. (2019). *Problems Faced by Ola and Uber Users - Business.* My India. https://www.mapsofindia.com/my-india/business/problems-faced-by-ola-and-uber-users

Khade, A., & Patil, V. (n.d.). A Study of customer satisfaction level of Ola and Uber paid taxi services with special reference to Pune city. *Int J Manag Technol Eng, 8*, 1596-1603.

Khan, A. W., Jangid, A., Bansal, A., & Tyagi, V. (2016). Factors Affecting Customer Satisfaction in the Taxi Service Market in India. *Journal of Entrepreneurship and Management, 5*(3), 46–53.

Lewis, R. C., & Booms, B. H. (1983). The marketing aspects of service quality. *Emerging Perspectives on Services Marketing, 65*(4), 99-107.

Parasuraman, A., Zeithaml, V. A., & Berry, L. (1988). *SERVQUAL: A multiple-item scale for measuring consumer perceptions of service quality.* Academic Press.

Surie, A., & Sharma, L. V. (2019). Climate change, Agrarian distress, and the role of digital labor markets: Evidence from Bengaluru, Karnataka. *Decision, 46*(2), 127–138.

Chapter 18
Understanding Investor Satisfaction of Financial Products Under the SLP Approach:
An Attempt to Understand Investor Priorities

Shradhanjali Panda
Ravenshaw University, India

Sanjeeb Kumar Dey
ⓘD https://orcid.org/0000-0002-1085-200X
Ravenshaw University, India

ABSTRACT

Financial product marketing requires the use of well-researched techniques to achieve investor satisfaction. The intention of this study is to examine elements that affect investor satisfaction while keeping the aforementioned debate as its central concept. Investor is the term used for customer of financial products. The factors that contribute most to it have been discovered to be safety, profitability, and liquidity. It was discovered after looking at a variety of schools of thought and literatures that there has been little research on investor satisfaction, and the work aims to examine the impact of financial products' liquidity, profitability, and safety (specifically, the SLP approach) on investors' satisfaction. Data is analysed using Tukey's test, principal component analysis, correlation, regression, and ANOVA. This study contributes that investor satisfaction is a valuable intangible asset that is primarily produced by the financial instrument's safety, security, and liquidity features using the SLP technique.

DOI: 10.4018/978-1-6684-5853-2.ch018

INTRODUCTION

Modern business strategies aim at considering the interest of the stakeholders shifting their goal from profit maximization to their satisfaction as protecting customers' interest is the primary objective now a days. Thus, the concept of customer satisfaction as loyal and pleased customers boost sales and thus growth of a company came into existence. However, the entire concept of customer satisfaction changes to investor satisfaction when it comes to marketing of financial instruments. The universal language of investment has the background meaning of an assured future return and ironically expansive factors are clubbed with the process starting from psychological to financial, behavioral to practical (Chen & Volpe, 1998). So, when it comes to the mode of investment, utmost care is taken by the financial institutions while offering them to the investors. Investor Satisfaction is not only limited to offering profit but also a range of causes like understanding investors' requirement, their financial goal, risk taking ability etc. Financial products or Instruments being claims against money demands a careful consideration and planning in its marketing strategy. The background reason being different risk return appetite of investors, uncertainty of future outcome prediction and changing guidelines by regulatory bodies, the whole marketing strategy relies on in-depth understating of financial instrument features. Understanding how marketing initiatives link to financial outcomes is crucial in the financial industry.

Many elements of the investor decision making process have previously been the subject of extensive investigation from a number of schools of thought. But when it comes to investor satisfaction, there is still a discrepancy. Sometimes, investors lack the expected outcomes from their investment. They fail to understand the basic aspects of investments and the factors they need to study thoroughly. Given its current relevance in the financial markets, financial contentment is commonly comprehending a key goal for financial managers and practitioners since it is vital to consider their clients' subjective perceptions of their situation. This objective necessitates a thorough research-based approach that examines the characteristics of an investment. Being this an emerging little explored of research, it is important to start by answering a few important questions, such as what factors contribute to financial satisfaction and why it is becoming a top priority for financial institutions. The current study attempts to further explore the topic in order to delve into these questions and logically respond to them. It makes an effort to identify and study the diverse determinants that influence financial satisfaction. This current study's intention is to investigate elements or aspects that affect investor satisfaction while retaining the aforementioned discussion as its main idea. By connecting the chosen determinants to financial satisfaction in one's life, the paper tests the impact on investor satisfaction (which takes into account the determinants i.e. safety, liquidity and profitability and thus suggests an SLP approach). So, the SLP approach that ascertains investor satisfaction by taking into account crucial elements including safety, liquidity, and profitability is being presented.

The study is divided into three parts. First part has tried to explore various research works conducted by economists, financial analysts, researchers and academicians in the field of investor satisfaction. In this literature review part, the primary determinants of financial products that affect investor satisfaction are tried to be identified. Once identified, they are used for further studying their inter-relationship and overall impact on investors. Second part of the study deals with data collection. Three districts (Cuttack, Khurda and Ganjam) are selected for the study. Population of these three districts represents around 12% of total population of the state. Moreover, capital of Odisha i.e., Bhubaneswar is covered by considering Khurda District in the present work. In this part of the work, data is collected and using statistical tools they are examined. Accordingly the result is derived. Third or last part of the study makes an attempt to interpret the result by analyzing the data and managerial implication is focused. In this segment, a model is proposed to discuss the above determinants linking them with each other. Overall outcome of the paper is thus concluded in this part.

LITERATURE REVIEW

There is a narrow line of difference between the concept of decision-making ability in personal investment plan and investment behavior of a person. Investors generally behave differently when it comes to implementing their money management skills. Application of this skill is relative as well as subjective in nature. Theoretical approaches of investment science are rarely adopted in this process. An investment strategy considers many factors like his future financial goal, ability to understand the financial product; costs associated with the process, his risk return appetite and last but not the least financial knowledge or financial literacy (Frey and Stutzer, 2000). The primary stage in the investment process is being mentally ready for commitment of one's hard-earned fund. Readiness of mind is closely associated with a robust understanding of available options and converting them into proper opportunities by correctly gauging the personal financial requirements. Unlike speculation, investment is not made in a hurry as an incorrect decision may lead to failure and insolvency. The fundamental aspects of investment therefore are comprehended in order to get optimum result from the assessment process for investment. So, marketers of financial products identify indicators for investment evaluation that greatly influence the decision-making ability of an investor. Shobha & Suman (2017) differentiated the theoretical and practical aspects of investment using separate methods of research. Their findings are mostly dependent on the basic understanding of investor behavior that concludes the study with selecting the major factor of it i.e. assured profitability from investment. The behavioral theory used in probable explanation of investor behavior supports the fact that investors seek maximum return from their investment irrespective of market condition and the adverse status of other macro-economic variables. More focus on this aspect is further studied by Barnes et al. (2011) using practical investment processes. Their study understands different group of investors classifying them into three segments like risk averse, risk takers and risk neutral. They found accordingly the goal changes. Priority of risk takers is profitability whereas risk avoiders seek safety and liquidity from their investment. The study supports the fact that investors' satisfaction has many reasons and from person to person it varies. In connection to risk, investors are influenced by psychological factors and emotions (Garrett & James, 2013). During a risky investment process, investors basically get carried away by feelings and sometimes behave irrationally to beat the market. In these situations, many opt for liquidating their investments rather than waiting for the risky situation to be passed (Rutkowska, 2022). This cognitive biasness is resulted by highly emotional reactions during a risky situation. Few other studies contradicted the logic by stating risky situations actually lead to best reaction as risk plays the role of an input (Grable et al., 2013) The emotional change during the risky situation helps the investors clearly forecast the future and make a correct decision in investment that at the end resulted in achieving investor satisfaction goal (Easterlin, 2006).

With regard to marketing of financial products, by demonstrating the requirements of investors, marketers previously controlled the market with limited instruments offered for investment. But, being forward in time, the market is currently being driven by the requirement of investors, which is the exact opposite of the previous scenario. Customer satisfaction is urgently needed, which depends on providing reliable information and excellent service. Consumers of financial products are referred to as investors, and businesses have cognitively constructed marketing by addressing the challenge of altering customers' risk-return choices (Barnes et al, 2011). Financial product suppliers provide investors' ecstasy (the highest level of delight) by being profitable (Shoba & Suman, 2017). Investor personality traits significantly influence their financial choices. There are several things that influence investor contentment. It has been found that safety, profitability, and liquidity are the main contributors to it. Regulatory requirements, ease of use, and financial stability are additional factors that have a big impact on investor satisfaction (Magnini, 2011). Because investor satisfaction is a psychological phenomenon with expectancy as its underpinning (Hicks et al, 2005). When the anticipated return is higher than the actual return, investors are more satisfied. A few studies also draw attention to the age of investors as a fascinating variable in investor satisfaction. Older investors are typically happier than younger investors in general (Arathy et al, 2015). Asset managers should focus on relationship management if they want to keep clients throughout periods of challenging financial performance. In this situation, investors' prior experience is crucial, and ultimately, this experience is what greatly adds to investor satisfaction (Oliver, 1996). Financial contentment is increasing for investors as behavioral finance gains traction since it focuses on happiness and wellbeing rather than just money (Plagnol, 2011). It is regarded as the most essential component of a person's pleasure and wellbeing in life (Hira & Mugenda, 1998). Financial assets are one of its main components. Financial instruments can be used to express those resources. According to some schools of thought, it is simpler for an investor to achieve financial contentment if he is free from variables like unwelcome financial obligations, stress, and debt (Frey & Stutzer, 2000). Financial contentment is influenced by external variables, but psychological elements also play a significant effect (Diener and Biswas-Diener, 2002). Many people believe that having a lot of money will make them happy financially. However, in actuality, a person's level of financial pleasure is determined by how they perceive their income and money management abilities (Grable et al, 2013). The experience and perception of investors cannot be ignored if financial service providers are to achieve the objective of the investors' financial satisfaction (Joo and Grable, 2004). Numerous research have attempted to pinpoint the elements or components of financial satisfaction. Different schools of thought identify a vast variety of reasons. Financial contentment is closely correlated with socio-demographic characteristics including financial conduct and attitude (Joo & Grabel, 2004). On the other hand, financial education is regarded as a significant contributor to financial satisfaction. "Ignorance is not bliss" in this situation, thus the investor needs to understand the fundamentals of the investment where his hard-earned money is being used (Robb, Babiarz, 2015). Financial happiness is correlated with investor welfare, financial knowledge, and financial attitude, according to a theoretical framework presented by Garret & James (2013). Allgood & Walstad (2013) feels that the most important component contributing towards financial pleasure is decision making competence in money problems. One needs to understand how to invest money and how a return can be guaranteed with a manageable risk.

RESEARCH GAP AND OBJECTIVES

Numerous research on investor attitudes, expectations, choices, and preferences have been done. Though a wide range of research works have been conducted on consumer satisfaction, yet when it comes to investor satisfaction in terms of financial products, a gap still exists. Logically consumer satisfaction and investor satisfaction are different from each other as the later deals with claims against money and not with consumables. There is a thin line of difference between consumer and investor. A person who purchases goods and services for their own personal satisfaction which they experience after using or consuming them is referred to be a consumer whereas a person who is willing to invest their resources like skill, fund, time etc in order to gain access to resources like money is known as an investor. However, there is still a difference in investor satisfaction. It was discovered after looking at a variety of schools of thought and literatures that there has been little research on investor satisfaction. After examination of different scholarly research articles on the above stated topic, it was realized that being a recent area, investors' satisfaction has not been properly addressed by economists and researchers. According to a study of the literature, there is still a room for research on investor satisfaction and the major factors influencing it. Few studies have been done to yet that examine the relationship between investor pleasure and the liquidity, safety, and profitability of financial products.

Thus, the current research work's research gap is classified into two parts. First part deals with identifying the determinants of investment. Second part deals with studying the impact of those identified determinants on investor satisfaction.

The current paper attempts to explore the highlighted components leading to financial satisfaction in light of the limitations in the research environment. Having identified the key determinants of investor's satisfaction, the aim of the present study is to find out how these key factors affect to it. The objectives can be stated as follows

- To identify the prominent determinants of financial instruments
- To study the impact of the identified determinants on investor's satisfaction
- To establish the inter relationship between these determinants.
- To assess the effect of individual determinant on investor's satisfaction.

Hypotheses of the Study

$H_1 1$: Investor satisfaction in safety of financial products is different across the districts
$H_1 2$: Investor satisfaction in liquidity of financial products is different across the districts
$H_1 3$: Investor satisfaction in profitability of financial products is different across the districts

RESEARCH METHODOLOGY

This research is empirical in nature. Both primary and secondary sources are used to gather evidence. Responses in form of Data have been collected as per necessity. Through the use of standardized questionnaires and interviews, primary data has been gathered. For this, a five-point Likert as well as interview method have been utilized. For the study, three districts are taken into account. They are Ganjam, Khurda, and Cuttack. Geographically, the eastern, central, and southern parts of the state are covered by the districts, which have a population that is close to 33% of the entire state. The study's sample size is 360. Tukey's test is followed by Factor Analysis, Correlation, Regression, and ANOVA, which are suggested for use in further analysis of the dataset.

Data and Period of Data Collection

The present paper devoted around 2 months to collect data. The month of June and July were used for collection of data from three districts of the state. Ganjam, Khurda and Cuttack districts are used for this purpose. According to 2011 Census report, literacy rate among all these states are highest in the state. Out of total literacy ratio of Odisha i.e. 72.87%, these three districts' average literacy rates are the highest ones. Literacy rate of Cuttack District stands at 85.5% whereas in urban literacy rate Khurda stands at around 91%. In case of male literacy rate, Khurda has around 94% that is the highest one in Odisha. Coming to Ganjam District, the literacy rate stands at 71%. In the process of data collection utmost care has been taken to cover all sectors of these three sectors for robustness of data analysis. So, along with urban, semi-urban and rural areas are too given equal weightage. Total 720 respondents were addressed at first phase of data collection. But, excluding unanswered and out layered responses, data filtering resulted in limiting the responses to 360 only.

Questionnaire Design

The adopted method for designing of the structured questionnaire follows a five point Likert Scale method. Maximum attention has been given for designing the questionnaire as it aims to touch different segments of the society. Simple language and easy format were adopted for this purpose. In time of need, interview method is also adopted to collect data. Different scholarly research works are used to adopt the above stated methods. The following table provides an insight for the sources of questionnaire designing.

Identified Variables

In depth study of different research works done in this area concludes the major determinants of Investor Satisfaction are safety of principal amount as well as return, liquidity of the financial products and profitability of financial products. Associated variables are explored accordingly. Understanding the background thought of the present work, investors' satisfaction is set as dependent variable whereas independent variables are primarily safety, liquidity and profitability of financial products. The following table offers a clear picture of identified variables and their source of research work. It also contains details of variables and their sources.

Table 1. Statement of variables and sources

Category	Variables	Source
Demography	Age, gender, location, qualification, work experience,	Krishnan, R. & Booker, M. (2002)., Oliver, R. (1996).
Determinants of Investors' Satisfaction (Independent Variables in 5 point Likert Scale)	SFP_1 SFP_1 SFP_1 LFP_1 LFP_1 LFP_1 PFP_1 PFP_1 PFP_1	Shoba, T. S., Suman, C. (2017)., Barnes, D.C. et al. (2011), Oliver, R. (1996) Chen, H. & Volpe, R.P. (1998), Robb, C. et al. (2015), Loureiro, S. M. C. (2014) Shoba, T. S., Suman, C. (2017), Arathy et al. (2015), Joo, S. (1998)
Investors' Satisfaction (Dependent Variable in 5 point Likert Scale)	IS_1 IS_1	Shoba, T. S., Suman, C. (2017), Joo & Grabel (2004)

- *The Author*
- Variable 1: The safety of an investment implies the certainty of return of capital without loss of money or time. Safety is the feature of investment which each investor desires as his expectation is to get back his capital on maturity without loss and without delay.
- Variable 2: An investment that is easily saleable or marketable without loss of money and without loss of time is said to possess liquidity. An investor generally prefers liquidity for his investments so that his need of money at a random point can be satisfied.
- Variable 3: All investments are characterized by the expectation of return. That creates the feature of profitability of an investment. In fact, investments are made with the primary objective of its profitability.
- Variable 4: Investor satisfaction goal can be achieved when all his preferences are fulfilled in terms of liquidity in his investments, safety of his fund, a good profitability in form of assured return with minimum risk.

ANALYSIS OF DATA

The questionnaire distributed among the respondents for data collection contains 21 questions to judge the responses on 5-point Likert scale starting from strongly disagree to strongly agree. Accordingly, the scores like 5, 4, 3, 2 and 1 are given. Factor analysis is done on the collected data using SPSS software and tried to interpret the factors affecting financial satisfaction. The following table shows the descriptive analysis of the sample using percentage analysis. For easy understanding and interpretation for the researcher, in this analysis measures of variables are computed.

Table 2. Statement of demographic factors

Specifications	Category	Number of respondents	In Percentage (%)
Gender	Female Male	194 166	53.88 46.12
Age	20-30 31-40 41-50 51-60	65 117 98 80	18 32.5 27.22 22.22
Location	Cuttack Khurda Ganjam	118 122 120	32.7 33.8 33.33
Marital Status	Unmarried Married	209 151	57.84 42.15
Qualification	10th standard or below 10th to Graduation Post Graduate & above	55 145 160	15.27 40.27 44.44
Work Experience	Less than 2 years 2-5 years 5-10 years More than 10 years	208 76 46 30	57.35 20.58 12.74 8.33
Income (Annual)	More than 10 lakhs 8-10 lakhs 5-8 lakhs 2-5 lakhs 0-2 lakhs	56 141 76 56 31	15 39.21 21.56 15.68 8.61
Investment on annual income	Above 10% 11% to 21% 22% to 33% Above 33%	124 154 60 22	34.4 43 16.6 6.1
Total		**360**	**360**

*Source: The Author

Table 2 represents the demographic features of the respondents. Total 360 salaried employees from Cuttack, Khurda and Ganjam are considered for the study. There is a gap of 6% between the number of male and women respondents. Similarly, the difference between married and unmarried respondents is around 5%. In case of age group, maximum respondents are of age group of 31 to 40 years i.e., 117 respondents. On the other hand, only 18% i.e. 65 respondents are of between the age group of 20 to 30. In location part, it was tried to give equal weightage to each three districts. However, data filtering resulted in small gaps and for Cuttack, Khurda and Ganjam districts the percentage of respondents are 32.7, 33.8 and 33.33 respectively. An analysis of qualification segment convey that around 160 respondents have either master degree or above qualification whereas number of respondents between the qualification range of 10th standard to Graduation is 145. Only 55 respondents belong to the qualification range of 10th standard or below. In earnings segment, primary mass of the respondents are earning 2-5 lakhs of annual income i.e. around 39%. More than 10 lakhs salary level, only 8.61% respondents are present. Majority of sample are falling under less than 2 years of work experience category i.e., 57%. As the study is about investors' satisfaction, the last row of the above table represents the percentage of investment out of total investment. Around 43% (highest) respondents invest between 11% to 21% of their total annual income.

Only 6% respondents invest more than 33% of their income i.e., the minimum. Interestingly out of this 6%, 3.5% belongs to unmarried segment.

Having analyzed the demographic profiles of the respondents, the following step is a Gap Test to identify the areas that need to be improved. The reason behind using a gap test is to draw a first- hand information from the respondents that can be helpful in further analysis of data and research. In behavioral aspects as emerging area of Management, gap analysis has already established its suitability by exploring the deviations between expectation and reality (Esterline, 2006). Here experienced performance of respondents is collected and compared with expected performances. The present work made an effort here by describing and identifying the discrepancies through comparing existing awareness level with that of optimal awareness level. The uniqueness of the test lies in its simplicity of natural method of benchmarking. Following table shows the result of gap analysis conducted on the responses of the respondents.

Table 3. Result of gap analysis

Sl No	Aspects of Investors' Satisfaction	Expected Mean	Estimated/ Actual Mean	Literacy Gap
1	Knowledge about Investment and saving	5	3.81	1.19
2	Aware about inflation and its impact	5	2.11	2.89
3	Knowledge on the concept of interest rate	5	2.92	2.08
4	Aware that Investment and speculation are different	5	2.11	2.89
5	Aware about the concept of return	5	3.67	1.33
6	Knows the concept of risk and its relationship with return	5	3.02	1.98
7	Knowledge about features of different financial products	5	2.31	1.69
8	Follows proper investment strategy	5	1.45	3.55
9	Knowledge about banking and insurance	5	2.95	2.05
10	Use of D-mat account	5	1.22	3.78
11	Planned for short term as well as long term investments	5	2.62	2.38
12	Knowledge about KYC	5	3.85	1.15

*Self Computed

The above Gap Analysis table provides a glimpse of Investors' Satisfaction under SLP approach. It can be traced out that in following proper investment strategy, the gap is widest and that is 3.55. It is followed by knowledge about inflation and its impact and a basic understanding between speculation and investment. In these both aspects gap stands at 2.89. Knowledge about interest rate, various financial products and their use, knowledge about the utility of Banking and Insurance and following a planned investment strategy, gaps lie between 1.5 to 2.5. They need moderate improvement for attaining the goal of Investors' Satisfaction. In remaining aspects, gaps are lowest i.e. below 1.5 and need no further improvement (Bhusan & Medury, 2014).

To evaluate the internal consistency or dependability of a group of scale or test items, the Cronbach's alpha statistic is used. Cronbach's alpha is a method to measure the potency of this consistency. Quoted differently, a measurement's reliability depends on how well it regularly captures a concept. As the most often used indicator in a Likert scale with numerous items, Cronbach's Alpha is used in the current study as a reliability test. The reliability test's alpha value is shown in the following table.

Table 4. Reliability test

Cronbach's Alpha	Cronbach's Alpha (on standardized items)	No of variables
.836	.839	21

• *The Author*

The score for each scale item is correlated with the overall score for each observation (often individual survey respondents or test takers), and the variation for all individual item scores is then compared: This total evaluation of a measure's reliability is given by the resulting coefficient of reliability, which has a range of 0 to 1. If all of the scale items are completely unrelated to one another (that is, if they are not correlated or have no shared covariance), then = 0, and if all of the items have high covariances, then will start to approach 1 as the scale's item count grows ever larger. In other words, the more the items have shared covariance and likely assess the same fundamental notion, the greater the coefficient. When an instrument was used to assign a score to an individual, a high value of alpha was "good," but the crucial factor should be that scores acquired when using an instrument had to be interpretable. Thus table 4 confirms the reliability of the scale items used in the questionnaire having Cronbach's Alpha value is 0.836 of 21 items.

Table 5. Tukey's test output for reliability

A. District	B. District	A-B (Mean Difference)	Std. Error	Sig	95% Confidence Interval	
					Lower Bound	Upper Bound
District₁	District₂	-12.100	.695	.000	-13.44	-10.04
	District₃	.955	.695	.362	-.71	2.61
District₂	District₁	12.100	.695	.000	10.058	13.44
	District₃	12.750	.695	.000	10.89	14.32
District₃	District₁	-.955	.695	.362	-2.31	.71
	District₂	-12.750	.695	.000	-14.32	-11.02

*Mean difference is significant at 0.05 level

For a pair wise comparison, Tukey's test is conducted and in the above table (table 5) the result is shown. Tukey's test in table 5 confirms the result between district 1 and 3 is significant. Same result is also applicable between districts 2 and 3.

Table 6. KMO (Kaiser-Meyer-Olkin) & Bartlett's Test

Kaiser-Meyer-Olkin Measure of sampling Adequacy		.789
Bartlett's Test of Sphericity	Approx. Chi-Square	561.845
	Df	210
	Sig	.000

● *The Author*

For testing of each variable and whole sampling efficacy, Kaiser-Meyer-Olkin test is used and suitability of data in factor analysis is checked. The acceptance criteria for more suitable data for factor analysis are estimated by its minimum proportion. As the KMO values have a limit from 0 to 1, values nearing to 0.8 and onwards are treated as appropriate for sampling (Klein, 2013). Table 6 suggests for further factor analysis as KMO statistics is 0.789 or 78.9%. It can be interpreted that the sample is adequate to 78%.

Table 7. Factor analysis

Sl No	Variables/ factors	Symbol	Factor Loadings	Determinants
1	Investment in Banks and fixed interest-bearing financial instruments are more safety than others	SFP_1	0.922	Safety in Financial Products (SFP)
2	Investments which are not subject to market risk are more safety	SFP_2	.918	
3	Investments bearing some security or guarantee by Government Regulating Agencies are more safety.	SFP_3	0.863	
4	Tenure and quantum of Investments are directly related to safety	SFP_4	0.851	
5	Rating Agencies help in assessing the safety associated with a particular investment.	SFP_5	0.819	
6	Investment protection and safety mechanism available are enough and effective	SFP_6	0.807	
7	Tenure and quantum of Investments are directly related to liquidity	LFP_1	0.903	Liquidity in Financial Products (LFP)
8	Investments with high liquidity are most preferred choice of investment	LFP_2	0.879	
9	Liquidity and return are inversely related	LFP_3	0.836	
10	Liquidity can be compromised with investment growth	LFP_4	0.782	
11	Stock market instruments offers more liquidity as compared to traditional financial investments	LFP_5	0.631	
12	Liquidity of investments play major determinants for selecting investment avenues	LFP_6	0.940	
13	Liquidity information are complete and accurately available for each financial products	LFP_7	0.917	
14	Priority in investment is always given to instrument offering more return	PFP_1	0.800	Profitability in Financial Products (PFP)
15	Profitability is considered net return received in hand after all expenses and taxes	PFP_2	0.656	
16	Possibility of more return is linked with stock market instruments as against traditional investment	PFP_3	0.888	
17	Profitability is inversely related with liquidity and safety	PFP_4	0.873	
18	Profitability is linked with movement of financial markets and economy at large	PFP_5	0.860	
19	High return results in more satisfaction	IS_1	0.721	Investors Satisfaction (IS)
20	High liquidity results in more satisfaction	IS_2	0.742	
21	Safety in investment results in more satisfaction	IS_3	0.644	

● *The Author*

Table 7 reveals that for the three identified determinants of investors' satisfaction, factor analysis with 18 factors has been conducted. Six factors under safety, seven factors under liquidity, five factors under profitability and three factors under investors' satisfaction are examined. Moreover, for the dependent variable (Investors' satisfaction), and three more factors are studied. The table depicts the detail about each factor, symbol used for them, corresponding factor loading and each determinant of these factors. A careful analysis of factor analysis can be interpreted as total 18 out of 21 factors have a loading more than 0.7 and this higher factor loading constitute ample variance from the factor or variable. Basically factor loading is the correlation coefficient and aims at reducing the data for a robust result using limited ones. In case of LFP_6, PFP_2 and IS_3, factor loadings are 0.631, 0.656 and 0.644 respectively. On the contrary, in case of SLP_1, SLP_2, LFP_1, LFP_6 and LFP_7 factor loadings are more than 0.9 i.e. 0.922, 0.918, 0.903, 0.940 and 0.917 respectively. Remaining factors have loadings between 0.7 to 0.9 that confirm robustness of the result.

Factor analysis is normally followed by correlation analysis as they are integral parts of the linearity test. So, following is the result of correlation analysis of identified determinants with that of dependent variable i.e., investors' satisfaction.

Table 8. Correlation analysis

Factor	SFP	LFP	PFP	IS
SFP	1			
LFP	0.811	1		
PFP	0.201	-0.614	1	
IS	0.592	0.014	0.726	1

*The Author

The above table states that correlation is present between some determinants whereas in others it is not. LFP has a positive correlation with all determinants and highest with SFP. The correlation between IS and LFP is minimum. Likewise, LFP has a significant negative relation with PFP, and it can be interpreted that liquidity of a financial product does not necessarily depends on profitability as investors who have a goal of making profit may exclude liquidity aspect from their investment planning. Similarly, investor satisfaction has positive correlation with SFP and PFP. It can be interpreted that satisfaction from an investment greatly comes from safety and liquidity of the financial products.

A regression test is conducted to test the effect of all independent variables over the dependent variable. Table 8 and table 9 show the results of regression analysis.

Table 9. Regression analysis

Model	R	R^2	Adjusted R^2	Standard Error pf	Durbin Watson
1	0.781	0.610	0.594	0.584	1.915

*The Author
**Dependent variable: Investors' satisfaction
***Independent Variables: Safety, Liquidity and Profitability of financial products

Table 8 shows R value of 0.781 that represents a presence of high correlation between dependent and independent variables. Added to it, R-squared value states that the independent variables are having around 61% of variability over the dependent variable. No auto correlation characteristics have been recognized in the analysis as Durbin Watson is 1.915 which should vary from 1.5 to 2.5.

Model	Un-standardized Co-efficient		Standardized Co-efficient	t	Sig	Co-linearity tolerance
	B	STD Error	Beta			
Constant	3.853	0.058		66.681	0.001	
Safety	0.115	0.058	0.125	1.973	0.051	1.00
Liquidity	0.008	0.058	-0.009	-0.143	0.885	1.00
Profitability	0.578	0.058	0.688	9.948	0.001	1.00

*The Author

Table 9 shows beta value of 0.688 which is highest standardized one relating to profitability. The given t-value is 9.948. It can be interpreted that there is a significant effect of profitability on Investors' Satisfaction. Liquidity (FDA) is significant too to the dependent variable i.e. financial satisfaction that has a t-value of -0.009. All the variance Influence Factors are below 2 that states low multi-co linearity in the model.

Table 11. ANOVA

Model	Sum of Squares	df	Mean Square	F	Sig
Regression	50.691	5	13.101	37.998	000
Residual	32.134	98	0.329		
Total	83.795	103			

*The Author

ANOVA result in table 10 shows an F –value of 37.998 and its related p-value is put forth as 0.000 < 0.05. So, fitting of multiple regression model is hence confirmed.

Along with ANOVA result, Tukey's test for output reliability is shown below.

Table 12. Tukey's test (output for reliability)

A. District Name	B. District Name	A-B (Mean Difference)	Std. Error	Sig	95% Confidence Interval	
					Lower Bound	Upper Bound
District$_1$	District$_2$ District$_3$	-1.271 3.787	.450 .450	.016 .000	-2.32 .76	-.21 4.89
District$_2$	District$_1$ District$_3$	1.271 5.084	.450 .450	.016 .000	.21 4.03	2.32 6.16
District$_3$	District$_1$ District$_2$	-3.827 -5.084	.450 .450	.000 .000	-4.89 -6.16	-2.76 -4.01

*Mean difference is significant at 0.05 level

FINDINGS AND THE PROPOSED MODEL

Having analyzed the above cited research works, for the present paper three determinants of investor satisfaction are identified. They are safety, liquidity and profitability of financial products. Having explored a wide list of factors, both internal and external, in this present study a model is proposed where in a framework that is being used in this work exploring financial satisfaction linking them with safety, liquidity and profitability. The following model depicts each determinant of financial satisfaction.

The following proposed model makes an attempt to explain the link of all these factors with financial satisfaction.

The Model

Investors' satisfaction is a multidimensional state of perception. Based on the survey, the present comprehensive research work proposes a model of satisfaction from respected outcomes from investment. An original model is proposed, which justifies the research topic of this study, as a result of the substantial literature survey pertaining to the stated objectives and the findings of this study

An in-depth analysis into an investor's alternative avenues of investment finds that the simple and basic aspects really play a great role in personal money management and investment strategies. Because investments are characterized by certain features. Though seems simple, safety and liquidity are two major features of an investment and every investor has that expectations from their money management (Peng, 2022)

Figure 1. SLP Approach leads to Investor Satisfaction
The Author

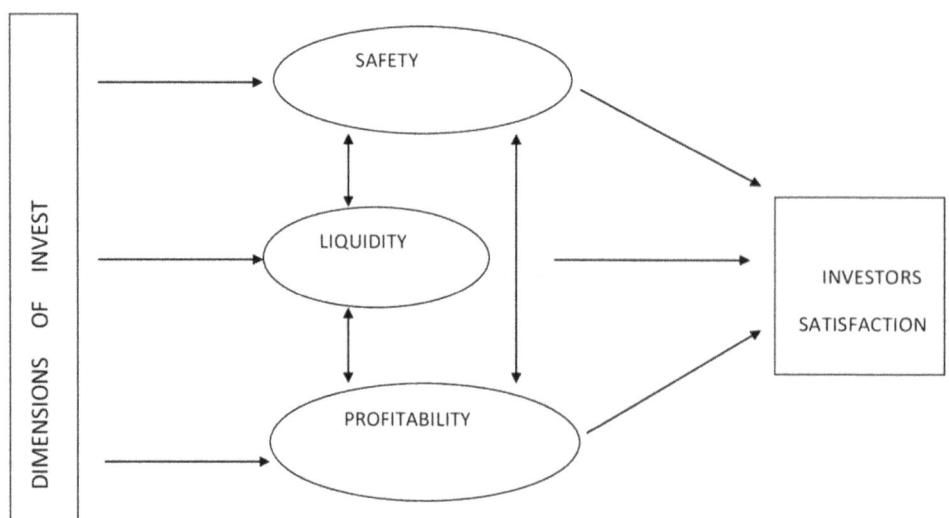

Discussion

Investors always seek the assurances in form of safety, liquidity, and profitability (return) from any financial products that are used as modes for investment. Considering the result extracted by using suitable statistical tools, it can be stated that safety is highly positively correlated with liquidity while liquidity is highly negatively correlated with profitability or return. The reason can be interpreted as liquidity obstructs the process of investment.

Financial Market is the largest sector of the nation with growing market pace, investor needs and innovative financial instruments. So, it leads to proper planning and adoption of suitable strategies for investors to put their hard-earned money. Financial Instruments deal with the crucial factors of investment and they are risk and return. This sensitivity leads to carefully consider the factors that affect or contribute to investor satisfaction in today's cutthroat competitive market. In view of the identified determinants of Investor Satisfaction, the present study proposes a model linking them all in one framework.

The primary and the indispensable factor being safety of the investment helps the investor to understand the market mechanism, features of financial instruments, their level of risk and the range of returns offered by them. Moreover, this understanding helps the investors to select suitable financial instruments for investment (Ahrholdt et al., 2017). But it must be followed by proper financial decision-making ability. For that effective financial attitude is needed. Interest to manage money related affairs and proper planning for a secured future are parts of financial attitude. It is possible only after the investor is financial literate and has the skill to take proper money related decision. All these above steps lead to financial wellbeing where a person can fully meet current and ongoing financial obligations can feel secure in their financial future and is able to make choices that allow them to enjoy life (Diener and Biswas-Diener, 2002). The last phase of the discussed steps is the goal of financial satisfaction where the investor is free from the fear of uncertain future and has a monetary secured future.

Managerial Implications

The above discussion related to outcomes of the present research work is three dimensional in nature. It is helpful for financial institutions offering financial products, investors as well as researchers. Financial institutions can adopt strategies and plan designing their financial products by considering the SLP approach explained in the paper. The targeted investors can be benefitted by understanding the basic requisites of personal investment strategies and identify each of these aspects in their selected investment alternative. SLP approach would help them in understanding the fundamental criteria required to meet the goal of financial planning and thus assist them to reach at the point of investor satisfaction where they take the optimum utilization of the financial instruments. It would create a positive reinforcement in their mind towards investment. Future practitioners and researchers can be benefitted by further exploring the approach empirically in a structured manner considering its practical implications.

Limitations of the Study

Though the current research work provides a strong conceptual, model and empirical based background to the findings and discussion part, yet few limitations cannot be avoided. The sample size and the locations are limited for the study and hence it can be increased further in future research works. Because of lack of some robust literatures, some variables on the relationship between investor satisfactions could not be established.

CONCLUSION

For the sake of examining the influence of selected determinants upon Investors' Satisfaction, the present study made an attempt to go through different research works in this context. Three determinants are identified and selected for the study. They are safety, liquidity, and profitability. The study reveals that all these three determinants affect investors' financial satisfaction, and they show a significant positive relation with the dependent variable. This study contributes in a number of ways. First, the study concludes that investor satisfaction is a valuable intangible asset that is primarily produced by the financial instrument's safety, security, and liquidity features. Second, the outcome offers a fresh insight into the relationship between investor pleasure and the safety, liquidity, and profitability of financial products using the SLP technique. Through a favorable correlation between the dependent variable (Investor satisfaction) and the independent variables, the study establishes a significant association (safety, liquidity and profitability). The study's findings indicate that financial product marketers must ensure the security of investment main amounts, investor funds' liquidity, and profitability in terms of favorable returns to investors. No investment decision is free from risk. Therefore, the investment decision making process is based on two major aspects: (a) a future financial goal with an expected return and a perfect time to invest (b) adverse market condition, risk and attitude of investor with correct state of mind (Allgood & Walstad 2013). Risk being the measurable uncertainty compels the investor to go through a difficult emotional phase that affects the investment process in pursuit of satisfaction. So, while exploring the goal of investor satisfaction, marketers of financial products should analyze investment risks from the viewpoint of an investor. Behavioral Finance suggests they should be addressed from the cognitive study angle so that the financial institutions being in the position of marketers of financial products can accurately check the pulse of investor satisfaction that may help them in acquiring more customer (investor) base. Having examined all the determinants of investor satisfaction it can be safely concluded that satisfaction from investment not only needs efficient money management skill but also basic knowledge in finance, proper attitude towards investment and meaningful understanding about one's risk return appetite. Thus, the present work contributes towards the strategy adopted by the financial institutions to achieve the goal of one's financial satisfaction by considering the determinants and their impact so that it can be a win-win situation for both financial institutions and investors. However, there is still room left for further research in this particular area that may put more lights on various other factors influencing investors' decision-making ability as well as investors' satisfaction.

REFERENCES

Ahrholdt, D. C., Gudergan, S. P., & Ringle, C. M. (2017). Enhancing service loyalty: The roles of delight, satisfaction, and service quality. *Journal of Travel Research*, 56(4), 436–450. doi:10.1177/0047287516649058

Allgood, S., & Walstad, W. (2013). Financial literacy and credit card behaviors: A cross-sectional analysis by age. *Numeracy*, 6(2), 1–26. doi:10.5038/1936-4660.6.2.3

Arathy, B., Aswathy, A. N., Anju, S. P., & Pravitha, N. R. (2015). A study on factors affecting investment on mutual fund and its preference of retail investors. *International Journal of Scientific and Research Publication, 5*(8), 1–4.

Barnes, D. C., Ponder, N. P., & Dugar, K. (2011). Investigating the key routes to customer delight. *Journal of Marketing Theory and Practice, 19*(4), 357–373. doi:10.2753/MTP1069-6679190401

Bhusan, P., & Medury, Y. (2014). An Empirical Analysis of Inter Linkages between Financial Attitude, Financial Behaviour and Financial Knowledge of salaried individuals. *Indian Journal of Commerce and Management Studies, 5*(3), 58–64.

Chen, H., & Volpe, R. P. (1998). An analysis of personal financial literacy among college students. *Financial Services Review, 7*(2), 107–128. doi:10.1016/S1057-0810(99)80006-7

Diener, E., & Biswas-Diener, R. (2002). Will money increase subjective well-being? *Social Indicators Research, 57*(2), 119–169. doi:10.1023/A:1014411319119

Easterlin, R. A. (2006). Life cycle happiness and its sources: Intersections of psychology, economics, and demography. *Journal of Economic Psychology, 27*(4), 463–482. doi:10.1016/j.joep.2006.05.002

Frey, B. S., & Stutzer, A. (2000). Happiness, economy, and institutions. *Economic Journal (London), 110*(466), 918–938. doi:10.1111/1468-0297.00570

Garrett, S., & James, R. N. III. (2013). Financial ratios and perceived household financial satisfaction. *Journal of Financial Therapy, 4*(1), 39–62. doi:10.4148/jft.v4i1.1839

Grable, J. E., Cupples, S., Fernatt, F., & Anderson, N. (2013). Evaluating the link between perceived income adequacy and financial satisfaction: A resource deficit hypothesis approach. *Social Indicators Research, 114*(3), 1109–1124. doi:10.100711205-012-0192-8

Hicks, J. M., Page, T. J., Behe, B. K., Dennis, J. H., & Fernandez, R. T. (2005). What Delighted customers buy? *Journal of Consumer Satisfaction, Dissatisfaction & Complaining Behavior, 18*, 94–104.

Hira, T. K., & Mugenda, O. M. (1998). Predictors of financial satisfaction: Differences between retirees and non-retirees. *Financial Counseling and Planning, 9*(2), 75–84.

Joo, S., & Grable, J. E. (2004). An exploratory framework of the determinants of financial satisfaction. *Journal of Family and Economic Issues, 25*(1), 25–50. doi:10.1023/B:JEEI.0000016722.37994.9f

Krishnan, R., & Booker, M. (2002). Investor's Use of Analysts' Recommendations. *Behavioral Research in Accounting, 14*(1), 129–158. doi:10.2308/bria.2002.14.1.129

Loureiro, S. M. C., Miranda, F. J., & Breazeale, M. (2014). Who needs delight? The greater impact of value, trust and satisfaction in utilitarian, frequent-use retail. *Journal of Service Management, 25*(1), 101–124. doi:10.1108/JOSM-06-2012-0106

Magnini, V. P., Crotts, J. C., & Zehrer, A. (2011). Understanding customer delight: An application of travel-blog analysis. *Journal of Travel Research, 50*(5), 535–545. doi:10.1177/0047287510379162

Oliver, R. (1996). *Satisfaction: a Behavior Perspective on the Consumer*. McGraw-Hill.

Peng, C. (2022). Investor sentiment, customer satisfaction and stock returns. *European Journal of Marketing*, *49*(5), 827–850.

Plagnol, A. C. (2011). Financial satisfaction over the life course: The influence of assets and liabilities. *Journal of Economic Psychology*, *32*(1), 45–64. doi:10.1016/j.joep.2010.10.006

Robb, C., Babiarz, P., Woodyard, A., & Seay, M. (2015). Bounded rationality and use of alternative financial services. *The Journal of Consumer Affairs*, *49*(2), 407–435. doi:10.1111/joca.12071

Rutkowska, A. (2022). *Investors' satisfaction in portfolio selection problem.* Conference paper. 10.2991/ifsa-eusflat-15.2015.23

Shoba, T. S., & Suman, C. (2017). Psychological Factors Contributing to the Financial Wellbeing of an Individual: A Review of Empirical Literature. *Indian Journal of Finance*, *11*(10), 51–65. doi:10.17010/ijf/2017/v11i10/118775

Compilation of References

Abbasi-Moghaddam, M. *A., Zarei, E., Bagherzade*h, *R.*, Dargahi, H., & Farrokhi, P. (2019). Evaluation of service quality from patients' viewpoint. Academic Press.

Abhijith, M., & Remya Vivek, M. (2018). Study on Customer *Satisfac*tion in Indian Banking Sector. International Journal of Pure and Applied Mathematics, 118(20), 4297–1302. http://www.ijpam.eu

Abraham, M. (2018) Apathy: Anxiety's Unusual Symptom. CalmClinic. https://www.calmclinic.com/anxiety/apathy

Acar, O. A., & Punton*i, S. (2016). Custome*r empowerment in the digital age. Journal of Advertising Research, 56(1), 4–8. doi:10.2501/JAR-2016-007

Accenture. (2016a). Global Fintech investment growth continues in 2016 driven by Europe and Asia, Accenture study finds. Available at https://newsroom.accenture.com/news/ global-Fintech-investme nt growth-continues-in-2016- drivenby- europe-and-asia-accen ture-study-finds.htm

Achille, A., & Zipser, D. (2020), A perspective for the luxury-goods industry during and after coronavirus. McKinsey & Company, https://www.m*ckinsey.com/ industries/retail/our-in*sights/a-perspective-for-the-luxury-goods-industry-during-and-after-coronavirus

Agnihotri, R., Rapp, A., & Trainor, K. (2009). Understanding the role of information communication in the buyer-seller exchan*ge process: Antecedents and out*comes. Journal of Business and Industrial Marketing, 24(7), 474–486. doi:10.1108/08858620910986712

Agolla, J. *E., Makara, T., & Monamet*si, G. (2018). Impact of banking innovations on customer attraction, satisfaction and retention: The case of commercial banks in Botswana. International Journal of Electronic Banking, 1(2), 150–170. doi:10.1504/IJEBANK.2018.095598

Agrawal, S. (2019). Effect of Governance, Piracy, and Investment on OTT Subscription Numbers [Doctoral dissertation]. *The Ohio State University.*

Ahmad, A. E. M. K., & Al-Zu'bi, H. A. (2011). E-banking functionality and outcomes of customer satisfa*ction: an em-pirical* investigation. International journal of marketing studies, 3(1), 50-65.

Ahmed, H. (2002). Financing Microenterprises : An Analytical Study of Islamic Microfinance Institutions. Islamic Economic Studies, 9(2), 27–64. *http://www.isdb.org/irj/go/km*/docs/documents/IDBDevelopments /Internet/English/IRTI/CM/downloads/IES_Articles/Vol 9-2.Hab ib Ahmed.Financing Microenterprises.dp.pdf

Ahmed, R. R., Romeika, G., Kauliene, R., Streimikis, J., & Dapkus, R. (2020). ES-QUAL model and customer satisfaction in online banking: Evidence from multivariate analysis techniques. Oeconomia Copernicana, 11(1), 59–93. doi:10.24136/oc.2020.003

Ahmed, S. M., Ahmad, K., & Jan, M. T. (2017). The impact of service quality on customer satisfaction and customer loyalty: An empirical study on Islamic banks in Bahrain. VFAST *Transaction of Education and Social Science, 5*(1), 39–47.

Ahrholdt, D. C., Gudergan, S. P., & Ringle, C. M. (2017). Enhancing service loyalty: The roles of delight, satisfaction, and service quality. Journal of Travel Research, 56(4), *436–450. doi:10.1177/0047287516649058*

Ajzen, I. (1985). From intentions to actions: A theory of planned behavior. In Action control (pp. 11–39). Springer. doi:10.1007/978-3-642-69746-3_2

Ajzen, I. (1991). The theory of planned behavior. Organizational Behavior and Human Decision Processes, 50(2), 179–211. doi:10.1016/0749-5978(91)90020-T

Ajzen, I. (2006). Behavioral interventions based o*n the theory of planned behavior. UMass.*

Akossou, A. Y. J., & Palm, R. (2013). Impact Data Structure on the Estimators R-Square and Adjusted R-square in Linear Regress*ion. Interna*tional Journal of Mathematics and Computation, 20(3), 84–93.

Akroush, M. N. (2009). Does service quality implementation mediate the *relationship between* technical service quality and performance : An empirical examination of banks in Jordan. Int. J. Services. Economics and Management, 1(3), 209–232.

Al-Hawari, M. (2006). The effect of automated service quality on bank financial performance and the mediating role of customer retention. Journal of Financial Services Marketing, 10(3), 228–243. doi:10.1057/palgrave.fsm.4770189

Al-hawari, M., & Ward, T. (2006). The effect of automated *service quality on Australian banks ' financ*ial performance and the mediating role of customer satisfaction. Marketing Intelligence & Planning, 24(2), 127–147. doi:10.1108/02634500610653991

Al-Jabri*, I. M. (2015). The intention to use mobile banking: Further ev*idence *f*rom Saudi Arabia. South African Journal of Business Management, 46(1), 23–34. doi:10.*4102ajbm.v46i1.80*

*Al-Omar*i, Z., Alomari, K., & Aljawarneh, N. (2020). The role of empowerment in improving internal process, customer satisfaction, learning and growth. Management Science Letters, 10(4), 841–848. doi:10.5267/j.msl.2019.10.013

Al-Somali, S., Gholami, R., & Clegg, B. (2009). An investigation into the acceptance of online ba*nking in Saudi Arabia. Technovation, 29(2), 130–1*41. doi:10.1016/j.technovation.2008.07.004

Aladwani, A. M. (2001). Online b*anking: A field study of drivers, development challenges, and expectations*. International Journal of Information Management, 21(3), 213–225. doi:10.1016/S0268-4012(01)00011-1

Alalwan, A. A., Dwivedi, Y. K., Rana, N. P., & Algharabat, R. (20*18). Examining factors influenci*ng Jordanian customers' intentions and adoption of internet banking: Extending UTAUT2 with risk. Journal of Retailing and Consumer Services, 40, 125–138. doi:10.1016/j.jretconser.2017.08.026

Alalykin-Izvekov, V. (2017). The anatomy of a sociocultural crisis: calamities in Pitirim A. Sorokin's philosophy of history. Biocosmology –neo-Aristotelism, 7(2), 204-228.

Alam, M. M. D., & Noor, N. A. M. (2020). The relationship between service quality, corporate image, and customer loyalty of Generation Y: An application of SOR paradigm in the context of superstores in Bangladesh. SAGE Open, 10(2). doi:10.1177/2158244020924405

Alam, S. L., & Campbell, J. (2017). Temporal motivations of volunteers to participate in cultural crowdsourcing work. Informa*tion Systems Research, 28(4), 744*–759.

Alauddin, M., & Ahsan, S., Md., Mowla, M., Islam, Md., Hossain, M. (2019). Investigating the relationship between service quality, customer satisfaction and customer loyalty in the hotel industry: Bangladesh perspective. Global Journal of Management and Business Research, 19(1), 29–35.

Aldaihani, F. M. F., & Ali, N. A. B. (2018). Impact of social customer relationship management on customer satisfaction through customer empowerment: A *study of Islamic Banks in Kuwait. International Re*search Journal of Finance and Economics, 170(170), 41-53. [.

Aldaihani, F. M. F., & Ali, N. A. B. (2018). The mediating role of customer empowerment in th*e effect of relationship market*ing on customer retention: an empirical demonstration from Islamic banks in Kuwait. Europ*ean journal of eco-nomi*cs, finance and administrative sciences, 99, 42-52.

Alemayehu, A., & Dalega, D. (2019). Impact of Service Quality on Customer Satisfaction in Insurance Companies: A Study Conducted on Wolaita Zone. Journal of Marketing and Consumer Research, 63, 1–6. doi:10.7176/JMCR/63-01

Alexander Hars, S. O. *(2002). Working for free? Motivations for participating* in open-source projects. International Journal of Electronic Commerce, 6(3), 25–39.

Alharthey, B. (2019). Impact of Service Quality on Customer Trust, Purchase Intention and Store Loyalty, with Mediat-ing Role of *Customers' Satisfaction on Customer Trust and Purchase. Briti*sh Journal of Marketing Studies, 7(2), 40–61.

Ali, F., Ryu, K., & Hussain, K. (2016). Influence of experiences on memories, satisfaction and behavioral intentions: A study of creative tourism. Journal of Travel & Tourism Marketing, 33(1), 85–100. doi:10.1080/10548408.2015.1038418

Alketbi, S., A*lshurideh, M., & Al Kurdi, B. (2*020). the influence of service quality on customers'retention and loyalty in the uae hotel sector with respect to the impact of custom*er'satisfaction, trust, and com*mitment: a qualitative study. PalArch's Journal of Archaeology of Egypt/Egyptology, 17(4), 541-561.

Allgood, S., & Walstad, W. (2013). Financial literacy and credit card behaviors: A *cross-sectional analysis by age. Num*eracy, 6(2), 1–26. doi:10.5038/1936-4660.6.2.3

Almeida-Santana, A., & Moreno-Gil, S. (2018). Understanding tourism loyalty: Horizontal vs. destination loyalty. Tour-ism Management, 65, 245–255. doi:10.1016/j.tourman.2017.10.011

Almohaimmeed, B. (2019). Pillars of customer retention: An empirical study on the influence of customer satisfac-tion, customer loyalty, customer profitability on customer retention. Serbian Journal of Management, 14(2), 421–435. doi:10.5937jm14-15517

Alolayyan, M. N., Al-Hawary, S. I. S., Mohammad, A. A. S., & Al-Nady, B. A. H. A. (2018*). Banking service quality provided by com*mercial banks and customer satisfaction. A structural equation modelling approaches. Interna*tional Journal of Productivity and Qu*ality Management, 24(4), 543–565. doi:10.1504/IJPQM.2018.093454

Alsajjan, B., & Dennis, C. (2010). Internet banking acceptance model: Cross-market examination*. Journal of Business* Research, 63(9-10), 957–963. doi:10.1016/j.jbusres.2008.12.014

Alumran, A., Hou, Y. X., Sun, J., Yousef, A., & Hurst, C. (2014). Assessing the construct validity and reliability of the parental perception on antibiotics (PAPA) scales. NCBI. https://www.ncbi.nlm.nih.gov/pmc/articles/PMC3909352/

Alvesson, M., & Kärreman, D. (2007). Constructing Mystery: Empirical Matters in Theory Development. Academy *of Management Review, 32(4), 126. doi:10.5465/amr.2007.26586822*

Alwi, S. (2021). Fintech as financial *inclusion: Factors affecting behavio*ral intention to accept mobile e-wallet during Covid-19 outbreak. Turkish Journal of Computer and Mathematics Education, 12(7), 2130–2141.

Amabile, T. M. (1988). A model of creativity and innovatio*n in organizations. Research in Organizational Behavior, 10*(1), 123–167.

Amankwah, O., Choong, W., & Mohammed, A. H. (2019). Modelling the influence of healthcare facilities management service quality on patients satisfaction. doi:10.1108/JFM-08-2018-0053

American Marketing Association. (2019). Resource library dictionary: Store *image. Author.*

Amin, M. (2016). Internet banking service quality and its implication on e-customer satisfaction and e-customer loyalty. International Journal of Bank Marketing, 34(3), 280–306. doi:10.1108/IJBM-10-2014-0139

Amin, M., & Isa, Z. (2008). An examination of t*he relationship between service quality perception and customer s*atisfaction: A SEM approach towards Malaysian Islamic banking. International Journal of Islamic and Middle Eastern Finance and Management, 1(3), 1*91–209. doi:10.1108/17538390*810901131

Amoah-Mensah, A. (2010). Customer Satisfaction in the Banking Industry: a Comparative Study of Ghana and Spain. Girona. http://hdl.handle.net/10803/22657%0AADVERTIMENT

Amorim, M., & Saghezchi, F. B. (2014). An investigation of service quality assessments across retail formats. International Journal of Quality and Service Sciences, 6(2/3), 221–236. doi:10.1108/IJQSS-02-2014-*0015*

Ampah, I. T., Ali, R. S., Ampah, I. T., & Ali, R. S. (2019). Measuring Patients (Customers) Perceptions and Expectations of Service Quality in Public Healthcare Institutions: Servqual Mo*del. Academic Press.*

Anat, K., Sandrine, C., & Silvia, B. (2016). Online Luxury Retailing: Leveraging Digital Op*portunities Research. In*dustry Practice, and Open Questions.

Anderson, J., & Gerbing, D. (1988). Structural equation modelling in practice: A Review and Recommended Two-Step Approach. Psychological Bulletin, 103(3), 411–423. https://psycnet.apa.org/buy/1989-14*190-001. doi:10.1037/0033-2909.103.3.411*

*An*derson, R. E., & Srinivasan, S. S. (2003). E-satisfaction and e-loyal*ty: A contingency framework. Psycholo*gy and Marketing, 20(2), 123–138. doi:10.1002/mar.10063

Ang, I. (1998). Doing cultural studies at the crossroads: Local/global negotiations. European Journal of Cultural Studies, 1(1), 13–31. doi:10.1177/136754949800100102

Angrave, D., Charlwood, A., Kirkpatrick, I., Lawrence, M., & Stuart, M. (2016). HR and analytics: Why HR is set to fail the big data challenge. Human Resource Management Journal, 26, 1–11. http://scholar.google.com/scholar_lookup?hl=en&publication_year=2016&pages=1-11&author=D.+Angrave&author=A.+Charlwood&author=I.+Kirkpatrick&author=M.+Lawrence&author=M.+Stuart&title=HR+and+analytics%3A+Why+HR+is+set+to+fail+the+big+data+challenge

Angur, M. G., Nataraajan, R., & Jr, J. S. J. (1999). S*ervice quality in the b*anking industry : An assessment in a developing economy. International Journal of Bank Marketing, 17(3), 116–125. doi:10.1108/02652329910269211

Anifa, M., Ramakrishnan, S., Jo*ghee, S., Kabiraj, S., & Bishnoi, M. M. (2022). Fintech Innovation*s in the Financial Service Industry. Journal of Risk and Financial Management, 15(7), 287. doi:10.3390/jrfm15070287

Anselmsson, J. (2006). Sources of customer satisfaction with shopping malls: A comparative study of different customer segments. Int*ernational Review of Retail, Distri*bution and Consumer Research, 16(1), 115–138. doi:10.1080/09593960500453641

Aoki, T. (2004). Teaching as indwelling between two curriculum worlds (1986/1991). In W. Pinar & R. L. Irwin (Eds.), Curriculum in a new key: The collected works of Ted Aoki (pp. 159–165). Peter Lang. doi:10.4324/9781410611390

Aral, S., Brynjolfsson, E., & Wu, L. (2012). Three-way complementarities: Performance Pay, human resource analytics, and information technology. Management Science, 58(5), 913–931. doi:10.1287/mnsc.1110.1*460*

Arathy, B., Aswathy, A. N., Anju, S. P., & Pravitha, N. R. (2015). A study on factors affecting investment on mutual fund and its preference of retail investors. International Journal of Scientific and Research Publication, 5(8), 1–4.

Arbuckle, J. L. (2012). IBM SPSS Amos *21. Amos Development Corpor*ation.

Aria, M., & Cuccurullo, C. (2017). Bibliometrix: An R-tool for comprehensive science mapping an*alysis. Journal of Informetrics, 11(4), 959–975. doi:10.1016/j.*joi.2017.08.007

Arnold, M. J., Reynolds, K. E., Ponder, N., & Lueg, J. E. (2005). Customer delight in a retail context: Investigating delightful and terrible shopping experiences. Journal of Business Research, 58(8), 1132–1145. doi:10.1016/j.jbusres.2004.01.0*06*

Arokiasamy, A., & Tat, H. (2014). Assessing the Relationship between Service Quality and Customer Satisfaction in the Malaysian Automotive Insurance Industry. Middle E*ast Journal of Scientific Researc*h, *20*(9), 1023–1030. doi:10.5829/idosi.mejsr.2014.20.09.12029

Attri, M. (2014). An empirical study on levels of customer satisfaction with retail service quality in a marketing haat. F*IIB Business Review, 3(2), 46–56. doi:10.1177/2455265820140209*

Auh, S., Menguc, B., Katsikeas, C. S., & Jung, Y. S. (2019). When *does customer parti*cipation matter? An empirical investigation of the role of customer empowerment in the customer participation–performance link. JMR, Journal of Marketing Research, 56(6), 1012–1033. doi:10.1177/0022243*719866408*

Awan, H. M., Bukhari, K. S., & Iqbal, A. (2011). Service quality and customer satisfaction in the banking sector: A comparative study of conventional and Islamic banks in Pakistan. Journal of Islamic Marketin*g.*

Awang, Z. (2012). Structural Equation Modeling Using Amos Graphic. Penerbit Universiti Teknologi MARA.

Ayadi, R., Arbak, E., Naceur, S. B., & De Groen, W. P. (2015). Financial development, *bank efficiency, a*nd e*c*onomic growth across the Mediterranean. In Economic and Social Development of the Southern and Eastern Mediterranean Countries. Springer International Publishing.

Baabdullah, A. M., Alalwan, *A. A., Rana, N. P., Kizgin, H., & Patil, P.* (2019). Consumer use of mobile banking (M-Banking) in Saudi Arabia: Towards an integrated model. International Journal of Informatio*n Managem*ent, 44, 38–52. doi:10.1016/j.ijinfomgt.2018.09.002

Babakus, E. and Boller, G.W. (1992) An Empirical Assessment of the SERVQUAL Scale. Journal of Business Research, 24, 253-268.

Baber, H. (2019). Financial inclusion and FinTech: A comparative study of countrie*s following Islamic finance and conventional finance. Qualitative Research i*n Financial Markets. doi:10.1108/QRFM-12-2018-0131

Bagchi, B., Chatterjee, S., Ghosh, R., & Dan*dapat, D. (*2020). Impact of COVID-19 on global economy. In Coronavirus Outbreak and the Great Lockdown. Springer Briefs in Economics. Springer. doi:10.1007/978-981-15-7782-6_3

Bagozzi, R. P., & Yi, Y. (1988). On the Evaluation of Structural Equation Models. Journal of the Academy of Marketing Science, 16(1), 74–94. doi:10.1007/BF02723327

Bagozzi, R. P., Gopinath, M., and Nyer, P., U. (1999), The Role of Emotions in Marketing. Journal of *the Academy of Market*eting Science, 27(2), 184-206.

Bahadori, M., Teymourzadeh, E., Faizy Bagejan, F., Ravangard, R., Raadabadi, M., & Hosseini, S. M. (2018). Fac*tors affecting the effectiveness of quality cont*rol circles in a hospital using a combination of fuzzy VIKOR and Grey Relational Analysis. Pr*oceedings of Singapore Healthcare, 27(3), 180–186. doi:10.1177/2010105818758088*

Bahadur, W., Aziz, S., & Zulfiqa, S. (2018). Effect of employee empathy on customer satisfaction and loyalty during employee–customer interactions: The mediating role of customer affective comm*itment and perceived service quality. Cogent Business & Management, 5(1), 1–21. doi*:10.1080/23311975.2018.1491780

Bahman, S. P., Nazari, K. & M. E. (2013). The effect of marketing mix in attracting *custome*rs: Case study of Saderat Bank in Kermanshah Province. AJBM, 7(34), 3272-3280,.

Bai, B., Law, R., & Wen, I. (2008). The impact of website quality on customer satisfaction and purchase intentions: Evidence from Chinese online visitors. International Jour*nal of Hospitality Managemen*t, 27(3), 391–402. doi:10.1016/j.ijhm.2007.10.008

Baines, P., Fill, C., & Rosengren, S. (2017). Marketing (4th ed.). Oxford University *Press.*

Bala, N., Sandhu, H., & Nagpal, N. (2011). Measuring Life Insurance Service Quality: An Empirical Assessment of SERVQUAL Instrument. International Business Research, 4(4), 176–190. doi:10.5539/ibr.v4n4p176

Balach*andran, I., & Hamzah, I. B. (2017). T*he influence of customer satisfaction on ride-sharing services in Malaysia. International Journal of Accou*nting and Business* Management, 5(2), 184–196. https://ftms.edu.my/journals/pdf/IJABM/Nov2017/184-196.pdf

Ballantyne, D., & Varey, R. J. (2006). Creating value-in-use thro*ugh marketing interaction: The e*xchange logic of relating, communicating and knowing. Marketing Theory, 6(3), 335–348.

Bansawl, H. S., Irving, P. G., & Taylor, S. F. (2004). A three-component model of customer commitment to service providers. Journal *of the Academy of Marketing Sci*ence, 32(3), 234–245. doi:10.1177/0092070304263332

Bao, Y., Bao, Y., & Sheng, S. (2011). Motivating purchase of private brands: Effects of store image, product signatureness, and quality variation*. Journal of Business Research, 64(2)*, 220–226. doi:10.1016/j.jbusres.2010.02.007

Bapat, D. (2017). Explor*ing the antecedents of loyalty in the context of multi-channel ba*nking. International Journal of Bank Marketing, 35(2), 174–186. doi:10.1108/IJBM-10-2015-0155

Baporikar, N. (2021). FinTech Challenges and Outlook in India. In Innovative Strategies for Impleme*nting FinTech in Bank*ing (pp. 136-153). IGI Global. doi:10.4018/978-1-7998-3257-7.ch008

*Barends, E., R*ousseau, D. M., & Briner, R. B. (2014). Evidence-based management: The basic principles. *Amsterdam: Center for Evidence-Based Managemen*t. http://scholar.google.com/scholar_lookup?hl=en&publication_year=2014&author=E.+Barends&author=D.+M.+Rousseau&author=R.+B.+Briner&title=Evidence-based+management%3A+The+basic+principles

Barnard, J. (2017). The Role of Comparative Law in Consumer Protection Law: A South African Perspective. South Africa Mercantile Law Journal.

Barnes, D. C., Beauchamp, M. B., & Webster, C. (2010). To delight, or not to delight? This is the que*stion service firms must* address. Journal of Marketing Theory and Practice, 18(3), 275–284. doi:10.2753/MTP1069-6679180305

Barnes, D. C., Ponder, N., & *Dugar, K. (20*11). Investigating the key routes to customer delight. Journal of Marketing Theory and Practice, 19(4), 359–376. doi:10.2753/MTP1069-6679190401

Barnes, S., & Vidgen, R. (2002). An Integra*tive Approach to the Assessment of E-Co*mmerce Quality. Journal of Electronic Commerce Research, 3, 114–127.

Bartlett, M. S. (1950). Tests of significance in factor analysis. British Journal of Psychology, 3(2), 77–85.

Bartlett, M. S. (1951). The effect of stand*ardization on a Chi-square a*pproximation in factor analysis. Biometrika, 38(3/4), 337–344. doi:10.2307/2332580

Baruh, L., Secinti, E., & Cemalcilar, Z. (2017). Online priv*acy concerns and privac*y ma*n*agement: A meta-analytical review. Journal of Communication, 67(1), 26–53. doi:10.1111/jcom.12276

Bassi, L. (2011). Raging debates in HR Analytics. People & Strategy, 34, 14–18. https://scholar.google.*com/scholar_ lookup?hl=en&pub*lica*tion_year=2011&pages= 14-18&author=L.+Bassi&title=Raging+debates +in+HR+Analytics

Basu, A. (2019). Viability assessment of emerging smart urban p*ara-transit solutio*ns*:* Case of cab aggregators in Kolkata city, India. Journal of Urban Management, 8(3), 364–376. doi:10.1016/j.jum.2019.01.002

Bauer, H. H., Falk, T., & Hammerschmidt, M. (2006). eTransQual: A transaction p*rocess-based approach for ca*pturing service quality in online shopping. Journal of Business Research, 59(7), 866–875. doi:10.1016/j.jbusres.2006.01.021

Baumann, C., Hoadley, S., Hamin, H., & Nugraha, A. (2017). Competitiveness vis-à-vis *service quality as* drivers of customer loyalty mediated by perceptions of regulation and stability in steady and volatile markets. Journal of Retailing and Consumer Services, 36, 62–74. *doi:10.1016/j.jretconser.2016.12.005*

Beckers, S. F., van Doorn, J., & Verhoef, P. C. (2017). Good, better, engaged? The effect of company-initiated customer engagement beha*vior on shareholder value. Jo*urnal of the Academy of Marketing Science, 45(3), 1–18.

Behdioğlu, S., Acar, E., & Burhan, H. A. (2019). Evaluating service quality by fuzzy SERVQU*AL: A case study in a physiothe*ra*py* and rehabilitation hospital. Total Quality Management & Business Excellence, 30(3–4), 301–319. doi:1 0.1080/14783363.2017.1302796

Be*langer, F., Hiller, J. S., & Smith,* W. J. (2002). Trustworthiness in electronic commerce: The role of privacy, security, and site attributes. The Journal of Strategic Information Systems, 11(3-4), 245–270. doi:10.1016/S0963-8687(02)00018-5

Bellou, V., & Andronikidis, A. (2008). The impact of internal service quality on customer service behaviour: Evidence from the banking sector. International Journal of Quality & Reliability M*anagement, 25(9), 943–954. doi:10.1108/02656710810908098*

Bente, C. (2011). Service Quality in Insurance Companie*s. The Annals of the* University of Oradea. Economic Sciences. http://anale.steconomiceuoradea.ro/volume/2021/n1/018.pdf

Berger, A. N., & Bouwman, C. H. (2009). Bank liquidity creation. Review of Financial Studies, 22(9), 3779–3837. doi:10.1093/rfs/hhn104

Berman, B. (2005). How to delight your customers. California Management Review, *48(1), 129–151. doi:10.2307/41166331*

Bernard, J. (2015). Consumer rights of the elderly as vulnerable consumers in South Africa: Some comparative aspects of the Consumer Protection Act (68 of 2008). International Journal of Consumer Studies, *39(3), 223–229. doi:10.1111/ ijcs.12170*

*Bernar*di, R. A. (1994). Validating Research Results when Cronbach'S Alpha is Below. 70: A Methodological Procedure. Educational and Psychological Measurement, 54(3), 766–775. doi:10.1177/0013*164494054003023*

*Berraies, S., & Ha*mouda, M. (2018). Customer empowerment and firms' performance: The mediating effects of innovation and customer satisfaction. International Journal of Bank Marketing, 36(2), 336–356. doi:10.1108/IJBM-10-2016-0150

Berry, L. L., Seiders, K., & Grewal, D. (2002). Understanding Service Convenience / 1 Understanding Service Convenience. Journal of Marketing, 66(3)*, 1–17. doi:10.1509/jmkg.66.3.1.*18505

Bhat, I. H. (2016). Validating a retail service quality instrument in grocery specialty stores. International Journal of Information, Business and *Management, 8(2), 205.*

Bhatiasevi, V. (2016). An extended UTAUT model to explain the adoption of mobile banking. Information Development, 32(4), 799–814. doi:10.1177/0266666915570764

Bhatt, K. (2020). Measuring service fairness and its impact on service quality and satisfaction: A study of Indian Banking Services. Journal of Financial Services Marketing, 25(1-2), 35–44. doi:10.105741264-020-00069-7

Bhattacherjee, A. (2001). Understa*nding information sys*tems continuance: An expectation-confirmation model. Management Information Systems Quarterly, 25(3), 351–370. doi:10.2307/3250921

Bhattacherjee, A. (2012). Social science research: Princip*les, methods, and practices.* CreateSpace Independent Publishing Platform.

Bhullar, A., & Chaudhary, R. (2020). Key factors influencing users' adoption towards OTT media platform: A*n empirical analysis. Int. J. Adv. Sci. T*echnol., 29(11), 942–956.

Bhusan, P., & Medury, Y. (2014). An Empirical Analysis of Inter Linkages between Financial Attitude, Financial Behaviour and Financial Knowledge of salaried individuals. Indian Journal *of Commerce and Management Studies, 5(3), 58–64.*

Bitner, M. J. (2010). Service scapes: The impact of physical surroundings on customers and employees. Journal of Marketing, 57–71.

Bitner, M.J., & Hubbert, A.R. (1994). Encounter Satisfa*ction versus Overall Satisfacti*on versus Quality: The Customer's Voice. Boulton and Drew.

Bitner, M. J., Booms, B. H., & Tetreau*lt, M. S. (1990). The service encounter: Di*agnosing favorable and unfavorable incidents. Journal of Marketing, 54(1), 71–84. doi:10.1177/002224299005400105

Blessinger, P., & Carfora, J. M. (2015). Innovative approaches in teaching and learning: An introduction to inquiry-based learning for multidisciplinary programs. In P. Blessinger & J. M. Carfora (Eds.), Inquiry-Based Learning for Multidisciplinary Programs: A Conc*eptual and Practical Resource for Educators (p*p. 3–22). Emerald Group Publishing Limited. doi:10.1108/S2055-364120150000003001

Blut, M. (2016). E-service quality: Development of a hierarchical model. Journal of Retailing, 92(4), 500–517. doi:*10.1016/j.jretai.2016.09.002*

*Blut, M., Cho*wd*hr*y, N., Mittal, V., & Brock, C. (2015). E-service quality: A meta-analytic review. Journal of Retailing, 91(4), 679–700. doi:10.1016/j.jretai.2015.05.004

Boateng, H., Adam, D. R., Okoe, A. F., & Anning-Dorson, T. (2016). Assessing the determinants of internet banking adoption intentions: A social cognitive theory perspective. Computers in Human Behavior, 65, *468–478. doi:10.1016/j. chb.20*16.09.017

Boateng, H., Kosiba, J. P. B., & Okoe, A. F. (2019). Determinants of consumers' participation in the sharing economy. International Journal of Contemporary Hospitality Management, 31(2), 718–733. doi:10.1108/IJCHM-11-2017-0731

Bobier, J. F., Merey, T., Robnett, S., Grebe, M., Feng, J., Rehberg, B., & Hazan, J. (2022). The Corporate Hitchhiker's guide to the metaverse. Boston Consulting Group.

Boldor, N., Bar-Dayan, Y., Rosenbloom, T., Shemer, J., & Bar-Dayan, Y. (2012). Optimism of health care workers during a disaster: A review of the literature. Emerging Health Threats Journal, 5(1), 7270. doi:10.3402/ehtj.v5i0.7270 PMID:22461847

Bolton, R. N., Lemon, K. N., & Verhoef, P. C. (2004). The theoretical underpinnings of customer asset management: A framework and propositions for future research. Journal of the Academy of Marketing Science, 32(3), 271–292. doi:10.1177/0092070304263341

Bonchek, M., & France, C. (2016). Build your brand as a relationship. Harvard Business Review, 5, 1–6. https://hbr.org/2016/05/build-your-brand-as-a-relationship

Boon-itt, S. (2015). Managing self-service technology service quality to enhance e-satisfaction. International Journal of Quality and Service Sciences, 7(4), 373–391. doi:10.1108/IJQSS-01-2015-0013

Boons, M., Stam, D., & Barkema, H. G. (2015). Feelings of pride and respect as drivers of ongoing member activity on crowdsourcing platforms. Journal of Management Studies, 52(6), 717–741.

Bose, S., & Gupta, N. (2013). Customer Perception of Services Based on the SERVQUAL Dimensions: A Study of Indian Commercial Banks. Services Marketing Quarterly, 34(1), 49–66. doi:10.1080/15332969.2013.739941

Boudreau, J. W. (2010). Retooling HR. Harvard Business Publishing. https://scholar.google.com/scholar_lookup?hl=en&publication_year=2010&author=J.+W.+Boudreau&title=Retooling+HR

Boudreau, J. W. (2012). Decision logic in evidence-based management: Can logical models from other disciplines improve evidence-based human resource decisions? In D. Rousseau (Ed.), The Oxford handbook of evidence-based management (pp. 223–248). Oxford University Press. https://scholar.google.com/scholar_lookup?hl=en&publication_year=2012&pages=223-248&author= J.+W.+Boudreau&title=Decision+logic+in+evidence-based+management%3A+Can+logical+models+from+other+disciplines+improve+ evidence-based+human+resource+decisions%3F doi:10.1093/oxfordhb/9780199763986.013.0013

Boudreau, J. W., & Ramstad, P. M. (2007). Beyond HR: The new science of human capital. Harvard Business School Pub. http://scholar.google.com/scholar_lookup?hl=en&publication_year=2007&author=J.+W.+Boudreau&author=P.+M.+ Ramstad&title =Beyond+HR%3A+The+new+ science+of+human+capital

Boudreau, K. J., & Lakhani, K. R. (2013). Using the crowd as an innovation partner. Harvard Business Review, 91(4), 60–69.

Braber, S. (2016). Security and privacy perceptions of Millennials (18-24) and Non-Millennials (36-50) on Facebook [Bachelor's thesis, University of Twente].

Brabham, D. C. (2008). Crowdsourcing as a model for problem solving: An introduction and cases. Convergence, 14(1), 75–90.

Brabham, D. C. (2010). Moving the crowd at Threadless: Motivations for participation in a crowdsourcing application. Information Communication and Society, 13(8), 1122–1145.

Brady, M. K., & Robertson, C. J. (2001). Searching for a consensus on the antecedent role of service quality and satisfaction: An *exploratory cross-national* study. Journal of Business Research, 51(1), 53–60. doi:10.1016/S0148-2963(99)00041-7

Broadus, R. (1987). Toward a definition of "bibliometrics.". Scientometrics, 12(5–6), 373–379. doi:10.1007/BF02016680

Brown, J. *(2002). The Cronbach alpha reliability estimate. Shiken:JALT Testing & Eval*uation SIG Newsletter, 6 (1), 17-19. https://hosted.jalt.org/test/bro_13.htm

Brown, R. D. (2001). E-commerce: Customer service success factors. Futurics, 25(3/4), 18.

Brown, T., Park, A., & Pitt, L. (2020). A 60-year bibliographic review of the Journal of Advertising Research: Per-s*pectives on trends in authorship, influences, and resear*ch impact. Journal of Advertising Research, 60(4), 353–360. doi:10.2501/JAR-2020-028

Browne, M. W., & Cudeck, R. (1989). Single sample cross-validation indices for covariance structures. Multivaria*te Behavioral Research, 24(4), 445–455. doi:10.1*20715327906mbr2404_4 PMID:26753509

Brownlee, J. (2019, November 5). A Gentle Introduction to Maximum Likelihood Estimation for Machine Learning. Machine Learning Mastery. https://machinelearningmastery.com/what-is-maximum-likelihoo d-estimation-in-machine-learning/

Bruning, R., Schraw, G., & Ronning, R. (1999). Cognitive psychology and instruction. Prentice Hall.

Bryant, A. (2011, M*arch 12). Google's 8-point plan to h*elp managers improve. The New York Times. https://www. nytimes.com/2011/03/13/business/13hire.html https://scholar.google.*com/scholar_lookup?hl=en&publicat*ion_year=2 011&author=A.+Bryant&title=Google %E2%80%99s+8-point+plan+to+help+managers+improve

Budiwan, V., & Efendi. (2016). The understanding of Indonesian Patients of Hospital Service Quality in Singapore. Procedia: Social and Behavioral Sciences, 224, 176–183. doi:10.1016/j.sbspro.2016.05.436

Bulgurcu, B., Cavusoglu, H., & Benbasat, I. (2010, January). Qualit*y and fairness of an information se*curity policy as antecedents of employees' security engagement in the workplace: An empirical investigation. In 2010 43rd Hawaii International Conference on System Sciences, (pp. 1-7). *IEEE.*

Bults, M., Beaujean, D. J. M. A., de Zwart, O., Kok, G., van Empelen, P., van Steenbergen, J. E., & Voeten, H. A. C. M. (2011). Perceived ris*k, anxiety, and behavioural res*pons*e*s of the general public during the early phase of the Influenza A (H1N1) pandemic in the Netherlands: Results of three consecutive online surveys. BMC Public Health, *11(1), 2. doi:10.1186/1471-2458*-11-2 PMID:21199571

Burks, D. M. (1966). Psychological egoism and the rhetorical tradition. Speech Monographs, 33(4), 400–418. doi:10.1080/03637756609375507

Burnham, T. A., Frels, J. K., & Mahajan, V. (2003). Consumer s*witching costs: A typology, a*ntece*d*ents, and consequences. Journal of the Academy of Marketing Science, 31(2), 109–126. doi:10.1177/0092070302250897

*Burns, A. C., V*eeck, A., & Bush, R. F. (2017). Marketing Research (8th Global Edition). Pearson Education Limited.

Burns, D. J., & Neisner, L. (2006). Customer satisfaction in a retail setting: The contribution of emotion. International Journal of Retail & Distribution Management, 34(1), 49–66. doi:10.1108/09590550610642819

Bussakorn, J., & Dieter, F. (2005). Internet banking adoption strategies for a developing country: The case of Thailand. Internet Research, 15(3), 295–311. doi:10.1108/10662240510602708

Butt, I., Ahmad, N., Naveed, A., *& Ahmed, Z. (2018).* Determinants of low adoption of Islamic banking in Pakistan. Journal of Islamic Marketing, 9(3), 655–672. doi:10.1108/JIMA-01-2017-0002

Calabrese, R., Girardone, C., & Sun, M. (2017). Access to Bank Credit: The Role of Awareness of Government Initiatives for UK SME*s*. *Financial Markets, SME Financing, and Emerging Economies*, *(J*anuary), 5–20. Advance online publication. doi:10.1007/978-3-319-54891-3_2

Calisir, F., & Gumussoy, C. A. (2008). In*ternet banking ve*rs*us* other banking channels: Young consumers' view. International Journal of Informa*tion Management, 28(3), 215–221. doi:10.1016/j.ijinfomgt.2008.02.00*9

Callon, M., Courtial, J.-P., & Penan, H. (1993). La scientométrie (Vol. 2727). Presses Universitaires de France.

Campbell, P. (2020). Guide to subscription business models for 2019. Available at: www. priceintelligently.com/subscription-business-model

Carman, J. M. (1990). Consume*r perceptions of service quality: An assessment of the* SERVQUAL dimensions. Journal of Retailing, 66(1), 33–55.

Caro, L., & Martinez, J. (2007). Measuring perceived serv*ice quality in urgent transport service. Journal of Retaili*ng and Consumer Services, 14(1), 60–72. doi:10.1016/j.jre*tconser.2006.04.001*

Carpenter, J. M., & Moore, M. (2006). Consumer demographics, store attributes, and retail format choice in the US grocery market. International Journal of Retail & Distribution Management, 34(6), 434–452. doi:10.1108/09590550610667038

Carr, N. (2010). A typology of crowds. http://www.roughtype.com/?p=1346

Carrel, A. L., & Li, M. (2019). Survey-based measurement of transit customer loyalty: Evalu*ation of measures and systematic biases. Tra*vel Behaviour & Society, 15, 102–112. doi:10.1016/j.tbs.2019.01.003

*Casaló, L. V., Flavián, C., & Guinalíu, M. (2008). The role of satisfac*tion and website usability in developing customer loyalty and positive word-of-mouth in the ebanking services. International Journal of Bank Marketing, 26(6), 399–417. doi:10.1108/02652320810*902433*

*Cascio, W., & Boudreau, J. (2010). Inv*esting in people: Financial impact of human resource initiatives. Ft Press. http://scholar.google.com/scholar_lookup?h*l=en&publication_year=2*010&author=W.+ Cascio&author=J.+Boudreau&titl e=Investing+in+people %3A+Financial+impact+of+ human+resource+initiatives

Castillo, J. (2017). The relationship between big five personality traits, customer empowerment and customer satisfaction in the retail industry. The Journal of Business and Retail Management Research, 11(2).

Catell, R. R. (1966). T*he screen test for a number of factors. Multivari*ate Behavioral Research, 1(2), 245–276. doi:10.120715327906mbr0102_10 PMID:26828106

Cha, J. (2013). Predictors of television and online video platform use: A *coexistence model of old an*d new video platforms. Telematics and Informatics, 30(4), 296–31*0.*

*Chahal, H., & Kumari, N. (2010). Development of multidimensi*onal scale for healthcare service quality (HCSQ) in Indian context. Journal of Indian Busi*ness Research, 2*(4), 230–255. doi:10.1108/17554191011084157

Chaia, B. B., See, P., & Shong, T. (2016). Banking Services *that Influence the Bank Performance. Procedia - Soci*al and Behavioral Sciences, 224(August), 401–407. doi:10.1016/j.sbspro.2016.05.405

Chan, S., & Lu, M. (2004). Understanding Inte*rnet banking adoption an*d use behavior: A Hong Kong perspective. Journal of Global Information Management, 12(3), 21–43. doi:10.4018/jgim.2004070102

Chan, Y. *H. (2004). Biostatistics 201: Linear Regression Analysi*s. Singapore Medical Journal, 45(2), 55–61. PMID:14985842

Chandar, V., & Ferraioli, J. (2021). Virtual Reality, Augmented Reality and the Metaverse—Opportunities in Digital Worlds. Morgan Stanl*ey*. *https://advisor.morganstanley.com/the*-irvin-and-bevack-group /documents/field/i/ir/irvin-and-bevack-group/Vr%20ar%20metav erse%20alphacurrents.pdf

Chaney, D., Gard*an, J., & De Freyman, J. (2021). A framework fo*r *the* relationship implications of additive manufacturing (3D printing) for industrial marketing: Servitization, sustainability and customer empowerment. Journal of Business and Industrial Marketing.

Chang, B., Kao, H., Lin, S., Yang, S., Kuo, Y*., & Jerng, J. (2019). ScienceDirect Qualit*y *ga*ps and priorities for improvement of healthcare service for patients with prolonged mechanical ventilation in the view of family. Journal of the Formosan Medical Association, 118(5), 922–931. doi:10.1016/j.jfma.2018.09.019 PMID:30301580

Chang, H. H. (2008). Inte*lligent agent*'s technology characteristics applied to online auctions' task: A combined model of TTF and TAM. Technovation, 28(9), 564–577. doi:10.1016/j.technovation.*2008.03.006*

*Chang, H. H., Wa*ng, Y. H., & Yang, W. Y. (2009). The impact of e-service quality, customer satisfaction and loyalty on e-marketing: Moderating effect of perceived value. Total Quality Management, 20(4), 423–443. doi:10.1080/14783360902781923

Chang, H. J.*, Cho, H. J., Turner, T., Gupta, M., & Watchraves*ringkan, K. (2015). Effects of store attributes on retail patronage behaviors: Evidence from activewear specialty stores. Journal of Fashion Marketing and Manageme*nt, 19(2), 136–153. doi:10.1108/JFMM-03-2014-0*019

Chang, H. J., Eckman, M., & Yan, R. N. (2011). Application of the Stimulus-Organism-Response model to the retail environment: The *role of hedonic motivation in impulse buyin*g *b*ehavior. International Review of Retail, Distribution and Consumer Research, 21(3), 233–249. doi:10.1080/09593969.2011.578798

Chang, L., Zhang, Z., Li, P., Xi, S., Guo, W., Shen, Y., & Wu, Y. (2022*). 6G-enabled Edge AI for metaverse*: Challenges, Methods, and Future Research Directions. arXiv:2204.06192.

Chatterjee, A. (2004). Credit Management: Practical Aprroach. SKYLARK.

Chatterjee, B. I., Küpper, J., Mariag*er, C., Moore, P., & Reis, S. (20*11). The decade ahead : Trends that will shape the consumer goods industry, Consum. Shopp. Insights. McKinsey Co.

Chatterjee, D., & Kamesh, A. V. S. (2020). Significance of Relationship marketing *in banks in terms of Customer Empowermen*t and satisfaction. European Journal of Molecular & Clinical Medicine, 7(4), 999–1009.

Chauhan, S., Akhtar, A., & Gupta, A. (2022). Customer exp*erience in digital banking: A review and fut*ure research directions. International Journal of Quality and Service Sciences, 14(2), 311–348. doi:10.1108/IJQSS-02-2021-0027

Chebat, J. C., & Kollias, P. (*2000). T*he impact of empowerment on customer contact employees' roles in service organizations. Journal of Service Research, 3(1), 66–81. doi:10.1177/10946705003100*5*

*Chege, C. (2021). E*xamining the influence of service reliability on customer satisfaction in the insurance industry in Kenya. International Journal of Research i*n Business and Social Scienc*e, *10*(1), 259–265. doi:10.20525/ijrbs.v10i1.1025

Chege, C., Wanjau, K., & Nkirina, S. (2019). Relationship between empathy dimension and customer satisfaction in the insurance *industry in K*e*n*ya. International Journal of Research in Business and Social Science, 8(6), 357–366. doi:10.20525/ijrbs.v8i6.577

Chen, C. M., & Liu, H. M. (2019). The moderating effect of competitive status on the relationship between customer satisfaction and retention. Total Quality Management & Business Excellence, 30(7-8), 721–744. doi:10.1080/147833 63.2017.1333413

Chen, H., & Volpe, R. P. (1998). *An analysis of personal* financial literacy among college students. Financial Services Review, 7(2), 107–128. doi:10.1016/S1057-0810(99)80006-7

Chen, S. C., & Quester, P. G. (2006). Modeling store loyalty: Per*ceived value in market orientation practice. Journal* of *S*ervices Marketing, 20(3), 188–198. doi:10.1108/08876040610665643

Chen, Y. N. K. (2019). Compet*itions between OTT TV platforms and* traditional television in Taiwan: A Niche analysis. Telecommunications *Policy, 43(9), 1–10. doi:10.1016/j.telpol.2018.10.006*

*ChenD.ZhangR. (2022). Exploring Research Tren*ds of Emerging Technologies in Health metaverse: A Bibliometric Analysi*s. Available at SSRN 3998068. doi:10.213*9/ssrn.3998068

Cheng, T. E., Lam, D. Y., & Yeung, A. C. (2006). Adoption of internet banking: An empirical study in Hong Kong. Deci*sion Support Systems, 42(3), 1558–1572. d*oi:10.1016/j.dss.2006.01.002

Chernikov, V., Kushch, S., & Tikkanen, H. (2015). Customer empowerment and firm performance: Benefits and potential harm. In Ideas in marketing: Finding the New and polishing the old (pp. 138–*138). Springer. doi:10.1007/978-3-319-10951-0_48*

*Chew, C., & Eysenbach, G. (*2010). Pandemics in the age of Twitter: Content analysis of Tweets during the 2009 H1N1 outbreak. PLoS One, 5(11), e14118. doi:10.1371/journal.pone.0014118 P*MID:21124761*

Chien, C.-J., & Tsai, H.-H. (2000). Using fuzzy numbers to evaluate perceived service quality. Fuzzy Sets and Systems, 116(2), 289–300. doi:10.1016/S0165-*0114(98)00239-5*

Chih, W. H., Wu, C. H. J., & Li, H. J. (2012). The antecedents of consumer online buying impulsiveness on a travel website: Individual internal factor perspectives. Journal of Tr*avel & Tourism Marketing, 29(5), 430–443. doi:10.1080 /10548408.2012.691393*

Child, D. (2006). The essentials of factor analysis (3rd ed.). Continuum Internationa*l Publishing Group.*

*Chimedtseren, E., & Safari, M. (2001). Servic*e quality factors affecting purchase intention of life insurance products. Journal of Insurance and Financial Management, 1(1), 1–12.

Chin, W. W., Marcolin, B. L., *& Newsted, P. R. (2003). A* Partial Least Squares Latent Variable Modeling Approach for Measuring Interaction Effects: Results from a Monte Carlo Simulation Study and an Electronic-Mail Emotion/Adoption Study. Informati*on Systems Research, 14(*2), 1. doi:10.1287/isre.14.2.189.16018

Chiou, J. S., & Shen, C. C. (2012). The antecedents of online financial service adopti*on: The impact of physical bank-ing serv*ices on Internet banking acceptance. Behaviour & Information Technology, 31(9), 859–871. doi:10.1080/0144 929X.2010.549509

Chitra, S., & Ramasethu, A. (2021). A Study on Customer *Satisfaction towards Banking Services* Provided by SBI in Reference with Coimbatore City. The International Journal of Analytical and Experimental Modal Analysis, 12(11), 306–315.

Chitturi, R., Raghunathan, R., & Mahajan, *V. (2008). Delight by design: The role* of *h*edonic versus utilitarian benefits. Journal of Marketing, 72(3), 48–63. doi:10.1509/JMKG.72.3.048

Chiu, C.-M., Chang, C.-C., Cheng, H.-L., & Fang, Y.-H. (2009). De*terminants of customer repurchase intention in online shopping. Onl*ine Information Review, 33(4), 761–784. doi:10.1108/14684520910985710

Chiu, C. M., Hsu, M. H., Sun, S. Y., Lin, T. C., & Sun, P. C. (2005). Usability, quality, value *and e-learning continuance decisions. Computers & Educa*tion, 45(4), 399–416. doi:10.1016/j.compedu.2004.06.001

Chiu, E. (n.d.). New realities Into the Metaverse and beyond. INTO THE METAVERSE, 2.

Chochoľáková, A., Gabčová, L., Belás, J., & Sipko, J. (2015). Bank custome*rs' satisfaction, customers loyalty, and additional purchase*s *of* banking products and services. A case study from the Czech Republic. Economia e Sociologia, 8(3), 82–94. doi:10.*14254/2071-789X.2015/8-3/6*

Choi, J., Yi, S., & Lee, K. C. (2011). Analysis of keyword networks in MIS research and implications for predicting knowledge evolution. Information & Management, 48(8), 371–381. doi:10.1016/j.im.2011.09.004

*Churchill, G. A. Jr, & Surpr*ena*n*t, C. (1982). An investigation into the determinants of customer satisfaction. JMR, Journal of Marketing Research, 19(4), 491–504. doi:10.1177/002224378201900410

Chwiałkowska, A. (2012). Crowdsourcing as a cu*stomer relationship building tool. Journal o*f Positive Management, 3(1). Advance online publication. doi:10.12775/JPM.2012.002

Clow, K. E., & Baack, D. (2018). Message strategies and execution framework', Integrated Advertis*ing, Promotion, and* Ma*r*keting Communications (8th ed.). Pearson Education Limited.

Coco, C. T., Jamison, F., & Black, H. (2011). Connecting people investments and business outcomes at Lowe's: Using value linkage analytics to link employee engagement to business performance. People & Strategy, 34, 28–33. http:// scholar.google.com/scholar_lookup?hl=*en&publication_year=2011&pag*es=28-33&author= C.+T.+Coco&author= F.+Jamison&author=H.+Black& title=Connecting+people+investments+ and+business+outcomes+at+Lowe%E2 %80%99s%3A+Using+value+linkage+ analytics+to+ link+employee+ engagement+to+business+performance

Cohen, J. B., Pham, M. T., & Andrade, E. B. (2007). The nature and role of affect in consumer behavior. In C. P. Haugtvedt, P. M. Herr, & F. R. Kardes (Eds.), Handbook of consumer psychology (pp. 297–348). Erlbaum.

*Cohen, W. A. (2013). Fowarded by Philip Kottle*r, *D*rucker on Marketing lessons from world's most influencial business thinker. Book, Tata McGra.

Colby, C. L., & Parasuraman, A. (*2003). Technology still matters. M*arketing Management, 12(4), *28–28.*

Colgate, Mark & Hedge, Rachel. (2001). An investigation into the switching process in retail banking services. International Journal of Bank Marketing, 19, 201-212. doi:10.1108/02652320110400888

Collier, J., & Bienstock, C. (2006). Measuring Service Quality in E-Retailing. Journal of S*ervice Research, 8, 260-275. . doi:10.1177/1094670505278867*

*Collins, C. (*2008). Looking to the future: Higher education in the Metaverse. EDUCAUSE Review, 43(5), 50–52.

Comninos, A., Esselaar, S., Nd*iwalana, A., & Stork, C. (2008). Towards ev*idence-based ICT policy and regulation m-banking the unbanked. Externo. http://externo.casafrica.es/aeo/pdf/english/ overview_part_2 _09_aeo_09.pdf

Comrey, L. A., & Lee, H. B. (1992). A first course in factor analysis (2nd ed.). Lawrence Erlbaum Associates.

Cong Do, P., Tan Phong, V., V*an Thuong, P., Hoang Tien, N., Van Du*ng, H., & Author, C. (2019). Factors Affecting Access to Finance By Small and Medium Enterprises In Vietnam. American International Journal of Business Management, 2(10), 69–79.

Constitution of the Republic of South Africa Act, No. 108 of 1996. Bill of Rights. (1996). https:*//www.justice.gov.za/legislation/*constitution/chp02.ht ml

Consumer Protection Act, No. 68 of 2008. (2008). https://www.gov.za/sites/default/files/gcis_document/201409/ 321864670.pdf

Cox, B., & Koelzer, W. (2004). Internet *Marke*ting in Hospitality. Pearson Prentice Hall.

Creswell, J. W., & Creswell, J. D. (2018). Research Design (5th ed.). Sage Publication Inc.

Cronbach, L. J. (1951). Coefficient *Alpha and the Internal Structure of Tests. Psy*chometrika, 16(3) 297–334. doi:10.1007/BF02310555

Cronin, J. J. Jr, Brady, M. K., & Hult, G. T. *M. (2000)*. Assessing the effects of quality, value, and customer satisfaction on consumer behavioral intentions in service environments. Journal of Retailing, 76(2), *193–218*.

*Cronin, J. Jr, & Taylor, S. (1992). Measuring Ser*vice Quality: A Reexamination and Extension. Journal of Marketing, 1992(56), 55–68. doi:10.1177/002224299205600304

Crotts, J. C., & Magnini, V. P. (2011). Is Surprise Essential? Annals of Tourism Research, 38(*2), 719–722. doi:10.1016/j. anna*ls.2010.03.004

Culnan, M. J. (1987). Mapping the intellectual structure of MIS, 1980-1985: A co-citation analysis. Management Information Systems Quarterly, 11(3), 341–353. doi:10.2307/248680

*Curran, J. M., & Me*uter, M. L. (2005). Self-service technology adoption: Comparing three technologies. Journal of Services Marketing, 19(2), 103–113. doi:10.1*108/08876040510591411*

Cyr, D., Kindra, G. S., & Dash, S. (2008). Web site design, trust, satisfaction and e-loyalty: The Indian experience. Online Information Review, 32(6), 773–790. doi:10.1108/14684520810923935

Dabholkar, P. A. (1996). *Consumer evaluations of ne*w technology-based self-service options: An investigation of alternative models of service quality. International Journal of Research in Marketing, 13*(1), 29–51. doi:10.1016/0167-8116(95)*00027-5

Dabholkar, P. A., Thorpe, D. I., & Rentz, J. O. (1996). A measure of service quality for retail stores: Scale development and validation. Journal of the Academy of Marketing Science, 24(1), 3–16. doi:10.1007/BF02893933

Dahlander, L., & Magnusson, M. *G. (2005). Relationships between open source software companies and communities:* Observations from Nordic firms. Research Policy, 34(4), 481–493.

Darian, J. C., Tucci, L. A., & Wiman, A. R. (2001). Perceived salesperson service attributes and retail patro*nage inten-tions. International Journal o*f R*e*tail & Distribution Management, 29(5), 205–213. doi:10.1108/09590550110390986

Darzi, M. A., & Bhat, S. A. (2018). Personnel capability and cus*tomer satisfaction as predictors of cust*om*e*r retention in the banking sector: A mediated-moderation study. International Journal of Bank Marketing, 36(4), 663–679. doi:10.1108/IJBM-04-2017-*0074*

Davenport, T. H., Harris, J., & Shapiro, J. (2010). Competing on tal*ent analy*tics. Harvard Business Review, 88, 52–58. http://scholar.google.com/scholar_lookup?hl=en&publication_year=2010&pages=52-58&author=T.+H.+Davenport&author=J.+ Harris&*author= J.+Shapiro&title=*Co*m*peting+on+talent+analytics

Davey, G., Sterling, C., Field, A., Sterling, C., & Albery, I. (2014). Complete Psychology. Taylor & Francis. doi:10.4324/9780203783979

Davis, *F. D. (1989). Perceived U*se*f*ulness, Perceived Ease of Use, and User Acceptance of Information Technology. Management Information Systems Quarterly, 13(3), 319–340. doi:10.2307/249008

Davis, F. D., Bagozzi, R. P., & Warshaw, *P. R. (1989). User acceptan*ce of computer technology: A comparison of two theoretical models. Management Science, 35(8), 982–1003. doi:10.1287/mnsc.35.8.982

De Bakker, F. G., Groenewegen, P., & Den Hond, F. (2005). A bibliometric analysis of 30 years of research and theory on corporate social *responsibility and corporate social perform*ance. Business & Society, 44(3), 283–317. doi:10.1177/0007650305278086

Debnath A. & Mazumdar. (2015). An Evaluative study on consumer rights in the context of business. International Journal of Humanities a*nd Social Science Studies, 1(4).*

Deodhar, S. B., & Aditi, A. A. (2012). Indian financial system. Himalaya Publishing House.

Department of Health & Human Services. (2020). Guidance on Preparing Workplaces for COVID-19. OSHA 3990-03 2020. https*://www.osha.gov/Publications/OSHA3990.pdf*

*De St*adler, E. B. (2016). The scope of the application of the Consumer Protection Act 68 of 2008 in the context of the sale of defective goods in comparative perspective. The University of Cape Town.

*Devaki, R. P. C., & Babu, S. D. (2021). The future of ov*er-*t*he-Top platforms after covid-19 pandemic. Annals of the Romanian Society for Cell Biology, 25(6), 11307–*11313. doi:10.1177/0972262921989118*

Devaraj, S., Fan, M., & Kohli, R. (2002). Antecedents of B2C channel satisfaction and preference: Validating e-commerce metrics. Information Syst*ems Research, 13(3), 316–3*33. *d*oi:10.1287/isre.13.3.316.77

Devda, S. S., Attri, A., & Attri, R. (2019). Need Gap Analysi*s of Online Taxi Ag-gregation* Business.https://www.semanticscholar.org/paper/Need-Gap-Analysis-of-Online-Taxi-Aggregation-Devda/cae2b71c64e329f2efcd227f8040bc9 26a265587

Devi, P., & P*rabhakar, C. (2018). Assessing the Servic*e Q*u*ality Gaps in the Life Insurance Sector. International Journal of Pure and Applied Mathematics, 119(15), 1639–1648.

Diaw, B., & Asare, G. (2018). Effect of innovation on customer satisfaction and customer ret*ention in the telecom-munication industry* in G*hana: Customers' Perspectives. European Journal of Research and Reflection in Management Sciences, 6(4), 15–26.

Dick, A. S., & Basu, K. (1994). Customer loyal*ty: Toward an integr*ated conceptual framework. Journal of the Academy of Marketing Science, 22(2), 99–113. doi:10.1177/0092070394222001

Diener, E., & Biswas-Dien*er, R. (2002). Will money increase subjective well-being? Soc*ial Indicators Research, 57(2), 119–169. doi:10.1023/A:1014411319119

Dillon, K. (2016). What Airbnb und*erstands about Customer "Jo*bs to be done". Harvard Business Review. https://hbr.org/2016/08/what-*airbnb-understands-about-custom ers-jobs-to-be-done*

*DiMag*gio, P., & Powell, W. W. (1983). The iron cage revisited: Collective rationali-ty and institutional isomorphism and collective rationality in organizational *fields. American Socio-logical Review, 48,* 147–160. http://scholar.google.com/scholar_lookup?hl=en&publication_year=198 3&pages=147-160&author=   P.+DiMaggio&author=W.+W.+Powell&titl e=The+iron +cage+revisited%3A+Coll*ective+rationality+   and+in stitutional*+isomorphism+and+collective+   rationality+in+organ izational+fields

Dinev, T., Xu, H., Smith, J. H., & Hart, P. (2013). Information privacy and correlates: An empirical attempt *to bridge and distinguish* privacy-related concepts. European Journal of Information Systems, 22(3), 295–316. doi:10.1057/ejis.2012.23

Directorate of Census Operations. (2011). District Census Handbook. DCO. https://gujecostat.gujarat.gov.in/uploads/mediafiles/2406-PART-B-DCHB-GANDHINAGAR.pdf

Dishaw, M. T., & Strong, D. M. (1999). Extending the technology acceptance model with task–technology fit constructs. Information & Management, 36(1), 9–21. doi:10.1016/S0378-7206(98)00101-3

Dixon, M., Freeman, K., & Toman, N. (2010). Stop trying to delight your customers. Harvard Business Review, 88(7/8), 116–122.

Djelassi, S., & Decoopman, I. (2013). Customers' participation in product development through crowdsourcing: Issues and implications. Industrial Marketing Management, 42(5), 683–692.

Dodgson, M., Gann, D. M., & Salter, A. (2008). The management of technological innovation: strategy and practice. Oxford University Press on Demand.

Donoghue, S., & de Klerk, H. M. (2014). Consumers' anger and coping strategies following appraisals of appliance failure. International Journal of Consumer Studies.

Donoghue, S., & van der Oordt, C. (2016). Consumers' subjective and objective consumerism knowledge and subsequent complaint behavior concerning consumer electronics. The University of Pretoria.

Donthu, N., & Yoo, B. (1998). Cultural influences on service quality expectations. Journal of Service Research, 1(2), 178–186. doi:10.1177/109467059800100207

Douthitt, S., & Mondore, S. (2014). Creating a business-focused HR function with analytics and integrated talent management. People & Strategy, 36, 16–21. http://scholar.google.com/scholar_lookup?hl=en&publication_year=2014&pages=16-21&author =S.+Douthitt&author=S.+Mondore&title= Creating+a+business-focused+HR+function+with+analytics +and+integrated+talent+management

Durbin, J., & Watson, G. S. (1950). Testing for Serial Correlation in Least Squares Regression, I. Biometrika, 37(3–4), 409–428. PMID:14801065

Dutta, M., & Sardar, S. (2021). Impact of covid-19 on the rise of OTT platforms in India. In Interdisciplinary Research in Technology and Management. CRC Press. doi:10.1201/9781003202240-99

Dwivedi, Y. K., Rana, N. P., Jeyaraj, A., Clement, M., & Williams, M. D. (2017). Re-examining the unified theory of acceptance and use of technology (UTAUT): Towards a revised theoretical model. Information Systems Frontiers. doi:10.100710796-017-9774-y

Díaz, E., & Koutra, C. (2013). Evaluation of the persuasive features of hotel chains websites: A latent class segmentation analysis. International Journal of Hospitality Management, 34, 338–347. doi:10.1016/j.ijhm.2012.11.009

Easterlin, R. A. (2006). Life cycle happiness and its sources: Intersections of psychology, economics, and demography. Journal of Economic Psychology, 27(4), 463–482. doi:10.1016/j.joep.2006.05.002

Eckersley, R. (2008). Nihilism, fundamentalism, or activism: Three responses to fears of the apocalypse. The Futurist, 42(1), 35.

Egala, S. B., Boateng, D., & Mensah, S. A. (2021). To leave or retain? An interplay between quality digital banking services and customer satisfaction. International Journal of Bank Marketing.

Elevating the insurance customer experience. (2020). IBM. https://www.ibm.com/downloads/cas/AAV81JLZ

El Haddad, R. (2019). *Exploring Service Quality of Low Cost Airlines Exploring* Service Quality of Low Cost Airlines. Services Marketing Quarterly, 0(0), 1–15. doi:10.1080/15332969.2019.1665901

Ellegaard, O., & Wallin, J. A. (2015). The bibliometric analysis of scholarly production: How great is the impact. Scientometrics, 105(3), 1809–1831. doi:10.100711192-015-*1645-z PMID:26594073*

Erdogan, A. I. (2018). Factors affecting SME access to bank financing: An interview study with Turkish bankers. Small Enterprise Research, 25(1), 23–35. doi:10.1080/13215906.2018.1428911

Eriksson, K., *& Nilsson, D. (2007). Determi*nants of the continued use of self-service technology: The case of Internet banking. Technovation, 27(4), 1*59–167. doi:10.10*16/j.technovation.2006.11.001

Eriksson, K., Kerem, K., & Nilsson, D. (2005). Customer acceptance of *internet banking in Estonia. International Journal* of Bank Marketing, 23(2), 200–216. doi:10.1108/02652320510584412

Ernst & Young. (2021). The winds of change Trends shaping India's FinTech sector. Author.

Eryand*ra, A., Sjabadhyni, B.,* & Mustika, M. D. (2018). How older consumers' perceived ethicality influences brand loyalty. SAGE Open, 8(2). doi:10.1177/2158244018778105

Estellés-Arolas, E., & Go*nzález-La*drón-De-Guevara, F. (2012). Towards an integrated crowdsourcing definition. Journal of Information Science, 38(2), 189–200.

Ettlinger, N. (2017). Open innovation and its discontents. Geoforum, 80, *61–71.*

Evren, S., & Kozak, N. (2*014). Bibliometric analysis of tourism and hospitality related articles published in Turkey. Anatolia, 25(1), 61–80. doi:10.1080/13032917.2013.824906

Eyal, I. (2017). Blockchain technology: Transform*ing libertarian cryptocurrency dreams to finance and banking realities. Computer, 50(9), 38–49. doi:10.1109/MC.2017.3571042

Eze, U. C., Manyeki, J. K., Yaw, L. H., & Har, L. C. (2011). Factors affecting internet banking adoption among young adults: Evidence *from Malaysia. In International Conference on Social Science* and Humanity, IPEDR (Vol. 11, pp. 377–381).

Falletta, S. (2014). In search of HR intelligence: Evidence-based HR Analytics practices in hig*h performing companies. People & Strategy, 36,* 28–37. https://scholar.google.com/scholar_lookup?hl=en&publication_year=2014&pages=28-37&au*thor= S.+Falletta*&title=In+search+of+HR+intelligence%3A+ Evidence-based+HR+Analytics+practices+in +high+ performing+companies

Farooq, M., Ali, W., Younas, W., Khalil-ur-Rehman, *F., & Qurashi, Q. A. (2019). The era of Transformative Market*ing: Service Quality of Mobile App Based Taxi Services in Kuala Lumpur. Proceedings on Engineering Sciences, 1(2), 49–58. doi:10.24874/PES01.02.006

Fatima, I., Hum*ayun, A., Iqbal,* U., & Shafiq, M. (2018). Dimensions of service quality in healthcare: A systematic review of literature. doi:10.1093/intqhc/mzy125

Fatima, T., Awan, T. M., & Kamr*an, M. (2021). Impact of Inte*ractive and supportive service innovation in customer retention: an interplay of value creation and participation. Foundation University Journal of Business & Economics, 6(1).

F*auzi, A., Widodo, T., & Djatmiko, T. (2018). Pengaruh Be*havioral Intention Terhadap Use Behavior Pada Penggunaan Aplikasi Transportasi [The Effect of Behavorial Intention on Use Behavior in the Use of Transportation Applications]. Studi Kasus Pad*a Pengguna Go-Jek Dan Grab Di Kalangan Mahasisw*a Te*l*kom University [On the Use of Online Transportaion Applications (Case Study on Go-Jek and Grab User*s Among Telkom U*niversity students]. E-Proceeding of Management.

Fauziah, F., Surachm*an, E., & Muhtadi, A. (2019). Integration of s*ervice quality and quality function deployment as an effort of pharmaceutical service improvement on outpatient in a referral hospital. Academic Press.

Fawad. (2021, November 26*). SEM|SPSS AMOS|Asse*ss Discriminant Validity|Heterotrait Monotrait Ratio [Video]. [Youtube]. https://www.youtube.com/watch?v=XlYU6z5f8a*I&t=70s*

Fawcett, S. E., & Waller, M. A. (2014). Can we stay ahead of the obsolescence curve? On inflection points, proactive preemption, and the future of supply chain management. Journal of Business Logistics, 35(1), 17–22.

*FCC. (2013). Annual assessment of the status of competi*tion in the market for the delivery of video programming. MB Docke*t No. 12-203. FCC 13*-99.

Featherman, M. S., & Pavlou, P. A. (2003). Predicting e-services adoption: A perceived risk facets perspective. International Journal of Human-Computer Studies, 59*(4), 451–474. doi:10.1016/*S*1*071-5819(03)00111-3

Feng, Y., Ye, H. J., Yu, Y., Yang, C., & Cui, T. (2018). Gamification artifacts and crowdsourcing participation: Examining the mediating role of intrinsic motivations. Computers in Human Behavior, 81, 124–*136.*

Ferreira, J. N. A. R., Fricton, J., & Rhodus, N. (2017). Orofacial Disorders: Current Therapies in Orofacial Pain and Oral Medicine. Springer In*ternational Publishing. doi:10.1*007*/*978-3-319-51508-3

Field, A. (2000). Discovering Statistics using SPSS for Windows. Sage publications.

Field, A. (2009). Discovering Statistics Using SPSS: Introducing Statistical Metho*d (3rd ed.). Sage Publications.*

*Fi*lh*o, D., B., F., Silva, J., A., & Rocha, E. (2011). What is R2 all About? Leviathan – Cadernos de Pesquisa Política, 3, 60-68.

Finzen, J., & Kin*tz, M. (2012, January). A Comparative Study of* Innovation-Related Crowdsourcing Projects in Germany. In ISPIM Conference Proceedings (p. 1). The International Society for Professional Innovation Management (ISPIM).

Fishbei*n, M., Ajzen, I., & Belief, A.* (1975). Intention and Behavior: An introduction to *theory and research. International Journal of Advanced Engineering and Science.*

*Fish*er, A., & Abram, D. (2013). Radical Ecopsychology. Psychology in the Service of Life (2nd ed.). State University of New York Press.

Flavián, C., Guinaliu, M., & Torres, E. (2006). How bricks-and-mortar attributes affect online banking ado*ption. International Journal of Bank Marketing, 24(6), 406–423. doi:10.1108/02652320610701735*

Flavián, C., Guinalíu, M., & Gurrea, R. (2006). The role played by perceived usability, satisfaction and consumer trust on website loyalty. Information & Management, 43(1), 1–14. doi:10.1016/j.im.2005.01.002

Fleming, L., & Waguespac*k, D. M. (2007). Brokerage, boundary spanni*ng, *a*nd leadership in open innovation communities. Organization Science, 18(2), 165–180.

Fornell, C., & Larcker, D. F. (1981). Evaluating structural equation models with unobservable Variables and Me*asurement Er*ror. JMR, Journal of Marketing Research, 18(1), 39–80. doi:10.1177/002224378101800104

Fortes, N., & Rita, P. (2016). Privacy concerns and online purchasing behaviour: Towards an integrated model. European Research on Management *and Business Economics,* 22(3), 167–176. Advance online publication. doi:10.1016/j.iedeen.2016.04.002

Foxall, G. (1993). Situated Consumer Behaviour: A behavioral interpretation of purchase and consumption. Research in Consumer Behaviour, 6, 113–152.

Fra*ndsen, T. F. (2017). Are predatory journals* und*ermining the credibility of science? A bibliometric analysis of citers. Scientometrics, 113(3), 1513–1528. doi:10.100711192-017-2520-x

Frey, B. S., & Stutzer, A. (2000). Happiness, economy, and institutions. Economic Journal (Lon*don), 110(466), 918–938. doi:10.1111/1468-0297.00570*

*Frey, K., Lü*thje, C., & Haag, S. (2011). Whom should firms attract to open innovation platforms? The role of knowledge diversity and motivation. Long Range Planning, 44(5-6), *397–420.*

Fuchs, C., & Schreier, M. (2011). Customer empowerment in new product development. Journal of Product Innovation Management, 28(1), 17–32. do*i:10.1111/j.1540-5885.2010.00778.*x

Fuchs, C., Prandelli, E., & Schreier, M. (2010). The psychological effects of empowerment strategies on consumers' product demand. Journal of Marketing, 74(1), 65–79. doi:10.1509/jmkg.74.1.65

Fuduri'c, M., Malthouse, E. C., & V*iswanathan, V. (2018). Keep it, shave* it, cut it: A closer look into consumers' video viewing behavior. Business Horizons, 61(1), 85–93. doi:10.1016/j.bushor.2017.09.008

Furu*nes, T., & Mkono, M. (2019). Service-delivery success an*d failure under the sharing economy. International Journal of Contemporary Hospitality Management, 31(8), 3352–3370. doi:10.1108/IJCHM-06-2018-0532

Füller, J. (2010). Virtu*al co-creation of new products and its impact on consumers' prod*uct and brand relationships. Academy of Management Annual Meeting Proceedings, 1, 1–6.

Galbreath, J. (2010). How does corporate social responsibility benefit firms? Evidence from Australia. Euro*pean Business Review.*

*Gamage, P. (2013). Determinants of acces*s *t*o bank finance for small and medium-sized enterprises: The case of Sri Lanka. Corporate Ownership and Control, 10(3), 314–321. doi:10.22495/cocv10i3c3art6

Gan, C., Clemes, M., Limsombunchai, V., & Weng, A. (2006). A logit analysis of electronic banking in New Zealand. Int. J. Bank Mark. 24 (6), 360–383. Gerrard, P., Cunningh*am, J. B., and Devlin, J. F.* (2006). Why consumers are not using Internet banking: A qualitative study. Journal of Services Marketing, 20(3), 160–168.

Ganesan, P., & Sridhar, *M. (2016). Service innov*ation and customer performance of telecommunication service provider: A study on mediation effect of corporate reputation. Corporate Reputation Review, 19(1), 77–*101. doi:10.1057/crr.2015.29*

Ga*nesh, J., Arnold, M. J., & Reynolds, K. E. (2000). Understanding the customer base of service providers: An examination of the differences between switchers and st*ayers. Journal of Marketi*ng, 64(3), 65–87. doi:10.1509/jmkg.64.3.65.18028

Garfield, E. (1955). Citation analysis as a tool in journal evaluation. Science, 122(3159), 108–*111. doi:10.1126cien*ce.*122.*3159.108 PMID:14385826

Garrett, S., & James, R. N. III. (2013). Financial ratios and perceived household financial satisfaction. Journal of Financial Therapy, 4(1), 39–62. doi:10.4148/jft.v4i1.1839

Garvin, D. A. *(2013). How google sold its enginee*rs *o*n management. Harvard Business Review, 91, 74–82. [PubMed], https://*scholar.google.com/scholar_look*up?hl=en&publication_year=2013&pages=74-82&author=D.+A.+Garvin&title=How+google+s old+its+engineers+on+management

Gaskin. (2013, October 13). Standardized Estimates and R-Sq*uare in AMOS [Video] Youtube. https://www.you*tube. com/watch?v=3KHULVuCSh0

Gatautis, R., & Vitauskaite, E. (2014). Crowdsourcing application in marketing activities. Procedia: Social and Behavioral Sciences, 110, 1243–1250.

Gaviria-Marin, M., Merigo, J. M., & Popa, S. (2018). Twenty years of the J*ournal of Knowledge Manageme*nt: A bibliometric analysis. Journal of Knowledge Management, 22(8), 1655–1687. doi:10.1108/JKM-10-2017-0497

Gazzola, P., Colombo, G., Pezzetti, R., & Nicolescu, L. (2017). Consumer empowerment in the digit*al economy: Availing sustainable p*urchasing decisions. Sustainability, 9(5), 693. doi:10.3390u9050693

Gengeswari, K., Padmashantini, P., & Sharmeela-Banu, S. A. (2013). Impact of customer retention practices on firm performance. I*nternational Journal of Academic Research in Business & Social Sciences, 3(*7), 68.

George, A., & Kumar, G. S. (2014). Impact of service quality dimensions in internet banking on customer satisfaction. Decision (*Washington, D.C.), 41(1)*, 73–85. doi:10.100740622-014-0028-2

Gera, R., Mittal, S., Batra, D., & Prasad, B. (2017). Evaluatin*g the Effects of Serv*ice Quality, Customer Satisfaction, and Service Value on Behavioral Intentions with Life Insurance Customers in India. International Jour*nal of Service Scienc*e, *M*anagement, Engineering, and Technology, 8(3), 1–20. doi:10.4018/IJSSMET.2017070101

Gerrard, P., Cunningham, J. B., & Devlin, J. F. (2006). Why consumers are not using internet b*anking: A qualitative stu*dy. Journal of Services Marketing, 20(3), 160–168. doi:10.1108/08876040610665616

Getnet, B. (2020). The Impact of Service Quality on Customer Satisfaction in Case of Selected Insurance Companies in Bale Robe Town. Research on Humanities and Social Sciences, *10(11), 40–48. doi:*10.7176/RHSS/10-11-04

Ghobadian, R., Speller, S., & Jones, W. (1994). Service Quality Concepts and Models. International Journal of Quality Management, 11, 43–66.

Gichuru, M. J., & Limi*ri, E. K. (2017). Market s*egmentation as a strategy for customer satisfaction and retention. International Journal of Economics. Commerce and Management. United Kingdom, V(12), 544–55*3.*

*Gijsbrechts, E., Campo, K., & Ni*s*ol*, P. (2008). Beyond promotion-based store switching: Antecedents and patterns of systematic multiple-store shopping. Internati*onal Journal of Research in Ma*rketing, 25(1), 5-21.

Giles, L. (2019). Learning to live together and a life worth living. In A*PCEIU reconciliation, peace and global citizenship education: Pedagogy and practice (pp. 12–19). Incheon: UN*ESCO Asia-Pacifc Centre of Education for International Unders*tanding (APCEIU). https://www.gcedclearinghouse.org/ sites/default/fles/resour ces/190516eng.pdf*

*GoG R*esolution. (2003). https://govinfo.me/kanya-kelavni-nidhi-gujarat/

Gogus, A., & Saygın, Y. (2019). *Privacy p*erception and information technology utilization of high school students. Heliyon, 5(5), e01614. doi:10.1016/j.heliyon.2019.e0*1614 PMID:31193323*

*Gomez, M. I., McLaughli*n, E. W., & Wittink, D. R. (2004). Customer satisfaction and retail sales performance: An empirical investigation. Journa*l of Retailing, 80(4), 265–278.* doi:10.1016/j.jretai.2004.10.003

Goode, E. (2017). Moral Panic. The Encyclopedia of Juvenile Delinquency and Justice, *pp. 1-3.*

*Gorsu*ch, R. L. (1983). Factor analysis (2nd ed.). Lawrence Erlbaum Associates.

Grable, J. E., Cupples, S., Fernatt, F., & Anderson, N. (2013). Evaluating the *link be*tween perceived income adequacy and financial satisfaction: A resource deficit hypothesis approach. Social Indica*tors Research, 114(3), 1109–1124.* doi:10.100711205-012-0192-8

Greco, P. (2005). Pandemic: How to Avoid Panic? Journal of Science Communication, 04. doi:10.22323/2.04040501

Greenland, S., Coshall, J., & Combe, I. (2006). Evaluating service quality an*d consumer satisfaction in emerging markets. Interna*tional Journal of *Consumer Studies, 30(6), 582–590. doi:10.1111/j.1470-6431.2005.00484.x*

Gronroos, C. (1988). Service quality: The six criteria of good perceived service. Rev*iew of Business, 9(3), 10.*

Gronroos, C., & Voima, F. P. (2013). Critical Service Logic: Making Sense of Value Creation and Co-Creation. Journal of the Acade*my of Marketing Science, 41(2), 1*33–150. doi:10.100711747-012-0308-3

Grosso, M., Castaldo, S., & Grew*al, A. (2018).* How store attributes impact shoppers' loyalty in emerging countries: An investigation in the Indian retail sector. *Journal of Retai*ling and Consumer Services, 40, 117–124. doi:10.1016/j. jretconser.2017.08.024

Grönroos, C. (1984). A service quality model and its marketing implications. European Journal of Marketing, 18(4), 36–44. doi:10.1108/EUM0000*000004784*

Grönroos, C. (2001). The perceived service quality concept–a mistake? Managing Service Quality, 11(3), 150–152. doi:10.1108*/09604520110393386*

G*u, J.* C., Lee, S. C., & Suh, Y. H. (2009). Determinants of behavioral intention to mobile banking. Expert System*s with Applications, 36(9), 11*605–11616. doi:10.1016/j.eswa.2009.03.024

Guadagnoli, E., & Velicer, W. F. (1988). Relation to sample size to the stability of component patterns. *Psychological Bulletin, 103(2), 265–275.* d*o*i:10.1037/0033-2909.103.2.265 PMID:3363047

Gupta, K. P., Manrai, R., & Goel, U. (2017). Factors influencing adoption of payments banks by *Indian customers: Extending* UT*A*UT with perceived credibility. Journal of Asia Business Studies, 2–29.

Gupta, T. K., & Singh, V. (2017). Measurement of service quality of automobile organisation *by artificial neural net*work. International Journal of Management Concepts and Philosophy, 10(1), 32–53. doi:10.1504/IJMCP.2017.081989

Hackl, P., Scharitzer, D., & Zuba, R. (2000). Customer satisfaction in the Austrian food *retail market. Total Quality Management, 11(7), 999–1*006. doi:10.1080/09544120050135524

Hadi, N. U., Abdullah, N., & Ilham, S. (2016). An Easy Approach to Exploratory Factor Analysis: Marketing Perspective. Journal of Educational and *Social Research, 6(1), 215–223.*

Haig, B. D. *(*2014). Investigating the psychological world: Scientific method in the behavioral sciences. MIT Press. doi:10.7551/mitpress/9780262027366.001.0001

Hair, J. F., Black, W. C., Babi*n, B. J., Ander*son, R. E., & Tatham, R. L. (2010). Multivariate Data Analysis (7th ed.). Pearson Education Inc.

Halinen, A., & Tähtinen, J. (2002). A process t*heory of relationship ending. International Journal of Se*rvice Industry Management, 13(2), 163–180. doi:10.1108/09564230210425359

Hall, C. M. (2011). Publish and perish? Bibliometric analysis, journal ranking and the assessment of research *quality in touris*m. *T*ourism Management, 32(1), 16–27. doi:10.1016/j.tourman.2010.07.001

Han, S. L., & Baek, S. (2004). Antecedents and consequences of service quality in o*nline banking: An application of the SER*VQUAL instrument. ACR North American Advances.

Han, X., Fang, S., Xie, L., & Yang, J. (2019). Service fairness and customer satisfaction: Mediating role of customer psychol*ogical empowerment. Jo*urnal of Contemporary Marketing Science.

Hanafizadeh, P., Behboudi, M., Koshksaray, A. A., & Tabar, M. J. S. (2014). Mobile-banking adoption by Iranian bank clients. Telematics and Informatics, 31(1), 62–78. doi:10.1016/j.tele.*2012.11.001*

Hand, C., Dall'Olmo Riley, F., Harris, P., Singh, J., & Rettie, R. (2009). Onl*ine grocery shopping: The influence of situational factors. European Journal of Marketing, 43(9/10), 1205–1219. doi:10.1108/03090560910976447*

Hanlon, A. (2022). Metaverse–together alone? LSE Business Review.

Hanna, R., Rohm, A., & Crittenden, V. L. (2011). We're all conn*ected: The power of the social media ecosystem. Business Horizons*, 54(3), 265–273.

Haque, M., & Sultan, Z. (2019). A Structural Equation Modeling Approach to Validate the Dimensions of SERVPERF in Insurance Industry of Saudi Arabia. Management Science Letters, 9, *495–504. doi:10.5267/j.msl.2019.1.012*

Harb, A., *Th*oumy, M., & Yazbeck, M. (2022). Customer satisfaction with digital banking channels in times of uncertainty.

Hare, C. (2003). The food-shopping experience: A satisfaction surve*y of older Scottish consumer*s. *I*nternational Journal of Retail & Distribution Management, 31(5), 244–255. doi:10.1108/09590550310472415

Hariyanti, A. O., Hidayatullah, S., & Prasetya, D. A. (2020a). Analysis of the Acceptance and Use of Mobile Banking Services Using the Unified Theory of Acceptance and Use of Technology International Research Journal of Advanced Engineering and Science, 5(1), 254–262.

Hariyanti, A. O., Hidayatullah, S., & Prasetya, D. A. (*2020*b). Analysis of the Acceptance and Use of Mobile Banking Services Using the Unified Theory of Acceptance and Use of Technology (Case Study of Bank Jat*im Pasuruan Branch). Research Journal of Advanc*ed Engineering and Science, 5(1), 254–262.

Harman, H. H. (1976). Modern factor analysis (3rd ed. revised). University of Chicago Press.

H*arris, J. G., Craig, E., & Light, D. A. (201*1). Talent and analytics: New approaches, higher ROI. The Journal of Business Strategy, 32(6), 4–13. http://scholar.google.com/sch*olar_lookup?hl=en&publicat*ion_year=2011&pages=4-13&author=J.+G+Harris&author=E+Craig&author =D.+A+L*ight&title=Talent+and+analytics%3A+New+approaches%2C+* higher+ROI. doi:10.1108/02756661111180087

Hartwick, J., & Barki, H. (1994). Explaining the role of user participation in information system use. Management Science, 40(4), 440–465. doi:10.1287/mnsc.40.4.440

Harzing, A. W., & Alakangas, S. (2016). Google Scholar, *Scopus and the Web of Science: A longi*tudinal and cross-disciplinary comparison. Scientometrics, 106(2), 787–804. doi:10.100*711192-015-1798-9*

*Heade*n, R. S., Klompmaker, J. E., & Rust, R. T. (1979). The duplication of viewing law and television media schedule evaluation. JMR, Journal of Marketing Research, 16(3), 333–340. doi:10.1177/002224377901600305

Heff*ernan, T., O'Neill, G., Tra*vaglione, T., & Droulers, M. (2008). Relationship Marketing. International Journal of Bank Marketing, 26(3), 183–199. doi:10.1108/*02652320810864652*

*Hegner-Ka*kar, A. K., Richter, N. F., & Ringle, C. M. (2018). The customer loyalty cascade and its impact on profitability in financial services. In Partial leas*t squares structural equation mo*deli*ng* (pp. 53–75). Springer. doi:10.1007/978-3-319-71691-6_3

Heidenreich, S., & Handrich, M. (2015). What about passive innovation resistance? Investigating adoption-related behavior from a resistance perspective. Journal of *Product Innovation Management, 32(6), 878–903.*

Hennig-Thurau, T., Gwinner, K. P., & Gremler, D. D. (2002). Understanding relationship marketing outcomes: An integration of relational benefits and relationship quality. Journal of Servic*e Research, 4(3), 230–247.* do*i:*10.1177/1094670502004003006

Herman, W. E., & Pinard, M. R. (2015). Critically examining inquiry-based learning: John Dewey in theory, history, *and practi*ce. In P. Blessinger & J. M. Carfora (Eds.), InquiryBased Learning for Multidisciplinary Programs: A Conceptual and Practical Resource for Educators (pp. 43–62). Emerald Group Publishing Limited., doi:10.1108/S2055-364120150000003016

Hicks, J. M., Page, T. J., Behe, B. K., Dennis, J. H., & Fernandez, R. T. (2005). What Delighted customers buy? Journal of Consumer Satisfaction, Dissatisfaction & Complaining Behavior, *18, 94–104.*

*Hienerth, C. (2*006). The commercialization of user innovations: The development of the rodeo kayak industry. Research Management, 36(3), 273–294.

Hira, T. K., & Muge*nda, O. M. (1998). Predictors* of financial satisfaction: Differences between retirees and non-retirees. Financial Counseling and Planning, 9(2), 75–84.

Hirsh-Pasek, K., Zosh, J., Hadani, H. S., Golinkoff, R. M., Clark, K., Donohue, *C., & Wartella, E. (2022). A whole new* world: Education meets the metaverse. Policy.

Ho, M. H. W., Chung, H. F., Kingshott, R., & Chiu, C. C. (2020). Custome*r engagement, consumption an*d firm performance in a multi-actor service eco-s*ystem: The moderating role of resource inte*gration. Journal of Business Research, 121, 557–566. doi:10.1016/j.jbusres.2020.02.008

Ho, S. H., & Ko, Y. Y. (2008). Effects of self-service technology on customer value an*d customer rea*dines*s: The case of Internet banking. Internet research. https://www.statista.com/

Hoelzle, J. B., & Meyer, G. J. (2013). Exploratory factor analysis: Basics and beyond. In I. *B. Weiner, J. A. Schinka, &* W. F. Velicer (Eds.), Research methods in psychology, 2 (2nd ed., pp. 164–188). Wiley.

Holland FinTech. (2015). The future of finance: The social*ization of finance. Author.*

Hollebeek, L. (2011). Demystifying customer brand engagement: Exploring the loyalty nexus. Journal of Marketing Management, 27(8), 785–807.

Holloway, B. B., & Beatty, S. E. (2008). Satis*fiers and dissati*sfiers in the online environment: A critical incident assessment. Journal of *Service Research, 10(4), 347–364. doi:10.1177/1094670508*314266

Hooper, D., Coughlan, J., & Mullen, M. (2008, September). Evaluating model fit: a synthesis of the structural equation modelli*ng literatu*re. In 7th European Conference on research methodology for business and management studies (pp. 195-200). Academic Press.

Hooper, D., Coughlan, J.*, & Mullen, M. R. (2008). Str*uctural equation modelling: Guidelines for determining model fit. Electronic J*ournal of Bus*iness Research Methods, 6(1), 53–60.

Horn, J. L. (1965). A rationale and test for the number of factors in factor analysis. *Psychometrika*, 30(2), 179–185. doi:10.1007/BF02289447 PMID:14306381

Hossain, M. (2012, May). Users' motivation to participate in online crowdsourcing platforms. In 2012 *International Conference* on Innovation Management and Technology Research (pp. 310-315). IEEE.

Howe, J. (2006). The rise of crowdsourcing. Wired. Retrieved from https://www.wired.com/wired/archive/14.06/crowds_pr.html

Howe, J. (2008). Crowdsourci*ng: How the power of the crowd is dr*iving the future of business. Random House.

Hsiao, C. H. (2018). The effects of post-adoption bel*iefs on the expectation–confirmation model in an electronics retail setting. T*otal Quality Management & Business Excellence, 29(7-8), 866–880. doi:10.1080/14783363.2016.1250621

Hu, L. T., & Bentler, P. M. (1999). Cutoff criteria for fit indexes in covariance structure analysis: Conventional criteria versus new alternatives. Structural E*quation Modeling, 6(1), 1–55. doi:10.1080/10705519909540118*

*Huber, F., Herrmann, A., & Wricke, M. (2001). Customer satisfaction as an antecedent of price acceptance: Results of an empirical study. Jour*nal of Product and Brand Management, 10(3), 160–169. doi:10.1108/10610420110395403

Hudon, M., Labie, M., & Szafarz, A. (Eds.). (2019). A research agenda for financial inclusion and microfinance.

Hue, L. T., Thuy, N. T., Huy, D. T. N., Nuong, L. N., Binh, N. V., Huyen, D. T. *T., & Thao, N. T. M. (2020). Factors affecting the access to bank cred*it of SMEs in northeastern region, Vietnam. International Journal of Entrepreneurship, 24(2), 1–12.

Hughes, D., Hughes, A., Powell, A., & Al-Sarireh, B. (2019). Hepatocellular carcinoma's 100 most influential manuscripts: A bibliometric analys*is. doi:10.5348/100083Z04DH2019OA*

Hui, E. C., Zhang, P. H*., & Zheng, X. (2013). Facilities management service and customer satisfaction in shopping mall sec*tor. Facilities. doi:10.1108/02632771311307070

Hunter, G., & Garnefeld, I. (2008). When does consumer empowerment lead to satisfied customers? Some *mediating and moderating effects of the empowe*rment-satisfaction link. Journal of Research for Consumers, 15, 1–14.

Hurst, J. L., Niehm, L. S., & Littrell, M. A. (2009). Retail service dynamics in a rural tourism community: Implications for customer relationship man*agement. Managing Service Q*uality, 19(5), 511–540. doi:10.1108*/09604520910984355*

Huy, L., Thinh, N., Pham, L., & Strickler, C. (2019). Customer T*rust and Purchase Intention: How Do Primary Website Service Qualit*y Dimensions Matter in the Context of Luxury Hotels in Vietnam? International Journal of E-Serʸices and Mobi*le Applications, 11(1), 1–23. doi:10.4018/IJESMA.2019010101*

Ibrahim, M. S., & Ahmed, M. S. (2019). SERVQUAL Reliability and Validity A Pilot Study to Evaluate Patients '. S*atisfaction in the Jordanian* Hospitals., 15(1), 56–67.

Id, X. Z., Estoque, R. C., Xie, H., Murayama, Y., & Id, M. R. (2019). Bibliometric analysis of highly cited articles on ecosystem services. Academic Press.

Ihtiyar, A*., & Ahmad, F. S. (2015). The impact of intercultural comm*unication competence on service quality and customer satisfaction. Services Marketing Quarterly, 36(2), 136–152. doi:10.1080/15332969.2015.101*4238*

*India, M. (2019). Problems Faced by Ola and Uber Users - Busi*ness. My India. https://www.mapsofindia.com/my-india/business/problems-faced-by-ola-and-uber-users

Ingledew, D. K., & Brunning, S. (1999). Personality, preventive health behaviour and comparative optimism about health problems. Journal of Health Psychology, 4(2), 193–208. doi:10.1177/135910539900400213 PMID:22021479

Ingraham, A., & Clair, J. S. (2020). The fourth industrial revolution of healthcare information technology: key business components to unlock the value of a blockchain-enabled solution. Blockchain.

IRDAI. (2021). The IRDAI Annual Report, 2020-2021. IRDAI. https://www.irdai.gov.in/admincms/cms/uploadedfiles/annual%20reports/Annual%20Report%202020-21.pdf

Irfan, W., Siddiqui, D. A., & Ahmed, W. (2019). Creating and retaining customers: Perspective from Pakistani small and medium retail stores. International Journal of Retail & Distribution Management, 47(4), 350–367. doi:10.1108/IJRDM-03-2018-0045

Irina, B. E. N. A. (2010). Evaluating customer satisfaction in banking services. Management & Marketing, 5(2), 143–150.

Islam, R., Ahmed, S., & Tarique, K. M. (2016). Prioritisation of service quality dimensions for healthcare sector. International Journal of Medical Engineering and Informatics, 8(2), 108–123. doi:10.1504/IJMEI.2016.075751

Ismail, A. (2006). Is economic value added more associated with stock return than accounting earnings? The UK evidence. International Journal of Managerial Finance.

Ittner, C. D., & Larcker, D. F. (1998). Are nonfinancial measures leading indicators of financial performance? An analysis of customer satisfaction. Journal of Accounting Research, 36, 1–35. doi:10.2307/2491304

ITU. (2019). OTT and related on-line services in Arab Region. Retrieved 24 May 2021 from International Telecommunication Union: https://www.itu.int/en/ITU-D/Regional-Presence/ArabStates/Documents/events/2015/EFF/OTT%20services%20in%20the%20Arab%20Region%2

Iwaarden, J., Ton, W., Ball, L., & Millen, R. (2003). Applying SERVQUAL to Web sites: An exploratory study. International Journal of Quality & Reliability Management, 20(8), 919–935. doi:10.1108/02656710310493634

Izquierdo, I., Olea, J., & Abad, F. J. (2014). Exploratory factor analysis in validation studies: Uses and recommendations. Psicothema, 26, 395–400. doi:10.7334/psicothema2013.349 PMID:25069561

Jacoby, L., & Jaccard, J. (2010). Perceived support among families deciding about organ donation for their loved ones: Donor vs nondonor next of kin. American Journal of Critical Care, 19(5), e52–e61. doi:10.4037/ajcc2010396 PMID:20810408

Jadil, Y., Rana, N., & Dwivedi, Y. (2022). Understanding the drivers of online trust and intention to buy on a website: An emerging market perspective. International Journal of Information Management Data Insights., 2(1), 1–12. doi:10.1016/j.jjimei.2022.100065

Jahantigh, F. F. (2019). Evaluation of healthcare service quality management in an Iranian hospital by using fuzzy logic. International Journal of Productivity and Quality Management, 26(2), 160. doi:10.1504/IJPQM.2019.097764

Jajaee, S., & Ahmad, F. (2012). Evaluating the Relationship between Service Quality and Customer Satisfaction in the Australian Car Insurance Industry. International Conference on Economics, Business Innovation, 38, (pp. 219-223). Macrothink.

Jansen, J. J., Van Den Bosch, F. A., & Volberda, H. W. (2006). Exploratory innovation, exploitative innovation, and performance: Effects of organizational antecedents and environmental moderators. Management Science, 52(11), 1661–1674. doi:10.1287/mnsc.1060.0576

Javed, S. A., & Nawaz, M. (2019). Patients ' satisfaction and public and private sectors' health care service quality in Pakistan: Application of grey decision analysis approaches. doi:10.1002/hpm.2629

Jebraeily, M., Safdari, R., Rahimi, B., Makhdoomi, K., & Ghazisaeidi, M. (2018). The application of intelligent information systems in hemo*dialysis adequacy promotion. Journal of Renal Injury Prevention, 7(2), 64–68. doi:*10.15171/jrip.2018.16

Jeon, H., Kim, C., Lee, J., & Lee, K. (2021). Understanding E-Commerce Consumers' Repeat Purchase Intention: The Role of Trust Transfer and the Mo*derating Effect of Neuroticis*m. *F*rontiers in Psychology, 12, 1–14. doi:10.3389/fpsyg.2021.690039 PMID:34140923

Jiang, K., Lepak, D. P., Hu, J., & Baer, J. C. (2012). How does human resource management influence *organizational outcomes? A meta-analytic* investigation of mediating mechanisms. Academy of Management Journal, 55, 1264–1294http://scholar.google.com/scholar_lookup?hl=en&*publication_year=201 2&pages=1264-1294&author=K.+Jiang&author=* D.+P.+Lepak&author =J.+Hu&author=J.+C.+Baer&title=How+does+human+resource+ mana gement+influence+ organizational+outcomes%3F+A+meta-analytic + in*vestigation+of+mediating+mechanisms*

*Jit, S., Liaq*at, K., Kabir, A. M., & Al, H. (2021). Adoption of digital banking channels in an em*erging economy: Exploring the role of in - branch efforts. Journal of Financial Serv*ices Marketing, 26(2), 107–121. doi:10.105741264-020-00082-w

Jones, D. E. (2015). The life arts project: Application of an inquiry-based learning model for adult learners. In P. Blessinger & J. M. Carfora (Eds.), Inquiry-Based Learning for Multidisciplinary Programs: A Conceptual and Practical Resource for Educators (pp. 275–288). Emerald Group Publishing Limited., doi*:10.1108/S2055-364120150000003031*

Jones, G., Hanton, S., & Connaughton, D. (2007). A Framework of Mental Toughness in the World's Best Performers. The Sport Psychologist, 21(2), 243–264. doi:10.1123/tsp.21.2.*243*

*Jones, M. A., & Da*vid, L. (2000). Switching barriers and repurchase intentions in services. *Kournal of Ret*ailing, 76(2), 259–274. doi:10.1016/S0022-4359(00)00024-5

Jong, J. (2016). Self-Administered Surveys. Cross Cultural Survey Guidelines. https://ccsg.isr.umich.edu/chapters/data-collection/self-adm inistered-surveys/

Joo, S., & *Grable, J. E. (2004). An ex*plo*ra*tory framework of the determinants of financial satisfaction. Journal of Family and Economic Issues, 25(1), 25–50. doi:10.1023/B:JEEI.0000016722.37994.9f

Joreskog, *K. G., & Sorbom, D. (1984). LISREL-VI User's* Guide (3rd ed.). Scientific Software.

Joseph, M., McClure, C., & Joseph, B. (1999). Service quality in the banking sector: The i*mpact of technology on servic*e *del*ivery. International Journal of Bank Marketing, 17(4), 182–193. doi:10.1108/02652329910278879

Jun, M., & Cai, S. (2001). T*he key determinant*s o*f* internet banking service quality: A content analysis. International Journal of *Bank Marketing, 19(7), 276*–291. doi:10.1108/02652320110409825

Järvinen, R. A. (2014). Consumer trust in banking relationships in Europe. International Journal of Bank Marketing.

*K*aiser, *H. (1970). A Second-Generation Littl*e *Ji*ffy. Psychometrika, 35(4), 401–415. doi:10.1007/BF02291817

Kalaja, R., Myshketa, R., & Scalera, F. (2016). Service quality assessment in health care sector: The case of Durres public hospital. Procedia: S*ocial and Behavioral Sciences, 235, 557–565. d*oi:10.1016/j.sbspro.2016.11.082

Kamran-Disfani, O., Mantrala, M. K., Izquierdo-Yusta, A., & Martínez-Ruiz, M. P. (2017). The impact of retail store forma*t on the satisfaction-*loya*l*ty link: An empirical investigation. Journal of Business Research, 77, 14–22. doi:10.1016/j.jbusres.2017.04.004

Kandpal, V., & Mehrotra, R. (2019). Financial *inclusion: The role of FinTech an*d *di*gital financial services in India. Indian Journal of Economics & Business, 19(1), 85–93.

Kano, N. (1984). Attractive quality and must-be quality. Hinshitsu (Quality, The Journal of Japanese Society for Qual*ity Control), 14, 39–48.*

Kant, R., & Jaiswal, D. (2017). The impact of perceived service quality dimensions on customer satisfaction: An empirical study on publi*c sector banks in India. International Journal of Bank Mark*eting, 35(3), 411–430. doi:10.1108/IJBM-04-2016-0051

Kaplan, R. S., & Norton, D. P. (2005). The balanced scorecard: Measures that drive performance. H*arvard Business Review, 83(7)*, 172. PMID:10119714

Kaur, B., Kiran, S., Grima, S., & Rupeika-Apoga, R. (2021). Digital banking in Northern India: The risks on customer satisfaction. Risks, 9(11*), 209. doi:10.3390/risks9110209*

Kaura, V., Prasad, C. S. D., & Sharma, S. (201*3). Customer Perception of Service Convenience: A Comparison between Public and New* Private Sector Banks. Global Business Review, 14(3), 529–547. doi:10.1177/0972150913496884

Kaynama, S. A., & Black, C. I. (2000). A propos*al to assess the service q*uality of online travel agencies: An exploratory study. Journal of Professional Services Marketing, 21(1), 63–88. *doi:10.1300/J090v21n01_05*

*Keaveney, S. M. (1995). Cu*stomer switching behavior in service industries: An exploratory study. Journal of Marketing, 59(2), 71–82. doi:10.1177/002224299505900206

Keaveney, S. M., & Parthasarathy, M. *(2001). Customer switch*ing behavior in online services: An exploratory study of the role of selected attitudinal, behavioral, and demographic factors. Journal of the Academy of Marketing Science, *29(4), 374–390. doi:10.1177/03079450094225*

Keller, K. L., & Swaminathan, V. (2020). Strategic Brand Management: Building, Measuring and Managing Brand Equity (5th ed.). Pearson Education Limited.

Keränen, J., *& Jalkala, A. (2014). Three s*trategies for customer value assessment in business markets. Management D*ecision, 52(1), 79–100. d*oi:10.1108/MD-04-2013-0230

Kesharwani, A., & Bisht, S. S. (2012). The impact of trust and perceived risk on Internet banking adoption *in India: An exten*sion of technology acceptance model. Internationa*l Journal of Bank Marketing, 30(4), 303–322. doi:10.1108/02652321211236923*

Khade, A., & Patil, V. (n.d.). A Study of customer satisfaction level of Ola and Uber paid taxi services with special reference to Pune city. Int J Manag Technol Eng, 8, 1596-1603.

Khan, A. W., Jangid, A., Bansal, *A., & Tyagi, V. (2016).* Factors Affecting Customer Satisfaction in the Taxi Service Market in India. Journal of Entrepreneurship and Management, 5(3), 46–53.

Khan, M. M., & Su, K. D. (2003). Service quality expectations of travellers visiting Cheju Island in Korea. Journal of Ecotourism, *2(2), 114–125. doi:10.1080/14724040308668138*

Khatoon, S., Zhengliang, X., & Hussain, H. (2020). The Mediating Effect of Customer Satisfaction on the Relationship between Electronic Banking Service Quality and Customer Purchase Intention: Evidence from the Qatar Banking Sector. SAGE Open, *10(2), 1–12. doi:10.1177/2158244020935887*

Khenfer, J., Shepherd, S., & Trendel, O. (2020). Customer empowerment in the face of perceived Incompetence: Effect on preference for anthropomorphized brands. Journal of Business Research, 118, 1–11. doi:10.1016/j.jbusres.2020.06.010

Khudzari, J. M., Kurian, J., Tartakovsky, B., & Raghavan, G. S. V. (2018). Bibliometric analysis of global research trends on microbial fuel cells using Scopus database. Biochemical Engineering Journal, 136, 51–60. doi:10.1016/j.bej.2018.05.002

Khurana, S. (2012). Relationship between Service Quality *and Customer Sati*sfaction: An empirical study of Indian Life Insurance Industry. Journal of Research in Marketing, 1(2), 35–42.

Kim, J. (2018). A Study on the Displacement of Mobile OTT Video Servic*es on Home TV.* J. *K*orea Contents Assoc., 18(8), 434–445. doi:10.5392/JKCA.2018.18.08.434

Kim, M., Kim, J. H., & Lennon, S. J. (2006). Online service attributes available on apparel retail we*b sites: An E-S-QUAL approach. Man*aging Service Quality, 16(1), 51–77. doi:10.1108/09604520610639964

Kim, S., & Jin, B. (2002). Validating the retail service quality scale for *US and Korean customers of discount st*ores: An exploratory study. Journal of Services Marketing, 16(3), 223–237. doi:10.1108/08876040210427218

Kim, S. S., Malhotra, N. K., & Narasimhan, S. (2005). Two Competing Perspectives on Automat*ic Use: A Theoretical and Empirical Comparison. In*formation Systems Research, 16(4), 418–432. doi:10.1287/isre.1050.0070

King, W. R., & He, J. (2006). A meta-analysis of the technology acceptance model. Information & Management, 43(6), 740–755. doi:10.1016/j.*im.2006.05.003*

*Kirca, A. H., Jayachandr*an, S., & Bearden, W. O. (2005). Market orientation: A meta-analytic review and assessment of its antecedents and impact on performance. Journal of Marketing, 69(2), 24–41. doi:10.1509/jmkg.*69.2.24.60761*

Kirkup, M., De Kervenoael, R., Hallsworth, A., Clarke, I., Jackson, P., & Del Aguila, R. P. (2004). Inequalities in retail choice: Exploring consumer experiences in suburban neighbourhoods. International Journal of Retail & Distribu*tion Management, 32(11), 511–522. doi:10.1108/09590550410564746*

Kitapci, O., Akdogan, C., & Dortyol, İ. T. (2014). The impact of service quality dimensions on patient satisfaction, repurchase intentions and word-of-mouth communication in the public healthcare industry. Procedia: Social and Behavioral *Sciences, 148, 161–169. doi:10.1016/j.sbspro.2014.07.030*

Kitchenham, B., & Charters, S. (2007). Guidelines for performing systematic literature reviews in software engineering. Academic Press.

Kleeman, F., Voss, G. G., & Rieder, K. (2008). Un(der)paid innovators: The commercial utilization of consumer work through crowdsourcing. Science. Technology and *Innovation Studies, 4(1), 5–26.*

K*l*ine, R. B. (1998). Software review: Software programs for structural equation modeling: Amos, EQS, and LISREL. Journal o*f Psychoeducational Assessment, 16(4), 343–364.* doi:10.1177/073428299801600407

Kline, R. B. (2011). Principles and Practice of Structural Equation Modeling. Guilford Press.

Knezevic, B., Renko, S.*, & Knego, N. (*2011). Changes in Retail Industry in the EU. Business. Management in Education, 9, 34–39.

Knox, S., & Walker, D. (2001). Measuring and managing brand loyalty. Journal of S*trategic Marketing, 9(2), 111–128.* doi:10.1080/713775733

Koc, E., & Boz, H. (2014). Triangu*lation in tourism research: A bibliometric study of* top three tourism journals. Tourism Management Perspectives, 12, 9–14. doi:10.1016/j.tmp.2014.06.003

*Koekemoer, L. (2014). Adverti*sing and Sales Promotion. Juta and Company Limited.

Koekemoer, M. (2017). South African Complaint Forums in the Retail Industry: a Survey of Literature and Some Lessons from the EU. Journal of consumer policy, 40. Springer Science Business Media.

Kohler, T., Fueller, J., Stieger, D., & Matzler, K. (2011). Avatar-based innovation: Consequences of the virtual co-creation experience. Computers in Human Behavior, 27(1), 160–168.

Kotler, P., & Keller, K. (2006). Marketing Management (12th ed.). Prentice Hall.

Kotler, P., & Keller, K. L. (2012). Marketing management. Pearson Education.

Kotler, P., Keller, K., Koshy, A., & Jha, M. (2013). Marketing Management—A South Asian Perspective (13th ed.). Pearson.

KPMG. (2022). Outlook for the year - Insurance sector in India. KPMG. https://home.kpmg/in/en/blogs/home/posts/2022/01/insurance-ecosystems-outlook-growth-mantra.html

Krishnan, R., & Booker, M. (2002). Investor's Use of Analysts' Recommendations. Behavioral Research in Accounting, 14(1), 129–158. doi:10.2308/bria.2002.14.1.129

Kukreja, G., Bahl, D., & Gupta, R. (2021). The Impact of FinTech on Financial Services in India: Past, Present, and Future Trends. IGI Global. doi:10.4018/978-1-7998-3257-7.ch012

Kumar, A., Olshavsky, R., & King, M. (2001). Exploring alternative antecedents of customer delight. Journal of Consumer Satisfaction, Dissatisfaction & Complaining Behavior, 14.

Kumar, P., Sharma, A., & Salo, J. (2019). A bibliometric analysis of extended key account management literature. Industrial Marketing Management, 82(January), 276–292. doi:10.1016/j.indmarman.2019.01.006

Kumar, R., & Singh, M. (2010, July). Using SERVQUAL Model for Comparative Service Quality Analysis of the Indian Non-Life Insurance Sector. Paradigm, 14(2), 56–63. doi:10.1177/0971890720100207

Kumar, R., Jothimurugan, T., & Anbuoli, P. (2018). Importance of SERVQUAL dimensions in leveraging service quality in insurance industry from the perspective of different cultural and socioeconomic environment – a SEM approach. International Journal of Services and Operations Management, 30(1), 98–119. doi:10.1504/IJSOM.2018.091442

Kumar, S. (2020, March 8). How to do Multi-collinearity test?|Tolerance test|VIF| [Video]. Youtube. https://www.youtube.com/watch?v=W4o_HWrnk2Q

Kumar, S., & Awasthi, P. (2018). Human resource accounting and organizational performance. Indian Journal of Accounting, 50, 1.

Kumar, S., Gupta, A., & Mishra, M. K. (2020). Human Resource Practice and Patient Empowerment: Mediating Role of Quality of Patient Care. Test Engineering and Management, 83, 22755–22764.

Kumar, V., & Reinartz, W. J. (2006). Customer relationship management: a databased approach. Wiley.

Kumar, V., Aksoy, L., Donkers, B., Venkatesan, R., Wiesel, T., & Tillmanns, S. (2010). Undervalued or overvalued customers: Capturing total customer engagement value. Journal of Service Research, 13(3), 297–310.

Kumar, V., George, M., & Pancras, J. (2008). Cross-buying in retailing: Drivers and consequences. Journal of Retailing, 84(1), 15–27. doi:10.1016/j.jretai.2008.01.007

Kwateng, K. O., Lumor, R., & Acheampong, F. O. (2017). Service quality in public and private hospitals: A comparative study on patient satisfaction. International Journal of Healthcare Management, 0(0), 1–8. doi:10.1080/20479700.2017.1390183

Kye, B., Han, N., Kim, E., Park, Y., & Jo, S. (2021). Educational applications of metaverse: Possibilities and limitations. *Journal of* Educational Evaluation for Health Professions, 18.

Kyei, D. A., & Bayoh, A. T. M. (2017). Innovation and customer retention in the Ghanaian telecommunication industry. International Journal of Innovation, 5(2), 171–183. doi:10.5585/iji.v5i2.154

Kyriazos, T. (2018). Applied Psychometrics: Sample Size and Sample Power Considerations in Factor Analysis (EFA, CFA) and SEM in General. Psychology (Irvine, Calif.), 9(8), 2207–2230. doi:10.*4236/psych.2018.98126*

Köseoglu, M. A., Sehitoglu, Y., Ross, G., & Parnell, J. A. (2016). The evolution of business ethics research in the realm of tourism *and hospitality: A bibliometric analysis. International Jo*urnal of Contemporary Hospitality Management, 28(8), 1598–1621. doi:10.1108/IJCHM-04-2015-0188

Ladhari, R. (2008). Alternative measures of service quality: A review. M*anaging Service Quality, 18(1), 65–86. doi:*10.1108/09604520810842849

Lai, I. K. W. (2019). Hotel image and reputation on building customer loyalty: An empirical study in Macau. Journal of Hospitality and Tourism Management, 38, 111–121. doi:10.1016/j.jhtm.2019.01.003

Lai, V. S., & Li, H. (2005). Technology acceptance model for internet banking: An invariance analysis. Information & Management, 42(2), 373–386. *doi:10.1016/j.im.2004.01.007*

Laininen, E. (2019). Transforming our worldview towards a sustainable future. In J. W. Cook (Ed.), Sustainability, human well-being, and the future of education (pp. 161–200). Palgrave Macmillan., *doi:10.1007/978-3-319-78580-6_5*

Lakhani, K. R., & Von Hippel, E. (2004). How open source software works:"free" user-to-user assistance. In Produktentwicklung mit virtuellen Communities (pp. 303–339). Gabler Verlag.

Lakhani, K. R., & Wolf, R. G. (2005). Why Hackers Do What They Do: U*nderstanding Motivation and Effort in Free/ Open Source Software Projects. Academic Press.

Landau, I. (2017). Finding Meaning in an Imperfect World. Oxford University Pre*ss. doi:10.1093/acprof:o so/9780190657666.001.0001

Lassar, W. M., Manolis, C., & Winsor, R. D. (2000). Service quality perspectives and satisfaction in private banking. Journal of Services Marketing, 14(3), 244–271. doi:10.1108/08876040010327248

Laukkanen, P., Sinkkonen, S., & Laukkanen, T. (2008). Consumer resistance to internet banking: Postponers, opponents and rejectors. International Journal of Bank Marketing, 26(6), 440–455. *doi:10.1108/02652320810902451*

Laukkanen, T. (2016). Consumer adoption versus rejection decisions in seemingly similar service innovations: The case of the Internet and mobile banking. Journal of Business Resea*rch, 69(7), 2432–2439.

Le, M. T. (2021). Examining Factors That Boost Intention and Loyalty to Use FinTech Post Covid-19 Lockdown As a New Normal Behaviour. Heliyon, 7(8), 1–9. doi:10.1016/j.*heliyon.2021.e07821*

Le Chi, C. (2016). A formative model of the relationship between destination quality, tourist satisfaction and intentional loyalty: An empirical test in Vietnam. Journal of Hospitality and Tourism Management, 26, 50–62. doi:10.1016/j.jhtm.2015.12.002

Lee, C., Lee, K., & Pennings, J. M. (2001). Internal capabilities, external networks, and performance: A study on technology-based ventures. Strategic Management Journal, 22(6-7), 615–640. doi:10.1002mj.181

Lee, D. (2017). HEALTHQUAL: A multi-item scale for assessing healthcare service quality. Service Business, 11(3), 491–516. doi:10.100711628-016-0317-2

Lee, D., & Kim, K. K. (2017). Assessing healthcare service quality: A comparative study of patient *treatment types. Int J Qual Innov, 3(1), 1. doi:10.118640887-016-0010-5*

Lee, H. W., Oh, H. G., & Choi, M. H. (2012). The formation process of public broadcasting audience's willingness to pay: Analysis through structural equation modeling (SEM). Korean Journal of Journalism & Communication Studies, 56(6), 101–126.

Lee, J. (2006). Measuring service quality in a medical setting in a developing country: The applicability of SERVQUAL. Services Marketing Quart*erly, 27(2), 1–4. do*i:*10.*1300/J396v27n02_01

Lee, K. C., & Chung, N. (2009). Understanding factors affecting trust in *and satisfaction with mobile ban*king in Korea: A modified DeLone and McLean's model perspective. Interacting with Computers, 21(5-6), 385–392. doi:10.1016/j.intcom.2009.06.004

Lee, K. C., & Chung, N. (2011). Exploring *antecedents of behavior intention to u*se Internet banking in Korea: Adoption perspective. In E-adoption and socioeconomic impacts: Emerging infrastructural effects. IGI global. doi:10.4018/978-1-60960-597-1.ch003

Lee, L. H., Braud, T., Zhou, P., Wang, L., Xu, D., Lin, Z., & Hui, P. (2021). All one needs to know about *metaverse: A complete survey on techn*ological singularity, virtual ecosystem, and research agenda. arXiv:2110.05352.

Lee, M. C. (2009). Factors influencing the adoption of internet banking: *An integration of TAM and TPB with perc*eived risk and perceived benefit. Electronic Commerce Research and Applications, 8(3), 130–141. doi:10.*1016/j.elera*p.2008.11.006

Lee, S., Han, H., Radic, A., & Tariq, B. (2020). Corporate social responsibility (CSR) as a customer satisfaction and retention strategy in the chain restaurant *sector. Journal of Hospitality and Touri*sm *Ma*nagement, 45, 348–358. doi:10.1016/j.jhtm.2020.09.002

Lee, T., Liu, C. H. S., & Li, P. H. (2021). The influences of cooperative climate, competitive climate and customer empowerment on service creativity. Journal of Retailing and *Consumer Services, 63, 1027*26. doi:10.1016/j.jretconser.2021.102726

Leimeister, J. M., Huber, M., Bretschneider, U., & Krcmar, H. (2009). Leveraging crowdsourcing: Activation-supporting compon*ents for IT-based ideas competition. Jou*rnal of Management Information Systems, 26(1), 197–224.

Lenka, U., Suar, *D., & Mohapatra, P. K. (2009). Service quality, customer satisfaction, and* customer loyalty in Indian commercial banks. The Journal of Entrepreneurship, 18(1), 47–64. doi:10.1177/097135570801800103

Levenson, A. (2011). Using targeted an*alytics to improve talen*t decisions. People & Strategy, 34, 34–43. https://scholar.google.com/scholar_lookup?hl=en&publication_year=2011&pages=34-43&author=A.+Levenson&title=Using+targeted+analytics+*to+im*prove+talent+decisions

Levenson, A., Lawler, E. E. III, & Boudreau, J. W. (2005). Survey on HR Analytics and HR transformation: Feedback report. Center for Effective Organiza*tions, University of Southern Califo*rnia., http://scholar.google.com/scholar_lookup?hl=en&publication_year=2005&author=A.+Levenson&author=E.+E.+Lawler&author=J.+W.+Boudreau&*title=Survey+on+HR+Analy*tics+and+HR+transformation%3A+Feedback+report

Lewis, R. C., & Booms, B. H. (1983). The marketing aspects of service quality. Emerging Perspectives on Services Marketing, 65(4), 99-107.

Li, F., Lu, H., Hou, M., Cui, K., & Darbandi, *M. (2021). Customer satisfaction with bank se*rvices: The role of cloud services, security, e-learning and service quality. Techno*logy in Society, 64, 1–11. doi:10.1016/j.techsoc.2020.101487*

Li, X., Ma, E., & Qu, H. (2017). Knowledge mapping of hospitality research– A visual analysis using CiteSpace. International Journal of Hospitality Management, 60, 77–93. doi:10.1016/j.ijhm.2016.10.006

Liang, D., *Ma, Z., & Qi, L. (2013). Service quali*ty *a*nd customer switching behavior in China's mobile phone service sector. Journal of Business Research, 66(8), 1161–1167. doi:10.1016/j.jbusres.2012.03.012

Liang, H., Wang, M. M., Wang, J. *J., & Xue, Y. (2018). How* intrinsic motivation and extrinsic incentives affect task effort in crowdsourcing contests: A mediated moderation model. Computers in Human Behavior, *81, 168–176.*

Liberati, A., Altman, D. G., Tetzlaff, J., Mulrow, C., Gøtzsche, P. C., Ioannidis, J. P., Clarke, M., Devereaux, P. J., Kleijnen, J., & Moher, D. (2009*). The PRISMA stateme*nt for reporting systematic reviews and meta-analyses of studies that evaluate health care interventions: Explanation and elaboration. Journal of Clinical Epidemiology, 62(10), e1–e34. doi:10.1016/j.jclinepi.2009.06.006 PMID:19631507

Lim, S., & Lee, Y. J. (2013). N screen servic*e users' mo*tivations for use and dissatisfying factors. Journal of Korea Contents Association, 13(3), 99–108. doi:10.5392/JKCA.2013.13.03.099

Lin, H. (2011). An empirical investigation of mobile banking adoption : The effec*t of innovation attributes and* knowledge-based trust. International Journal of Information Management, 31(3), 252–260. doi:10.1016/j.ijinfomgt.2010.07.006

Ling, K., Chai, L., & Piew, T. (2010). The Effects of Shop*ping Orientations, Online Trust* and Prior Online Purchase Experience toward Customers' Online Purchase Intention. International Busin*ess Research, 3(3), 63–76. do*i:10.5539/ibr.v3n3p63

Littler, D., & Melanthiou, D. (2006). Consumer perceptions of risk and uncertainty and the implications for behaviour towards innovative retail services: T*he case of internet bank*ing. Journal of Retailing and Consumer Services, 13(6), 431–443. doi:10.1016/j.jretconser.2006.02.006

Liu, A. H., & Leach, M. P. (2001). Developing loyal customers with a value-adding s*ales force: Examining custome*r *s*atisfaction and the perceived credibility of consultative salespeople. Journal of Personal Selling & Sales Management, 21(2), 147–156.

Liu, C., Arnett, K. P., & Litecky, C. (2000). D*esign quality of websites for* electronic commerce: Fortune 1000 webmasters' evaluations. Electronic Markets, 10(2), 120–129. doi:10.1080/10196780050138173

Liu, *W., Wang, J., Li, C., Chen,* B., & Sun, Y. (2019). Using Bibliometric Analysis to Understand the Recent Progress in Agroecosystem Services Research. Ecological Economics, 156(October), 293–305. doi:10.1016/j.ecolecon.2018.09.001

Lloret, S., Ferreres, A., Hernan*dez, A., & Tomas, I. (2017). The exploratory factor analy*sis of items: Guided analysis based on empirical data and software. Anales de Psicología, 33, 417–432. doi:10.6018/analesps.33.2.270211

Lochab, A., Kumar, S., & Himanshi. (2020). Dilemma to decision: Human resource analytics for organizational performance-*an empirical analysis. Asian Journal of M*u*lt*idimensional Research, 9(2), 143–151. doi:10.5958/2278-4853.2020.00028.2

Lochab, A.*, Kumar, S., & Tomar, H. (2018). Impact of Human Resource Analytics on Organiza*tional Performance: A Review of Literature Using R-Software. International Journal of Management. Technology And Engineering, 8, 1252–1261.

Lochab A., & Kum*ar S. (2019). "HR Analytics: The Winding Pa*th Ahead," Journal of the Gujarat r*esearch society, 21(11), 1215-1261.*

Loiacono, E. T., Watson, R. T., & Goodhue, D. L. (2002). WebQual: A measure of website quality. Marketing theory and applications, *13(3), 432-438.*

Lopes, E. L., de Lamônica Freire, O. B., & Lopes, E. H. (2019). Competing scales for m*easuring perceived quality in t*he electronic retail industry: A comparison between ES-Qual and E-TailQ. Electronic Commerce Research and Applications, 34, 100824. doi:10.1016/j.elerap.*2019.100824*

Loubser, M., & Reid, E. (2012). Product Liability in South Africa. Juta and Company.

Loureiro, S. M. C., & Kastenholz, E. (2011). Corporate reputation, satisfaction, delight, and loyalty towards rural lodging units in Portugal. International Journal of Hospitality Management, *30(3), 575–583. doi:10.1016/j.ij*hm.2010.10.007

Loureiro, S. M. C., Miranda, F. J., & Breazeale, M. (2014). Who needs delight? The greater impact of value, trust and satisfaction in utilitarian, fre*quent-use retail. Journal of Se*rvice Management.

Lovelock, C., & Wirtz, J. (2007). Services Marketing: People, Technology, Strategy. Prentice Hall.

Lu, S., Rajavi, K., & Dinner, I. (2021). The effect of over-the-top med*ia services on piracy search: Evidence from a natural experi*ment. Marketing Science, 40(3), 548–568.

Lubis, A., Dalimunthe, R., Absah, Y., &Fawzeea, B. K. (2020). "The Influence of Customer Relationship Management (CRM) Indicator*s on Customer Loyalt*y of Sharia Based Banking System," Lubis, A, 84-92.

Lundvall, B. Å., Rasmu*ssen, P., & Lorenz, E. (2008). Education in th*e Learning Economy: A European Perspe*ctive. Policy Futures in Education, 6(6), 681–700.* doi:10.2304/pfie.2008.6.6.681

Ma, Z., & Zhao, J. (2012). Evidence one-banking customer satisfaction in the China commercial bank sector. Journal of Software, 7(4), 927–933.

MacCallu*m, R. C., Browne, M. W., & Sugawa*ra, H. M. (1996). Power analysis and determination of sample size for covariance structure modelling. Psychological Methods, 1(2), 130–149. doi:10.1037/1082-989X.1.2.130

MacKenzie, S. B., Podsakoff, P. M., & Podsakoff, N. P. (2011). Construct measurement and validation procedures in MIS and behavioral research: Integrating new and existing techniques. Management Information Systems Quarterly, 35(2), 293–334. doi:10.2307/23044045

Madhani, P. M. (2020). Effective rewards *and recognition strategy: Enhancing employee engagement, customer retent*ion and company performance. The Journal of Total Rewards, 29(2), 39–48.

Madnani, D., Fernandes, S., & Madnani, N. (2020*). Analysing the impact of COVI*D-19 on over-the-top media platforms in India. International Journal of Pervasive Computing and Communications, 16(5), 457–475. doi:10.1108/IJPCC-07-2020-0083

Magnini, V. P., Crotts, J. C., & Zehrer, A. (2011). Understanding customer delight: An application of travel-blog analysis. Jour*nal of Travel Research, 50(5), 535–545. doi:10.1177/0047287510379162*

Mahmoud, M. A., Hinson, R. E., & Anim, P. A. (2017). Service innovation and customer satisfaction: The role of customer value creation. European Journal of Innovation Management.

*Makany*e*za*, C., & Chikazhe, L. (2017). Mediators of the relationship between service quality and customer loyalty: Evidence from the banking sector in Zimbabwe. International Journal of Bank Marketing, 35(3), 540–556. d*oi:10.1108/ IJBM-11-2016-016*4

Malar, D. A., Arvidsson, V., & Holmstrom, J. (2019). Digital transformation in banking: Exploring value co-creatio*n in online banking se*rvices in India. Journal of Global Information Technology Management, 22(1), 7–24.

Mani, Z., & Chouk, I. (2017). Drivers of consumers' resistance to smart products. Journal of Marketing Management, 33(1-2), 76–97.

Manrai, L. A., & Manrai, A. K. (2007). A field study of customers' switching behavior for bank services. Journal of Retailing and Consumer Services, 14(3), 208–215. doi:10.1016/j.jretconser.2006.09.005

March, J. (1995). Cognitive-behavioral psychotherapy for children and adolescents with OCD: A review and recommendations for treatment. Journal of the American Academy of Child and Adolescent Psychiatry, 34(1), 7–18. doi:10.1097/00004583-199501000-00008 PMID:7860461

Marimon, F., Gil-doménech, D., & Bastida, R. (2017). Total Quality Management & Business Excellence Fulfilment of expectations mediating quality and satisfaction: the case of hospital service. doi:10.1080/14783363.2017.1401458

Markovic, S., & Raspor, S. (2010). Measuring Perceived Service Quality Using SERVQUAL: A Case Study of the Croatian Hotel Industry. Management, 5, 195–209.

Markus, M. L. (2007). The governance of free/open source software projects: Monolithic, multidimensional, or configurational? The Journal of Management and Governance, 11(2), 151–163.

Marsden, P. (2009). Crowdsourcing: Your recession—Proof marketing strategy? Contagious Magazine, 18, 24–28.

Marsrurul, M. (2019). Impact of service quality on customer satisfaction in Bangladesh Tourism Industry: An empirical study. Advances in Management, 12(1), 136–140.

Martenson, R. (2007). Corporate brand image, satisfaction and store loyalty: A study of the store as a brand, store brands and manufacturer brands. International Journal of Retail & Distribution Management, 35(7), 544–555. doi:10.1108/09590550710755921

Martineau, E. (2012). A typology of crowdsourcing participation styles [Doctoral dissertation]. Concordia University.

Martinelli, E., & Balboni, B. (2012). Retail service quality as a key activator of grocery store loyalty. Service Industries Journal, 32(14), 2233–2247. doi:10.1080/02642069.2011.582499

Martinez, M. G. (2015). Solver engagement in knowledge sharing in crowdsourcing communities: Exploring the link to creativity. Research Policy, 44(8), 1419–1430.

Martins, C., Oliveira, T., & Popovič, A. (2014). Understanding the Internet banking adoption: A unified theory of acceptance and use of technology and perceived risk application. International Journal of Information Management, 34(1), 1–13.

Materla, T., & Cudney, E. A. (2017). Identifying Factors Affecting Patient Satisfaction using the Kano Model. Academic Press.

Mathew, J. (2020). Post COVID-19. Will consumer behaviour patterns mutate? BrandEquity. https://brandequity.economictimes.indiatimes.com/news/marketing/post-Covid-19-will-consumer-behaviour-patterns-mutate/75369733

Mathew, S., Jose, A., Rejikumar, G., & Chacko, D. P. (2020). Examining the relationship between e-service recovery quality and e-service recovery satisfaction moderated by perceived justice in the banking context. Benchmarking. International Journal (Toronto, Ont.).

Mathieson, K. (1991). Predicting user intentions: Comparing the technology acceptance model with the theory of planned behaviour. Information Systems Research, 2(3), 173–191.

Matos, C. A., Ituassu, C. T., & Rossi, C. A. (2007). Consumer attitudes toward counterfeits: A review and extension. Journal of Consumer Marketing, 24(1), 36–47. doi:10.*1108/07363760710720975*

Maxwell, L. K., & David, C. H. (1995). The Application of the Durbin-Watson Test to the Dynamic Regression Model Under Normal and Non-Normal Errors. Econometric Reviews, 14(4), 487–510. doi:10.1080/07474939*508800333*

*Mbama, C. I., Ezep*ue, P., *Alboul, L., &* Be*er,* M. (2018). Digital banking, customer experience and financial performance: UK bank managers' perceptions. Journal of Research in Int*eractive Marketing.*

McCain, K. W. (1990). Mapping authors in intellectual space: A technical overview. Journal of the American Society for Information Science, 41(6), 433.

McCain, K. W. (1996). Dictionary of bibliometrics. Academic Press.

*McDougall, G. H., & Lev*esqu*e,* T. (2000). Customer satisfaction with services: Putting perceived value into the equation. Journal of Services Marketing.

Meesala, A., & Paul, J. (2018). Service quality, consumer s*atisfaction and loyalty in hospitals: Thinking for the future. Journal* of Retailing and Consumer Services, 40(November), 261–269. doi:10.1016/j.jretconser.2016.10.011

Meißner, M., Haurand, M. D., & Stummer, C. (2017). With a little help from my customers: The influe*nce of customer empowerment on consumers'perc*ep*tion*s of well-established brands. International Journal of Innovation Management, 21(06), 1750048. doi:10.1142/S1363919617500487

Meleddu, M., Pulina, M., & Scuderi, R. (2019). Socio-Economic Planning Sciences *Public and private healthcare services: Wha*t drives the choice? Socio-Economic Planning Sciences, 100739(October). doi:10.1016/j.seps.2019.100739

Menon, G. (2020). KPMG India- Media and entert*ainment po*st-COVID: The best of times, the worst of times. Available at: https://home.kpmg/in/en/home/insights/

Mercier, C. R. (1996). *Sufficiency Ratings for Secondary Roads: Model* Development. International Journal of Bank Marketing, 14(7), 12–20.

Meyer, T., Barnes, D. C., & Friend, S. B. (2017). The role of deligh*t in driving repurchase inte*ntions. Journal of Personal Selling & Sales Management, 37(1), 61–71. doi:10.1080/08853134.2016.1272052

Michel, S., Brown, S. W., & Gallan, A. S. (2008). An expanded and strategic view of discontinuous innovations: Deploying a service-*dominant logic. Journal of the* Academy of Marketing Science, 36(1), 54–66. doi:10.100711747-007-0066-9

Mir, R. A., Rameez, R., & Tahir, N. (2022). Measuring Internet banking service quality: An empirical evidence. The TQM Journal.

Miranda, M. J., Kónya, L., & Havrila, I. (2005). Shoppers' satisfaction levels are not the only key to store loyalty. *Marketing Intelligence & Plann*ing, 23(2), 220–232. doi:10.1108/02634500510589958

Mishra, S., Sarkar, U., Taraphder, S., & Datta, S. (2017). Principal Component Analysis. International Journal of Livestock Research, 7(5), 60–78.

Modi, N. (2019). Aboout NFSU. Nationa*l Forensic Sciences U*niv*e*rsity. https://www.nfsu.ac.in/about

Mohammad, A. A. (2020). "The effect of customer empowerment and customer engagement on marketing performanc*e: the mediating effect of brand comm*unity membership," Verslas: teorijair praktika, 21(1), 30-38.

Mohammadi, H. (2015). Investigating users' perspectives on e-learning: An integration of TAM and IS success model. Computers in Human Behavior, 45, 359–374.

M*ohammadi-Sardo, M., & Salehi, S. (*2019). Emergency Department Patient Satisfaction Assessment using Modified Servqual Model; a Cross-sectional Study. Advanced Journal of Emergency Medicine, 3(1), e3–e3. doi*:10.22114/ajem. v0i0.107 PMID:31388652*

Mohammed, T., Mustapha, K. B. J., Godsell, Z., Adamu, K. A., Babatunde, D. D., Akintade, A., Acquaye, H., Fujii Ndiaye, M. M., & Yamoah, F. A. (2021). A critical analysis of the impacts of COVID-19 on the global economy and ecosystems and opportun*ities for circular economy strategies. Reso*urces, Conservation and Recycling, 164, 105169. Advance online publication. doi:10.1016/j.resconrec.2020.105169 PMID:32982059

Mohan, D. (2017). A Study on Customer Satisfaction Towards Services Provided by S*tate Bank Of India- With* Special Reference To Nagappattinam District. Aarhat Multidisciplinary International Education Research Journal, 6(5), 180–190.

Moher, D., Liberati, A., Tetzlaff, J., & Altman, D. G. (2009). Preferred reporting items for systematic reviews an*d meta-analyses: The PRISMA statement. Annals* of *I*nternal Medicine, 151(4), 264–269. doi:10.7326/0003-4819-151-4-200908180-00135 PMID:19622511

Mondare, S., Douthitt, S., & Carson, M. (2011). Maximizing *the impact and effe*ctiveness of HR Analytics to drive business outcomes. People & Strategy, 34, 20–27. http://scholar.google.com/scholar_lookup?hl=en&publication_y ear=2011&pag*es=20-27&author=S.+Mondare&author=S.+Douthitt&au thor=M.+*Carson&title=Maximizing+the+impact+and+effectiveness +of+HR+Analytics+to+drive+business+outcomes

Montero-Díaz, J., Cobo, M.-J., Gutiérrez-Salcedo, M., Segado-Boj, F., & Herrera-Viedma, E. (20*18). Mapeo científic*o *de* la Categoría «Comunicación» en WoS (1980-2013). Comunicar, 26(55), 81–91.

Moon, J. W., & Kim, Y. G. (2001). Extending the TAM for a World-W*ide-Web context. Information & Manage*ment, 38(4), 217–230. doi:10.1016/S0378-7206(00)00061-6

Morris, M. G., Venkatesh, V., & Ackerman, P. L. (2005). Gender and Age Differences in Employee Decisions about New Technology: An Extension to the T*heory of Md Masum Miah – Users' Satisfaction of* Digital Banking Services in Finland Planned Behaviour. IEEE Transactions on Engineering Management, 52(1), 69–84.

Morschett, D., Swoboda, B., & Foscht, T. (2005). Perception of store attributes and overall attitude towards grocery retailers: The role of shopping motives. In*ternational Review of Retail, Distribution and Co*nsumer Research, 15(4), 423–447. doi:10.1080/09593960500197552

Mostafa, R., Elseidi, R. (2018). Factors affecting consumers' willingness to buy private label brands (PLBs). Spanish Journal of Marketing-ESIC, 22 (3), *341-361. . doi:10.1108/SJME-*07-2018-0034

Moyler, A., & Hooper, M. *(2009). Over the Top TV (OTT TV) Platform Tech*nologies. BCi Ltd. and Endurance Technology Ltd.

Mugobo, V., & Malunga, P. (2015). Consumer Protection Act in South Africa. Chall*enges and Opportunities for* Furniture Retailers in Cape Town, South Africa. [MC Ser Publishing Rome, Italy.]. Mediterranean Journal of Social Sciences, 6.

Muir, K. W., Bosworth, H. B., & Lee, P. P. (2010). Healt*h Services Resear*ch *a*nd How It Can Inform the Current State of Ophthalmology. American Journal of Ophthalmology, 150(6), 761–763. doi:10.1016/j.ajo.2010.07.006 PMID:21094708

Mukherjee, A., Nath, P., & Pal, M. (2003). R*esource, service quality and performance* triad : A framework for measuring efficiency of banking services. The Journal of the Operational Research Society, 54(7), 723–735. doi:10.1057/palgrave.jors.2601573

Muthukannan, P., Tan, B., Gozman, D., & Johnson, L. (2020). The emergence of a FinTech ecosystem: A case study of the Vizag FinTech Valley in India. Information & Management, 57(8), 103385. doi:10.1016/j.im.2020.103385

Muñoz-Leiva, F., Porcu, L., & del Barrio-García, S. (2015). Discovering prominent themes in integrated marketing communication research from 1991 to 2012: A co-word analytic approach. International Journal of Advertising, 34(4), 678–701. doi:10.1080/02650487.2015.1009348

Mystakidis, S., & Christopoulos, A. (2022). Teacher Perceptions on Virtual Reality Escape Rooms for STEM. Education for Information, 13(3), 136.

Nambiar, B. K., Ramanathan, H. N., Rana, S., & Prashar, S. (2019). Perceived Service Quality and Customer Satisfaction: A Missing Link in Indian Banking Sector. Vision: The Journal of Business Perspective, 23(1), 44–55. doi:10.1177/0972262918821228

Nasri, W., & Charfeddine, L. (2012). Factors affecting the adoption of Internet banking in Tunisia: An integration theory of acceptance model and theory of planned behavior. The Journal of High Technology Management Research, 23(1), 1–14.

Nataraajan, R., & Bagozzi, R. P. (1999). The Year 2000: Looking Back. Psychology and Marketing, 16(8), 631–642. doi:10.1002/(SICI)1520-6793(199912)16:8<631::AID-MAR1>3.0.CO;2-N

Naude T. (2018). Dissemination of Consumer Law and Policy in South Africa. Journal of Consumer Policy. Springer Science and Business Media. doi:10.1007/s10603-018-9381-4

Negi, R. (2009). Determining Customer Satisfaction through Perceived Service Quality: A Study of Ethiopian Mobile Users. International Journal of Mobile Marketing, 4, 31.

Neufeld, D. J., Dong, L., & Higgins, C. (2007). Charismatic Leadership and User Acceptance of Information Technology. European Journal of Information Systems, 16(4), 49.

Ng, J. H. Y., & Luk, B. H. K. (2018). Patient satisfaction: Concept analysis in the healthcare context. Patient Education and Counseling, 102(4), 790–796. doi:10.1016/j.pec.2018.11.013 PMID:30477906

Ngo, L. V., & O'cass, A. (2013). Innovation and business success: The mediating role of customer participation. Journal of Business Research, 66(8), 1134–1142. doi:10.1016/j.jbusres.2012.03.009

Ngobo, P. V. (2017). The trajectory of customer loyalty: An empirical test of Dick and Basu's loyalty framework. Journal of the Academy of Marketing Science, 45(2), 229–250. doi:10.100711747-016-0493-6

Nguyen, H. L., Cao, T. K., & Phan, T. T. H. (2016). The Influence of service quality on customer loyalty intentions: A study in the Vietnam retail sector. Asian Social Science, 12(2), 112–112. doi:10.5539/ass.v12n2p112

Nguyen, H. T. (2020). An application of the Kano model and retail service quality scale to Vietnamese supermarkets. International Journal of Productivity and Quality Management, 31(2), 189–206. doi:10.1504/IJPQM.2020.110025

Nguyen, N. P., Yan, G., Thai, M. T., & Eidenbenz, S. (2012). Containment of misinformation spread in online social networks. Paper presented at The 4th Annual ACM Web Science Conference, Evanston, Illinois. 10.1145/2380718.2380746

Nippatlapalli, A. R. (2013). A Study On Customer Satisfaction Of Commercial Banks:Case Study On State Bank Of India. IOSR Journal of Business and Management, 15(1), 60–86. doi:10.9790/487X-1516086

Novemsky, N. (2020), Why a Pandemic Leads to Panic Buying. Yale Insights. https://insights.som.yale.edu/insights/why-pandemic-leads-to-panic-buying

Noyes, R., Reich, J., Clancy, J., & O'Gorman, T. W. (2018). Reduction in Hypochondriasis with Treatment of Panic Disorder. The British Journal of Psychiatry, 149(5), *631–635. doi:10.1192/bjp.149.5.631* PMID:3814956

Nunnally, J. C. (1978). Psychometric Theory. McGraw-Hill Publishing.

Nunnally, J. C., & Bernstein, I. H. (1994). Psychometric theory (3rd ed.). McGraw-Hill.

Nunnally Jr, J. C. *(1970). Introducti*on *to* psychological measurement.

Nuriddin, A. J. (2018). Help Yourself to Ultimate Health: Know the Causes, Symptoms, and Solutions to Optimal Health. iUni*verse.*

Nysveen, H., & Pedersen, P. E. (2014). Influences of cocreation on brand experience. International Journal of Market Research, 56(6), 807–832.

Odriozola-fernández, I., & Berbegal-m*irabent, J. (2019). Open innovation in small* and medium enterprises: A bibliometric analysis. doi:10.1108/JOCM-12-2017-0491

OECD. *(2005). Enhancing the performance of the services sector.* Paris: OECD.

Oh, H., & Kim, K. *(2017). Customer satisfacti*on, service quality, and customer value: Years 2000-2015. International Journal of Contemporary Hospitality Management, 29(1), 2–29. doi:10.1*108/IJCHM-10-2015-0594*

*Olive*ira, T., Faria, M., Thomas, M. A., & Popovic, A. (2014). Extending the understanding of mobile banking adoption: When UTAUT m*eets TTF and ITM. International Journal of Inf*ormation Management, 34(5), 689e703.

Oliver, M. (1992). Changing the Social Relations of Research Production? Disability, Handicap & Society, 7(2), 101–114.

Oliver, R. (1996). Satisfaction: a Behavior *Perspective on the Consumer. McG*raw-Hill.

Oliver, R. L. (1980). A cognitive model of the antecedents *and consequences of satisfaction decisions. JMR, Journal of Marketing Research, 17(4)*, 460–469.

Oliver, R. L. (1993). Cognitive, affective, and attribute bases of the satisfaction response. The Journal of Consumer Research*, 20(3), 418–430. doi:10.1086/209358*

*Olive*r Richard, L. (1997). Satisfaction: A behavioral perspective on the consumer. Irwin-McGraw-Hill.

Osborne, J. W. (201*4). Best Practices in Exploratory Factor Analys*is. Scotts Valley, CA. CreateSpace Independent Publishing., ISBN-13, 978–1500594343.

Otto, A. S., Szymanski, D. M., & Varadarajan, R. (2020). Customer satisfaction and *firm performance: Insights from* over a quarter century of empirical research. Journal of the Academy of Marketing Science, 48(3), 543–564. doi:10.100711747-019-00657-7

Otto J., Van Heerden C.*, and Barnard J*. (2014). Redress in terms of the National Credit Act and the Consumer Protection Act for d*efective goods sold and financed in terms of* an instalment agreement. The Sou*th African M*ercantile Law Journal, 241.

Overview of Community Token Economies. (n.d.). Outlier Ventures. https://outlierventures.io/research/overview-of-ctes/

Ozatac, N., Saner, T., & Sen, Z. S. *(2016). Customer Satisfacti*on in the Banking Sector: The Case of North Cyprus. Procedia Economics and Finance, 39(November), 870–878. doi:10.1016/S2212-5671(16)30247-7

OziliP. K.ArunT. (2020). *Spillover of COVID-19: impact on the* global economy. doi:10.2139/ssrn.3562570

Ozturk, A. B., Bilgihan, A., Nusair, K., & Okumus, F. (2016). What keeps the mobile hotel booking users loyal? Investigating the roles of self-efficacy, compatibility, perceived ease of use, and perceived convenience. International Journal of Information Management, 36(6), 1350–1359.

O'Cass, A., & Ngo, L. V. (2011). Achieving customer satisfaction in services firms via branding capability and customer empowerment. Journal of Services Marketing, 25(7), 489–496. doi:10.1108/08876041111173615

O'Mahony, S. (2003). Guarding the commons: How community managed software projects protect their work. Research Policy, 32(7), 1179–1198.

Paauwe, J., & Boselie, P. (2005). 'Best practices … in spite of performance': Just a matter of imitation? The International Journal of Human Resource Management., 16, 987–1003. http://scholar.google.com/scholar_lookup?hl=en&publication_year=2005&pages=987-1003&author=J.+Paauwe&author=P.+Boselie&title=%E2%80%98Best+practices+%E2%80%A6+in+spite+of+ performance%E2%80%99%3A+Just+a+matter+of+imitation%3F

Painoli, G., Dhinakaran, D., & Vijai, C. (2021, June). Impact of FinTech on the Profitability of Public and Private Banks in India. Annals of the Romanian Society for Cell Biology, 25(6), 5419–5431.

Pais, A., & Costa, M. (2020). An ideology critique of global citizenship education. Critical Studies in Education, 61(1), 1–16. doi:10.1080/17508487.2017.1318772

Pakurár, M., Haddad, H., Nagy, J., Popp, J., & Oláh, J. (2019). The Service Quality Dimensions that Affect Customer Satisfaction in the Jordanian Banking Sector. Sustainability, 11(4), 1113. doi:10.3390u11041113

Pallant, J. (2013). SPSS Survival Manual. A step-by-step guide to data analysis using SPSS (4th ed.). Allen & Unwin. www.allenandunwin.com/spss

Palmatier, R. W., Houston, M. B., & Hulland, J. (2018). Review articles: Purpose, process, and structure. Journal of the Academy of Marketing Science, 46(1), 1–5. doi:10.100711747-017-0563-4

Panda, P., Mishra, S., & Behera, B. (2021). Developing a Research Methodology with the Application of Explorative Factor Analysis and Regression. IOSR Journal of Business and Management, 23(4), 23-34.

Panda, T., & Das, S. (2014). The Role of Tangibility in Service Quality and Its Impact on External Customer Satisfaction: A Comparative Study of Hospital and Hospitality Sectors. The IUP Journal of Marketing Management, 13(4), 53–69.

Panigrahi, S., Azizan, N., & Waris, M. (2018). Investigating the Empirical Relationship Between Service Quality, Trust, Satisfaction, and Intention of Customers Purchasing Life Insurance Products. Indian Journal of Marketing, 48(1), 28. doi:10.17010/ijom/2018/v48/i1/120734

Pant, S. (2020, September). FinTech: Emerging Trends. Telecom Business Review, 13(1), 47–52.

Panter-Brick, C., & Fuentes, A. (2009). Health, Risk, and Adversity. Recommendations for the Management of the Coronavirus Disease 2019 (COVID-19). Berghahn Books.

Paposa, S., Ukinkar, V., & Paposa, K. (2019). Service Quality and Customer Satisfaction: Variation in Customer Perception Across Demographic Profiles in Life Insurance Industry. International Journal of Innovative Technology and Exploring Engineering, 8(10), 3767–3775. doi:10.35940/ijitee.J9970.0881019

Parasuraman, A., Berry, L., & Zeithaml, V. (1991). Refinement and reassessment of the SERVQUAL scale. Journal of Retailing, 67(4), 420–450.

Parasuraman, A., Berry, L. L., & Zeithaml, V. A. (1991). Understanding customer expectations of service. Sloan Management Review, 32(3), 39–48.

Parasuraman, A., Zeithaml, V., & Malhotra, A. (2005). E-S-QUAL a multiple-item scale for assessing electronic service quality. Journal of Service Research, 7(3), 213–234.

Parasuraman, A., Zeithaml, V. A., & Berry, L. (1988). SERVQUAL: A multiple-item scale for measuring consumer perceptions of service quality. 1988, 64(1), 12-40.

Parasuraman, A., Zeithaml, V. A., & Berry, L. (1988). SERVQUAL: A multiple-item scale for measuring consumer perceptions of service quality. Academic Press.

Parasuraman, A., Zeithaml, V. A., & Berry, L. L. (1985). A conceptual model of service quality and its implications for future research. Journal of Marketing, 49(4), 41–50. doi:10.1177/002224298504900403

Parasuraman, A., Zeithaml, V. A., & Berry, L. L. (1988). SERVQUAL: A multiple item scale for measuring customer perceptions of service quality. Journal of Retailing, 64(1), 12–40.

Parasuraman, A., Zeithaml, V. A., & Malhotra, A. (2005). E-S-QUAL: A Multiple-Item Scale for Assessing Electronic Service Quality. Journal of Service Research, 7(3), 213–233. doi:10.1177/1094670504271156

Parikh, D. (2006). Measuring retail service quality: An empirical assessment of the instrument. Vikalpa, 31(2), 45–56. doi:10.1177/0256090920060203

Park, J. (2019). Service Quality in Tourism: A Systematic Literature Review and Keyword Network Analysis. Academic Press.

Park, W., Lee, S., Park, C., Jung, S., & Kim, H. (2021). The Effect of Service Quality of Internet Insurance on Intention to Purchase Online. International Journal of Smart Business and Technology, 9(1), 63–70. doi:10.21742/IJSBT.2021.9.1.06

Paswan, A. K., & Ganesh, G. (2005). Cross-cultural interaction comfort and service evaluation. Journal of International Consumer Marketing, 18(1-2), 93–115. doi:10.1300/J046v18n01_05

Pathak, B. (2018). Indian Financial System. Pearson Education.

Pee, L. G., Koh, E., & Goh, M. (2018). Trait motivations of crowdsourcing and task choice: A distal-proximal perspective. International Journal of Information Management, 40, 28–41.

Pei, X.-L., Guo, J.-N., Wu, T.-J., Zhou, W.-X., & Yeh, S.-P. (2020). Does the Effect of Customer Experience on Customer Satisfaction Create a Sustainable Competitive Advantage? A Comparative Study of Different Shopping Situations. Sustainability, 12(18), 7436. doi:10.3390u12187436

Pekkaya, M., İmamoğlu, Ö. P., & Koca, H. (2017). Evaluation of healthcare service quality via Servqual scale: An application on a hospital. doi:10.1080/20479700.2017.1389474

Peng, C. (2022). Investor sentiment, customer satisfaction and stock returns. European Journal of Marketing, 49(5), 827–850.

Petzer, D. J., & Van Tonder, E. (2019). Loyalty intentions and selected relationship quality constructs: The mediating effect of customer engagement. International Journal of Quality & Reliability Management, 36(4), 601–619. doi:10.1108/IJQRM-06-2018-0146

Pham, M. T. (1998). Representativeness, relevance, and the use of feelings in decision making. The Journal of Consumer Research, 25(2), 144–159. doi:10.1086/209532

Phora, J. S. (2017). Developing a legal framework for e-commerce in South Africa. University of Pretoria.

Pikkarainen, T., Pikkarainen, K., Karjaluoto, H., & Pahnila, S. (2004). Consumer acceptance of online banking: An extension of the technology acceptance model. Internet Research, 14(3), 224–235.

Pilkington, A., & Liston-Heyes, C. (1999). Is production and operations management a discipline? A citation/co-citation study. International Journal of Operations & Production Management, 19(1), 7–20. doi:10.1108/01443579910244188

Pilkington, A., & Meredith, J. (2009). The evolution of the intellectual structure of operations management—1980–2006: A citation/co-citation analysis. Journal of Operations Management, 27(3), 185–202. doi:10.1016/j.jom.2008.08.001

Pinto, P., Hawaldar, I. T., & Pinto, S. (2020). Impulse buying behavior among female shoppers: Exploring the effects of selected store environment elements. Academic Press.

Pires, G. D., Stanton, J., & Rita, P. (2006). The internet, consumer empowerment and marketing strategies. European Journal of Marketing.

Piyathasanan, B., Mathies, C., Patterson, P., & de Ruyter, K. (2013). The Value of Crowdsourcing: Antecedents and Value Creation of Creative Process Engagement. ANZMAC 2013.

Piyathasanan, B., Mathies, C., Patterson, P. G., & de Ruyter, K. (2017). Continued value creation in crowdsourcing from creative process engagement. Journal of Services Marketing.

Plagnol, A. C. (2011). Financial satisfaction over the life course: The influence of assets and liabilities. Journal of Economic Psychology, 32(1), 45–64. doi:10.1016/j.joep.2010.10.006

Poetz, M. K., & Schreier, M. (2012). The value of crowdsourcing: Can users really compete with professionals in generating new product ideas? Journal of Product Innovation Management, 29(2), 245–256. doi:10.1111/j.1540-5885.2011.00893.x

Poon, W. C. (2008). Users' adoption of e-banking services: The Malaysian perspective. Journal of Business and Industrial Marketing.

Pornpitakpan, C., & Han, J. H. (2013). The effect of culture and salespersons' retail service quality on impulse buying. Australasian Marketing Journal, 21(2), 85–93. doi:10.1016/j.ausmj.2013.02.005

Potey, D., & Soni, J. (2019). A Study on How Digital Payments have Revolutionized the Customer Experience. The Management Quest, 2(1).

Potra, S., Pugna, A., Negrea, R., & Izvercian, M. (2018). Customer perspective of value for innovative products and services. Procedia: Social and Behavioral Sciences, 238, 207–213. doi:10.1016/j.sbspro.2018.03.025

Pouragha, B., & Zarei, E. (2016). The effect of outpatient service quality on patient satisfaction in teaching hospitals in Iran. Materia Socio-Medica, 28(1), 21. doi:10.5455/msm.2016.28.21-25 PMID:27047262

Poynter, R. (2013). Crowdsourcing lessons for market research. Academic Press.

Prakash, N., Somasundaram, R., & Krishnamoorthy, V. (2018). An empirical study on apparel retail service quality and its impact on customer loyalty in specialty store. International Journal of Services and Operations Management, 30(4), 505–519. doi:10.1504/IJSOM.2018.10014628

Pranic, L., & Roehl, W. S. (2012). Rethinking service recovery: A customer empowerment (CE) perspective. Journal of Business Economics and Management, 13(2), 242–260. doi:10.3846/16111699.2011.620137

Pretorius, L. S. (2016). Rural consumers' consciousness and use of the Consumer Protection Act in the Valspan community within the Phokwane Municipality. University of the North West.

Priem, R. L., Li, S., & Carr, J. C. (2012). Insights and new directions from de*mand-side approaches to te*chnology innovation, entrepreneurship, and strategic management research. Journal of Management, 38(1), 346–*374.*

Pritchard, A. (1969). Statistical bibliography or bibliometrics. The Journal of Documentation, 25(4), 348–349.

Priya, P., & Anusha, K. (2019, September). FinTech Issues and Challenges in India. International J*ournal of Recent Technology and Engineering, 8(3), 904–908.*

Pyle, D. H. (1999). Bank risk management: theory. In Risk Management and regulation in banking (pp. 7–14). Springer.

Pérez, M. S., Abad, J. C. G., Carrillo, G. M. M., & Fernández, R. S. (2007). Effects of s*ervice q*uality dimensions on behavioural purchase intentions: A study in pu*blic-sector transport. Managing Service Quality: An International Journal Pitt, L. F.,* Watson, R. T., &Kavan, C. B. (1995). Service Quality: A Measure of Information Systems Effectiveness. Management Informati*on Systems Quarterly, 19(2),* 173–187. doi:10.2307/249687

Pétavy, F., Céré, J., Tan, C., & Roth, Y. (2012). Online co-creation to accelerate m*arketing and innovati*on, Academic Press.

Rabbani, M. A., Qadri, F. A., & Ishfaq, M. (2017). Service Quality, Customer Satisfaction and Customer Loyalty: An Empirical Study On *Banks In India. VFAST T*ransaction of Education and Social Science, 5(1), 39–47.

Rahman M.S. (2017) The Advantages and Disadvantages of Using Qualitative and Quantitative Approach and Methods in Language Testing *and Assessment Resea*rch: A literature Review. Journal of Education and Learning, 6(1). Canadian Center of Science and Education.

Rajeswari, P., & Vijai, C. (2021). Fin*Tech Industry In India: The* Revolutionized Finance Sector. European Journal of Molecular & Clinical Medicine, 8(11), 4300–4306.

Ram, S. (1987). A model of innovation resistance. ACR North American Adv*ances.*

Ram, S., & Sheth, J. N. (1989). Consumer resistance to innovations: The marketing problem and its solutions. Journal of Consumer Mark*eting, 6(2),* 5–14.

Ramachandran, A., & Chidambaram, V. (2012). A revi*ew of customer satisfaction towards service quality of banking sector. Periodica Polyte*chnica Social and Management Sciences, 20(2), 71–79. doi:10.3311/pp.so.2012-2.02

Ramadhan, A., & Soegoto, D. (2020). The Factor Influencing Customer Satisfacti*on in Health Insurance Companies. Advances in Economics. B*usiness and Management Research, 112, 117–121. doi:10.2991/aebmr.k.200108.028

Ramos Rodríguez, A. R., & Ruiz Navarro, J. (2008). Base inte*lectual de la investigación en creación de e*mpresas: Un estudio biométrico. Revista europea de dirección y e*conomía de la empresa,* 17(1), 13-38.

Ramos-Rodríguez, A., & Ruíz-Navarro, J. (2004). Changes in the intellectual structure of strategic management research: A bibliom*etric study of the Strategic Management Journal, 1*980–2000. Strategic Management Journal, 25(10), 981–1004. doi:10.1002mj.397.

Ranaweera, C., & Prabhu, J. (2003). The influence of satisfaction, trust and switching barriers on customer retention in a continuous purchasing setting. Internation*al Journal of Se*rvice Industry Management, 14(4), 374–395. doi:10.1108/09564230310489231

Ranganathan*, C., & Ganapathy, S. (2002). Key dimensions of business-to-consumer web sites. Informatio*n & Management, 39(6), 457–465. doi:10.1016/S0378-7206(01)00112-4

Rani, M. S. B. A. (2021). Study on customer sat*isfaction, adoption, percepti*on, behaviour, and Security on financial technology (fintech) services. In International Conference on Multidisciplinary Innovation and Economics (Vol. 8). Academic Press.

Rasmussen, T., & Ulrich, D. (2015). Learning from practice: How HR Analytics avoids being a management fad. Organizational Dynamics, 44, 236–242. http://scholar.google.com/scholar_lookup?hl=en&publication_year=2015&pages=236-242&author=T.+Rasmussen&author=D.+Ulrich&title=Learning+from+practice%3A+How+HR+Analytics+avoids+being+a+management+fad

Raza, S. A., Umer, A., Qureshi, M. A., & Dahri, A. S. (2020). Internet banking service quality, e-customer satisfaction and loyalty: The modified e-SERVQUAL model. The TQM Journal.

Reddy, N. S. (2019). The profitability interlinkage model of retail store management. International Journal of Mechanical Engineering and Technology, 10(2).

Reeves, C. A., & Bednar, D. A. (1994). Defining quality: Alternatives and implications. Academy of Management Review, 19(3), 419–445. doi:10.2307/258934

Reinchheld, F. F. (1996). The loyalty effect: The hidden force behind growth, profits, and lasting value. Long Range Planning, 29(6), 909–909. doi:10.1016/S0024-6301(97)82843-9

Reserve Bank of India. (2018). Report of the Working Group on FinTech and Digital Banking. Retrieved from https://www.rbi.org.in/Scripts/PublicationReportDetails.aspx?UrlPage=&ID=892

Reynolds, K. E., Ganesh, J., & Luckett, M. (2002). Traditional malls vs. factory outlets: Comparing shopper typologies and implications for retail strategy. Journal of Business Research, 55(9), 687–696. doi:10.1016/S0148-2963(00)00213-7

Rhee, H., & Bell, D. R. (2002). The inter-store mobility of supermarket shoppers. Journal of Retailing, 78(4), 225–237. doi:10.1016/S0022-4359(02)00099-4

Ribeaux, P. (1978). Psychology and Work. Macmillan Education.

Riffai, M. M. M. A., Grant, K., & Edgar, D. (2012). Big TAM in Oman: Exploring the promise of on-line banking, its adoption by customers and the challenges of banking in Oman. International Journal of Information Management, 32, 239–250.

Rita, P., Oliveira, T., & Farisa, A. (2019). The impact of e-service quality and customer satisfaction on customer behavior in online shopping. Heliyon, 5(10), e02690. doi:10.1016/j.heliyon.2019.e02690 PMID:31720459

Ritchie, J., Lewis, J., Nicholls, C., McNaughton, J., & Ormiston, R. (2014). Qualitative research practice: A guide for social science students and researchers. SAGE Publications. doi:10.4135/9781452230108

Rivas, R. (2020). Hoarding, overpricing would lead to criminal charges, warns DTI. Rappler. https://www.rappler.com/business/254286-dti-warning-hoarding-overpricing-would-lead-criminal-charges

Robb, C., Babiarz, P., Woodyard, A., & Seay, M. (2015). Bounded rationality and use of alternative financial services. The Journal of Consumer Affairs, 49(2), 407–435. doi:10.1111/joca.12071

Robinson, J., Whyte, J., & Segura, C. (2022). Exploring the metaverse and the digital future. Groupe Special Mobile Association Intelligence (GSMA), 1-27.

Rod, M., Ashill, N. J., & Gibbs, T. (2016). Customer perceptions of frontline employee service delivery: A study of Russian bank customer satisfaction and behavioural intentions. Journal of Retailing and Consumer Services, 30, 212–221. doi:10.1016/j.jretconser.2016.02.005

Rod, M., Ashill, N. J., Shao, J., & Carruthers, J. (2009). An examin*ation of the relationship between service quality dimensio*ns, overall internet banking service quality and customer satisfaction: A Ne*w Zealand study. Marketing Intelligence & Planning.*

*Rodríguez-lópez, M. E., Alcántara-pilar, J. M., Del Barrio-garcía, S., & M*uñoz-leiva, F. (2019). International Journal of Hospitality Management A review of restaurant research in the last two decades: A bibliometric analysis. International Journal of Hospitality Management, 102387(Sep*tember). doi:10.1016/j.ij*hm.2019.102387

Rogers, E. M. (2003). Diffusion of Innovations (5th ed.). Simon *and Schuster. https://scholar.google.com/scholar_lookup?hl=en&publication_* year=2003&author=E.+M+Rogers&title=Diffusion+of+Innova*tions*

*Rokonuzzaman, M. D., Harun, A., Al-Emran, M. D., & Pr*ybutok, V. R. (2020). An investigation into the link between consumer'*s product involvement and store loyalty:* The roles of shopping value goals and information search as the mediating factors. Journal of Retailing and Consumer Services, 52, 101933. doi:10.1016/j.jretconser.2019.10193*3*

*Rompho, N., & Unyathanakorn, K. (2014). Factor*s Affecting Customer Satisfaction in Online Banking Service. Journal of Marketing Development and Competitiveness, 8(2), 50–60. http:// www.digitalcommons.www. na-businesspress.com/JMDC/R ompho*N_Web8_2_.pdf*

Roth, Y., & Kimani, R. (2014). Crowdsourcing in the production of video advertising: The emerging roles of crowdsourcing platforms. In International perspectives on *business innovation and disruption in the creativ*e industries. Edward Elgar Publishing.

Roth, Y., Brabham, D. C., & Lemoine, J. F. (2015). Recruiting individuals to a crowdsourcing community*: Applying motivational categories to an ad copy test. In* Advances in crowdsourcing (pp. 15–31). Springer.

Rousseau, D. M., & Boudreau, J. W. (2011). Sticky findings: Research evidence practitioners find usefu*l. In S. A. Mohrman & E. E. Lawler III, (Eds.), Useful re*search: Advancing theory and practice. Berrett-Koehler. https://scholar. google.com/scholar?hl=en&q=Rousseau%2C+D.+M.%2C+%26+Boudreau%2C+J.+W.%282011%29.+ Sticky+fi ndings%3A+Research+*evidence+practitioners+find+useful.+In+S.+A.+Mohrman%2C+%26+E.+E.+Lawler* %2C+ III+%28Eds.%29%2C+Useful+research%3A+ Advancing+theory+and+practice+ %28ch.+14%29.+Berrett-Koehler

Rousseau, D. M., Manning, J., & Denyer, D. (2008). 11 Evidence in management and *organizational science: Asse*mbling the field's full weight of scientific knowledge *through syntheses. The Academy o*f Management Annals, 2, 475–515. http://scholar.google.com/scholar_lookup?hl=en&publication_year=200 8&pages=475-515&author= D.+M.+Rousseau&author=J.+Manning&aut hor=D.+ Denyer&title=11+Evidence+in+ management+and+organiza tional+science%3A+Assembling+the+field %E2%80%99s+full+weigh t+of+scientific+ knowledge+through+syntheses

Rowley, J. *(2006). An analysis of the e-service literature: To*wards a research agenda. Internet Research, 16(3), 339–359.

Rowley, J. (2006). An analysis of the e-service literature: Towards a research *agenda. Internet Resear*ch, 16(3), 339–359. doi:10.1108/10662240610673736

Rubera, G., & Kirca, A. H. (2017). You gotta serve somebody: The effects of firm innovation on customer satisfaction and firm value. Journal of the Acade*my of Marketing Science, 45(5), 741–761. doi:10.100711747-016-0512-7*

Ru*ssell,* C. (2005). An overview of the integrative research review. Progress in Transplantation (Aliso Viejo, Calif.), 15(1), 8–13. doi:10.1177/152692480501500102 PMID:15839365

Rust, R. T., & *Alpert, M. I.* (1984). An audience flow model of television viewing choice. Marketing Science, 3(2), 113–*124. doi:10.1287/mksc.3.2.113*

*Rutkowska, A. (2022). Investor*s' *s*atisfaction in portfolio selection problem. Conference paper. 10.2991/ifsa-eus-flat-15.2015.23

*Saeedpoor, M., Mobin, M., & R*astegari, A. (2015). A SERVQUAL Model Approach Integrated With Fuzzy Ahp and Fuzzy Topsis Methodologies to Rank Life Insurance Firms. Proceedi*ngs of the American* Soc*i*ety for Engineering Management 2015 International Annual Conference. Research G*ate. https://www.researchgate.net/publication/282819370_A_*SERVQUA L_MODEL_APPROACH_INTEGRATED_WITH_FUZZY_AHP_AND_FUZZY_TOPSIS_ METHODOLOGIES_TO_RANK_LIFE_INSURANCE_FIRMS

Saeidi, S. P., Rasli, A. B. M., Saeidi, P., Saaeidi, S. A., & Saeidi, S. P. (2017). How service quality results in customer satisfaction of *large-scale retailers in Mal*aysi*a.* Advanced Science Letters, 23(9), 9050–9054. doi:10.1166/asl.2017.10021

Saha, P., & Zhao, Y. (2005). Relationship between online *service quality and* cu*s*tomer satisfaction: a study in internet banking. Academic Press.

Sahoo, S, Misra,S., Ray, K. (2019). Customer Perception of Service based on Servqual Dimensions: A Study of Indian Life Insurance Companies. Parikalpana - KIIT *Journal of Management. 166-182. . doi:10.23862/kii*t-parikalpana/2019/ v15/i1-2/190181

Saleem, A., Ghafar, A., Ibrahim, M., Yousuf, M., & Ahmed, N. (2015). Product Perceived Quality and Purchase Intention w*ith Cons*umer Satisfaction: Global Journals Inc. USA. Global Journal of Management and Business Research, 15(1).

Salim, T., Onyia, O., Harrison, T., & Lindsay, V. (2017). Effects of perceived c*ost, service quality, and custo*mer satisfaction on health insurance service continuance. Journal of Financial Services Research. Macmillan Publishers.

Samantaray, A., *Mishra, U. S., Das, J. R., & Mahapatra, J. (2017). An*alysing the mediating effect of customer satisfaction on the relationship between service quality and customer loyalty in indian organized retail sector. International Journal of Applied *Business and Economic Research, 15(25), 243–251.*

Sampaio, C. H., Ladeira, W. J., & Santini, F. D. O. (2017). Apps for mobile banking and customer satisfaction: A cross-cultural study. International Journal of Bank Marketing.

Sandhu, B. (2011). Customers' Perception towards Service Quality of Life Insurance Corp*oration of India: A Factor Analy*tic Approach. International Journal of Business and Social Science, 2(18), 219–231.

Santos, J. (2003). E-service quality: A model of virtual service quality dimensions. Managing Service Quality, 13(3), 233–246.

Santos, J. (2003). *E-service quality: A model of virtual service qu*ality dimensions. Managing Service Quality, 13(3), 233–246. doi:10.1108/09604520310476490

Saraswathy, C., & Suganya, R. V. (2018). A Study on Customer's Satisfaction Of Banking Services In Pudukkottai District. International Journal of Pure and Applied Mathematics, 119(7), 1027–1038.

Saricam, C. *(2022). Analysing Service Quality and Its R*ela*t*ion to Customer Satisfaction and Loyalty in Sportswear Retail Market. AUTEX Research Journal, 22(2), 184–193. doi:10.2478/aut-2021-0014

Sarkodie, S. A., *& Strezov, V. (2019). Science of the Total Environm*ent A review on Environmental Kuznets Curve hypothesis using bibliometric and meta-analysis. The Science of the Total Environment, 649, 128–145. doi:10.1016/j. scitotenv.2018.08.276 PMID:30172133

Sathish, D., & VenkatramaRaju, D. (2010). The growth of Indian retail industry. Advances in Management.

Saunders, M., Lewis, P., & Thornhill, A. (2016). Research Methods for Business Students (7th ed.). Pearson Education India.

Sawhney, M., Verona, G., & Prandelli, E. (2005). Collaborating to create: The Internet as a platform for customer engagement in product innovation. Journal of Interactive Marketing, 19(4), 4–17.

Schleicher, A. (2018). Insights and Interpretations. PICA. https://www.oecd.org/pisa/PISA%202018%20Insights%20and%20Int erpretations%20FINAL%20PDF.pdf

Schlossberg, H. (1990). Satisfying customers is a minimum; you really have to 'delight'them. Marketing News, 24(11), 10–11.

Schumacker, R. E., & Lomax, R. G. (2010). A Beginner's Guide to Structural Equation Modeling (3rd ed.). Routledge. https://usermanual.wiki/Pdf/ABeginnersGuidetoStructuralEquationModeling3rded.967768708/help

Schumpeter, J. A. (2013). Capitalism, socialism and democracy. Routledge.

Schwarz, N., & Clore, G. L. (1983). Mood, misattribution, and judgments of well-being: Informative and directive functions of affective states. Journal of Personality and Social Psychology, 45(3), 513–523. doi:10.1037/0022-3514.45.3.513

Scott, D. (2014). Knowledge and the curriculum. Curriculum Journal, 25(1), 14–28. doi:10.1080/09585176.2013.876367

Seemiller, C., & Grace, M. (2017). Generation Z: Educating and engaging the next generation of students. About Campus: Enriching the Student Learning Experience, 22(3), 21–26.

Sehgal, S., Singh, H., Agarwal, M., & Shantanu, V. B. (2014). Data Analysis Using Principal Component Analysis. International Conference on Medical Imaging, m-Health and Emerging Communication Systems, 45–48.

Seth, R., & Seth, K. (2005). Creating Customer Delight: The How and Why of Customer Relationship Management. SAGE Publications. https://books.google.co.in/books?id=cwAKAQAAMAAJ

Severin, V., Louviere, J. J., & Finn, A. (2001). The stability of retail shopping choices over time and across countries. Journal of Retailing, 77(2), 185–202. doi:10.1016/S0022-4359(01)00043-4

Shafiq, M., & Naeem, M. A. (2017). Service Quality Assessment of Hospitals in Asian Context: An Empirical Evidence From Pakistan. doi:10.1177/0046958017714664

Shamash, D., & Nordnes, R. A. (2022). The Open Metaverse 2021/22. Outlier Ventures.

Shankar, A., Datta, B., & Jebarajakirthy, C. (2019). Are the Generic Scales Enough to Measure Service Quality of Mobile Banking? A Comparative Analysis of Generic Service Quality Measurement Scales to Mobile Banking Context. Services Marketing Quarterly, 40(3), 224–244. doi:10.1080/15332969.2019.1630176

Sharanya, E., & Kumari, K. V. (2019). Structural Relationship between Dimensions of Psychological Empowerment, Customer Oriented Behaviour and Job Satisfaction of Employees in Public Sector Banks. Indian Journal of Public Health Research & Development, 10(11), 101. doi:10.5958/0976-5506.2019.03432.6

Sharma, A., & Stafford, T. F. (2000). The effect of retail atmospherics on customers' perceptions of salespeople and customer persuasion: An empirical investigation. Journal of Business Research, 49(2), 183–191. doi:10.1016/S0148-2963(99)00004-1

Sharma, D. (2014). Examining the influence of service quality on customer satisfacti*on and patronage intentions* in convenience store industry. Academic Press.

Sharma, S. (2014). Internet banking adoption in India Structural equation modeling approach. Journal of Indian Business Research, 6(2*), 155–169. doi:10.1108/JIBR-02-2013-0013*

Sharma, S., Srivastav, S., Gupta, A., & Manglick, A. (2022). Application of Technology and Innovation in FinTech *and it's Adaptability in Ind*ia. In 2nd International Conference on Innovative Practices in Technology and Management (ICIPTM) (p*p. 305-311). 10.1109/ICIP*TM54933.2022.9753933

Sharma, V. (2021). Examination of Service Quality of Digital Payments among Working Professionals. Turkish Journal of Computer and Mathematics Educ*ation, 12(2), 777–783.*

Sharrock, R. (2016). The Law of *B*anking and Payment in South Africa. Juta and Company Ltd.

Shen, Q. L., & Li, Y. T. (2010). Explore antecedent factors of switching costs and inten*tions and their impact o*n customer loyalty. The 13th Conference on Interdisciplinary and Multifunctional Business Management, 13, (pp. 271-288). Semantic Scholar.

Sheppard, B. H., Hartwick, J., & Warshaw, P. R. (1988). The theo*ry of reasoned action: A meta-analys*is o*f* past research with recommendations for modifications and future research. The Journal of Consumer Research, 15(3), 325–343.

Sheridan, E., Ng*, M., Czura, L., Steig*er, A., Vegliante, A., & Campagna, K. (2021). Framin*g the Future of Web 3.0– Metaverse Edit*ion. Goldman Sachs.

Sheth, J. (2020). Impact of covid-19 on consumer behaviour: Will the old habits return or die? Journal of Business Research, 117, 280–283. doi:10.1016/j.jbusres.202*0.05.059*

Shieh, J., Huang, K., & Wu, H. (2019). Service quality evaluation of a geriatric long-term *care:* A combination of SERVQUAL model and importance-performance analysis. doi:10.1080/09720510.2018.1555080

Shieh, J. I., Wu, H. H., & Huang, K. K. (2010). A DEMATEL method in identifying ke*y success fact*ors of hospital service quality. Knowledge-Based Systems, 23*(3), 277–282. doi:10.1016/j.knosys.2010.01.013*

*Sh*im, S., Eastlick, M., Lotz, S., & Warrington, P. (2001). An online prepurchase intentions model: The role of intention to search. Journal of Retailing, 77, 397–416.

Shin, J., Park, Y., & Lee, D. (2016). Strategic management of over-the-top services: Focusing on Korean consumer adoption behaviour. Technological Forecasting and Social C*hange, 112, 329–337. doi:10.1016/j.techfore.2016.08.004*

*Sh*in, K., Kim, E., & Jeong, E. (2018). Structural relationship and influence between open innovation capacities and performance*s. Sustainability, 10(8), 2787. doi:10.3390u10082787*

Shoba, T. S., & Suman, C. (2017). Psychological Factors Contributing to t*he Financial Wellbeing of an Individual: A Review of Empirical Literature. Ind*ian Journal of Finance, 11(10), 51–65. doi:10.17010/ijf/2017/v11i10/118775

Shree, S. V., Pugazhenthi, R., & Chandrasekaran, M. (2017). Statistical Investigation of the Performance Evaluation i*n Manufacturing Envir*onment. International Journal of Pure and Applied Mathematics, 114(12), 225–235.

Shree*nivasan, K., Thiyagarajan, S., Kasthuri, A., & Abinaya, J. (2018). Customer Perception of Ser*vice Quality in the Insurance Sectors. International Journal of Pure a*nd Applied Mathematics, 1*19(10), 1307–1316.

Siami, S., & Gorji, M. (2012). The measurement of service quality by using SERVQUAL and quality gap model. Indian Journal of Science and Technology, 5(1), 1956–1960. doi:10.17485/ijst/2012/v5i1.30

Siddiqui, M., & Sharma, T. (*2010*). *Analyzing customer satisfa*ction with service quality in life insurance services. Journal of Ta*rgeting. Measurement and Analysis for Marketing, 18(3/4), 221–238. doi:10.1057/jt.2010.17*

*Siddiqui, M., & Sharma, T. (201*0). Measuring the Customer Perceived Service Quality for Life Insurance Services: An Empirical Investigation. International Business Research, 3(3), 171–186. doi:10.5539/ibr.v3n3p171

*Silvestri, C., Aquilani, B., & Ru*ggieri, A. (2017). Service quality and customer satisfaction in thermal tourism. The TQM Journal, 29(1), 55–81. doi:10.1108/TQM-06-2015-0089

*Singh, A., & Prasher, A. (2019). Measu*ring healthcare service quality from patients" perspective: Using Fuzzy AHP application. Total Quality Management & Business Excellence, 30(3–4), 284–300. doi:10.1080/14783363.2017.1302794

Sin*gh, P. (2014). Social media crowdsourcing: Supporting user-driven innovation by generating* ideas. International Journal of Online Marketing, 4(2), 1–14.

Singh, S., & Arora, R. (2011). A Comparative Study of Banking Services and Customer S*atisfaction in Public, Private and Foreign Banks. Jou*rnal of Economics, 2(1), 45–56. doi:10.1080/09765239.2011.11884936

Sirdeshmukh, D., Singh, J., & Sabol, B. (2002). Consumer trust, value, and loyalty in relational exchanges. Journal of Marketing, 66(1), 15–37.

Sirdeshmukh, D., Singh, J., & Sabo*l, B. (2002). Consumer trust, value and loyalty in relational exchanges. Journal* of Marketing, 66(1), 15–37. doi:10.1509/jmkg.66.1.15.18449

Siu, N. Y., & Cheung, J. T. H. (2001). A measure of retail service quality. Marketing Intelligence & Planning, 19(2), 88–96. doi:10.1108/02634500110385327

Sivadas, E., & Baker-Prewitt, J. L. (2000). An examination of the relationship between service quality, customer satisfaction, and stor*e loyalty. International Journal of Retail & Di*stribution Management, 28(2), 73–82. doi:10.1108/09590550010315223

Sivapalan, A., & Jebarajakirthy, C. (2017). A*n application of retailing ser*vic*e* quality practices influencing customer loyalty toward retailers. Marketing Intellig*ence & Planning, 35(7), 842–857. doi:10.1108/MIP-09-2016-0178*

*Sivesan, S. (2019). Impact of Service Quality on Customer Satis*faction in Life Insurance Companies in Sri Lanka. Global Journal of Management and Business Research: E Marketing. 19 (5).

Slu, N. Y. M., & Mou, J. C. (2003). A st*udy of service quality* in *i*nternet banking. Hong Kong Baptist University.

Smith, D., Manesh, M. M. G., & Alshaikh, A. (2013). How can entrepreneurs motivate crowdsourcing participants? Technology Innovation *Management Review, 3(2).*

Snyder, H. (2019). Literature review as a research methodology: An overview and guidelines. Journal of Business Research, 104, 333–339. doi:10.*1016/j.jbusres.2019.07.039*

Solutions, S. (n.d.). Identifying Multivariate Outliers in SPSS. Statistics Solutions. https://www.statisticssolutions.com/identifying-multivariate -outliers-in-spss/?__cf_chl_jschl_tk__=3f161d0bfbc0bb2f449f3 b6184*003a98e29964ca-1624273684-*0-*A*a4yMWgrdSqehH0tXjJ2w0ze4u3 u1fsu4LyudGXWzrsL7N58ett1pw70Vq83Y07EQrgLUMG6xTOHw7PFoQdj9LE xjbWvByaDMsQQj9

Spearman, C. E. (1904). "General intelligence," objectively determined and measure*d. The American Journal of Psychiatry, 15, 201–293.*

Spreng, R. A., & Singh, A. K. (1993). An empirical assessment of the SERVQUAL scale and the relationship between service quality and satisfaction. Enhancing knowledge development in marketing, 4(1), 1-6.

Srivastava, N., & Goel, S. (n.d.). A Study of Patient Satisfaction Level in Inpatient Spine Department of a Tertiary Care Multispecialty Hospital. doi:10.15419/jmri.147

Stanoevska-Slabeva, K. (2011). Enabled innovation: Instruments and methods of internet-based collaborative innovation. Conference Draft, 1st Berlin Symposium in Internet and Society.

Steils, N., & Hanine, S. (2019). Recruiting valuable participants in online IDEA generation: The role of brief instructions. Journal of Business Research, 96, 14–25.

Sterling, S. (2014). Separate tracks or real synergy? Achieving a closer relationship between education and SD, post-2015. Journal of Education for Sustainable Development, 8(2), 89–112. doi:10.1177/0973408214548360

Sterling, S. (2017). Assuming the future: Repurposing education in a volatile age. In B. Jickling & S. Sterling (Eds.), Post-Sustainability and Environmental Education (pp. 31–45). Palgrave Macmillan., doi:10.1007/978-3-319-51322-5_3

Sterling, S. (2019). Planetary primacy and the necessity of positive dis-illusion. Sustainability, 12(2), 60–66. doi:10.1089us.2019.29157

Stewart, J. (1994). The psychology of decision making. In D. Jennings & S. Wattam (Eds.), Decision Making: an Integrated Approach. Pitman.

Stix, G. (2020). Attempts at Debunking "Fake News" about Epidemics Might Do More Harm Than Good. Scientific American.

Ström & Martinez. (2013). The determinants of customer satisfaction, loyalty and willingness to pay in subscription based streaming services. Stockholm School of Economics.

Subalakshmi, S., Grahalakshmi, S., & Manikandan, M. (2018). Financial Ratio Analysis of SBI. ICTACT Journal on Management Studies, 4(1).

Suh, B., & Han, I. (2002). Effect of trust on customer acceptance of Internet banking. Electronic Commerce Research and Applications, 1(3-4), 247–263.

Suhada, T. A., Ford, J. A., Verreynne, M. L., & Indulska, M. (2021). Motivating individuals to contribute to firms' non-pecuniary open innovation goals. Technovation, 102, 102233.

Suhartanto, D., Brien, A., Primiana, I., Wibisono, N., & Triyuni, N. N. (2020). Tourist loyalty in creative tourism: The role of experience quality, value, satisfaction, and motivation. Current Issues in Tourism, 23(7), 867–879. doi:10.1080/13683500.2019.1568400

Sui, D., & Shaw, S. L. (2022). New Human Dynamics in the Emerging Metaverse: Towards a Quantum Phygital Approach by Integrating Space and Place (Vision Paper). In 15th International Conference on Spatial Information Theory (COSIT 2022). Schloss Dagstuhl-Leibniz-Zentrum für Informatik.

Suki, N. (2013). Customer Satisfaction with Service Delivery in the Life Insurance Industry: An Empirical Study. Jurnal Pengurusan, 38, 101–109. doi:10.17576/pengurusan-2013-38-09

Sum, C. Y., & Hui, C. L. (2009). Salespersons' service quality and customer loyalty in fashion chain stores: A study in Hong Kong retail stores. Journal of Fashion Marketing and Management.

Sumaedi, S., Yarmen, M., & Yuda Bakti, I. G. (2016). Healthcare service quality model: A multi-level approach with empirical evidence from a developing country. International J*ournal of Productivity and Performance Management,* 65*(8),* 1007–1024. doi:10.1108/IJPPM-08-2014-0126

Summers, T. A., & Hebert, P. R. (2001). Shedding some light on *store atmospherics:* Influence of illumination on consumer behavior. Journal of Business Research, 54(2), 145–150. doi:10.1016/S0148-2963(99)00082-X

Surie, A., & Sharma, L. V. (2019). Climate change, Agrarian distress, and the role of digital labor markets: Evidence from Bengaluru, Karnataka. Decision, 46(2), 127–138.

Swain, S. (2018). Do patients really perceive b*etter quality of service in privat*e ho*s*pitals than public hospitals in India? doi:10.1108/BIJ-03-2018-0055

Swana, J., Bowers, M., & Richardsona, L. (1999). Customer Trust in the Salesperson: An In*tegrative Review and Meta-Analysis of the Empir*ical Literature. Journal of Business Research, *44(2), 93–107. doi:10.1016/S0148-2963(97)00244-0*

*Szymanski, D. M., & Hise, R. T. (2000). E-satisfaction: An i*nitial examination. Journal of Retailing, 76(3), 309–322. *doi:10.1016/S0022-4359(00)00035-X*

*Sánchez-Pérez, M., Sánchez-Fernández, R., Marín-*Carrillo, G. M., & Gázquez-Abad, J. C. (2007). Service quality in public services as a segmentation variable. Service Industries Journal, 27(4), 355–369. doi:10.1080/02642060701346771

Söderlu*nd, M. (2006). Measuring cus*tom*e*r loyalty with multi-item scales: A case for caution. International Journal of Service Industry Management, 17(1), 76–98. doi:10.1108*/09564230610651598*

Tahai, A., & Meyer, M. J. (1999). A revealed preference study of management journals' direct influences. Strategic Management Journal, 20(3), 279–296. doi:10.1002/(SICI)1097-0266(199903)20:3<279::*AID-SMJ33>3.0.CO;2-2*

Tan, M., & Teo, T. S. H. (2000). Factors influencing the adoption of Internet banking. Journal of the Association for Information Systems, 1(1).

Tanniru, M., & Sandhu, K. (2*019). Engageme*n*t l*eading to empowerment-digital innovation strategies for patient *care continuity. Journal of Hospital Management and Health Policy, 3, 28. doi:10.21037/jhmhp.2019.09.01*

Tapscott, D., & Williams, A. D. (2006). Wikinomics, how mass collaboration changes everything. Penguin Group.

Taylor, S., Nicholson, J., *Milan, J., & Martinez, R. (1997). As*sessing the Roles of Service Quality and Customer Satisfaction in the Formation of the Purchase Intentions of Mexican Consumer. Journal of Marketing Theory and *Practice, 5(*1)*, 78–90. doi:10.1080/10696679.1997.11501752

Teas, R. K. (1994). Expectations as a comparison standard in measuring service quality: An assessment of a reassessment. Journal of Marketing, 58(1), 132–1*39. doi:10.1177/002224299405800111*

Terblanche, B., Corbishley, B., Nel, F., & Venter, P. (2016). Retail Management SA Perspective (2nd ed.). Oxford University Press.

*Terblanche, N. S., & Boshoff, C. (2006). T*he relationship between a satisfactory in-store shopping experience and retail loyalty. South African Journal of Business Management, 37(2), 33–43. doi:10.4102ajbm.v37i2.600

Teshome *K., A. K. (2020). Ethiopian MicroFinance Institutions Performance Analysi*s Report. Academic Press.

Thang, D. C. L., & Tan, B. L. B. (2003). Linking consumer perception to preference of retail stores: An empirical assessment of the multi-*attributes of sto*re image. Journal of Retailing and Consumer Services, 10(4), 193–200. doi:10.1016/S0969-6989(02)00006-1

Thenmozhi, S. P., & Dhanapal, D. (2011). Unorganised retailing in India–A study on retail service quality. *European Journal of Social Sciences, 23(1), 71-78.*

Theodoridis, P. K., & Chatzipanagiotou, K. C. (2009). Store image attributes and customer satisfaction across different customer profiles within the supermarket sector in Greece. European Journal of Marketing, *43(5/6), 708–734.* *doi:10.1108/03090560910947016*

The State of Crowdsourcing in 2015: How the world's biggest brands and companies are opening up to consumer creativity. (n.d.). *eYeka. https://en.eyeka.co*m/resources/analyst-reports#CSreport2015? utm_campaign=csr&utm_content=1&utm_medium=act&utm_source=prc &utm_term=en

The value of getting personalization right—or wrong—is multiplying. (2021). McK-insey. https://www.mckinsey.com/capabilities/growth-marketing-and-s ales/our-insights/the-value-of-getting-personalization-right -or-wrong-is-multiplying

Thinh, N., Huy, L., & Son, N. (2017). The Impact of Website Service Quality on Customer Trust and Purchase Intentions in the Hotel: Theoretical Approach. International Journal of App*lied Business and Economic Rese*arch, 15(23), 479–498.

Thomason, J. (2021). MetaHealth-How will the Metaverse Change Health Care? Journal of Metaverse, 1(1), 13–*16.*

Thompson, R. R., Garfin, D. R., Holman, E. A., & Silver, R. C. (2017). Distress, Worry, and Functioning Following a Global Health Crisis: A National Study of Americans' Res*ponses to Ebola. Clinical Ps*ychological Science, 5(3), 513–521. doi:10.1177/2167702617692030

Thomson, W., Mahanti, A., & Gong, M. (2017, October). Understanding uploader motivations and sharing dynam*ics in the one-click hosting ecosystem. In 2017 IE*EE 42nd Conference on Local Computer Networks (LCN) (pp. 520-522). IEEE.

To, W. M., Tam, J. F., & Cheung, M. F. (2013). Explore how Chinese consumers evaluate retail service quality and satisfaction. Service Business, 7(1), 121–142. doi:10.100711628-012-0149-7

Torres, E. N., & Kline, S. (2013). From customer *satisfaction to customer delight: Creati*ng a new standard of service for the hotel industry. International Journal of Contemporary Hospitality Management.

Tranfield, D., Denyer, D., & Smart, P. (2003). Towards *a methodology for develo*ping evidence-informed management knowledge by means of systematic review. British Journal of Management, 14*(3), 207–222. doi:10.1111/1467-*8551.00375

Tsoukatos, E., & Rand, G. (2017). Path analysis of perceived service quality, satisfaction and loyalty in Greek insurance. Managing Service Quality, 16(5), *501–519. doi:10.1108/09604520610686746*

Tsouk*atos, E., Simmy, M., & Rand, G. (2004). Quality Improvement in the G*reek *and Kenyan Insurance Industries. Archives of Economic Histo*ry, 16(2), 93–116.

Tsourela, M., & Roumeliotis, M. (2015). The moderating role of technology readiness, gender, and sex in consumer acceptance and actual use of Technology-based servi*ces. The Journal of High Technology Managem*ent Research, 26(2), 124–136.

Tucker, L. R., & MacCallum, R. C. (1997). Exploratory factor analysis. Retrieved from https://www.unc.edu/~rcm/ book/factor.pdf

Tuzkaya, G., Sennarog*lu, B., Kalender, Z. T., & Mutlu, M. (2019). Socio-Economic Planning Sciences Hospital service quality evaluation with IVIF-PROMETHEE and a cas*e study. Socio-Economic Planning Sciences, (September), 100705. *do*i:10.1016/j.seps.2019.04.002

Tyler, R. (1949). Curriculum Development: The Tyler Model. Educational Research Techniques. https://educationalre-searchtechniques.com/2014/07/01/curriculum-development-the-tyler-model/

Udo, G. J., Bagchi, K. K., & Kirs, P. J. (2010). An assessment of customers' e-service quality perception, satisfaction and intention. International Journal of Information Management, 30(6), 481–492. doi:10.1016/j.ijinfomgt.2010.03.005

Ueltschy, L. C., & Krampf, R. F. (2001). Cultural sensitivity to satisfaction and service quality measures. Journal of Marketing Theory and Practice, 9(3), 14–31. doi:10.1080/10696679.2001.11501894

Ulaga, W. (2011). Investigating customer value in global business markets: Commentary essay. Journal of Business Research, 64(8), 928–930. doi:10.1016/j.jbusres.2011.04.005

Ullah, I., & Narain, R. (2020). The impact of customer relationship management and organizational culture on mass customization capability and firm performance. International Journal of Customer Relationship Marketing and Management, 11(3), 60–81. doi:10.4018/IJCRMM.2020070104

Umar, A., & Bahrun, R. (2017). The mediating relationship of customer satisfaction between brand trust, brand social responsibility image with moderating role of switching cost. Advanced Science Letters, 23(9), 9020–9025. doi:10.1166/asl.2017.10015

UN. (2015). Sustainable Development Goals knowledge platform. UN. https://www.un.org/sustainabledevelopment/sustainable-development-goals/

UNESCO – United Nations Educational, Scientific and Cultural Organization. (2019). A stepping stone towards monitoring progress towards measuring progress towards SDG 4.7. UNESCO. https://en.unesco.org/news/stepping-stone-towards-measuring-progress-towards-sdg-47

Upadhyai, R., & Roy, H. (2019). A Review of Healthcare Service Quality Dimensions and their. Measurement, 21(1), 102–127. Advance online publication. doi:10.1177/0972063418822583

Upadhyay, J., & Adhikari, P. (2021). Impact of Service Quality on Customer Satisfaction and Firm Performance in Nepalese Life Insurance Companies. International Journal of Engineering and Advanced Technology, 10(3), 110–115. doi:10.35940/ijeat.C2191.0210321

Upton, C. L. (2009). Virtue ethics and moral psychology: The situationism debate. The Journal of Ethics, 13(2/3), 103–115. doi:10.1007/10892-009-9054-2

Ursach, G., Horodnic, I., & Zait, A. (2015). How reliable are measurement scales? External factors with indirect influence on reliability estimators. Procedia Economics and Finance, 20, 679–686. doi:10.1016/S2212-5671(15)00123-9

Usman, D.J., Yaacob, N. and Ralman, A. (2015). Lack of Awareness: A major challenge for electricity consumers in Nigeria: Canadian Center of Science and Education. Asian Social Science. doi:10.5539/ass.v11n24p240

Van Der Linde, S. (2017). Product liability: The common law and the consumer protection act 68 of 2008. University of Pretoria.

Van der Oordt, C. (2015). Consumers' knowledge and attitudes towards consumerism and subsequent complaint behavior concerning consumer electronics. University of Pretoria.

Van Dijk, J. (2011). Co-creation in practice: Exploring practitioner views on co-creation. Retrieved from http://issuu.com/joycediscovers/docs/article_interviews

van Dyke, T. P., Kappelman, L. A., & *Prybutok, V. R. (1997)*. *Measuring inform*ation systems service quality: Concerns on the use of the SERVQUAL questionnaire. Management Information Systems Quarterly, 21(2), 195–208.

Van Schalkwyk P. J., Beven-Dye A. and Akpojivi U. (2015). South African independent reta*ilers' knowledge of the* Co*nsumer Protection Act. The Retail and Marketing Review 11 *(2).

Vargo, S. L., & Lusch, R. F. (2004). The four service marketing myths: Remnants of a goods-based, manufacturing model. Journal of Service Research, 6(4), 324–335.

Varian, H. R. (2003). Innovation, compone*nts, and complements. October.*

*Vazifehdust, H., & Farokhian, S. (2013). Factors influe*ncing customer satisfaction with the success factors identified in the insurance industry. African Journal of Business Management, 7(21), 2026–2032. doi:10.5897/AJBM11.2051

Vazquez, R., R*odríguez-De*l *Bo*sque, I. A., Díaz, A. M., & Ruiz, A. V. (2001). Service quality in supermarket retailing: Identifying critical service experiences. Journal of Retailing and Consumer Services, 8(1), 1–14. doi:10.1016/S0969-6989(99)00018-*1*

*Venkatesan, R. (2017). Executing on a customer engagemen*t st*rategy. Journal of the Academy of Marketing Science,* 45(3), 289–293.

Venkatesh, V., & Davis, F. D. (2000). A theoretical extensio*n of the technology a*ccep*tance model: Four longitudinal field studies. Management Science, 46(2), 186–204.

Venkatesh, V., & Morris, M. G. (2000). Why Do not Men Ever Stop to Ask for Directions? Gender, Social Influence, *and Their Role in Technology *Acceptance and Usage Behavior. Management Information Systems Quarterly, 24(1), 115.

Venkatesh, *V., Morris, M., Davis, G., & Davis, F. (2003). User acceptance of information technology: Toward a unified view. MIS *Q. 27 (3), 425–478. .

Venkatesh, V., Ramesh, V., & Massey, A. P. (2003). Un*derstanding usability in mobile commerce. Communications of the ACM, 46, 53*–56.

Venkatesh, V., Thong, J. Y. L., Xu, X., Walker, *R. H., & Johnson, L. W. (2006). Why consumers use and do not use technology-enabled services. Journal of Services Market*ing, 20(2), 125–135.

Verma, S., & Chaudhuri, R. *(2009). Effect of CRM on Customer Satisfaction in Service Sector in* India. Journal of Marketing Communications, 5(2).

Vijayasarathy, L. R., & Jones, J. M. (2000). Intentions to shop using internet catalogues: Exploring the effects of product types, shopping orientations, and attitudes towards compu*ters. Electronic Markets, 10(1), 29*–38.

V*irk*, N., & Mahal, P. K. (2012). Customer satisfaction: A comparative analysis of public and private sector banks in India. In Information and Knowledge Ma*nagement (Vol. 2, No. 3, pp. 01-07)*.

Wachter, K. (2002). Longitudinal assessment of web retailers: Issues from a consumer point of view. Journal of Fashion Mark*eting and Management, 6(2), 134*–145. doi:10.1108/13612020210429476

Walchek, S. (2015). The unbundling of fi*nance. TechCrunch.*

*Walsh, K. (2020). Should we use fear in o*ur public health messages about pandemics? MDPI.

Walter, C. G., & Paul, G. W. (1970). Consumer Behaviour: An Integrated Framework. In Home Wood, IL*L (p. 7). Richard* D I*r*win.

Wang, J., Shahzad, F., Ahmad, Z., Abdullah, M., & Hassan, N. M. (2022). Trust and Consumers' Purchase Intention in a Social Commerce Platform: A Meta- Analytic Approach. SAGE Open, 12(2), 1–15. https://journals.sagepub.com/doi/pdf/10.1177/21582440221091262. doi:10.1177/21582440221091262

Wang, L., Fan, X., & Willson, V. (1996). Effects of non-normal data on parameter estimates and fit indices for a model with latent and manifest variables: An empirical study. Structural Equation Modeling, 3(3), 228–247. doi:10.1080/10705519609540042

Wang, Y., Su, Z., Zhang, N., Xing, R., Liu, D., Luan, T. H., & Shen, X. (2022). A survey on metaverse: Fundamentals, security, and privacy. IEEE Communications Surveys and Tutorials.

Warrillow, J. (2016). The Automatic Customer; Creating a Subscription Business in Any Industry. Penguin.

Watkins, M. W. (2018). Exploratory Factor Analysis: A Guide to Best Practice. The Journal of Black Psychology, 44(3), 219–246. doi:10.1177/0095798418771807

Weick, K. E. (1976). Educational organizations as loosely coupled systems. Administrative Science Quarterly, 1–19.

Weijo, H. A., Martin, D. M., & Arnould, E. J. (2018). Consumer Movement and Collective Creativity: The Case of Restaurant Day. Journal of Consumer Research. https://academic.oup.com doi:10.1093/jcr/ucy003

Wells, B. P., & Stafford, M. R. (1995). Service Quality in the Insurance Industry. Journal of Insurance Regulation., 13(4), 462–478.

West, J., & Gallagher, S. (2006). Challenges of open innovation: The paradox of firm investment in open-source software. Research Management, 36(3), 319–331.

Wheatley, O., & Bakthavatchalam, S. (n.d.). What Does the Metaverse Mean for the Banking and Financial Services Industry? ISG. https://isg-one.com/articles/what-does-the-metaverse-mean-for-the-banking-and-financial-services-industry

Wheaton, M. G., Abramowitz, J. S., Berman, N. C., Fabricant, L. E., & Olatunji, B. O. (2012). Psychological Predictors of Anxiety in Response to the H1N1 (Swine Flu) Pandemic. Cognitive Therapy and Research, 36(3), 210–218. doi:10.100710608-011-9353-3

White, K. (1992). The Durbin-Watson Test for Autocorrelation in Nonlinear Models. The Review of Economics and Statistics, 74(2), 370–373. doi:10.2307/2109675

White, L., & Yanamandram, V. (2007). A model of customer retention of dissatisfied business services customers. Managing Service Quality, 17(3), 298–316. doi:10.1108/09604520710744317

Wieringa, J., & Verhoef, P. (2007). Understanding Customer Switching Behavior in a Liberalizing Service Market: An Exploratory Study. Journal of Service Research, 10(2), 174–186. doi:10.1177/1094670507306686

Wind, Y. (2008). A plan to invent the marketing we need today. MIT Sloan Management Review, 49(4), 21–28.

Winter, D. G., John, O. P., Stewart, A. J., Klohnen, E. C., & Duncan, L. E. (1998). Traits and motives: Toward an integration of two traditions in personality research. Psychological Review, 105(2), 230.

Wire, B. (1995). Stanford federal credit union pioneers online financial services. Business Wire, June, 21.

Wirtz, J., & Lovelock, C. (2016). Service Marketing (8th ed.). World Scientific Publishing Co. Inc. doi:10.1142/y0001

Woker T. (2016). Consumer protection and alternative dispute resolution. South African Mercantile Law Journal, 21.

Wolfinbarger, M., & Gilly, M. (2002). comQ: dimensionalizing, measuring, and predicting quality *of the e-tail experience. Marketing Sc*ience Institute Report, (02-100).

Wong, A., & Sohal, A. (2003). Service quality and customer loyalty perspectives on two levels of retail relationship*s. Journal of Services M*arketing, 17(5), 495–513. doi:10.1108/08876040310486285

Wong, A., & Sohal, A. S. (2006). Understanding the quality of relationships in consumer services: A study in a retail environm*ent. International Journal* of Quality & Reliability Management, 23(3), 244–264. doi:10.1108/02656710610648215

Wong, D. H., Rexha, N., & P*hau, I. (2008). Re-examini*ng tr*a*ditional service quality in an e-banking era. International Journal of Bank Marketing, 26(7), 526–545. doi:10.1108/02652320810913873

Wright, D. B. (2019, December). Research method*s for education with* tec*h*nology: Four concerns, examples, and recommendations. In Frontiers in Education (Vol. 4, p. 147*). Frontiers Media SA.*

Xavier, P., & Ypsilanti, D. (2008). *Switching costs* and consumer behaviour: Implications for telecommunications regulation. Info, 10(4), *13–29*. doi:10.1108/14636690810887517

Yalley, A. A., & A*gyapong, G. K. Q. (2017). Measuring serv*ice quality in Ghana: A Crossvergence cultural perspective. Journal of Financial Services Marketing, 22(2), 43–53. doi:10.105*741264-017-0021-x*

Yang, Z., & Fang, X. (2004). Online service quality dimensions and their relationships with satisfaction: A content analysis of customer reviews of *securities brokerage service*s. *I*nternational Journal of Service Industry Management, 15(3), 302–326. doi:10.1108/09564230410540953

Yang, Z., & Jun, M. (2002). Consumer perception of e-service quality: from i*nternet purchaser and non-purchaser perspectives. Journal o*f Business strategies, 19(1), 19-42.

Yavas, U., Benkenstein, M., & Stuhldreier, U. (2004). Relationships between service quality and behavioral outcome*s: A study of private bank customers in* Germany. International Journal of Bank Marketing, 22(2), 144–157. doi:10.1108/02652320410521737

Ye, H. J., & Kankanhalli, A. (2015). Investigating the antecedents of organizational task crowdsourcing. Information & Management, 52(1), 98–110.

Yen, Y., & Horng, D. (2010). Effects of satisfaction, trust and alternative attractiveness on switching intentions in i*ndus*trial customers. International Journal of Management and Enterprise Development, 8(1), 82–101. doi:10.1504/IJMED.2010.029762

Yin, X., Zhu, K., Wang, H., Zhang, J., *Wang, W., & Zhang, H. (2022). Motivati*ng p*a*rticipation in crowdsourcing contests: The role of instruction-writing strategy. Information & Management, 59(3), 103616.

Yin, Y., Wang, Y., & Lu, Y. (2019). Why firm*s adopt empowerment practices and* how such practices affect firm performance? A transaction cost-exchange perspective. Human Resource Management Review, 29(1), 111–124. doi:10.1016/j.hrmr.2018.01.002

Yiu, C. S., Grant, K., & *Edgar, D. (2007). Factors affecting the adoption of* Internet banking in Hong Kong – Implications for the banking sector. International Journal of Information Management, 27(5), 336–351.

Yong, A. G., & Pearce, S. (2013). A Beginner's Guide to Factor Analysis: Focu*sing on Exploratory Factor Analysis. Tu*torials in Quantitative Methods for Psychology, 9(2), 79–94. doi:10.20982/tqmp.09.2.p079

Yoo, B., & Donthu, N. (2001). Developing and validating a multid*imensional consumer-base*d br*a*nd equity scale. Journal of Business Research, 52(1), 1–14. doi:10.1016/S0148-2963(99)00098-3

Yoon, C. (2010). Antecedents of customer satisfaction with *online banking in China: The effects of experience. Computers in* Human Behavior, 26(6), 1296–1304.

Yu, C. S. (2012). Factors affecting individuals to adopt mobile banking: Empirical evidence from the UTAUT model. Journal of Electronic Commerce Research, 13(2), 104.

Yu*Sheng, K*Ibrahim, M. (2019). Service innovation, service delivery and customer satisfaction and loyalty in the banking sector of Ghana. International Journal of Bank Marketing.

Zadeh, A. H*., & Sharda, R. (2014). Modeling brand post popu*larity dynamics in online social networks. Decision Support Systems, 65, 59–68.

Zainuddin, A. (2012). Research Methodology and Data *Analysis (2nd ed.). Selangor: UiTM Press.*

*Zeitham*l, V., Berry, L., & Parasuraman, A. (1996). The Behavioural Consequences of Service Quality. Journal of Marketing, 60(2), 31–46. doi:10.1177/*002224299606000203*

Zeithaml, V. A., Bitner, M. J., & Gremler, D. D. (2013). Services Marketing: Integrating customer focus Across the firm. Sixth.

Zeithaml, V. A., Parasuraman, A., & Malhotra, A. (*2002). Service quality delive*ry through web sites: A critical review of extant knowledge. Journal of the Academy of Marketing Science, 30(4), 362–375. doi:10.1177/*009207002236911*

Zeithaml, V. A., Rust, R. T., & Lemon, K. N. (2001). The customer pyramid: Creating and serving profitable customers. California Management *Review, 43(4), 118–142.* d*oi*:10.2307/41166104

Zeithaml, V. *A., Wilson, A., Jo Betner, M., & Greml*er,[D]. D. (2016). Services marketing (3rd European ed.). McGraw Hill Education.

Zephaniah, *C. O., Ogba, I. E., & Izogo, E. E. (2020). Examining the effec*t of customers' perception of bank marketing communication on customer loyalty. Scientific American, 8, 1–22. doi:10.1016/j.sciaf.2020.e00383

Zhang, *H., & Xiao, Y. (2020). Customer involvement in* big data analytics and its impact on B2B innovation. Industrial Marketing Management, 86, 99–108. doi:10.1016/j.indmarman.2019.02.020

Zhang, M., Di Fan, D., & Z*hu, C. J. (2014). High-Perfo*rma*nc*e Work Systems, Corporate Social Performance, and Employee Outcomes: Exploring the Missing Links. Journal *of Business Ethi*cs,[1]20(3), 423–435. doi:10.100710551-013-1672-8

Zhao, X., Lynch, J. G. Jr, & Chen, Q. (2010). Reconsidering Baron and Kenny: Myths and truths a*bout mediation analysi*s. The Journal of Consumer Research, 37(2), 197–206. doi:10.1086/651257

Zhao, Y. C., & Zhu, Q. (2014). Effects of extrinsic and intrinsic motivation on participation in crowdsourcing contest: A per*spective of self-dete*rmination theory. Online Information Review.

Zhou, L. (2004). A dimension-specific analysis of performance- only measurement of service quality and satisfaction in China's retail banking. Journal of *Services Marketing, 18(7), 5*34–546. doi:10.1108/08876040410561866

Zhou, T., Lu, Y., & Wang, B. (2010). Integrating TTF and UTAUT to explain mobile banking user adoption. Computers in Human Behavior, 26(4), 760–767.

Zhu, W. (2000). Which *Should it Be Called: Con*vergent Validity or Discriminant Validity? [PubMed]. Research Quarterly for Exercise and Sport, 71(2), 190–194. doi:10.1080/02701367.2000.10608897

About the Contributors

Sarmistha Sarma is a Professor at the Institute of Innovation in Technology and Management (affiliated to Guru Gobind Singh Indraprastha University, Delhi (India)) in the Department of Business Management. She has a PhD in Management from Fakir Mohan University, Balasore, Orissa, (India) along with a Master of Business Administration (M.B.A) from Gauhati University Assam (India). She likes to analyze the various factors leading to purchase decisions. Her research focuses on the ways lifestyle, culture, and ethnicity impact buying decisions. She is a founding member of the Center for Promotion of Multidisciplinary Research (CPMR), a society dedicated to the promotion of applied research in various disciplines.

Neha Gupta is an Assistant Professor at IBCS, SOA University (Deemed), Buubaneswar, Odisha in the Department of Business Management. She has a PhD in Management from Utkal University, Bhubaneswar, Orissa, (India) along with a Master of Business Administration (M.B.A) from GGSIPU Delhi. She is also UGC -NET qualified in Management stream. Her research focuses on study related to consumer behaviour on financial products, studies on technology acceptance using TAM based model.

* * *

Demissie Admasu has been a PhD scholar at KIIT Deemed to be University in School of Management since 2020. Executive Director of Gamo Development Association since 1 Nov. 2022, Ethiopian KHC South West Zone Development Commission as planning, Monitoring, and Evaluation Officer and Branch Manager of Omo Micro finance Institution Arba Minch from 1999-2022 for 23 years. He earned his MBA in Marketing from Hawassa University Ethiopia in 2018. Demissie's current research projects include the performance of Ethiopian Microfinance, and its Marketing strategies. He got an acceptance for the first article in prestigious journal: Journal of Jilin university. His research interests lie in the area of microfinancing business and marketing.

Ankita Agarwal completed her graduation in Commerce from BJB Autonomous College, Utkal University, Odisha (India) in 2010. She received her MBA from IBS, Hyderabad (India) in 2012 and was awarded a Ph.D. in Management from KIIT University, Odisha (India) in 2021. She is currently working as Assistant Professor (Marketing-cum-Skills Development) at Biju Patnaik Institute of Information Technology and Management Studies (BIITM), Bhubaneswar, Odisha (India). She has 7 years of teaching experience and 3 years of corporate experience. She has previously been associated with Oriental Bank of Commerce as Marketing Officer. She also holds JAIIB from the Indian Institute of Bankers. She has attended various national and international seminars and conferences held at prominent educational institutes and presented papers in the areas of Sustainable Production, Marketing and Digitalization. She has also published research papers in several journals of national and international repute. Her research interests are in the areas of Retail Marketing, Online Buying Behaviour and Services Marketing.

Varun Agarwal has done his graduation in Commerce from BJB Autonomous College, Utkal University, Odisha (India) in 2010. He completed his MBA from IBS, Hyderabad (India) in 2012 and received his Ph.D. in Management from Utkal University, Odisha (India) in 2021. He is currently working as Assistant Professor (Marketing) at Biju Patnaik Institute of Information Technology and Management Studies (BIITM), Bhubaneswar, Odisha (India). He has rich experience of 8 years in academics and 2 years in corporate. He has previously worked as Assistant Manager at IDBI Bank. His case study titled "Patanjali's Marketing Mix – The Monk's New Ferrari" was published by Emerald Emerging Markets Case Studies in 2017. He holds interest in soft skills training and has conducted various training programmes at reputed educational institutes including KIIT University, CTTC and Confidence Factory among others. He has also published research papers in various journals of national and international repute. His areas of interest in research include Services Marketing, Banking and Retail Marketing.

Devesh Bathla is a fourth-generation educationist! An analytical thinker and strategic planner evangelizing the future of learning analytics. Ambitious Researcher with 09 patents filed, a proud Industry Practitioner and a skilled Analytics Trainer to Working professionals and Management students who demand innovation & continuous improvement. Experienced in marketing analytics, consistently achieved business objectives, reduced marketing / operating costs and improved productivity. Rise faster, earn more, have fun, change the world! Areas of expertise - Industry: Marketing Analytics, Predictive Modelling, Data Visualization, Future Forecasting, ATL&BTL campaigns, Digital Marketing, Business Strategy, New business development, New product ideation, Innovative Campaigns, Product launches, P&L responsibility, Sales & Marketing. Tools: SAS, IBM - MMFA, Cognos, Tableau, Power BI, Google Analytics.

Dhananjay Beura has 7 years of industry experience and 11 years of teaching experience. He is a pharmacy graduate and completed his post graduate diploma in management from one of top rated B School in India, i.e. Jaipuria Institute of Management Lucknow. He has completed his PhD in marketing management. He has worked with Eli Lilly & Co as brand manager and ICICI Bank as Manager, International trade finance and derivatives looked after corporate branch, Nariman point Mumbai. He is currently working as a Professor in marketing at BIITM, Bhubaneswar. He is also engaged in consulting activities related to strategic advisory with some of the Indian companies and advertising agency. There are eight trademark registered brands and one patent into his credit and few more in the pipeline to be registered. He is also engaged in conducting training program with few corporate and Govt. Institutions for sales force effectiveness and managerial effectiveness. He has published many articles in national and international journal.

Sanjeeb Kumar Dey, Assistant Professor, Department of Commerce, Ravenshaw University, has 15 years of industry and teaching experience in the field of Corporate Finance and Taxation. He is the life member of ICA, IAA, OCA, etc. He has published more than 10 text books and 50 research papers in various indexed journals of National and International repute publishers. He has also successfully guided more than 17 scholars in M.Phil. and Ph.D. degree. His present research interest includes corporate taxation, behavioral finance, investment management, etc. He can be reached at <u>ravenshawuniversity.ac.in</u>.

Sudeshna Dutta has five years of industry experience and seven years of teaching experience. With Centurion University, IAM and currently with BIITM. She has worked with eminent banks like HDFC Bank and Kotak Mahindra and Indusind Bank as Senior Manager. Over the course of time, she has developed an avid interest in banking and financial services. She received the Ph.D. degree for her doctoral research work "Evaluating Service Quality with Customer Satisfaction- A study of Private Sectors Banks in Bhubaneswar". Keen interest in research, she has published research paper in valuable Scopus indexed journal. She is a Certified member of NSDL(The National Security Depository Ltd).She has provided consultancy services related to financial products to many Pvt. Limited Companies. Sudeshna Dutta is first a student, and then a teacher. She firmly believes that learning is an ongoing process and one who stops learning fails that moment.

Pruthiranja Dwibedi is currently working as a research scholar at Department of Commerce, KIIT University. He has been awarded with UGC- NET JRF in Commerce.

Jyotisankar Mishra is currently serving as an Assistant Professor at KIIT University, Bhubaneswar, India. His research interest area includes Organizational Behaviour, Leadership, Human Resource Accounting and consumer behaviour.

Manoj Kumar Mishra is currently working as an Assistant Professor in School Management at O P Jindal University, Raigarh. He is pursuing his Ph.D from Jagannath University Jaipur, India on "Green Entrepreneurship". He did his MBA from VTU with specialization in marketing and graduation from AKTU. He has presented several research papers in many national and international conferences including presentations at IITs and IIMs. His papers are published in various journals of National Repute which includes Scopus indexed and UGC –Care Listed Journals. Mr. Mishra has conducted two workshops and six FDPs on research methodology across different institutes in India.

Sagarika Mohanty has a B.COM (Accounting hons) from Rourkela Municipal College, Rourkela, M.COM (finance and control) from BJB (Auto) College, Bhubaneswar, Qualified UGC NET in Commerce in 2019, M.COM from IGNOU, Pursuing PhD in Management from KIIT University, Bhubaneswar.

Lingam Naveen is an ex-corporate turned academician working as assistant professor in operations and marketing area. He is a doctorate scholar from KIIT School of Management, Bhubaneswar, India. His research interests include retail marketing, tourism and banking. He is keenly interested in learning new research methodologies and statistical techniques and implement them in his research work.

Priyabrata Panda is working as an Assistant Professor and Head, School of Commerce, Gangadhar Meher University, Sambalpur, Odisha, India. He is the Assistant Editor of Orissa Journal of Commerce which is listed in UGC-CARE. He is also the Managing Editor of Odisha Journal of Commerce and Management.

Shradhanjali Panda is currently working as Assistant Professor at Department of Business Administration, Ravenshaw University, Cuttack. Her core area is Finance. She has twelve years of teaching experience as well as three years of industry experience. Dr. Panda has published more than forty research articles in different National and International journals of repute. She has authored two books to her credit and presented papers in more than sixty National and International Conferences. Her research areas are Equity Valuation, Portfolio Management, Value & Growth Investment strategies and Market Efficiency. She is reviewer of Journal of Education, Society & Behavioural Science and Consulting Ahead, Consulting Development Centre, Govt. of India. She is life member in different bodies like All India Commerce Association, Odisha Economic Association, All Odisha Commerce Association and ISTD.

Sasmita Samanta, Hon'ble Vice-Chancellor and President World Leadership Academy, has been featured on The Education. She is an accomplished academician and academic administrator with more than 25 years of experience in strategizing excellence in professional and technical education. Currently donning the mantle of Professor of Management and Vice-Chancellor of KIIT Deemed to be University, Bhubaneswar, India, she is leading the institution's transformation into a world-class university. Prof. Samanta's intellectual capabilities is manifested in distinctions as Ph.D. (Management); a Stanford LEAD Alumna and Stanford Distinguished Scholar, Stanford Graduate School of Business, Stanford University, USA; Fellow of Royal Society of Arts (FRSA, UK); and Fellow of Computer Society of India (FCSI, India). She has been trained in leadership from the University of Nebraska Omaha (UNO), USA. and CSC Leaders programme, Common Purpose Charitable Trust, UK. Her academic areas of interest and specialisation include Organisational Behaviour, Human Development, Spiritualism and Leadership. Her research areas focus on competency in corporate management, Entrepreneurial mind set, gender roles and mainstreaming, sustainable finance, risk management. She has published 69 articles in a wide range of academic journals such as European Journal of Academic Essays, International Journal of Social Economics, International Journal of Asian Business and Information Management, Psychology And Education Journal, The Indian Journal of Commerce, Journal of Medicinal and Chemical Sciences, Journal of Medicinal and Chemical Sciences, International Journal of Innovation Science, Emerging Dimensions of Business & Management in the Present-day Competitive. Moreover, in leadership, her key contributions have been the maintenance of a participative and transparent governance system, the introduction of an Activity-based Learning System in all programmes across the university and the development and maintenance of a student-centric ambiance on the campus.

Mathews Smangaliso Shange lives in KwaZulu-Natal, South Africa. He has received most of his education from the South African higher learning institutions where he achieved the following qualifications: Academic Achievements: Master of Commerce specializing in Marketing- University of KwaZulu-Natal, BComm Honours in Marketing Management-Mancosa, Post Graduate Diploma in Business Management- Mancosa, Advanced Diploma in Marketing Management- Mangosuthu University of Technology and National Diploma in Marketing Management- Pietermaritzburg Technical College He has conducted a research study in marketing where his research focus was on determining attitudes, awareness and use of Consumer Protection Act among furnisher retail consumers in Umlazi township, South Africa. Currently, he is doing his PhD in Management Sciences and working on a research study that intends to assess the impact of five forces on the retail sector post Covid-19 in South Africa. His work experience and expertise are in sales and marketing functions as he has worked in the FMCG , Chemicals, Banking and Construction industries for a number of years. His passion is in research particularly in the field of marketing, digital marketing, advertising, consumer behavior, market and product development, and management. He has contributed to the field of higher education research through participating in academic research projects. He is willing to collaborate with other academics or research organizations in any of the research projects. He is presently working as a Marketing Lecturer at Mangosuthu University of Technology where he teaches Marketing Leadership and Planning, and Analysis and Strategic Decisions.

Areej Siddiqui is a Faculty of International Trade and Business. She has been teaching courses on Trade Documentation and Global Sourcing to MBA students as well as industry executives over the last decade. She has also been actively involved in training of Bankers, Customs Officials, Trade Officials and Government Officials involved in Export-Import processes in India on matters related to Trade Documentation, Custom Procedures and Trade Facilitation and is an expert in the domain. Her research work on key areas of Trade Facilitation, Trade Operations, Emerging Economies, Foreign Direct Investment and Trade Agreements have been published in top journal and she has also worked on projects on implications of Trade related aspects.

Amandeep Singh holds a Doctorate in Management specializing in Marketing and he is also UGC-NET qualified. He holds more than 16 years of teaching experience. His main area of research is Consumer Sciences and Business Innovations. Currently, he is working as Professor at Chitkara Business School, Chitkara University, Punjab, India handling Marketing and General Management subjects at the Post Graduate level. Specifically, he has delivered Marketing Management, Consumer Behaviour, Services Marketing, and Marketing Research courses in the field of Marketing. He has also delivered courses in the field of General Management such as Social Entrepreneurship, Managing Family Business, Business Innovations and Organizational behaviour in his teaching career. He has published 48 research papers in various journals and conferences which are indexed in Scopus, Web of Science and Google Scholar. He has edited 7 books published by IGI Global, De Gruyter and Wiley. He has also chaired many National and International Conferences. He is on the editorial board of 3 International Journals. He was awarded the Best Teacher in 2008. He is also part of the Board of Studies of various B-Schools and leading universities in Northern India.

Amrinder Singh is having more than 12 years of experience in the teaching field. He has done MBA PhD in Marketing from Punjabi Iniversity Patiala.He is currently working as Head Chandigarh Group of Colleges Jhanjeri. Prior to that he has was working as Head CT University, Ludhiana. He has 15 papers to his credit till date. He has also chaired many national and international conferences. He is on the advisory board of many universities.

Leena Singh, MBA (H R), Ph.D (Eco), Associate Professor, School of Management Studies, IGNOU, New Delhi, teaching post graduate students Managerial Economics, Entrepreneurship and Business Ethics and CSR. Nine years corporate experience and 19 years teaching experience.

Shikta Singh has a great passion for Teaching & Research. Presently she is serving as an Associate Professor in KIIT School of Management, KIIT University, an institution of eminence. She is also the MBA Chairperson of Healthcare management at the Institute. She is a successful corporate trainer, training industry people on finance & technical skills. She has been an alumnus of Utkal University,

Ravenshaw University, and Pune University. She has completed her PhD in the area of Applied & Analytical Economics and presently continuing an advanced Program in Applied Finance at IIM Calcutta. She brings with her more than 13 years of rich teaching experience in universities like-KIIT University, Utkal University, Abhinav Institute of Management & Research, Pune. She is also a Visiting Professor to a few reputed institutions of Odisha & outside viz. Symbiosis School of Economics, Pune, XIMB, Savitri Phule University, Pune, R.D University. Her current research interest lies in various Macro Economic issues, Behavioral Finance, International Financial Management, Industrial Economics and Development Economics. She has authored around 30 research papers of national and international repute in the area of macroeconomics, industrial economics, behavioral finance, Stock market dynamics, and management as published 7 Book chapters and One Book. She has been guiding 5 research scholars, of which three scholars have been awarded. She is the recipient of multiple awards and is a gold medalist. She has worked on two research projects for RBI Bulletin and on Health care for a Consultancy. She also has written blogs on economic significance, news columns. She has successfully bagged various projects approved by ATAL, AICTE, ICSSR & MHRD, GOI. Presented papers in various International Conferences viz. in Singapore 2014, ERAZ Conference held at Belgrade 2017, and ICOM 2017 Conference at Abu Dhabi, ICOM 2019 MICA, and IMC 2020 held at Delhi. She has been a position holder in her 12th, Post graduate and M.Phil. level and has received gold medal for the same. Apart from that she has got 0.1 merit certificate and gold medal for being the All India Topper in Economics during 12th board.

Bindiya Soni holds a graduate and post graduate degrees in Management (Five Years Integrated MBA) from Gujarat University, Ahmedabad. She holds a doctoral degree from S.P. University, Vallabh Vidyanagar, Anand. She is associated as Professor in Management department at Ananad Institute of Management and Information Science, Anand which is affiliated to Gujarat Technological University (GTU). She holds two years of corporate experience, and eight years of teaching experience. She holds the credit of presenting papers at various international and national level conferences. She has more than 25 research papers published at national level journal. Some of the papers were also published in reputed referred journal. Her interest areas consist of Entrepreneurship, Strategic Management, and Finance. She holds the recognition of guiding award winning business plan. She has actively contributed in organizing various co-curricular activities like state level and national level seminars. She is regularly appointed as In-Charge Director of Anand Institute of Management. She is associated as an Associate Editor of Pezzottaite Journals of Jammu and Kashmir.

Rabi Subudhi is a Senior Professor at KIIT School of Management, KIIT University, India. With over 34 years of teaching experience, he has published 12 books and over seventy research papers in the area of quantitative research methodology. He is an active member of many reputed international academic societies, like, American Society of Engineering Management (ASEM), International Sociology Association (ISA-RC), ORSI, ICA and ICAS. He has supervised 10 scholars for their PhD degrees and received a senior research fellowship (SRF) award from CSIR, Govt. of India, for his doctoral research. He was chapter president of ORSI Bhubaneswar. He is presently the Editor of KIIT Management Research Journal, Parikalpana. He is also a reviewer for many international journals. He has published many articles in regional languages and takes interest in Children's literature.

Sai Sundaram is an accomplished customer-oriented technology executive with strong management consulting and transformation advisory experience across organisations, their extended supply chains, executing complex M&A transactions and enabling people growth. Futurist, understand how emerging technologies can impact and transform industries in terms of business models, their extended supply chains, people and customer engagement. Significant experience in driving complex commercial deals and understanding how newer commercial models are likely to evolve in the future due to technological disruptions.

Jigna Trivedi holds a graduate and post graduate degrees in Management from Gujarat University, Ahmedabad. She holds a doctoral degree from S.P. University, Vallabh Vidyanagar, Anand. She had received the fellowship from Entrepreneurship Development Institute, Ahmedabad, during her course of doctoral research work. She is associated in the capacity of Professor in Management department at Shri Jairambhai Patel Institute of Business Management and Computer Applications (formerly known as National Institute of Cooperative Management-NICM), Gandhinagar. She was given the charge of director to oversee the administrative responsibilities for the period of one year. She is a recognized guide of Gujarat Technological University (GTU), Ahmedabad. She holds one year of corporate experience, and fifteen years of teaching experience. She holds the credit of presenting seven and fourteen papers at various international and national level conferences, respectively. She has attended more than ten training programmes, faculty development programme and workshops at national and state Level. She has more than 60 research papers published in national and international level referred journal of repute. She has received many best paper awards for paper presentation in various national level conferences. She holds the credit of working as a Co-Principal Investigator/Coordinator of District Human Development Report for Porbandar and Navsari district. She was Principal Coordinator in the preparation of DHDR of Botad district. The policy document or project was funded by Gujarat Social Infrastructure Development Society (GSIDS)-Government of Gujarat, Gandhinagar. She has contributed in newspaper articles too. Her two books titled-'New Paradigms of Business Plan for Select Horticulture Crops-A Practical Textbook for Entrepreneurship' and 'Sugar Cane Growers and Sugar Cooperatives of Gujarat' is currently under published. Her major achievement includes receipt of Research Fellowship from Entrepreneurship Development Institute (EDI) and receipt of seven best paper award in various National level Conference. Her expertise of knowledge is shared through visiting or guest assignments with various institutes of national importance. She has also imparted research training to doctoral students and Class 1 and 2 level government officials. Her interest areas consist of Accounting for Managers, Cost Accounting for Managers, Corporate Taxation, Risk Management and Mergers and Acquisitions. She holds the recognition of guiding award winning business plan. She has actively contributed in organizing various co-curricular activities like state level and national level business plan competition- Advitiya at the institute. Recently three research scholars have been awarded doctoral degree under her able guidance.

Index

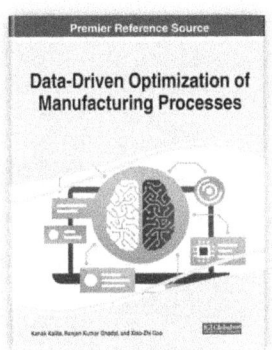

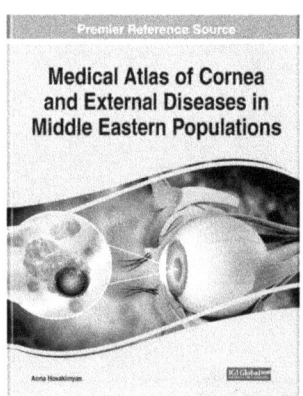

9 781668 458532